Cultural Anthropology

Cultural Anthropology: Global Forces, Local Lives is an accessible, ethnographically rich, cultural anthropology textbook which gives a coherent and refreshingly new vision of the discipline and its subject matter – human diversity. The fifteen chapters and three extended case studies present all of the necessary areas of cultural anthropology, organizing them in conceptually and thematically meaningful and original ways.

A full one-third of its content is dedicated to important global and historical cultural phenomena such as colonialism, nationalism, ethnicity and ethnic conflict, economic development, environmental issues, cultural revival, fundamentalism, and popular culture. The more conventional topics of anthropology (language, economics, kinship, politics, religion, race) are integrated into this broader discussion to reflect the changing content of contemporary courses.

This well-written and well-organised text has been trialed both in the classroom and online. The author has extensive teaching experience and is especially good at presenting material clearly matching his exposition to the pace of students' understanding. Specially designed in colour to be useful to today's students, *Cultural Anthropology: Global Forces, Local Lives*:

- supports study with chapter case studies on subjects as diverse as "Doing anthropology at Microsoft" and "Banning religious symbols in France"
- explains difficult key terms with marginal glosses and links related topics with marginal cross-references
- assists revision with boxed chapter summaries, an extensive bibliography and index
- illustrates concepts and commentary with a vivid range of photographs drawn from the most contemporary anthropological sources
- provides a support website which includes study guides; Powerpoint presentations; chapter supplements; multiple-choice, essay, and assignment questions; a model course mapped to the textbook; a flashcard glossary of terms; and links to useful maps.

Jack David Eller is Assistant Professor of Anthropology at the Community College of Denver. He is the author of *Introducing Anthropology of Religion* (Routledge 2007).

Cultural Anthropology

Global Forces, Local Lives

JACK DAVID ELLER

Routledge
Taylor & Francis Group

NEW YORK AND LONDON

First published 2009
by Routledge
711 Third Avenue, New York, NY 10017

Simultaneously published in the UK
by Routledge
2 Park Square, Milton Park, Abingdon, Oxon OX14 4RN

Routledge is an imprint of the Taylor & Francis Group, an informa business

© 2009 Jack David Eller

Typeset in Berkeley by Keystroke, 28 High Street, Tettenhall, Wolverhampton
Printed and bound in Great Britain by Bell & Bain Ltd, Glasgow

British Library Cataloguing in Publication Data
A catalogue record for this book is available from the British Library

Library of Congress Cataloging-in-Publication Data
Eller, Jack David, 1959–
    Cultural anthropology : global forces, local lives / Jack David Eller.
        p. cm.
    1. Ethnology. I. Title.
    GN316.E445 2009
    306—dc22   2008048585

ISBN10: 0–415–48538–X (hbk)
ISBN10: 0–415–48539–8 (pbk)
ISBN10: 0–203–87561–3 (ebk)

ISBN13: 978–0–415–48538–8 (hbk)
ISBN13: 978–0–415–48539–5 (pbk)
ISBN13: 978–0–203–87561–2 (ebk)

Contents

Illustrations and Acknowledgements

PLATES

FIGURES

MAPS

TABLES

Boxes

Introduction

"The world has come to the conclusion – more defiantly than should have been needed – that culture matters. The world is obviously right – culture does matter" (Sen 2006: 103). Indeed, culture has entered public consciousness and political discourse, often, literally, with a vengeance. This fact demands examination.

Human beings have always had culture, that is, learned and shared ways of living; even some non-humans can and must learn essential skills and habits. And human cultures have always been diverse: humans in disparate groups in disparate places and times have inevitably developed different – sometimes strikingly, even shockingly different – tendencies and codes of thought and behavior. Yet, people have not always, in fact until recently generally have not, appreciated the significance and value of these differences and certainly have not actively and systematically set out to study and explain these differences. Instead, "our kind" was deemed to be truly human, and other kinds were judged as less so. This is clearly not a position that anyone can afford to hold.

Cultural anthropology is the modern science of human behavioral diversity. While it aimed initially to describe "primitive cultures," it always had the ambition and the potential to be a complete subject of human ways of life, including "modern," urban, technological life. In recent years, cultural anthropology has begun to realize that potential, at the same time narrowing the distance between "others" and "ourselves." For instance, there is no such thing as a "primitive" culture. It is to introduce and celebrate the achievements of cultural anthropology, and to indicate the contributions that it can and will make to our understanding of contemporary and future cultural circumstances, that this book was written.

PHILOSOPHY AND HISTORY OF THE BOOK

I have taught cultural anthropology for over twenty years, yet I have been frustrated from the very start of my teaching career with the structure of most courses and texts on the topic. All of them naturally include a discussion of the concept of culture and its major components, like language and gender and personality. All of them present an analysis of the important areas of culture – economics, politics, kinship, and religion. However, virtually all offer at most a couple of concluding chapters on "culture change" and "the modern world" as if these matters are tangential, almost anathema, to anthropology and barely within its purview. This is simply not true: change is an inherent part of culture, and the modern world is the most critical matter for all of us, since it is the world that we, modern nation-state populations and indigenous peoples alike, inhabit.

So, I found teaching a course with thirteen weeks dedicated to the basics of cultural anthropology and a couple of weeks devoted to "the modern world" to be akin to spending thirteen weeks learning the grammar and vocabulary of a foreign language and only two weeks actually speaking (that is, *applying* or *using*) the language. That is inadequate. If cultural anthropology cannot be applied usefully to contemporary life, then its utility is fatally limited. Happily, it can be. Of course, in the days before the internet, it was more difficult to provide students with information that was not already integrated into textbooks. It was possible, although costly, to photocopy materials for distribution; often, as a teacher, I was compelled to talk about topics for which the students had no readings at hand.

In response, I created my own addendum to formally published books, covering crucial issues like colonialism, nationalism and ethnic conflict, economic development and "Third World" poverty, indigenous peoples, and cultural movements. That addendum evolved into the third section of this book, which was obviously composed first. Subsequently, based on my years of teaching, I realized that I had a worthwhile perspective on the entire discipline of cultural anthropology, one that would allow me to craft an entire textbook embodying the same principles throughout the presentation as I had established in the final section. The result is the book you are holding in your hands.

COVERAGE OF THE BOOK

There are many fine and venerable textbooks on cultural anthropology. The world does not need another one unless it has something new to offer. The student and instructor, and anyone interested in the discipline, will find that this book covers more topics more deeply than rival texts, and in so doing immerses the reader in the worldview, the history, the literature, and the controversies of cultural anthropology like no other.

Certainly, this book includes all of the standard and necessary subjects of a cultural anthropology text, as mentioned above. Even these are presented in novel and usefully organized ways. However, it also provides original and nuanced coverage of a number of topics which are customarily given insufficient attention or no attention at all, such as:

- a sophisticated and subtle discussion of cultural relativism
- an integrated analysis of the biological/evolutionary basis of culture
- a meaningful description of the emergence of anthropology out of the intellectual traditions of the Western world
- details on culturally relevant genres of language behavior, such as political speech, jokes and riddles, and religious language, based on the notion that language is social action
- a refined discussion and critique of the race concept
- the presentation of gender not only in relation to women but also to the construction of maleness and of alternate genders across cultures
- the inclusion of consumption as part of the anthropology of economics
- the integration of kinship-based groups into a more general analysis of social group formation
- a contribution to an anthropology of war
- a cutting-edge description of the composite nature of religions, set within the question of social legitimation
- extended discussion of colonialism and post-colonialism
- serious presentations on nationalism, ethnicity, and other forms of identity politics
- major attention to development policies and practices and the role anthropology has played and can play in them
- the recognition and inclusion of indigenous sources and voices
- a balanced analysis of possible futures of culture based on integrative and disintegrative processes
- inclusion of state-of-the-art anthropological concepts including globalization and glocalization, multi-sited ethnography, world anthropologies, microfinancing, diaspora, cultural tourism, popular culture, and multiple modernities.

FEATURES OF THE BOOK

The book also incorporates a number of features, within specific chapters and across the structure of the entire book, which enhance the readability and the utility of the text. Each chapter, for example, includes:

- an opening vignette introducing the topic
- at least two boxed case-studies or discussions to pursue issues in more depth
- a concluding box concerning a "Contemporary Cultural Controversy" to indicate the relevance of the topic and to spark analysis and debate
- a brief but meaningful summary

- a list of key terms
- notes in the margins of pages, providing definitions, intra-text references, and resources (books, videos) for further research.

In addition to chapter-specific features, the overall construction of the book includes:

- an intentionally graphically simple design, leaving more room for text and reducing the cost to buyers
- organization into three sections of equal length, with one-third dedicated explicitly to contemporary cultural processes
- chapters of virtually equal length
- extensive intra-textual references, so that readers may find links between subjects discussed in more than one chapter
- three in-depth case-study/discussions, entitled "Seeing Culture as a Whole," distributed evenly through the text (one-third, two-thirds, and end point) to summarize and integrate the preceding chapters
- a glossary
- an unusually thorough bibliography.

All of these features are supported by a rich and dynamic companion website, with resources for student and instructor alike, including additional original material which will be continuously added to the site, making the book a living and growing product.

My hope is that this textbook, the fruit of two decades of my teaching experience and more than a century of the experiences of cultural anthropologists, will convey the relevance, urgency, and excitement of cultural anthropology that I feel and that I try to communicate to my students. Culture *does* matter, and there is no more pressing task for professional anthropologists and for the educated public than to realize that most if not all of the present problems and challenges facing humanity are cultural problems and challenges – related to how we identify ourselves, how we organize ourselves, and how we interact as members of distinct human communities. Cultural anthropology has made significant contributions to these questions, and it is my heart-felt hope that this book will help future anthropologists and world citizens make even more significant contributions.

1. Ainu
2. Albanians
3. Anang
4. Angola
5. Anuta
6. Apache
7. Argentina
8. Bali
9. Barabaig
10. Basseri
11. Burmese
12. Burundi
13. Brazilians
14. Cambodia
15. Cameroon
16. Cheyenne
17. China
18. Cree
19. Dani
20. Dinka
21. Dusun
22. French
23. Gisu
24. Hidatsa
25. Hua
26. Huron
27. Igbo
28. Ilongot
29. Iroquois
30. India
31. Japanese
32. Konyak Nagas
33. Kuna
34. !Kung or Ju/hoansi
35. Kurds

36. Maasai
37. Malagasy
38. Mali
39. Maroons
40. Mayotte
41. Menomini
42. Navajo
43. Qemant
44. Quebec
45. Sambia
46. Semai
47. Senegal
48. Sierra Leone
49. Sikhs
50. Sinhalese
51. South Africa
52. Soviet Union/USSR (former)
53. Tamils
54. Thai
55. Tikopia
56. Tiwi
57. Ulithi
58. Utka
59. Wana
60. Warlpiri
61. Yanomamo
62. Yugoslavia (former)
63. Zimbabwe
64. Zuni

MAP Major societies mentioned in the text

Understanding Anthropology

During his inaugural parade in January 2005, the American President, George W. Bush, made a gesture with his raised hand, holding down the second and third fingers with his thumb and extending his first and fourth fingers. As a Texan, his gesture was a salute to the University of Texas Longhorns football team. However, when the event was reported in Norway, some people were shocked to see what they considered to be a salute to Satan. In February he was visiting Slovakia on a cold winter's day and shook hands with Slovak leaders while wearing gloves. This was "unheard of" behavior for many Slovaks, who consider shaking hands through one's gloves an offense, equivalent to not shaking hands at all. (When leaving the following day, he removed his gloves for the parting handshake.) Finally, in April while hosting Saudi Crown Prince Abdullah, the President was photographed walking with the Prince and holding his hand. The reactions in the United States varied from amused to scandalized by the "gay" appearance of it, whereas in Saudi Arabia holding a man's hand in public is a sign of respect and friendship. Lest you think that only a head of state can commit an international faux pas, I was traveling in Europe in the mid-1980s when I found myself trying to cross a busy street in Athens, Greece. Athens is notorious for its traffic, and crossing a main thoroughfare is no easy feat. Happily, a motorist slowed down for me, and I dashed across the street. As I did so, I threw out my hand, palm toward him, and waved briskly to show my appreciation. Only afterward did I remember that an open palm thrust at a person in Greece is a rude and even obscene gesture. I felt horrible, hoping that I had not insulted a kind stranger through my thoughtlessness.

Everywhere humans are found, they live in groups. And everywhere human groups are found, these groups have worked out unique ways of living, complete with a language, a form of organization, a body of knowledge, a set of values, and a code of behavior. Members coordinate their actions in terms of these rich "cultural" resources – as must non-members who want to interact with or understand and be understood by the group.

In a word, humanity is a remarkably and inherently diverse species. Not only are there differences between groups, but there are differences within groups: members are differentiated by age, gender, class, occupation, region, specialization, and poten-tially other qualities such as race, ethnicity, and religion. The human species is not homogeneous, nor are its constituent groups homogeneous. But neither are they isolated and independent. From the beginning of human history, groups have had contact with each other and exchanged ideas, technologies, and genes. Trade, travel, and conquest circulated cultural items regionally, then continentally, and today globally.

The world of the twenty-first century (by Western time-reckoning; it is the fifteenth century by the Muslim calendar and the fifty-eighth century by the Hebrew calendar) is a complex world of difference and connectedness. The much-discussed processes of "globalization" have linked human communities without eliminating human diversity; in fact, in some ways they have created new kinds of diversity while injecting some elements of similarity. The local and particular still exists, in a system of global relationships, for a result that some have called "glocalization" (more on this below). But above all else, the conditions of the contemporary world virtually guarantee that individuals will encounter and deal with others unlike themselves in various and significant ways. This makes awareness and appreciation of human diversity – and one's own place in that field of diversity – a critical issue. It is for exploring and explaining this diversity that anthropology is made.

THE SCIENCE(S) OF ANTHROPOLOGY

Anthropology has been called the science of humanity. That is a vast and noble calling but a vague one and also not one that immediately distinguishes it from all the other human sciences. Psychology and sociology and history study humans, and even biology and physics can study humans. What makes anthropology different from, and a worthy addition to, these other disciplines?

Anthropology shares one factor with all of the other "social sciences": they all study human beings in action and interaction. However, all of the other social sciences only study *some kinds* of people and/or *some kinds of things* that people do. Economics studies the economic things people do, political science studies the political things people do, and so on. Above all, they tend to study the political, economic, or other behaviors of certain kinds of people – "modern," urban, industrialized, literate, usually "Western" people. But those are not all the people in the world. There are very many people today, and over the ages there has been a vast majority of people who are not at all like Western people today – not urban, not industrialized, not literate. Yet they are people too. Why do they live the way they do? Why do they not live the way we do – or more to the point, why do we not live the way they do? In a word, why are there so many ways to be human? Those are the sorts of questions that anthropology asks.

Any science, from anthropology to zoology, is distinguished by three features: its *questions*, its *perspective*, and its *method*. The questions of a science involve what it wants to know – why it was established in the first place and what part of reality it is intended to examine. The perspective is its particular and unique way of looking at reality, the "angle" from which it approaches its subject, or the attitude it adopts toward it. Its method is the specific data-gathering activities it practices in order to apply its perspective and to answer its questions.

As a distinct science, anthropology has its own distinguishing questions, ones that no other science of humanity is already asking or has already answered. Some sciences, like psychology, suggest in their very name what their questions will be: psychology, from the Greek *psyche* meaning "mind" and *logos* meaning "word/study," announces that it is interested in the individual, internal, and "mental" aspects of humans and human behavior. Sociology, from the Latin *socius* for "companion/ ally/associate" and *logos*, implies the study of humans in groups. The name anthropology does not speak as clearly, and in fact many readers, and many members of the public, may have little notion of what anthropology is or what anthropologists do. Anthropology is a fairly new word for a fairly new science, asking some fairly new questions. Derived from two Greek roots, *anthropos* for "man/human" and *logos*, anthropology was named and conceived of as the study of humanity in the widest and most inclusive possible sense.

Anthropology's uniqueness is thankfully not in its name but in its unique questions about humans, which include:

- How many different ways are there to be human? That is, what is the "range" of human diversity?
- What are the commonalities across all of these different kinds of humans and human lifeways?
- Why are humans so diverse? What is the source or explanation of human diversity?
- How do the elements of a particular human lifeway fit together and influence each other?
- How does one way of being human develop into another way over time?

Given these questions, we may think of anthropology as not just the study of humans but *the study of human diversity*. Humans are diverse along two dimensions. The first dimension is the chronological, the past versus present. The second dimension is the physical and the behavioral, our bodies versus the things we do and the ways we organize ourselves. Therefore, the definition of anthropology may be refined or expanded to *the study of the diversity of human bodies and behavior in the past and the present*. We can now see that there are several possible subfields of anthropology, depending on exactly what area of this diversity each focuses on – what specific anthropological questions it seeks to answer. These subdisciplines give conventional anthropology its "four-fields" character.

Physical or biological anthropology

Physical anthropology

The study of the diversity of human bodies in the past and present, including physical adaptation, group or "race" characteristics, and human evolution.

Physical or biological anthropology is the area that specializes in *the diversity of human bodies in the past and present*. It is plain to see that humans differ in their physical appearance: there are different skin colors, different hair colors, different body shapes, different facial forms, and so on. What may we hope to learn from it? First and foremost, we learn that *there is more than one way physically to be human*. All of the various human body shapes and facial features are human. Physical anthropologists can also relate those physical traits to the natural environment: is there a reason why people in some parts of the world, for instance, in some climates, have this or that physical characteristic? This is the question of physical adaptation, and it is entirely possible that a group, if it has lived in a particular environment for long enough, could develop traits that fit well in that environment. Finally, physical anthropologists can discover things about human migrations, intermarriages, and such phenomena from the distribution of traits like blood type, gene frequency, and so on. We will return to the question of "race and ethnicity" below.

See Chapter 6

In addition to the present diversity of human bodies, there is considerable historical diversity as well. The evidence indicates clearly that humans have not always had the bodies we have today. This evidence is fossils. Anthropologists have found no human bodies quite like ours that are older than a couple of hundred thousand years at most, and even during that time there have been other "humans" who looked remarkably different from us. If you saw a Neandertal (who lived between 130,000 and 40,000 years ago) on the street today, you would recognize him or her as human but not exactly "normally" human. As we look further back in time, human-like beings become progressively less human-like while still retaining certain critical human features, such as upright walking, a relatively large brain, and a human-like face. How then did we humans come to have the bodies that we have today, and what other forms did our human ancestors take in the past on their way to becoming us? That too is a question for physical anthropology – the question of human evolution. Some scientists even specialize in the physical characteristics of other species that are similar and related to our own, the primates, for which their science is called **primatology**. We will examine the subject of human evolution later.

Primatology

The study of the physical and behavioral characteristics of the category of species called primates.

See Chapter 2

Archaeology

One common image of the anthropologist is a sort of "Indiana Jones" figure: the researcher who digs up pyramids in Egypt or ancient cities in Mexico. In fact, the researchers who conduct this kind of study are archaeologists. From the root *archae-* for "beginning," **archaeology** is *the study of the diversity of human behavior in the past.* Archaeologists may do their work in the company of physical anthropologists, who examine the actual anatomical remains of past humans. However, the archaeologists do not focus on the bodies but on the behaviors of those humans. How can they do that, when those people are all dead and their ways of life have vanished? The answer is that they examine the things those humans left behind – their tools, their homes, their art, their writing if they had it, and so on. Archaeologists divide this evidence approximately into two categories: artifacts and features. **Artifacts** are the more or less portable objects that people made and used; things like pottery, clothing, jewelry, tools and weapons, and the like are considered artifacts. **Features** are the larger, more or less immovable objects like buildings, walls, monuments, canals, roads, farms, and so on. To understand more about the environmental setting of these societies and how the humans made use of them, archaeologists also consider **ecofacts** such as plant (wood, seeds, pits, pollen) and animal (bones, shells) remains.

Studying artifacts and features is fascinating, but archaeologists do not study them just to learn about them. They search and interpret this evidence for the thoughts, the ideas, the feelings, and the social patterns of the people who made them. How did those past people make these things? Why did they make them?

Archaeology
The study of the diversity of human behavior in the past, based on the traces left behind by past humans or societies.

Artifacts
Physical objects created by humans, often specifically the "portable" objects like tools, pottery, and jewelry (as opposed to the non-portable ones like buildings and roads).

Features
In archaeology, the large and non-portable objects or structures created and left by humans, including walls, buildings, roads, canals, and so on.

Ecofacts
The environmental remains from past human social contexts, including wood, seeds, pollen, animal bones, and shells.

PLATE 1.1 Archaeologists study at the sites of past societies, such as Teotihuacan near Mexico City

How did they use them? What did the objects mean to the makers and users? Archaeologists try to go from the objects themselves to the minds and hearts of the people who lived among those objects long ago. It is a creative, interpretive activity, but the artifacts and features are often the only traces that those people and their ways of lives have left behind.

Archaeologists do not look exclusively at the ancient past. They can also study the recent past, such as medieval European or early colonial American sites. And since modern humans also make and leave remains behind them, archaeologists have found that their methods can be practiced on living societies to learn how contemporary humans exploit and affect their environments. One recent form of this work has been dubbed **garbalogy**, since it sifts through contemporary trash to discover what kinds of objects humans produce, consume, and discard today.

Garbalogy
The study of contemporary trash to examine how humans make, consume, and discard material objects in the present.

Linguistic anthropology

Linguistic anthropology
The study of the diversity of human language in the past and present, and its relationship to social groups, practices, and values.

Linguistic anthropology focuses on *the diversity of human language in the past and present*. Linguistic anthropologists study the similarities and differences between present-day languages, looking into their grammar, their vocabulary, and their everyday use. This will not only shed light on each language but also on the possible relationships between languages. Are there, for instance, language "families" that are related historically, by migration or intermixing or other processes? Linguistic anthropologists can also investigate changes within a language over time. Anyone who has read Shakespeare or even older English literature knows that English has evolved fairly dramatically over the recent centuries. All languages undergo similar processes, and linguistic anthropologists can analyze the reasons for and the particular directions of this change. They can also attempt to reconstruct "ancestral" languages – ones that link, say, English to German and both to ancient Greek or Sanskrit – even to the point of reconstructing the very first language.

More essentially, linguistic anthropology attempts to understand language use in its relation to social life and social practices. How are values and concepts captured in and expressed by language? How is language employed to structure and communicate social differences, for example, of status and rank or age or gender? Linguistic anthropology has increasingly emphasized the element of "performance" in language, discovering specialized forms for various purposes (for example, speech-making as opposed to story-telling) and the role of language in forming and maintaining social relationships, including power relationships. Language in anthropological perspective will be the subject of another chapter.

See Chapter 4

Cultural anthropology

Cultural anthropology
The study of the diversity of human behavior in the present.

Cultural anthropology, also sometimes called social anthropology, is *the study of the diversity of human behavior in the present*. The large majority of anthropologists are cultural anthropologists, and they have one tremendous advantage over both physical anthropologists and archaeologists: they have living people to talk to. The goal of cultural anthropology is still to learn about the thoughts and feelings of people that lead to their behavior, but now we can ask them, "Why did you do that?" or "How did you make that?" or "What does that mean to you?" Cultural anthropology is the activity that many people associate with *National Geographic* magazine, the Discover Channel, or similar media, where strange-looking (to us) people are portrayed doing exotic or unfamiliar or maybe even shocking (to us) things. Of course, observers can appreciate the sheer spectacle of such people and their behavior, but cultural anthropology is more than the observation and collection of behavioral curiosities. It is about making humans unlike oneself seem less "exotic" and more human – in fact, just as human as each of us is. It is about getting to the heart and mind of people very different from oneself in at least some ways. But it is also about getting to one's own heart and mind, since "we" are one of the diverse kinds of human as surely as "they" are. In so doing, cultural anthropology penetrates to the very nature of humanity. What separates one kind of human from another yet unites us all? What makes one group's hearts and their minds different from another group's and yet similar and related?

Please remember, as the first lesson in cultural anthropology, that others may appear strange and incomprehensible, even abnormal, to you, but that you may appear just as strange, incomprehensible, and abnormal, to them.

TRADITIONAL ANTHROPOLOGY AND BEYOND

You have now seen the traditional four subfields of anthropology. However, in important ways, anthropology has outgrown this narrow categorization, if it was ever actually constrained by it. For instance, a number of well-developed subdisciplines have emerged under the general heading of cultural anthropology, including, among others:

- Urban anthropology, or the study of humans in urban settings, the effects of urbanization on previously non-urban societies, and the relationships between cities and their surrounding hinterlands (such as labor migration).
- Medical anthropology, or the study of knowledge systems and practices concerning health and medical treatment cross-culturally.
- Forensic anthropology, or the use of anthropological knowledge and methods to solve crimes (e.g. identify murder victims, determine time and cause of death).
- Visual anthropology, or the study of the production, presentation, and use of material or "artistic" media such as painting, body art, clothing designs, and so on. It can include not only the arts that other societies make but the arts that anthropology employs to study them, such as film and photography.
- Ethnomusicology, or the study of musical forms and their relation to culture.

■ Ethnobotany, or the study of knowledge and uses of plants in various cultures.

■ Development anthropology, or the study of as well as the practical contribution to how "modern" forces affect and change societies. This can include attempting to minimize the negative impact of change on traditional societies and even in some cases advocating for the rights and wishes of those societies.

■ Feminist anthropology, or the study of women's issues and roles across cultures. This is often expanded to include gender issues and roles more generally, particularly how gender is defined, practiced, and controlled through language, values, and power.

Applied anthropology

See Chapters 3 and 11–15

Boas, Franz. 1928.
Anthropology and Modern Life. New York: W. W. Norton & Company, Inc.

Anthropology is not and never has been a purely "academic" pursuit, disconnected from the real world. In its pre-modern form it was to be found in the early European colonial encounters with non-Western peoples, providing data and often service in the colonial enterprise, for better or for worse. Some of the first anthropologists, such as Franz Boas (1858–1942) in his 1928 book *Anthropology and Modern Life*, were deeply concerned with practical social issues, like racism, nationalism, eugenics, criminology, and education. Of course all anthropological findings may be used for real-world policy- and decision-making, but many anthropologists overtly practice a kind of "applied anthropology" intended to bring the concepts, perspectives, and methods of the science to non-academic initiatives.

Anthropology is a lively, diverse, and growing discipline. According to a survey undertaken by the primary professional organization of the field in the United States, the American Anthropological Association, the number of Bachelor degrees earned in anthropology nearly doubled from 1992–3 to 2001–2, from 5,945 to 9,728; the number of Master degrees rose by around 50 percent (1,049 versus 1,519), while almost three times as many Ph.D.s were awarded (367 versus 1,025) (Boites, Geller, and Patterson n.d.). Significantly, more than half (up to 60 percent) of anthropology graduate degrees are earned by women. Another study (Givens, Evans, and Jablonski 2000) happily discovered that the vast majority of anthropology graduates (85 percent) would choose anthropology again as their major and career if they had to do it again.

What exactly do anthropologists do for a living? Many are teachers and scholars (researchers and writers) of anthropology, but by no means all. Givens, Evans, and Jablonski calculated that only a little over half (59 percent) of all anthropology Ph.D.s worked in academia in 1990, with somewhat more (71 percent) holding academic jobs in 1997. The Society for Applied Anthropology estimates that actually most anthropologists work outside of colleges and universities, if Master degree-holders are included, and no doubt the number would be greater still for Bachelor degree-holders. The authors conclude: "Presently, there is no discernible ceiling or cap . . . for Ph.D. anthropologists targeting the nonacademic realm of employment." An anthropology major or minor can in fact be a fine preparation for a

www.sfaa.net

non-anthropological career, in education, business, law, journalism, and medicine, especially if one expects to be working with diverse populations or in an international setting.

Even within the confines of professional anthropology, there are many important and even critical applications of the discipline. Applied anthropology as a specialty within the field seeks to use anthropological knowledge and techniques to address real-world problems and to contribute to social or other improvements. The National Association for the Practice of Anthropology promotes the use of anthropology "to address social issues related to public health, organizational and community development, information technology systems, housing, social justice, law, the media, marketing, environmental management, and the arts." The Society for Applied Anthropology urges that the "occupation of 'Anthropologist' should be promoted as a satisfying and important professional role whether as an independent consultant, an employee of public agencies, corporations, or private organizations, or as a university faculty member or administrator." In fact, as Box 1.1 shows, companies like Microsoft have begun to appreciate the value of anthropological skills, whether applied to their own operational culture, their partners and competitors, or to the consuming public.

www. practicinganthropology.org

BOX 1.1 DOING ANTHROPOLOGY AT MICROSOFT

There are two underappreciated facts about the modern business world. The first is that small businesses generate over half of the economic activity in the United States and employ almost 40 percent of the high-tech workers (Murphy 2005). The second is that every company, as a human social group, has its own "corporate culture." These two facts add up to one major insight: the more a sales team knows about its potential small business customers, the more business it can do with them. That is why leading companies like Microsoft have brought anthropology into the business world.

To better understand the software needs of entrepreneurs, Microsoft has been undertaking detailed field studies of small firms all over the U.S. Its executives refer to this sort of qualitative research as "anthropology," a term that has become a popular buzzword at the company in recent years. . . . Microsoft employs numerous social scientists, including two credentialed anthropologists, to work on projects such as the development of Office SBA. Their fieldwork is far removed from the popular perception of the anthropologist. . . . But there is a certain correspondence between Microsoft's research agenda and the work of those old-time anthropologists. . . . The modern version of this knowledge–power dynamic is Microsoft, a multinational technology colossus that hires anthropologists who study the natives in order to sell them more software.

Doing anthropology at Microsoft means understanding the "culture," habits, practices, and values of their business partners better so that the two can interact more successfully – and profitably – for both.

Ervin (2000), in his substantial analysis of applied anthropology, mentions a wide variety of ways for putting anthropology into practice. He specifically names policy-making in such areas as health, education, social-economic problems, environment and resource management, and technology. Anthropologists can perform functions in needs assessment (determining what problems need to be solved and what inputs will be required), program evaluation (determining the effectiveness of programs), and social impact analysis (determining the effects of programs on people). Some of the specific tasks that anthropologists can perform include training, supervision, administration, consultation, interviewing, grant-writing, and expert-witness testimony. A few anthropologists have even started their own consulting companies, like Robert Winthrop's Cultural Solutions firm in Ashland, Oregon (Ervin 2000: 50).

See Chapters 14 and 15

One particular arena where anthropologists can make and have made a contribution is in advocacy for indigenous peoples, bringing cultural considerations to the attention of governments and corporations. Organizations like Cultural Survival (which publishes a magazine by the same name) in the U.S. or Survival International in the U.K. promote awareness of indigenous issues. The American Anthropological Association maintains a Department of Government Relations which "works to increase public understanding of anthropology" and to lend an anthropological voice to political discourse. Some of its activities include initiating and responding to governmental policies, working with federal agencies, preparing briefings from the anthropological perspective, serving in advisory positions, and developing testimony to support funding allocations. Participation and advocacy can take many other forms as well, such as working for indigenous groups like Native American communities and societies to help them advance their practical claims (e.g. water or land rights) and cultural interests. When I was doing my fieldwork in Australia, there were anthropologists assisting Aboriginal groups to collect and present their tradition-based land claims in Australian courts; they would conduct the research, brief the lawyers, and sometimes even testify themselves in court. Others were helping them produce and sell their art.

The continuing evolution of cultural anthropology

One question that may be asked and has been asked is: Who are the subjects of cultural anthropology's investigation? The conventional impression, virtually the stereotype, of the science is that it concerns exclusively small, "traditional," even "primitive" groups. Indeed, one of the great early anthropologists, A. R. Radcliffe-Brown, defined anthropology as "the study of what are called primitive or backward peoples" (1965: 2). The equally esteemed E. E. Evans-Pritchard admitted that anthropology was the branch of social science "which chiefly devotes itself to primitive societies" (1962: 11). However, Evans-Pritchard situated the emphasis on remote exotic peoples within the context of anthropology's greater subject which "embraces all human cultures and societies, including our own" (4).

Radcliffe-Brown, A.R. 1965 [1952]. *Structure and Function in Primitive Society*. New York: The Free Press.

Evans-Pritchard, E.E. 1962. *Social Anthropology and Other Essays*. New York: The Free Press.

If you consider the questions posed by anthropology generally and cultural anthropology specifically, you will realize that there is nothing about them that limits them to any particular kinds of peoples or cultures. Accordingly, as the human world has changed – especially becoming more interconnected, more fluid, more "modernized" – cultural anthropology has changed too, partly because it can, partly because it must. Cultural anthropology was never really exclusively the study of small, isolated, traditional societies, although it did occupy the "savage slot" (Trouillot 1991), for tactical reasons (because it is easier to analyze compact and unfamiliar cultures), and for the simple reason that no other science did. But anthropology could not and did not aspire to remain in that slot, if only because there are no more isolated and "primitive" societies and probably never were.

See Chapters 11–15

The three main phenomena that have forced a reconceptualization of cultural anthropology are colonialism, post-colonial independence and nationalist and indigenous movements, and modernization and globalization. Colonialism brought far-flung societies within the political, economic, and cultural sphere of the West, imposing changes and inequalities. Independence, nationalism, and indigenous movements have transformed the sometimes "passive" objects of anthropological scrutiny into active subjects, actors, and producers of culture who speak for themselves. Finally, modernization and globalization have threatened and attempted to integrate cultures into a single world system which is, Thomas Friedman (2005) notwithstanding, anything but "flat," if only because they are driven from centers of wealth and power and generate uneven outcomes. In the contemporary world, globalization is the most heralded cultural force, regarded as "processes that take place within [groups] but also transcend them, such that attention limited to local processes, identities, and units of analysis yields incomplete understanding of the local" (Kearney 1995: 548). But the local does not disappear, nor is it bleached of all its unique characteristics; rather, in each location and occasion, a distinct combination or manifestation of the local and the global emerges, leading to a result that some observers have wryly called **glocalization**, linking local or small-scale changes to large-scale or global factors. The message is that even within a global context cultural realities are local, and therefore cultural anthropology's questions, perspectives, and methods still apply.

See Chapter 12

See Chapters 13 and 14

See Chapters 14 and 15

Glocalization
A combination of the words "globalization" and "local," which suggests the unique local and situated forms and effects of widespread and even global processes.

In response to "glocal" realities, some anthropologists have taken "big picture" approaches to the world, as in Eric Wolf's (1982) *Europe and the People without History* and the various works of Ernest Gellner (e.g. 1988). Others have explored specialized aspects of human behavior, such as war and violence (e.g. Wolfe and Yang 1996; Scheper-Hughes and Bourgois 2004; Eller 1999, 2005), globalization (e.g. Lewellen 2002), consumption and shopping (e.g. Howes 1996; Counihan and Van Esterick 1997; Miller 1998), conservation and parks (Igoe 2004), undocumented migration (Chavez 1998), homelessness (Finkelstein 2005), casino gambling (Darian-Smith 2004), natural disasters (Hoffman and Oliver-Smith 2002), the media (Askew and Wilk 2002), and even the meat industry (Stull and Broadway 2004).

Wolf, Eric. 1982. *Europe and the People without History*. Berkeley: University of California Press

Finally, cultural anthropologists are no longer the exclusive owners and practitioners of "anthropological" concepts and methods; other social scientists (in established fields like sociology or psychology and new fields like media studies or cultural studies), or merely talented amateurs, have explored unlikely corners of American society to bring back stories of life in areas like Mexican illegal workers (Conover 1987), New York State prison guards (Conover 2001), the working poor or those doing little-known work (Ehrenreich 2002; Levison 2002), and even prison life (Lerner 2002). I have had students in my classes write research papers on skateboarding, tattooing, computer hacking, online computer gaming, and exotic dancing. There is no theoretical limit to what cultural anthropology can put under its microscope, and the more examples of human cultural diversity it comes to include, and the more practitioners it enlists, the more complete will be our understanding of humanity – that is, of ourselves.

THE "ANTHROPOLOGICAL PERSPECTIVE"

Anthropological perspective
The unique "angle" or point of view of anthropology, consisting of cross-cultural or comparative study, holism, and cultural relativism.

Cultural anthropology is distinct among sciences for the questions it asks. However, it also stands out in its approach to or its way of thinking about its subject, that is, its perspective. The **anthropological perspective** has three components. The first is obvious, the second less obvious but fairly uncontroversial, and the third is not at all obvious and quite controversial. They are:

1. Comparative or cross-cultural study
2. Holism
3. Cultural relativism.

Comparative or cross-cultural study

Cultural anthropology does not look at just one kind of culture, certainly not just the anthropologist's own kind of culture. A cross-cultural perspective or emphasis means that anthropologists are curious about human behavior in a wide and inclusive sense, embracing many or potentially all human ways of being. Anthropologists are perhaps particularly interested in cultures that are *unlike* their own. After all, people already know their own culture pretty well – or think they do. One premise of human sciences is that most people in fact are not as aware of the causes and consequences of their own behavior as they often like to think that they are. This is a reason why sociologist C. Wright Mills (1959) referred to the "sociological imagi-nation": researchers must learn to see meanings, rules, relationships, institutions, and such phenomena that are "invisible" to or outside the attention of group members even as those phenomena influence human behavior, individually and collectively. Therefore, one reason why cultural anthropology has insisted on a comparative perspective is that it is often easier to see what is unfamiliar than what is familiar; familiar things tend to be taken for granted or overlooked, whereas the unfamiliar demands attention. Anthropology if anything serves to question assumptions and to expose the taken-for-granted.

However, even if anthropologists knew their own culture very well, that would not be sufficient. Anthropologists, like all scientists, cannot use a sample of one to draw conclusions about other cases. Whether it is plants, planets, or people, it is not acceptable to assume that they are all alike. In fact, it is wise to assume exactly the opposite. Anybody who is truly interested in knowing and understanding humans needs a bigger sample than one. We cannot know ourselves, no matter how thoroughly, and claim that now we "know humanity." Actually, in almost every way, Western culture in general or American culture in particular is quite atypical and non-representative. But then, there is no "typical" culture. Since no culture pertains to all humans, or even a majority or close to it, every culture is a minority. *Whatever you do or think or feel, in the human world you are in the minority.*

So it should be apparent why **cross-cultural or comparative study** is a valuable part of anthropology. The first reason is that the diversity is there. There simply *are* other cultures than one's own. But more, by exposing ourselves to the plethora of human cultures, we can make two important discoveries:

Cross-cultural study
The examination of a wide variety of societies when considering any particular cultural question, for purposes of comparison.

- The commonalities or "universals" that occur across cultures – that is, is there anything that most or all cultures do that seems to be *necessary* for humans?
- The full range of variation between cultures – that is, just how different can humans be? How many different kinds of language, personality, economics, religion, and so on are there? Just how many ways are there to be human? In other words, what is *possible* for humans?

I like to think of anthropology, then, as the study of what is possible and what is necessary for humans.

Holism

Holism refers to "the whole," the entirety. Each particular culture is and must be approached as a whole, not just as a single trait (say, a political system or an economy) or as a disconnected list of traits. A whole, cultural or otherwise, is a system containing multiple parts in some kind of integrated relationship with each other. The first significance of this fact is that a culture *has parts*, and anthropologists discover these parts and the different forms they can take. If, for instance, kinship is a part of culture, then what different kinds of kinship are there? What are the possibilities of marriage, child-rearing, household residence, descent, and so forth? The second significance is that the parts are interconnected in some way. If an anthropologist wants to study, say, the religion of a particular society, s/he cannot study the religion in isolation; rather, s/he must consider the language, the politics, the kinship, the gender roles. Potentially – and actually – every part of a culture relates in some way to every other part. The parts may not be as tightly integrated as the parts of a car engine, but they are interrelated. The third significance is that each part has its unique function and each contributes to the function of the whole. Just like an organ in the

Holism
The part of the "anthropological perspective" that involves consideration of every part of a culture in relation to every other part and to the whole.

body or a part in a car, each has its own "job to do" and each contributes to the overall job of the whole. So, wherever we enter a culture to begin to analyze it or whatever we care to focus on, we will find ourselves swept into considering all of its parts and the whole which those parts constitute.

The holistic perspective has helped lead cultural anthropology into a "case-study" approach. In a traditional or classic anthropological description of a specific culture – known as **ethnography** – the writer would typically begin with a discussion of the environment in which the group lives (mountain, desert, jungle, island) and then proceed to provide details on each aspect of the culture. Sometimes these accounts would center on a particular part of the culture, depending on what was most noteworthy, but all of the parts required analysis. In some instances an entire book was written on one aspect of culture, as in the case of *Nuer Religion* (Evans-Pritchard 1956), but even then it was a contribution to a body of literature on and including all facets of that particular society. In other words, any single ethnography prepared by a cultural anthropologist may not cover every single aspect of the culture, but collectively the research on the culture would.

Cultural relativism

It is a fact that cultures are different; that is why anthropologists study them. Cultures are different in how they see, interpret, value, and respond to the world, including the other humans in their world. What is done in one culture may not be done in another. What is important or valuable in one culture may not be in another. What is good or right in one culture may not be in another. For example, in mainstream American culture, polygamy is deemed to be bad, immoral, and illegal (there are of course minority sections of America that practice and value polygamy, such as the sect of "fundamentalist" Mormons). However, in many cultures – in fact, in most cultures – polygamy has been not only acceptable but normal or even preferred. Who is right about this?

Actually, that is not the correct question to ask. In fact, it is not even a possible question to ask. But let us say this for now: *different cultures can and do have different notions of what is good, normal, moral, valuable, legal, and so on.* An anthropologist investigating a headhunting society would find men with human heads in their possession, perhaps displayed on their walls or hung from their ceilings. The tendency may be to judge them with the anthropologist's own values and norms: "Those men are all immoral criminal killers!" An outsider might want to call the authorities and have the "deviants" and "murderers" arrested. The visitor may, then, be surprised when the authorities ask us why s/he is bothering them; in fact, the owners of heads may be the authorities – the chiefs, the priests, or other leaders. That may be hard to accept, but imagine this: a man from the same headhunting society comes to your society and sees that you do not have heads on display. What would he think? He might think you are weak or inconsequential, a person of no courage, fame, or prominence, or that you are just "deviant" from the ideal of

See Chapter 2

See Chapter 8

Ethnography
A written account or description of a particular culture, usually including its environment, economic system, kinship arrangements, political systems, and religious beliefs, and often including some discussion of culture change.

headhunting. If the headhunter visited the White House or 10 Downing Street and observed no heads, he might assume that the resident has no political authority, since great men collect heads.

Notice that the headhunter got Western people wrong, just as Western people got him and his culture wrong. What do we learn by thinking this way? Not very much, at least not very much about them. We do learn about ourselves (that we disapprove of headhunting), but we already knew that. Clearly, understanding – let alone judging – others by our standards is not helpful. We might call them bad or immoral or criminal, but that does not explain why they do what they do – and they could just as easily say the same thing about us from their point of view. If anthropologists therefore want to understand the behavior of members of another culture, we cannot apply *our* norms and morals and values and meanings to them, because they do not use ours. They use their own. That would be like trying to apply the rules of chess to poker. The rules of chess are neither bad nor good; they just don't pertain.

If anthropologists want to understand another culture, then *we must understand or judge them in terms of their own notions of good, normal, moral, valuable, meaningful, and so on*. That is cultural relativism. **Cultural relativism** asserts that an observer cannot apply the standards of one culture to another culture, at least not in an informative way. Rather, a phenomenon in a culture must be understood and evaluated *in relation to, relative to*, that culture. Why? First, it is always tempting and easy to conclude that different is bad: they do not do it my way, so they are wrong. Scientific observers must avoid this arrogance and shortsightedness. Second, it is quite likely to breed misunderstanding. If you impose your own cultural outlook on a cross-cultural encounter, you may misjudge the whole situation. This happens, for instance, in international business. A meeting of Western and non-Western businesspeople might easily end with each side thinking it understands what occurred in the meeting. Later, if one side does not respond as the other expected it would, there may be confusion, anger, even real financial loss. What went wrong? Each side interpreted the meeting from its own cultural point of view, not realizing that the other side had a different point of view – until it was too late.

Accordingly, any judgment about norms, morals, values, meanings, laws, and so on is a cultural judgment, made "in relation to" some standard of norms, morals, values, meanings, and laws. That is what cultural relativism means. Sticking out one's tongue is an insult here, a greeting there. If an anthropologist gets mad or offended when members of a society where tongue-sticking is a greeting stick their tongues out at him or her, those members will be quite surprised and confused by our response. This experience is called **culture shock** – the surprise, confusion, and actual pain that one feels in the presence of the profoundly unfamiliar and unexpected. This is probably the most common experience in the world. So is the reaction: to judge people from other cultures by the standards of one's own culture. This is called **ethnocentrism** (from *ethno-* for a way of life or culture and *center* for putting it in the center or pride of place), the attitude or practice of assuming that one's own cultural point of view is the best, the right, or even the only point of view. Of course, ethnocentrism is possible – it is the easy, even the automatic, thing – but it is simply

Cultural relativism
The reaction to the fact of cultural diversity in which one attempts to understand and judge the behavior of another culture in terms of its standards of good, normal, moral, legal, etc. rather than one's own.

Culture shock
The surprise, confusion, and pain we feel when we encounter a way of life that is very foreign to our own.

Ethnocentrism
The attitude or belief that one's own culture is the best or only one, and that one can understand or judge another culture in terms of one's own.

not helpful. One can be ethnocentric from one's own cultural perspective, but others can be ethnocentric from their cultural perspective. Nothing is gained by this except mutual (and probably negative) judgment.

Every judgment, then, of good/bad, moral/immoral, normal/abnormal, valuable/valueless, is made from some cultural point of view – in relation to some standard of good, moral, normal, valuable. And a culture is precisely a set of standards for such judgments. Cultural relativism says that we need to take this fact into account when we confront and interact with other cultures; it must be part of our perspective on cultural difference. However, there are many fallacies and misconceptions that people, both relativists and non-relativists, have about cultural relativism.

1. Cultural relativism *does not mean* that "anything goes" or judgment is impossible. Some critics of relativism insist that it means, or leads to, a position of no standards at all, a "do what you want to do," "if it feels good, do it" ethic or anti-ethic. That is not at all what cultural relativism advocates. It does not say, "Anything goes" but rather, "Here this goes, and there that goes." It is *descriptive*. It does not tell us what moral or value judgments to make, only that diverging moral or value judgments are made. And it certainly does not conclude that value judgments are impossible. Rather, it is a description of exactly how such judgments are made – in relation to some standard of judgment – and investigators should find out what that standard of judgment is. But there is no such thing as a "standardless" judgment, and there does not appear to be a single standard that all cultures share. Instead, there are multiple standards.

2. Cultural relativism *does not mean* that anything a culture does is good/moral/valuable/normal. Some critics of relativism claim that taking a relativistic stance toward another culture is essentially condoning it. But to condone means to judge favorably, and relativism is not about judging but about understanding. If we encountered a culture that practiced polygamy or infanticide or "honor killing," cultural relativism would not require us to say, "Those attitudes and behaviors are good or acceptable." What it would require us to do is determine where those attitudes and behaviors come from and what they mean to the people who practice them. One certainly does not have to approve in order to understand. In fact, not only do anthropologists not have to but they cannot "condone" these or any other behaviors, because *condoning, like condemning, is a value judgment*. To say a behavior is good or bad is to judge it, and that means judging by some particular value standard. That would mean abandoning the relativistic perspective and referring to one's own community of values, one's own culture. As an anthropologist it is possible to understand a behavior without judging – in fact, it is *only* possible to understand without judging – while as a member of one's own culture one can say that one does not share or condone that behavior. But you must always remember that your judgment is a product of your culture and may not be shared by all cultures.

See Chapter 5

3. Cultural relativism *does not mean* that anything a culture believes is true. Some critics of relativism assert that relativism compels us to accept as valid any belief or "knowledge" that a culture asserts. If, for instance, a culture believes that the earth is flat, then it is flat *for them*, even while it is round for us. This is of course nonsense and has nothing whatsoever to do with cultural relativism. There is a philosophical position known as "epistemological relativism" which does actually hold that all knowledge and truth is relative, but that is not the claim made by cultural relativism and is quite beyond the ability or need of anthropology to address. Let us consider the problem of knowledge by contrasting two different kinds of statements:

Polygamy is good.   The Earth is round.

Both take the superficial form of *noun-is-adjective*. But the similarity ends there. The latter is a fact statement, or rather a fact claim. Is it true or false? More importantly, how do we determine? We make observations and measurements, that is, we check against reality. We find that the Earth really is round, not flat, and verify the initial statement. How about the statement on polygamy? Is it true or false that polygamy is good? The answer is – neither. It is culturally relative. That is, in Warlpiri (Australian Aboriginal) or in fundamentalist Mormon culture, polygamy is good. In mainstream American society, polygamy is bad. So "polygamy is good" is not the same kind of statement as "the Earth is round." Again, the latter is a fact claim (either true or false), but the former is a *value claim*. It is neither true nor false.

Value claims are judgments and therefore must be made by reference to, relative to, some value standard. But what standard? Shall we use mainstream Western standards, or Warlpiri standards, or Japanese standards, or Yanomamo standards, *ad infinitum*? The answer is that any of those standards is equally usable – and equally used by somebody. Therefore, a value statement like "polygamy is good" is not, cannot be, true or false because *it is not even a complete statement yet*. Before we can

PLATE 1.2 Warlpiri (Australian Aboriginal) women preparing ritual objects

evaluate the statement, we need to know more: good *for what*, good *according to whom*? If one says, "Polygamy is good among the Warlpiri," an anthropologist can respond, "That is true." If one says, "Polygamy is good," the anthropological response is not "True" or "False" but "Please finish your statement." It is not clear yet which cultural value standard the speaker is applying, so the statement is unfinished and meaningless as formulated.

Since there are multiple potential and actual value standards that may be used to evaluate the claim, the final judgment will be *relative to* whichever standard one ultimately uses. In other words, value statements are culturally relative, whereas fact statements are not. Or, we might say that fact statements are relative to a single standard (reality) that is objective and universally shared. The acceleration of gravity on Earth (thirty-two feet per second) is the same for all people in all cultures because they share a single common physical reality. If all people in all cultures shared a single common standard – a single common cultural reality – for evaluating polygamy, then they would all come to the same evaluation, but then there would not be many different cultures for it to be relative to.

4. Cultural relativism *does not mean* that cultures are different in every conceivable way, that there are no cultural universals. Cultural relativism does not rule out the possibility of any commonalities or universals among humans. Relativism does not say that commonalities cannot exist; it merely correctly asserts that we cannot *assume* they exist. The question of cultural universals is an empirical question: that is, if we find them, then they exist. If we do not find them, then they do not exist. But the lack of *universal meanings or values* is not the same thing as the lack of *meanings or values*. Even if there are not universal ones, there are "local" ones geographically and historically – very many local ones, in fact – and if that is all there is, then that has to be enough.

5. Cultural relativism *does not mean* that "everything is relative," including cultural relativism itself (cultural relativism is not self-contradictory). Some things are culturally relative, and some things are not. Cultural relativism is simply an awareness and acknowledgment of differences in human judgment about norms, values, meanings, and so on. It amounts to saying, "Different cultures have different notions of good/normal/moral/valuable." But that statement is not a value statement itself; it is a fact claim. It is not saying culture is good, or cultural relativism is good, or multiple value standards are good. Perhaps from certain viewpoints, multiple value standards – multiple cultures – are not good at all. They definitely make the human world more complicated and contentious. Still, culture *is*; multiple value standards *exist*. That is a fact. How we respond to it, what sense we make of it, is the important question.

6. Cultural relativism *does not mean* that cultures cannot be compared. Cultural relativism does not mean that comparison is impossible, any more than it means that judgment is impossible. What it means is that when any comparison is being made, the terms or criteria of the comparison must be specified. One cannot say

culture X is "better than" culture Y without specifying "better at what?" Some cultures are certainly larger than others, and some cultures are certainly better at hunting or making war than others. As long as the standards of comparison are stated (and perhaps it is also explained *why those particular standards* were selected) comparisons may of course be made. In fact, recall that the first part of the anthropological perspective was "comparative" study. We can compare two or more cultures on any variable without making value judgments about them.

THE RELEVANCE OF ANTHROPOLOGY

Besides its questions and perspective (which we have just seen) and method (which we will see in the next chapter), any science worthy of the name has relevance, something to say that people need to hear, that can and probably is beneficial in some way. There are at least four ways in which anthropology is relevant, each sufficient to qualify it as a worthwhile endeavor, but together making it one of the most important and urgent things that people in the modern world can do.

1. Anthropology has immediate bearing on our decisions, actions, and policies on the domestic and the international scene. When any nation or group of people is acting on the world stage (and even on the domestic stage), it is acting in a multicultural environment. The first thing they must know and deeply incorporate in their thinking is that other groups and societies are not like them and do not have to be. No person or group can assume, expect, or demand that their ways of seeing and understanding things be shared by everyone. If those understandings are shared, fine. However, no one can assume that they are. Thus, if one nation or group tries – even with the best of intentions – to impose its values or beliefs or standards on other people, it may encounter unexpected (and unexpectedly fierce) resistance or surprising and undesirable outcomes. If one nation or group simply forges ahead with behaviors that make sense to its members or uses words or gestures that seem familiar to those members (for example, when Christians talk about a war against Muslim enemies as "a crusade"), it should not be shocking to find those meanings misunderstood and those goals unshared. Even more so, when one society chooses a course of action toward another society, there are specific cultural particulars about that society that it would strongly behove the actor to know and use. Much failure of communication, not to mention failure of goals, can be avoided with a little cultural knowledge of the people with whom one interacts.

BOX 1.2 CULTURE AND INTELLIGENCE GATHERING

A recent controversy has concerned the possible use of intensive physical means, including torture, to obtain information from enemy prisoners such as suspected terrorists. The question of the legality and morality of coercive interrogation and torture is not one we can or want to open here, but a question we can open is its effectiveness. An "anthropological" lesson was learned in 1943, when Marine Major Sherwood Moran wrote a report on his remarkably successful technique of interrogating the characteristically difficult-to-interrogate Japanese prisoners of war. He determined that coercion and torture, including indignities and intimidations, do not produce useful information. His alternate approach had two prongs. The first was to redefine the situation – to consider the subject, and to get the subject to consider himself, "as out of the war, out of the picture, and thus, in a way, not an enemy" (quoted in Budiansky 2005: 34). The second was to know the subject's culture and language, not just superficially but deeply. "If you know anything about [their] history, art, politics, athletics, famous places, department stores, eating places, etc. a conversation may be relatively interminable" (35). Technical/ military knowledge was less important than familiarity with "idiomatic phrases and cultural references" which establish a rapport and social relationship – which demonstrate that the interrogator really knows them and wants to know more.

2. **Anthropology shows us what human beings really are**. All of the social sciences and humanities have one aim: to know humanity. However, almost all efforts to "know humans" before anthropology suffered from one fatal flaw: they took only one type of human – the researcher's own type – as typical. The only meaningful way to study a subject is to study the *range* of the subject. If the subject is human beings, then the only way to study them is to study them in all their diversity, physically and culturally. All of the diverse ways of being human are ways of being human. One's own way is not the only way, certainly not the natural way, not even the "best" way, since "best" is a judgment – and one that not all people share. The other flaw that has limited previous attempts to know humanity is the lack of awareness or concern for the "learning" or developmental aspect of human knowledge and behavior. Too many intelligent scholars of humanity have assumed, or written as if they assumed, that human individuals essentially invent their own realities independently or abruptly turn into spontaneous philosophers on their eighteenth birthday, after an irrelevant childhood. However, humans *become humans* very gradually and not at all independently, and the kinds of humans they ultimately become vary enormously. Only a view of humanity that emphasizes enculturation and cross-cultural comparison can grasp the true extent of human nature.

See Chapter 5

3. **We all live "anthropological" lives, whether we know it or want it or not**. Most people reading this book or taking an anthropology course will not go on to become professional anthropologists. Most students who take psychology or history courses do not become professional psychologists or historians either. But all of us living in the world today are and will be amateur anthropologists – every day, whether we like it or not, whether we know it or not. We can simply no longer assume that we will spend our lives in the company of people who think and feel and value and behave like we do. We will be neighbors, co-workers, friends, perhaps even spouses, but certainly co-inhabitants of the world, with people who are very different from

PLATE 1.3 The author standing in front of the Besaki Temple in Bali, 1988

us – who speak a different language, follow a different religion, have a different ancestry, belong to a different race, hold a different political view, and so on. We cannot eliminate this diversity, and we cannot condemn it, since that would encourage them to condemn us too. We have no choice but to accept it, appreciate it, and perhaps even enjoy it. This is not merely a matter of "foreigners" or people from obviously different countries and cultures than one's own. Americans cannot assume that all other Americans think and feel exactly as they do. Modern multicultural societies like the U.S.A. or the U.K. are too large and complex to expect everyone to have the same views, the same tastes, and the same understandings. Every encounter with another human being is (or has the potential to be) an anthropological encounter, one in which each participant has to determine what the others mean and how to communicate across the meaning gap. This may seem exhausting – and it often is – but it can also be invigorating and eye-opening. But mostly, it is just unavoidable. So, "culture" is not merely out there in remote villages and desert islands. Culture is what you do, and what I do, and what each human being does. And anthropology is how we make sense of it all.

4. Anthropology allows us – and compels us – to think about ourselves differently. The most natural thing in the world is to take one's own way of life as good, natural, even universal. Perhaps this was possible in the past, but no longer. Having seen that there are many ways to be human, each of us recognizes, has no choice but to recognize, that our way is only one of many. Other people, very different from us in numerous ways, get along fine without our beliefs and values and norms and rules. Further, we discover that, but for the grace of culture, we would have their beliefs and values and norms and rules: if we were born and raised in their society, we would be like them. We would be them. Even more, if culture is human-made, then *our* culture is human-made. Humans made it this way, humans keep it this way, and humans could (and did and will) make it some other way. Anthropology did not start out as "culture criticism," but it quickly opens that avenue. One's own culture, as certain and secure and "right" as it feels to oneself as a member of that culture, now appears as a fragile, ephemeral, relative, *constructed* "social reality" that is maintained only by transmission and by the concerted efforts of all its members. As Shakespeare said, we are all mere players on a stage, but we work together to keep the reality of the act (and the stage) going – and convincing.

BOX 1.3   CONTEMPORARY CULTURAL CONTROVERSIES: BANNING RELIGIOUS SYMBOLS IN FRANCE

As a consequence of its colonial history in Africa, France has a large resident population of North African Muslims. France also has a national history of stern separation of religion and state. On March 15, 2004 the French President enacted a law to ban from public primary and secondary schools the wearing of any religious symbol or garb that indicates the wearer's religious affiliation. The policy applied specifically to Jewish yarmulkes, Sikh turbans, large Christian crosses, and Muslim headscarves. Although the law was not aimed at any particular religion, Muslims – particularly Muslim women – viewed it as a direct attack on their religion, sparking street protests and national and international complaints about violations of religious freedom. Nevertheless, a member of the Australian Parliament, Bronwyn Bishop, recommended similar action in 2005, arguing that the Muslim headscarf "has become the icon, the symbol of the clash of cultures" – although Bishop stated no objections to crosses and yarmulkes. What do you think?

SUMMARY

Humans are diverse. Anthropology did not create this diversity but emerged as a response to and an investigation of it. Anthropology is thus the science of human diversity; it takes as its "question" or subject matter the full spectrum of human forms and ways and the explanation of that spectrum. The diversity that anthropology observes takes the form of bodily and behavioral differences, for which specialties within the field have been established:

- Physical anthropology to study diversity of the human body in the past and present.
- Archaeology to study diversity of human behavior in the past.
- Linguistic anthropology to study diversity of human language in the past and present.

■ Cultural anthropology to study the diversity of human behavior in the present.

In addition to its question, anthropology is distinguished by its perspective, or the approach or attitude it takes toward its subject. This "anthropological perspective" includes:

■ Comparative or cross-cultural study, or the description and analysis of the complete range of variation of humans and our ways.
■ Holism, or the interrelatedness of all of the "parts" of culture and of the culture to its natural environment.
■ Cultural relativism, or the awareness that we can make (useful) judgments of a culture only in terms of its own standards of good and normal and moral and meaningful and legal.

Most people in the modern world are not professional anthropologists (and none were until fairly recently in history). However, all of us today live "anthropological lives" in the sense that we will experience and deal with human physical and cultural diversity continuously, both locally and globally. Cultural anthropology can and should be more than an academic exercise in the examination of exotic or extinct peoples; it must also be a relevant and constructive commentator on and contributor to human existence in the twenty-first century.

Key Terms

Anthropological perspective	Ethnocentrism
Archaeology	Ethnography
Artifacts	Features
Cross-cultural study	Glocalization
Cultural anthropology	Holism
Cultural relativism	Linguistic anthropology
Culture shock	Physical anthropology
Ecofacts	Primatology

2 Understanding and Studying Culture

When I was in Australia for the first time, it took me a while to make my way into an Aboriginal community. In the meantime, I was fairly circumspect about who I told what I was doing there. One day when I was staying in a travelers' hostel, I told two older gentlemen also staying there that I had come to Australia to study Aboriginal culture. In response, one of them said, and I will never forget, "Aboriginals do not have culture, and they never did." I did not discuss my work with him any further. There are several possibilities about why he said what he said. One is that he was totally uninformed about Aboriginal peoples. Another is that he was a racist. A third – and the one that I hope is true – is that he was operating with a different definition of culture than I was and than anthropology does. Before anthropology was developed, and often still today, people tended to think of culture as referring to opera, symphony, and proper table manners: to be "cultured" was to have refinement or sophisticated taste. Even quite recently, scholars like the historian Matthew Arnold (1869) could characterize culture as "the best which has been thought and said in the world." This, however, is not the view that cultural anthropology takes, nor is it one that cultural anthropology can take. First of all, it is elitist: who is to say what is the "best"? Aboriginals do not have or perhaps care for opera, but they have corroborees and didgeridoo music. Second, it is exclusivist: on that definition, many – in fact, most – things that humans do would be excluded, since they are not the "best." Even the "second best" would not count, and "low" or "folk" or "popular" culture would certainly not count – and such was Arnold's intent.

"Culture" is an old word, derived from the Latin root *cultus* for "cultivated" and related to such words as cult and agriculture and other usages such as a bacteria culture. The common thread among them involves raising something or growing it into a particular form. In human society (which itself can be an elitist and exclusivist term, as in the "society page" of a newspaper, which reports the doings of "high society"), culture refers to how people are raised and formed to become the kinds of individuals who can take their place in that society. Therefore, anthropology uses the term in a non-elitist and inclusive way, to refer to all of the things humans do that are acquired during the process of maturing in a particular society. Sometimes scholars have used it in an even more inclusive sense, as the total social heritage of the human species, capitalized as Culture. But no single human being, nor even any single human society, possesses the sum total of the heritage of humanity. Rather, each person and group holds a part or version of that heritage, a culture that is similar to yet different from every other. Cultural anthropology focuses on these cultural particulars, without losing sight of the bigger question of the range and common-alities of particular cultures or of the forces and processes outside of a culture that impinge on it.

DEFINING CULTURE

Part of the methodology of every science is its vocabulary, its set of core terms and concepts. In physics these include mass, force, velocity, and momentum. Cultural anthropology too has its core terms and concepts, which, according to Evans-Pritchard (1962: 2), include "society," "custom," "structure," "function," and of course culture. Of these, culture is the most central. The problem is that there is no single official definition of culture. There are almost as many definitions of culture as there are cultural anthropologists; in fact, there are different fundamental approaches to a definition. One approach understands culture as primarily ideas or beliefs; that is, as essentially "in people's heads." From this perspective, we cannot really "see" culture but we can infer it from the behaviors people engage in. Another approach perceives culture as a set of real facts, albeit "social facts," regarding observable behavior and the products of that behavior, including the rules, groups, and institutions that shape people's lives. Culture can even refer to material objects like tools and houses. Ultimately, culture undoubtedly encompasses all three.

So there is no authoritative or universally shared definition of culture. But if there is a most influential and widely quoted definition of culture in anthropology, it is the one given by the early anthropologist/ethnologist E. B. Tylor in his 1871 book *Primitive Culture*. It is quoted here not because it is perfect or final but because it captures most of the components of culture and of cultural anthropology.

Tylor, E.B. 1958 [1871]. *Primitive Culture*. New York: Harper Torchbooks.

> Culture or Civilization, taken in its wide ethnographic sense, is that complex whole which includes knowledge, belief, art, morals, law, custom, and any other capabilities and habits acquired by man as a member of society.
>
> (1958: 1)

Culture, then, may be understood as those ways of thinking, feeling, and behaving, and the social and material products of those ways, which are shared among a group of people not on the basis of innate or physical traits but rather on the basis of common experience and mutual learning. This and Tylor's characterization of culture include several key notions which we could consider the classic qualities of culture:

- learned
- shared
- symbolic
- integrated
- adaptive.

Contemporary encounters with culture in the modern globalized context suggest that these standard features do not quite capture its full richness. In particular, culture is and always has been characterized by its "mobility (geographical and social), complexity, fragmentation, contradiction, risk, and disembedding" (Coupland 2007: 29). Therefore, we could and should add that culture, at all times and places but especially and crucially in the present moment, is produced and practiced through situated human action and that it circulates across social and national borders. This means that "a culture" cannot be simply and unproblematically ascribed to "a society" nor restricted to some clearly bounded territory.

Culture is learned

Culture is not something in our genes or brain or blood, or any other aspect of our body. No one is born with a particular language or religion or gender role or political persuasion or economic skill. Neither is any particular language or religion determined in any way by human biology. The evidence for this is simple: any human baby, given the experience, can speak any language, believe any religion, or practice any skill. Culture is not "in" humans in the sense that skin color, eye color, blood type, or height are "in" humans.

So, if culture is not "inside" the individual at birth, where is it? The obvious answer is "outside" the individual. Culture, at the moment of birth, is what is going on around the individual, what the people in his/her social environment are doing. Think of culture as a great, ongoing conversation (which to a large extent it is). When a person is born, the conversation is already in progress all around him/her. The new member does not create it and does not initially know how to participate in it. Gradually, s/he begins to participate – haltingly and imperfectly. Eventually, the person becomes a competent member and joins in the conversation. Perhaps in small or large ways s/he affects the content or direction of the conversation. Then, ultimately, each individual leaves the conversation for good. However, during his/her time, the person "kept it going." Even more, each individual served as part of the social environment for members born afterward, who experienced what the individuals in the group did and said and who learned to be competent and full participants in their turn, they too keeping the conversation going – maybe in old channels, maybe in new ones.

Humans, then, are not born with a culture but acquire one. That is easy to say but not so simple to grasp. What does it mean to acquire a culture? What process takes place from the learner's point of view – and from the teacher's? Anthropologists refer to it most often as **enculturation**, although it is also known as **socialization**. Basically, enculturation or socialization is the process by which a person masters his/her culture, ordinarily as a child.

While culture is not "in" humans at birth, it is "in" humans by the time they reach maturity. That is, culture "gets in" over time and by some means. Until recently, many scholars thought that the means was a straightforward process of observation, imitation, and reward and punishment. However, this account is insufficient. What humans appear to do is observe behavior, surely, not simply to imitate it but rather somehow to actively extract meaning from it, derive the rules or principles by which good language or good behavior is produced. In other words, culture learners are not passive recipients of cultural lessons but active constructors of their own cultural competence. Clearly, adults do not model every possible behavior for a child, nor do they directly and explicitly describe every rule and principle; adults do not have the time, and often they themselves do not know the principles or "grammar" of their own culture. Instead, they provide an environment in which and from which children actively "learn." In other words, to paraphrase Hans Freudenthal (1973), the acquisition of culture consists of a **guided reinvention of culture**. New humans must essentially reconstruct culture for themselves from their experiences, with of course the assistance and guidance of fully competent members of the group, who correct "mistakes."

What would happen if a human did not learn culture? What would a human without a culture be like? To conduct such an experiment would be unethical. However, a few "natural experiments" have occurred in which children were somehow separated or excluded from society and later discovered. Sometimes they were "lost in the woods" and grew up as "feral children"; sometimes they were deliberately abused, isolated, and allowed minimal human contact (see e.g. Maclean 1979). Regardless of the source, such children grow not into "natural" humans and certainly not into any particular kind of human – i.e., you would not expect to leave a child in a French forest and have him/her emerge as French – but rather as something "incomplete," not quite socially functional. They do not speak any language, profess any religion, or possess any social skills. And if they are discovered too late, they may never be able to fully acquire these human capabilities.

What this suggests is that culture is not an option, a superficial extra for a human like a coat that can be put on or taken off at will and without consequence. The American anthropologist Clifford Geertz has argued that culture is *necessary*: humans are "incomplete or unfinished animals who complete or finish ourselves through culture – and not through culture in general but through highly particular forms of

---

Enculturation
The process by which a person learns or acquires his or her culture, usually as a child. *Also known as socialization.*

Socialization
From an anthropological point of view, a synonym for enculturation.

See Chapter 5

Guided reinvention of culture
The process by which individuals, ordinarily children, "acquire" ideas, concepts, and skills actively by observing the behavior of others, extracting meanings and rules, and testing those meanings and rules in social situations; fully competent members "guide" the learning by providing models of behavior and correction for inappropriate behaviors.

Geertz, Clifford. 1973. *The Interpretation of Cultures.* New York: Basic Books.

it" (1973: 49). Other beings come more or less ready-made with a set of instinctive behaviors that suffice for them, although often not quite as completely as we think: predators like lions and birds of prey can and must learn how to hunt, and primates like monkeys and apes can and must learn how to parent. So humans are not the only species that depend on learning to complete their behavioral possibilities; humans just depend more urgently on this learning.

BOX 2.1   LIVING WITHOUT CULTURE – THE "WILD BOY OF AVEYRON"

In 1797 a boy was seen running, naked and on all fours, alone through the French forest. In 1799 he was captured and brought to Paris for observation and training. The boy, eventually named Victor, was described by Pierre-Joseph Bonnaterre, who, like others at the time, knew that they had come across something unique and important. In his report (Lane 1977: 35–54), Bonnaterre claimed that, while Victor did not walk on all fours, he also did not walk normally and "steadily" but rather rocked "from one side to the other" and that he never seemed to tire, no matter how long he ran. The boy's senses were "more like an animal than a man"; his senses of smell and taste were the most developed, the observer reasoned, because Victor would sniff foods before deciding what to eat or refuse. He seemed indifferent to cold. He had no language at all, making only "cries and inarticulate sounds."

> His expressive sounds, rarely emitted unless he is emotional, are rather noisy, especially those of anger and displeasure; when joyful, he laughs heartily; when content, he makes a murmuring sound, a kind of grunting. He does not utter raucous or frightening cries; almost all of them are guttural and depend only slightly on the movement of the tongue.

He was an intelligent child: presented with a mirror "he looked immediately behind it, thinking to find there the child whose image he perceived." However, he lacked "conventional" knowledge or morality: "While not wicked, he is not good, for he is unaware of both." He showed no glimmer of a religious or spiritual nature. Emotionally, he displayed excitement and agitation and anger but not love:

> he loves no one; he is attached to no one; and if he shows some preference for his caretaker, it is an expression of need and not the sentiment of gratitude: he follows the man because the latter is concerned with satisfying his needs and satiating his appetites.

Society

A group of humans who live in relative proximity to each other, tend to marry each other more than people outside the group, and share a set of beliefs and behaviors.

Culture is shared

Since culture is learned, it obviously cannot be a trait or possession of only one individual. Culture is "outside" the individual before it is "inside," and so it depends fundamentally on a community that "has" it or "does" it. We call such a community a society; that is, a group of humans who live in relative proximity to each other, are more likely to marry each other than members of different groups, and share a set of beliefs and behaviors. Culture, then, becomes the learned and shared ways of thinking, feeling, and behaving of the group.

It is not quite so simple, though. Surely, a single individual can originate something – a new behavior, a new word, a new style, a new invention, a new religion – that becomes culture. Surely also, an item of culture need not be *completely* shared within a society to qualify as culture. "Cultural" does not mean "shared by 100 percent of a society." But if not 100 percent, what is the quantitative cut-off point? Perhaps we must accept that culture is not exactly a quantitative thing. It is what is "more or less shared" within a society. The anthropologist Ralph Linton (1936) has suggested that culture consists of a variety of "modes" or "degrees" of shared-ness. Or rather, culture may not be so much shared as *distributed* (Figure 2.1). Some individuals and subgroups in a society know or do some parts, others know and do other parts. Yet it is all still culture.

Universals ←→ Alternatives ←→ Specialties ←→ Individual Peculiarities

FIGURE 2.1 Ralph Linton's modes of cultural distribution

Linton used the term "universals" to designate those things that all or the vast majority of a society do in generally the same way; a common language may be an example. "Alternatives" refer to things that some individuals or subgroups do in one way but other individuals or sections do in another way; different religions or cuisines within a society would qualify. Even less widely shared, "specialties" are things that some individuals or subgroups do while others do not do them (playing the guitar, for instance, which must be learned but is not learned by everyone). Finally, some capabilities and habits are very narrowly shared; such "individual peculiarities" may be practiced by one person or at most a small number of people. Some members of the group may even perceive such practices as "abnormal," but they are still cultural.

In this view there are many ways to be cultural. Culture need not be and often is not thoroughly shared within a society. For instance, priests probably know a lot more about religion than laymen do. Professional chefs know a lot more about cooking than amateurs do. Western societies are accustomed to the idea that cultural knowledge is "public" and available to all. However, not every society holds this view. Knowledge is often exclusive to a subgroup, a particular category of people, or even a single individual. In many religions there is the "popular" version of doctrines or rituals and the "esoteric" version for the worthy or the fully initiated. Among Australian Aboriginal societies like the Warlpiri, knowledge is systematically distributed. First of all, there is male knowledge and female knowledge. Some aspects of religion are public and open to all, but others are highly closed, to the point of death for revealing them. The secrets of male ritual knowledge are not only limited to men but to adult circumcised men. The secrets of women are likewise limited to fully initiated women. Of course, such knowledge is also stratified by age: young people will not and cannot possess it all, and they will achieve greater and greater "sharing" as they mature and prove their ability and worthiness. Finally, even knowledge that one is qualified to "hear" one may not be qualified to "speak." Some

Subculture
A group or subset within a society that is distinguished by some unique aspects of its behavior (such as clothing styles, linguistic usages, or beliefs and values).

knowledge is virtually private property, and no one but the rightful owner may perform it or transmit it. Certainly it must be transmitted if it is to endure, but only the owner may confer rights to others to perform it. Accordingly, no man or woman could in theory ever possess all the religious knowledge of a society, if s/he could in practice remember and master it all (see e.g. Morphy 1991; Bell 1993; Keen 1994; Dussart 2000).

Society then – especially a society of greater size and complexity – will consist of subgroups and sections with their own distinct knowledge, beliefs, values, norms, and so on. In traditional Plains Indians societies like the Cheyenne, various warrior associations had their own names and traditions and symbols and interests (Hoebel 1960). In modern Western society there are many **subcultures** and even

Counterculture
A group or subset within a society that more or less intentionally adopts behaviors, beliefs, or practices that are at odds with or opposed to the mainstream of society.

countercultures that vary from – often deviate from – each other and the "mainstream" culture. Certainly, an anthropologist would not want to study only tattooed and pierced skateboarders to learn about American or Canadian culture, but neither would an anthropologist want to ignore them. They would represent one "tributary" or "rivulet" or "current" in the cultural stream – one that belongs to the culture as much as any and sheds light on it as do all the others.

Culture is symbolic

Earlier we likened culture to a conversation. The analogy immediately suggests language; however, not all human communication is linguistic, and not all language is verbal (hearing-impaired people have a rich manual language in such forms as American Sign Language). What is really interesting and important about language in particular, and culture in general, is that it is a set of meanings based on the human capability and need to create and assign meaning.

Humans are beings who can and must "mean." No doubt other beings also "mean" sometimes. When a cat snarls and hisses, it means something. However, a cat apparently does not have to learn to snarl and hiss, nor do different cats in different places snarl and hiss differently. The gesture is natural or instinctive. When a fire gives off smoke, the smoke "means" that there is fire below, but the fire hardly has an intention to mean. The meaning is natural and objective, directly connected to the event that causes it.

Symbol
An object, gesture, sound, or image that "stands for" some other idea or concept or object. Something that has "meaning," particularly when the meaning is arbitrary and conventional, and thus culturally relative.

Symbols are things with meaning too. However, unlike the smoke of a fire or the hiss of a cat, the meaning of a symbol is added on, "bestowed upon it by those who use it," and this meaning "is in no instance derived from or determined by properties intrinsic in its physical form" (White 1940: 453). That is, a symbol's meaning is *arbitrary and conventional*, not immediate, natural, or necessary. As a symbol, the sound "dog" represents or means the familiar domesticated animal. However, the symbol does not sound or look like a dog. There is no obvious or objective connection between the sound and the creature. The proof of this is that different societies use different verbal symbols for the same creature – *chien* in French, *Hund* in German, *perro* in Spanish, *maliki* in Warlpiri, and so on. Any of these symbols

PLATE 2.1 Culture is composed of symbols, like these Australian Aboriginal artworks

works equally well, as long as users know the symbol and know that others know it. Similarly, a shake of the head can mean "yes" in one culture and "no" in another – and nothing at all in a third.

Certainly in many cases there is a contingent relationship between the symbol and its meaning. The cross as a symbol for Christianity is not utterly arbitrary, but it is not the necessary or only possible symbol, nor was it the first. Even more importantly, the cross *does not always* mean Christianity: other societies have used cross-like designs without "meaning" Christianity. Clifford Geertz called a symbol a "vehicle for a conception" (1973: 91), but what precise conception is loaded into what precise vehicle depends on the society and even the historical moment of that society. A dramatic example is the swastika, a symbol with very distinct meaning for most modern Western people. However, this ancient symbol has not always had its association with Nazism and Hitler; long before National Socialism was imagined, South Asians and some Native Americans used a similar design to convey radically different meaning.

Culture, thus, is a great meaning system – a "web of significances" in which we are suspended, as Geertz said. The symbols of a culture act like a lens, shaping the reality that is refracted through them. No human experiences the natural or social world except through the symbol-lens of culture, which no doubt affects how different peoples perceive and respond to their world.

Culture is integrated

Tylor opened his definition of culture by calling it a "complex whole." Any particular culture, that is to say, is not a single item or a homogeneous mass. Neither is it a jumble of loose parts. Rather, a culture is a system composed of many elements in some functional interrelation. Some of the early analogies for culture were highly "organismic," depicting culture as an organism with internal organs and organ systems. Although the metaphor goes a bit too far, it may be useful. Each part or domain of a culture, like each organ in a body, has its own particular function to perform, its own "job to do," even as each part contributes to the functioning of the whole. This position is known as **functionalism**. As a model it provides a way to conceptualize culture – internally differentiated, multiply functional, and structured. The specific structure in any particular culture may differ from another, but a structure of some sort is always present. That is, culture is a (loose) system – or better yet, a set of systems, a system of systems. As a research method it gives anthropologists something to look at or look for. Researchers can aim to identify the various parts, examine their separate functions or contributions, and relate them to the functioning of the whole.

Cultural anthropology has analyzed cultural systems into four rough areas of functionality. This does not mean necessarily that all cultures have equally articulated and formalized institutions of all four kinds, but it does mean that all cultures have four kinds of functions that must and will be performed by some means in the system. These areas of functionality or "domains" of culture include *economics*, *kinship*, *politics*, and *religion*. One way to visualize them and their interconnections is as four circles within the larger circle of culture (Figure 2.2).

Functionalism

The method, and eventually the theory, that a cultural trait can be investigated for the contribution it makes to the survival of individual humans, the operation of other cultural items, or the culture as a whole.

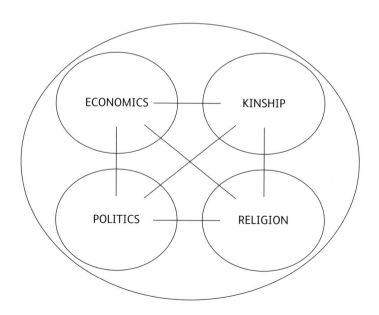

FIGURE 2.2 A model of cultural integration

Each domain is analytically distinct, but each is integrated with every other just as the parts of a car or the organs of a body are interrelated. In fact, the domains probably actually overlap each other, such that sharp lines between them cannot be drawn. No matter where cultural anthropology starts its research and analysis, it will be unavoidably drawn into consideration of all of the other domains. Even more importantly, the addition, removal, or modification of a part can and sometimes will have consequences for the functioning of the other parts and the whole – often unforeseen and undesired consequences.

Culture is an adaptation

Cultures and the societies that "have" them do not float in space. Every society and its culture exists in a specific physical context, an environment. That environment may be desert or jungle, volcanic island or arctic tundra, but each presents its unique practical challenges and opportunities. There may be too little water or too much, certain kinds of plants and animals, harsh and unpredictable or gentle and consistent climates, and so on. Most living species are highly specialized to live in a particular environment; even our primate cousins tend to need forest habitats to survive. Humans, on the other hand, are the most non-specialized, the most "generalized" of beings (see below). Because humans come with so little genetic or instinctive pre-programming (as Geertz stated), humans can be culturally programmed in nearly infinite ways. Where most living creatures adapt to their environments with their bodies, humans adapt with their behavior.

The adaptive power of behavior is a quantum leap above physical/genetic adaptation. Physical adaptation is slow; behavioral adaptation is fast. Physical adaptation is "chance" or random – that is, a species cannot will itself to have thicker fur or a bigger brain. Behavioral adaptation is intentional and "free" at least to an extent – that is, humans can innovate where they perceive a need. Anthropologists must not overestimate the creativity of humans: most people in most places and times have been much more imitative than inventive. Still, the overall creativity of humans makes it possible and inevitable that there will be many ways to be human. Finally, behavioral adaptations and inventions are simple to transmit across group boundaries and require nothing more than mutual observation.

So, the diagram of culture given in Figure 2.2 should set the society that bears it within some environmental context. Perhaps we should draw another, larger circle that encloses the circle of culture. Then, we can relate not only the domains of culture to each other but each of them and the cultural whole to its environmental setting. Again, without major inputs of energy and technology, the environment will be a limiting and shaping factor on how the society works, organizes itself, and even relates to the natural and supernatural world. In a word, culture is how humans get along in and with their external circumstances.

As with so many claims, anthropologists must be cautious about the adaptive quality of culture. For one thing, human societies are not always in harmony with their environments. It is something of a romantic fallacy to assert that pre-modern societies lived in perfect ecological balance, and it is clearly impossible to believe that modern industrial ones do. Australian Aboriginal hunters burned the desert flora, and Easter Islanders stripped their island bare. For another, when societies migrate, as they often do, they bring with them practices and values that may have been adapted to a former environment but are less adapted to the new one; over time, they may conform themselves more to the requirements of their new location, but not always or quickly enough. Finally, it cannot be said that culture is always advantageous for all of its members. Societies have engaged in practices and activities from war to slavery to human sacrifice to the destruction of twins that were certainly not beneficial to the victims of such behaviors. The perpetrators of such actions may have felt that the actions were good, even necessary (as in Aztec sacrifice, to keep the sun alive and strong), but this does not mean that the actions were good for all involved. In short, the "freedom" of humans enables them to engage in activities that are not always rational or healthful.

Culture is produced, practiced, and circulated

Too often social scientists and the public have labored under a static view of culture – static historically as fixed and unchanging (i.e., "traditional"), and static geographically as tied and limited to one "local" group or society. Members of a society tended then to seem like passive recipients of a discrete and settled culture, which we realize from our discussion above is untrue. Individuals and groups are active, in conjunction with larger scale entities, like corporations, organizations, and governments, in producing and reproducing – or altering or eliminating – aspects of culture.

The production of culture calls our attention to "how the symbolic elements of culture are shaped by the systems within which they are created, distributed, evaluated, taught, and preserved" (Peterson and Anand 2004: 311). This is easiest to see in the realm of arts, which are obviously produced, usually by a single person or small collection of people; however, it is equally relevant to science, technology, language, law, and religion – indeed, to all areas of culture. These production processes also link our descriptions of culture to issues of media- and culture-making and culture-disseminating technologies (e.g. recording, publishing, broadcasting), of markets (for the sale and purchase of cultural products), and of power (in terms of who owns and/or dominates these media, machines, and markets). Anthropologists have examined, for example, the uses of cinema in Peru (Himpele 2008), radio among the Ojibwe of Canada (Valentine 1995), and television in Aboriginal Australia (Michaels 1986; Deger 2006), among many others. The Warlpiri, to name one society, maintain an arts center (Warlukurlangu) and a television station (Imparja).

The production and reproduction of culture has consequently shifted focus away from "traditions" and "rules" to the *practice* of culture; that is, culture is presently seen less as a fixed body of knowledge or as a set of coercive rules than as socially structured action. Geertz was one of the first to suggest that culture is best understood not as abstract ideas nor as concrete behavior but "as a set of control mechanisms – plans, recipes, rules, instructions (what computer engineers call 'programs') – for the governing of behavior" (1973: 44). In this view, human activity and the groups and institutions that emerge from it are not simple instantiations of cultural "rules" but neither are they random results of "free" humans. Rather, according to Pierre Bourdieu (1977), who attempted to formulate a theory of practice, human behavior is an outcome of predispositions and strategies – acquired capabilities and habits, as Tylor put it – which are produced in the individual by culture and enculturation and then usually reproduced by the individual in culturally informed and culturally situated action.

Bourdieu, Pierre. 1977. *Outline of a Theory of Practice*. Cambridge: Cambridge University Press.

Cultural anthropology has been strongly influenced by the practice and production perspectives, which are clearly intimately linked. Together they offer to transcend oppositions like individual/culture and action/structure. The other common dualism is local/global, which is transcended by the notion of cultural circulation. Indisputably, an item of culture (a work of art, a piece of technology, a clothing style, a word, a song, a religion) is not trapped within the boundaries of a particular society. Culture circulates within a society – between regions, classes, generations, and so on – and between societies. Culture is mobile, along chains of migration and chains of exchange, and this is no recent fact: in pre-contact Australia, societies traded not only materials like stone and objects like axes but entire religious complexes (sets of rituals, myths, songs, and dances) and kinship systems. In the modern globalized world, the paths of exchange are only extended and accelerated, so that one finds blue jeans and rock'n'roll music in Aboriginal Australia and sushi and Buddhism in the U.S.A. and Europe. Culture flows, blending with or beating against elements already in place, and cultural anthropology has discovered that it must go with the cultural flow (see below).

See Chapter 11

Biocultural
The mutual interaction between physical/biological and behavioral/cultural factors, in which physical traits make certain behaviors possible, and behavior feeds back to influence physical traits.

THE BIOCULTURAL BASIS OF HUMAN BEHAVIOR

The diversity of human behavior proves that this behavior is not programmed in the human body in any precise way. However, the fact that all humans can and must learn culture, and that no other beings do or can learn culture fully, means that there is something about human beings that makes culture possible and necessary. Culture, that is, is constructed on a foundation of physical characteristics which, while they do not determine behavior in detail, set the general outlines for the kinds of behavior that humans can and must perform. This feedback relationship between biology and culture makes humans **biocultural** beings – not merely biological, but not merely cultural either.

The distinctive human physical traits are not entirely uniquely human but are generally shared by a category of species known as **primates**, which includes apes like the chimpanzee and gorilla, monkeys of various kinds, and the most "primitive" of

Primate
The term for the classification of mammals, including prosimians, monkeys, apes, and humans, that share a collection of physical characteristics including a distinct tooth pattern, five-fingered hands, a tendency toward erectness of the spine, large eyes and good vision, and a relatively large brain in relation to body weight, among others.

Prosimian

The category with the classification *Primate* that includes the least derived or "most primitive" species, such as lemurs, lorises, bush babies, galagas, and so on. Most have long tails and protruding snouts, but they exhibit other basic features of primates.

primates classified as **prosimians**. Primates are grouped together in the first place on the basis of these common characteristics, such as:

- Hands with five fingers and (usually) fingernails instead of claws, with an opposable thumb that makes grasping possible. The fingers have sensitive tactile pads on the tips, and the hands and feet (which are also "grasping" in orangutans) come at the end of very flexible limbs capable of a wide range of motion.
- Teeth that are varied and generalized, with cutting teeth in the front and grinding teeth in the back. There is even a regular pattern of teeth, consisting of two incisors, one canine, two premolars, and two or three molars on each side, top and bottom. The variety of teeth makes a varied and omnivorous diet possible.
- Large brains relative to body weight, with special development of the frontal and back areas. There is also an emphasis of eyes over noses on the face. Vision is acute, while the sense of smell is weaker. The result is a flattened face with large eyes.

Erectness

The tendency to have an "upright" posture based on a spine that is vertical rather than parallel to the ground.

- A tendency toward spinal **erectness**, with the head "on top of" rather than "in front of" the spine. This gives primates a relatively upright posture and a tendency toward **bipedalism** or walking on two feet.
- Relatively long lifespan, with a lengthy period of immaturity or "childhood," during which youths are highly dependent on and very interactive with parents as well as other members of the group.

Bipedalism

The ability and tendency to walk on two feet.

The combined effect of this constellation of traits is a kind of "freedom" or "openness" of behavior, an adaptability which most other species lack; primates are not highly physically specialized for any single way of life, which means that they – and we – are capable of diverse ways of life. The biocultural approach, and the evidence discovered through this approach, suggest not only that human physical characteristics make human behavioral characteristics (culture) possible but that *culture is not an "all or nothing" thing*. Humans have a great deal of it, but other species may have some measure of it too, depending on how human-like their biology is.

BOX 2.2 PRIMATE CULTURE?

In 1949 Japanese scientists began observing a troop of small monkeys called macaques on the Japanese island of Koshima and providing them with food. In 1953 one young female, whom the researchers called Imo, was seen carrying a sweet potato to a stream where she rubbed it in the fresh water. On subsequent trips to the stream, she waded deeper into the water and held the food with one hand while washing it with the other. Within three months, three other individuals began practicing the behavior, and by the end of five years 75 percent of the younger members of the group were habitual potato-washers. Only the old males did not adopt the behavior. But sweet potatoes are a big food that allows them to eat fast and flee. So observers decided to give them small foods like wheat or rice which the macaques would have to laboriously pick out of the sand. Imo once again outsmarted the scientists, inventing a new behavior in which she scooped a handful of sand and grains and carried it to the water, tossed it all in, and quickly skimmed the food off of the surface. This new solution also spread among most members of the group (Kawai 1965). No other population of macaques had ever been observed engaging in this behavior. What appeared to be going on here was the innovation and then learning and sharing of a new behavior as an adaptation to a novel environmental circumstance – the key qualities of culture. Since that time scientists in the field have noted many other kinds of "cultural" behaviors, such as tool-use and tool-making, and even some that appear to be "symbolic." For instance, in 1993 a young male chimpanzee dubbed Kakama was watched moving through the forest in Uganda with his mother and clutching a small log. At first he handled it the way a female handles a baby. He went to considerable trouble to bring the log along as they traveled, eventually stopping to build a nest in the branches, in which he placed it. Over the course of two hours, Kakama took the log everywhere he went, carrying it on his back or on his hip. At one point it fell to the forest floor, but he retrieved it. Wrangham and Peterson concluded that they "had just watched a young male chimpanzee invent and then play with a doll" (1996: 254–5).

Beings with bodies like primates are prone to engage in behaviors like primates. The most fundamental primate behavior is living in social groups. Other animals (and even plants) live in groups, but social groups are distinguished by their internal diversity of rules and roles – that is, different parts to play or "kinds of individuals" to be. One particularly clear and important expression of social behavior is **dominance** or hierarchy, in which some individuals have more status or social power than others. This can of course be based on sheer strength, but it typically is not. Such factors as age, sex (males are often but not always dominant), family relations, and "alliances" with other individuals can all enhance status and the likelihood of achieving leadership and enjoying its benefits, such as more and better food and mates. Indeed, as Frans de Waal's chimp "ethnography" *Chimpanzee Politics* (1998) suggests, primates engage in distinctly "political" actions when they are seeking or exercising power. There are even data to support the notion that sex roles in some primate societies are learned. Hamadryas baboons, for instance, live in male-dominated harems, while savannah baboons do not. When Hans Kummer (1995) transplanted Hamadryas females into savannah troops, the females initially acted submissive, only to discover that the males did not herd and bite them, and they quickly became as "free" as native female savannah baboons; on the other hand, freedom-loving savannah females placed in Hamadryas troops were bitten and herded by males and eventually "learned their place," although they still remained rebellious and hard to control.

There is reason to believe that primates not only enjoy being social but *need to be* social. The famous primatologist Robert Yerkes went so far as to claim that one primate is no primate at all (Lorenz 1963: 100). A series of experiments by Harry Harlow (1959) supports this position. He took baby rhesus monkeys and raised them in isolation. The result was often a "neurotic" monkey who cringed in the corner of

Dominance
The social relationship in which certain individuals have higher prestige or power in the group, allowing them to enjoy more or better resources as well as the deference of lower ranked members.

de Waal, Frans. 1998 [1982]. *Chimpanzee Politics: Power and Sex among Apes*, revised edn. Baltimore: Johns Hopkins University Press.

his cage and even rocked back and forth the way some disturbed humans do. When introduced to other monkeys, the response tended to be either fear or aggression but hardly ever successful social interaction. And if an isolated female became a mother (difficult enough, since mating behavior itself appears to be learned), she usually had little or no idea what to do with the infant; she would either be neglectful or actually aggressive toward it, often ending in its death.

Nonhuman primates demonstrate a range of other behaviors that are familiar and similar to humans. Among these behaviors are the following.

1. Aggression and territoriality. Primates tend to defend a specific territory or "home range" within which they move about but generally remain. Essentially, each local group within the species has its "borders" which it patrols and polices. Other local groups of the same species that infiltrate these borders may encounter aggressive resistance. An important aspect of primate aggression is intergroup or intraspecies aggressive behavior (IAB), which is defined as aggressive or violent interactions between two or more spatially separate, distinct, and identifiable groups by individuals acting as members or representatives of such groups. Johan van der Dennen (2002) has identified sixty-four species practicing IAB, of which fifty-four are primates. Most such aggression is "ritualized" and not fatal. Individuals will "display" with threatening gestures or sounds and perhaps tussle for a few moments until one realizes he is the loser of the encounter and runs away or displays submissive behavior, which ends the face-off. However, not all aggression concludes so peacefully, and the more human-like the primate, the more human-like the aggression. Jane Goodall, the pioneering primatologist who has observed chimps in the wild since the 1970s, reported what could only be called a war between two groups of chimps that had recently split apart. Over a period of years, the larger group hunted down the smaller splinter group and killed the males and killed or captured the females until the latter group was exterminated. She even calculated that approximately 30 percent of male chimp deaths were due to violence (Goodall 1986).

Goodall, Jane. 1986. The Chimpanzees of Gombe: Patterns of Behavior. Cambridge: Harvard University Press.

See Chapter 4

2. Communication and social interaction. While all animals communicate, primate communication is also unique in many aspects. For one, primates communicate visually much more than other species, given their evolved vision. When a primate encounters a novel situation, it explores the situation by *looking* rather than smelling. Primates also interact with each other and their world by touch more than most species, employing the sensitive pads on their fingers. One classic primate behavior is grooming or running their fingers through each other's hair. This is no doubt both hygienic and pleasurable, but it also has a social component: grooming shows and establishes affiliation, even affection. Friends groom each other, adults groom infants, and males groom females as part of courtship. Grooming behavior indicates or creates social ordering: lower ranking individuals tend to groom more dominant ones, unless the dominant one is seeking allies, in which case dominant ones may groom subordinates to win their favor. Chimps in particular will put their arms around others or pat them on the back to comfort them. They even appear to hold or shake hands and kiss hands, especially as an introduction between strangers. Bonobo or pygmy chimps are famous for their much more sexual touching which has little or nothing to do with reproduction; this touching even takes place within the same sex. Finally, primates communicate "orally" or with sound. Apes have even been shown experimentally to communicate "linguistically" (that is, to use "language symbols" like sign language or meaningful shapes and objects).

3. Eating and hunting meat. It was believed prior to the 1970s that chimpanzees were primarily vegetarian and that they might occasionally eat a small animal or bird but would not deliberately and systematically kill larger animals for meat. However, as Goodall witnessed, they not only eat and relish meat but also hunt for meat. In particular, they hunt monkeys, which are not easy to catch for the larger and more terrestrial chimps. Hunting such prey requires cooperation and coordination, foresight and planning. The hunters usually divide the assignment between those who will give chase through the branches and those who will pursue along the ground below. Together they try to steer the prey to a congenial spot for capture. A successful hunt is often followed by sharing or "politicking" with the resultant meat. Hunters may bring meat back to share with females and young, and they may share it with (or steal it from) other males to form or secure alliances. Successful males may occasionally keep all their catch to themselves, but the dietary advantage of such behavior is set against the social disadvantage of the selfish and "unfriendly" aspect of it.

4. Tool use and production. For a long time, it was supposed that humans are the only primates that use tools; in fact, the accepted definition of human was based on tool-use A few species here and there appeared to use tool-like objects as well, including otters that bash open mollusks with a stone, but these are not full tools. A tool is a natural object that is not only used but is made or modified for use to accomplish some task that the body cannot do or cannot do as effectively. So, when we smash a can of beans with a rock to open it, that is tool-like, but when we sharpen the rock to make a cutting edge for slicing open a dead zebra, we are making a true tool. Goodall was the first to document that chimps use and make simple tools. Chimps like to eat termites, but termites retreat inside their hard hills. Another animal would wait patiently or dig or try to insert a claw or tooth into the hole – that is, use its body – but chimps will search for a good-sized and -shaped branch or stem, trim and fashion it just so, and stick it into the hole, pulling it and the clinging termites out. This kind of "fishing" behavior requires not only mental skills like imagination and foresight but a dexterous and grasping hand. Since that time, primatologists have watched chimps and a few other primates using stones or sticks to hammer nuts, leaves to scoop water, and chewed leaves to soak up juices from their meat. Even more interestingly, they have noticed regional diversity within a given species of primate; that is, chimps in one location have been seen learning and practicing one set of behaviors, while members of the same species in other locations have their own distinct local "cultures." In the laboratory, chimps have shown powerful cognitive abilities in using and combining objects to achieve goals (e.g. stacking boxes to reach bananas hanging from the ceiling, or using keys to unlock

Australopithecus

A genus of the category Hominid, closely related to and earlier than genus Homo, to which modern humans belong.

Homo habilis

An extinct human species that lived from over 2 million years ago until less than 2 million years ago. They are also known as the first stone toolmakers.

Homo

The genus that contains the modern human species (*Homo sapiens*) as well as several other extinct human species.

Oldowan

The earliest known stone tool technology, associated with *Homo habilis* and named for the location of its discovery, Olduvai Gorge in East Africa.

Homo erectus

An extinct human species that lived from approximately 1.8 million years ago until a few hundred thousand years ago or perhaps even more recently.

Acheulian

The stone tool technology associated with *Homo erectus*, which involves a more complex flaking of bifacial implements.

Homo sapiens

The species name for modern humans.

chests with food inside). There is little doubt that the more we give primates to think about and do, the more they will surprise us with their intelligence and ability.

Finally, just as culture as a general phenomenon or capability is apparently not all-or-nothing, neither is human culture in particular all-or-nothing. Rather, what we see in the fossil and archaeological record is that as humans developed into their present-day physical form, something like present-day culture gradually but inexorably emerged. For instance, the most ancient well-documented category of pre-human species is called **Australopithecus**, which includes the famous Australopithecus afarensis, known popularly as "Lucy." Living three or four million years ago, these pre-humans already had some key human traits like upright bipedal walking and smaller teeth but also some primitive traits like a small brain (no larger than an ape). There is no firm evidence that they made or used tools.

Around 2.5 million years ago, a new species, designated **Homo habilis**, commenced the category or genus called **Homo**, which would eventually include modern humans. This species, its descendants, and their key physical and behavioral characteristics are as follows.

1. **Homo habilis**. They possessed a larger brain than Australopithecus afarensis, up to half of modern size (600–700 cubic centimeters versus 1,200–1,400 for moderns). They showed the first firm evidence of stone tool-use and manufacture, based on a simple stone chopper, called **Oldowan**, made by hammering one stone with another to produce a cutting edge.

2. **Homo erectus**. First appearing around 1.8 million years ago, **Homo erectus** is another advance in brain size, reaching two-thirds or more of modern brain mass (1,000 cc). They were also the first species of fossil humans to migrate out of Africa, eventually reaching most of Eurasia (where they are popularly known as "Peking Man" and "Java man"). They developed a more sophisticated stone tool technology called **Acheulian** in which the entire surface of the stone was chipped to yield a symmetrical "bifacial" tool. They apparently used fire and may have also constructed rudimentary shelters.

3. **Archaic Homo sapiens**. By around 600,000 years ago, the first **Homo sapiens** appeared, although they were not quite the modern human species of today. Their brains were equal to or larger than modern, and their bodies were similar enough to be placed in the same species. They lived in many parts of Eurasia, where they had regionally diverse behavior and in some cases probably language. The best known of the archaic Homo sapiens populations is the **Neandertals**, a local group that inhabited Europe and the Middle East starting about 130,000 years ago. They had large bodies and brains, and their behavior was remarkably sophisticated. They made new and better tools, called **Mousterian**, which included a variety of implements specialized for particular purposes, with more "finishing" of the tools. Most notably, there is evidence from various sites of intentional burials, suggesting some symbolic abilities and perhaps some "beliefs" about death and after death. Some anatomists conclude that they had the anatomy for speech.

4. Modern Homo sapiens (anatomically modern humans). As long ago as 200,000 years, the first fully modern Homo sapiens appeared, probably in Africa. They migrated to the rest of the world, displacing the Neandertals in Europe by 35,000 to 40,000 years ago. Their tools and culture were no more advanced than other species originally, but since 30,000 years ago or so, their – or our – cultural development has been rapid. Soon they were producing realistic paintings, often on cave walls, as well as carving and jewelry and other "arts." New "composite tools" (made of multiple parts, like an arrow or a spear) distinguished their technology, as well as fast-changing and regionally diverse technologies and cultures. No doubt they had fully functional languages and belief and meaning systems comparable to those found in any society today. Students of early modern humans agree that, if one of them could be brought to the present day, he or she would resemble and learn to act like a normal modern human.

Neandertal
The species or subspecies of Homo that first appeared around 130,000 years ago and is associated with the cold climate of Europe. They became extinct in the last 35,000 to 40,000 years and are generally not regarded as direct human ancestors, although this interpretation is still somewhat controversial.

Mousterian
The stone tool technology associated with Neandertals, first appearing less than 130,000 years ago.

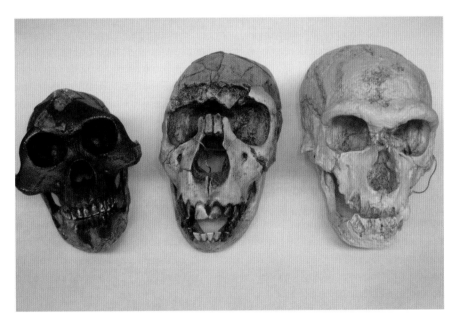

PLATE 2.2 Hominid fossil skulls (from left to right): Australopithecus afarensis, Homo erectus, Neandertal

STUDYING CULTURE: METHOD IN CULTURAL ANTHROPOLOGY

The discussion of anthropology in this book began by introducing its distinct questions, its distinct perspective, and its distinct set of terms and concepts. But in order to answer its questions, to put that perspective into action, and to employ those terms and concepts, cultural anthropology also needs a method. How exactly do cultural anthropologists go about answering their questions, in particular collecting the data they require to solve the problems that they have set themselves? The social sciences have a battery of tried-and-true data-collecting techniques. These include surveys, interviews, questionnaires, experiments, and of course analysis of the data that other social scientists have already collected. Cultural anthropology would be remiss to ignore these techniques. However, none of them, nor all of them in concert, are adequate to accomplish what cultural anthropologists want to accomplish. Imagine, for example, that you wanted to learn about Nuer cattle-herding culture in Africa or the Japanese tea ceremony. What would you do? You would probably first read every available book, watch every available movie, talk to every available researcher and traveler that/who might provide some information. One vast limitation of this procedure is that you would not learn anything new; there would be no opportunity for original discovery.

Seeking new knowledge, you might design a survey or a questionnaire to probe the issues you want to understand. So now what do you do with it? There being so few Nuer or Japanese nearby, you would have to send it to them by mail or e-mail. You might find that very few receive mail or e-mail, even fewer read it, and fewer still respond. Besides, they may not speak your language, and they definitely do not know who you are or why you are asking these strange and perhaps personal questions. Even if they did receive it and cared to respond, they might find the questions invasive, or they might be inclined to tell you what they think you want to hear or what makes them look good. It is possible that you would not ask the right questions to begin with, and it is highly possible that you would not understand the information you received anyway.

Or, to bring the example even closer to home, imagine that a cultural anthropologist wanted to learn about the life of students at a college. The problems are roughly the same. Students at the college might not respond, or perhaps only the "good" ones will respond (giving a skewed sample). Knowing that the researcher plans to publish and share the results, and that the findings may come back to affect them, the students may lie or admit only the positive parts of their behavior. And the anthropologist still may not really understand the results that come back from the subjects. In order to overcome the limitations of these techniques – whether in remote or familiar contexts – a cultural anthropologist has only one real choice: to go and live among the subjects.

Fieldwork

The anthropological method of traveling to the society one wants to study and living there for a prolonged period of time to collect data first hand.

Anthropology solves this problem with **fieldwork**. All sciences depend on some manner of fieldwork. Geologists go out and dig rocks. Paleontologists go out and excavate fossils. Marine biologists go out and observe ocean life. The thing they have in common is *going out*. Accordingly, anthropologists cannot complete their research in a library or classroom; a person can study *cultural anthropology* in the classroom (that is, what anthropologists have done and learned from it) but not *culture*. Culture is where the practitioners of that culture are.

So anthropologists go to the "field." They could take their surveys and questionnaires with them, recruit a sample of volunteers, and administer the tests to them. The researcher could get closer, perhaps find a house near the subjects and sit on the porch and watch them go by, perhaps even invite them to sit on the porch too. The researcher would see where the people are going and what they are doing, but would that necessarily provide any understanding of what is going on?

Cultural anthropologists have discovered that the only way to acquire a serious, deep understanding of the lives of other people is to place themselves as much as possible within those lives. This is known as **participant observation**. Participant observation is the truly unique and original aspect of cultural anthropology. Anthropologists go to live among the peoples they study, but more than that, they go to live *like* the peoples they study. No other social science does quite the same thing, although some have adopted the method on occasion. The first step in successful anthropological fieldwork is learning the local language. This is critical not only because most of the locals will probably not know the anthropologist's language but because even if they do, their ideas and concepts possibly cannot be properly conveyed in another language. A language, like the cultural whole of which it is part, is a lens for seeing the world. Forcing them to function in the anthropologist's language is forcing them to reshape, perhaps fatally distort, their thinking into something that is familiar to an outsider. For instance, it would be easier for an English-speaking anthropologist to force the local people to interact in English, but there would be something – maybe something critical – "lost in translation." It is much better to learn their words for things, their concepts, and their realities. There are often no exact equivalents for their words and ideas in English or other foreign languages.

Learning the language is not only a necessary step but it is a good way to earn one's way into the society and to spend time with them. An anthropologist will eventually want, and if lucky be able, to visit with them, travel with them, work with them, even live with them. They are not coming to the anthropologist's world; the anthropologist is going to theirs. The goal is to eat their food, perform their tasks, participate in their rituals. In this way, cultural anthropology is the most intense and personal of the sciences. No other research takes such a commitment of one's life. An astronomer may spend every night for weeks peering through a telescope, but at least s/he goes home, takes a shower, and sleeps in his or her own bed. Anthropologists may not even have showers or beds where they do their studies. Often there is no going home for a long time. A typical fieldwork experience may take a year or more. And usually, a professional anthropologist goes back to the field periodically to see what new things have transpired, what s/he missed before, or simply what one cannot learn in such a "short time." Some anthropologists take their families with them, but most travel alone. Depending on how far away the society is, the anthropologist may not see friends or family during the entire period. The work can also be physically challenging: climate extremes (most of the world's small-scale societies live today in the most inhospitable environments), natural dangers, strange food, exotic diseases, few amenities, few or no facilities in the event of injury. It can be lonely and isolating.

But if all goes well, the anthropologist slowly wins his or her way into the confidence and friendship of the people. S/he may even be "adopted" into a family, given a kinship name, and assigned local responsibilities. This is not easy to achieve or to perform. Generally the local people do not know the anthropologist when s/he first arrives. It would be like someone coming to your neighborhood, knocking on

Participant observation
The anthropological field method in which we travel to the society we want to study and spend long periods of time there, not only watching but joining in their culture as much as possible.

Structured interview

A fieldwork method in which the anthropologist administers a prepared set of questions to an informant/consultant.

Unstructured interview

A fieldwork method in which the anthropologist conducts a relatively free-flowing conversation with an informant/consultant, either without prepared questions or unconstrained by these questions.

Genealogy

Kinship or "blood" and "marriage" information about a society.

Shostak, Marjorie. 1983 [1981]. *Nisa: The Life and Words of a !Kung Woman*. New York: Vintage Books.

your door, and asking to live in your house for a year or two. New people are always strangers first, friends later (if they are lucky). And anthropologists depend on that friendship – sometimes to keep them fed, always to keep them informed. An anthropological fieldworker needs at least a few good informants or consultants, people who will take the time and effort to explain their culture. That sounds very scientific, but it is not. Informants/consultants are the people who like and trust the fieldworker well enough to want to take time from their busy lives to talk to the stranger, answer silly questions, and teach their ways. In an essential way, the informant/consultant is a teacher. Likewise, anthropologists in the field are students, virtually children. Many local people consider anthropologists to be literally like children – petulant, demanding, prone to error (see e.g. Briggs (1970) for an unusually honest account of the foibles of fieldwork). The analogy is not bad: if anthropologists are like children, then anthropological fieldwork is like enculturation. The fieldworker is learning the culture "from the inside."

Once in the field, there is a variety of activities in which the researcher can engage. S/he may still administer his or her surveys and questionnaires. Interviews are a standard technique in the field, either in a **structured** (with the questions prepared in advance) or an **unstructured** (unplanned and free-flowing) format. It is always important to collect genealogical information, not only because anthropologists need to know who is related to whom and how, but because kinship and **genealogy** are so central to the organization of most societies. Commonly anthropologists will collect oral histories, either biographies of individuals or accounts of the history of the group; a well-told life story can shed light on a society far beyond the experiences of that single individual (see e.g. Shostak (1983) for a classic biography of a hunter-gatherer woman). And a few anthropologists, especially in the early twentieth century, carried formal tests (for instance, psychological and "projective" tests, like the Rorschach "ink blot" test) into the field to measure specific cognitive or perceptual tendencies and to compare these with other traditional societies and with their own.

Often enough, even the best-prepared anthropologist will encounter two surprises: (1) the things that s/he came to study are not the really important things, and/or (2) s/he does not even know what the right questions are at first. By jumping into the society and its culture, by taking his or her place in its structure, the researcher gets a better idea "on the ground" of what should really be studied. Most fieldwork diverges from its initial plans when it confronts the reality of the new culture, and this is fine: one cannot know what one will find, or what will be important to consider, before arriving in the field. But if there is one critical fact to remember, it is that anthropological fieldwork is a relationship, and the knowledge an anthropologist takes home is a product of those relationships. S/he will have talked to specific people at specific times in specific contexts, and each anthropologist as an individual brings a certain quality to the experience. Cultural anthropology is science, but it is also a personal encounter between human beings.

Fieldwork in a globalized world: multi-sited ethnography

The classic image of anthropological fieldwork is the solitary researcher sitting in the forest or desert with an isolated "primitive" tribe. This approach may have been, and may still be, appropriate in certain times and places. However, increasingly this sort of "village anthropology" – or what we might call more technically "the intensively-focused upon single site" style of observation (Marcus 1995: 96) – is inappropriate and inadequate in many contexts. Local cultures, or subcultures or classes or ethnic groups and so on, are affected by and implicated in wider networks of institutions and relations, including "media, markets, states, industries, universities" (97), from the regional to the national to the global level. In a real sense, not all of the culture that influences the people under investigation, and therefore not everything that the anthropologist wants or needs to know, is "in" the local society. Accordingly, "in response to empirical changes in the world and therefore to transformed locations of cultural production," fieldwork methods have also changed.

The most interesting and important shift is toward "multi-sited ethnography," which literally takes the fieldworker to multiple physical locations in order "to examine the circulation of cultural meanings, objects, and identities in diffuse time–space" (96). For instance, the anthropologist may move from the village to the city to the factory and beyond, even to the national and international levels.

Multi-sited research, Marcus writes, is premised not on enclosed societies and cultures but on "chains, paths, threads, conjunctions, or juxtapositions of locations in which the ethnographer establishes some form of literal, physical presence" (105). The fragmented and mobile quality of such work reflects the fragmented and mobile quality of modern global culture. Instead of becoming rooted in one place, the anthropologist travels through a discontinuous sequence of "positions" or "scapes," guided by a set of imperatives – to follow the people as they migrate and circulate, the "things" (commodities, money, cultural products such as art), the ideas and metaphors and narratives, the lives and life stories, and the conflicts (106–10). In this practice, fieldwork itself, and the reporting on culture, becomes both local and global, truly glocal.

The ethics of fieldwork

Anthropological fieldwork is a "social" activity in a way that no other science's method is. The fieldworker has injected him/herself into the lives of other people – often people who do not know him or her, want him or her there, or particularly want to help him or her. In an earlier era an anthropologist could often rely on a colonial administrator to order the "natives" to accept and assist a stranger. Those days are for the most part long gone. In many parts of the world, local peoples have acquired at least some modicum of control over their lives, so outsiders cannot just barge in and expect the locals to do their duty as "anthropological subjects" and informants. At the very least, they may ask, "What's in it for us?" and at the very most they may say, "Go away!" I was personally told to get the Warlpiri's permission before entering their community or face the prospect of being marched straight out of town.

Participant observation by definition puts researchers skin to skin, life to life, with "subjects" who are living people. That fact demands a particularly self-conscious code of ethical behavior. At the minimum, this includes "Do no harm," and increasingly includes "Ask first." At the highest level, it includes "Make a contribution" (perhaps an opportunity and call for more applied anthropology) and "Consider your own impact on them."

In the contemporary context, fieldwork usually commences with some form of permission from the local society; for such purposes, institutions like community governments or the regional associations, such as the Aboriginal "Land Councils" in Australia, have been established. By now most well-known traditional societies have been studied repeatedly, and the locals know what anthropologists want and what the arrangement will be like. Some members are warm to the idea, some not. An anthropologist should never expect to make friends with every member of the society, any more than people expect to make friends with every member of their own society. A few friends are worth the world in the field.

In the field, it will be necessary, and desirable, to abide by their rules and norms as much as possible. They usually understand that the foreigner is not one of them; the anthropologist is an outsider, a stranger, a child. Sometimes a fieldworker will arrive with the reputation (often nothing to do with that individual personally) of an oppressor, colonizer, or at least of the last bad anthropologist who passed through. On the other hand, s/he may benefit from a previous positive experience with an anthropologist, as I did in one community: the famous Jane Goodall had been there long before, and they assumed that I knew and worked with her. Accordingly, one evening a man walked me around the settlement, introducing me as the "anthropology man" and friend of Ms. Goodall. At any rate, the local people frequently know that anthropologists come to learn their secrets and publish those secrets for the world to see. They may understand that anthropologists come for their own career advancement. They know that the fieldworker will stay for a while and leave, maybe never to return again. In ways, they know the outside world better than the outside world knows them.

Having obtained permission somehow (the "somehow" will depend on the circumstances of each field experience), it is obligatory to be as honest as possible about why the anthropologist is there. If s/he has come to study religion, the locals should not be told that s/he merely wants to "learn the language" or some other neutral excuse. Some anthropologists have shown their research notes to the local people before leaving or before publishing them, but that is not always possible or politic, especially in the case of sensitive or personal data. But one must always remember that some of them can read English or other world languages and will see what is written about them – in case the writer ever wants to come back again. In addition, there is value in showing them these notes and analyses in advance, because they may be able to correct or interpret certain items that have been misunderstood or misinterpreted.

There is no ignoring the fact that much of the world today is a battleground and that many fieldwork settings are tense and dangerous. If an anthropologist wants to do fieldwork among refugees, for example, or in a war zone, or among a "terrorist" or insurrectionist population, life will be more complicated and research will be more sensitive. They may perceive the outsider – rightly or wrongly, intentionally or unintentionally – as a threat, a "security leak," even a spy. I was personally accused by one man of being a spy for the CIA on one occasion (falsely, as it turns out), but their concern is real enough. They never know who foreigners are really sent by, what foreigners will do with the information, or who else might see it.

One way that anthropologists have traditionally handled the problem of "co-operation" is by giving gifts, trading, or paying for information. All of these practices have their issues. Giving gifts to some people and not others can create jealousy and hurt feelings, as well as inequalities in the society that may have never existed before. Trading is a good idea but can become expensive, and saddle the researcher with lots of stuff that s/he doesn't really want; it can also upset the local economy, as they begin to produce goods for trade rather than for consumption. And paying for information can undermine the friendship aspect of fieldwork, although it is some-times necessary and desirable. Fieldworkers may even want to "hire" an informant, translator, or travel companion.

In the contemporary context, one of the best exchanges for information – while also being a great way to learn – is offering some useful service that the local people need. (Ironically, this can also foster dependence and resentment.) For example, many indigenous societies have been involved in land claims or "development" struggles (for example, over dam projects or mining, or similar related issues) for decades, and many anthropologists have helped by researching culture (land tenure, political organization, kinship structure) and organizing these data for presentation to courts or governments. Along the way, scholars have learned many valuable things about these and other aspects of the culture by being so intimately involved with real-life practical matters. It has been good for the local people and for scholarship. At the same time, it is important that the fieldworker not "go native" and lose him/herself among the locals. This means, among other things, that visitors should probably not get too intimately involved in their daily lives, especially sexually. Like any professional, one must maintain a certain distance from one's clients or subjects. Often this is hard: one may be inclined to intervene in domestic matters, to introduce one's values, medicines, or other practices. Each situation will be a judgment call, and each person must be his or her own judge. But there are lines that should not be crossed, and a trusty rule of thumb is this: after the anthropologist has left, the local people still have to live there. We can walk away, but they cannot. Do not leave things worse for them and for the next anthropologist who may visit.

See Chapters 14 and 15

In the end, it is unavoidable that one will have some impact on the society one lives with. These days, the impact may be fairly light, as many major changes have already long since occurred. The introduction of new tools and technologies, new ideas and concepts, new diseases, even the mere awareness that there is a bigger world out there with strange-looking and strange-acting people in it irretrievably

See Chapter 11 and beyond

PLATE 2.3
Bronislaw Malinowski
conducting fieldwork with
Trobriand Islanders

www.aaanet.org/
committees/ethics/
ethics.htm

changes local peoples. Anthropologists can neither force them to alter their ways of life nor prevent them from doing so, but anthropologists and all other outsiders can never forget the fact that we ourselves are agents of change. The ethical guidelines that have been adopted by the American Anthropological Association are available on their website.

BOX 2.3 CONTEMPORARY CULTURAL CONTROVERSIES: STUDYING KENNEWICK MAN

"Kennewick man" consists of a skull and a few bones discovered on the banks of the Columbia River in Washington State in 1996, but he touched off a scientific, political, and cultural firestorm. Some anthropologists (e.g. Chatters 2002) concluded that the remains were those of an ancient Caucasian – much more ancient than any known in North America. This announcement was met with concern by Native American activists, who saw it as an attempt to debunk their claim to original settlement of the continent. The local Umatilla society filed a claim to take possession of the bones, since the Native American Graves Protection and Repatriation Act (NAGPRA, 1990) allows Indian societies to demand return of their artifacts and physical remains. Scientists insisted it was their right and duty to study the materials and that NAGPRA did not apply, since the skeleton was not Native American. The Umatilla and others countered that such treatment was desecration of their ancestors, that science was invasive and disrespectful, and that the political uses of Kennewick man could be detrimental to their rights. What do you think?

SUMMARY

The questions and the perspectives of anthropology lead almost inevitably to its concepts and methods. Central to cultural anthropology is the idea of culture – that humans are not born knowing and doing all of the things that we see them do. Rather, from the experience of human diversity, anthropologists have determined that culture is

- learned
- shared and distributed
- symbolic
- integrated
- an adaptation.

In the modern global context, it is increasingly clear and important that culture is also produced, practiced, and circulated.

While culture is not "in" the body in any particular way, human physical characteristics make cultural behavior possible – that is, human behavior has a two-part biocultural basis. Therefore, culture is potentially not exclusive to humans. Beings with physical traits similar to humans have behavioral traits similar to humans, and as humans gradually acquired their present traits, their behavior became more recognizably cultural.

Anthropology has developed special methods for collecting the information that it needs to answer its questions. The most fundamental method is participant observation, during which researchers may perform a variety of activities. Everything that anthropologists do includes some degree of interaction with "subjects" who are real human beings, and fieldworkers must conduct that interaction ethically, aware that they are humans too and that their actions will have impacts on the people in that society.

Key Terms

Acheulian	Genealogy	Oldowan
Australopithecus	Guided reinvention of culture	Participant observation
Biocultural		Primate
Bipedalism	Homo	Socialization
Counterculture	Homo erectus	Society
Enculturation	Homo habilis	Structured interview
Erectness	Homo sapiens	Subculture
Fieldwork	Mousterian	Symbol
Functionalism	Neandertal	Unstructured interview

3

The Origins of Cultural Anthropology

The Persian Empire under Darius encompassed a wide variety of different peoples and cultures, as did all ancient and modern empires. According to a story recounted by the Greek historian Herodotus, Darius once summoned some Greek and some Callatian (Indian) subjects to appear before him to explain their burial practices. The Greeks said that they cremated their dead, whereas the Callatians reportedly consumed theirs. Darius asked the Greeks if they would ever eat their dead, which mortified the Greeks. He then asked the Callatians if they would ever burn their dead, at which suggestion they "uttered a cry of horror and forbade him to mention such a dreadful thing." Herodotus concluded from this and similar experiences:

> if anyone, no matter who, were given the opportunity of choosing from amongst all the nations in the world the set of beliefs which he thought best, he would inevitably, after careful consideration of their relative merits, choose that of his own country. Everyone without exception believes his own native customs, and the religion he was brought up in, to be the best; and that being so, it is unlikely that anyone but a madman would mock at such things. . . . One can see by this what custom can do, and Pindar, in my opinion, was right when he called it "king of all."

> (Herodotus 1972: 219–20)

No doubt Herodotus was not the first person to notice that humans differ in their beliefs, their values, and even their bodies over space and time. However remote and "backward" they may seem, no society in the history of the human race has probably been so isolated that they did not have neighbors who varied from them in language, religion, and other customs. Even so, as abundantly obvious as human diversity is, and as attentive to such details as Herodotus was, neither he nor most societies went a step further to organize a systematic study, a science, of human diversity. Herodotus came very close, and his insights seem convincing to this day, but no such thing as anthropology was created in his day or for many days afterward. Finally, in passing, Herodotus was wrong about one thing: given a choice between one's own customs and some other society's, usually there is no "careful consideration of their relative merits." If you were given the choice between burying and eating your dead, would it really require – or even allow – weighing the two options? Rather, our customs are often so deeply ingrained in us that the preference is automatic and strong – like "second nature."

WHAT MAKES CULTURAL ANTHROPOLOGY POSSIBLE – AND NECESSARY

Strangely, or not so strangely, humans have only recently thought to do such a thing as cultural anthropology: for most of human history (and most human societies today), there has never been anything even remotely like cultural anthropology. This is not to say, as mentioned above, that humans were never before aware of behavioral differences between themselves and other groups, nor that they never pondered these differences. However, mere awareness of the otherness – of what we sometimes call the "Other" (remembering that each of us is the other to everyone else) – is not cultural anthropology, and throughout history most societies have not proceeded from acknowledgment of other humans to a science of human otherness.

Let us begin, then, with two statements that are true and important: anthropology is a very new science, and anthropology is a very unlikely science. The first of these claims is easy enough to understand and defend. Until about a hundred and fifty years ago (and maybe considerably less), there was nothing like cultural anthropology, or any other kind of anthropology, in the pantheon of human sciences. Some social and natural sciences, from history and philosophy to mathematics and physics, are ancient. Anthropology is easily the last of the major social sciences to emerge, and what we recognize as modern cultural anthropology assumed its form only about a century ago. Why was this discipline so late to appear on the horizon of human inquiry?

The answer relies on the second statement: something about anthropology must be very unlikely. That is, anthropology is an unlikely thing to do, an unlikely way to think. Philosophy is fairly unlikely, yet recognizable philosophy was being done over two thousand years ago as a result of certain people making certain kinds of observations and asking certain kinds of questions. By looking around at the various cities and states and their political forms, something like political science was fairly obvious. By looking around at the events occurring before and during one's lifetime, something like history was fairly obvious. By looking at the sky and the stars, something like astronomy was fairly obvious. By looking at objects in motion, something like physics was fairly obvious. But by looking at other human societies, something like anthropology was apparently not fairly obvious.

Why is this? Why did observation of human diversity not lead to a science of human diversity? The best way to think about this is to consider not the observations themselves but the responses to the observations. Human diversity has always been an acknowledged fact, but what humans do with – or about – that fact is another matter entirely. Clearly, anthropology is not the default response. Rather, the default or first response seems to be some combination of:

- indifference toward the Other
- fear and hostility toward the Other
- judgment and condemnation of the Other
- desire and/or effort to eradicate the Other, either through conquest or "conversion"
- rejection of the Other as less than one's own kind – and sometimes less than completely human.

These attitudes are immanent in most of the surviving records we have from past societies, ancient and not so ancient. Other societies were typically regarded as "savages," "barbarians," "infidels," "primitives," "uncivilized," "evil," and so on. To be different was to be bad, to be wrong. This is distinctly not a perspective from which cultural anthropology will grow.

As with Herodotus, there were some near-misses in the ancient world. The Greek philosopher Xenophanes observed the difference and the relativity of religion across cultures:

Ethiopians have gods with snub noses and black hair, Thracians have gods with gray eyes and red hair. . . . If oxen or lions had hands which enabled them to draw and paint pictures as men do, they would portray their gods as having bodies like their own; horses would portray them as horses, and oxen as oxen.

(quoted in Wheelwright 1966: 33)

Ultimately, the ancient Greeks never developed an anthropological science, rather seeing people unlike themselves as "barbarian" and "uncivilized." This situation is much more common than one might think. In the contemporaneous Torah/Old Testament, non-Jews were idolaters, sinners, and evil-doers; no serious possibility of acceptability without believing in the "right" god and practicing the "right" culture was entertained. Medieval Christianity and Islam, as well as most other religious and cultural traditions, did no better. In fact, there are probably two recurring obstacles to the very possibility of something like cultural anthropology:

- Absolute certainty in the truth and goodness of one's own culture (ethnocentrism).
- Lack of information about other societies, or poor or patently false information about them.

Certainty in one's own truth and goodness, a kind of "one-possibility thinking," is characteristic of most societies, traditional or modern. Cultural certainty is a barrier to relativism and thus to cultural anthropology, since only one kind of thought is permitted or at least valued highly; all others are by definition false or unacceptable. Why then would you want to know more about those barbarians, those infidels, those blasphemers?

Lack of information or possession of poor information poses its own challenge. If you do not know much about another society and culture, it will be difficult to say anything meaningful and useful about it. The first thing you will naturally try to do is to assimilate the Other into your own schemes of understanding. This led to some amusing if not depressing results. For example, even the most hard-headed medieval Europeans could not ignore the fact of anomalous archaeological features in their own territories. Saxo Grammaticus, writing in the twelfth century about the enormous stone edifices of Denmark, opined that "the country of Denmark was once cultivated and worked by giants. . . . Should any man question that this is accomplished by superhuman force, let him look up at the tops of certain mountains and say, if he knows how, what man hath carried such immense boulders up to their crests" (quoted in Slotkin 1965: 6). Even into the sixteenth century men of good conscience still struggled with the signs of otherness in their midst; of the Paleolithic and Neolithic artifacts scattered around Europe, Ulisse Aldrovandi said that "they were natural accretions developed by geological processes," Conrad Gesner "that they were thunderbolts. Stone projectiles were usually called 'elf arrows' or 'thunderbolts' by laymen" (quoted in Slotkin 1965: 44). In yet other cases, unexplainable but obviously non-Christian phenomena were either ignored or dismissed as demonic. Much more recently, the devoutly Muslim Taliban destroyed enormous Buddhist statues rather than allow those idols to corrupt Afghanistan.

Now, attribution of stoneworks and artifacts to giants and elves might launch a science of giants and elves, but it is not likely to launch a science of human diversity. In fact, it *cannot* do so, since no connection is drawn between those objects and humans; rather, such opinions led observers *away from* humanity and from a science like cultural anthropology. Humans do what we do; giants and elves – non-humans – do those odd and remarkable things. And if that is not bad enough, the reports of "monstrous races" that persisted from ancient times right up to the late Middle Ages in Europe were the tombstones of a stillborn anthropology.

Slotkin, J.S., ed. 1965. *Readings in Early Anthropology*. London: Methuen & Co.

BOX 3.1 THE "MONSTROUS RACES" OF THE PRE-MODERN WORLD

From the Greeks through the Romans to the medieval Europeans, travelers and scholars spoke and wrote about various pseudo-human if not non-human races such as:

PLATE 3.1 A Blemmyae, one of the "monstrous races" of ancient and medieval literature

- Amazons, warlike women who amputate their right breast so as to better draw a bow
- Amyctyrae, beings with such large lower lips that they can use them for umbrellas
- Androgini, who have the sex organs of both men and women
- Antipodes, beings who walk upside-down
- Astomi, people who have no mouths and are covered with fur. They survive by smelling food.
- Blemmyae, creatures who have no heads but have faces in their chests
- Bragmanni, who stand all day in fire staring at the sun
- Cyclopes, beings with one large eye
- Cynocephali, people with dog-heads
- Panotii, beings with ears that dangle down to their feet
- Sciopods, people with a single huge leg and foot, who lie on their backs and shade themselves with their foot
- And the usual panoply of pygmies, giants, hairy men and women, and cannibals.

More amazing still, writers described them as if they were real, as if the reporters had seen them for themselves, even producing maps illustrating where each monstrous race dwelt – Astomi in east India, Blemmyae in Libya, Bragmanni in India, Cyclopes in Sicily and India, and so on. A full accounting would show that these races tended to inhabit the East (India), the North (the Baltic and Arctic regions), and the South (Africa) – everywhere that was remote and exotic to Europeans except the West, where no people lived since the world was believed to end there (see e.g. Friedman 2000).

ENCOUNTERING THE OTHER

As colorful as these descriptions are, it must be apparent that such a state of knowledge is not conducive to a serious discipline like cultural anthropology. First, if these beings are as weird and unpleasant as they sound, no one is going to be inclined to study them. Second, if they are not human at all, there is little light they could shed on humanity. Third and most dramatically, fear and revulsion will tend to keep people far away from them.

At some point this all had to change if anthropology was ever to emerge. So the question for us is, what is it that makes a science like anthropology possible? And more than just possible but necessary? What kind of society can, and must, enter upon a line of inquiry that will end with the birth of anthropology – and not specifically the science of anthropology so much as the anthropological perspective described previously? Obviously, it will be a society that has lost or at least shaken its own cultural certainty as well as one that has accumulated a body of accurate and useful information about the Other. This will inevitably depend on and follow from a new and sustained kind of encounter with the Other. That is, someone does not say, "Let's invent anthropology" and then start to seek out different forms of humans. Instead, one first bumps against different forms of humans and then, gradually and grudgingly, comes to a point where one is doing anthropology.

The time and place where these conditions began to coalesce was Europe *circa* 1500. Around then and around there, a series of discrete yet interrelated developments began to force not just an awareness but a curiosity, even an appreciation, of otherness on observers. Among these new experiences were the following.

The "voyages of discovery" and the rise of colonization

The most familiar and prominent new factor in late medieval Europe was the "discovery" of new lands and new peoples in places where lands and people were not known or even imagined. Europeans had long known of other societies – Muslim, African, Asian – but the encounter with Native Americans and the vastly greater number of African, Asian, and eventually Australian peoples met by European travelers opened their eyes to a diversity that was previously undreamed of. Yet, as exciting (and profitable) as all this discovery was, it presented a psychological and cultural challenge. Who were these people? How did they get all the way out there? In fact, were they people at all? As incomprehensible as that question sounds to us, to early explorers it made sense and even forced itself on them. For the Christian Bible did not mention these natives. Were they descendants of Adam and Eve, like the Western Christians and supposedly all humans? If so, why did they look and act so differently? But if they were not descendants of Adam and Eve, then what were they? Animals? Degraded humans? Creations of Satan? Or, just as bad, creations of some other god?

The question of the humanity of the "Indians" was quite a serious one. Within decades of Columbus' arrival in America, there was a significant debate within the

Catholic Church as to the identity of the natives. Were they human or not? What this meant was, did they have souls or not? The "conservative" position was that they did not have souls and therefore were not human; if this were the case, then they could be classified and treated as animals (also believed to have no souls) – chased off, carried away, enslaved, or killed as suited the conquerors. The "liberal" position, championed by Bartolome de las Casas, was that they did have souls and therefore were human. If this were the case, then they deserved "humane" and "Christian" treatment – they could not be killed or enslaved wantonly. But neither could they be left alone; their human souls required "saving," and they deserved and needed the benefits of the "true" culture and the "true" religion. The Church finally decided in 1537 that the Indians were humans and ordered that they be dealt with in a humane way, but this did not stop the ravages and abuses to which they were

See Chapter 12 and beyond

subjected by administrators, missionaries, soldiers, traders, and settlers.

The exploration of the late 1400s and early 1500s, which continued into the late 1800s, brought new otherness to the attention of Europeans who were well satisfied with the truth and goodness of their own society. This was the kind of otherness that is "out there," far away and intellectually manageable, but still an ideological and religious problem. The sheer volume of it – hundreds and hundreds of new societies with their own languages, religions, and complete cultures – was daunting but thought-provoking.

Encounters with other Eurasian civilizations

"Primitive" societies were a problem of sorts but the kind of problem that visitors could ignore or excuse most of the time. Other "advanced" societies were a bigger problem. Since at least the 1300s, European adventurers had been traveling to and bringing back reports from distant civilizations like China, the Islamic world, and India. Marco Polo is a well-known example, whose descriptions of splendor in China were at first taken as fiction. Even earlier, the Crusades (in the twelfth and thirteenth centuries) had gotten Europeans far from home and into exotic new places where they saw the wonders of Constantinople, Syria, and Mesopotamia. They could not help but notice that these societies were not only different but in some inescapable ways superior to their own. The Eastern civilizations were often more urban, more literate, richer, more "cultured," and more powerful than anything in Europe. This should not be: Europe supposedly had the "true" religion and culture. The foreigners were idolaters, infidels, devil-worshippers. Yet they had things that Europeans valued and desired and would acquire and utilize – not the least of which were block printing and gunpowder.

So, the experience of these travels and conflicts showed not only that other civilizations existed and were different but that they were "better" in some ways. Otherness could not be laughed away as inferiority; there were things the Other did better and things the newcomers needed to learn from them.

The "Renaissance"

The so-called Renaissance of the fifteenth and sixteenth centuries refers to a "rebirth." What was coming "back to life," and what had been dead or moribund for centuries in Europe was city life, literacy, long-distance trade, and the widespread exchange of ideas that marks the modern world and marked the ancient world. After the fall of Rome, cities had dwindled and disappeared, literacy had retreated to the monasteries (or at least books had – often monks could not read them but copied them by rote), and a subsistence level of agriculture tying serfs to the land and to the lords who owned the land ossified culture and stultified diversity. What little art and literature existed was made for and about the dominant class, culture, and religion.

The Renaissance was thus a rebirth of a specific cultural model and progenitor, namely ancient Greece and Rome. Europe had always maintained a vague dream of Rome but knew little about it. Ancient texts had long been lost, and the ability to read what remained suffered as well. Meanwhile, the Islamic world had preserved the works of Plato and Aristotle and others, studied them, advanced them, and incorporated them into their civilization. With the Crusades and the subsequent (ambivalent) trade relations with Islam, Europe rediscovered its ancient texts and began to familiarize itself with its own ancestry. Of course, the assumption had always been that, while the Greeks and Romans could not possibly be Christians, they were in some way "pre-Christians" or "proto-Christians." Medieval Europeans knew that Plato talked about an ideal world of perfect forms, which sounded a lot like heaven to them. They simply presumed that the ancients were a lot like them.

However, the reality was considerably different – and considerably more disturbing. Greeks and Romans had their own very distinct, and very non-Christian, religions. They had their own political systems, kinship systems, economies, and so on. Reading ancient texts was not like reading texts from one's own time; the ancients lived in a very different mental and cultural world. Many of the ideas and styles were very appealing, but they were most definitely foreign and other. But this meant that Europe's own ancestors, their own forebears, exhibited otherness. It was one thing to face the Other across the ocean; Europeans could disregard or belittle that difference. It was worse to face the Other in a rival civilization; they could not be ignored, but they could be resisted. But it was deeply troubling to face the Other in one's own ancestry, in one's own family tree. Early modern Europeans found that their own ancestors were Other to them.

The "Protestant Reformation"

Since the establishment of Christianity as the official religion of Rome and then of post-Roman Europe, there had been only one official truth about religion, which was the Roman Catholic truth. All other opinions about religion were "heresy," from the Greek word *hairesis* meaning "to choose." One did not choose one's own views and truths but received them from authority. Of course, there had always been disagreements about those truths, but those disagreements were always settled by and in favor of authority. So, reform had been repeatedly attempted and thwarted over the centuries, but Martin Luther's movement escaped that fate. It caught on, much to the consternation of the authorities. Luther claimed (often in the most shocking language) that the Church was wrong about many of its beliefs and was actually anti-Christian. He called the Pope and all Catholics blasphemers and atheists, and he said he could prove it: just go back to the "source," to the Bible itself. To assist, he produced a German translation of the Bible.

The Protestant Reformation introduced a schism into Christian Europe that would not go away, no matter how hard anyone tried. And they tried hard. Religious wars tore apart Europe for years, until a peace was declared, allowing the two "religions" to co-exist. Note that the peace did not allow all religions to exist, only Catholicism and Lutheranism. Other "protestant" sects such as Unitarians, Shakers, Quakers, Anabaptists, as well as non-Christian religions like Judaism, were still out of bounds. But two religions are much more than twice as many as one: one is monopoly, two (or more) is diversity. When the compromise broke down, resulting in the Thirty Years War (1618–48) and millions of deaths, a new peace recognized *three* religions – Catholicism, Lutheranism, and Calvinism. Europe was never again to be a homogeneous, one-possibility place. Religious diversity was here to stay, despite everyone's best efforts. No one had wanted multiple religions; the Catholic Church wanted just one (Catholicism) while Luther wanted just one (Lutheranism). Instead, what they got was not two, not three, but hundreds and hundreds. Westerners were now, and would forever be, the Other to each other.

The scientific revolution

The so-called scientific revolution drew its inspiration from many of the same sources as the above and had many of the same consequences. Like Luther, people were taking it upon themselves to "go to the source" and verify the claims and beliefs of the time. In this case, the source is the natural world. Science did not say then, and does not say now, that all authorities are wrong. It merely says (1) that you must cross-examine authority or tradition, that you cannot accept a position simply because it comes from an authority or tradition (in other words, you must be skeptical, no matter what the source of the claim); and (2) that you must base your conclusions on careful and sustained observations of external reality. This can mean experimentation, or it can mean merely the collection of empirical data from the natural world.

While the intent was not and is not to challenge and defeat all received opinion and tradition, the consequence was and is to stop taking mere authority as an authority. They have been wrong before, and they could be wrong again. The ultimate authority is one's own experience and observation: if traditions or rulers say one thing but experience suggests another, then a person should trust experience. So, if tradition says there are dog-headed people out there but observation reveals none, we should conclude that there are not dog-headed people out there.

RETHINKING SOCIETY: SEVENTEENTH- AND EIGHTEENTH-CENTURY SOCIAL THEORY

By the middle and end of the seventeenth century, European scholarship and society were in ferment. The old certainty, while not vanquished, had been shaken and cracked. It was no longer possible to delude themselves that theirs was the only society in the world nor even the best society in the world. It was perfectly obvious that their own society was full of problems – crime, vice, inequality, injustice, hunger, poverty, war, and other socially undesirable circumstances. Criticizing one's own society became an increasingly common thing to do, although often in indirect and fictional ways, like Thomas More's *Utopia* or Jonathan Swift's *Gulliver's Travels*. One necessary prerequisite of any social criticism, let alone any social change, is an alternative. If not this, then what? Is it possible for society to be better? Is it even possible for society to be different? And where would a model for another possibility come from?

A model appeared at that moment: all those "primitive societies" that had just been "discovered." Actually, two views or models of the primitives eventually emerged based on the same experiences – the "brutish savage" and the "**noble savage**." The former model is represented by the political philosopher Thomas Hobbes. A pivotal moment in European history arrived when one of those "Protestant" sects, the Puritans, staged a revolt against King Charles I that led to his execution (1649). No contemporary European society had ever attempted such a radical social experiment, and many thought it could not succeed, including Hobbes, who argued for the need for a strong central government like the old monarchy. To prove his point, he employed primitive societies as his example of a world without govern-ment. In his famous *Leviathan* (1651) he characterized primitives as living "in a state of nature" without society or government, which might sound like a good thing: everyone was equal, but they were also solitary. Humans did not interact with other humans, not peacefully at any rate. Because all were equal, and totally independent from each other, competition and conflict naturally followed.

Hobbes never set foot in a "primitive society," and his judgments of them are at best based on second-hand accounts if not pure fantasy. His opinion was clearly negative: probably the most quoted phrase in his entire work describes the quality of primitive life as "solitary, poor, nasty, brutish, and short." Whether it is true or false (and it is mostly false), it is important for taking non-Western societies seriously. Hobbes had established that those remote and exotic societies are not irrelevant, not mere objects of curiosity and derision, but important windows on to the human condition – perhaps into the past of our own condition. This was not anthropology just yet, but it was a real (if troubled) step in that direction.

The "noble savage" model is most closely associated with Jean Jacques Rousseau, author of *The Social Contract* (1762). In certain ways, he compared "savages" favorably to his own countrymen and institutions, finding in them the very archetype of free and natural humanity. He too saw them as living in a "state of nature," independent and equal, enjoying "the peacefulness of their passions, and their ignorance of vice." He contrasted their "natural existence," distinguished by instinct,

Noble savage

The notion, often associated with Rousseau, that non-Western or "primitive" people are actually happier and more virtuous than Westerners. Based on the idea that humans are free and equal in "a state of nature" but that social institutions deprive them of that freedom and equality.

amorality, appetite, natural liberty, and individual strength, to his own "civil society," with its formal justice, morality, reason, civil liberty, and public will.

Of course, Rousseau's image of primitive society is as simplistic and stereotyped as Hobbes'; there is no such thing as "natural man," since all humans are cultured and none live in a state of raw nature, and there is no such thing as "savage society" but a rather a staggering variety of traditional cultures – from the happy to the miserable, from the peaceful to the warlike. In addition, he was by no means recommending a return to the primitive state but merely pointing out the two possible states of humanity and the costs of evolving from one to the other.

BOX 3.2 BRUTISH SAVAGE VERSUS NOBLE SAVAGE

In *Leviathan* Hobbes wrote:

From this equality of ability arises equality of hope of attaining of our ends. And therefore if any two people desire the same thing, which nevertheless they cannot both enjoy, they become enemies; and . . . endeavor to destroy or subdue one another.

Hereby it is manifest, that during the time men live without a common power to keep them all in awe, they are in that condition which is called war; and such a war, as is for every man, against every man.

In such a condition, there is no place for industry; because the fruit thereof is uncertain; and consequently no cultivating of the earth; no navigation, nor use of the comfortable buildings; no instruments of moving, and removing, such things as require much force; no knowledge of the face of the earth; no account of time; no arts; no literature; no society; and which is worst of all, continual fear, and danger of violent death; and the life of man solitary, poor, nasty, brutish, and short.

In *The Social Contract* Rousseau wrote:

Although, in this state [civil society], he deprives himself of some advantages which he got from nature, he gains in return others so great, his faculties are so stimulated and developed, his ideas so extended, his feelings so ennobled, and his whole soul so uplifted, that, did not the abuses of this new condition often degrade him below that which he left, he would be bound to bless continually the happy moment which took him from it for ever, and, instead of a stupid and unimaginative animal, made him an intelligent being and a man.

Rousseau was clearly not doing anthropology – we would never call our subjects "stupid and unimaginative" – but his perspective was different from anything we have seen before. Rousseau and Hobbes and others like them took the Other seriously, declaring them a worthy – even a necessary – subject of study and discussion. And Rousseau's view, while not much more realistic than Hobbes', was definitely more positive: not only were there things to learn about distant societies, there were actually things to learn *from* them. Contemporary Westerners could admire them and wish that Western culture was, in some ways, more like them.

TOWARD AN ETHNOLOGICAL SCIENCE IN THE NINETEENTH CENTURY

Approaching the nineteenth century, we do not find anything yet that is quite recognizable as modern anthropology. We do, however, begin to see the foundations on which such a science will grow. First, the cultural certainty of Europe has been challenged, though not destroyed. In fact, the nineteenth century was a particularly ethnocentric period, partly a cause and partly an effect of the new phase of industrial colonialism and the relations between (white) Europe and the (non-white) colonies. But even that was a mixed blessing for what would become anthropology, since this prolonged contact between the two worlds provided the second ground for the new science – more and higher quality observational information about non-European societies. It is no coincidence that a discipline like anthropology – or "ethnology," the study of culture or ways of life – would develop at this moment, in relation to colonial administration, which provided the access to other societies and the practical utility of knowledge about them.

See Chapters 12 and 13

   Out of the wealth of new information came a desire if not the need to classify it and arrange it in some sensible order, and thus to "explain" it. Writing years later, Evans-Pritchard defined ethnology as the project "to classify peoples on the basis of their social and cultural characteristics and then to explain their distribution at the present time, or in past times, by the movement and mixture of peoples and the diffusion of cultures" (1951: 4). The questions asked by early ethnologists, then, were largely *historical and geographical*: how are cultures related to each other (and to Western culture), where did these relations come from, and what was the ultimate source from which they all flowed? In other words, how did Culture as a whole or particular cultures or specific institutions and practices within cultures originate, and how did those things change over time into their various manifestations, including the "modern" Western one?

   Two similar but different answers emerged. One was **diffusionism**, the idea that Culture (with a capital "C") had originated once or at most a few times and then spread from that center or those centers of origin outward to other locations on the globe. This approach was expressed in the German *Kulturkreis* ("culture circle") school of thought that envisioned culture as one or more circles emanating out from their center(s) like ripples on a pond. The greater the proximity between societies in space, the greater the similarity in culture. The center was identified sometimes as Egypt, sometimes elsewhere, but the idea of following the ripples "backward" in space suggested the possibility of following them backward in time as well – back to the first culture.

   The other approach, especially after the mid-nineteenth century, was evolutionism. In this view, the observed cultures descended from one or more

Diffusionism
The early ethnological or anthropological position or theory that Culture, or specific cultural practices, objects, or institutions had appeared once or at most a few times and spread out from their original center.

"ancestral" cultures, passing through various stages or phases of cultural development along the way. Whether there was a single (unilinear) series of cultures or several independent (multilinear) series was an open question. Either way, cultures had a "history" which could and should be reconstructed. The goal was to arrive at a set of cultural types or stages that would describe the actual process by which cultures evolved from one state to another – something like a timeline with different cultural types attached to certain moments in time.

However, how would nineteenth-century ethnologists go about this research? It was impossible to board a time machine and return to selected moments to observe the culture. All that was available was the present. Fortunately for cultural researchers, they thought they saw all around themselves "survivals," traces, virtual living fossils of those earlier days still in existence – "primitive societies." Since they could not study time, they could study space and project it onto time, that is, convert geography into chronology. By taking the various primitive peoples of the world today as representatives, if not actual frozen specimens, of days gone by, they could rebuild the history of culture.

Different ethnologists arrived at different solutions to the problem at hand, but all of the solutions shared certain features. For one, they arranged the observable societies "in order" of evolutionary progress. The "simplest" or "most primitive" naturally filled the "lower" and earlier spots; Australian Aboriginals were a common candidate for that honor, as Emile Durkheim concluded in *The Elementary Forms of the Religious Life* (1915). What, he asked, was the first kind of religion, or what is the most minimal, elementary form? It is the Aboriginals, who have totems and rituals but no gods or institutionalized practices and offices like modern European/Christian ones. Ethnologists would disagree on the precise order of stages and the precise choice of representative for each stage, but the general idea was fairly standard. Thus, Lewis Henry Morgan (1877) distilled the stages of cultural evolution down to three – savagery, barbarism (each subdivided into lower, middle, and upper), and civilization – characterized by certain diagnostic cultural features (e.g., bow and arrow, farming, writing). "Progress" was based on technological achievement (the threshold from savagery to barbarism was the invention of pottery, for instance), a standard which was important to Westerners and in which Westerners excelled. And of course, "civilization" was his own society – nineteenth-century Euro-American culture.

Durkheim, Emile. 1965 [1915]. *The Elementary Forms of the Religious Life*. New York: The Free Press.

Morgan, Lewis Henry. 1877. *Ancient Society, or Researches in the Lines of Human Progress from Savagery, through Barbarism to Civilization*. New York: Henry Holt and Company.

THE TWENTIETH CENTURY AND THE FOUNDING OF MODERN ANTHROPOLOGY

There are a number of objections to the ethnological, diffusion/evolution approach to culture. That it is ethnocentric is one: observers took themselves as the "end" or "goal" of culture, and compared all other cultures to themselves. The more unlike "us" they were, the further down the scale they went. That it is not particularly useful is another: even if the evolutionary order is correct, *why* do cultures evolve, and why did those surviving fossil cultures *not* evolve? Both of those objections troubled subsequent scholars, but another objection that bothered them as much or more was that it is so speculative: theorists did not know anything concrete about the past of those societies (or, at the time, even much about the current cultures of those societies), so they were merely speculating or worse. Other later critics would complain that, more than guessing, (white European) ethnologists/anthropologists were *using* (non-white non-European) natives as objects for their own selfish ends. There is some merit to that complaint. But for now, the point is that by the turn of the twentieth century, a few observers were despairing of the ethnological/historical approach. Two men in particular would turn from it vehemently and put their stamps on the new science of cultural anthropology. They are Franz Boas and Bronislaw Malinowski.

Boas (1858–1942) is widely regarded as the father of modern cultural anthropology. Trained originally in Germany in the late 1800s as a physicist and geographer, he brought a keen observer's eye and a strict scientist's method to the new science he shaped. In the 1880s he came to the Arctic coast of North America to study the color of sea water. While working there, he inevitably became acquainted with the local Inuit (Eskimo) people; soon, he realized that they were even more interesting than sea water, and not at all "primitive." He soon turned his back on the nineteenth-century "comparative" model as inaccurate and ethnocentric; as a scientist, he knew that to judge or evaluate your subject is to not observe or understand it adequately. By this decision, he essentially invented cultural relativism.

PLATE 3.2 Franz Boas, one of the founders of modern anthropology, posing for a museum exhibit around 1895

One of Boas' first and most important statements about what would become anthropology was his 1896 paper "The Limitations of the Comparative Method of Anthropology," first published in the journal *Science*. In this classic essay, still read in anthropology, he proposed that there are no "higher" or "lower" cultures and that all such judgments are merely relative to one's own standards of culture. Thus, any "ranking" of cultures is suspect from the outset and probably says more about the student than about the cultures studied. He went on to state that the similarities or differences between cultures are not as significant as diffusionists and evolutionists think because widely separated cultures can arrive at similar adaptations due to environmental factors. Rather than ordering cultures on the basis of supposed progress or similarity, he recommended actually observing each single culture in maximal detail and each single part of a culture within the context of the whole. Thus, he gave voice to holism. He emphasized that the goal of this science should not be the construction of elaborate and speculative cultural histories but rather the careful and accurate description of individual cultures through intense and objective observation. This observation would require personal, close-up experience with the culture for prolonged periods of time. When he settled into his academic position in America, he became the teacher and mentor of the first generation of American anthropologists. Thus, he essentially invented American anthropology.

Bronislaw Malinowski (1884–1942) did his work slightly later than Boas but has probably had an equally profound influence on the discipline, if only because Boas was so resistant to the idea of making any theories of culture. Boas in particular insisted that the data required to make good theories were still lacking, so any proposed theory would be premature. It would be better to collect data now – do the "science" now – and make theories later. But of course a science, even in its infancy, cannot proceed without theory. Theory helps to identify the question, suggest the method, and organize the evidence. Accordingly, Malinowski proposed one that would become extremely influential in the first half of the twentieth century.

Malinowski got his start in anthropology by accident, as did Boas. Originally trained in math and physics in Poland, he turned to the science of humanity after reading James George Frazer's ethnological classic *The Golden Bough* in 1910. *The Golden Bough* has affected many readers since it appeared in 1890 and is perhaps the "gold standard" of the nineteenth-century comparative project. Frazer took examples of myth and religion from all around the world and juxtaposed them in a fascinating but decontextualized way; on any one page, he could alternate from Mexico to Madagascar to India to Greece and back again. However, the cultural setting or context of each of these references was not and could never be developed by this procedure and in the space allotted to it.

Malinowski's exposure to the comparative and evolutionary method came at a time when a few scholars had begun to call for more in-depth knowledge and description of particular societies. Boas had helped inspire this approach, and by the turn of the century expeditions were setting out intentionally to collect cultural data – a team from Cambridge to the Torres Straits in 1898 to 1899, another to India in 1901 to 1902, still another to Melanesia in 1907 to 1908. The future anthropological star, A. R. Radcliffe-Brown, made such a trip to the Andaman Islands in 1906 to 1908. However, most of these visits were extremely short (often only a few days), were conducted by people who were not specially trained in anthropological field methods (since such methods did not really exist yet), and necessarily involved working through interpreters and acculturated local people.

However, by this time some scholars like W. H. R. Rivers were beginning to recognize the need for and to call for more "intensive" research, which he defined as research:

> in which the worker lives for a year or more among a community of perhaps four or five hundred people and studies every detail of their life and culture; in which he comes to know every member of the community personally; in which he is not content with generalized information, but studies every feature of life and custom in concrete detail and by means of the vernacular language. It is only by such work that one can realize the immense extent of the knowledge which is now awaiting the inquirer, even in places where the culture has already suffered much change. It is only by such work that it is possible to discover the incomplete and even misleading character of much of the vast mass of survey work which forms the existing material of anthropology.
>
> (quoted in Kuper 1983: 7)

Kuper, Adam. 1983. *Anthropology and Anthropologists: The Modern British School*, revised edn. London and New York: Routledge.

Malinowski was one of the main figures to accept the challenge thrown down by the likes of Boas and Rivers. Malinowski started his fieldwork career at age 30 with six months in New Guinea. He returned to the Trobriand Islands for two more years of work in 1915 to 1916 and 1917 to 1918. In so doing, he helped establish the modern fieldwork methods of cultural anthropology.

Malinowski determined that there were three general types of cultural data, each requiring its own collection technique. The first was the description and analysis of institutions, which were to be studied by thorough documentation of concrete evidence. More precisely, this meant the creation of charts of activities and customs associated with a particular institution, based on accounts given by the natives as well as on observations by the investigator. This method would yield a literal visible representation of the "mental chart" that members of the society possess. The second type of data, constituting another dimension of cultural reality, was the minutiae of everyday life, which filled out and deepened (if complicated) the analysis of general institutions. As he noted, the emphasis on rules and structures and institutions left an impression of more precision and consistency than is actually seen in real life. So, abstract or generalized presentations of social structures had to be complemented with particular and personal instantiations or uses of those rules and structures in the details of everyday life, anticipating the distinction between "structure" and "action" that anthropologists like Raymond Firth would elaborate. The third type of data included cultural content like narratives, utterances, folklore, and other conventional sayings and activities. The immediate result of his methods was his epic ethnography *Argonauts of the Western Pacific* (1922), in which he modeled what a sensitive and informed fieldworker could do with the data he collected.

Malinowski, Bronislaw. 1984 [1922]. *Argonauts of the Western Pacific*. Long Grove, IL: Waveland Press, Inc.

Cultural evolutionism
The early ethnological or anthropological position or theory that Culture started at some moment in the past and evolved from its "primitive" beginnings through a series of stages to achieve its "higher" or more modern form.

The other profound influence of Malinowski on the fledgling field of anthropology was his theoretical approach, which was significantly connected to his method. Like Boas, he rejected **cultural evolutionism** and speculative historical reconstructions. As he wrote: "I still believe in evolution, I am still interested in origins, in the process of development, only I see more and more clearly that answers to any evolutionary questions must lead directly to the empirical study of the facts and institutions, the past development of which we wish to reconstruct" (quoted in Kuper 1983: 9). Thus, anthropologists should study the present with all possible attention and clarity before they indulge in speculations about the past. What a fieldworker sees today is institutions, the individuals acting within them, and standard "narratives" or "scripts" which those individuals produce and reproduce in the process. These investigators can hunt for – and perhaps only for – the *function* of institutions and practices today, in the present. Hence, he recommended an approach known as functionalism. Rather than pursue its history (a potentially vain pursuit), the anthropologist can observe its function here and now. What is the function, for example, of marriage, or political systems, or religion?

For Malinowski, the essence of function was to be found in the needs of the individuals who comprise a society. Society, he asserted, is ultimately a collection of individual human beings. So, culture "functions" according to the needs and nature of those individuals, who have two kinds of needs – physical and psychological. Each item of culture, or culture as a whole, must serve to fill one or more of these needs. It is the job of the ethnographer to determine what needs it fills and how.

Functionalism became a reigning idea during the early twentieth century and not only in anthropology (Durkheim had already elaborated it in sociology). However, others began to turn the idea in new directions, if not turn against it altogether. Radcliffe-Brown argued that culture does in fact function, but not in the way that Malinowski imagined. Radcliffe-Brown maintained, rather, that individuals are relatively trivial; what is important – and enduring – is society itself, the community, the social whole. In opposition to Malinowski's functionalism, he advocated a "social" or "structural" functionalism, the social function of institutions defined by him as "the contribution that they make to the formation and maintenance of a social order" (Radcliffe-Brown 1965: 154). Radcliffe-Brown's focus on institutions versus individuals and on order versus action was hugely influential on the British tradition of social anthropology, which came to emphasize law, kinship systems, and so on. Social order or social structure was not a mere idea, an abstraction in the mind of the anthropologist, in this view, but a real and concrete thing. He went so far as to assert that society can be studied, but culture cannot:

> You cannot have a science of culture. You can study culture only as a characteristic of a social system. . . . If you study culture, you are always studying the acts of behavior of a specific set of persons who are linked together in a social structure.

> (quoted in Kuper 1983: 55)

THE ANTHROPOLOGICAL CRISIS OF THE MID-TWENTIETH CENTURY AND BEYOND

Just as approaching maturity often entails a life crisis and a rebellion against tradition in individuals, so cultural anthropology suffered a disciplinary crisis and rebellion in the mid-twentieth century that was perhaps a sign of maturation and a break-through to a deeper level of understanding – and self-understanding. The sources of this crisis and the call to "rethink" or "reinvent" anthropology probably included the aging and passing of the founding generation, as happens in all disciplines. However, even more important was the change in the subjects of cultural anthro-pology themselves, the "primitive peoples" and small traditional societies, which forced a change in the science that purported to study them. Not the least of these changes was the rush of independence movements that ended the centuries-old European project of colonialism and empire. Finally, perhaps a critical point had been reached which compelled anthropology to look at itself in new and sometimes uncomfortable ways – not only at what it was doing but even at the very tools and concepts it was using to do it.

See Chapter 13

One of the first and most important moves in this "new anthropology" was the announcement by Edmund Leach that societies are not always as discrete and traditional as we think they are. In his seminal *Political Systems of Highland Burma* (1954) he described a situation in which societies overlapped each other without clear and permanent boundaries and in which the very politics and culture of the multicultural system fluctuated over time. Given the realities of highland Burmese social relations, he concluded that "ordinary ethnographic conventions . . . are hopelessly inappropriate" (281). In fact, he went so far as to argue that the entire notion of discrete societies was an "academic fiction": "the ethnographer has often only managed to discern the existence of 'a tribe' because he took it as axiomatic that this kind of cultural entity must exist" (291). At almost the same moment J. S. Furnivall published his study of Burma and Indonesia entitled *Colonial Policy and Practice* (1956) in which he introduced the concept of "plural society" to describe the mixed yet segregated social realities in those locations. Burma and Java were not homogeneous societies at all but a jumble of "separate racial sections" which "mix but do not combine" (304), linked (and stratified) by sheer economic interests.

Leach, Edmund R. 1954. Political Systems of Highland Burma. Boston: Beacon Press.

See Chapter 12

One of the other conventions of early anthropology – the peacefulness and stability of traditional societies – was upset by ongoing researches in Africa. Meyer Fortes and E. E. Evans-Pritchard had already discovered that various supposed tribes "appear to be an amalgam of different peoples, each aware of its unique origin and history" (1940: 9) and are not always on easy terms with each other. Max Gluckman even more decisively burst the fiction of simple integration of societies in his aptly named *Custom and Conflict in Africa*, which found that not only are societies not as integrated and harmonious as was once thought but that conflict could actually be the social structure of a society: by way of the contours and variations within a society, "men quarrel in terms of certain of their customary allegiances, but are restrained

Wagner, Roy. 1975. *The Invention of Culture.* Englewood Cliffs, NJ: Prentice-Hall, Inc.

Hobsbawm, Eric and Terence Ranger, eds. 1983. *The Invention of Tradition.* Cambridge: Cambridge University Press.

Hymes, Dell, ed. 1972 [1969]. *Reinventing Anthropology.* New York: Random House, Inc.

from violence through other conflicting allegiances which are also enjoined on them by custom" (1956: 2). The simple view of primitive order was forever dashed.

These reports from the field heralded an identity crisis within anthropology that was expressed in such subsequent titles as *The Invention of Culture* (Wagner 1975), *The Invention of Tradition* (Hobsbawm and Ranger 1983), *The Invention of Primitive Society* (Kuper 1988), and first and perhaps most dramatically *Reinventing Anthropology* (Hymes 1972). These books and others like them shone the spotlight directly on cultural anthropology itself, identifying clearly anthropology's own "culture" and how its methods, concepts, and assumptions had influenced its findings and conclusions. Anthropology would subsequently become more self-reflective as it discovered that it was at least in a sense not only science but also literature – that is, a tradition of writing – as in James Clifford and George Marcus' (1986) *Writing Culture: The Poetics and Politics of Ethnography.*

Along the way, cultural anthropology split into more schools and theoretical camps than ever, as some practitioners returned to the roots of the discipline to reform them while others took inspiration from fields and advances outside of anthropology. Among these elaborations of anthropology are the following.

Neo-evolutionism

The mid-twentieth-century revival of focus on the historical development of cultures and societies, as in the work of Leslie White and Julian Steward, which generally sought to repair the failings of nineteenth-century evolutionism by proposing specific processes and a "multilinear" path of change.

1. Neo-evolutionism. Leslie White (1949, 1959a, 1959b) and Julian Steward (1950, 1953) are considered the most prominent thinkers to reintroduce a more sophisticated version of cultural evolution. White suggested a principle behind the evolutionary progress of societies, namely the amount and kind of energy it could harness and exploit. As societies developed newer and greater sources of energy (from domesticated animals to electricity and nuclear power), not only their economic but also their other social characteristics would change in correspondence. Steward contributed the notion of "multilinear" evolution to combat the impression that all societies evolved in the same manner or that all societies were part of some grand cultural evolution. In this view, each particular culture pursued its own developmental course, and societies at similar points in their evolution (perhaps due to their similar environments) would exhibit similar cultures.

Structuralism

The theory (associated most closely with Claude Lévi-Strauss) that the significance of an item (word, role, practice, belief) is not so much in the particular item but in its relationship to others. In other words, the "structure" of multiple items and the location of any one in relation to others is most important.

2. Structuralism. Instead of looking back into the heritage of anthropology, Claude Lévi-Strauss looked across at the developing discipline of linguistics for a new approach to vexing problems like kinship and religion (e.g., the analysis of myth). Drawing on the work of Ferdinand de Saussure in particular, Lévi-Strauss took the notion of culture as a language seriously: language has "bits" or elements (sounds, words, and so on) in structural relationships with each other (that is, "grammar"). The grammatical relations between linguistic elements determine their meaning more than the individual elements themselves. Therefore, he proposed that we might approach anthropological problems in the same way. Rather than looking for the "meaning" of some cultural element – totemism, mother-in-law avoidance, a particular theme in a myth – in the thing itself, he proposed that we look for it in the relations between the elements. In other words, if a society has the crocodile for a totem animal, the meaning of that totem is not to be found in the properties of the crocodile but in the system of relationships between the various totem animals and,

more importantly, the system of relationships between the social groupings associated with those species.

3. **Ethnoscience**. Combining two interests of American anthropology in particular – personality or cognition and classification – ethnoscience, also known as cognitive anthropology, sought to examine and expose the mental classification systems that shaped local people's experiences and actions. As formulated by Goodenough (1956), Frake (1962), and Tyler (1969) among others, ethnoscience aimed to be more scientific while also pursuing the psychological side of culture, which had always been a focus in American cultural anthropology. The point was to bring to light the intellectual models of reality that humans have in their heads (often if not usually implicitly) that organize their world in specific ways. Thus, the scientific anthropologist would reconstruct the "folk taxonomy" or the "knowledge structure" of a society, which was the skeleton and structure of its entire meaning and action system.

Ethnoscience
The anthropological theory or approach that investigates the native classification systems of societies to discover the concepts, terms, and categories by which they understand their world.

4. **Symbolic/interpretive anthropology**. In some ways moving in the opposite direction and in other ways very comparable, symbolic anthropology also sought to gain access to the deeper meanings of other societies, but it tended to do this through "symbols" rather than through taxonomies. Influenced heavily by the philosophies of Suzanne Langer (1942) and Ernst Cassirer (1954) who saw all human thought and action as mediated by symbols, the meanings of which could not always be described rationally, anthropologists like Victor Turner (1967, 1981 [1968]), Clifford Geertz (1973), and Sherry Ortner (1973) attempted to identify the "key symbols" that functioned as lenses through which people perceived their worlds. It was at least in part a reaction against Lévi-Straussian structuralism, which posited a single mental structure for all human beings and stripped away all of the particulars and context from anthropological analysis. Geertz coined the phrase "thick description" for the practice of trying to penetrate to the deep meaning of people's realities and to present that meaning in all of its richness and complexity. Anthropological analysis and description thus became an interpretive or "hermeneutic" exercise, aiming to "read" a culture and to render its symbols and meanings understandable to us without washing out all of the uniqueness and particularity of the society in question.

Symbolic anthropology
The school of thought (often associated with Clifford Geertz and Victor Turner) that the main goal of anthropology is to elucidate the meanings within which humans live and behave. Rather than focusing on institutions and rules, it focuses on symbols and how symbols shape our experience and are manipulated by people in social situations.

Turner, Victor W. 1967. *The Forest of Symbols: Aspects of Ndembu Ritual.* Ithaca and London: Cornell University Press.

5. **Marxist/critical anthropology**. In the second half of the twentieth century especially, Marxist or "critical" theory exerted a strong pull on cultural anthropology. In the works of Maurice Bloch (1983), Maurice Godelier (1978), and many others, there was a new concern for issues of economics, class, power, and domination. Working from the Marxian claim that the culture of a society is the culture of the dominant class of that society, they looked for practical and material relationships that shaped the ideologies and institutions of any social group. A key concept was "mode of production," the means and relationships of the production of goods and wealth, which led to and shaped the "relations of production," that is, the actual social relationships between individuals and groups like ownership and property relations, kinship and gender relations, and so on. This perspective emphasized and actively looked for competitive or conflictual relations in society in a way that early

Marxist/critical anthropology
The theory, based on the work of Karl Marx, which emphasizes the material and economic forces that underlie society, relying on notions of power and inequality, modes of production, and class relations and conflicts.

See Chapter 7

Cultural materialism
The theory that practical/material/economic factors can explain some or all cultural phenomena.

Harris, Marvin. 1974. *Cows, Pigs, Wars, and Witches: The Riddles of Culture.* New York: Random House.

Feminist anthropology
The anthropological theory or approach that focuses on how gender relations are constructed in society and how those relations subsequently shape the society. Also examines how gender concepts have affected the science of anthropology itself – the questions it asks and the issues it emphasizes.

Rosaldo, Michelle and Louise Lamphere, eds. 1974. *Women, Culture, and Society.* Stanford: Stanford University Press. Reiter, Rayna, ed. 1975b. *Toward an Anthropology of Women.* New York: Monthly Review Press.

World anthropologies
The perspective that anthropology as developed and practiced in the West is not the only form of anthropology, and that other societies may develop and practice other types of anthropology based on their specific experiences and interests.

www.wcaanet.org

anthropology did not and perhaps could not, with its perspective of integration and homogeneity. While it claimed to be scientific and practical, it also tended to be abstract and "theoretical" (even inventing a new word for practice – "praxis") and often openly partisan and critical of existing values and institutions.

6. Cultural materialism. Championed especially by Marvin Harris in popular writings like *Cows, Pigs, Wars, and Witches* (1974) and technical books like *The Rise of Anthropological Theory* (1968) and *Cultural Materialism: The Struggle for a Science of Culture* (1979), this perspective extended the ecological views of White and Steward as well as the Marxist view, basing cultural behaviors firmly on "the practical problems of earthly existence" posed by the encounter between "womb and belly" on one hand and the material world of food, climate, and competition for territory or offspring on the other (Harris 1979). Like ethnoscience it aimed at a more scientific anthropology, exposing the "causes" of human action.

7. Feminist anthropology. A feminist approach to anthropology also appeared in the 1970s as a reaction to male-centered perceptions of the field and its literature ("man the hunter" type approaches, and so on). Happily, from early in its history women have played a prominent role in cultural anthropology (as evidenced by Margaret Mead, Ruth Benedict, and Cora Dubois, to name a few), but a literature on women and their activities across cultures had been lacking, partly because many cultures have sex-segregated knowledge which male anthropologists could not access. Michelle Rosaldo and Louise Lamphere (1974) and Rayna Reiter (1975b) were three of the early founders of the movement to explore gender relationships, gender inequalities, and the participation of women in cultures where that participation had been overlooked or minimized. Feminist anthropology does not focus exclusively on women but rather on gender diversity and gender issues broadly conceived.

Finally, one of the most exciting and promising new directions is the emergence of a **world anthropologies** perspective, the recognition that, just as there are many diverse cultures in the world, there are many diverse ways to do anthropology. The fact is, as the editors of the recent volume entitled *World Anthropologies* explain, the existence and practices of various local anthropologies, especially in the non-Western world, means that "the idea of a single or general anthropology is called into question" (Ribeiro and Escobar 2006: 1). Indeed, anthropology as it has been traditionally known and done has, it turns out, been distinctly Western, and world anthropologies promises to expand anthropology while "provincializing Europe" – not denying or denigrating the Western perspective but showing conclusively that Western thought, and with it anthropological thought as it has so far existed, "are particular and historically located, not universal as is generally assumed" (3–4). Happily, organizations like the World Council of Anthropological Associations, representing anthropologists from Africa, Latin America, Europe, North America, and Asia, embody and advance just such a global prospect.

BOX 3.3 CONTEMPORARY CULTURAL CONTROVERSIES: THE AMERICAN "SOCIAL CONTRACT"

The U.S. Declaration of Independence states that humans are born with certain rights; that "to secure these rights, governments are instituted among men, deriving their just powers from the consent of the governed"; and that "whenever any form of government becomes destructive of these ends, it is the right of the people to alter or to abolish it, and to institute new government, laying its foundation on such principles and organizing its powers in such form, as to them shall seem most likely to effect their safety and happiness." These words may be seen as asserting that government and perhaps society in general is a contract – political and other institutions are not natural or divinely inspired but made by humans. So, if a prior contract becomes unsatisfactory, or if it is abused and usurped by those in power, it can be modified or even replaced. Some people respond that at least certain institutions (like marriage or family) are too important or "real" to tamper with, while others think that the whole notion of the human construction of culture undermines the authority of society and tradition. What do you think?

SUMMARY

Anthropology is a new science and an unlikely science, and it is new because it is unlikely. If people had thought to do anthropology – that is, the study of human diversity – as easily as they thought to do history or algebra, then they would have done it long ago. The two main barriers to an "anthropological perspective" were always, and continue to be:

- certainty in one's own correctness and goodness
- no information or poor information about others.

Western civilization like all others suffered from these two limitations, although there had always been a somewhat dissatisfied and self-critical tendency in it. However, a series of experiences around the early 1500s shattered forever that certainty while providing a new quantity and quality of experience of the Other. These included:

- voyages of discovery to new lands
- encounters with other "advanced" civilizations
- the Renaissance
- the Protestant Reformation
- the scientific revolution.

While European societies first struggled with and tried to assimilate these new cultures, they also began to use them for purposes of their own imagination – in particular, to imagine alternatives (whether positive or negative) to their own contemporary social and cultural realities. Hobbes and Rousseau were two of the first to do so, with diametrically opposed results. Even so, the first steps toward taking other cultures seriously were taken.

Early "anthropological" thinkers typically came from a historical and "progressivist" direction, interested in the origins of culture (or Culture) and the stepwise "progress" of culture from "primitive" to "modern." However, the first modern anthropologists, like Franz Boas and Bronislaw Malinowski, rejected this approach and adopted a more empirical, relativistic, holistic, and humanistic stance. The main thing was to collect good data and use those data to understand cultures as we found them – not as they (allegedly) once were or as we would like them to be. Since those early days, anthropology has altered as its subjects have altered, referring back to its origins, looking for models from other fields, and studying itself with the same tools and the same intensity as it studies other cultures. Anthropology will continue to grow and change for these same reasons. What the anthropology of the future will look like is as hard to predict as – and will depend critically upon – the cultures of the future.

Key Terms

Cultural evolutionism

Cultural materialism

Diffusion

Ethnoscience

Feminist anthropology

Marxist/critical anthropology

Neo-evolutionism

Noble savage

Structuralism

Symbolic anthropology

World anthropologies

Language and Social Relations

In Malagasy, a language spoken on the island of Madagascar, there are three styles or "voices" in which to phrase a sentence. Two of these correspond to the active and passive voices in English, but the third is known as the circumstantial voice and has no precise English equivalent. The circumstantial voice shifts the subject of the sentence from the person being addressed to the object that will be used to perform an action. The difference between the three speech forms appears in the various ways to give an order:

Active: *Manasa ny lamba amin'ny savony* or "Wash the clothes with soap."

Passive: *Sasaa ny lamba anim'ny savony* or "Have the clothes washed with the soap."

Circumstantial: *Anasao lamb any savony* or "The soap is to be used to wash clothes."

(Ochs 1996: 105–6)

The question for a speaker is, when do you use each particular form, and what difference does it make? In simple declarative sentences as well as imperatives, it is always preferable to use the circumstantial voice if possible. According to Ochs, Namaizamanga village in central Madagascar was an egalitarian and non-violent place, with no formal leaders and few differentiated statuses, where it was regarded as impolite to express direct anger, disagreement, or criticism. So the active voice was considered to be "harsh and abrupt, without respect" (106). Indirect speech was regarded as appropriate as well as sophisticated – a quality of the formal and stylized speech style known as *kabary*.

One of the most conspicuous areas of difference between human groups is their language. Sometimes language difference has been taken as the defining feature of a distinct society, although not always: two or more societies can speak the same language (e.g., the U.K. and the U.S.A.), and one society can speak two or more languages (e.g., Flemish and Walloon in Belgium). The overt qualities of language – the specific sounds, words, and grammars of each – are easy to observe and clearly fall within the prerogative of anthropology. In fact, language is such a vast subject that anthropology has developed a specialized subdiscipline to investigate it, namely linguistic anthropology. However, linguistic anthropology is interested in more than the sounds and grammar of languages. It is also concerned with what kinds of variations and choices exist within a language, how people use those variations and choices to convey social information and to express and maintain social relations, and how the concepts and values in a language shape the experience of its speakers. That is, linguistic anthropology holistically relates language to other aspects of society and culture.

PLATE 4.1 Linguistic anthropologists began collecting language in the field in the late 1800s

HUMAN LANGUAGE AS A COMMUNICATION SYSTEM

Humans are hardly the only species to communicate. All species, even plants, communicate in various ways, in the sense of transmitting and receiving "information," for example, by exchanging chemical markers. Bees are famous for their "dance" that communicates the distance and direction to flowers. Humans are not even the only species that communicates "orally." Cats, dogs, and birds, and of course monkeys and apes, make sounds that carry meaning for others of their kind. In the laboratory we have discovered that the primates related most closely to us are the most like us linguistically; they cannot speak, but they can understand speech and can communicate through linguistic media such as hand signals, shapes and objects, and buttons and keyboards. That non-human primates have some linguistic ability is no surprise, given their physical and behavioral similarity to us.

Most of what we consider human language is performed in the medium of speech, but not all of it. People who are completely without speech ability can communicate linguistically, as with American Sign Language. Beyond that, all humans communicate non-verbally all the time, using hand gestures, facial expressions, body postures, and so on. Regardless of the medium, however, language has a set of distinct characteristics, referred to as "design features" (Hockett 1958; 1977). Among these features are:

- rapid fading – the communication lasts for only a brief time (except for writing)
- interchangeability – individuals can be both senders and receivers of messages
- feedback – language users can monitor their own messages and correct errors in them
- semanticity – the elements of language have "meaning" or reference to the world
- arbitrariness – the connection between a linguistic signal and its "meaning" is not "natural" or "given"
- discreteness – language is composed of small, separate, and reusable "bits"
- **displacement** – language can refer to things that are not "present" in time or space
- **productivity** – language users can make and understand new messages using old familiar "bits"
- reflexiveness – language users can employ language to communicate about language
- prevarication – language use can be false, deceptive, or meaningless
- learnability – users of one language can learn another language
- cultural transmission – the rules or conventions of language are the property of a social group and are acquired or learned by interacting with that group.

Clearly, then, language is profoundly connected to culture. The human abilities or skills or tendencies that make culture possible also make language possible. In fact, many of the features of language on Hockett's list are also features of culture in general.

Displacement

The linguistic feature that allows for communication about things that are "not here" in the sense of absent or out of view, past or future, conceptual or even imaginary.

Productivity

The capacity of language to combine meaningless sounds to create new words or to combine words to create new utterances.

Language first of all consists of symbols; it depends on the capacity to engage in symbolism, to think symbolically. Language is a set of acts or gestures – largely but not essentially verbal – that "mean something." Many things "mean something": when a dog barks, it means something to the dog, to other dogs, and to us. When dark clouds appear on the horizon, it means something (that it might rain, for example). But no one would call the dog barking, or the clouds appearing, symbolic. The difference between such *signs* and real symbols is that symbols are *conventional and arbitrary* vehicles for their meanings. There is no necessary or "natural" relationship between a symbol and its meaning. We could use any sound or hand gesture or facial expression or picture to represent any meaning, as long as we all agree to use it and understand its use. In a sense, we are "free" to make and use symbols, including language symbols, in a way that the dog, let alone the cloud, is not. There are of course certain words in any language that sound like the thing they mean, such as the word "boom" for an explosion or the child's word "choo-choo" for a train, but these are a special class of words called onomatopoeia and are not typical of human language.

See Chapter 2

One of the marvelous aspects of human language is that a relatively small number of basic linguistic units can be combined in various ways to produce a theoretically unlimited number of meanings or utterances. There are two ways to look at this. The first is that meaningful language at bottom consists of meaningless bits, that is, sounds. The sound "d" has no meaning, nor the sound "o" nor the sound "g," but together in a particular arrangement (d-o-g) they have meaning in a particular language. Together in a different arrangement (g-o-d) they have a very different meaning. Together in any other arrangement (say, g-d-o) they have no meaning in that language.

The second is that we can use our newly meaningful sound groups ("words") in novel combinations to generate original and previously unheard utterances – phrases, sentences, speeches, stories, entire books like this one. This is not to assert that all or even most of human speech is particularly original; in fact, very much of what humans say during a day is highly conventional, virtually "script-like," whether they are exchanging greetings or quoting a proverb or famous saying. However, while a line like "A rose by any other name would smell as sweet" is conventional today, perhaps no one ever combined those words in quite that way before Shakespeare did.

Finally and remarkably, humans can talk about things that are "not here" in a variety of senses. For example, humans can talk about things that are not immediately in front of us – behind us or in another room or on the other side of the planet. We can also talk about things that do not exist in the present at all, that is, the past and the future. Humans can talk about things that are blocked from view, invisible, or even completely abstract or general – things like ideas or concepts or relationships, such as "justice" or "same/different." We can even talk about things that are purely imaginary or fictional: we can talk about dragons and leprechauns and elves and Hamlet or Harry Potter just as easily and surely as about dogs and cats and clouds. In fact, in a certain important way, it does not really matter whether these things are real or not; if people think they are real and act as if they are real, then those things have real social consequences.

The point is that human language ultimately and crucially exploits some unique human cognitive or mental abilities. Humans could not produce symbols unless they were cognitively "free" to make meaning. Similarly, our kind of language would be impossible without the human talents of creativity, imagination, and even fantasy. In language, as in culture in general, humans invent their own worlds and live in them. Humans can create their own cognitive, "meaningful," world, and they *must* create it.

THE STRUCTURE OF LANGUAGE

Any particular language has a finite set of elements and a finite set of rules for combining those elements into larger and more complex units. The speaker of the language must learn and master these elements and rules, achieving linguistic **competence**, the ability to make intelligible utterances. To learn a language – and for anthropology to study the cultural phenomenon of language – we must start with the smallest bits and build up higher and more complex linguistic behavior out of these lower order units. Language thus proceeds from sound to meaning to utterance, and finally to practical use.

Competence
In language, the mastery of the elements (sounds, semantics, and grammar) of a language to be able to make intelligible utterances.

Phonology

The most basic bits in any human language are its sounds, and **phonology** (from the root *phone* for sound) is the study of how those sounds are combined and used in language (*phonetics* is usually understood to refer to the processes of the physical production and sensory reception of sounds). More specifically, phonology is the study of which sounds are used in a language and how those sounds are used to generate words. We are not talking yet about meaning; we are still at the pre-meaningful stage of language.

Humans can make very many different sounds, but no language employs all of them. Any particular language will contain some sounds and not others; it will use sounds that other languages do not and will use them in ways that other languages do not. English contains *th* and *ʃ* and *sh* sounds that do not occur universally, and some speakers of other languages have difficulty distinguishing or producing such sounds. French, for example, does not contain the *th* sound, which is often replaced with a *z* sound, rendering the word "the" as "ze." Japanese speakers struggle with the *r* and *l* sounds in English. Other languages use sounds that are foreign to English. The !Kung or Ju/hoansi in Africa's Kalahari Desert use a set of click sounds in their words that English speakers can make but would never pronounce as parts of English words. (Even the names for their society include sounds that are not part of any possible English word and for which English has no alphabetic symbol, which is why we use punctuation symbols to represent them.) The total number of sounds available in a language can vary widely: Warlpiri (Australian Aboriginal) has only

Phonology
The study of the sounds used in a language.

three vowel sounds – "ah," "ee," and "oo." Nuer (African) reportedly has fourteen vowels, each with at least three "lengths," two degrees of "breathiness," and three "tones," producing over two hundred possible combinations (Needham 1972: 18). Some languages, like English, use stress or emphasis to modify their sounds, and others, like Chinese, use tone. When a person pronounces the words of one language with the phonology of another, it is known as "speaking with an accent."

Phoneme

The smallest bit of sound in a language.

Beyond the simple matter of which sounds are used in a language, there is the matter of how those sounds are used. **Phonemes** are the smallest bits of linguistic sound. For example, [b] and [p] (phonemes are usually written within square brackets) are two distinct phonemes in English, which can be verified by asking a native speaker if "bit" and "pit" are the same word. These different phonemes make a linguistic difference. The phonemes [r] and [rr] (a "rolled" r) do not make a difference in English ("ruffles" and "rruffles" are not different words), but they might make a difference in some other languages. An example is Warlpiri, which actually has not two but three forms of the "r" sound – [r], [rr], and [rd] (a kind of "flapped r" sound). The difference – and the significance of the difference – can be noticed in the Warlpiri suffix -*kurra* as opposed to the word *kura*. The first means "toward" while the second means "sex" – a difference in meaning that an English speaker attempting Warlpiri would surely want to pay attention to. On the other hand, Warlpiri does not distinguish between the sounds [b] and [p]. In fact, the Warlpiri sound is neither [b] nor [p] but something in between. "Bit" and "pit" would be the same word to them, but neither would be pronounced quite correctly. Try making a sound intermediate between [b] and [p] and you will see how elusive these skills can be.

The second issue is how those sounds are used in combination. There are often rules, for instance, for which sounds may occur together or where a sound may occur in a word. English allows for clusters of consonants, as in the word "straight," with its initial string of three consonants, [s], [t], and [r]. Abbreviating "consonant" with C and "vowel" with V, linguists would represent the sound structure of the word "straight" as CCCVC. Not every language can do this, and some do not do it at all. English also allows many other variations, such as CVC ("sat"), CV ("so"), VC ("is"), VCV ("away"), V ("a"), and even CCCVCCC ("squirts"), some of which are difficult or nearly impossible for other language speakers to master. Languages like Tahitian and Hawaiian only allow CV or V syllables; that is, every consonant must be followed by a vowel, and a vowel can occur alone.

There are also linguistic norms governing where a sound can occur in a syllable or word. The sound [ng] (as in "sing") exists in English but has specific (if implicit) rules for its use: it may come at the end of a word (like "sing") or in the middle of a word (like "singer") but never at the beginning of a word. Any word that started with the sound [ng] would be immediately recognizable as a non-English word. Warlpiri, on the other hand, uses the [ng] phoneme as an initial sound in many words, such as *ngapa* (water), *ngarni* (to eat), *ngaka* (after), and *ngarlarrimi* (to laugh). Most English speakers, while they can make the sound, cannot pronounce these words easily; the initial [ng] is just too unfamiliar. Conversely, the Shoshone (Native

American) language contains several consonant sounds (including but not limited to [ch], [f], [j], [k], [p], [sh], [t], and [z]) that cannot be used as initial sounds.

The appearance of a sound in a syllable or word may affect its surrounding sounds. One example from Warlpiri requires that an [i] sound not be followed by an [u] sound. In English, a noun that starts with a vowel will be preceded by an article that ends with a consonant and vice versa ("an apple" versus "a banana"). In French, explicit standards of *liaison* and *elision* link one syllable or word with another: *ils ont* ("they have") is pronounced "eel zon" ("on" pronounced nasally, not as in English), somewhat similar to the English tendency to run sounds together ("the mall" sometimes sounds like "them all"). Back to French, *je* ("I") and *ai* ("have") are spoken as *j'ai*, and *de* ("of") and *les* ("the"-plural) are combined as *des*. Turkish practices a form of vowel harmony, in which different kinds of vowels (called "front vowels" or "back vowels") never occur in the same word: a word will contain all front vowels or all back vowels but not both. Sounds can also be employed for semantic (meaningful) or grammatical effect, as discussed below.

Morphology or semantics

Speakers can begin to build a set of meanings on the foundation of orderly sound, depending on the structural relations between these sounds; the form or shape of the combination of (meaningless) sounds carries us to meaning. Therefore, linguists call the study of the "meaningful bits" of language **morphology** (from the root *morph* for form or shape) or **semantics**.

Just as phonemes are the smallest bits of usable sound in a language, **morphemes** are the smallest possible bits of meaning. Words constitute a class of morphemes called **free morphemes** – that is, morphemes that can stand on their own to convey meaning. "Dog" is a free morpheme, since it is independently meaningful. There is another class, however, called **bound morphemes** which convey meaning but only in combination with another morpheme. In English, these usually take the form of prefixes and suffixes. The morpheme *-s* "means" plural, just as the morpheme *un-* "means" not, when used in conjunction with a free morpheme and in the right orientation. For instance, if an English speaker simply said "-s," others would not know what it meant. But if the speaker attached the sound to "dog" and said "dogs," other speakers would understand perfectly. In the wrong order ("sdog" or "happyun") they would find the words erroneous, unclear, or nonsensical.

Not all languages function the same way morphologically. In English there is only one semantic plural form, which means "two or more" (although there are two phonetic forms, [-s] and [-z], depending on what sound precedes it, e.g., [dog][-z] but [cat][-s]). However, Warlpiri has two plural forms, neither of which use *-s*. To say "two dogs" in Warlpiri the suffix *-jarra* is added to the word for dog, *maliki*; this means exactly two dogs. To say "three or more dogs" the suffix *-patu* is used. German tends to use *-en* as the suffix to indicate plural (*Frau* for "woman" becomes *Frauen* for "women"). Languages with "gender" like French and Spanish and German add

Morphology

The area of language dealing with how meaningful bits (usually but not exclusively words) are created and manipulated by the combination of language sounds.

Semantics

The study of meaning in language. *See morphology.*

Morpheme

The smallest bit of meaningful sound in a language, usually a word but also a prefix or suffix or other meaning-conveying sound that may be used in conjunction with a word.

Free morpheme

A morpheme that has meaning in its own right, that can stand alone as a meaningful sound (for the most part, a word).

Bound morpheme

A morpheme that has meaning but only when it is used in conjunction with a word.

another wrinkle: for instance, French words tend to attach an *e* at the end of feminine words, which is not pronounced but changes the pronunciation of the syllable before it. Thus, *chien* (male dog) becomes *chienne* (female dog), changing the nasal -*ien* of the first word into a more familiar *n* sound for English speakers.

Many languages apply stress or emphasis to certain parts of words, either typically or to alter their semantic form. English is a stress language, with every word given its unique emphasis pattern, producing a kind of "rhythm" in speech which can be exploited in poetry (known technically as "meter"). There is no consistent rule on how English stress operates, but one frequent pattern is emphasizing the final vowel (by stressing or "lengthening") in verbs but other vowels in nouns or adjectives; thus "to elaborate" or "to articulate" stresses the final [a] sound, while "elaborate" or "articulate" as adjectives shorten it. Old Irish, by comparison, always stresses the first syllable of nouns and adjectives, with stress on the second syllable for some adverbs. In Tagalog, a language spoken in the Philippines, sound stress has more profound morphological consequences, changing the word's meaning completely: for instance, *gabi* with emphasis on the second syllable refers to a particular starchy root but with emphasis on the second syllable means "night."

Another class of languages does not use stress/emphasis but rather "tone" to convey meaning; that is, the meaning of the word depends on the pitch, or change of pitch, in which it is spoken. Instead of rhythm this gives the language a melodic quality. While rare in Western languages, this practice is common in Eastern and African ones; in fact, more than half of the world's languages incorporate tone in some way (Crystal 1987: 172). Some, like Zulu, use only two tones (high and low), others, like Yoruba, use three (high, middle, and low), and Cantonese Chinese uses six (middle, low, high-then-falling, low-then-falling, high-then-rising, and low-then-rising). Thus a single "syllable" like *si* in Cantonese can mean "poem," "to try," "matter," "time," "to cause," and "city" depending on how it is intoned. The Tai-Kadai language family of Southeast Asia and southern China reportedly contains eleven different tones.

Grammar or syntax

Syntax

The rules in a language for how words are combined to make intelligible utterances or speech acts (for example, sentences). Also known as grammar.

Grammar or **syntax** refers technically to the rules by which a language combines words (and other morphemes) into meaningful and intelligible utterances, like sentences. Obviously, being able to say "dog" or "dogs" is necessary, but it would not be very useful if that was all a speaker could say. Hopefully speakers can use the words in more sophisticated and informative utterances to convey complete ideas or statements.

There are some basic grammatical rules in each language that organize the "structure" of normal "good" speech. In English, the most fundamental rule or variable in sentences is word order. That is, English speakers make and understand sentences based on the sequence of the words: in a regular declarative sentence, they know to put – and expect to hear – the "subject" word first, then the "verb" word, then the "object" word (notated as SVO). Of course, things can get much more complicated, with dependent clauses and participial phrases and such, but this is the skeleton of a basic sentence. So, the sentence "The man hit the dog" has a specific meaning. The sentence "The dog hit the man," with exactly the same words in a different sequence, has a specific but different meaning. And any other sequence – like "The the hit man dog" – yields no meaning at all.

Up to 75 percent of the world's languages follow a SVO or SOV pattern (Crystal 1987: 98). However, other orders exist. Standard Turkish sentences place the subject first and the verb last. Old Irish typically took the VSO order. Tagalog can give the predicate before the topic (according to the Philippine Center for Language Study (1965: 13), concepts of "subject," "verb," and "object" do not quite apply to Tagalog grammar, since a verb can be a subject) or in reverse order with the addition of the morpheme *ay*. Thus "The dress is beautiful" can be said as *Maganda ang damit* ("beautiful" + "is" + "dress") or as *Ang damit ay maganda* ("is" + "dress" + *ay* + "beautiful").

Some languages do not depend on word order at all or do not have to provide every grammatical element for a sentence. The order of words in a Warlpiri sentence does not determine its meaning. For instance, to communicate that a man hit a dog, in Warlpiri one would use the words *wati* ("man"), *pakarnu* ("hit" – past tense), and *maliki* ("dog"), but to make the appropriate sentence one cannot simply say *wati pakarnu maliki*. The subject word in a Warlpiri sentence is identified not by its location in the sentence but by a bound morpheme that indicates "subject," in this case the suffix *-ngki*. The correct utterance thus is *wati-ngki pakarnu maliki*. In any order the meaning is the same. To change the meaning so that the dog is doing the hitting, the suffix must go on *maliki*, the correct suffix being not *-ngki* but *-rli* (based on the number of syllables and the terminal syllable of the word). Now the sentence is *maliki-rli pakarnu wati*, which can be arranged in any order. Latin is similar in using suffixes to indicate a word's role in a sentence, rather than the order of words.

Spanish does not even require that all of the elements of a "good" English sentence be included. The Spanish equivalent of the English "I love you" can take the form OV, without a "subject": *Te amo* ("you" – object + "love"). If an English speaker said "You love," the meaning would be ambiguous, since "you" can be a subject pronoun or an object pronoun (unlike "I" and "me"). However, Spanish makes clear the reference through the verb and its conjugation (*amo* is "love"-first person, as opposed to *amas* ("love"-second person). While this might seem confusing to English speakers, English does something similar in imperative sentences, like "Go to the store!" in which the subject is not spoken but understood ("you-understood").

Syntax/grammar can of course be much more intricate than these simple matters, and grammatical principles found in English may be absent in other languages and vice versa. For instance, English contains articles ("a" and "the"), but Turkish and Warlpiri do not. At the same time, many languages, including French, Spanish, and German, contain the concept of "gender" in which every noun is assigned one of two (or in the case of German, three – masculine, feminine, and neuter) genders. So, *chat* ("cat") in French is masculine, and *television* is feminine. Then, articles and adjectives must agree with the noun in gender and in number: *le chat, la television, les chats, les televisions, le grand chat, la grande television.*

In English, nouns and pronouns are distinguished by "case," that is, their role in a sentence (basically, subject and object). In other languages the situation is considerably elaborated. For instance, German has four cases ("nominative" or roughly subject, "accusative" or roughly direct object, "dative" or roughly indirect object, and "genitive" or roughly possessive), each of which requires a modification of articles; added to three genders and two numbers (singular and plural), many people find German declensions maddeningly difficult. In Russian, nouns have cases – six of them, depending on the noun's function in the sentence (as subject, direct object, possessive/quantity/negation, indirect object, location, or means (i.e., by/with)) – and must be conjugated with the proper suffix (also considering gender, of which there are three).

Finally for our purposes are "person" and "tense." "Person" is the grammatical category that indicates who the speaker and the audience of an utterance are; in English this includes the first (I/we), second (you/you all), and third person (he/she/it/they), divided into singular and plural. Verbs are conjugated somewhat differently for each person (although not as differently as in Spanish). Warlpiri contains more person forms than English, including a second- and third-person inclusive and exclusive (that is, "we-but-not-you" and "we-all," and "they-but-not-you" and "they-all"), each taking a different verb ending. "Tense" is, generally speaking, the time element in speech – present, past, and future – although this can be joined with "aspect" – that is, the relation of the action to other facts or events (e.g., completed in the past, ongoing in the present, simultaneous with some other actions). Not all languages can fit neatly into the tense and aspect categories of English. For example, Shoshone verbs can take progressive (ongoing over time), continuative (happening over and over), customary-habitual, resultative (resulting from some previous action), future, completive (finished in the past but having effects in the present), and expective (expected to occur) tenses and aspects, each with different suffixes and other rules of use (Gould and Loether 2002).

Pragmatics or sociolinguistics

Pragmatics
The rules or practices regarding how language is used in particular social situations to convey particular social information, such as the relative status or power of the speakers.

Sociolinguistics
See pragmatics.

Our speech choices have social meanings and social consequences. There may be grammatical ways to say things that are not *appropriate* ways to say things. This indicates something very important: language does much more than exchange factual information. As in the alternatives of Malagasy "voice," all of which convey the same factual data – that I want you to wash the clothes – each conveys other critical information as well and may elicit a very different response. It may actually be, in the end, that most of what language conveys is not facts but other kinds of "social" information.

Pragmatics (from the root *pragma* for practical or practice) or **sociolinguistics** (literally, society + language) refers to the rules or conventions for using language appropriately in social situations – that is, for saying the right thing to the right person in the right circumstances. The point is that *a language is a "code" not only for factual information but for social information as well*. The kinds of social information encoded, and how, will depend upon the society and the distinctions it makes between "different kinds" of people and situations. There is no society in which all individuals are exactly equal in status or in which all situations are exactly the same in meaning and value. Minimally, some people are "higher" than others and some situations are "more important" than others. Different speech forms will be appropriate in regard to these different people and conditions.

One good example of the social use of language is the area of **honorifics** or language forms specialized to indicate the relative social status or relationship of the speakers. In French, there are two forms of the pronoun "you" – the singular or familiar *tu* form (for friends and equals) and the plural or formal *vous* form (for strangers and superiors). Employing the *tu* form in talking with your superiors would either indicate closeness, disrespect, or error, just as employing the *vous* form with your spouse or friends would seem overly formal or distant. English lacks such basic vocabulary distinctions, but there are ways to convey respect, from "polite" terms of address like "sir" and "ma'am" to more specialized ones like "your honor" and "your majesty," as well as semantic additions like "please" and "may." We might even use a respectful syntax, like a question rather than a command, and a deferential tone of voice.

Other languages can go much further. For instance, in Thai there are thirteen different forms of the first-person pronoun ("I") depending on whom one is addressing. *Phom* would be an appropriate polite word to use between equals, while *kraphom* would sound better when talking to someone higher in rank (say, a monk or a government official), and the most formal *klaawkramom* would be correct for addressing a member of the royal family. Japanese also has an extensive set of linguistic choices, expressed most simply in the distinction between *tatemae* (polite forms for strangers or people outside your in-group) and *honne* (familiar forms for close friends and family). The idea "Sakai drew a map for Suzuki" can take the following forms for the following reasons (Foley 1997: 319–21):

Honorifics
Language forms specialized to indicate the relative social status or relationship of the speakers.

Foley, William A. 1997. *Anthropological Linguistics: An Introduction*. London: Blackwell Publishers.

1. *Sakai ga Suziki no tame ni chinzu o kai-ta* (used if the two people mentioned, Sakai and Suzuki, are familiar or inferior to the speaker).
2. *Sakai san ga Suzuki san ni chizu o kai-ta/kaki-mash-ta* (used if Sakai and Suzuki are equal to the speaker).
3. *Sakai san ga Suzuki san ni chizu o o-kaki-ni nat-ta/nari-mashi-ta* (used if Sakai is considerably higher in status than the speaker).
4. *Sakai san ga Suzuki san ni chizu o o-kaki shi-ta/shi-mashi-ta* (used if Suzuki is considerably higher in status than Sakai).
5. *Sakai san ga Suzuki san ni chizu o kai-te kudasai-ta/kudasai-mashi-ta* (used if Suzuki is considerably lower in status than Sakai but the speaker wants to show his solidarity/familiarity with Suzuki).

And so on. Clearly, learning Japanese involves much more than simply learning the Japanese translations for English words. Indeed, it would be difficult to render the Japanese connotations of these sentences into everyday English at all.

Overall, the style variations in a language are codes for the important social distinctions made by the society. These can include such social factors as age, gender, power, office, education, interpersonal relationship, class, title, race, geographical region, and many others. No doubt if a non-native speaker said any of the five Japanese sentences above, all Japanese speakers would understand the factual content of the utterance: somebody drew a map for somebody. However, all but the correct form would "feel wrong" to the native speakers and perhaps evoke negative reactions.

As we noted, English has a set of possibilities for communicating relative status and prestige and the formality of the situation, albeit limited compared to those of Thai and Japanese. In the U.S.A. in particular, there are not many honorific forms because there is no use for them. Americans do not make the same distinctions, or attach the same importance to them, that, say, the Japanese do. If Americans made such distinctions, they would have to have a way to talk about them. At the same time, British English includes forms of address to nobility and royalty, because nobility and royalty exist in that society. The fact that Americans do not have regular linguistic forms for such social distinctions means that they do not make those distinctions: there is no royalty in the U.S.A. It is probably fair to say that America, as a society with an egalitarian ideology, deliberately and consciously avoids making many social distinctions in its speech. For example, the fact that students usually speak in a comparatively informal style to teachers indicates that the "social distance" between students and teachers is not great. Americans would even address their president with the informal "you" because they have no other semantic choice (although they might express respect in other ways, including polite forms, tone of voice, and body language).

Much of the remainder of this chapter will explore the forms and occasions for pragmatic language use. Language will be seen not only to describe social (and of course "objective") facts but also to create, sustain, and contest those facts as well.

MAKING SOCIETY THROUGH LANGUAGE: LANGUAGE AND THE CONSTRUCTION OF SOCIAL REALITY

The previous discussion of speech styles and social status barely scratches the surface of the complex and intimate relationship between language and society. Language is much more than a set of words for things. It also fundamentally expresses and constructs social relationships, including political and religious as well as gender and age and other status relations, not just in terms of what different individuals and groups talk about but how they talk. We should think of language and its skillful manipulation as a social resource that both is produced by and produces interpersonal and intergroup bonds and fractures.

Language as performance

One of the best ways to introduce the social efficacy of language is in terms of what J. L. Austin called **performatives**. In *How to Do Things with Words* (1962), Austin distinguished between speech acts that describe the world and ones that change the world in some way. For example, there is a big difference between a declarative sentence ("You are getting married") or an imperative sentence ("Get married!") and a performative sentence ("I now pronounce you man and wife"). In such utterances, the saying of it makes it so – the words are more than words but a real social act that accomplishes some social effect. Put another way, speaking in such cases is not just saying something but doing something.

There are many kinds of linguistic performatives in any society. When a judge says, "Case dismissed" or a king says, "I knight thee," a social change has been worked. Notice that only certain kinds of people can perform certain linguistic acts; issuing performative statements is part of the role they occupy. Ordinary citizens cannot dismiss court cases or bestow knighthoods (in fact, no one in the United States can bestow knighthoods). Furthermore, the social context must be correct: a priest cannot walk down the street marrying people by saying, "I pronounce you man and wife." In extreme situations, the proper people must be present, the proper rituals must be observed, perhaps even the proper clothing must be worn. The speech act is part of a much more comprehensive social setting or "ritual."

Austin distinguished a variety of kinds of performatives, including "verdictives" in which a "ruling" of some sort is made, "exercitives" in which power is exercised such as to appoint or advise or warn, "commissives" in which a commitment is made, such as a promise or agreement (e.g., an oath), and "behabitives" that express a socially recognized behavior, such as an apology or a congratulation. Two other interesting aspects of performatives are interrelated. One is that the "sincerity" of the utterance does not determine its effectiveness: if I am still angry with you but I say, "I forgive you," the words can be just as socially "successful." However, as in other dimensions of language, performatives allow for the possibility of deception or failure; that is, I can say, "I promise to do so and so" and never intend to do it, and I can attempt to apologize and fail, either because the recipient sees through my false sentiment or because I do not execute the verbal behavior correctly. Then they might say, "No, give a *real* apology!" or "Apology not accepted."

Performatives have what Austin called "illocutionary force" in that they do not convey meaning so much as bring about a social outcome – actually making someone a knight or a married person. Other kinds of utterances can have "perlocutionary force" in that they can have an effect on the audience and lead them to have certain feelings or to take certain actions. Persuading is a key perlocutionary effect; others include frightening and upsetting. Perlocutionary acts do not directly change the social world, but they change people's attitudes, prompting them to put those changes into action.

Performatives
Linguistic utterances that do not merely describe but actually accomplish a transformation in the social world.

Austin, J.L. 1962. *How To Do Things with Words*. Oxford: Clarendon Press.

Language and political power

One thing that gets a leader elected in a democracy is the ability to give a good speech; sometimes it is the main thing. Pericles in ancient Athens and Marc Anthony in Shakespeare's *Julius Caesar* swayed the crowd with skillful oration. Language is central to obtaining, exercising, and challenging power in many societies.

Michelle Rosaldo describes the Ilongot of the Philippines as a society that took linguistic abilities very seriously; for them, "true verbal art has social force" (Rosaldo 1984: 140). Oratory or *purung* was a highly prized and formally structured speech form in which "art and politics are combined" (138). It was contrasted to ordinary forms such as gossip or *berita*, myths or *tadek* or *tudtud*, and tales, where the content was more important than the style; in *purung* the most important thing was how things were said rather than what was said.

PLATE 4.2 Masterful use of political speaking is a path to power in many societies, as for American President Barack Obama

One of the characteristics of good Ilongot *purung*, as in many societies, was a certain amount of indirectness and wit (*beira* or elaboration, *'amba'an* or witty flourish, *'asasap* or "crooked" speaking). This was possible because the community already shared knowledge and memories of past actions and events, and it was important to prevent emotions from becoming too enflamed. In practice, *purung* was delivered in the form of verbal exchanges, in which the speakers claimed that they were "giving" or even "feeding" each other words. The target of a speech would repeat the words of the speaker, insisting that they "will not 'hide' their hopes, that in their hearts are no ill thoughts, that in their breath they know that they are kinsmen" (143). The ultimate purpose of these performances was to restore the kin bonds of the two speakers or sides, but this was accomplished "through deception, pretense, wit, and the display of unity and strength by 'sides' that are, initially, opposed" (143). As in this and most such instances, a kind of verbal negotiation not only of interests but of statuses was taking place, and neither side could afford to totally dominate or humiliate the other.

From the holistic perspective of anthropology, it is clear that the style and substance of political speaking would be related to the general quality of politics and to the hierarchies or lack thereof in the society. Box 4.1 illustrates a clear contrast between the form and the intent of public oratory based on the political relations within the society.

BOX 4.1 SPEECH AND POWER – A CULTURAL COMPARISON

In the descriptions by Atkinson and Firth, the Wana of Sulawesi (Indonesia) and the Tikopia had very different manners of public speaking, reflecting their very different social and political systems. The Wana were an acephalous (i.e., without a head or leader) and mostly egalitarian society in which no enduring political roles or groups existed. Tikopia was a highly stratified society with a formal system of chiefs with coercive power.

When Wana men met for the purpose of public speaking, they practiced *kiyori*, an extremely stylized poetic form broken into stanzas with rigid principles about syllabification, emphasis, and rhyme. They might also use specialized terminology, especially as part of religious or legal occasions. It was ordinarily addressed to one man by one man, and the listener might repeat the speech several times as if memorizing it. Sometimes the receiver of the *kiyori* would answer with his own, setting off an exchange of lines. The intentions of speaking *kiyori* varied from establishment of alliances to advice to strong criticism. One of the key features of *kiyori*, however, was the use of ambiguous or conventional references, like aphorisms and metaphors. In fact, it was "an expressive form well suited for speaking in oblique and clever ways" (Atkinson 1984: 57), and skillful speakers took full advantage of the potential for ambiguity.

In Tikopia, a public assembly or *fono* might have a very different quality. The occasion of a *fono* was usually an announcement by a chief or one of his functionaries; it was for proclamation, not discussion. As Firth (1975) describes it, the speaker addressed the crowd with restraint, possibly standing still or walking back and forth. He spoke in a forceful staccato voice, issuing direct commands and declarations, without personal opinion or ingenious proverbs and allusions. There was no attempt to avoid directness.

The difference between the two oratorical styles relates to the two political contexts in which they occurred. Wana speakers, without permanent status or followers, could not afford to be abrupt. They had to appear to be intelligent and wise even while they avoided conflict and open opposition, because they were actively and precariously recruiting their allies via the speech act. Tikopia speakers did not have any such reticence, because their political positions were already firm. Being the dominant members of officially stratified societies, they did not have to spare any feelings or circumvent any conflict: they had the social right and duty to issue orders and expected the compliance of their listeners.

Oral literature and specialized language styles

There are many other areas where language and social relationships intersect, including gender, to which we will return in the next chapter. However, one more that calls for our attention at this point is "cultural knowledge" and the specialized language styles that communicate it. Anthropologists and others often refer to this body of knowledge and the genres in which it occurs as **folklore**, a society's primarily oral and traditional knowledge which is "told" or "performed" in specific, appropriate ways. To gain some idea of the range of linguistic activities that may be regarded as folklore, consider Alan Dundes' list:

Folklore

The "traditional," usually oral literature of a society, consisting of various genres such as myth, legend, folktale, song, proverb, and many others.

> Folklore includes myths, legends, folktales, jokes, proverbs, riddles, chants, charms, blessings, curses, oaths, insults, retorts, taunts, teases, toasts, tongue-twisters, and greeting and leave-taking formulas. . . . It also includes folk costume, folk dance, folk drama, folk instrumental music . . . , folksongs . . . , folk speech . . . , folk similes . . . , folk metaphors . . . , and names. Folk poetry ranges from oral epics to autograph-book verse, epitaphs, latrinalia (writings on the walls of public bathrooms), limericks, ball-bouncing rhymes, jump-rope rhymes, finger and toe rhymes, dandling rhymes (to bounce children on the knee), counting-out rhymes . . . , and nursery rhymes. The list of folklore forms also contains games; gestures; symbols; prayers (e.g., graces); practical jokes; folk etymologies; food recipes; quilt and embroidery designs; house, barn, and fence types; street vendor's cries; and even the traditional conventional sounds used to summon animals or to give them commands.
>
> (Dundes 1965: 3)

See Chapter 10

Myth will be discussed in more detail in the context of religion, and there are too many others to explore them all here, but a few of these oral literature styles will highlight the variety and social importance of specialized linguistic performances.

1. **Proverbs.** In many societies, much "conventional wisdom" is contained in proverbs and other such traditional sayings. They tend to be brief, pithy, and often metaphorical. American English is full of them – "A penny saved is a penny earned," "A leopard can't change its spots," and so on. Other societies have their own culturally specific sayings as well as socially appropriate occasions for using them. Ilongot *purung* or Wana *kiyori* may incorporate apt proverbs, as well as original metaphors. John Messenger notes that the Anang in Nigeria employed proverbs for a variety of purposes, including entertainment and education but also more serious ones like rituals and court hearings. Particularly in the traditional courts known as *esop*, Anang litigants "take every opportunity to display their eloquence and constantly employ adages" (Messenger 1965: 303–4). A well-met proverb could make the case and determine the outcome of the proceedings. Of course, many of these maxims do not make much sense outside of their cultural context, for example:

> "If a dog plucks palm fruits from a cluster, he does not fear a porcupine."

> "A single partridge flying through the bush leaves no path."

PLATE 4.3 Herbert Jim, a contemporary Seminole (Native American) story teller

"If you visit the home of the toads, stoop."

"The crayfish is bent because it is sick."

To use and understand such utterances well requires an understanding of the society's world of meaning.

2. Riddles. Like a proverb, a riddle "seems to depend on *metaphor*, on a kind of poetic comparison drawn between the thing actually described and the referent to be guessed" (De Caro 1986: 178). In contemporary American society, riddles are mostly told for fun and most often by or to children. However, in other societies they can have other and more serious functions. De Caro notes six contexts in which riddling takes place across cultures, including leisure, education (for instance, the famous Buddhist *koan*), courting and mating, greeting, initiations and funerals, and folk narrative. In Dusun society, riddles could be combative as well as humiliating, and Turkish society used riddles in festivals such as weddings and actually had professional riddlers and neighborhood riddling teams.

Beuchat (1957) tells that the Bantu made riddles for fun and to demonstrate intelligence and wit. The riddles were characteristically short verbal analogies which required a "solution" or answer, such as:

"I have built my house without any door." Answer: an egg.

"The little hole full of grass litter." Answer: the teeth.

"Two little holes that refuse to be filled; there enter people, oxen, goats, and other things." Answer: eyes.

3. Ritual languages. In many societies, one or more specialized linguistic genre(s) may exist for specific purposes. Sherzer (1983), for instance, identifies three quite distinct speaking styles in Kuna society in Panama, associated with a particular ritual activity and distinguished from everyday speech or *tule kaya*. Political or chiefly speech (*sakla kaya*), curing song or "stick doll language" (*suar miimi kaya*), and girls' puberty rite language (*kantule kaya*) each had different pace and tone qualities, as well as specialized vocabularies and other aspects of increasing formality. Latin served the same general purpose in medieval Europe, conveying a gravity that ordinary vernacular languages did not. The use of archaic forms like "thee" and "thou" in English still confers an artistic and even religious aura. Richard Bauman (2001) proposes eight characteristics or "devices" that set specialized or ritualized speech apart from everyday talk: unique "codes" including archaic or esoteric terms, formulas like conventional openings and closings (e.g., "Once upon a time"), figurative language like metaphors, stylistic alternatives like rhyme or repetition, patterns of tempo or stress or pitch, "paralinguistic" usages (see below), overt appeals to tradition, and "disclaimers of performance."

Bauman, Richard. 2001. "Verbal Art in Performance." In Alessandro Duranti, ed. *Linguistic Anthropology: A Reader*. Malden, MA and Oxford: Blackwell Publishing, 165–88.

Paralanguage and non-verbal language

Not all of human communication, or even of language, is verbal, and verbal language is not limited to its "words" or morphemes. Non-verbal gestures of various kinds can have meaning independent of spoken language, and they can be added to alter the meaning of speech. At the same time, the ways that speakers modulate speech can also affect its meaning.

Paralanguage includes the vocal features that shape the delivery of spoken language, such as tone, pitch, speed, rhythm, and volume. Saying the same thing rapidly or slowly, or in a high- or low-pitched voice, can change its meaning. Some specialized forms of speech, like the Tikopia *fono* mentioned above, are associated with particular paralinguistic variations. We can also communicate emotion and sincerity through voice qualities, as well as advanced skills like irony and sarcasm. Other paralinguistic features include sounds that are not strictly linguistic but that convey meaning; called **vocalizations**, some examples are "um" and "shhh" and "tsk-tsk."

The vocal apparatus is not the only part of humans involved in the construction of meaning, including linguistic meaning. The entire human body can be a meaning-conveying medium. **Kinesics** is the general name for the bodily movements or gestures that augment and modify verbal communication (sometimes called "body language"). Among kinesics issues are facial expressions, hand gestures, and the physical distance between speakers. For example, a wink in America can suggest dishonesty or conspiracy between speakers. Raised eyebrows indicate surprise, and lowered brows can express doubt or displeasure. In some societies there is a more

Paralanguage
The qualities which speakers can add to language to modify the factual or social meaning of speech, such as tone of voice, volume, pitch, speed and cadence, and "non-linguistic" sounds like grunts and snickers.

Vocalizations
Non-linguistic sounds that can accompany and affect the meaning of speech.

Kinesics
The study of how body movements are used to communicate social information, sometimes referred to as "body language."

or less complete "language" of hand signs, as in the Warlpiri system known as *rdaka rdaka* (literally, "hand hand"). There are hand signs for many common words, used by hunters to maintain silence, by mourners when certain words are forbidden, and most widely by women. In many other societies, there are less complete but still important culturally relative gestures.

BOX 4.2 GESTURES ACROSS CULTURES

Like so much else, gestures are culturally relative; the same gesture can have a different and even opposite meaning in different cultures. For instance (based on Axtell 1991):

Sticking out your tongue is an insult in the U.S.A. but a greeting in Tibet.

In the U.S.A., the thumb and forefinger circle means "OK," but in Russia, Germany, and Brazil it is an insult. In Japan it is the sign for money (a round coin).

In Holland, tapping your forefinger on your forehead means "You are stupid."

In Iran and Australia, the "thumbs up" signal is rude.

In Bulgaria, Greece, Turkey, Iran, and Bengal, nodding your head means "no" and shaking your head means "yes."

In England, the two-fingered "V" gesture is an insult if the back of the hand is facing the audience; in that case, it means "Up yours."

Finally, **proxemics** looks specifically at the use of personal space in interactions. Different societies maintain different degrees of physical distance between members, depending on their relationship. American casual speakers keep a twenty-four-inch or so zone between them, while Japanese maintain more distance and Middle Easterners less (the latter may even hold hands, as we noted at the opening of Chapter 1). Diverging from these standard distances can communicate intimacy, respect, avoidance, or invasiveness depending on the culture and the distance.

Proxemics
The study of how cultures use personal space (or "proximity").

Language change, loss, and competition

Like everything else in the cultural world, language is dynamic, constantly changing, and available for humans to manipulate and compete over and through. One important aspect of real-world language use is the multilingual situation in many societies. In places from Belgium to New Guinea, multiple languages co-exist side by side, with various relationships, from cooperative to hostile. "Linguistic nationalism" can threaten to pull societies apart, as in Canada, where the French-speaking Quebecois have tried several times to pass a referendum separating Quebec from Canada to form

Diglossia

The use of two varieties of a language by members of a society for distinct functions or by distinct groups or classes of people.

Pidgin

A simplified version of a language that is usually used for limited purposes, such as trade and economic interactions, by non-native speakers of the language (as in Melanesian pidgin versions of English). Usually an incomplete language that is not the "first" language of any group.

Creole

A pidgin language that has become elaborated into a multi-functional language and distributed into a first language of the community.

Anti-language

A speech style used by individuals or groups in the performance of roles opposing or inverting the society outside of their group.

their own officially French-speaking country. When two languages share a social space, the choice of language may be a "political" or "symbolic" statement, as Leach (1954) noted in Burma: which language you speak, at any given time or habitually, can indicate "whose side you are on." Even within a single language, there may be two or more forms treated as "high" and "low" or "prestigious" and "common." This phenomenon is known as **diglossia** and is found in distinctions of function (say, lower form for "popular" or casual uses and higher form for official or formal uses) as well as class and stratification.

In situations of sustained and, particularly, imbalanced culture contact, changes may occur to one or both of the contact languages. Often a simplified working version of the dominant language, showing certain features of the subordinated language, will emerge for basic purposes like trade. Such a hybrid language is called a **pidgin** and tends to have a significantly reduced vocabulary and grammar; one defining feature is that a pidgin is not the first or primary language of either party. However, over time a pidgin may become more sophisticated and multi-functional, even becoming the first language of a community. When a new or hybrid language has achieved this level of sophistication and use, it is called a **creole**. Another possible and common consequence of language contact is language loss, which can occur when the members of a speech community adopt a foreign language to the exclusion of their previous one, whether voluntarily or not. Young people may cease learning it, and elders may be the last to speak it. In the worst cases, the entire language-bearing society dies or is exterminated.

Finally, language may be a focus of struggle between two societies, communities, or subcultures, or it may be a medium for staking out distinct and competitive or resistant identities *vis-à-vis* the dominant society. Technical or subcultural jargons or argots can signal differentiation from or even rejection of other segments of society. Halliday (1976) coined the term **anti-language** to refer to the most dramatic form of this behavior, a speech style (specialized phonetics, vocabulary, grammar, and/or pragmatics) used by individuals or groups in the performance of roles opposing or inverting the society outside of their group.

LANGUAGE ACQUISITION AND THE LINGUISTIC RELATIVITY HYPOTHESIS

No one is born knowing and speaking any particular language, yet we all have one within a few years of birth. Language is learned and shared like the rest of culture. For some researchers, this has profound implications.

It seems evident that language is not "in the brain" at birth; if language was innate, all humans ought to speak the same language. It also seems evident that there is something in or about the human brain that extracts or constructs language from experienced speech, some neurological capacity to acquire and use language. There is nothing contradictory in accepting both of these realities. Whatever the biological substrate, different societies speak different languages; language is relative to a particular society. However, theorists like Edward Sapir and Benjamin Lee Whorf went far beyond that obvious truth. They suggested that not just the words and the sounds but the very minds that produce those words and sounds are quite different. As Whorf wrote:

> the background linguistic system (in other words, the grammar) of each language is not merely a reproducing instrument for voicing ideas but rather is itself the shaper of ideas, the program and guide for the individual's mental activity, for his analysis of impressions, for his synthesis of his mental stock in trade. Formulation of ideas is not an independent process, strictly rational in the old sense, but is part of a particular grammar, and differs, from slightly to greatly, between different grammars. We dissect nature along lines laid down by our native languages. The categories and types that we isolate from the world of phenomena we do not find there because they stare every observer in the face; on the contrary, the world is presented in a kaleidoscopic flux of impressions which has to be organized by our minds – and this means largely by the linguistic systems in our minds.
>
> (Whorf 1940: 231)

Edward Sapir, one of the great early professional anthropologists, joined Whorf in this assessment of the role and power of language. As he said:

> Human beings do not live in the objective world alone nor alone in the world of social activity as ordinarily understood, but are very much at the mercy of the particular language which has become the medium of expression for their society. It is quite an illusion to imagine that one adjusts to reality essentially without the use of language and that language is merely an incidental means of solving specific problems of communication or reflection. The fact of the matter is that the "real world" is to a large extent unconsciously built up on the language habits of the group. No two languages are ever sufficiently similar to be considered as representing the same social reality. The worlds in which different societies live are distinct worlds, not merely the same world with different labels attached.
>
> (Sapir 1949:162)

This quotation explains what is known as the **linguistic relativity hypothesis** or the Sapir-Whorf hypothesis. The idea is that a language is not just a list of words for things, not just vocabulary. It is also a code for concepts, ideas, relationships (and not just social ones but "natural" ones like cause, similarity and difference, time, and such), and even values and meanings. Humans are not born with any vocabulary, nor are we born with any concepts, ideas, relationships, values, or meanings. Then, as we acquire the "linguistic code" of our society's language we acquire these concepts, ideas, relationships, and so on. If so, speakers of different languages (especially radically different ones) acquire different concepts, ideas, relationships, values, meanings, and so on and come to experience the world through them. In the ultimate formulation of the hypothesis, speakers of different languages live in very different

Linguistic relativity hypothesis
The claim that language is not only a medium for communication about experience but actually a more or less powerful constituent of that experience. Language consists of concepts, relations, and values, and speakers of different languages approach and interpret reality through different sets of concepts, relations, and values. Also known as the Sapir-Whorf hypothesis.

mental worlds. As Whorf defines it, then, the linguistic relativity hypothesis "means, in informal terms, that users of markedly different grammars are pointed by their grammars toward different types of observations and different evaluations of externally similar acts of observation, and hence are not equivalent as observers but must arrive at somewhat different views of the world" (1956: 221). This is clearly a controversial suggestion and can probably be taken too far. Some concepts, like causality or space, for instance, can at least partially arise from embodied experience in the physical world. Yet even in these "basic" concepts, some cultural variation can and does occur.

Whorf, Benjamin Lee. 1956. *Language, Thought, and Reality: Selected Writings of Benjamin Lee Whorf.* Cambridge, MA: The Massachusetts Institute of Technology Press.

Attempts to test the linguistic relativity hypothesis empirically have yielded mixed results. One area of testing has been color perception and terminology. While some cultures have as few as two color terms (essentially "black" and "white"), many have no more than four. Does the presence or absence of color terms affect the actual perception of color? The comparative work of Berlin and Kay (1969) suggests not: they discovered what they regarded as a set of standard hues that societies (although not all societies) recognize and name, as well as a universal sequence of named hues, starting (and sometimes ending) with black and white, followed by red, then yellow or green, then blue. But the fact that not all societies get beyond black and white, and that many do not get beyond black and white and red and yellow, makes the research inconclusive.

A much more recent experiment, however, suggests the power of the linguistic effect on thought. Ross, Xun, and Wilson (2002) studied bilingual Chinese-Canadians on a series of psychological and personality items. Some individuals were given the test in Chinese, and others were given the same questions in English. An even more provocative version of this investigation was conducted by Ramirez-Esparza et al. (2006), in which they surveyed the same bilingual English-Spanish individuals twice, once in each language. Both studies found that the language of response affected the responses. Chinese-born individuals writing in Chinese showed significantly more typically Chinese views and self-perceptions than the same population writing in English. Likewise, English-Spanish bilinguals evinced personality traits that were more consistent with Spanish speakers when functioning in Spanish and more consistent with English speakers when functioning in English. Ramirez-Esparza et al. attribute the results to "cultural frame switching," a phenomenon in which individuals "change their interpretations of the world, depending upon their internalized cultures, in response to cues in their environment . . . as subtle as language" (2006: 20). Ross et al. go so far as to propose that "East-Asian and Western identities are stored in separate knowledge structures . . . in bicultural individuals, with each structure activated by its associated language" (2002: 1048).

The place of language in experience is most immediate and obvious in the area of social and cultural concepts, which may have no correlate at all in other cultures. The concepts may be embedded in language, or they may be lexical items themselves. As an embedded case, one cannot speak Japanese well without learning to make and express major culturally specific social distinctions, like those mentioned above.

Likewise, in Ilongot or Tikopian society, the use or understanding of different speech styles attunes a speaker to matters of egalitarianism and hierarchy, fixed and fluid roles.

On the other hand, there are some ideas and concepts captured by words in any given language and culture that are divergent, if not absent altogether, from others. The Warlpiri religious concept of *jukurrpa* has no cognate in English or any other non-Aboriginal language; it is not just another name for God or heaven or even for dreams, although its literal translation is "dream" or "dreaming." The "field" of this key term includes dreams as well as the creation time at the beginning of the world, sacred designs and objects, and rituals; no single English word does or can convey all these meanings. Even when a society has a word that we might render as "god" or "spirit" or "soul," we cannot assume that their meaning is identical to ours or each others'. Culturally specific words like *brahma* in Hinduism, *nirvana* in Buddhism, *diyi* ("luck") in Apache, even *jihad* in Arabic, as well as many others, cannot be simplistically translated into some supposed "equivalent" in another language; yet these terms and concepts are central and motivational in their societies. This presents a fascinating challenge to cross-cultural translation and understanding: the key terms and concepts of another culture, expressed in language and also in practice, may be constitutive of a very different social experience, a very different "cultural reality."

See Chapter 10

BOX 4.3 CONTEMPORARY CULTURAL CONTROVERSIES: THE POLITICS OF LANGUAGE IN THE U.S.A.

In George Orwell's prophetic novel *1984*, the philosophy of the regime was "Who controls the past controls the future. Who controls the present controls the past." And the regime understood that control of the present rests in the language, which was why it devised "Newspeak," a form of language in which it was easy to say and think certain things and difficult or impossible to say or think others. Opinion-makers and politicians of all points on the spectrum have equally understood that language may be used not only to inform but to persuade, motivate, and even "disinform" – usually to propagate their power or policies (hence the term "propaganda"). Recently, a figure named Frank Luntz has been using this insight to reframe the political discourse in American society. Acting primarily as an advisor for the political "Right," he has conducted "market research" on different words and phrases to determine which will best influence public opinion. It was his idea to replace "estate tax" with "death tax" and "global warming" with "climate change." He has actually advocated dropping certain terms like "globalization," "drilling for oil," and even "government" completely. Some people see this as blatant and dangerous manipulation. What do you think?

SUMMARY

Language is both a medium of human communication and interaction and a shaping influence on that communication and interaction. Humans are not the only species that communicate, nor even communicate linguistically. However, humans have unique linguistic skills, which are also the same skills that make culture in general possible:

- symbolism
- productivity
- displacement.

Language takes the form of a set of basic items and combinatory rules, from sound units to meaning units to utterances to socially appropriate speech acts. Each of these dimensions is studied by a specific area of linguistics:

- phonology
- morphology or semantics
- syntax or grammar
- pragmatics or sociolinguistics.

Language in its social production and use is much more than a list of names for things. It is a code for social information and social relationships. Any language includes a variety of specialized speech forms for different individuals and groups, different occasions, and different relationships. Language as a social phenomenon can express or determine functions such as:

- changes of social status and role
- politics and power relations
- performance of specific linguistic genres, such as ritual or story-telling
- blending, stratifying, or differentiating of social groups.

Language, as a set of concepts or categories, may also influence the way in which humans experience and interpret, and therefore respond to, their world – both physical and social. The linguistic relativity hypothesis suggests that language mediates human thought and experience such that members of different speech communities think and experience differently. This is an area of controversy and ongoing research.

Key Terms

Anti-language

Bound morpheme

Competence

Diglossia

Displacement

Folklore

Free morpheme

Grammar

Kinesics

Linguistic relativity hypothesis

Morpheme

Morphology

Paralanguage

Performatives

Phoneme

Phonology

Pidgin

Pragmatics

Productivity

Proxemics

Semantics

Sociolinguistics

Symbol

Syntax

Vocalizations

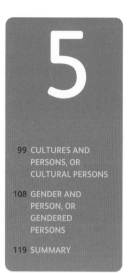

5

Learning to be an Individual: Personality and Gender

The Utku of northern Canada (Briggs 1970) have been described as a generally non-violent group living in a harsh arctic environment where intimacy of residence and interdependence of economics were a necessity. They highly valued a mild and steady temperament and disliked expressions of negative emotion – anger (*urulu* or *huaq*), resentment, and mere unhappiness. But blatant displays of positive emotion were troubling too. The ideal Utku person exhibited *kanngu*, restraint or shyness or a satisfaction with being appropriately inconspicuous. A good, even morally good, person possessed *naklik* or love, concern, and protectiveness; the worst thing a person could be was bad-tempered and selfish. Small children were especially lavished with *naklik* and administered few punishments. Adults thought it would be pointless, since children below the age of 5 did not possess enough *ihuma* or sense/reason to learn self-control. However, at around age 5, a child became capable of *ihuma* and learned his or her first tough lesson: that he or she was really not so important after all. Parents would ignore the child's cries and rather abruptly withdraw affection. This might be accompanied by teasing, occasional destruction of the child's property (and pets), and open preference for the new baby that may have come along to receive the parents' *naklik*. Gradually the older child learned to restrain his or her emotions and to accept his or her place in the family and society – a place of interpersonal equality, but a place in which no one was particularly special and where emotions were not overtly expressed.

A society is a system of human individuals in some structured relationships with each other, relationships that are informed and shaped by beliefs and values and meanings. More than that, a society is a set of "kinds of persons to be": individuals occupy culturally defined roles and positions, and they act within a universe of concepts and categories that make their actions meaningful and appropriate. Gilbert Herdt has referred to this universe of categories and meanings as a **cultural ontology**. Ontology is the study of being, of what kinds of things exist. Herdt defines cultural ontology as "local theories of being and metaphysics of the world; of having a certain kind of body and being in a certain kind of social world, which creates a certain cultural reality; and of being and knowledge combined in the practice of living" (1994: 61). Culture posits many different kinds of beings, a great number of which pertain to what we would call "religion." However, a culture also contains an ontology of human beings – what kinds of humans are there, what makes them different kinds of humans, and how does the society treat and value them? As Herdt adds,

> For a collective ontology to emerge and be transmitted across time, there must be a social condition, eventually a stable social role, that can be inhabited – marking off a clear social status position, rights and duties, with indications for the transmission of corporeal and incorporeal property and status.

(Herdt 1994: 60)

Humans, even within a single society, are born diverse, but culture provides a combination of increased diversification through enculturation and of categorization of innate and acquired differences. We might say that humans *learn how to be individuals in the presence of culture* and that culture assigns meaning and value to different kinds of individuals. The study of the individual in a cultural context raises fundamental questions about "human nature": to what extent is human behavior given by nature or shaped by culture? This is a debate that rages to this day. Two particularly important and interrelated aspects of the argument are the questions of personality and gender. Here, as in all other areas that it surveys, anthropology finds that the answers – or at least the facts – are more complicated but at the same time more interesting than mere dualities.

CULTURES AND PERSONS, OR CULTURAL PERSONS

Since different cultures have different categories and definitions of persons, the anthropologist must be careful to understand theirs and not impose his or her own culture. One indicative area is the concept of "self." **Self** is a key concept in Western cultures. In a way it is taken for granted: self is real, everybody has one, and it is a good thing. Society keeps the self-concept front and center by constantly invoking it and even "working on it." Self or person was characterized by Geertz as "a bounded, unique, more or less integrated motivational and cognitive universe, a dynamic center of awareness, emotion, judgment, and action organized into a distinctive

Cultural ontology
A society's system of notions about what kinds of things (including kinds of people) exist in the world and their characteristics and social value. A socially specific way of categorizing and valuing the physical and social world.

See Chapter 10

Herdt, Gilbert, ed. 1994. *Third Sex, Third Gender: Beyond Sexual Dimorphism in Culture and History.* New York: Zone Books.

Self
The more or less enduring, bounded, and discrete part of an individual's identity or personality, and the reflexive awareness of this aspect of oneself.

whole and set contrastively both against other such wholes and against its social and natural background" (1976: 225). Particularly in American culture, people are encouraged to cultivate and develop the self, to become very "self-aware" and to improve the self, through physical exercise (equating the self with the body in some way) or more often through "psychological growth" or "self-actualization." Americans even talk about their "self-image" and "self-esteem" and how it can be askew from the "reality" of the self; that is, people can imagine or see themselves to be worse than they really are or occasionally better than they really are. But if one's self-concept can be so elusive and problematic, then self is not quite as simple or self-evident as it may seem.

Two points have surfaced from the cross-cultural analysis of the self. First, self is not as solid and certain as we like to think; it may not even be a universal human concept. Second, self may not be as exclusively human as we like to think. That is, not all humans may have the modern Western sense of self, and not only humans may have some sense of self. To take the first point, a fair amount of research has gone into the question of whether all societies conceive of and experience the self as Westerners do – as a bounded, enduring, private personal essence. There is at least some reason to conclude that they do not. Buddhism teaches explicitly, for instance, that there is no self. *Anatta* or selflessness (not in the sense of unselfishness but literally of having no self) is a central and formal concept in high Buddhism: there is no "you" that endures from moment to moment, let alone for a lifetime or an eternity. Instead, in each moment the person is remade, the previous moment lighting the candle that is the "self" for this moment. So, while there is some continuity for the individual, it is much less than and very different from the Western view.

In other cultures, the enduring and bounded self has been called into question. Nancy Munn's *Walbiri Iconography* (1973) examines the Warlpiri sense of self. She claims to find evidence that they did not have a persistent, concrete self of the familiar Western kind. By looking at their mythology and especially their symbolism, as in their sand-drawings that accompany story-telling, she concludes that they did not have a permanent unchanging sense of self but rather one that was ever transmutable – from human to animal or plant and back, or from human to "spirit" and back. In fact, a "person" could be two things at once rather than "just" himself or herself – human and animal simultaneously, for instance. And for them, the individual was never fully differentiated from the tribe or society; the individual was not really "an individual" but part of a social mass that never completely extricated itself from the society or looked at itself in isolation.

Lee, Dorothy. 1959. *Freedom and Culture.* Englewood Cliffs, NJ: Prentice-Hall, Inc.

Lutz, Catherine A. 1998. *Unnatural Emotions: Everyday Sentiments on a Micronesian Atoll and their Challenge to Western Theory.* Chicago and London: The University of Chicago Press.

Other anthropologists have described self-concepts in other societies – Dorothy Lee among the Wintu (1959), A. Irving Hallowell among the Ojibwa (1967), and Catherine Lutz among the Ifaluk (1998), to name but a few. Lee makes some intriguing claims: based on Wintu linguistic practices, she suggests that the Wintu did not share the Western sense of "an established separate self." Rather, "a Wintu self is identical with the parts of his body and is not related to them as 'other' so long as they are physically part of him" (135). Nor was the self-concept nearly so crucial for the Wintu: "with the Wintu the universe is not centered in the self" (138). Likewise,

PLATE 5.1 Enculturation: Warlpiri elder men showing boys sacred knowledge and skills

Lutz' study of Ifaluk indicated that for these Pacific islanders "the person is first and foremost a social creature and only secondarily, and in a limited way, an autonomous individual" or distinct self; the Ifaluk "are oriented toward each other rather than toward an inner world of individually constituted goals and thoughts" (1998: 81). Therefore, they think of themselves as "more public, social, and relational, and necessarily more dyadic than we do" (82).

Western society may overestimate the solidity of its own selves, as is shown by the ease with which that self is manipulated and even re-formed in such circumstances as brain-washing and conversion. The well-known "Stockholm Syndrome" is a phenomenon in which kidnap victims or captives come – sometimes fairly quickly – to identify and empathize with their captors; by a few simple devices, a person's sense of self can be eroded and replaced with another, more pliant one. Interrogators are all too familiar with the requirements for this pliability, and domestic abusers often count on it tacitly. The taken-for-granted sense of self appears to need constant reinforcement. Disrupt this process (with sleep deprivation, disturbances of natural rhythms, detachment from friends and family and everything familiar, and disinformation from "re-programmers"), and the self quickly collapses and can be reshaped by the right techniques.

Finally, the self may not be uniquely human. Just as anthropologists find "a little culture" in closely related species, so we find "a little self" in these same beings. The question is whether a non-human animal can have an experience of "me-ness" – an awareness of what is and is not its particular individuality. Chimpanzees seem to possess it, at least to a degree. In 1970 the psychologist Gordon Gallup conducted experiments to determine if a chimp knows who s/he is. He placed chimps in front of a mirror, and eventually they discovered that the image in the glass was "themselves." They related their motions to the motions in the mirror, and they even began to examine themselves for the first time, looking at parts of themselves that they had never seen before, like their ears and the inside of their mouths. Going a step further, once the animals had become familiar with themselves, Gallup made subtle changes in their appearance, such as putting a spot of paint on their foreheads. Back in front of the mirror, they quickly realized that "they" were different and explored the spot, including touching it and sniffing their fingers to figure out what was going on. Chimps that had never seen a mirror before did not react to the spot at all – they had not yet acquired a "sense of self." Other experiments have suggested that chimps may also have a sense of "intersubjectivity" – that is, an awareness that other beings have minds and even what may be in those minds. Chimps that are shown the secret hiding place of a key to locked-up food, and are then shown humans who behave as if they do not know where the key is, will guide the humans to the key with facial and hand gestures, indicating that they know that they know that the humans do not know and that the humans need to know it.

Blank slates, elementary ideas, and human nature

The quintessential question of all social sciences and humanities is, what does it mean to be human? The two major competing perspectives in Western civilization have been the "idealist" one (that our ideas or nature are in us from birth) and the "empiricist" one (that experience fills in our mind or personality over time). This dichotomy is popularly known as the "nature-versus-nurture" question. The empiricist or nurture position is known by the analogy of the *tabula rasa*, the blank slate, which is inscribed by experience. The idealist or nature position would then be associated with a full slate of some sort, with the "writing" already given by such sources as blood or genes or brains.

Psychology and anthropology were born at roughly the same time, attempting to answer roughly the same questions, although with very different interests and foci. Psychology quickly became the study of the "inner" life of individual humans, of that allegedly secret and invisible realm of "mind." Anthropology, and its related field of sociology, became the study of external and collective realities and behaviors. Of course, psychology is interested in behavior too, and anthropology is drawn into questions of mind, since mind and behavior, psyche and society, are inextricably linked. In fact, a few enterprising fieldworkers like A. Irving Hallowell (1967) measured mental traits among non-Western peoples by taking Rorschach (ink blot) or other psychological tests into the field.

Meanwhile, anthropology was approaching the question of human nature and the universal structures of mind from its own angle. One of the first important anthropological ideas was offered by Adolph Bastian (1826–1905), who used the term *elementargedanken* to designate the elementary thoughts or ideas that he believed were found in all humans in all places and times. The *elementargedanken*, few in number and completely universal, were expressed in various forms in various times and places as *volkergedanken* or folk ideas. Thus, the Aboriginals or the Utku or the Japanese or the Americans would have local versions of religion or kinship, but underneath these particular manifestations was a common shared humanity that merely "came out" in different ways due to local environmental or historical circumstances. One phrase to describe this notion was the "**psychic unity of humanity**." Lucien Lévy-Bruhl (1857–1939), on the other hand, argued that there were two radically different ways of being and thinking among humans – the modern or rational mentality and what he called a "**primitive mentality**" that was prelogical and mystical or mythical. How else, he queried, could we explain the "odd" and ultimately "false" things that people did or thought in "primitive" societies? Lévy-Bruhl eventually withdrew his concept of primitive mentality, but ideas like it have persisted over the years to distinguish what appears (to the foreign observer) to be practical from impractical (symbolic? false?) beliefs and behaviors.

Psychic unity of humanity
The attitude that all humans regardless of culture share the same basic thought processes.

Primitive mentality
The idea, associated with Lucien Lévy-Bruhl, that non-Western and "primitive" peoples possessed a distinctly different, "pre-logical" mode of thought.

American "culture and personality"

American soil is where the seed of psychological anthropology took firmest roots. Recall that anthropology emerged in the early 1900s, when social changes were occurring in Western societies, not the least of which were the civil rights movement and the first battles in the "sexual revolution." So, when Margaret Mead (1901–78) conducted the fieldwork that would culminate in her book *Coming of Age in Samoa: A Psychological Study of Primitive Youth for Western Civilization* (1928), it is clear not only that she was conducting psychologically inspired research but she intended it to have ramifications for Western society. She expected to find that the maturation process as we know it, in particular the turbulence of adolescence, was not a universal one but a culturally particular one. In Samoans (specifically Samoan adolescent girls), she claimed to find the happy, sexually free, well-adjusted youths that she believed Americans could and should be. The implication was not only that humans are psychologically quite malleable – that there are few if any real universals – but that Westerners could stand to learn a thing or two from other, in some ways "better," societies. Mead's work has come under intense fire from Derek Freeman, who argues that her methods were inadequate, her conclusions wrong, and her agenda too heavy-handed.

Mead, Margaret. 1928. *Coming of Age in Samoa: A Psychological Study of Primitive Youth for Western Civilization*. New York: W. W. Morrow.

Closely behind Mead came another influential female anthropologist who wrote the most popular book ever published in the field, *Patterns of Culture* (1934). Ruth Benedict (1887–1948) was perhaps even more explicitly psychological in her approach and interests, and became a leading force in the culture-and-personality school of thought. In *Patterns of Culture* she treated three different societies as each a unique and complete human reality or "configuration." A society, she concluded, has a culture with its specific values and ideals, and it aims to create – and generally succeeds in creating – individuals who manifest those values and ideals. While the process of individual creation is not perfect (a certain "range" of personalities emerges in the end), it is effective enough to produce a recognizable "type" of person or

Benedict, Ruth. 1934. *Patterns of Culture*. New York: The New American Library.

personality that is distinctly "Kwakiutl" or "Zuni" or "Dobuan" – or, by implication, American. Thus she could sum up a culture with a few key personality or tempera-ment traits, such as "egocentric," "individualistic," and "ecstatic" for the Kwakiutl, "restrained" and "non-individualistic" for the Zuni, and "fearful" and "paranoid" for the Dobuans. It might be instructive to think of what the key personality traits of one's own culture would be.

Such sweeping psychological characterizations have largely been abandoned by anthropology, partly because they are too general and partly because they overlook other, more large-scale structural aspects of culture. The interest in the effects or marks of culture on the individual has not been lost completely, though, as subse-quent writers have offered new terms and descriptions of the individual-level effects of culture. Anthony Wallace suggested the word "mazeway," by which he meant "the entire set of cognitive maps of positive and negative goals, of self, others, and material objects, and of their possible dynamic interrelations in process, which an individual maintains at a given time" (1961: 15–16). Later, Pierre Bourdieu (1977) offered *habitus* as the linking concept between the structures of society and the behaviors of individuals. The *habitus* is the personal precipitate of experience with social realities such that individuals in their actions tend to reproduce those very social realities. Finally, any culture itself contains certain key terms and concepts through which the people understand their own practices and values and communicate and transmit those practices and values to each other – what has been called an ethnopsychology. *Naklik* and *urulu/huaq* are two such key concepts in Utku society, and *punan*, *lirima*, and *liget* are central notions in Semai, Gisu, and Ilongot societies, respectively (see Box 5.1).

Personality as a cultural construction

Personality
The ways of thinking, feeling, and behaving characteristic of a particular individual.

Culture and personality
An early twentieth-century school of anthropology which investigated the relationship between individual/psychological processes and culture, often but not always from a psychoanalytic perspective, focusing on childhood experiences and childrearing practices.

The individual exists, then, in a complex and dynamic relation to society and culture. Persons are not carbon copies of society, but they are not utterly free agents from it either. In the course of their interactions with each other and the social systems they have erected, individuals develop a personality. Let us define **personality**, rather casually, as the distinctive ways of thinking, feeling, and behaving of an individual. Two things are clear. First, humans are not born thinking or feeling or behaving in any specific way; so, by this definition, one's personality is not exactly or entirely innate. Second, humans within a group or society share certain tendencies of think-ing or feeling or behaving. After all, my personal thought or emotion or behavior patterns are not completely unique to me; I share them with others around me, and I mostly got them from those others. I think and feel and act like most Americans, and Warlpiri or Kwakiutl or Japanese or Samoan individuals think and feel and act much like other Warlpiri or Kwakiutl or Japanese or Samoans around them.

We might express the relation between **culture and personality** as an analogy: *personality is to the individual as culture is to the society*. Personality is a quality or disposition of the individual in the same way that culture is a quality or disposition of a society. If so, culture and personality are intimately, essentially, necessarily linked. If humans are not born with it, and if humans share important and major portions of it with others around them, then where does it come from? The answer is that very much, maybe the vast majority, of it comes from outside the individual – from what other people are doing and what they teach or influence the individual to do. And the process that links these external (to the individual) realities with the internal realities of personality is enculturation. Enculturation, as discussed earlier, is the process by which an individual learns his or her society's culture – that is, by which culture gets "in" the individual. During enculturation the ideas, beliefs, values, norms, meanings, and so on that exist before, apart from, and outside of the individual are *internalized* and become part of and "inside of" the individual. To repeat: during enculturation, culture becomes part of the individual's personality. The fact that, as seen earlier, acquiring culture is an active and imperfect process guarantees that individuals will not be mere cookie-cutter versions of some cultural template.

See Chapter 2

One way to conceive the processes by which enculturation is accomplished is to think of the "goals" of the society. What kind of person does it value and want to produce? Or perhaps we should rephrase that: what kind of person(s) does it value (or devalue) and want (or not want) to produce? Most people never ask themselves this question, even as parents. When pushed, they can probably name a few characteristics that they would like to instill in their children or that they themselves would like to have. But people usually do not do this and do not need to do it. The entire process can occur tacitly, implicitly, subconsciously. The members of society *are* certain kinds of persons, and their children will be certain kinds of people, whether they think about and plan for it or not.

The ways that a society transmits its "lessons" about normal or appropriate personality can be identified as its **childrearing practices**. These are the things that adults do to or with or in front of children that provide them with a "learning environment" within which they reinvent, with adult guidance, the personality traits of the society. Some of these practices are very formal and intentional, some are informal and unintentional (see e.g. Whiting and Child 1953; Whiting 1963). We can think of these practices as falling within three broad categories.

Childrearing practices
The methods employed by members of a society to care for children and to prepare those children to become future members of that society.

1. **Explicit instruction**. There are times and ways in which adults sit children down and say, "Around here we do this," like "Boys don't cry" or "It is good to share." Some societies give more explicit instruction than others. The Western educational system is obviously an institution devoted to explicit instruction, as well as to implicit instruction (for example, youths learn lessons of obedience, self-discipline, competition, and so on). Other institutions, including the church, also perform explicit instruction ("X is true; do Y"). Most societies have never had institutions like schools or churches and so have had little specialized and formal explicit instruction, and in any society it is not the only and often not the most important medium of enculturation.

2. **Modeling**. Parents and other adults (and even other children) in the child's behavioral environment serve as models for the child's own behavior and personality. Even

if a father never gives his son any explicit instruction, once the son realizes that he is a male too, the father becomes a role-model for maleness in that society. The boy thinks (or more likely unconsciously infers), "That is what a male is supposed to be/do." Throughout their lives, people may and will learn the expectations of many different roles and types of person to be: "This is what an adult/female/American/New Yorker/African American/college student/anthropologist (and so on) is supposed to be/do." All of the co-members of one's society are models for each other. Often, of course, the words (the explicit instruction) may contradict the modeled behavior: a society might say, "You should not fight" even as it engages in violence. And people may not think at all about the behavior that they model. Still, they are modeling – and new members are learning.

3. "Exercises." Children (and adults as well) are not only allowed and encouraged to learn and take notes and to observe and imitate but also to practice it for themselves. Society must give people an opportunity to develop the skills or habits that it wants them to have. For instance, if a society wants to instill independence, it provides situations and rewards for individuals, including children, to make their own decisions. If it wants to instill competitiveness, it provides opportunities and incentives for them to compete and win. In the end, people can only acquire skills and abilities by practicing them; just as you would not expect to prepare a great soccer player simply by having him or her read about kicking and passing and watch others kick and pass, so you would not expect to prepare a member of society just by having him or her passively absorb instructions about how to act or observe others acting. They must be given the chance to rehearse their abilities and to master them; accordingly, it is a fact that active learning is stronger and faster than passive learning.

BOX 5.1   LEARNING TO BE VIOLENT OR NON-VIOLENT

Are humans naturally violent or non-violent? This is a question that has long interested humans, perhaps more urgently today than ever before. The cross-cultural data suggest that the answer may not be a simple dualistic choice. Around the world we encounter many more societies that exhibit some form of violence than not; Bonta (1997) in his survey counts a mere twenty-five societies that deserve to be called generally non-violent. But what makes one society violent and another non-violent?

Dentan (1968) described the Semai of Malaysia as one of the least violent societies in the world. Part of the explanation was their large-scale social arrangements: as hunters and gatherers living in kinship-based communities without private property, they had little cause or opportunity to engage in aggression. Their gender relationships were also harmonious, and there was little competition of any kind. And at the heart of their culture was the concept of *punan*, the condition of being unhappy or frustrated, as well as the condition of making someone else unhappy or frustrated. It was bad to be *punan*, and individuals went to great lengths to avoid it. *Punan* was uncomfortable and potentially dangerous: someone in a state of *punan* could have or cause accidents and misfortune. The Semai took the adage "It hurts me as much at it hurts you" quite seriously.

According to Heald (1986), the Gisu of Uganda had a well-earned reputation for violence. Even they bemoaned their level of aggression, condemning themselves as bad people. At the same time, they prized, and actively promoted, a quality they called *lirima*. *Lirima* was the manly aspect of powerful emotion, linked to anger, jealousy, and hatred. But when harnessed, it provided males with the strength, courage, and determination to overcome fear – and enemies. Men, it turns out, did not possess *lirima* by nature; it had to be inculcated. So they performed initiations in which youths were allowed and encouraged to acquire *lirima*, thus becoming exactly the kind of people they criticize themselves for.

The Ilongot illustrate an even more anomalous kind of personality and violence. Most of the time, they lived their lives in relative tranquility. At other times, they hunted human heads. Central to their sense of themselves and of the institution of headhunting was their concept of *liget* or passion. Men had much *liget*, more so than women. They also had more *beya* or knowledge or experience. *Liget* and *beya* were not opposed though: "good" *liget* was focused and disciplined by knowledge, but unfocused passion was frightening and ugly. Accordingly, the Ilongot believed that as a man's knowledge grew, his passion subsided. There was a critical moment in early manhood when each was at its peak, and killing an enemy for his head was the "peak experience" of life, the moment of life lived to its fullest. After that event, which might occur only once in a man's life, he "settled down" and began his domestic life, with waning *liget* but expanding *beya*.

Whatever human nature may be, it appears to be diverse and malleable; as Benedict framed it, human possibilities fall along a "great arc," and different societies select specific human qualities to groom and value. Thus, culture is not opposed to the individual or personality, and nurture is not opposed to nature. Both contribute to the shaping of human individuality.

The observation that societies do typically have recognizable personality traits – the Semai peaceful, the Gisu violent – led mid-twentieth-century anthropologists to devise terms to describe these commonalities. **Basic personality**, for instance, has been used to refer to the "structure of articulated personality characteristics and processes attributable, non-statistically, to almost all members of some culturally bounded population" (Wallace 1961: 106). That is, we might say that the basic personality of Americans is competitive, independent, materialistic, and so on. A similar term is **national character**, which has tended to be applied to modern state-level societies, as in Benedict's famous World War II study of Japanese "national character" (1946). Again, the results of such work would be "The Japanese are X and Y," where X and Y are allegedly shared personality traits.

This approach has been rightly criticized as too generalizing: "all Japanese" do not share one or any particular set of personality traits, nor are "all Americans" the same psychologically. In its place, some observers have suggested **modal personality** as a statistical concept; that is, the most frequently occurring personality traits in a society. So, we might say that one modal personality trait of Americans is competitiveness, although not all Americans are equally competitive and some are not competitive at all. We also might want to think not exactly of the "actual" personality traits of a society but of the "ideal" or most highly valued ones. In other words, the

Basic personality
The psychological traits common to most or all of the members of a society (roughly synonymous with modal personality).

Wallace, Anthony. 1961. *Culture and Personality.* New York: Random House.

National character
The alleged common personality characteristics of an entire society or country; especially applied to modern societies or nation-states.

Modal personality
The statistically most commonly occurring personality traits in a society.

Gisu were widely violent but did not idealize violence; they wished they committed less of it. Something similar might be said about Americans: the ideal is domestic tranquility, but the reality is a high level of domestic violence. What Americans want to produce and what they actually produce diverge, and there must be something in the culture and the enculturation process that leads, even unwittingly, to that outcome.

A final, and one of the most interesting and profound questions, is whether emotions are culturally structured. Until fairly recently, most Westerners assumed that they were not – and not even within the reach of scientific examination. As Lutz emphasizes in her comparative analysis of Ifaluk and Western ethnopsychologies, emotions tend to be viewed as *natural, physical, and subjective*: they are seen as "private" and therefore inaccessible to others (like anthropologists) and "factual," sometimes literal bodily states like a racing heart or a tearing eye. She further suggests that Western society generally considers emotions irrational, uncontrollable (we are "carried away" by our feelings), dangerous, and frequently female.

Not all societies share this conception of emotions nor, so it seems, precisely the same emotions. Lutz, for instance, argues that the Ifaluk experience a number of emotions that are not quite translatable into Western categories. Among these are *fago* which conveys compassion and love and sadness simultaneously, especially in reaction to the suffering or need of others; it cannot be translated as "love," for instance, since it has no romantic connotations, and it implies an inequality or dependence not always included in "love." *Song*, another Ifaluk emotional concept, refers to anger but to a particular form of anger, "justifiable anger" or "righteous indignation," and some people are more entitled to feel and express this emotion than others, notably chiefs and parents. *Metagu* or "fear/anxiety" is seen as a positive emotion and social force: "fear is what keeps people good" (Lutz 1998: 201).

Other observers have commented on the meaning and social use of emotions in other societies. According to Schieffelin (1983), anger, sadness, and shame play a special role, and form a special nexus of emotions, in Kaluli cultural life. Keeler (1983) re-examines the Javanese feeling of *lek* which Geertz characterized as "stage fright" but which Keeler likens more to "respectful self-restraint" as a consequence of social status differences. Perhaps most suggestively, Abu-Lughod (1985) reports that emotions such as *tahashshum* (embarrassment/modesty/shame) among Egyptian Bedouins not only have strategic functions – as they do in Kaluli, Javanese, and Western societies – but that the distinction between "real" and "conventional" or "private" and "public" emotions cannot be sustained. Some of the most intimate feelings in Bedouin life are communicated in conventional media like songs and poems; that is, even private emotions are conventionalized.

Sexual dimorphism
The occurrence of two physically distinct forms of a species, based on sexual characteristics as well as non-sexual ones such as body size.

GENDER AND PERSON, OR GENDERED PERSONS

Wherever we find humans, we find male and female. **Sexual dimorphism** (the occurrence of two discrete body forms based on sex) would seem to be a natural, biological, and universal feature of human existence. American culture in particular and Western culture in general tends to reinforce this impression: there are two kinds of humans – men and women – and two proper codes of behavior – male and female. A person is born a man or a woman, remains so for life, and acts accordingly. Even if things were as simple and universal as this, it would still be within the power of culture to "culturize" the physical differences, with relative values, meanings, and role assignments for the sexes. There is cross-cultural evidence to suggest that here too things are even more complicated.

Surveying the cultures of the world, anthropologists find exceptions to all of these notions. Not all societies believe that there are only two kinds, even two *physical* kinds, of humans to be. Not all believe that one's sex is set at birth and immutable. And not all assign the same names, tasks, or values along the same sex-line divisions. This is an even clearer case of cultural ontology, each specific society's understanding of what kinds of beings, including human beings, exist, why they exist, and what we are supposed to do about it. As an introductory example, Roscoe (1994) tells us that traditional Zuni culture held that a child's physical sex was a social construction – that is, that it required social action (in the form of rituals and offerings) to ensure that a child had any sex at all, let alone a particular one, and that a child's sex was not firmly fixed until birth if not later; if a woman fell asleep during labor, the baby's sex might change. So the "settling" of a person's physical sex was the result of culture, not nature.

Further, a person's sex is not always determined in the same way (by what genitals they possess) or in a binary way. In fact, there are several related but independent variables in the arena of sex and gender, including sexual anatomy, sexual identity (what sex one "feels like" or "identifies with"), sexual preference (what sex one wants to have sex with, and how), and **gender**. By gender we typically mean the social or cultural characteristics – rules, roles, tasks, values, and meanings – that are assigned to people on the basis of (some or another) sexual characteristics. But if sex is not exactly a natural fact, then gender certainly is not. Indeed, Roscoe defines gender as

Gender
The social categories based on physical sexual characteristics and the meanings, behaviors, and values associated with these categories.

> a multidimensional category of personhood encompassing a distinct pattern of social and cultural differences. Gender categories often draw on perceptions of anatomical and physiological differences between bodies, but these perceptions are always mediated by cultural categories and meanings.
>
> (Roscoe 1994: 341)

Gender divisions and differences

Even in societies that simply and firmly assign human beings to one of two sex or gender categories, there is no absolute reason why those two categories should be segregated and/or valued unequally. Yet, Rosaldo asserts that "what is perhaps most striking and surprising is the fact that male, as opposed to female, activities are always recognized as predominantly important, and cultural systems give authority and value to the roles and activities of men" (1974: 19). This is not entirely universally true, but it is widespread enough to be noteworthy. Several students of Iroquois culture, for instance, have commented on the power and status of women in that society, but more often than not women and women's activities are held in lower esteem than men's – sometimes extremely so.

See Chapter 7

Rosaldo's explanation for this fact, which had great influence for a time, was to distinguish between the "domestic" and "public" spheres of a society. Women, she suggested, are typically consigned to a private/domestic space (e.g., the household), based partly on an essentialist view of their "nurturing" tendencies, which is closed off from the economically and politically important public space where men function. As appealing and intuitive as this notion is, other observers have questioned it. Nelson (1974), for example, argues that women in the Middle East, one of the more patriarchal culture areas, still exercise more power in the public sphere than is usually appreciated. She names such prominent roles as marriage mediator, counselor to her sons, and sorceress/magician/healer as effective positions of power, not to mention their control over food, hospitality, and the family's reputation and honor, as well as over other women via informal friendships and formal women's organizations.

Reiter (1975a) takes the case a step further. She suggests that in the French village she examined, there was no real public/private segregation at all. Rather, she refers to what she calls a "sexual geography" of the village, such that men occupied and used certain spaces at certain times and women occupied and used some of those same spaces at other times. Women did indeed predominantly inhabit the home and a few other locations, such as the three shops in the village as well as the church (where no "self-respecting man" was going to be seen), and most of their interests and activities centered on the family. Men, who did almost all of the outside-the-home labor, possessed the village square, the cafés, and the mayor's office in the evenings. However, Reiter found that when the men were working in the fields at midday, women took over the public village spaces: "The village is then in female hands" (257). Even more, women did not feel downtrodden or inferior at all. Rather, she depicts them as viewing men "as overgrown children strutting around and holding onto places and roles that are really quite silly; these have less value than their own homes and roles as family-cores. They even consider men's space to be inferior to their own" (258).

It may be useful to take the advice of these researchers and consider the relations between the sexes more in terms of a "gendered geography" than a simple and complete division or opposition. This geography may be and often is literally spatial. Herdt (1987) notes that the Sambia of New Guinea, a highly sex-segregated society, actually had separate buildings and even separate footpaths for men and women. However, this geographic exclusion may also be and probably more often is conceptual or cognitive, that is, in terms of knowledge and language rather than space. For instance, until a few decades ago it was widely believed that men in Australian Aboriginal societies had all of the ritual knowledge and responsibility; earlier studies described male rituals and statuses in detail. However, a new generation of anthropologists like Diane Bell (1993) discovered a whole parallel world of religious knowledge and ritual activity among women, which led others to explore the relations to groups and to land which individuals can trace through fathers or mothers.

One of the more well-studied domains of gender diversity is in language. Many attempts, both popular and scholarly, have been made to distinguish how men and women communicate, including whimsical associations between the sexes and different planets (Mars for men, Venus for women (Gray 1992)). Maltz and Borker (1996) summarize the state of the research into cross-gender communication, which finds that women ask more questions, encourage responses, interject more conversation-promoting utterances like "uh huh" and "yes," allow themselves to be interrupted, and use interactional pronouns like "you" and "we." Men are more likely to interrupt, to argue, to ignore the other's comments, to try to control the topic, and to offer opinions or declarations. Lakoff (1975) among others has interpreted this as an effect of male domination and female subordination in society. Maltz and Borker propose, instead, that men and women constitute "different sociolinguistic subcultures, having learned to do different things with words in a conversation" (1996: 84). Boys and girls, they argue, learn to speak differently "because of the very different social contexts in which they learn how to carry on friendly conversation" (87). Why there are divergent male and female conversational contexts, they do not explain.

While not universal by any means, there is evidence of linguistic segregation by sex/gender across cultures. In many societies, the "status" or "high" styles or genres of language are the exclusive province of males. The Wana *kiyori* form mentioned in the last chapter was used solely by men, as was the *kabary* style that comprises formal Malagasy; in fact, Ochs (1996) says that skilled speech and traditional speech types, distinguished by indirectness, relate to men, while plain speech types, distinguished by directness, relate to women. Finally, in the Hindi Fijian village studied by Brenneis (1984), the "high" or "sweet" mode of speech called *parbacan*, used for religious occasions and characterized by indirectness, more traditional (Sanskrit) vocabulary, and a more complex grammar, was the unique province of men.

The oppression of women across cultures

As Rosaldo and just about everyone else have noticed, in the great majority of human societies, males exercise predominant social power. This does not always and inevitably lead to the actual disadvantage, oppression, and even harm of women. However, it can and often does. Some of these practices center on women's activities, political and economic and especially sexual. Others weigh on their very bodies and lives, to the point of disfigurement and death. Probably in at least some if not all cases, men's power and dominance is achieved by the control over women that these institutions afford. Some of the more conspicuous and important examples include the following:

Female infanticide

The overt killing or neglect until death of female babies. It may also take the form of preferential abortion.

See Chapter 8

Purdah

The practice of "wearing the veil" in many Muslim countries, in which women are expected to keep some parts of their body covered in public – in some instances the head, in other instances the entire body other than the eyes.

Honor killing

The killing, usually of females, when their behavior has brought shame or dishonor on a family, such as premarital sex or "dating" outside the preferred categories.

1. Female infanticide. When male children are much more valued than female children, female babies (and with new technologies, increasingly female fetuses) may be overtly killed or allowed to die from neglect. This practice occurs most often in societies where male children are needed as warriors or where males will bring wealth into the home at marriage but females will take wealth out of the home – that is, where dowry is practiced. In addition, if male heirs are important for continuing the family line or performing rituals for dead ancestors, boys will be prized over girls.

2. Purdah. Purdah is the practice of "wearing the veil" that is found in many Muslim societies. In these cultures, family honor and female virginity are important and closely related. One way that a man and his family express and maintain honor is by controlling the sexuality of the family's women. Together with general notions of female physical modesty, and in extreme cases the exclusion of women from public activities like education and work, the purdah complex seeks to "protect" women by shielding them from the lecherous eyes of other men.

3. Honor killing. In societies in which honor is a prime concern, honor offended must be restored, often through extreme action. Affronts to honor are often related to inappropriate sexual behavior of women, such as dating or marrying outside the religion or having premarital sex. In more than a few instances, the women have been punished for being raped – an ironic case of blaming the victim. Most common in Muslim societies, honor killings are not unknown in Christian and Sikh societies or wherever honor is a serious matter. One high-profile case in England involved a Kurdish Muslim who killed his 16-year-old daughter for being "too Westernized" and dating a Lebanese Christian boy.

PLATE 5.2 Muslim women in "purdah" or veil

4. **Foot-binding**. In traditional China, a woman's feet were often tightly wrapped in her youth to prevent them from growing normally. The result, after many years of binding, was a small but also twisted foot that hardly allowed her to wear shoes or to walk. Small feet were considered beautiful, and women with large feet might be mocked. Not all agricultural families could afford to hobble their women this way; it was often practiced by and on the upper classes. Interestingly enough, American women also value and are valued for their ability to wear unnaturally small and unnaturally shaped shoes, and some have recently resorted to surgery to reduce their feet – literally have bone removed – to fit into them.

Foot-binding
A traditional Chinese practice of tying a young girl's feet tightly so that her feet remained small (and often painful) into adulthood.

5. **Sati**. In India, widows have been traditionally encouraged to follow their husbands into death. Bodies are ordinarily cremated as a means of disposal and of releasing the spirit from the body. A woman who voluntarily threw herself into her husband's funeral pyre was considered a "pure one," a *sati*, and venerated for her selfless enactment of a famous mythical event. In recent times, there have been accounts of women going involuntarily to their premature deaths, either by compulsion or drugging. The alternative to self-immolation in parts of India today is often destitution as a homeless widow living in a "widow ghetto," begging, stealing, or prostituting herself to stay alive (Sen 2001).

Sati
The traditional Indian practice in which a widow commits suicide by throwing herself on her dead husband's funeral pyre.

6. **Dowry death or bride burning**. In parts of northern India, a living wife often does not have it much better. Men marry to acquire a dowry, which traditionally consisted of a circumscribed amount of handmade goods. Today, men demand goods like electronics and jewelry, and of course cash. The husband may return to his father-in-law after the marriage and request additional dowry, which the latter can seldom afford. As a threat, or a follow-through on a threat, or as genuine homicide, the husband – or his mother, who often lives with the couple – may push the wife into the cooking fire or actually douse her with kerosene and set her alight. If she lives but is disfigured, he may divorce her and re-marry, gaining another dowry. Of course, if she dies, he is free to seek another wife and dowry.

Dowry death
The killing of wives because the husbands were not satisfied with the dowry payment they received, or else to free them to marry again and collect another dowry.

7. **"Female circumcision" or female genital mutilation**. In a number of societies, many in Africa, an operation or series of operations is conducted on girls and young women that can range from a fairly minor trimming of the external genitals to a complete excision of the clitoris and the sewing up of the organs, as some combination of aesthetics and sexual control. The physical result is often deemed to be more beautiful than the natural body. It is also commonly believed that removing parts of the female genitalia reduces sexual desire and pleasure, enhancing chastity. In the situation where the organs are sewn together completely, the main goal is the maintenance of virginity; in such societies, "proof" of virginity at marriage may be demanded, and serious consequences befall the woman who does not pass the test of premarital abstinence. Older women, again, are typically the performers of these operations and are often strong advocates for the continuation of the "tradition."

Female circumcision
Also known as female genital mutilation, the practice of cutting off some or all of a female's external genitalia, for purposes of "beauty" or the regulation of sexual sensations.

The construction of masculinity

Much of the attention in the discussion of gender focuses on women, which is an important corrective to the disregard of them in much of the past literature. However, in any gender system, men are a gender too, and their gender identity is just as culturally defined as women's. In fact, in some ways it appears to be more precarious. This is suggested by the fact that, in many societies, there is either an explicit belief or an implicit message that men are "made" whereas women are "born." To put this another way, there is a recurring cross-cultural theme that girls naturally mature into women but that boys must be "made" into men: femininity is seen as a "natural" fact but masculinity is seen as a "social" fact.

One of the persistent manifestations of this notion is male initiation rituals. In Aboriginal Australia, boys were "made into men" through physical operations – circumcision, subincision (cutting a slit in the underside of the penis), scarification, nose perforation, and/or tooth removal – which may take place over a series of ceremonies covering many years. As we saw above, the Gisu performed a ritual to instill the manly virtue of *lirima* in youths, and the headhunt was the culmination of the path to maleness for the Ilongot. This is not to say that female-oriented rituals never occur – of course they do – including scarification and the aforementioned female circumcision. Such practices seem to occur more widely in reference to men, but both sexes can be identified and even "created" by literal alterations of the body, which give individuals the culturally correct physical features for their sex. Harold Garfinkel (1967), the founder of ethnomethodology, has referred to modified sex organs as "cultural genitals," in which physical facts like the possession of genitalia become "cultural facts" either through interpretation or alteration of them. I, for instance, was told to keep it a secret from the Aboriginal men if I was uncircumcised, since only circumcised men were fully men and eligible to see the most secret of male rituals.

One practice that has been included in the ritual conception of men in some cultures is what the Western world would call "ritual homosexuality." (The very term suggests the problem with imposing foreign cultural categories – a foreign cultural ontology – on another society.) For example, in a variety of Melanesian societies, boys were occasionally or routinely exposed to the genitals and even semen of elders (but not always adults). The Etoro (Kelly 1977) and the Sambia (Herdt 1987) had young boys ingest semen by oral sex performed on adolescent males, while the Kaluli introduced semen by anal sex and the Onabasulu by manual stimulation of males on to the skin of boys. It is interesting that they sometimes found each other's practices offensive: the Kaluli disapproved of the Etoro behavior and vice versa (Kelly 1977: 16).

For the Sambia, as Box 5.2 discusses, ritualized and routine juvenile homosexuality was (it has since stopped) an acceptable and necessary part of their gender creation, based on their unique cultural ontology of maleness and femaleness. In other unrelated cultures, including ancient Sparta, male homosexuality served other functions, including the establishment of corporate spirit within armies. Men in Sparta, as in Sambia culture and elsewhere, were not "habitual" or exclusive

Garfinkel, Harold. 1967. *Studies in Ethnomethodology*. Englewood Cliffs, NJ: Prentice-Hall.

homosexuals; in fact, Spartan men married and had children, and Sambians "graduated" from homosexuality to an adolescent bisexuality to adult heterosexuality. It is not the case in all cultures that "homosexuality" is a total and permanent identity or "lifestyle"; it may be a temporary situation or a cultural performance that does not define the man nor constitute an alternative or deviant gender role.

BOX 5.2 THE CONSTRUCTION OF MALENESS IN SAMBIA CULTURE

The Sambia were a horticultural society in the eastern Highlands of New Guinea in which males were highly valued and a strict segregation, even tension, existed between the sexes. Their villages were divided into male and female spaces, and prior to marriage "all heterosexual relationships, intrigues, and even casual conversations among boys and girls are blocked and forbidden" (Herdt 1987: 3). Women were regarded as not only inferior but dangerous and polluting to men, and with marriage men claimed to own women. Masculinity was a prized quality among men, expressed most fully in the aggressive warrior or war leader, the *aamooluku*. No man wanted to be a *wusaatu* or rubbish man (literally, "soft person"). In the past, troops of men would raid neighboring villages, killing every man, woman, and child before burning it to the ground (53).

Masculine identity and power was based on the central concept of *jerungdu*, which was both a physical substance and the concept of male strength and prowess. One medium of this power was semen, which they believed was not naturally produced in a man's body but must be placed there. Male children also, obviously, had a female influence – physical and spiritual – on them by virtue of emergence from the womb, contact with the mother's skin, and the childhood diet of "soft" foods. It was of critical importance to remove this polluting and weakening female contamination from young males and convert them into real men.

One of the principal means for doing so, and for resolving the semen-shortage problem, was to inseminate the young boys orally, starting at their first initiation around age 6. They would fellate older boys who were at a higher initiation status (boys passed through six initiations to achieve manhood). This might occur daily but in secret; adult men did not participate. It was believed that a boy would not grow, and would not become a man, without it. At about age 14, boys changed from the fellators to the fellated, and with marriage in late teens or early twenties, they discontinued the behavior altogether.

Oral insemination was not the only behavior intended to transform the youth's body from one that was mixed male/female to one that was all male. Boys were also rubbed with scratchy objects to "open" or "stretch" their skin, causing bleeding that washed out female pollutants. They were induced to vomit or defecate to "purge" their internal female contaminants, and they pierced their noses to draw blood (adult men continued to nosebleed themselves, especially after their wives' periods). They observed food rules and taboos, avoiding "soft" foods that would reintroduce femaleness, and they performed other rituals involving the placement of saliva and hair in ritually selected trees.

In Sambia culture, maleness was a social accomplishment. Being born with male organs did not guarantee successful achievement of adult manhood. Only the ingestion of manly substances – symbolically and literally – and the removal of inherent womanly ones could build a proper man out of the natural raw materials of maleness.

The construction of "alternate" genders

Attitudes, practices, and beliefs regarding sex, sexuality, and gender – indeed, the very categories on which these ideas and behaviors are based – vary across cultures. Readers might be prepared to learn, then, that not all cultures share the notion of two and only two sexes or genders at all. In fact, Thomas Laqueur (1990) has suggested that the idea of two sexes/genders is actually recent in Western cultures; he asserts that until the eighteenth century there was only *one* sex – male – and that females were regarded as incomplete or damaged males (Freud's theories echo this sentiment, with his "penis envy" view). On the other hand, a story told in Plato's *Symposium* relates that in the beginning there were three sexes, each dual – one androgynous (male/female), one male/male, and one female/female – which were split in half by the gods, sending each person in search of his or her "other half" (which might be the "opposite" sex or the "same" sex).

Be that as it may, in more than a few cultures there are categories of third or even fourth genders – and even sexes – based on beliefs and concepts that may not exist in other cultures. A few examples of such identities include the following.

1. **Berdache**. In many Native American societies there is or was a tradition of males who adopted certain female roles and traits. In fact, Roscoe (1994) indicates that almost a hundred and fifty societies had the third gender, and almost half of those had a fourth gender for women playing more masculine roles. Early Western observers deemed them "transvestites" or "homosexuals," partly judgmentally and partly because those were the only categories the observers possessed. However, within the societies, berdaches were members of a distinct and often highly regarded gender. Some were assigned to the category based on physical features, particularly hermaphrodite genitals. Others chose the role. One of the best cases of a berdache institution is the Navajo *nadleehe*, or "one who changes continuously." Like the Zuni, they believed that sex or gender was not entirely fixed, nor was it always related to external/bodily traits. The Navajo *nadleehe* was greatly respected, often given control of the family's wealth and active as a religious specialist. They performed female economic roles and might dress as males, females, or neither. The Mohave *alyha* and the Lakotah *winkte* are two of the better known examples (see Roscoe (1998: 213–47) for a more complete listing). Commonly, berdache status was not believed to be about bodies at all but about spirit – about having "two spirits," both male and female, in one body.

2. **Eunuch**. The common image of eunuchs is castrated males in ancient and medieval societies who were assigned specific roles and tasks, most famously guarding the harems of polygamist leaders. However, eunuchs were not always castrated; they might be sterile or celibate or simply lacking in sexual desire. The defining feature of the eunuch status was not absence of male parts but absence of "manliness," based on their non-generativity (i.e., they would or could not have children). Ringrose (1994) indicates that they were a legitimate third gender, neither male nor female, and that they performed functions that neither males nor females could do.

Laqueur, Thomas. 1990.
Making Sex: Body and Gender from the Greeks to Freud. Cambridge, MA: Harvard University Press.

Berdache
A gender concept in some Native American societies for biological males who adopt certain behavioral and personality characteristics of females.

Eunuch
A gender category involving non-sexual individuals (usually men), who may be castrated or merely celibate, sterile, or lacking sexual desire.

Interestingly, these jobs often involved positions of mediation and transaction across boundaries, such as doorkeepers, guards, messengers, servants, secretaries, and masters of ceremonies – suggesting that their own anomalous circumstances made them fit for dealing with anomalous boundary-crossing circumstances.

3. **Hijra**. In northern India, a virtual subsociety of individuals regarded as "neither man nor woman" – but also "man plus woman" – exists and participates in the greater society (Nanda 1999). *Hijras* may be born with male or hermaphroditic body parts; either way, they share the quality of impotence. The ultimate mark of a true *hijra*, though, is to have the male genitals removed completely (in a ritual called *nirvana*), so that the person truly is neither man nor woman but a third distinct type. *Hijras* typically live in their own communal groups under the leadership of a guru or teacher, forming a surrogate kinship system. Local groups are organized into "houses" (of which there are seven with names and histories and rules); each house has a regional leader or *naik*, and the regional leaders occasionally meet at the national level. *Hijras* are most known for their musical performances at weddings and births. Ironically to Westerners, *hijras* as non-sexual beings and ascetics are associated in Hindu tradition with fertility and procreation. They are sexually ambiguous, but in a culturally specific way: the god Shiva possesses androgynous traits and is ascetic, blurring the Western lines not only between male and female but between sexuality and asceticism.

Hijra
A gender concept in India for biological males who regard themselves as neither male nor female; they often play a social role at weddings and childbirths.

Nanda, Serena. 1999. *Neither Man nor Woman: The Hijras of India* (2nd edn). Belmont, CA: Wadsworth Publishing Company.

4. **Travesti**. In Brazil, there is a type of effeminate male who actively attempts to achieve more female-like physical features and often works as a male prostitute. They are not transsexuals and do not claim to be women; rather, they say that they want to be "feminine" or "like women" (Kulick 1997). To that end, they take female hormones and undergo surgery to modify their bodies to a more culturally appropriate

Travesti
An alternate gender role in Brazil, in which males take on certain physical traits and sexual behaviors typically associated with females.

PLATE 5.3 *Hijras* in India often sing and dance at weddings and childbirths

female shape. They are often appreciated for their beauty, by female standards. They do not, however, undergo sex-change operations, since they do not want to be women or to lose their male genitals. Sexually, they act as receivers of anal sex with men but never as penetrators. Kulick argues that *travesti* do not constitute a third gender but rather represent the Brazilian dualistic view of gender identity – two genders, "men" and "not-men" (including women and *travestis*), based not on bodies but on behavior. In this case, the behavior is partly the role in sexual intercourse (men penetrate, non-men are penetrated) and partly on more general qualities of dress, manner, and so on. A "real man" could have sex with a *travesti* and remain a real man, so long as he was the penetrator. In fact, *travestis* thought it would be offensive to have sex with each other, since they were the "same kind."

There are a few documented cases of "cross-gender" female institutions in various cultures. Schwimmer (1984) mentions female transvestism in four Melanesian societies. A number of Native American societies had female correlates of the male berdache status, including the Mohave *hwame* role. According to Grémaux (1994), there was a custom by which women could become "social males" in the Balkans. One process involved a biological female who renounced her femaleness in adulthood, often via a vow of abstention from sex and marriage. A second process involved the decision of the parents to raise a baby girl as a son, giving her access to property and inheritance and even training her as a soldier (especially when the family had no sons). However, around the world, "alternate" or "third" genders tend to be institutions for what the West would consider "biological males," although not all societies, as we have seen, make the same assessment of that fact as do Western societies. Ultimately, the main difference between Western cultures and others that permit and value gender alternatives may be the latter's toleration of ambivalence, ambiguity, and even contradiction in sex, identity, and other factors.

Finally and not surprisingly, modernization and globalization have left impressions on cultural conceptions of sex and gender. In the "transcultural junctures created by science, modernization, and development programs" (Pigg and Adams 2005: 21), foreign, especially Western, notions of sex and gender have circulated around the globe. The media for these cultural notions and images have included of course movies and music but also political discourse about human rights and even scientific discourse about contraception, abortion, homosexuality, sexually transmitted diseases, and other "sexual health" issues. This supposedly neutral "medicalization" of sexuality has affected local concepts and practices in disparate ways. Readers may recall that the President of Iran recently denied that homosexuality even exists in Iran. Meanwhile, according to Cohen (2005), the Western or "cosmopolitan" category of "gay" has been introduced into India, vying with traditional categories like *hijra* or *kothi*. According to Nguyen, the "new version of the 'facts of life'" is reorganizing male–female and male–male relationships in the Ivory Coast (2005: 245), and ideas of women's rights and practices like birth control are sparking reconstructions of the role of women, the nature of marriage, and the understanding of "morality" from Russia and India to China and Africa – and the West as well.

BOX 5.3 CONTEMPORARY CULTURAL CONTROVERSIES: GENDER AND MENTAL ILLNESS

One point of convergence between gender and psychological concepts is the issue of "gender deviance." Proof of this claim is that the American Psychiatric Association only removed homosexuality from its list of mental disorders in 1973 (Naphy 2004: 208). The term "homosexual" had only been introduced in 1848 by Karoly Maria Benkert, who opined that it represented "a direct horror of the opposite sex" (quoted 206). Homosexuals and other "deviants" were subjected to medical and surgical "therapies" including castration and lobotomy: Norway reportedly lobotomized 2,500 patients, Sweden 3,300, and Denmark 3,500, including its last case in 1981 (209). Homosexuality was a literal crime in most of the U.S.A. into the 1970s. Meanwhile, women in the U.S.A. in the 1940s and 1950s who did not conform to conventional roles of housewife and mother were condemned as bad or sick. Failure to have children was regarded as a "quasi-perversion," and women "who had trouble adjusting" to the life of a housewife and mother were labeled "neurotic, perverted, or schizophrenic" (Coontz 1992: 32). Maladjusted women were given drugs and electroshock treatment. Gender and sexual nonconformists are still stigmatized and discriminated against in many societies. What do you think?

Coontz, Stephanie. 1992. *The Way We Never Were: American Families and the Nostalgia Trap.* New York: Basic Books.

SUMMARY

Human beings are individuals, but they must and do learn to be particular kinds of individuals, and this occurs under the influence of culture. Psychological anthropology or culture and personality bridges the gap between the poles of "nature" and "nurture" – humans have an individual and a species nature which is nurtured in specific ways to achieve specific outcomes.

- ■ Enculturation is the process that links the individual to his or her society and its expected and desired psychological and behavioral characteristics.
- ■ Personality is the individual product or precipitate of a person's experience in a social context, based on more or less explicit and intentional practices aimed at raising the proper kind(s) of people.
- ■ Modal personality is the cumulative or statistical result, the most common personality traits in a society, where personality traits may or will be distributed according to factors such as age, sex, class, and so on.

In the final analysis every society contains a unique cultural ontology or theory/system of what kinds of entities and beings – human and otherwise – exist, what their natures are, and how society should respond to them.

- Some societies, but not necessarily all, posit a "self" that distinguishes the individual.
- Humans may not be the only species capable of "self"-awareness, any more than we are the only species capable of "language" or "culture."

Part of a society's ontology includes its sex/gender system. A society may:

- identify two sexes or genders based on physical traits
- identify two sexes or genders based on other than physical traits
- identify three or more sexes or genders based on physical or other than physical traits.

That is, human individuals come with particular physical/bodily configurations, but how society interprets and values – culturizes – those physical facts is relative.

Key Terms

Basic personality	*Hijra*
Berdache	Honor killing
Childrearing practices	Modal personality
Cultural ontology	National character
Culture and personality	Personality
Dowry death	Primitive mentality
Eunuch	Psychic unity of humanity
Female circumcision (FGM or female genital mutilation)	Psychological anthropology
	Purdah
Female infanticide	Sati
Foot-binding	Sexual dimorphism
Gender	*Travesti*

Individuals and Identities: Race and Ethnicity

In the interior of Suriname, one of three small countries on the north coast of South America, live six "black tribes" sometimes called collectively "Maroons" – the Ndyuka, the Matawai, the Saamaka, the Aluku, the Pamaka, and the Kwinti (van Velzen and van Wetering 2004). Numbering more than 100,000 people in total, they are clearly not "native" to Suriname; that is, there were traditionally no black tribes in South America. The ancestors of the Maroon societies were brought to South America from Africa as slaves by the Dutch, to labor in the new Dutch colony. Predictably, many African slaves escaped into the southern jungle, often welcomed or aided by local native South American peoples. By the early 1700s, independent named black societies were established inland, and in 1760 the Ndyuka even signed a treaty with the colonial administration. Over the years, each Maroon tribe developed its own unique culture, reflecting a combination of influences including but not limited to European, African, and Native American. And the Maroon peoples are only part of a much more complex multicultural Suriname which is also home to Asian Indians, Javanese, Creoles, and Native Americans. Interestingly, Suriname's neighbor, Guyana, "never evolved black tribes" (2004: 8).

Human beings belong to a single species. However, it is an incredibly diverse species, behaviorally and physically – a "polytypic species," one that comes in a variety of different forms. Long before anthropology existed, people were trying to make sense of this diversity, and one enduring concept invented by Western societies to categorize and explain human diversity is race. More recently, observers suggested the concept of "ethnic group" to refer to the same, or sometimes quite different, human variables. Both terms, but especially race, have a troubled history, fraught with confusion and abuse. Both terms, like gender, are also ways to classify humans and, even more importantly, to assign value and tasks to humans. In other words, like gender, race and ethnicity are examples of an ontology or a taxonomy, a classification and evaluation system. As anthropologists, we are indeed interested in human difference – the characteristics of distinct human groups – but we are equally if not more interested in the systems by which those groups are conceived, the relations between those groups, and the social practices by which, and the social purposes for which, those groups and relations are created, perpetuated, contested, or changed.

THE ANTHROPOLOGY OF RACE

Every English speaker has a general sense of what race means: physical differences (usually and especially surface differences, like skin color) between humans, or more often between major "types" or divisions, even "breeds," of the human species, generally geographically separated, and the groups characterized by those differences. Although race thus relates to physical or biological factors, there is a wide (though not quite universal) consensus that races are not "real" or "objective" entities but are rather social constructs. As Audrey Smedley asserts, the "reality of race" resides in "a set of beliefs and attitudes about human differences, not the differences themselves" (1999: xi). This is not to declare that there are no differences between human individuals or groups – there obviously are – but rather to draw attention to the fact that the differences that matter and precisely how and why they matter are cultural and not natural issues. Smedley explains that biological variations between groups of human beings "have no social meanings except what we humans give them. This is what is meant when we claim that races are culturally constructed. It is the social meanings imposed on the varying human populations that we must investigate to understand race" (xii).

Smedley, Audrey. 1999. *Race in North America: Origin and Evolution of a Worldview* (2nd edn). Boulder, CO: Westview Press.

It is not difficult to show that race is a slippery and problematic term: for instance, when a "black" person and a "white" person have a child, what race is the child? Does it matter if it is the father or the mother who is "black"? Does it matter exactly what the child looks like, that is, how "black" or "white" s/he appears? The talented "black" golfer Tiger Woods has publicly declared that he is not "black" since his ancestry includes African, Caucasian, Asian, and Native American; he even invented a new race term for himself – Cablinasian – despite the fact that most Americans still consider him "black."

The truth is that different societies, or even the same society at different times in its history, have answered these questions differently. Part of the problem is that the term "race" has been chronically imprecisely defined, if it has been defined at all. Francis Collins, head of the Human Genome Project, insists that "it is essential to point out that 'race' and 'ethnicity' are terms without generally agreed-upon definitions. Both terms carry complex connotations that reflect culture, history, socioeconomic and political status, as well as a variably important connection to ancestral geographic origins" (2004: S 13). Brazilian anthropologists Sergio Pena and Telma de Souza Birchal insist that race is not a scientific idea; rather, "The notion of race has been imported from the common sense to science since its appearance" (2005–2006: 3).

Five obvious and fatal objections to the concept of race have been raised. First, no one has been able to specify exactly how many races there are. Common estimates range from three to five or as many as nine. Second, race classifications select certain physical characteristics (most often skin color) and not others on which to base the categories, and it is not explained how and why these particular traits were chosen as the relevant ones: why skin color instead of blood type or height or shoe size? Third and related to the first two, the classifications, evaluations, and applications of race change over time. For example, not so long ago English speakers used (and sometimes still use) the term *race* in reference to "the French race" or "the Scandinavian race" or "the Jewish race" or "the Arab race," or even "the human race." Groups that never regarded themselves as a single identity ("the Native American race") are subsumed under one category, as are people who are physically quite diverse, like the "Hispanic race" which includes "white" people, "black" people, "Indian" people, and every conceivable mixture of these and more. Fourth, some researchers have calculated that there is more physical and genetic variation *within* race groups than between them: according to Richard Lewontin (1972), for the eight race categories he considered, 85.4 percent of genetic diversity was found inside the categories and only 6.3 percent between the categories. Fifth and finally, race classifications have not always, if ever, been content to stop at physical characteristics but have attributed psychological, emotional, intellectual, and even moral qualities to the purported races as well. For instance, Madison Grant wrote in 1916 that "moral, intellectual, and spiritual attributes are as persistent as physical characters and are transmitted substantially unchanged from generation to generation" (226).

The evolution of the race concept

According to Dante Puzzo, a historian of Western ideas, race (and its evil concomitant racism) "is a modern conception, for prior to the sixteenth century there was virtually nothing in the life and thought of the West that can be described as racist" (1964: 579). Michael Banton (1987) found that the word "race" did not appear in English until 1508. However, as Europeans acquired more experience with peoples from other parts of the world, and as they acquired power over those peoples, differences in body and behavior became more interesting to them – and frequently became intertwined for them.

See Chapter 3

The familiar system of race categories appeared in the work of Linnaeus (1707–1778), the great classifier of natural species. In the first edition of his *Systema Naturae* published in 1740 he divided the human species into four subtypes based

PLATE 6.1 Children in Central Australian Aboriginal societies have straight, often blond, hair, challenging the simple racial categories of the West

on color – white, black, red, and yellow. By the tenth edition (in 1758–1759), these types had evolved into Homo europaeus, Homo afer, Homo americanus, and Homo asiaticus, acquiring not only geographical but (often quite offensive) mental and behavioral features:

■ Homo europaeus: "white, sanguine, muscular. Hair flowing, long. Eyes blue. Gentle, acute, inventive. Covered with close vestments. Governed by laws"
■ Homo afer: "black, phlegmatic, relaxed. Hair black, frizzled. Skin silky. Nose flat. Lips tumid. Women without shame. Mammae lactate profusely. Crafty, indolent, negligent. Anoints himself with grease. Governed by caprice"
■ Homo americanus: "reddish, choleric, erect. Hair black, straight, thick; nostrils wide; face harsh; beard scanty. Obstinate, merry, free. Paints himself with fine red lines. Regulated by customs"
■ Homo asiaticus: "sallow, melancholy, stiff. Hair black. Eyes dark. Severe, haughty, avaricious. Covered with loose garments. Ruled by opinions."

(quoted in Slotkin 1965: 177–8)

The pseudoscientific conflation of physical, psychological, and cultural traits was only amplified by the inclusion of other fallacious species of humanity such as Homo ferus, a hairy and mute quadruped, and Homo monstrosus, a race of cavemen who roamed about at night.

The elastic quality of race categories is seen again in the work of Johann Friedrich Blumenbach (1752–1840), who proposed the standard four races in his *On the Natural Variety of Mankind* in 1770 – European (for whom he introduced the term "Caucasian"), African, American, and Asian. Subsequently, he added a fifth race, Malayan, for southern Asian people. Interestingly, Blumenbach made several important qualifications to his race system, not the least of which was that each of the "five principal races" was actually composed of "one or more nations which are distinguished by their more or less striking structure from the rest of those of the same division. Thus the Hindoos [sic] might be separated as particular subvarieties from the Caucasian; the Chinese and Japanese from the Mongolian; the Hottentots from the Ethiopian," and so on. In other words, he admitted considerable variation *within* "primary races." He also conceded that races were not entirely discrete: although the race types were "so many different species of man, yet when the matter is thoroughly considered, you see that all do so run into one another, and that one variety of mankind does so sensibly pass into the other, that you cannot mark out the limits between them" (quoted in Slotkin 1965: 189). Finally and most consequentially, the races were not only distinguished but ranked in terms of antiquity and perfection, the first race in time and quality being the white/Caucasian race. As the original, "primeval" form of humanity, Caucasians were the most "beautiful," at the middle of a spectrum of races with Asians and Africans at the opposite extremes, Americans/Indians intermediate between Caucasians and Asians, and Malayans intermediate between Caucasians and Africans. The non-Caucasian races were deemed a product of *degeneration* from the first, ideal type and the admixture of the higher and lower types.

Race typologies multiplied and morphed over the centuries. George Cuvier (1769–1832) managed to condense them to three – Caucasian, Mongolian, and Negroid – with white Caucasians as the optimal form of humanity and black Negroids as "the most degraded race among men, whose forms approach nearest to those of the inferior animals, and whose intellect has not yet arrived at the establishment of any regular form of government, nor at anything which has the least appearance of systematic knowledge" (quoted in Green 1959: 235). Most whimsically of all, Carl Gustav Carus (1789–1869) created a four-race system consisting of Day People (Caucasian), Eastern Twilight People (Mongolians, Malayans, Hindus, Turks, and Slavs), Western Twilight People (American Indians), and Night People (Africans and Australians).

Measuring and managing mankind

The failure to achieve any accord on the number or nature of races, yet the persistence with which theorists have sought racial systems, alerts us to the urge toward race typing in Western societies: while thinkers have not settled on a uniform race classification, they have certainly believed that such classification was possible and important. None seemed to stop and ask the question that Sherwood Washburn posed only in the 1960s: what is a race classification for? What is its social origin and – still more significantly – its social function or effect?

The question of why people want and need to identify races and to build race classifications is indeed the central question of race. Several scholars have directed attention less toward race itself or any particular race system than toward what we could call "racial thinking," the (erroneous) belief that humanity is divided into scientifically observable, homogeneous, and mutually distinct biological "types." Importantly, it assumes that these types exist transhistorically, that is, that these categories exist . . . as natural facts, and that these categories existed throughout time, whether people in a particular era realized it or not.

(Eissenstat 2005: 239–40)

More crucial than the concept of race for describing physical differences between kinds of humans, then, is the use of those descriptions for *explaining and justifying* certain behaviors of and relationships among these kinds.

See Chapter 12

It cannot be overemphasized that Western societies developed their racial thinking in the context of political and cultural domination over non-Western societies. Far beyond the neutral or pure-scientific activity of cataloging and organizing human physical variety (a not illegitimate project), Western travelers and theorists were led to ask why the people they encountered acted and thought in unfamiliar and (often to Western eyes) nonsensical or reprehensible ways. And as this contact became increasingly exploitative, including conquest and slavery, Westerners were further led to ask why these other people were so "weak" or "backward" or "inferior." One possible and appealing answer was a sort of biological determinism – that humans with particular biological traits also had particular behavioral or mental traits that inhibited their "progress." The persistence of "backward/inferior" behavioral and psychological qualities after exposure to the "superior" ways of the West, and the failure of these other peoples to "improve" and "succeed" in the Western sense, gave rise to the notion that physical characteristics were a sign and a cause of mental and even moral deficiencies – most critically, that the physical and the mental/moral were inseparably connected and that both were innate and permanent.

Thus the conventional English-language, especially North American, concept of race arose, with its five key components (Smedley 1999: 28):

1. a race is an "exclusive and discrete biological" entity;
2. races are fundamentally unequal, and the relations between races are necessarily hierarchical (some are "better" than others);
3. "the outer physical characteristics" of races are "but surface manifestations of inner realities [such as] behavioral, intellectual, temperamental, moral, and other qualities";
4. all of the qualities of a race are "natural" and genetically inherited – and inherited as a single indivisible bundle;
5. therefore, the differences and hierarchies between races are immutable, "fixed and unalterable, [and] could never be bridged or transcended."

In the end, race was not simply a classification of human physical differences but a *bio-moral* judgment (Wolf 1994) on certain types of humans who were ranked inherently and eternally "higher" or "lower" than other types of humans. Race thinking accomplished the valuable task of "naturalizing" political, economic, and cultural status or class inequalities and ascribing them as intrinsic properties of the victims of these inequalities.

The obvious task then was to specify and quantify these natural differences. Accordingly, the nineteenth century became the great era of measuring mankind. In fact, in his study of the science of race, John Haller proposes that "The hallmark of anthropology in the nineteenth century was anthropometry" (1971: 7). **Anthropometry** was and is a practice of measuring the bodies of human beings for the purpose of describing individual and collective physical characteristics. In itself, recording people's height and weight and head size is neither unacceptable nor absurd; however, the generalizations and interpretations of this research could be problematic, distasteful, and patently false.

Certain traits emerged as central to race classification, including hair form and color, skin color, eye form and color, nose form, face form, overall height and body form, and especially head size and shape. One of the earliest notions, developed in the 1700s, was **facial angle**, or roughly the amount that the lower face and jaw protrudes, deviating from the flat face of the ideal Caucasian. It was noticed that apes and even more so dogs and other animals had very acute facial angles, which was linked to their lower intelligence; by extension, humans with acute facial angles (resulting from sloping foreheads and/or large jaws or lips) were deemed more animalistic and less intelligent. Darker skin color was also taken as a lower and more primitive feature, as was short stature or especially long or short limbs.

However, the major factor then, as for many people today, was the head and brain. "Scientific" measures like brain volume and cephalic index purported to quantify racial differences. **Cephalic index**, introduced by the great neurologist Paul Broca, was a ratio of the width of the head from ear to ear relative to the depth of the head from front to back; a higher index suggested a rounder head and a superior intelligence. Determining brain volume was fairly straightforward, on the assumption that larger brains meant greater intelligence. Happily for scientific racists, Caucasians scored well on both tests, with a cephalic index and a brain weight and volume higher than all other races. Samuel Morton ranked the brains of races in the descending order of Caucasian, Mongoloid, Malay, Native American, and African, further arguing that brains had not altered in 4000 years and thus could be deemed fixed and permanent. In the skull and in numerous other characteristics, Africans consistently ranked lowest, indicating to racial thinkers "a far closer relationship to the ape" than any other human species (Haller 1971: 34).

The implications of such racial thinking are obvious: if some races were naturally and permanently higher or lower than others, it made little sense to preach the equality of races or to attempt to raise the lower races. It even seemed reasonable to subordinate and restrict the lower ones, and certainly interbreeding (**miscegenation**) was to be avoided as deleterious to the more perfect races – or, ironically, sometimes to be promoted as a means to "improve" the more degraded races. Nineteenth- and early twentieth-century racial thinking was thus an ideal justification for slavery, segregation, colonialism, and genocide. Influential figures like Edward Drinker Cope

Anthropometry
The measurement of human bodies to determine individual and group ("racial") physical characteristics.

Facial angle
The slope of the lower face and jaw away from the flatness of the forehead, used by "scientific racists" to measure the difference between races (the sharper the angle, the more "primitive" the face).

Cephalic index
A measurement of the skull/brain volume and shape, based on a ratio of the width of the head from ear to ear relative to the depth of the head from front to back.

Miscegenation
A term for the undesirable effects of the mixing of different genetic types or populations, especially race groups. Often refers to the very notion of mixing the races.

insisted that the "inferior character of the Negro mind in the scale of evolution made him unfit for American citizenship" (Haller 1971: 198), while Nathaniel Southgate Shaler went so far as to excuse lynching as a legitimate form of race self-defense (ibid.: 184–5).

It should be noted, in conclusion, that biological-deterministic, bio-moral explanations and recommendations were not limited to race groups. In the nineteenth and even more so in the twentieth century, biological causes were often proposed for behavioral, temperamental, moral, or social circumstances. Measurements of brain size, cephalic index, and facial angle, or less "scientific" attributes like stature and skin color, were applied to the new immigrants arriving in the United States from Eastern and Southern Europe around 1900 – Caucasians all, by the standard typology. Various immigrant groups were regarded as congenitally prone to drunkenness or idleness or crime or violence. Predictably, all sorts of vices and social improprieties were explained in biological terms, including poverty: some people, it was held, were naturally unable to compete or succeed, and a few social engineers went so far as to recommend that the poor not be allowed to breed, since poverty was a transmissible condition. Criminals were subjected to bio-moral analyses in the hope that a "criminal type" might be identified that would make the capture and punishment of outlaws easier (a kind of biological "profiling"). Mental illness was often associated with physical imperfections and therefore with physical therapies: the "insane" were often thought to be animal-like in their insensitivity to heat, cold, pain, and exhaustion (which is not even true of animals), and somatic "cures" like bleeding, blistering, near-drowning, swinging and spinning, or immobilization were practiced. This attitude extended to those with disabilities, such as the deaf who were also regarded as lacking sense or intelligence, like wild animals, and were not allowed to vote in the United States until the early 1800s. Advocates of the **eugenics** movement like Victoria Woodhull echoed the sentiments of the racial miscegenists when she insisted that all such people, "imbeciles, criminals, paupers, and the otherwise unfit . . . must not be bred."

Eugenics
The scientific practice of "improving" a population or species by selective breeding or genetic engineering, to breed out "bad" traits and breed in "good" ones.

THE MODERN ANTHROPOLOGICAL CRITIQUE OF RACE

The confusions, abuses, and outright falsehoods surrounding racial thinking could not forever escape criticism, and cultural anthropology contributed significantly to this critique. The elaboration of the anthropological concept of "culture" combined with the growing body of observational data of non-Western peoples and the inclusive and relativistic attitude of anthropology provided it with a unique and authoritative perspective from which to judge the discourse of race.

One of the first and strongest voices to challenge racial thinking was Franz Boas. Much of his work was targeted specifically at the reigning ideas and practices of race, as in his 1928 *Anthropology and Modern Life*, as well as his 1940 *Race, Language, and Culture* and his 1945 *Race and Democratic Society*. Starting from the premise that there "is little clarity in regard to the term 'race'" (1928: 19), he took the key step of separating physical from psychological and cultural phenomena, concluding that "it is well-nigh impossible to determine with certainty the hereditary traits in mental behavior" (50). Rather, the variability of intelligence and personality within a group, and the rapidity and ease with which individuals change in new circumstances, convinced him that "cultural experience" was as important as if not more important than "racial descent."

Having placed learning above biology for explaining behavior, Boas went further to unpack the race concept itself. A race was not a closed, fixed physical type but something more akin to a family line, with its common but by no means immutable traits; mix in other family lines and the race type dissolves. Still worse, a race is not a homogeneous unit but a vague division of humanity with much internal variety: obviously not all Caucasians or Homo europaeus have blond hair and blue eyes, and the alleged "race traits" of any race are a statistical abstraction from a diverse distribution of features. At best, the stereotype of a race is the *extreme or ideal* form, but these extreme forms "are not pure racial types. We do not know how much their descendants may vary from themselves and what their ancestry may have been" (22–3). Most devastating of all, Boas asserted that physical traits, as much as mental/behavioral ones, are plastic and subject to environmental pressures, not fixed, permanent inheritances. Some of his most influential (and controversial) research argued that the children and grandchildren of immigrants differed measurably from their ancestors in head shape, cephalic index, and height and conformed more to the standards of their newly adopted land – indicating that "race traits" were highly changeable and only appeared stable as long as environmental conditions remained the same.

Under the tutelage of Boas, anthropology was academically and politically active on the question of race, even condemning Nazi racism in a 1938 resolution which stated that "Anthropology provides no scientific basis for discrimination against any people on the ground of racial inferiority, religious affiliation or linguistic heritage" (American Anthropological Association 1939: 30). Melville Herskovits attacked racism against African Americans directly in *The Myth of the Negro Past*, which refuted five lies about the "Negro race": that they "are naturally of a child-like character"; that they are unintelligent since "only the poorer stock of Africa was enslaved"; that because slaves came from all parts of Africa they had no common culture; that whatever culture they did have was "so savage and relatively so low in the scale of human civilization" that they would have quickly given it up; and that "the Negro is thus a man without a past" – and presumably therefore only a man (and woman) with a racial body (1958: 1–2).

Herskovits, Melville J. 1958 [1941]. *The Myth of the Negro Past*. Boston: Beacon Press.

But arguably the most vociferous critic of racial thinking was Ashley Montagu, calling it "man's most dangerous myth," not only as an error but as a tragedy (1945: 1). Races in the everyday sense do not exist, he explained, as it is a fact "that all human beings are so much mixed with regard to origin that between different groups of individuals intergradation and 'overlapping' of physical characters is the rule" (3). Worse still, as we have seen, the concept of race implies much more than physical similarity but "a compound of physical, mental, personality, and cultural traits which

Montagu, M. F. Ashley. 1945. *Man's Most Dangerous Myth: The Fallacy of Race* (2nd edn). New York: Columbia University Press.

determine the behavior of individuals inheriting this alleged compound" (6). However, "Such a conception of 'race' has no basis in scientific fact or in any other kind of demonstrable fact. It is a pure myth, and it is the tragic myth of our tragic era" (8).

For Montagu, racial thinking was a way of translating cultural differences into physical differences; the real and crucial issues are status and caste issues, in which resources, opportunities, and social value are differentially assigned to groups and these groups are then "closed" to each other spatially (by segregation) and sexually (by rules of **endogamy**). Race is thus, he concluded, "a term for a social problem which is created by special types of social condition and by such special conditions alone. In terms of social relations so-called 'race problems' are, in the modern world, essentially of the nature of caste problems" (67). In a racial system, physical characteristics "are merely the pegs upon which culturally generated hostilities are made to hang" (66). Accordingly, following a suggestion in the 1935 book *We Europeans* by Julian Huxley and A. C. Haddon, Montagu advocated the use of the term "ethnic group" (see below) to name these socially and culturally distinguished collections of humans – and rejection of the term "race" completely.

Like Montagu, Frank Livingstone insisted on the "non-existence" of races in the human species, claiming that "there are excellent arguments for abandoning the concept of race with reference to the living populations of *Homo sapiens*" (1962: 279). The physical anthropologist Sherwood Washburn, who raised the central question of the purpose of race classifications, seconded the analysis that race is a cultural construction and that there is "no possibility of studying human raciation, the process of race formation, without studying human culture" (1963: 522). The physical evidence tells us that there are "no three primary races, no three major groups. The idea of three primary races stems from nineteenth-century typology" (523). Rather, "Since races are open systems which are intergrading, the number of races will depend on the purpose of the classification" (524) – or, if no social purpose is served by it, no racial distinction might be made in the first place.

These and many other anthropologists have deflated the concept of race as a natural, objective, scientific tool and have redirected attention to the social phenomenon that Manning Nash calls the "ideology of race." Recognizing that the "non-existence" of races in the natural/objective sense does not mean the non-existence or irrelevance of race as a cultural force, Nash defines race ideology as

> a system of ideas which interprets and defines the meanings of racial differences, real or imagined, in terms of some system of cultural values. The ideology of race is always normative: it ranks differences as better or worse, superior or inferior, desirable or undesirable, and as modifiable or unmodifiable. Like all ideologies, the ideology of race implies a call to action; it embodies a political and social program; it is a demand that something be done.

(1962: 285)

Perhaps we should add that it is also a justification for things that are already being done, such as discrimination, slavery, or genocide.

Endogamy

The marriage principle in which an individual marries someone who is in the same cultural category as himself or herself (e.g., marrying someone in one's own race or religion).

Nash goes beyond the identification of race ideology to theorizing about when such an ideology will appear, since not all societies in all times have possessed it. A race ideology, he hypothesizes, is likely to coalesce when there is a conflict between two or more groups distinguishable in physical terms; when there is a division of labor based on this distinction which results in the "subordination or systematic deprivation of one group"; when the subordinate group resists or refuses its sub-ordination; and interestingly when there is dissent within the dominant group over the "prevailing facts of disprivilege" (288). In such conditions, the ideology of race serves not only to subjugate the "lower race" but to justify to the "dominant race" its own advantages and privileges. If he is correct, then the appearance and elab-oration of a race system should come *after* the social inequalities which it explains, legitimates, and perpetuates rather than before.

BOX 6.1 AMERICAN ANTHROPOLOGICAL ASSOCIATION STATEMENT ON "RACE" (1998)

In the United States both scholars and the general public have been conditioned to viewing human races as natural and separate divisions within the human species based on visible physical differences. With the vast expansion of scientific knowledge in this century, however, it has become clear that human populations are not unambiguous, clearly demarcated, biologically distinct groups. . . .

Historical research has shown that the idea of "race" has always carried more meanings than mere physical differences; indeed, physical variations in the human species have no meaning except the social ones that humans put on them. Today scholars in many fields argue that "race" as it is under-stood in the United States of America was a social mechanism invented during the 18th century to refer to those populations brought together in colonial America: the English and other European settlers, the conquered Indian peoples, and those peoples of Africa brought in to provide slave labor. . . .

Early in the 19th century the growing fields of science began to reflect the public consciousness about human differences. Differences among the "racial" categories were projected to their greatest extreme when the argument was posed that Africans, Indians, and Europeans were separate species, with Africans the least human and closer taxonomically to apes.

Ultimately "race" as an ideology about human differences was subsequently spread to other areas of the world. It became a strategy for dividing, ranking, and controlling colonized people used by colonial powers everywhere. But it was not limited to the colonial situation. . . .

"Race" thus evolved as a worldview, a body of prejudgments that distorts our ideas about human differences and group behavior. Racial beliefs constitute myths about the diversity in the human species and about the abilities and behavior of people homogenized into "racial" categories. The myths fused behavior and physical features together in the public mind, impeding our comprehension of both biological variations and cultural behavior, implying that both are genetically determined. Racial myths bear no relationship to the reality of human capabilities or behavior. Scientists today find that reliance on such folk beliefs about human differences in research has led to countless errors.

At the end of the 20th century, we now understand that human cultural behavior is learned, conditioned into infants beginning at birth, and always subject to modification. No human is born with a built-in culture or language. Our temperaments, dispositions, and personalities, regardless of genetic propensities, are developed within sets of meanings and values that we call "culture." Studies of infant and early childhood learning and behavior attest to the reality of our cultures in forming who we are.

The "racial" worldview was invented to assign some groups to perpetual low status, while others were permitted access to privilege, power, and wealth. . . . Given what we know about the capacity of normal humans to achieve and function within any culture, we conclude that present-day inequalities between so-called "racial" groups are not consequences of their biological inheritance but products of historical and contemporary social, economic, educational, and political circumstances.

THE ANTHROPOLOGY OF ETHNICITY

Most English speakers are not only familiar with the concept of ethnicity or ethnic group but commonly associate it with race, as in "race and ethnicity" or "racial and ethnic groups." Many may even consider the two terms synonymous, although they are not. Nevertheless, race and ethnicity are closely related in certain ways. Both are practices for categorizing people – by physical characteristics for "race" and by cultural or behavioral characteristics for "ethnicity." Often, a group that shares physical traits also shares behavioral ones; as shown above, racialist thinkers tended to link the behaviors of the group causally to its biology, while anthropologists realize today that behavior is learned and shared and, therefore, that groups of people who are genetically related will inevitably tend to interact more and to share more cultural characteristics as well. Furthermore, like races, ethnic groups are not objective or natural "things" but social concepts with social meaning and function. Accordingly, as with race, anthropological attention has shifted from the reputed qualities of particular ethnic groups to the relations between these groups (frequently competitive and sometimes combative, including discrimination, oppression, and genocide) and to the processes by which the groups are formed and sustained.

When Huxley and Haddon proposed "ethnic group" as a replacement for "race," they were explicitly reviving a very old notion, one employed by the ancient historian and traveler Herodotus, who "found human beings divided into a number of groups, *ethnea*, and the *ethnos* forms his practical basis of classification" (Huxley and Haddon 1935: 30). However, the term *ethnos*, roughly translated as "a people," "a nation," or "a cultural group" (and incorporated into anthropology in terms like ethnology, ethnography, and various subdisciplines such as ethnobotany and ethnopsychology), was then as today a slippery and vague concept: "Thus, his *ethnos* is at times a tribe, at times a political unit, at times a larger grouping, and in using the word he guards himself against treating either type of unit as necessarily or even probably of common descent" (31).

So the root *ethnos* and the English words derived from it, including "ethnic group" and "ethnicity," entered the language with wide but various and uncertain meaning; they could refer to numerous kinds of groups with imprecise qualities and porous boundaries. Even so, or perhaps for exactly that reason, the concept of ethnic group has stuck and even grown in popular and scholarly usage. Max Weber wrote about it in the early twentieth century, defining the term as a human group

> that entertain[s] a subjective belief in their common descent because of similarities of physical type or of customs or both, or because of memories of colonization and migration; this belief must be important for the propagation of group formation; conversely, it does not matter whether or not an objective blood relationship exists.
>
> (1968: 389)

Weber, Max. 1968. *Economy and Society*, Vol. 1, ed. Guenther Roth and Claus Wittich. New York: Bedminster Press.

Notice in this definition that physical and cultural traits are still both included, yet neither is necessarily "real": membership in an ethnic group, he asserted, is distinct "precisely by being a presumed identity, not a group with concrete social action. . . . [Ethnicity] does not constitute a group; it merely facilitates group formation of any kind, particularly in the political sphere." This led Weber to three crucial realizations about ethnic groups: first, that they need not be very culturally different from each other (that is, a small cultural difference is sufficient to construct an "ethnic" difference); second, that they need not be very internally culturally homogeneous (that is, there may be considerable diversity *within* the ethnic group); and third, that any cultural trait – language, religion, clothing, cuisine, and so on – can suffice to distinguish one ethnic group from another.

Since the reintroduction of "ethnic group" by Weber, and by Huxley and Haddon (and the later invention of the noun "ethnicity"), the concept has become essential to discussions of and developments in human group relations. While there is no single authoritative definition for ethnic group or ethnicity, the definitions that have been offered share important common features and indicate important cultural processes. Thus, ethnicity has been defined as the "subjective symbolic or emblematic use of any aspect of culture [by members of a group], in order to differentiate themselves from other groups" (DeVos 1975: 16), or as the

> character, quality, or condition of ethnic group membership, based on an identity with and/or consciousness of group belonging that is differentiated from others by symbolic "markers" (including cultural, biological, or territorial), and is rooted in bonds to a shared past and perceived ethnic interests.
>
> (Burgess 1978: 270)

Rather than crafting definitions, another and more fruitful course is to identify the characteristics of the groups that are produced. Fredrik Barth suggests that an ethnic group has four key qualities: it is "largely biologically self-perpetuating" generally through endogamous marriage, "shares fundamental cultural values," "makes up a field of communication and interaction," and "has a membership which identifies itself, and is identified by others, as constituting a category distinguishable from other categories of the same order" (1969: 10–11). Andrew Greeley (1971: 120–1) offers a list of six features of an ethnic group:

1. A presumed consciousness of kind rooted in a sense of common origin.
2. Sufficient territorial concentration to make it possible for members of the group to interact with each other most of the time and to reduce to a minimum interaction with members of other ethnic groups.
3. A sharing of ideals and values by members of the ethnic group.
4. Strong moralistic fervor for such ideals and values, combined with a sense of being persecuted by those who do not share them and hence are not members of the ethnic group.
5. Distrust of those who are outside the ethnic group, combined with massive ignorance of them.
6. Finally, a strong tendency in members of an ethnic group to view themselves and their circle as the whole of reality, or at least the whole of reality that matters.

Ethnic culture, ethnic boundary, and ethnic mobilization

Whether or not all ethnic groups possess all the qualities highlighted by Greeley, such analyses raise two relevant points. First, ethnicity and ethnic groups bring together a set of powerful forces, summarized by Manning Nash (1989) as "blood, bed, and cult," to which we might add "soil" or "land" as well. In other words, there is, to some extent, a biological or genetic component: an ethnic group may be endogamous or intermarrying, so that the group is more or less genetically "closed." Some ethnic groups place a strong value on marrying within the group, and some practically or even legally prohibit marriage outside the group. When ethnic groups are thus sexually isolated, they necessarily come to share a biological bond with each other, like a family; some go so far as avowing an ineffable and almost mystical "essence" that sets them apart from – and often above – other groups. Pierre van den Berghe has likened ethnic groups to extended kin groups: an ethnic group, he argues, always contains at least a core "made up of people who know themselves to be related to each other by a double network of ties of descent and marriage. Ethnicity is thus defined in the last analysis by *common descent*" (1987: 24). Still, he admits that, "in many cases, the common descent ascribed to an ethny [his term for ethnic group] is fictive. In fact, in *most* cases, it is at least *partly* fictive" (27). We should conclude that ethnicity is based not so much on ancestry as on "a myth of ancestry" (Horowitz 1985: 52) which may involve stories of the origin and struggles of the group.

The mention of myth brings us to the Nash's "cult," which here means not just religious belief (although certainly religious belief too) but all of the cultural factors

Nash, Manning. 1989. *The Cauldron of Ethnicity in the Modern World.* Chicago: The University of Chicago Press.

that unite the group and which serve more than instrumental functions for the group. Orlando Patterson has explicitly stated that certain aspects of its culture have "the functions of . . . rituals for the group – the ways in which they are used to maintain group cohesiveness, to sustain and enhance identity, and to establish social networks and communicative patterns" (1975: 305). Finally, "soil" or "land" is important literally and symbolically – literally as a place for the group to live and as a physical/territorial boundary around the group, and symbolically as a homeland where formative events occurred and/or where the forefathers lived and died.

See Chapters 13 and 14

The problem of ethnicity and ethnic groups can perhaps be distilled to two issues – the *culture* of the group and the *boundaries* that enclose the group; both serve to distinguish and even segregate groups from each other. To begin, surely ethnicity is "about" culture, in the same way that race is "about" biology. However, in the same way that biological difference does not make straightforward or exclusive race classifications possible, cultural difference does not make straightforward or exclusive ethnic classifications possible. First, as DeVos noted earlier, an ethnic group does not use *all* of its culture in defining its ethnic identity; in fact, as Weber explained long ago, an ethnic group is not different in every cultural regard from neighboring ethnic groups. In Rwanda the Hutu and the Tutsi speak the same language, while in Northern Ireland the Protestants and the Catholics belong to the same major religion (Christianity). Any ethnic group is unlike other groups in some ways and like other groups in other ways.

Furthermore, there is potentially considerable cultural variation within an ethnic group. Anthropological studies of supposed African "tribes" in the 1940s illustrated conclusively that many such groups were highly internally heterogeneous and frequently appeared "to be an amalgam of different peoples, each aware of its unique origin and history" (Fortes and Evans-Pritchard 1940: 26). That is to say, not only were "societies" or "ethnic groups" often internally diverse, but many had only recently come into existence, through a process that anthropologists call **ethnogenesis**, the construction of ethnic identity out of the "raw material" of culture and history. On those grounds, it is accurate to conclude that "it would be misleading to state simply that ethnic groups are identical with cultural groups" (Eriksen 2002: 36).

Ethnogenesis
The process by which ethnic groups come into being and/or attain their cultural characteristics.

For these reasons, anthropologists like Fredrik Barth have redirected the discussion away from the "contents" or traits of particular ethnic groups and toward the boundaries between them, which emphasizes the fact that ethnicity is a relationship and process. Criticizing the notion that there really are discrete "aggregates of people who essentially share a common culture" (1969: 9) – aggregates that can be identified by a trait list of cultural characteristics (a specific language, religion, history, name, territory, and such) – Barth insists that the key to ethnicity and ethnic groups is "the ethnic *boundary* that defines the group, not the cultural stuff that it encloses" (15). This shift in focus allows us to see that ethnicity is a form of social organization, not merely a fact of timeless and immutable cultural difference. It therefore compels us to analyze the processes by which groups develop and preserve boundaries, even while individuals or culture traits within the boundary change over time.

Barth, Fredrik, ed. 1969. *Ethnic Groups and Boundaries*. Boston: Little, Brown & Co.

Finally and critically, it answers a question implied by DeVos' definition above: if ethnicity is the use of aspects of a culture, why are some aspects used and not others, and what are they used for? In this new view, particular elements of culture function as "markers," "signs," "flags," or "badges" of membership and non-membership, of inclusion and exclusion. Even more, members who "wear" the markers signal their solidarity with other members – and their preparedness for common action.

In the ultimate analysis, ethnicity is a style of social action, specifically and commonly political and economic action. An ethnic group may be an identity group, but it is also, in most cases, an interest group and often a competitive group. Ethnic groups do not exist in isolation; a group by itself is not an ethnic group in the proper sense. Two or more ethnic groups share a social space where they are in some particular (if shifting) social, political, or economic relation to each other. Like races, they are regularly separated by territory or neighborhood, class or profession, and politics or power – and unequally at that. While ethnicity does not imply hierarchy as inherently as race, in practice it often has precisely that effect. Thus ethnicity can be a means to press the group into action, to mobilize it to strive for some goal, which may include or entail "closing ranks" and acting jointly as a group and *in the interests of* the group.

Types of ethnic organization and mobilization

Eriksen, Thomas Hylland.
2002 [1993]. *Ethnicity
and Nationalism:
Anthropological
Perspectives*. London:
Pluto Press.

Since ethnicity does not refer to any specific and universal kind of cultural difference or cultural goal, it follows that ethnic groups come in many diverse forms and relations to each other. In fact, not all cultural groups are fully and equally organized and "incorporated" as ethnic groups; in a word, not every cultural difference is the basis for an ethnic difference or an ethnic group. Eriksen (2002: 43) proposes that, at the lowest level of awareness and mobilization, an ethnic label might be no more than a "category," a name to call a certain people or for a certain people to call themselves. When such people begin to interact in terms of their common identity, they constitute a "network." Once the group becomes not only organized but goal oriented, it transforms into an "association," and when that association develops a territorial base, it evolves into a "community." Not all (potential) ethnic groups, of course, achieve this complete evolution.

Among groups that attain ethnic awareness and organization, there is still great diversity. Eriksen (2002: 14–15) offers five different types of ethnic groups/relations:

1. urban ethnic minorities (usually as the result of migration)
2. indigenous peoples (usually as the result of colonialism and conquest)
3. proto-nations, that is, groups that "claim that they are entitled to their own nation-state"
4. ethnic groups in plural societies
5. post-slavery minorities.

Gurr and Harff (1994: 15–23) give a similar but somewhat different analysis, including four types which they call:

1. ethnonationalists, "relatively large and regionally concentrated ethnic groups that live within the boundaries of one state or of several adjacent states; their modern political movements are directed toward achieving greater autonomy or independent statehood";
2. indigenous peoples, "the descendants of the original inhabitants of conquered or colonized regions";
3. communal contenders, "ethnic groups whose main political aim is not to gain autonomy but is, rather, to share power in the central government of modern states";
4. ethnoclasses, "culturally distinct minorities who occupy distinct social strata and have specialized economic roles in the societies in which they now live. They are, in other words, ethnic groups who resemble classes."

RACIAL AND ETHNIC GROUPS AND RELATIONS IN CROSS-CULTURAL PERSPECTIVE

The characteristics of race and ethnic groups are less interesting or important than the relations among these groups. In fact, it is appropriate and useful to think of racial and ethnic relations as a subset of group relations more generally, whether those relations are based on race, ethnicity, gender, age, class, or any other criteria. It is never the differences between groups that matter as much as the social/cultural meanings of those differences and the relationships and inequalities between the bearers of the group "markers."

First and foremost, race and ethnic systems are not only methods for classifying and explaining human differences but for establishing (more or less) sharp and permanent separation among the groups distinguished by these differences. In a word, the concepts and practices of race and ethnicity create "distance" between socially defined and socially defended bounded groups. There are various ways to conceptualize and quantify this "social distance," such as the Social Distance Scale developed by Emory Bogardus (1933), a set of questions to test the willingness of people to enter into relationships (from superficial to intimate) with members of other groups. At the minimal level of acceptance, the scale asks whether the subject is willing to allow group X to inhabit or even visit his or her country; at increasingly intimate levels, questions assess whether the subject would accept members of group X in his or her town, neighborhood, workplace, circle of friends, or very family (through intermarriage). Obviously, the more exclusions raised against a group, the greater the "social distance" between the group in question and one's own.

But the relations between groups are not merely individualistic and subjective. There are large-scale, structural relationships as well, ones that persist despite the attitudes and actions of particular individuals. George Simpson and Milton Yinger

Assimilation
The social process by which individuals and groups are absorbed into another, usually dominant, cultural group.

Cultural assimilation
A type of assimilation which refers specifically to the loss of distinctive cultural traits, such as language or religion.

Racial assimilation
A form of assimilation in which the physical traits of a group are lost through intermarriage.

Social assimilation
A form of assimilation in which groups are integrated into the society (for instance, sharing the same jobs or the same neighborhoods), whether or not they share the same culture.

Structural assimilation
See social assimilation.

(1972) constructed a useful typology of group relations, comprising six types arrayed from relatively benign to highly malignant.

1. Assimilation. The process by which a group loses some or all of its unique characteristics and adopts the characteristics of another or the dominant group. **Cultural assimilation** refers specifically to the loss of distinctive cultural traits, such as language or religion, while **racial assimilation** occurs when the physical traits of a group are lost through intermarriage. (Some analysts have also proposed a category of **social** or **structural assimilation** for groups that are integrated into the society – say, sharing the same jobs or the same neighborhoods – whether or not they share the same culture. Significantly, a group may be culturally assimilated, that is, possess more or less the qualities of another or the dominant culture, but still not be socially assimilated.)

2. Pluralism. The co-existence in the same country or society of groups with distinct cultures. Rather than adopting a foreign or dominant culture, a group retains some distinct behaviors or values, possibly as a source of ethnic or racial pride, and may even maintain loyalty to their group (or, if migrants, to their former homeland) rather

PLATE 6.2 Human faces of many races

than to the wider society in which they live. (Other theorists have recommended distinguishing cultural from structural **pluralism** as well.)

3. **Legal protection of minorities**. Since the personal interactions and attitudes between groups may be influenced by discrimination and hostility, a society may institute formal protections for the rights of subordinated groups. Examples would include the 1964 Civil Rights Act in the United States and the 1965 Race Relations Act in the United Kingdom, followed by many other measures to attempt to guarantee equality between groups and to reduce or eliminate the prejudice and animosity against disadvantaged groups.

4. **Population transfer**. A policy or practice of physically moving groups from one location to another, ostensibly to reduce tensions and hostilities. For instance, Native Americans were "removed" from parts of the southeast in 1830 and resettled in "Indian country" (present-day Oklahoma) for their (and white Southerners') benefit; the surviving "reservation" system in the U.S.A. or "reserve" system in Australia is a product of such policies. At the partition of India in 1948, large populations were also transferred to the "correct" side of the India/Pakistan (i.e., Hindu/Muslim) border.

5. **Continued subjugation**. Dominant groups may have no desire, and no awareness of a need, to change the subordinate position of other groups in the society or country. In such cases, the dominant group may institutionalize hierarchical relations (like slavery or ghetto neighborhoods), pass laws and adopt entire systems of exclusion (like segregation in the U.S.A. or **apartheid** in South Africa), or even use force to suppress groups and any resistance they might organize.

6. **Extermination**. The "final solution" to racial and ethnic "problems" may be the physical destruction of disfavored groups. Also known as **genocide**, the most familiar case is the killing of millions of Jews by Nazi Germany in the 1940s, but many other instances have been recorded in history (and no doubt many more unrecorded), including the eradication of Armenians by Turkey, of Hottentots by Dutch settlers in South Africa, of Aboriginals by Euro-Australians, and of Native Americans by Euro-Americans. Short of all-out extermination of ethnic groups is the outbreak of "ethnic conflict."

Pluralism
The co-existence of multiple social/cultural groups in the same society or state.

Apartheid
In twentieth-century South Africa, the official policy of separating the races within their society legally and socially.

See Chapter 11

Genocide
The destruction of a group or society by harming, killing, or preventing the birth of its members.

See Chapter 13

BOX 6.2   DEAFWORLD: THE CULTURE OF THE DEAF

Most people do not think of the disabled as a cultural group; however, many among the nearly one million deaf and nearly eight million hearing-impaired Americans disagree. Indeed, as Owen Wrigley stresses in his *The Politics of Deafness*, at least some representatives of the deaf community "vigorously refuse the identity label 'disabled,' seeing themselves strictly as a linguistic minority" (1996: 7–8), even as "a distinct 'ethnic identity'" (13). They promulgate a conception of deafness not as a physical deficit but as a cultural difference. No doubt many a reader will find this use of "ethnic" and "cultural" to be a stretch of those terms: how is it that "a group of people who do not have any distinctive religion, clothing, or diet – or even inhabit a particular geographical space they call their own – could be called 'cultural'" (Padden and Humphries 2005: 1)? And while the use of these terms does at first appear to challenge or distort them, in reality the anthropological value of "ethnicity" and "culture" does not lie in any particular "distinctive" marker or location but rather in the creation and transmission of beliefs, practices, values, and relations. True, not all deaf (or, as some prefer, Deaf) are born deaf, nor is deafness passed from person to person in the deaf community. All the same, there is a Deaf community, sometimes named Deafworld or even "Deaf country," with its own traditions, most especially its (sign) language. American Sign Language (ASL) is more than a manual version of spoken English; it has its own style (characterized by candor and direct-ness), its own practices for greetings, leave-takings, attention-getting, turn-taking, and so on, and even its own literature of stories, poems, plays, and jokes (Lane et al. 1996). It has a social network with social institutions, from clubs to schools and colleges (most prominently Gallaudet University), and national and international organizations, like the National Association of the Deaf, the American Athletic Association of the Deaf, the National Theater of the Deaf, and the World Federation of the Deaf. More than a few members of Deafworld are protective of their unique identity, some going so far as to demand that members use ASL and not try to "pass" as Hearing by reading lips; the most militant citizens of Deafworld reject hearing aids and surgery on the basis that such efforts are genocidal – akin to forcing black people to change their bodies to conform to white biological standards.

The race regime of South Africa

The most complete and rigid race system ever practiced by humanity probably reigned in South Africa in the second half of the twentieth century. A large region on the southern tip of the African continent, it was the home to diverse native people before the arrival of Europeans, first in 1652 but mainly in the 1800s. The original Dutch colonists established a racial division of labor, with themselves as the merchant and ruling class over African manual and slave labor; against some native groups, like the hunting-and-gathering Ju/hoansi, the Dutch or "Boers" conducted a virtual genocide, while they fought hard wars with societies like the Zulu. When the British arrived in the early nineteenth century, conflicts followed between the two white groups and between them and the black peoples of the area, leading to the utter defeat and displacement of the native populations.

See Chapter 7

In 1931 South Africa became independent, with the white minority governing the large non-white majority. But racial differences and inequalities were formalized after 1948, when the newly elected Nationalist Party began to implement its apartheid program. Afrikaner for "apartness" or essentially segregation, apartheid structured life in South Africa for almost half a century. With it came official registration of the "races" of South Africa, including "white," "Asian," "colored," and "African." Race labels were applied without regard to cultural assimilation:

PLATE 6.3 Racial divisions, racial tensions, and racial violence were high during the apartheid era of South Africa

"coloreds," for instance, were generally fully Westernized and Christian like whites but were still legally and structurally set apart. Likewise, "westernized Indians and Africans [could] not lose their ascribed caste status. Membership in one of the four castes [was] by birth and for life" (van den Berghe 1967: 102).

Of course, the four race castes were carefully separated and ranked in terms of wealth, power, and status, with the whites dominating in all three realms; each race had "a legally defined set of privileges or disabilities" (ibid.), with strong sanctions against race fraternization and intermarriage. Africans were at the bottom of the system, with coloreds second only to whites in most regards, and Asians (mostly Asian Indians) "subjected to a more hostile government policy and to more restrictions" than the coloreds although generally economically better off. The African majority (over two-thirds at the height of apartheid) was largely relegated to slums or to nominal "homeland" areas. In 1994, the long-jailed leader of the African National Congress, Nelson Mandela, became the first elected black president of South Africa, thus ending the utter political domination by whites but hardly solving all of the economic and structural problems caused by centuries of colonial and racial oppression.

Interestingly, Dunbar Moodie finds that the "tribal identity" of many South African black groups is a recent development largely shaped by colonialism. Before European intervention, he explains, lower level collectivities like "homestead and lineage groupings, more or less structured into chiefdoms . . . were the standard forms of social organization" (Moodie 2005: 320). "Tribes" and "tribalism" were to a significant extent products of colonial administration, with Europeans introducing the notion of tribe (as some primordial, distinct, culturally bounded system) and even creating "tribal authorities" like "chiefs" for "tribes" that had never had chiefs before.

van den Berghe, Pierre L. 1967. *Race and Racism: A Comparative Perspective.* New York: John Wiley & Sons, Inc.

Finally, the circulation of labor, especially the migration of men to cities, induced them to organize and to find native leaders in totally non-traditional ways, inventing "ethnicity" or "tribal identity" in the process. Predictably, then, some groups like the Xhosa are highly diverse, even amalgamations of numerous peoples such as Thembu, Bomvana, Mfengu, and Mpondo, to name just a few. In other words, not only the "races" but the "native tribes" of South Africa are at least partly constructions of modern forces.

Racial democracy in Brazil?

Clearly not all regions of the world suffer from the same level of race consciousness and racism. Some, in fact, claim to be "race blind"; that is, to have no race problems and virtually no race consciousness at all. Among these, Brazil is sometimes held up – and sometimes holds itself up – as a "racial paradise," a "racial democracy" where the races are equal and where "race" in the English-language sense of the word does not even quite exist. It is true, as various observers have commented, that Brazilian society is not based on the rigid and highly binary (white/black) categories of European and American race thinking. Although colonial Brazil was characterized by the same "racial" composition as the United States (white colonists, African slaves, and Native indigenous people), interbreeding was more condoned and common, and "mixed-race" children more accepted and highly placed in the social structure.

Frequent blending of the "races" in Brazil "made the line between Black and White imprecise" (Daniel 2005: 89), and race categories "displayed fluid racial markers, such that Blackness and Whiteness represented merely polar extremes on a continuum" (91). Accordingly, Brazilian race thinking includes many more fine distinctions of color and other physical features: the Brazilian Institute of Geography and Statistics found that people used an incredible 134 different color terms to describe themselves and others, including *alva* (pure white), *alva-escura* (off-white or dark white), *esbranquecimento* (mostly white), *acastanhada* (cashew- or caramel-colored), *trigueira* (wheat-colored), *amarelo* (yellow), *verde* (greenish), *roxa* (purplish), *preta* (black), *queimada* (burnt), *quase-negra* (almost Negro), *pretinha* (light black), *meio-preta* (mid-Negro), *mulatinha* (lighter skinned white Negro), and of course *mulatta* (mixed white and black). The importance of this complicated and continuous terminology is that it has precluded the emergence of two or three closed and absolute race categories.

However, complexity is not necessarily equality. Contemporary researchers question the "myth of racial democracy" in Brazil, finding that physical appearances, while diverse, are not without social consequences. There may be more subtle distinctions in the Brazilian typology, but there nevertheless exist

> distinct aesthetic canons [that] lead one to regard certain types as more attractive than others. For example, light brown skin is valued over both pale and dark

skin; straight hair is considered 'better' than curly or kinky hair, and facial features approximating the Negroid type are generally regarded as ugly.

(van den Berghe 1967: 71)

In addition and more seriously, social opportunities are distributed in racially meaningful ways: individuals with more "African" characteristics disproportionately fill the lower rungs of income, jobs, and education. And, particularly in the interior of the country, many indigenous peoples live on the periphery of Brazilian society, their land and lives at risk from exploitation and latter-day colonialism.

Finally, while Brazil has traditionally avoided the simple dualistic race system of black versus white, there are some signs of change in that direction. Daniel refers to an ideology of "whitening" that encourages the increase of white physical traits in the population along with a purge of African and Native ones, through such means as expanded European immigration, restricted African immigration, and the promotion of marriage to partners "more culturally and **phenotypically** European" than oneself (2005: 91). At the same time, another movement operates in the opposite direction, to "raise black consciousness" and to unify darker skinned Brazilians into a self-aware race group: the effect would be, and the goal is, to replace the spectrum of non-white color categories with a single one (negro or black), thus supplanting the loose Brazilian system with a more rigid, American-like system.

Phenotype

The observable physical traits of an individual, based on the expression of the internal and not directly observable genetic make-up of the individual (the genotype).

Mestizaje: the future of race in Mexico

The mixing of diverse populations has been a fact (although not always an equally welcome or statistically significant fact) whenever two groups come in contact for any appreciable length of time. However, in some times and places, "race mixing" has been positively encouraged, even praised. The part of the world in which this sort of mixing has perhaps been most common – and most lauded – is Latin America, especially Mexico. The local term for the fact of historical mixing and the positive value of such mixing is *mestizaje*, from the Spanish word *mestizo*, a person of dual (especially Caucasian and Native American) ancestry.

Mestizaje may be defined as "the claim – both scientific and ideological – that racial mixture throughout the [South American] continent has affected both genetic and cultural blending to the point where any racial distinction has become meaningless" (Tilley 2005: 54). For those who acknowledge the process, some bemoan it as a corruption of the "real" races, some accept it as a neutral fact, and others celebrate it as the undermining of the entire race concept – and even as the emergence of a single unified super-race. The most memorable spokesman for this position was José Vasconcelos, whose 1925 essay *The Cosmic Race* explicitly pits the English attitude of race exclusiveness against the race inclusiveness of the Spanish and Portuguese – and the future belongs to the inclusivists:

> The days of the pure white, the victors of today, are as numbered as were the days of their predecessors. Having fulfilled their destiny of mechanizing the world,

they themselves have set, without knowing it, the basis of a new period: The period of the fusion and mixing of all peoples.

(1979: 16)

Recognizing that the Spanish people themselves are "but a conglomeration of different types and races" (19) and therefore amenable to blending, he not only expects but desires the birth of a "fifth race" (after white, black, Asian, and Native American) which, created through "well-being, sympathy, and beauty" will be "a type infinitely superior to all that have previously existed" (31).

In some ways the *mestizaje* of Vasconcelos and others is accurate and tolerant, noting in a very modern manner that "No contemporary race can present itself alone as the finished model that all others should imitate" (Vasconcelos 1979: 32), or as a finished model at all; all "races" are a moment in the flux of human diversity. Still, there is covert and occasionally overt racism in the message as well. The white race, or more specifically yet the Latin race, is seen as the only one capable of civilization and of transcending current race limitations; the traits of the white race are also expected to predominate in the new cosmic race. Black traits will diminish and disappear, which is the only way that

> the Black could be redeemed, and step by step, by voluntary extinction, the uglier stocks will give way to the more handsome. Inferior races, upon being educated, would become less prolific, and the better specimens would go on ascending a scale of ethnic improvement, whose maximum type is not precisely the White, but that new race to which the White himself will have to aspire.
>
> (Ibid.)

Even the tolerant Latin must prevent "an unrestrained influx of Asians," since the Chinese, who "multiply like mice," would "come to degrade the human condition" by overwhelming the better races (19).

But if there is a real target of the cosmic race, it is the "Indians," the native peoples of the Americas. *Mestizaje* is a way of "undefining Indians" (Tilley 2005) by submerging them into a hybrid population in which Indianness or indigenous identity no longer exists or matters. Vasconcelos is blunt that the Indian race is a retarded race, a thing of the past, which, "by grafting onto the related race, would take the jump of millions of years" (1979: 32). Accordingly, the Indian race "has no other door to the future but the door of modern culture, nor any other road but the road already cleared by Latin civilization" (16). Nor was Vasconcelos the only person nor Mexico the only country to adopt such thinking: "in both El Salvador and Nicaragua, *mestizaje* facilitated the dominant claim that 'Indians' had vanished altogether" (Tilley 2005: 65), washed away by the tide of race mixing.

The Burakumin of Japan

Japan is widely regarded, by scholarly and popular opinion both inside and outside the country, as a homogeneous, mono-racial or mono-ethnic society: in 1986, then-

Prime Minister Nakasone Yasuhiro asserted that, in contrast to such societies as the U.S.A., "Japan has one ethnicity (*minzoku*), one state (*kokka*), and one language (*gengo*)" (quoted in Lie 2001: 1). Of course, other peoples and cultures reside within the territory of the Japanese state, including Koreans, Chinese, Ainu, Okinawans, Iranians (usually as guest workers), even some Americans, and a group known as the Burakumin. However, the Japanese anthropologist Hasebe Kotondo nonetheless argued that the Japanese "race" was unique and that "the Ainu, Koreans, and others were completely different races from the Japanese" (Yonezawa 2005: 124).

The Burakumin are the most interesting case in Japan, because like many groups encountered already, as well as the Deaf, they challenge the conventional concepts of race and ethnicity. With a label derived from the word *buraku* meaning village (Burakumin thus meaning "people of the village"), they are also known as *eta* (extreme filth) or *hinin* (non-human), strongly indicating their separate and inferior status; they are also sometimes less prejudicially called *Hisabetsu*. The special problem of conceiving the Burakumin is that they are essentially physically indistinguishable from other Japanese; that is, they do not have the ordinary biological markers of a distinct "race." In fact, George DeVos and Hiroshi Wagatsumo (1966) have called them Japan's "invisible race," which seems like an oxymoron: how can a group be a race without racially specific physical features?

The origins of the Burakumin are unclear and controversial. While some Japanese think they are of Korean or indigenous ancestry, the dominant view is that they are descendants of workers in lower class and "polluting" professions such as leather-making and butchering. Their status was certainly recognized by the seventeenth century, when the three classes of warrior, peasant, and townsperson were established, leaving them as outcastes at the bottom of society (like the outcastes or *pariah* of India, who incidentally did much the same work). Officially, the status of and discrimination against Burakumin was banished in 1871 through the Eta Emancipation Act, but little changed in the short run and negative attitudes toward them linger today.

Many of the Burakumin lived and live in several thousand formal *buraku* villages in Japan, but many others do not; many are listed on the official registry of Burakumin, but many others are not. Most importantly, as Lie suggests, with their "emancipation" the Burakumin began a process of transition from a caste to an ethnicity: no longer (at least legally) required to perform certain economic tasks or to marry within the group, in a classic case of ethnogenesis they began to think of themselves – and to be thought of by others – as a "people" rather than as a class. An important development in their ethnic consciousness was the promulgation of government policies (like the *yuwa* or assimilation plan) that recognized and handled them as a distinct group. In addition, the twentieth century saw the formation of pro-Burakumin organizations, such as *Suiheisha* (Leveling Society) in 1922 and *Buraku Kaiho Domei* (Buraku Liberation League) in 1955, which attempted to unify and advance them as a group.

All the same, interpersonal and structural discrimination against the Burakumin continues. Negative stereotypes persist, such as that they are "rough in speech, crude or brutal in relations with each other, having a low boiling point, quarrelsome, highly sensitive to insult, born traders, and relatively much more cohesive than any other community" (quoted in Lie 2001: 88); they have even been accused of possessing unseen physical differences like one less rib or the bone of a dog, deformed sexual organs, or the inability to cast a shadow in moonlight (86). Many still live in segregated and substandard housing and work in limited low-paying jobs; they are sometimes explicitly excluded from higher status work through name lists and ancestry registries. Some even adopt noticeable behavioral markers, like a particular kind of sandal. The irony is that a Burakumin can be sitting next to a "regular" Japanese person on a bus without the latter even realizing the difference between them – which is why Burakumin sometimes exit the bus a stop or two before it reaches their segregated and lower class neighborhood.

We will encounter other examples of racial and ethnic groups, relations, and problems in future chapters, particularly the Hutu and Tutsi, the Serbs and Bosnian Muslims, and various indigenous peoples.

See Chapters 12, 13, and 15

BOX 6.3   CONTEMPORARY CULTURAL CONTROVERSIES: "MULTICULTURALISM" IN THE U.S.A.

In a society as diverse as the United States (with six race categories, approximately sixty racial combinations, and almost forty languages reported in the 2000 census), it is inevitable that culture and cultural diversity would be a social and political issue, perhaps especially in the institution most tasked to prepare and unify the citizens of the country – the education system. In the 1990s this issue came to a head in the controversy over "multiculturalism" in schools and other facets of American society. Non-white and non-European people insisted that American institutions were "Euro-centric," focusing on European or Caucasian history and accomplishments and promoting the views of "dead white males," with the outcome that "the rest of us are pushed to the periphery, occupying the restricted category of 'other'" (Reagan 1993: 71). One of the key demands of the multiculturalists was the inclusion of more non-European materials in the curriculum and "canon" (the list of officially approved readings) to represent blacks, Latinos, Asians, women, gays, and other neglected voices. Anti-multiculturalists responded with two main arguments: first, that the curriculum and the canon included what they included for good reason, because those items (e.g., Plato, Shakespeare) were the best that humanity had produced and that other items were "trendy" and substandard; and second, that a society required a common unifying body of knowledge and tradition, and that multiculturalism would fragment society or – worse – literally bring about the "end of American civilization" (Auster 1994: 61). Certainly there is a danger of replacing Euro-centrism with some other centrism, like Afro-centrism, or of fostering a kind of "identity politics" that could lead to the "disuniting of America" (Schlesinger 1992). On the other hand, no culture or canon is ever closed, and all groups have a right to struggle over what is included in the education and experience of its citizens. What do you think?

SUMMARY

Like gender, race and ethnicity are cultural interpretations and utilizations of "facts," namely the facts of physical and behavioral difference, respectively. Racial and ethnic classifications are ways in which popular opinion – and scholarly analysis – in some cultures have made sense, and made use, of human difference.

Race has been an especially salient concept in Western societies, imposing a purportedly scientific order on the human physical variation. However, efforts to make race more scientific only made it more problematic. Ultimately, the imprecision and disagreement in the practice of race categorization, together with the discovery of the role of learning independent of biological inheritance, leads anthropology to criticize the notion of race and to focus on the social creation and function of racial thinking and racial systems.

For some observers, ethnic categories take a place alongside, or take the place of, racial categories. Ostensibly based on cultural, historical, and actual kinship characteristics, ethnic groups have proved to be every bit as vague and socially constructed – and socially exploited – as race groups. Cultural differences are actually not always great among ethnic groups, and the relationships among groups emerge as more crucial than the cultural qualities within groups. Accordingly, a number of different kinds of ethnic groups, and of relations among such groups, have been identified, from segregation and violent conflict to peaceful co-existence and amalgamation. Still, race and ethnicity continue to be salient organizational concepts in the modern world.

Key Terms

Anthropometry

Apartheid

Assimilation

Cephalic index

Cultural assimilation

Endogamy

Ethnogenesis

Eugenics

Facial angle

Genocide

Miscegenation

Phenotype

Pluralism

Racial assimilation

Seeing Culture as a Whole #1: The Relativism of Motherhood, Personhood, Race, and Health in a Brazilian Community

Alto de Cruzeiro is a hillside shanty town hovering above the town of Bom Jesus da Mata in northeastern Brazil, a sugar-cane-producing region. The poor live at the higher altitudes, the opposite of arrangements in Western societies, where the rich tend to live on the hills. Most of the men of the Alto are seasonal cane-cutters, and some women work, though not all, most often as domestic servants and launderers. Many women live alone with their children in the *favela* after the men abandon their families, eking out a marginal existence in poverty.

Until the 1950s, laborers could supplement their incomes with food grown in family gardens; however, as the sugar industry expanded and modernized, that land too was converted into cane production, leaving the locals more impoverished and hungry than ever. One fallout of these changes has been rising infant mortality. In 1965, 44 percent of all deaths in the Alto were children under 5; by 1989 49 percent of deaths were babies less than 1 year old (Scheper-Hughes 1992: 296). Since the cost of feeding a family of six was four times the minimum wage, many people were chronically undernourished.

Yet, the attitude of the upper classes in town is that there is no hunger problem locally or nationally. One official said that "the people eat poorly. They have bad dietary habits. For instance, the rural workers don't have the custom of eating fresh vegetables, fresh meat . . . or even fresh fruits. Their diet is all carbohydrates" (63). Why are people struggling, then?

> There is not so much poverty in Brazil as there is poverty of spirit, which is worse. Poverty of spirit – which you find among the rural workers – means that one is unwilling to improve one's condition. It means that one does not hunger after the finer things in life, that one is content to live and let live. The *matuto* [peasant or "forest person"] is soft; he doesn't like to work hard. He is not ashamed to ask for things, to beg.

(63)

Despite the fact that cane-cutting is a strenuous life, the workers have internalized this evaluation. They see themselves as weak and sickly, even in racial terms: they are an inferior race or type who are physically smaller, always ill, always hungry. They even admit that they eat more than the rich because "their 'inferior' constitutions require it" (166). When they give birth to low birth-weight babies who often do not live very long, it just seems to prove the point.

The *matutos* cannot help but notice that they suffer from a variety of physical and psychological ailments. In their "folk medicine" terminology, they attribute this to a condition called *nervos*, the symptoms of which include headache, dizziness, muscle weakness, mental confusion, shaky hands, insomnia, and loss of appetite. Diagnosing this condition as a medical rather than a nutritional one, they visit doctors, who prescribe tranquilizers instead of food. Nancy Scheper-Hughes has called this concept of *nervos* a "social illness," in two senses; first, it is a social concept applied to a constellation of

Scheper-Hughes, Nancy. 1992. *Death without Weeping: The Violence of Everyday Life in Brazil.* Berkeley: University of California Press.

symptoms that can be (and perhaps should be) understood another way, and second, the syndrome is caused by the social situation in which the poor find themselves. The rich do not experience *nervos* – either because they are better bred or because they are better fed.

When the poor do eat, they indeed do not eat well. This is partly a result of too little money to afford high-quality foods and partly it is a circular effect of seeking out "filling" foods with little nutritional value. Fruits and vegetables are categorized as "weak" or "light" foods that do not satisfy. Starchy foods like beans, rice, and pasta "kill hunger," but when people cannot even afford those, they eat substances that "fool hunger," such as flour and mere sugar-water. They also feed children and babies the same way, sometimes substituting *farinha* (manioc flour) for powdered milk in infant formula.

Babies born from starving mothers are born starving too. Mothers comment that babies often arrive small, shriveled, discolored, and feeble. Some infants are too weak even to eat, which is not blamed on hunger – after all, the hungry eat – but on *nervos*. Some babies are just born *nervos*, they believe. Worse yet, many such babies do not even want to live. "Our babies [are] born already *wanting* to die," one mother stated (315). "They come into the world with an aversion to life . . . food doesn't interest them; it doesn't hold their attention. You see, they are neither here nor there" (386). Scheper-Hughes calls this "Doomed Baby Syndrome," in which mothers allow their babies to starve and die because that is what the mothers believe the babies want: "It is better to let the weak ones die," a mother claimed, because the babies are "little angels" who come into the world solely for the purpose of dying (368). So mothers may underfeed or completely neglect the weakest infants, allowing the self-fulfilling prophecy to come true.

How can a mother watch her child die? One way is to think that it is "natural" – the child's own wish and nature. The other way is by becoming accustomed to infant mortality: mothers there and elsewhere do not become too attached to newborns, since they know the little ones are so likely to perish. It is not an absence of "maternal instinct" but a social construction of it: children who live are the object of intense joy and affection. However, after a woman has five of her nine pregnancies end in mortality, she reserves that affection until the baby proves its "will to live." "Motherlove," Scheper-Hughes concludes, is not lacking but rather "grows slowly, tentatively, and fearfully" (359) as a reaction to brutal experience.

7

Economics: Humans, Nature, and Social Organization

Before contact with European-Australians, the Warlpiri, like other Australian Aboriginals, were a foraging society, where the fruits of the day's hunting-and-gathering activities were shared with the local group. No one would be denied food, no one would accumulate food, and kin were looked after. When I arrived in the field, the majority of Warlpiri had been settled in the town of Yuendumu for a few decades. In the community there was a general store owned and operated by a resident white man, who tried to hire local Aboriginals to work the cash registers. These workers, usually younger and at least basically literate in English and in numeracy, faced an interesting dilemma. They were in a position to "distribute" food and other goods, but they were instructed to do so consistently and impersonally: everyone who comes through the check-out line pays the same price. That was the new "market" practice. However, when their family members appeared with an armload of groceries and little or no money, there was a traditional pressure on them to look after their kin by sharing – in this case, offering a discount if not giving the food away for free. This was an awkward and painful situation. What do they do: conform to new economic expectations and charge their kin the same as everyone else (including strangers), and risk alienating their relatives, or conform to the old economic expectations and charge their kin less or nothing at all, and risk losing their jobs? Many solved the quandary by simply quitting: "Hire a *kardiya* (white person)," they would say, "they can say no."

All societies face a fundamental challenge – to feed and clothe and otherwise provision their members based on the available resources in their environment. Different societies met this challenge in different ways, depending on their environment, but all shared one factor in common: they solved the problem of survival collectively. It might be possible for humans to satisfy their needs totally individually, but it would be difficult and is essentially never done. So humans acquire, prepare, distribute, and consume goods and services in groups, and the means by which they do so will have ramifications for those groups. The economic practices of a society will be significantly influenced by the physical possibilities of their environment (the amount and quality of land, water, plants and animals, and other materials), and the economic practices that emerge will significantly influence other aspects of the culture – not in a deterministic, cause-and-effect way, but in specific and observable ways. Further, economic facts are seldom purely "practical"; they also have value and prestige and even "symbolic" and ritual significance that affect the social meaning of the products and of the relationships within which those products are made, distributed, and used.

ECONOMICS AS THE BASE OR CORE OF CULTURE

The mention of economics usually conjures up images of factories and money and stores and profit and many other familiar concepts. These are indeed all economic phenomena, but they are more properly examples of one type of economy than a definition of economy. Some economies have factories, money, and so on, but the vast majority across cultures and throughout history have done without them. In order to be anthropologically relevant, the study of economics must be cross-cultural and inclusive, as well as holistic and relativistic. This means that we cannot assume that one kind of economy is the *right* and certainly not the *only* kind of economy for humans.

Holism or cultural integration dictates that all of the aspects of a culture, including its environmental context, will be interrelated and interdependent. As we said previously, anthropologists can visualize a holistic cultural system as containing four domains of culture like networked spheres within the cultural whole. Understanding the relations between the domains of culture begins with the notion of adaptation. **Adaptation** is the process by which humans (or any species) fit themselves into and cooperate with their surroundings. Although humans adapt physically like all other beings, most of human adaptation takes the form of behavioral modification. Culture is the uniquely human adaptation. So human cultural adaptation starts with the environment which a group or society of humans inhabits. Any environment is a particular combination of physical factors – climate, water and food supplies, natural resources, large-scale natural formations (rivers, mountains), and so on. These factors will set the limits (technology notwithstanding) of what the culture can and cannot, must and must not, do. In other words, the environment will set the fundamental terms of *what is possible and what is necessary*

See Chapter 1

Adaptation
Changes in a system, including a species, in response to changes in its context or environment so as to make that system or species more fit to survive in the context or environment.

for the humans living in it. The environment is a challenge that must be met. Yet "nature" is not a completely absolute or independent variable: through culture, humans bring the world of nature within the world of culture, *culturizing* nature and integrating it into the cultural system. In the process, both culture and nature are mutually reshaped.

It is worth remarking that two quite different environments can pose quite similar adaptive challenges. For instance, few environmental settings seem less alike than a desert and the Arctic, yet some of the conditions they present to humans or any life-forms located there are actually comparable. There is little liquid water as well as a relatively short supply and variety of potential foods and of potential tool-making and building materials. Plant life is scarce, so agriculture is virtually impossible. Thus, while they look superficially very dissimilar, the adaptations they will call for are actually surprisingly alike.

Therefore, the primary and overarching challenge that a human society will face is adapting – behaviorally and, over the long run, physically – to its environment. In the extreme short term, this means getting sustenance from this environment. The first problem, then, for humans is and will always be how to transform their environment into the things that they need to support their life. In other words, the first problem for humans is and will always be *economic*.

If we think again now about how to model the relations between the domains of culture, we would want to start with an environment and then establish first a means of livelihood that is adapted to that environment. That is, if we were to "build" a culture from the "ground up," the environment would be the ground, and the "base" of the culture would be the part that "touches the ground." It is the economic system that not only metaphorically but literally makes contact with the Earth and its resources and converts them into human-usable goods.

Imagine building any house or other structure. The first thing you need is a piece of land. The nature of that land – its size, quality, climate – will (hopefully) suggest to you the kind of house to build. The "ground floor" of the house, shaped as it is by the environment, would subsequently shape the floors above it. If you built a square ground floor, you would likely not build a triangular second floor; then the two lower floors will set the terms for the third floor, and all the floors will set the terms for the top floor. Of course, this is not a purely "one-way" process. There is a kind of feedback relation between the upper and lower levels too: the upper floors exert pressure on the lower floors in particular ways, and once they have been formed, they will influence the levels "below" them, such that the politics or the religion can affect the economics and even the very environment. There is, in the final analysis, a bidirectional relationship but one in which economic adaptation is still the base or core.

Thus, although our house model appears somewhat static, it is necessary to understand that the relationship between the economy and the other aspects of a culture is quite dynamic. One other dynamic quality that the model does not convey is the inevitable presence of neighboring societies which may have more or less impact on the society in question. In some cases, there may be neutral or friendly exchange relations between the two (or more), while in others there may be competitive or hostile relations. Societies may be completely surrounded or even engulfed by other, larger and more dominant societies, and they may be highly dependent on these external social structures. The society itself, finally, may be more internally complex than the model indicates, with multiple "layers" or subgroups/classes or even subcultures in various (and often unequal) relations with each other. All modern societies are and many pre-modern societies were actually composite systems of social groupings in diverse and problematic arrangements.

See Chapter 13

At any rate, a society's life begins with its practical, productive activities, which may be referred to as its **mode of production**. The mode of production is the tasks, the tools, and the knowledge and skills that humans use to get their daily bread (or kangaroo or whatever). It is labor and all that is required for labor. This may be as simple as picking a nut off a tree or as elaborate as working in an office or on an assembly line. Humans must engage in productive, practical, material activity in order to survive.

Mode of production
The activities and tools a society employs to satisfy its material needs. The form of "work" or "labor" that is performed in a society.

However, work cannot be done in social isolation – not in isolation from other humans, nor in isolation from other facets of society. Economic activity is always social – with and for other people too. Therefore, the mode of production leads to and generates some **relations of production** – that is, ways that humans organize themselves to get the work done and the products distributed and used. The general factors involved in the relations of production include division of labor, ownership, "property," power, often class, and usually the family, as well as sharing and selling and the status or prestige that comes with having, consuming, displaying, and giving the goods and services. These relations give shape and content to the rest of society. These two features – mode and relations of production – in tandem make up what we would call the economy of a society.

Relations of production
In Marxist theory, the social roles and relationships that are generated by the mode of production, including such things as class, ownership, "management," and in some lines of thinking "family."

THE ANTHROPOLOGY OF ECONOMICS

An anthropological approach to economics, then, must be inclusive rather than exclusive – considering and encompassing all of the actual forms of economic behavior in the human world, not just one's own or others similar to one's own – as well as holistic and relativistic. Therefore, economics for anthropologists must mean not just capitalism or industrialization and mass production but all of the processes and practices by which humans transform the natural environment into usable goods and services for humans and then put those goods and services to use. Any economy, from a hunting one to an industrial one, will have certain components:

Economy = natural resources + labor + tools + knowledge/skill + "capital" (in some form)

In addition, we can see that any economic system has, from "start to finish," three phases:

1. Production. This is the phase of operation on the environment in which "raw" materials are transformed into human (and therefore "social" or "cultural") goods.
2. Distribution. This is the phase of moving goods and services from the people who produce them to the people who use them.
3. Consumption. This is the phase of actually using or "consuming" (eating, wearing, burning) products.

Anthropology has traditionally put very much emphasis on the production phase of the economy, considerable emphasis on the distribution phase, and less emphasis on the consumption phase. In the following sections we will discuss production and distribution and try to make some contribution to the growing anthropology of consumption. We will begin by offering the customary typology of the phases of economy; that is, the "types" of production or distribution that have been identified. However, in the real world, things are not as clean as that. Types are always abstractions or generalizations from reality; what we see in the field is often variation or even hybridization of these ideal types, as we will indicate below. Second, even within types, there is a fair amount of freedom for humans to vary; the "pure" foraging or pastoralist society often took different shapes depending on the environment, the history of the group, or simply the indeterminacy of human beliefs and behaviors. Third, as we noted, groups with a particular economy were often in contact, if not integrated into a single system, with groups practicing very different economic forms, further complicating the picture. Finally, in the case of most of the "traditional" economic systems, either no society practices them any more or no society practices them in a thoroughly "traditional" way any more. We will return to examine the contemporary condition of many of these societies in the final chapters of this book.

Systems of production

If a culture is a "four-story" structure with economics as the "base," then production is the "base of the base," the first level of the first floor. It precedes and sets the stage for subsequent economic activities, which in turn shape and influence non-economic activities, institutions, and values. Anthropology has identified four general systems or ideal types for the production of basic goods and services. These types are:

■ Foraging
■ Pastoralism
■ Horticulture
■ Intensive agriculture.

In characterizing any actual society's economic system, anthropologists want to accomplish two things. First, we want to understand their "mode of production" and how it is anchored to the environment(s) they dwell in. Second and more profoundly, we want to see what kind of culture and social order they produce – what specific relationships, values, beliefs, and so on flow from the economic base and how those things are related to and shaped by their economic activities. If what we have said already is true, then we should detect regular patterns of economics and culture – things that tend to go together and things that do not or cannot go together. That is, we should see patterns emerge that link particular types of economic factors with particular types of non-economic (kinship, political, and even religious) factors.

Foraging

Foraging was the first human economic system, chronologically and conceptually. Also known as "hunting and gathering," it is the type of procurement that all humans practiced and depended on from the very first humans until some 10,000 to 12,000 years ago. Even since that time, when other production systems emerged and spread, foraging continued to be practiced in at least some places – and occasionally in contact with other, later systems – until modern times. In the earlier days of foraging, it was practiced in all environments of the Earth. In more recent ages, it has tended to be relegated to the most "marginal" environments where other systems cannot be practiced or where societies that practice them cannot or have not chosen to penetrate. Examples of recent and well-known foraging societies include the !Kung or Ju/hoansi of the African Kalahari, all Australian Aboriginal societies, and the various Inuit or Eskimo peoples of the Arctic. While their environments could be quite different, the economic adaptations they made to them tended to be quite similar.

Foraging is a mode of production involving minimal technologies to acquire food and other goods through a combination of hunting animals and collecting plants. Although it appears to entail the least transformation of the environment, still transformation it is, since humans did not simply walk up and take a bite out of a kangaroo or a tree. Foraging peoples had to apply some technology, skill, knowledge, and capital to their natural environment in order to make the benefits of that environment usable or "edible" for them. In some cases, as in Australia, foragers routinely burned the landscape, undoubtedly affecting the local plant and animal life.

Therefore, at its most basic, foraging included the "work" of hunting and of gathering, two distinct skills or methods of food provision. This implies a potential and usually actual **division of labor** between the hunting/animal work and the gathering/plant work. The classic or stereotypical version of foraging involved a gender-based division of labor with male hunting and female gathering. This arrangement did indeed exist: the Warlpiri in the Central Desert of Australia tended to follow the pattern of male hunting and female gathering, although with two warnings. First, not all "animal work" was necessarily viewed as hunting; catching small lizards and insects might be done by women or children. Second, a man might "gather" materials of particular interest to him, such as bush tobacco, so even here the gender division was not absolute.

Ernestine Friedl (1975, 1978) has identified three other foraging arrangements. In one, men hunted and both men and women gathered; the Hadza people of

Foraging
Also known as hunting and gathering, the production of food by collecting wild (undomesticated) animals and plants.

Division of labor
The differentiation of the economy into a set of distinct production tasks, which are assigned to different individuals, groups, or classes, usually creating economic and political inequalities.

Friedl, Ernestine. 1975. *Women and Men.* New York: Holt, Rinehart, and Winston.

PLATE 7.1 Koya hunter
from central India

Tanzania (Woodburn 1968) and a few other societies were reputed to organize this way. In a second variation, men and women shared both hunting and gathering. Estioko-Griffin and Griffin (2002) described the Agta of the Philippines as nearly undivided in economic activities by sex: women participated in the same productive behaviors as men, including hunting and fishing, and they gathered plants irregularly and only when more desirable food was not to hand. Turnbull (1962) also presented the Mbuti pygmies of the Congo forest as working together, male and female, to net game. In the third style, men hunted but women handled the catch of the men.

Because women's labor often produced a large proportion (if not the majority) of the group's food, there tended to be relative gender equality in foraging societies. In fact, they tended to be generally egalitarian, due to the inability of any individual to accumulate a surplus or to possess skills that other people did not. Concepts of "ownership" or "private property" were often limited if not lacking, particularly in regard to land. Foraging environments often prohibited economic surpluses, since there was not enough food available to accumulate it, and foraging values usually discouraged a person from trying to become superior to or richer than anyone else; values of sharing within the community provided no opportunity to hoard personal wealth. Some status differences existed, based on age, skill, ritual knowledge, and sometimes gender, but these statuses were often more interdependent than stratified. Without wealth and power differences, formal leadership and especially "government" were absent and unnecessary.

Other social features of foraging societies followed from their environmental and productive situation. For example, local groups, especially in marginal environments, tended to be small; in many instances the residential group was only a dozen or fewer,

Turnbull, Colin. 1962. *The Forest People*. New York: Simon & Schuster.

or at most a few dozen, and ordinarily composed of kin. The entire society seldom if ever formed a single community. There was simply not enough food and water to support large populations. The society was accordingly dispersed over a large territory and would only assemble as one in times of plenty or for special occasions like rituals. This meant that groups also tended to be mobile, moving continuously in search of provisions. The groups may have lacked any permanent settlements or houses, but they migrated within an established "range" or territory. So, they could still have a sense of "home area" but one within which they circulated constantly. They might stop (or "sit," as the Warlpiri say) in one place so long as resources permitted, but the general ethos of society was a mobile one.

One common misconception about foragers is that they were poor and miserable, living on the edge of starvation. No doubt there were times of hardship in their history, as there have been in modern industrial societies. However, surprisingly, foraging peoples tended to have a very positive attitude toward their lives and their environments. The Warlpiri told me that their desert country was *ngurrju*, good. They enjoyed their way of life and had plenty of time for leisure. Traditional food collecting took up a few hours a day, a few days a week; the rest of the time they spent visiting and socializing, doing ritual "business," or merely napping.

Since generosity and equality were the general rule, the place of war and violence was limited. Therefore, foragers tended to be comparatively peaceful peoples. This is not to say that they never had conflicts and even violent outbursts, because they did and do, but these usually occurred over ritual concerns or marriage or other personal issues, and were usually settled ritually, even if that ritual involved some symbolic or real violence.

Finally, because the life of foragers was so "close to the ground," they tended to have a major emotional and "spiritual" connection to their environment. For many foragers, the land itself was alive or was the handiwork of living beings – spiritual, mixed spiritual-human, mixed human-animal/plant, and so on. They may have had "totemic" or other social relations between human individuals or groups and other natural beings or forces. They often regarded themselves and their cultures as essentially autochthonous – that is, literally rising up out of the ground they inhabited – like the Warlpiri, who believe that their personal spirit or "soul" comes from the spirit power in the earth and returns there when they die.

BOX 7.1 THE AINU FORAGERS OF NORTHERN JAPAN

The Ainu are an indigenous people of Japan who traditionally lived a life resembling Inuit or Eskimo societies. They were dependent on a harsh environment where small scattered habitations were demanded. At the time of Ohnuki-Tierney's research (1974), the Ainu of northwest Sakhalin Island were living mostly in settlements of twenty families containing around 150 people. Each house in the settlement consisted of a single room, although its internal space and overall orientation were organized by religion, for example, with the sacred side facing the mountains. In the winter, men hunted and trapped land and sea mammals and also fished, while women stayed mostly at home. Large animals, especially bears, had a distinctly spiritual quality, and hunting them was as much a religious as an economic activity; in fact, she writes that "there is no demarcation between activities relating to the obtaining of animal meat and those dealing with the deities" (20), since most animals were deities. Hares were not deities, so women were allowed to trap them but not to do any other type of hunting.

In the summer, men would turn their attention to fishing, spearing larger fish like trout and salmon and catching smaller fish in baskets. This was also the season in which women's economic contribution expanded. Plants would bloom, providing as much or more food than hunting, and women did most of the plant-gathering work. They knew about and collected bulbs of various plants, as well as leeks, berries, mushrooms, and a hundred other species for food or medicines.

Pastoralism

Domestication

The process of modification of plants and/or animals to establish human control over them, leading to agriculture and pastoralism.

Neolithic

The "New Stone" age, beginning around 10,000 to 12,000 years ago with the first animal and plant domestication.

Pastoralism

A productive system based on domesticated animals as the main source of food.

Somewhere around 10,000 to 12,000 years ago, one or more groups of humans in one or more locations discovered that they could control and **domesticate** certain species for human consumption. Thus, instead of having to roam in search of their food sources, they could bring the sources "home" to them. This is sometimes referred to as the "**Neolithic**" or New Stone Age revolution, and it was revolutionary not only for how humans worked and provided food but for every aspect of their cultures and social relationships, as well as for the species they fed on. The revolution of domestication actually culminated in not one but two new economic systems. The first we will describe is pastoralism. **Pastoralism**, from the word "pasture," is the production of food predominantly from the exploitation of domesticated animals. It is what might conventionally be called "herding" or "ranching." Thus, the primary "work" to be done was tending and exploiting – milking, bleeding, and slaughtering – such animals as cattle, sheep, goats, llamas, horses, pigs, and other, smaller creatures, depending on the locally available species.

In the vast majority of these societies – and they were spread across the world, from the grasslands of east Africa to the mountains of Central Asia and the plains of North America – the ownership and control of herd animals was the prerogative of men. Women and children might do the day-to-day work of tending the animals – milking the cattle and so on – but it was men who decided when one would be slaughtered or traded or "sold" for some purpose. Thus, in terms of production and even more so control of production, pastoralism was a man's world, and the gender division of labor devolved into a gender inequality. Men's status was much higher than women's in typical pastoral societies. Men accordingly tended to be the heads of family and household; again, women might wield real "domestic" power in the home, but their political power was limited compared to men.

Since a man's herd was his surplus and therefore his wealth, he usually tried to avoid killing his animals but rather consumed them in "sustainable" ways, such as

PLATE 7.2 Tuareg pastoralist with his camels, North Africa

drinking their milk or blood. Herds in some cases might be quite large; Klima (1970) reports that the average Barabaig (east Africa) cattle herd was around seventy head, and a very large herd could number more than 500. If one individual or household had a larger herd than another, he or it was wealthier, and wealth meant differential access to status and opportunities. One such opportunity might be marriage – to marry well or to marry often. A wealthy Barabaig man would have four or more wives and many sons, and he would also actively seek to increase his animal holdings through a variety of social institutions. Barabaig society contained an assortment of rule-governed livestock transactions, such as the *gefuryed* in which a man would lend a bull to another man in exchange for rights to the future calf of his trading partner's cow; Klima also notes that men were not above deliberately manipulating and exploiting these arrangements for their benefit (30). Another way of adding to one's wealth was by marrying one's daughters or sisters to men with mighty herds in exchange for a payment in cattle.

See Chapter 8

The differences in wealth and power and prestige in pastoral societies were not immense, because the wealth itself was not immense. Still, there could be men or families or households that were higher in rank or status than others. In Barabaig society, a man "who is successful in raising a large herd of cattle is socially recognized as being more knowledgeable and powerful than a person with a small herd" (Klima 1970: 32), and the man who was poor in cattle might have to work for a wealthier man. There might be "leaders" with some power to command the efforts and allegiances of other men, at least members of their family, lineage, village, or "tribe." Formal government was still often lacking, but the rudiments or precursors of government were observable. Further, the existence of some surplus and a larger and more dependable food supply led to larger societies as a whole, sometimes with hundreds or even thousands of people (some of the enormous and important societies in history like the Mongols were pastoralists). On the other hand, not all pastoral societies were huge, and they often still had to disperse into smaller local communities. In addition, migratory patterns, sometimes called transhumance, sometimes had to continue, as herds required new sources of land, water, and pasturage. So pastoralists may or may not have achieved settlements in semi-permanent villages.

BOX 7.2   LIMITS TO GROWTH IN BASSERI PASTORALISM

As described by Barth (1965), the Basseri lived in a mountainous region of southern Iran, where they raised sheep, goats, and donkeys; each household owned around 100 sheep and up to a dozen donkeys. Pasture rights were obtained through membership in an *oulad*, a kinship group consisting of about ninety families. There were no limits to how many animals a man or household could put on his *oulad's* land. There were, however, other kinds of limitations he faced. One was the size of the herds of his *oulad* mates. Another was the inverse relationship between the size of a herd and its productivity: that is, the larger a herd became, the harder it was to manage and protect it. A large herd might have to be trusted to hired or temporary help, who could cheat him or simply take less care of the animals than the owner would. The near-total lack of any kind of communal labor pitted each man against every other. Natural conditions like fluctuating weather and fertility introduced unpredictable variations in herd size. Finally, sons took a share of the father's herd as inheritance, while daughters could not provide the labor needed to expand the herd.

To protect themselves against these threats, men took a variety of steps. A father might attempt to postpone a son's marriage to delay the transfer of inheritance, sometimes until after age 30 or 35. Men also saw the value of converting animals into "real" wealth like land; thus large animal-holders became landowners and landlords to tenant farmers, who paid the owner with one-third to two-thirds of their crop. Such a landowner had special status and privilege. However, the wealth-accumulation process could also run in reverse: a man with a small herd, many sons, heavy debts, and bad luck could watch his herd decline below the sustainable level (about sixty sheep), in which case he was forced to work for wealthier men and eventually settle as a property-less villager, becoming one of those tenant farmers hired by landowners. Barth refers to this process as "sedentarization by impoverishment."

The presence of "wealth on the hoof," in tandem with the requirement for access to land and the dominance of males and maleness in society, almost inevitably led to a more warlike stance than anything found in foraging societies. Foragers had little to fight over, but pastoralists had a lot. They could fight to control water and pasture resources. They could fight to raid other societies and steal their herds or to defend their own herds from theft; they could also steal women. They could fight over previous marriage exchanges and grievances about unsolved property disputes, and they could fight just to show they were men – tough, honorable, powerful. In fact, some of the most violent and warlike pre-modern peoples have been pastoralists, and it was pastoralists who were often most effective in fighting off colonial advances when Europeans arrived. Foragers, like the Aboriginals, tended to succumb quickly and easily.

Pastoralists, being mobile, aggressive, and organized, also tended to encounter other, non-pastoral peoples in their travels. In some instances, like the Bedouins of North Africa, they became the "traders" and entrepreneurs (literally, "between-carriers") of goods over long distances. In other instances, however, they engaged in conflict with and often conquest of their neighbors. Sometimes they decimated these other societies, even pushing them to extinction; at other times they ruled them from afar, extracted wealth from them in the form of tribute, or even settled among them as a dominant "class." This phenomenon is so common in human history that it deserves much more attention than it usually gets from anthropology and history. For instance, the impact of the Mongols on Eurasian society, especially China and Russia, cannot be overestimated. In Europe, it was pastoral tribes like the Germanic peoples who came to populate much of the continent, and it was pastoral tribes that finally toppled the Roman Empire. Similarly, pastoral peoples were on the move in India (the "Aryans"), the Middle East, and Africa, and many of today's "composite" societies like the ones in Rwanda and Burundi are products of this pervasive force. Even in the U.S.A. there was the classic confrontation between the "cattlemen" or pastoralists and the "sod busters" or farmers that played out and largely shaped the life of the western states.

Finally, understandably, pastoral attitudes and values reverberated through their religion as well. They tended to have male gods – often sky gods – such as the male god of the ancient pastoral Hebrews. Like that god, pastoral gods tended to require sacrifices, particularly of male animals, killed and roasted for the gods' pleasure. The gods too were warlike and authorized the people to raid and fight, sometimes with a sense of tribal superiority or even an ideology that all cattle or other animals actually belonged to them and needed rounding up. Males tended to be the chief officiates of these religions, holding roles like priest or diviner or even "negative" ones like witch. Religion was still "decentralized," as was the economy and society as a whole, but this merely emphasized the point that what transpired in nature and society also transpired in the supernatural realm.

Interestingly, the dividing line between foraging and pastoralism was not entirely clear or absolute. In his study of Melanesian societies, Paul Sillitoe discusses the production of pigs, a staple food. Some societies tended their pig herds as essentially domesticated animals, while others left "their creatures more to forage and root for themselves"; the latter also did not so much breed animals as allow animals to breed in the wild. This "unsupervised" form of "pig herding" leads Sillitoe to conclude that "it is sometimes difficult to decide whether a group preys on wild pigs or herds semi-domesticated ones" (1998: 47).

Horticulture

Horticulture

A production system based on low-technology farming or gardening, without the use of plows, draft animals, irrigation, or fertilizers.

The other economic system to evolve out of domestication entailed the production of domesticated plants and is known as horticulture. **Horticulture** may be defined as farming without the use of technologies like the plow, irrigation, fertilizer, or draft animals. The absence of these inputs also generally tended to limit outputs and to prevent the permanent use of farmlands, since the soil became exhausted of nutrients after a few years' tilling. Horticulture was once practiced in a wider variety of climate types but has recently been found most often in and is most suited to hilly inland areas and tropical environments, like the rainforests of New Guinea or the Amazon, where soils are actually relatively thin, heavy rains can damage fragile soils, but growth rates are fairly high, such that displaced wild vegetation can quickly recover.

Slash-and-burn

A horticultural practice in which trees and underbrush are cut, left to dry, and then burned as preparation for planting a garden. Also known as swidden.

In fact, this is exactly the strategy in one of the more common forms of horticulture, known as **"slash-and-burn"** or **swidden** agriculture. In this technique, areas of future farm fields were cleared of vegetation by cutting away brush and "slashing" trees to cause them to die and dry out; some time later, the horticulturists returned and set fire to all of the undergrowth, opening the fields for planting while restoring the nutrients in the native plants back to the soil in the form of ash. Sowing the fields could be as simple as tossing a few seeds into holes poked by digging sticks or could be more complex and labor intensive. Either way, stumps, rocks, and other debris were usually left in place; no attempt was made to plow the fields or to contour the land in any appreciable way; that is, the farmers basically "worked around" the obstacles in their fields. As you might imagine, a horticultural community would need to have a number of such territories in various states of readiness, from "in production" to recently burnt to recently slashed to fallow. After two or three harvests, the fertility of the land was often depleted, and it was necessary to allow it to "return to nature," only to be slashed and burned again in the future.

Swidden

See slash-and-burn.

Horticultural labor, then, consisted of a sequence of stages which might be assigned to members in various ways; one common division of labor was to have men do the heavy work of clearing the land and women the subsequent work of planting and harvesting. The Dani of New Guinea were an example of this classic pattern (Heider 1979). This labor plan was by no means universal. Among the Semai of Malaysia the women and children slashed the trees before the men chopped them down; then the men and boys made the planting holes, and the women and children followed behind placing the seeds in the holes (Dentan 1968). The Yanomamo (South America) reserved both forest clearing and planting for men (Chagnon 1992). And the Konyak Nagas of India had a very mixed arrangement: older men and women would clear the undergrowth while younger men did the slashing. Then men sowed rice and millet, with women coming after to cover the grains with

Chagnon, Napoleon. 1992. *Yanomamo* (4th edn). Fort Worth, TX: Harcourt Brace College Publishers.

earth. Boys and girls weeded together, and men and women harvested together (Von Fuerer-Haimendorf 1969).

The diversity of productive relationships within horticultural societies guaranteed a diversity of cultural systems emerging from them. For instance, in some cases land was private property, in other cases not. The Konyak Nagas maintained very old links with ancestral lands, and almost all farm plots were individually owned; in fact, one person would own multiple scattered plots, as many as 250 in an extreme case. Among the Semai there was no permanent ownership of land; the "owner" of a tract was simply the person or family who cleared and currently used it. If they abandoned or simply neglected it for too long, others would move in and occupy it (but still not acquire "title" to it); the same was true of houses.

The relationship with and productivity of the land also affected settlement or mobility. Some societies built fairly permanent villages and farmed the land in the vicinity on some kind of rotation. Other societies moved frequently to open new land and establish new temporary residences for a few months or years. Likewise, cultural values and practices like gender stratification and violence were diverse. The Iroquois (eastern North America) represented one of the most female-centered societies on record.

> Iroquois women controlled the factors of agricultural production, for they had a right in the land which they cultivated, and in the implements and the seeds. Iroquois agricultural activities, which yielded bountiful harvests, were highly organized under elected female leadership. Most important, Iroquois women maintained the right to distribute and dispense all foods, even that procured by men. This was especially significant, as stored food constituted one of the major forms of wealth for the tribe. Through their control of the economic organization of the tribe, Iroquois matrons were able to make available or withhold food for meetings of the Council and for war parties, for the observance of religious festivals and for the daily meals of the household. These economic realities were institutionalized in the matrons' power to nominate Council Elders and to influence Council decisions. They had a voice in the conduct of war and the establishment of treaties. They elected "keepers of the faith" and served in that capacity. They controlled life in the longhouse.
>
> (Brown 1975: 250–1)

At the other end of the spectrum, some horticultural societies, like the Sambia mentioned in the previous chapter, maintained tense and profoundly unequal, even segregated, relations between the sexes. The Yanomamo were also highly male-dominated. Even so, of all the economic systems, horticulture was the most likely to provide prominent female status: according to one analysis, more than a quarter of horticultural societies attached children primarily to their mother's kin group, compared to 10 percent of foraging groups and even less of pastoral and intensive agricultural societies (Lenski and Lenski 1982).

Violence varied as well, but somewhat independently from other variables. The Yanomamo reportedly were male-dominated in their economics and their gender roles and also warlike, and the Semai were egalitarian in their economics and their gender roles and peaceful. However, the Iroquois and many other societies mixed these traits in many combinations – being male-dominated but non-violent or (more commonly) not male-dominated but violent.

Even such "low-intensity" farming could produce a noticeable surplus, allowing for two outcomes. One was larger societies. Society could become so large that it included multiple local communities or villages. These communities might or might not feel any significant affiliation with each other as members of the "same" society: for instance, the Yanomamo were infamous for conducting raids and warfare against other Yanomamo villages. The other outcome was enhanced notions of, and competition for, wealth, power, and prestige. Horticultural societies sometimes developed more elaborate ranking and stratification systems and even "governments," up to chiefs and other political institutions. They certainly had more problems to solve and disputes to settle, with more people living in closer contact and potentially getting into squabbles about property. In some places, like Melanesia, complicated status contests such as the *kula* eventually took shape, in which individuals or families strived to achieve and express status through trading and gift-giving and displays of wealth.

The weaknesses or vulnerabilities of horticulture were compensated by the new opportunities it offered. Among these opportunities was one of the prerequisites for further cultural elaboration – specialization. A small number of people could be "freed" from food production due to the surplus that others created. These people could practice other activities and develop new skills and techniques, including pottery and metalworking as well as more full-time religious and artistic roles. The "blacksmith" or iron-worker in particular often played not only an important economic but a ritual role in society. In addition to these seminal technologies, other arts and crafts like weaving were possible with the economic surplus, not to mention the "intellectual" arts like teaching, priestcraft, and even "timekeeping" (the builders of Stonehenge were, after all, horticulturists).

Speaking of priestcraft, horticultural religion tended to reflect and reinforce the practical modes and relations of horticultural life. Religion often focused on fertility and the cycle of natural processes, from the "birth" (planting) to "death" of the plants. Gods or spirits of various species or natural forces (e.g., rain, sun) or moments in the planting cycle were important for organizing economic activity, as was an awareness of the timing of the seasons. Seasons did not make much difference to foragers, and little more difference to pastoralists, but for horticulturists there was "a time to plant" and "a time to reap." Doing things at the wrong time could leave the plants, and the planters, dead. So, for instance, knowledge of the solstices appeared, along with "calendrical" (annual) rituals to demarcate them and the key activities undertaken around those times. A "harvest" ritual (not unlike Thanksgiving in the U.S.A.) was common, or even a ritual recognizing the "season of death" (not unlike Halloween in the U.S.A. or the *Dia de los Muertos* in Mexico) at the end of the farming season. The winter solstice (late December), when the days started to get longer in the Northern Hemisphere, and the spring equinox (late March) were both commonly associated with birth or rebirth and moments for important rituals. Note that the two major Christian holidays fall at precisely those times.

By the way, Sillitoe also indicates that the distinction between foraging and horticulture was not always certain. The Gidra and Kiwai people of New Guinea engaged in "limited management of plant resources" (27), for instance, claiming sago and coconut palm trees but only minimally tending them until harvest time. Men might "dig them up and replant them elsewhere or leave them to self-propagate into dense stands." "There is not much difference between these activities and those of nearby Australian Aboriginals, customarily labeled hunter-gatherers," Sillitoe concludes (27).

Intensive agriculture

Approximately 5,000 or 6,000 years ago, a second revolution in human economics and culture occurred that eventually had even more profound and lasting effects on the species and the planet. **Intensive agriculture** is high-input, high-yield farming employing such technologies as the plow, irrigation, fertilizer, and draft animals (all the ones missing from horticulture), allowing for something else that horticulture cannot provide – permanent farmlands. Given this "base," intensive agriculture made possible not only more of what we have seen before but entirely new dimensions of culture not previously possible (Figure 7.1).

The most obvious difference between horticulture and intensive agriculture is the vast surpluses achievable with the latter; farmers were able to produce crops – sometimes two or three per year in extremely well-watered locations like Bali – sufficient to feed enormous populations, measuring into the tens of thousands even in ancient times and into the hundreds of millions today. The earliest environments for this new practice tended to be centered on river valleys, which provided the requisite water and alluvial soils; however, not every early intensive agricultural society lived along a river (for instance, the Inca and Aztec). Rather, what river-based and non-river-based intensive agriculture really seemed to share was a proscribed territory of arable land, such that the only possible response to increasing populations was intensification of production, not expansion of productive land.

Intensive agriculture
The production of food by use of complex and high-yield methods like irrigation, fertilizer, draft animals, and permanent fields.

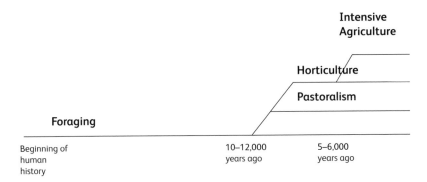

FIGURE 7.1 A timeline of production systems

PLATE 7.3 Intensive agricultural societies use all available land, as in Nepal where hillsides are cut into terraces

The work of intensive agriculture was and is arduous and incessant, and required the efforts of the entire farming family; men, women, and children alike were enlisted as farm labor. However, in contrast to horticulture, ownership and control of land, production, and surplus were usually concentrated in the hands of men, leading back to a male-centered and -dominated society. Fathers tended to be heads of families, and membership, inheritance, and such issues were settled among and between males. This pre-eminence of males, together with the accumulation of sometimes vast surpluses, made raiding, plunder, and inter-society aggression attractive. Accordingly, intensive agricultural societies tended and tend to be warlike, even promoting a social institution of professional soldiers on permanent military stand-by.

In fact, a key aspect of the form of society made possible – and probably necessary – by intensive agriculture was a high degree of social differentiation and social specialization. First of all, the enormous surpluses translated to enormous differences in wealth and power; while most people were still food producers (which was true until very recently), a small but important class of wealth expropriaters existed to "rule" and "manage" the economy and society. This class constituted and constitutes an elite or an actual government over the equally new political institution, the territorial state. There might be other classes intermediate between the elite and the agricultural **peasants**, the latter now not independent subsistence producers but providers of surplus to a "center" of society. As this suggests, the second possibility of intensive agriculture was an elaboration of the number of different kinds of jobs to do or literally different kinds of people to be. In addition to peasants and rulers, there could be professional priests, scribes, craftsmen, artisans, and naturally soldiers. All of this variation was financed by the surplus production of the laboring classes, often including slaves.

See Chapters 9 and 13

Peasant

An out-of-favor term for rural and agricultural peoples who live in but are peripheral to a centralized and often urbanized society. The peasants provide the food for the society but generally have the least power and wealth in the society.

BOX 7.3 ENSURING POWER IN AN INTENSIVE AGRICULTURAL SOCIETY

As described by Hilda Kuper (1963), the Swazi of South Africa stood on or just across the line of intensive agriculture. They cultivated maize and millet with a combination of old and new technologies: women used a simple hoe to sow small plots of maize and also reaped it, but men used ox-drawn plows to prepare land as well. There was no irrigation or crop rotation, however. Both men and women processed the harvest, shucking corn and threshing millet. Overall, farming was a low-status activity. Land was not owned or leased by individual farmers but was rather available to them through personal (what we might call "feudal") relationships with landowners. According to Kuper, "land, the basis of subsistence, is 'served' to the people by their political overlords" (42). This created a system of economic and political inequality, which was not only normal but desirable – but only when the advantages accrued to the overlords. Lower ranking people, the "commoners," were not expected or allowed to accumulate wealth; a man with more – whether more animals or more wives – was open to accusations of witchcraft, for which the penalty was death. Then, the property that he had illicitly acquired "was legally 'eaten up' by chiefs" (49), adding to their already superior position.

Where intensive agriculture first appeared – in the Middle East (so-called "Mesopotamia"), Egypt, India, and China – we find a new type of society and culture normally referred to as **civilization**. Civilization is a social formation centered on, although not exclusively consisting of, cities – large, densely populated, and at least somewhat "unproductive" communities. Most of the population still lived in the hinterland, but the power and decision-making for the society emanated from the city; it was the "seat of power." Along with, or perhaps because of, cities came a constellation of new skills, technologies, and species of knowledge. Among these were the state, the first writing systems, mathematics, monumental architecture (e.g. pyramids and palaces), and representational art.

Civilization

A form of society based on cities as the centers of administration and the focus of social life, usually dependent on intensive agriculture in the surrounding countryside.

Another new institution created by intensive agriculture was the market (see below), a place and practice for exchanging goods based on their economic value. Eventually money was invented to symbolize that value and facilitate exchange. To make the market function, a professional class of merchants evolved, who extracted a share of the value in order to mediate the exchange. This market, and the long-range trading that sustained it, introduced a circulation not only of goods but of ideas and cultures, as travelers from distant lands brought their produce and their languages, religions, and other cultural elements to the city. Cities thus, from the beginning, were sites for the mixing and transmitting of culture and thereby for the creation of new cultures and of new cultural awareness like "cosmopolitanism" (*cosmos* for world or universe, and *polis* for city) and "multiculturalism" – and ultimately globalization.

Religion predictably reflected social changes on the ground in these societies. Just as economics and politics were "centralized," so religion and the "spiritual realm" could become centralized too. There was often a single "high god" or a pantheon of gods (like the Greek "Olympian" gods) of the city or civilization that was believed to own and control the affairs of the society. The human rulers and the god or gods might be in close communication – or in the case of ancient Egypt, be one and the same. Professional priests ran the cult of the god(s) from the city center, collecting tribute (what we would call taxes) for the benefit of the god(s) which was used to fund all of the activities of the society. The god(s) was/were often judgmental and warlike, identical to the rulers themselves, who sat in judgment over the people and led the "defense" of society. Religion was so central to the function and identity of many of these ancient civilizations that they have been referred to as "temple communities."

At any rate, in the last couple of centuries, improvements to agricultural techniques, culminating in machine power and the "industrial revolution," have changed the nature of farming and the relationship between the farm and the city. In particular, in the industrialized world, cities really do contain the majority of the society; in the U.S.A. today, less than 2 percent of the population produces the food that the other 98 percent consume. "Urbanized" societies find most of their population living in small or large cities, engaged in other activities than food production. Much of the rest of the world is urbanizing too, undergoing even now the revolution that began thousands of years ago for others. This introduces problems for them that already "modernized" societies experienced and generally solved long ago, such as an exploding population, the degradation and pollution of the environment, and a shift from subsistence-related to surplus-related production. We will return to this situation in the final chapters of this book.

See Chapter 14

Surveying the progression of economic systems and the cultural institutions and relations they engendered, a few broad conclusions may be drawn. First, where an economy produces a surplus, there is "wealth," whether that wealth is in food, money, cattle, or land. And where there is wealth, there are differences in wealth; wealth is not evenly distributed. And where there are differences in wealth, there are differences in status and power. Second, in terms of gender relations, when women make significant productive contributions to the society – and even more so, when they control their own work and its rewards – their social status is comparatively high. When they cannot contribute to production or control their own wealth, their status tends to be lower. Finally, overall the trade-off in the evolution of economies and cultures has consisted of more productivity based on more control of the economy and the environment in exchange for less social equality and less freedom of action within that society: foragers could work when they were hungry and walk away from groups they did not like, but farmers – and industrial and post-industrial workers – are more constrained both by their jobs and their societies.

Systems of distribution

Once goods are produced, there is the task of providing them to the people who need them – or at least to the people who will consume them, which is not necessarily the same thing. This second phase is distribution. Unlike the tendency for a society to have a single dominant system of production, it may have more than one distribution system or all three systems in operation simultaneously, sometimes in different realms of the culture. The three systems (as first proposed by Polanyi (1957)) are:

- Reciprocity
- Redistribution
- Market exchange.

Reciprocity

Reciprocity is an informal type of back-and-forth exchanging, of giving and taking. This does not particularly distinguish it from other distribution methods, where someone always gives and someone else takes. We might do better to think of it as a style of exchange in which individuals or groups of relatively equal power and status, and who know each other personally, mutually give and take goods as part of and as a commentary on their ongoing social relationship. Reciprocity really exists in three sub-forms, namely:

Reciprocity
A form of exchange that involves giving and receiving between relative equals and as part of a larger ongoing social relationship.

1. **Generalized reciprocity**. In this form, goods are given without any particular calculation of the value of the goods or any particular expectation for a "return" of equal value in any particular time frame. That is, if I have something to give, I give it, not worrying whether I will receive something in exchange any time soon but assuming that, if you have something to give, you will give it. In some societies, especially foraging ones, this may be the predominant or even sole distribution system; if one man had meat today as the result of a successful hunt, he shared the meat with everyone in his social group, and he did not expect compensation or praise for his behavior. Maybe tomorrow someone else would have meat, and he would share likewise. The person who does not share, or who demands credit or acclaim for doing so, is simply impolite and socially inappropriate. Clearly, this type of sharing will only occur between people who know and trust each other and who have a long-term social relationship – during which "reciprocity" will eventually and "generally" be achieved.

2. **Balanced reciprocity**. In this form, goods are given with some calculation of their value and some expectation of an equal return within some reasonable time. It still entails a long-term and meaningful relationship between the exchangers but ordinarily transpires between individuals who are not quite as close as those who would do generalized reciprocity; after all, you would not give a friend or loved one a gift and then wait impatiently for an equal return.

3. **Negative reciprocity**. In this final form, goods are given with calculation of their value but also with an expectation or intention of receiving more value than one gives. This resembles most closely the modern "market" principle, except that it is characterized by the ongoing relationship found at the heart of all reciprocity, even if that relationship is more distant and tenuous than in other forms of reciprocity. Perhaps the most famous and well-researched example of negative reciprocity is the

"kula" institution described by Malinowski in Melanesia. Men traveled great distances at considerable inconvenience and risk in order to trade necklaces and armbands with their partners, each man hoping to receive the "best" necklace for his armband or vice versa. However, the point was not to get and hold a piece but to get it, display it, and eventually trade it for an even more prized piece. This way, a man achieved and expressed his status in society, his skill as a trader, and ultimately, if all went well, his elevation to "kula master." In the end, however, his success depended not only on his tough bargaining and skillful manipulation of the game but on his relationships with other traders who could just as easily pass their prestigious objects to other partners.

BOX 7.4 THE *HXARO* EXCHANGE

According to Richard Lee (1984), the !Kung or Ju/hoansi practiced a form of reciprocity called *hxaro*, a "delayed form of nonequivalent gift exchange" that had the effect of "circulating goods, lubricating social relations, and maintaining ecological balance" (97). All sorts of things were exchanged by *hxaro*, including tools and jewelry and weapons and utensils, and both men and women entered into such exchanges. Two things that were never traded in this manner were food and people. The range of *hxaro* trade relations could be quite extensive, and every visit between individuals and communities was an occasion for exchanging – starting new trades or completing old ones. In their self-effacing, egalitarian way, givers would downplay the quality of their gift with comments like "I couldn't find a really good thing, I just brought you this" (100). What was important, and explicitly so, was not the object itself but the social relationship between the participants: Ju/hoansi understood that a deficient reciprocation "could mean a *hxaro* partner was losing interest in maintaining the relationship and was allowing it to lapse" (101), and while such partnerships could end by agreement, they were also often the source of arguments and conflicts – although the lapse was usually a symptom of a changed relationship more than a cause of it.

Lee, Richard. 1984. *The Dobe !Kung*. New York: Holt, Rinehart, and Winston.

Redistribution

A form of exchange that involves collection of surplus or wealth by a "central" individual, group, or institution that controls how the wealth is redistributed and used.

Redistribution

One of the key characteristics of reciprocity is that it has no "center." No one person or group controls or oversees the exchange. In redistribution, on the other hand, a center is implicit and necessary, and the social implications of this fact are serious. **Redistribution** may be defined as exchange in which wealth is collected by a central person, group, or institution who/which then hands it out to the people who need it and/or "spends" it for purposes that are (ideally) beneficial to all in the exchange arrangement but which also reflect the power and interests of the distributor.

A classic example of redistribution also comes from Melanesia, where a "big man" might erect a redistribution system around himself. A man was not born a big man, even if his father was one. Rather, this was a status that each man had to gain individually. The point was to develop a coterie of followers or contributors who would turn their surplus over to you, which you could redistribute according to the needs and interests of the system. So, a potential big man first had to generate his own surplus, which he displayed and gave away in a very public gesture resembling a party. If his hard work and generosity were seen and appreciated, others might opt to associate themselves with him; like finding a good "patron," it was always desirable to attach oneself to a powerful and generous man. The more people who joined his "team" and contributed their surplus, the more the big man could display and redistribute. Eventually, he might become the center of an important and powerful exchange network. Like a feudal lord (another center of redistribution), his favor was valuable and his support good or even necessary, and a follower was likely to return deference for various kinds of benefits.

In intensive agricultural and industrial societies, the "government" is effectively the center of redistribution. Whether this takes the form of king or priest or state, the center can compel and even coerce participation in the form of taxes or tithes or other expropriation of private wealth. This wealth goes to "social services" (e.g., unemployment or retirement benefits) but also to large-scale projects which individuals could not afford alone (e.g., roads), to "security" systems such as the police or military, and to finance the government itself, which often enough meant and means the luxurious lifestyle of the leaders.

Market exchange

Market exchange was the last of the three distribution systems to appear historically and is still not the only existing system even in "modern" societies. However, it is increasingly defining the modern world and penetrating and displacing other systems. In Western society, even when people practice reciprocity or redistribution, it is usually in terms of goods and services acquired by market practices: people give gifts bought at the store and paid for with money.

We may think of market exchange as distribution which involves a specialized location or institution – the "market" – where people bring their goods or their symbols of wealth (e.g., money) for the purpose of exchange based on self-interest and maximization of value ("profit") determined by "supply and demand" and where ongoing social relationships are reduced, not significant, or an actual impediment to exchange. Modernity or capitalism hardly invented the market principle; ancient intensive agricultural societies generally had markets, and many traditional African horticulturists, for instance, held markets but on a more limited scale and schedule. Villages might organize a "market day" once every several days, at which time people gathered to exchange foods or handicrafts or whatever they produced. After market day, people would not do market exchange until the next market day, leaving lots of occasions for reciprocity or redistribution.

In pre-modern marketing arrangements, it was of course the case that people usually knew each other over long periods of time. It is possible in modern Western market practices that participants know the people they "buy from" or "sell to" or even that they develop a personal relationship with them. Humans are humans and

Market exchange
A form of distribution based on the use of a specialized location (the "marketplace") and relatively impersonal principles of supply and demand and the pursuit of profit.

tend to make social bonds over time. This can facilitate the market "deal," as trust can grow between traders. However, in capitalist societies, friendship is not enough and can be positively detrimental; that is why contracts and courts exist. And it is entirely possible and even preferable sometimes to have a minimal social relationship with one's market partner: most modern shoppers do not seek out or particularly want to know and befriend their car salesman or grocery check-out clerk, and the system certainly does not depend on it. In fact, as many people have discovered, "doing business" with friends or family can be a vexing undertaking.

BOX 7.5 A PRE-MODERN MARKET

Like many traditional societies, the Igbo of Nigeria held rural markets in which not only local people but traveling merchants and traders gathered to exchange goods. Actually, Igbo society (Uchendu 1965) contained two parallel market systems. Village markets were owned and operated by sets of villagers and were dominated, as buyers and sellers, by women; long-distance markets in exotic goods such as salt, slaves, cattle, and manufactured goods were the province of men. The village market was not only a place of business but a place to exchange news and gossip, to observe or participate in ceremonies and parades, and to meet friends, pay or collect debts, and make marriages and divorces. Inside the marketplace, sellers were "zoned" into areas of similar commodities (e.g., all the sellers of corn were grouped together), and prices were arrived at by bargaining and supply/demand. A "market ring" system existed between markets, such that nearby markets staggered their days or times, allowing traders to circulate between them. And the "market peace," essential to any large public gathering, was assured by three devices: a weather magician who "drove away the rain," a market court with police and judges to punish offenders who disturbed the peace, and a market god who punished those who escaped the arm of the human authorities.

Again, the market principle does not depend on money, nor certainly on capitalism. Capitalism is one way of doing markets (even communists "went to the market" to buy bread), and money is a convenient "medium" or symbol of wealth and value: it is easier to carry some money to the market than some corn, and of course "service" workers like teachers do not produce material goods to take to market anyway. Nevertheless, money and capitalist modes of production and exchange are increasingly pervading the economic and social world – not just in the U.S.A. or the West but globally – and they appear to be the future (at least the short- to mid-range future) of economics and culture. Either way – with or without money (or credit cards, symbols of symbols of wealth) and with or without capitalism – market exchange, intensive agriculture, and industrialization/urbanization will continue to transform not only economies and politics but the social relations within which all humans live their lives.

PLATE 7.4 Modern markets, like this one in downtown Tokyo, can generate great wealth

Consumption

The third and most neglected phase of any economic system is consumption – the actual use of goods and services. It has received less attention in anthropology at least partly because it has received less attention in Western economic thinking in general. Gregory writes that, "The consumption sphere is very much a subordinate sphere under capitalism, and as such was not subjected to any systematic analysis by the classical economists. . . . The methods of consumption under capitalism are disorganized relative to the methods of production" (1982: 75–6). Many cultural anthropology textbooks make little or no mention of it, which is regrettable, not only because it too is a cultural activity but because it is the "end" of the system, where goods meet real humans and their lives.

Anthropologists in the field have not ignored consumption, and a few prominent economic theorists have given it some thought. Marx, who was most concerned with the "mode of production," did also identify a "mode of consumption," but it was a secondary issue for him that received little elaboration beyond the distinction between subsistence consumption and luxury consumption, associated with the working class and the owning class respectively. The first scholar to take consumption seriously was perhaps Thorstein Veblen, whose *Theory of the Leisure Class: An Economic Study of Institutions* (published in 1899) introduced the concept of "conspicuous consumption." Veblen's idea was that the drive to consume certain kinds of goods was based on the desire to create and display differences between people and on the capacity of goods to do so. In other words, products do not just have "uses" but they also have "values," and the people who possess – and can display – more of certain kinds of products have *their* social value enhanced as well. He imagined that the "upper classes" set the tone in a society, which the lower classes tried to emulate in order to acquire some of the status and prestige of their betters. One of the marks of high status in the past, he argued, was leisure itself (free time and freedom from labor), but now it was objects.

While the study of consumption has progressed since then, a theory of consumption really has not appeared. To my knowledge, there is no system or typology of consumption available, comparable to those of production and distribution discussed above; there is certainly no standard and established such typology. Still, we can begin to lay out some of the issues that would be part of any systematic anthropological study of consumption. First, consumption entails a variety of sub-processes, from acquisition to preparation to presentation to use. This leads to a series of research questions:

- Who acquires goods and services for consumption by the group, and how/where (i.e., the cultural phenomenon of "shopping")?
- Who prepares products for consumption, and how?
- How and why are products presented to potential consumers – and to potential audiences?
- When (for instance, at what time of day or on what occasions) and by whom are particular goods consumed?
- How are goods consumed in ritual contexts?
- Are different products consumed by different types of people, and are they consumed in different ways?
- Who can consume together, and who cannot?
- How does consumption indicate, perpetuate, and comment on social relationships and institutions? How can consumption be used to challenge and change social relationships and institutions?

The essence of an anthropology of consumption is that consumables are not neutral things, even when they are minimally processed natural commodities (e.g., kangaroo meat). Even food, as Roland Barthes asserts, "is not only a collection of products that can be used for statistical or nutritional studies. It is also, and at the same time, a system of communication, a body of images, a protocol of usages, situations, and behaviors" (1997: 21). That is, like all other parts of culture, consumable goods are *symbols* with meanings and effects. Any object – food, clothing, a house, a car – "sums up and transmits a situation; it constitutes information; it signifies" (ibid.)

Mary Douglas was one of the first anthropologists to think about consumption systematically. In her famous essay "Deciphering a Meal" from her book *Implicit Meanings* (1975), she discussed the social construction of various kinds of food-sharing. Central to her analysis was the distinction between the categories of "meal" and "drinks." Anyone in Western society knows that "having drinks" is a more casual social affair than "having dinner." The social dynamic involved is "intimacy and distance": "The meal expresses close friendship. Those we only know at drinks we know less intimately."

Barthes, Roland. 1997. "Toward a Psychosociology of Contemporary Food Consumption." In Carole Counihan and Penny van Esterick (eds) *Food and Culture: A Reader*. New York and London: Routledge, 20–7

Douglas, Mary. 1975. *Implicit Meanings: Essays in Anthropology*. London and Boston: Routledge & Kegan Paul.

Since we have limited space here, and since food is such a ready medium for observing consumption, let us remain with it. The Barabaig, pastoralists from earlier in the chapter, consumed milk, but the preferences of the sexes differed: men liked raw milk, whereas women preferred churned or curdled milk. More significantly, a husband lived and ate in his own room in his homestead, apart from wives and children. A wife cooked in her room (*ged*) and delivered the food to his room (*huland*); if he had multiple wives, each woman cooked for him in turn, and he had to eat the same amount from each or cause dissension in his family (Klima 1970: 37).

As Douglas opined, consumption speaks to basic cultural notions of categorization – what is food, and what kinds of foods are there? The Semai distinguished between four categories of "real food," which were, in their view, natural and not cultural types; in other words, the natural order came in four types, and it would be unnatural to mix food types. This sort of thinking leads easily enough to various kinds of consumption rules and taboos. The Hua of Papua New Guinea had rules for what foods could and could not be eaten by different kinds of people. For instance, a pregnant woman could not, according to Meigs (1997), eat cat or dog or possum because those animals speak in babble, which would negatively affect the child; likewise, a warrior should not eat sharp or scratchy food because such foods could draw blood. More profoundly, people could not eat food prepared by a "stranger," where strangeness was defined by not sharing the person's *nu* or spiritual substance. *Nu* was passed between people directly by physical contact as well as indirectly through food exchanges. "Food in Hua thinking contains the self and the feelings of its producer" (103); thus, "To eat a food . . . is not only an economic, social, and nutritive event but also an emotional and mystical one" (104).

The idea that food is more than food, and that goods are more than goods, is a common one, and is closely tied to individual and group identity. In the village of Gopalpur, as in many parts of India, humans were classified according to social and spiritual qualities. One of the manifestations of the "caste system" was restrictions on who could sit with and eat with whom. The various castes or *jatis* did not "eat together," although this had a culturally specific meaning: it applied to certain kinds of foods more than to others (especially rice) and to certain acts more than to others (especially eating off the same plate or bowl and sitting in a line to do so). Thus, different castes could eat together if they used separate plates and either faced each other or at a slant, but then, by their cultural definition, they were not "eating together" (Beals 1980).

See Chapter 8

Let us briefly mention one other arena, which is the ritual and status aspect of food consumption. Obviously many societies have food taboos, such as the Hua rules about what kinds of food men and women should eat. Rituals and culturally significant occasions not only tend to call for different food behaviors (such as feasts and sacrifices) but for different foods; Americans eat more turkey at Thanksgiving than at any other time of the year. It is the "right food" for the occasion. One of the best-known food regulations in Western civilization is the Torah/Old Testament proscription against shellfish and various other potential foods. Douglas (1966) analyzed this too as it related to categories (e.g., animals that chew their cud and split the hoof versus those that do not), some of which are fit to eat and some of which are not. Thus, "purity" and cultural or religious "fitness" enter the calculation as to what people may eat and how and when (for instance, no calves boiled in their mother's milk). Finally, Allison (1997) has investigated the high-stakes game of packing nursery school *bento* lunch boxes for Japanese children, in which a mother's social status and aesthetic sense are on trial. She goes so far as to insist that making and eating *bentos* (since children are under pressure to eat them in particular ways) are ideological systems that enculturate both children and mothers into socially appropriate roles and principles of proper order, appearance, style, and "naturalness" – but, like all of culture, a kind of "naturalness made artificial" and perfected by humans, that is, a kind of culturized nature (299).

BOX 7.6　CONTEMPORARY CULTURAL CONTROVERSIES: STUDYING CONSUMPTION OR MANIPULATING CONSUMPTION?

Modern market practices have not only come to dominate economic activity in industrialized Western societies but have become worldwide forces, shaping a national and global "buyosphere" (Hine 2003). The power of market concepts and behaviors to reconfigure social relations has been noted, from Max Weber's seminal study of the relation between capitalism and Protestantism to anthropologist Daniel Miller's *A Theory of Shopping* (1998). In fact, according to George Ritzer, consumption not only "plays an ever-expanding role in the lives of individuals around the world" (2003: 1); it permeates activities and institutions from obviously economic (stores, restaurants, casinos, and cruise ships) to less obviously economic or superficially non-economic (education, medicine/health care, museum and charity organizations, and religion). Consuming, Ritzer claims, has become a form of entertainment in its own right. The explosive popularity and cultural importance of consumption has made it a worthwhile subject for anthropological investigation, including into what has been called "consumer behavior." Consumer behavior has actually been a topic of analysis for many decades, at least since the 1950s, and represents a sort of applied anthropology. It is certainly a valid endeavor to study the behaviors, meanings, and consequences of consumer action; however, in more than a few cases this kind of knowledge can be and has been employed to manipulate such action – to produce more effective marketing strategies, to perfect advertising campaigns, and ultimately to induce people to consume *more* of *certain kinds* of goods. Anthropologists could participate in these investigations, and/or our research could be used by others for their own purposes. What do you think?

SUMMARY

Every society has an economic system as part of its culture, even if it does not have factories and money and supermarkets. Those are specific ways of doing an economy, not the definition of economy. An economy is the practices and institutions, and the associated beliefs and values and roles, involved in transforming the environment into usable products for humans. As such, the economic behaviors of a society will dramatically influence other aspects of that society, including how humans organize themselves and assign tasks and values and meanings to work, objects, and humans themselves.

An economic system comprises three phases:

- Production
- Distribution
- Consumption.

Within each of these phases is a variety of possible arrangements or systems for accomplishing the functions of the economy. There are four major production systems, although a specific society's economy may combine or modify them in various ways:

- Foraging
- Pastoralism
- Horticulture
- Intensive agriculture.

There are three major distribution systems, which may co-exist in a society:

- Reciprocity
- Redistribution
- Market exchange.

Finally, although it has not been studied and systematized like the other phases, consumption is the final and important stage in which the roles, values, statuses, and meanings of goods and people converge in the actual use of cultural products.

Key Terms

Adaptation

Civilization

Division of labor

Domestication

Foraging

Horticulture

Intensive agriculture

Market exchange

Mode of production

Neolithic

Pastoralism

Peasant

Reciprocity

Redistribution

Relations of production

Slash-and-burn

Swidden

Kinship and Non-kin Organization: Creating Social Groups

In February 2004, a Frenchwoman named Christelle Demichel married her fiancé Eric. The only thing unusual about the wedding is that the groom was absent, since he was dead, having been killed in a motorcycle accident in 2002. Ms. Demichel was able to marry him anyway owing to a 1959 French law legalizing wedding ceremonies between a person and his or her deceased partner. Prior to 1959, a flood resulting from the failure of Malpasset Dam had taken the life of Irene Jodard's fiancé, and she had asked the government to allow her to proceed with the wedding. From this request came the new law, giving the French President the power to authorize a marriage if the wedding had already been planned and the parents of the deceased approved. The legal marriage date would be backdated to before the death, and while no inheritance rights or other financial advantages could come from such a marriage, any child born from the couple would be regarded as legitimate.

There is no society on Earth in which humans live, work, and fill all of their needs in isolation from each other. In fact, such would be the very opposite of a society. Rather, humans form relationships and groups to accomplish their ends and enjoy their lives. The kinds of relationships and groups they may form, as in the case above, are incredibly diverse, but they form them for various and particular reasons, love and companionship being just two. Humans also collectively produce and distribute and consume wealth, establish residences, solve problems and exercise power, and create and perpetuate identities. The lone individual could not make or perpetuate these social arrangements and institutions. It is groups of people who share in tasks, results, and interests.

There are many types of human groups, including crowds and classrooms. Each has its own dynamics and its own "culture." However, the most socially significant groups are what we may call **corporate groups**. A corporate group is a collection of humans who act and to an extent think as a single "body" (*corps*) in terms of such practical activities as production, distribution, consumption, ownership, decision-making, **residence**, inheritance, and ultimately "identity" or "destiny." They are the ones who see themselves as "in this together," who "look out for their own kind," who "keep it in the family." Accordingly, family or kinship is one – in fact, the predominant – way to provide this structure, but clearly not the only way. In this chapter, then, we will consider the cross-cultural possibilities and necessities of kinship – the diverse ways in which people arrange themselves into "family" groups and assign those groups not only tasks but meaning. In addition, we will investigate other principles by which virtually all societies at least supplement if not replace kinship by other, either cross-cutting or more inclusive kinds of corporate identities.

Corporate group

A social group that shares some degree of practical interest, identity, residence, and destiny.

Residence

The kinship principle concerning where people live, especially after marriage, and therefore what kinds of residential and corporate groups are found in the society and what tasks and values they are assigned.

CORPORATE GROUPS: THE FUNDAMENTAL STRUCTURE OF HUMAN SOCIETIES

A society is not only a group of humans but a group of groups, a structured collection of collectivities. The most important and enduring of these intra-societal groups are corporate groups. Corporate groups are the basic organizational and functional units of a society. The kinds of functions they provide vary by the society and by the specific corporate group, but they may include the following.

1. **Regulating behavior or establishing rights for members, as well as between members of disparate groups**. Like a business corporation, each group is a system of interrelated roles, with rules for their interaction.

2. **Owning property**. A corporate group is often if not ordinarily an ownership entity, collectively possessing rights or title to land, buildings, wealth, and other resources.

3. **Producing and distributing wealth**. A corporate group is frequently a "work" group, which accomplishes productive tasks together and shares the fruits of that labor among its members.

4. **Inheriting property**. A corporate group often aims to keep its wealth and resources within the group when members pass away. Thus, it may establish a sequence of ownership and rights for the transference of property from current to future members.

5. **Consuming and residing**. A corporate group, since it may produce and distribute together, may also consume together. It may give members a place to eat and in most cases a place to sleep (although it is not necessary that all the functions of the members are conducted together). It may be their "home" in figurative or literal ways.

6. **Providing for the social and emotional needs of members**. As human beings, the individuals in corporate groups have needs other than physical and material ones. The group may satisfy those needs through meaningful social interactions, camaraderie, and even affection.

7. **Creating a sense of identity**. A corporate group regularly shapes the sense of self of the members, giving them a common "name" and a feeling of belonging to something greater and more enduring than themselves. This identity can translate into a sense of destiny as well – that they have a future *as* a collectivity and will collectively face that future.

8. **Perpetuating the group by providing new members**. Any group has a future only if it can persist beyond the lifetime of current members. A corporate group has some mechanism for obtaining new members (e.g., reproduction, adoption, capture, hiring) and inculcating them with the skills or values of the group. Perpetuating groups often equates to perpetuating social statuses – and differences in social status – in the society: in other words, poor or subordinate groups tend to reproduce poverty or subordination, and rich or powerful groups tend to reproduce wealth and power.

9. **Establishing alliances between groups**. No group exists in isolation, so there must be some system or standard for making (and breaking) relationships between groups with different members, interests, and identities. Corporate groups can enter or find themselves in diverse connections with each other over the short or long term. These relations can be mutually beneficial, mutually exploitative, or beneficial for one and exploitative for the other.

No particular corporate group must fulfill all of these conditions. Some are very important and meaningful to members, while others are more trivial. Such groups may consequently be constructed on the basis of any number of natural or cultural characteristics of their members. Of the wide array of possible corporate foundations, we can distinguish two general types: groups that are based on family or kinship ties or relations, and those that are based on other, non-kinship qualities or characteristics. In any society, both of these types of groups will exist simultaneously, such that any single individual is a member of one (or more than one) kinship group as well as multiple non-kinship groups. This creates bonds with kin and non-kin alike, often of different types and functions and sometimes competing or conflicting with each other.

KINSHIP-BASED CORPORATE GROUPS

Kinship is a virtually universal way of organizing people into corporate groups, although it is by no means the only way. We can think of kinship as roughly what English speakers mean when they talk about "family," although, like everything else in the cultural world, "family" is a culturally relative term. The physical or "blood" relations between individuals are of course exactly the same from one society to another; for instance, the man who is your father's brother's son or the woman who is your mother's sister's husband's sister is exactly the same person in every society. However, what is important is not the "objective" fact but its meaning for society. This is another case of how society culturizes physical facts to give them cultural meaning, value, and use.

Any kinship system is a product of three distinct but interconnected principles or concepts, namely:

- Marriage
- Residence
- Descent.

Marriage may be thought of as the "horizontal" principle, which links individuals (and groups) together and establishes new groups. Residence is literally the geographic or spatial principle – in what location people actually live or perform their corporate functions. Descent would provide the "vertical" or temporal principle, linking individuals and groups through time and "down" between the generations. Each of these principles or concepts comes in diverse forms and in various combinations, giving the society's kinship system its unique contours.

Marriage

Marriage
A cultural institution joining two or more persons into a socially recognized, long-term relationship for personal, sexual, childbearing, political, and/or economic purposes.

Marriage is the first step in assembling kinship-based corporate groups. Marriage brings together individuals from different kin and corporate groups and binds them into one, or the other, or a new group. This is the "horizontal" nature of marriage. In considering the meaning of marriage, as always anthropologists must build a definition that is inclusive, not simply impose their own cultural notion of marriage on all societies and assert that how their culture does marriage *really is* marriage and that if another culture does it differently, theirs is not "really marriage." Even in Western societies marriage is a contentious issue. Is marriage only between a man and a woman? That is, can members of the same sex marry? Is marriage between only one man and only one woman? Is marriage only between two *living* people?

Marriage across cultures has certain core characteristics but a great degree of flexibility. Wherever it is found, it is a socially recognized relationship between individuals (two or more) and often between their families as well. It has enduring if not permanent qualities (it is expected to last for more than a few days, although not necessarily forever), and it establishes various kinds of rights and obligations. These functions of marriage can and usually do include economic ones (shared labor or other productive activities, distribution and consumption, ownership, inheritance, and so on), political ones (establishment and enforcement of rules, decision-making, and problem-solving for members), and of course sexual ones. Societies universally culturize the physical act of sex by elaborating rules and norms for who, how, when, where, and so on. In some societies, this is more critical than in others: some have fairly lax norms about sex and "fidelity" (including "premarital" sex) and some have harsh restrictions, down to premarital virginity sanctioned with the death penalty. The fundamental "rule" of human societies is the famous **incest taboo**, that members of the same "family" do not ordinarily have sexual access to each other, although again "family" is a cultural term.

One of the key aspects of marriage relates to children. Children are of course required in order to "staff" a new family or to perpetuate an existing one. Child-bearing is an important function of marriage in virtually all societies, although not of all marriages, since many married people choose not to have children. It goes without saying that marriage is not necessary for making babies – it is again a way that society culturizes and "normalizes" child-bearing. Many societies do deem that marriage is a prerequisite to produce "socially acceptable" or "legitimate" children. But birth is hardly the end of the member-making process. Children must be cared for and instructed, that is, *enculturated*, which is a typical though never exclusive function of family. Children must learn the social and practical skills they need to participate in society – from language and "manners" to gender roles and economic skills. Some societies feature full-time professional institutions to contribute to this process (e.g., schools), but the family is always a place where it occurs first if not most. We can think, more broadly, of the care and teaching of children as one crucial part of the general concern of **social reproduction**; that is, keeping society going over time, including over generations.

Another major and often overlooked element of social reproduction is the reproduction of labor. In the short term, laborers must be prepared to do the next day's labor. The marriage relationship and resultant family is where much of this work occurs, including feeding the laborers, cleaning their clothes, providing them with a place to sleep, and so on. In what has become known as the "anthropology of

Incest taboo
The near universal rule against marrying or having sex with "kin."

Social reproduction
The maintenance and perpetuation of society beyond mere childbearing, including enculturation and teaching of members to take their place in society and day-to-day activities to allow members of the society to perform their specified tasks (including what is sometimes called "housework").

PLATE 8.1 Two mothers and their children from the Samantha tribe, India

housework," researchers in recent decades have investigated all the activities that are required to insure that the group and the society can continue from day to day – activities that are overwhelmingly associated with women but that have become more problematic in societies where women are also wage laborers.

Finally, marriage can be effective in establishing alliances between families. Marriage agreements and exchanges suggest that marriage is often more than a relationship between the individuals entering into the marriage. Often, and explicitly in many cases, the marriage is actually a bond or alliance between families. Royal marriages in European history were regularly quite self-conscious in their intentions to unify powerful or rich "houses" or noble families, and entire countries have been created through such marriages. On a more mundane level, families may seek to marry their children to other specific families for economic, political, or status reasons. The alliance between families may be more important to both sides than the particular marriage at hand, as indicated by ways in which they may strive to sustain the alliance even if the marriage fails in some way, as we will see below.

We should not ignore the pleasant emotional potential of marriage for partners. Neither should we overestimate it. In Western societies, love is regarded as the best reason and reward for marriage, but this opinion is not universally shared. Many marriages are arranged cross-culturally, between individuals who may not even know each other, let alone love each other. If the marriage grows into love that is wonderful, but the marriage does not depend on it. Westerners tend to privilege the emotional

PLATE 8.2 A traditional wedding ceremony on the island of Vanuatu

aspect of marriage, even thinking of the "practical" aspects as "unromantic." However, marriage is also if not mostly a lot of daily trivia – paying the bills, washing the dishes – that cannot be ignored or neglected. And many people realize they are in, and even choose to remain in, "loveless" marriages for various reasons – "for the children," out of fear or dependence, or out of mere convenience or inertia.

BOX 8.1 LOVE AND MARRIAGE IN ANCIENT GREECE AND ROME

While American people and politicians argue about "traditional marriage," it is interesting to consider some of the actual traditions of marriage in the West. John Boswell in his study of relationships in pre-modern Europe writes that "nothing in the ancient world quite corresponds to the idea of a permanent, exclusive union of social equals, freely chosen by them to fulfill both their emotional needs and imposing equal obligations of fidelity on both partners" (1994: 38). This is partly due to the rigid gender inequalities of those societies as well as to their economic and emotional expectations. In fact, Boswell finds that there were four types of heterosexual relationships (with their homosexual counterparts). Marriage was one, in its monogamous and polygamous forms. Its function was largely to provide children and to establish property rights, which were often the same thing, since children (and wives) were the property of men. Love and sex were not essential features of marriage: "Spouses who were actually 'in love' with each other were thought extraordinary and odd" until late antiquity (39). Love and sex were often sought in other partners, specifically concubines, lovers, and sex-objects. Concubines were typically women of lower social standing who were "kept" by men, sometimes for years, as non-marital or extramarital partners, sometimes in the family household. A lover was a person chosen for love or sex but without the long-term and economic implications of concubinage. A sex-object tended to be a servant or slave (regarded as the man's property) who was used for sex. All three of the latter relationships could be and frequently were in addition to, not instead of, marriage.

So, obviously, marriage is not only a central social institution – one upon which many other relationships and institutions are built – but a diverse one.

The first question that a society's marriage practices must address is who one can or should marry (that is, who is an eligible partner), which leads to a basic distinction between **exogamy** and **endogamy**. These terms are elusive, because they do not apply to a society as a whole but to groups or categories within society: any particular marriage will be exogamous with regard to some groups/categories and endogamous with regard to others. Put simply, exogamy (*exo* for outside and *gamy* for marriage) means marriage to someone who is "outside" or not a member of one's own group or category, while endogamy (*endo* for inside) means marriage to someone who is "inside" or a member of one's group or category. For instance, a society may have an exogamous rule or preference – even a quite strong one, sometimes a formal or "legal" one – applied to sex or gender: you should marry someone who is not a member of your own gender. Almost all societies observe a fundamental "kinship

Boswell, John. 1994. *Same-Sex Union in Premodern Europe*. New York: Villard Books.

Exogamy

The marriage principle in which an individual marries someone who is not in the same cultural category as himself or herself (e.g., marrying someone of a different sex/gender).

Endogamy

The marriage principle in which an individual marries someone who is in the same cultural category as himself or herself (e.g., marrying someone in one's own race or religion).

exogamy" – that is, you should marry someone who is not a member of your kin group, although how "kin group" is defined differs by culture. Some may practice exogamy with regard to the village: you should marry someone from another village than your own.

Similarly, there may be a tendency (more or less explicit or formal) toward endogamy in terms of age group or social class or race/ethnicity or religion or locality. It is certainly possible for a very old person to marry a very young person in a modern Western society, but it is not the norm and draws some degree of social judgment (think of Anna Nicole Smith and her aged – now deceased – husband). Members of the same social class or religion or region not only have a greater chance of meeting but also of having things in common, and some religions quite strenuously urge that members marry "within the faith." And, while the U.S.A. does not have a "race endogamy" law, it did in times and places in the past, and most marriages there today are still racially endogamous, even if most Americans do not disapprove of "interracial" marriages.

Exogamy and endogamy set the most general limitations on who is an "eligible" or "acceptable" candidate for marriage. However, societies typically provide much more structure for the practice than this. A second basic question then is how many people an individual can marry. There are really only two choices: one or more than one. Anthropologists refine this distinction, identifying three systems.

Monogamy

The marriage rule in which an individual may have only one spouse.

Serial monogamy

The marriage practice of having only one spouse at a time but perhaps having more than one spouse, at different times, during one's life.

1. Monogamy (*mono* for one). The individual can only marry one person. The most common form of **monogamy** is one man married to one woman; homosexual marriage could of course also be monogamous. We should further distinguish between what we might call "absolute" or "lifetime" monogamy and **serial monogamy**, the distinction being whether a person can have only one spouse in an entire lifetime or just one spouse at a time. In strict traditional Christian doctrine, marriage was a one-time thing; remarriage was forbidden. Most modern Americans will probably marry more than once in their lives; monogamy then prohibits multiple *simultaneous* marriages, not multiple *consecutive* marriages. As "natural" as monogamy seems to modern readers, it is actually not the most common marriage rule in the world cross-culturally, although it may be the most common form in practice; even when societies allow or prefer multiple marriages, individuals may not desire them or have the resources to accomplish them. And, since there is a rough balance of population between the sexes globally, there cannot be enough members of the opposite sex for each person to have multiple spouses.

Polygyny

The marriage rule in which a man marries two or more women.

2. Polygyny (*poly* for many and *gyn* for woman). A man may or should marry two or more women. While this seems undesirable, even perverse, to many Westerners, it is in fact the most common marriage rule or preference cross-culturally. Somewhere between 70 and 80 percent of the world's known societies have condoned multiple wives for men. This can be seen as, and often is, a means of male domination or at least a manifestation of male status and power. However, women are not always the helpless victims of **polygyny**; women in many societies welcome co-wives into the home (or sometimes a homestead consisting of multiple households, one for each

woman and her children) for purposes of shared housework, female companionship, and division among them of the man's sexual demands. Women often feel that it is bad for a woman to sit alone in the household, and "first wives" may go so far as to play a role in selecting subsequent co-wives for their husbands. Men may marry sisters, termed **sororal polygyny**, which promises (but does not guarantee) to provide more domestic tranquility. Finally, in many polygynous societies, one or a few dominant males may monopolize the women, leaving other men with one wife or none. The Tiwi of Melville and Bathurst Islands north of Australia, a foraging society in which a few old men monopolized the young women, found an ingenious solution: a man was not allowed to marry at all until he reached the age of 30 or over, and his first wife would usually be an older woman, widowed from her own previous marriage to a much older man. Thus, every man and every woman married several times at various stages of life to spouses at various stages of their own lives (Hart and Pilling 1960).

3. Polyandry (*andro* for man). A woman may or should marry two or more men. This marriage form is particularly rare, practiced in less than 1 percent of known societies. Among the few cases are the Toda of southern India, the Pacific island Marquesans, and the Tibetans. Often, a woman will marry a set of brothers, bearing children for all of them. The children may be assigned "social fatherhood" to the senior brother, since physical fatherhood cannot be known and is culturally irrelevant, or social fatherhood may be assigned to various husbands for various children. The "problem" of paternity might be one reason why **polyandry** is so rare.

A third question in marriage is how precisely the marriage will be made. In some societies, the procedure was as informal as a man leaving gifts of food or other goods at the household of a woman; if she accepted the gifts and welcomed him in, they took up residence and were regarded as married. Among the Cheyenne, a man announced to his kin his desire to marry. If they approved, they would gather wealth and deliver it to the woman's parents. If her kin accepted the pairing, the wealth was distributed among her family, and the following day her kin would return gifts of equal value (Hoebel 1960). However, in many societies marriage is a much more elaborate business which occupies the interest of entire families if not entire communities. Many societies traditionally practiced – and many still practice today – **arranged marriage**, in which the families of prospective marriage partners make the selection and plan the event. The partners may not know each other at all, may never have even seen each other, and typically do not "date" before the marriage; unchaperoned dating is a particularly unique characteristic of Western courtship, and a relatively modern one at that. Arranged marriages are often handled by the men of the respective families, who make strategic alliances between themselves by exchanging sons and daughters for marriage. This practice illustrates quite clearly not only that marriage is an alliance-building institution in many cases but also that it is a device and field for male social dominance. Especially in situations of **hypergamy** (*hyper* for up or high), families may be seeking to raise their overall social status by marrying their daughter to a richer or more prestigious family, which may lead them

Sororal polygyny
The marriage practice in which a man marries two or more sisters.

Polyandry
The marriage rule in which a woman marries two or more men.

Hoebel, E. Adamson. 1960. *The Cheyennes Indians of the Great Plains*. New York: Holt, Rinehart, & Winston.

Arranged marriage
A practice where family members (often parents) choose the partner for marriageable youths, sometimes with little or no input from or option for the partners themselves.

Hypergamy
The marriage practice of marrying "up" with a spouse in a higher status, class, or caste than oneself.

See Chapter 5

to do reckless things such as expose their women to potential abuse and even "dowry death," as mentioned before.

Marriages, whether arranged or not, are often accompanied or even accomplished by property exchanges. This signals both the economic/contractual and the alliance aspects of marriage. Of course, while in American society there are minor wealth exchanges at weddings (e.g., guests bring gifts), some societies hand over substantial amounts of wealth in planning or consummating a marriage. The main forms this can take are as follows.

1. **Bridewealth/brideprice**. In this practice, a man gives wealth to the bride's family, usually her father or brother(s), in order to make the marriage. Nearly half of all recorded societies have done this, and it correlates to male social power and prestige, since men are not only giving and receiving wealth, but women are often not included in the negotiations nor are they recipients of the wealth themselves. This may sometimes be construed as "buying a wife," virtually treating women like property. However, it is viewed more often as compensation to the woman's family for the loss that her departure will mean – particularly the loss of her production (household work) and of her reproduction (any children she will bear). The woman's status in her marital family is often quite low, at least until she bears a child, preferably a son. However, in some cases today even a child does not enhance her status much. **Bridewealth** is especially closely associated with pastoral societies, where men dominate and have transferable wealth to offer, namely their herds. Thus, a man will typically offer a woman's male kin a certain number of animals in exchange for her hand in marriage, and a father may search for the best bridewealth offer for his daughter, meaning that men with great wealth will be able to arrange more and "better" marriages for themselves and their sons than can less wealthy men.

2. **Bride service**. In societies where men are expected to give something in exchange but real "wealth" does not exist, they may be required to provide **bride service** instead. For example, in foraging societies a man may be obligated to bring meat from his hunts to the woman's family for a period of years before the marriage is considered fully made or before he can remove her to his family. The Torah/Old Testament story of Jacob and his efforts to marry Rachel is an example of the institution of bride service, wherein he was asked to labor for her father (Laban, his own mother's brother, making Rachel his first cousin; see Genesis 29) before he could marry her.

3. **Dowry**. In a minority of societies that practice substantial property exchange, the woman or her family give wealth to the man (occasionally to the married pair as a couple) in order to make the marriage. In some societies this is interpreted as an "early inheritance" of her parents' property; however, when the wealth is transferred to her husband or his parents, it is hard to see how this constitutes an inheritance to her. In fact, the system of **dowry** can be a real disadvantage to the woman or her family and can be yet another path of male domination; not surprisingly, it is found in societies such as pre-revolutionary China, parts of India, and even traditional U.S.A., where men were or are dominant. The heavy burden of providing a dowry can lead parents to disdain having female children; as one advertisement for an India

Bridewealth

The marriage wealth-exchange practice in which a man or his family must pay an amount of property to his wife's kin before he may assume rights over his wife.

Bride service

The marriage wealth-exchange practice in which a man must labor for his wife's kin for a certain period of time before he may assume rights over his wife.

Dowry

The marriage wealth-exchange practice in which the woman's family is required to provide the husband with property (e.g., money, land, household goods) in order to make the marriage.

abortion clinic starkly framed it, "Pay 500 rupees now [for an abortion] or 50,000 in 18 years [for a dowry]" (Sen 2001). China's government recently outlawed extravagant dowries (although they still occur), and not so long ago an American girl might be expected to bring a trousseau or "hope chest" of goods, money, and even land to her marriage; the last vestige of this practice is the "tradition" that the bride's family pays for the wedding.

These basic forms of exchange are not entirely mutually exclusive. The Barabaig pastoralists practiced a sort of combination of bridewealth and dowry, each with exceptional qualities. Bridewealth was important, but was more symbolic than economic: in fact, only one cow was paid to the woman's family, but it had to be a heifer (young female) and all one color. In addition, the married couple received "marriage cattle" to start their own herd. The woman would bring a dowry of two to forty cattle which remained hers until she had a son (when they were transferred to him), and the man received donations of animals from his kinsmen as well (Klima 1970).

It is worth mentioning a few other noteworthy marriage practices that put the institution in perspective. For example, one practice – or pair of practices – found across cultures is the levirate/sororate. In both, families are expected to provide a "substitute spouse" if for some reason the original marriage ends in certain ways, particularly with a death. The **levirate** specifically entails that another man from the groom's family, ideally a brother, should marry the widow if her husband dies. From the woman's point of view, she is expected to marry her dead husband's brother or other kinsmen after she is widowed. This practice tends to be associated with male-dominated societies and families and with the high value of male children; in fact, in many cases any children issuing from the "second marriage" may still be attributed to the first (dead) husband. The practice also says something about the contractual and alliance nature of marriage, where the alliance outlives its human members. The **sororate** is the mirror-image, in which a widower is provided with a sister or other female relative of his dead wife. In another form of marriage known among the Nuer of east Africa and sometimes called "ghost marriage," a woman could be married to a man who had already died, particularly if he died young without children. As her ghost-husband, any children she later had (not by him, obviously) were looked upon as his children, who would continue his male line and perform rituals and ceremonies for him (Evans-Pritchard 1951). Perhaps most anomalously of all, the Na or Moso people of western China did not traditionally practice marriage at all: males and females engaged in a series of "furtive visits" or "secret romantic encounter[s] . . . without any consanguineal relatives knowing about it" (Hua 2001: 185), and the roles of "husband" and "father" were conspicuously absent.

English speakers tend to think of the "first cousin" relationship as "too close" for marriage. However, not all societies share this sentiment, since not all societies define "kin" and "cousin" in the customary English way (see the discussions of lineage and kinship terminology below). In fact, in many societies, cousins are the preferred marriage partners, constituting **preferential cousin marriage**. Some cousins are more

Sen, Mala. 2001. *Death by Fire: Sati, Dowry Death, and Female Infanticide in Modern India*. New Brunswick, NJ: Rutgers University Press.

Levirate
A marriage practice in which the brother of a deceased man is expected to marry his brother's widow.

Sororate
A marriage practice in which a woman is expected to marry the husband of her sister in the event of the married sister's death.

Evans-Pritchard, E. E. 1951. *Kinship and Marriage among the Nuer*. New York: Oxford University Press.

Preferential cousin marriage
The marriage principle that a person ought to marry a "cousin," that is, a child of one's mother's sibling or one's father's sibling.

preferred than others, and it is important to make a distinction between "cross-cousins" and "parallel cousins." Cross-cousins are children of the opposite-sex siblings of one's own parent – that is, father's sister's children or mother's brother's children. Parallel cousins are children of a parent's same-sex sibling – that is, father's brother's children or mother's sister's children. To English speakers, there is no significant social difference between these various cousins, but to other societies there may be a crucial difference. It is relatively common for societies to designate cross-cousins as good marriage selections, since, in certain descent systems, cross-cousins are not in the same kin group at all. Much less often, parallel cousins – who are regarded as kin – will be the preferred marriage partners, with the overt intention of keeping property, name, and honor in the family.

Residence

The second principle within kinship systems involves who actually lives together in local domestic groups. Residence is not essential for corporate behavior, but it is definitely a convenience; furthermore, people who do form a residential unit will almost necessarily act corporately. We can thus think of residence as the spatial or geographic element of kinship.

There is a difference between a family or kindred and a household. A family or a **kindred** is roughly all the people to whom a person considers him or herself "related" by blood or marriage. It is not probably or even possibly a residential group, since it is too large and dispersed to live in one house, or even one compound or neighborhood or town. A **household** is all the people who live together "under one roof" and act corporately within that residence. Obviously, just as not all of a family or kindred shares one household, not all of the people who share a household need be family or kindred; people can and do live in non-kin residential groups, as when a collection of roommates share a house or apartment. They may still be corporate in the sense of preparing and consuming food, owning property, and sharing responsibility for expenses, though they are not related by kinship.

Nevertheless, kinship and residence tend to overlap, and undoubtedly most residential groups are also kin groups. Anthropologists, therefore, regard residence as one of the building blocks not only of kinship but of corporateness in general. The kinds of corporate residential groups formed by residence practices will significantly shape society. There is a finite set of possibilities, although they can be mixed and modified in various ways.

1. **Patrilocality or virilocality (*patri* for father or *viri* for man).** The vast majority of societies (approaching 70 percent) normally settled married couples in or near the residence of the man and his family. Men brought their wives into the household, and women left their childhood homes to reside in their husband's household. The resulting household under such a system consisted of related men (fathers and sons, brothers, uncles and nephews, and so on) and their "in-married" wives as well as

Kindred

An ego-centered (that is, reckoned from the perspective of some particular individual) category of persons related by kinship, especially in bilateral societies, including members from "both sides" of the family in older and younger generations.

Household

All the people who live in the same house or compound of houses and act for some or all purposes as a corporate group.

the children they produced together. They might literally all live in one big house, perhaps with separate corners or cooking areas for "nuclear families," or more often in separate houses in a family "compound." Either way, though, it should be no surprise that **patrilocality** tended to enhance male status and power, since daughters left their parental, patrilocal household to move into their husband's. Thus, men remained to own and control the property, and women lived in places where they did not own and control much of anything. Worse yet, women were sometimes distantly separated from their male kinsmen who could protect and defend them; alone in their husband's household, surrounded by his male kin, women were at a distinct disadvantage.

2. **Matrilocality or uxorilocality** (*matri* for mother or *uxori* for wife). A much smaller percentage (less than 15 percent) of societies advocated that people live in or near the residence of the woman and her family. Women brought their husbands into the home, and men left for their wives' homes. Here, the resulting household contained related women (mothers and daughters, sisters) and their "in-married" husbands and their joint children. **Matrilocality** tended to enhance female status, since, being the consistent factor in the household, women tended to own and control the property, land, and wealth. Men were separated from their own families and allies and cast among related females, and their access to wealth and property might depend on their wife's family. Such an arrangement would be conducive to horticultural economies, where women often formed important land-holding and farm-laboring corporate groups.

3. **Avunculocality** (*avuncu* for uncle). In a distinctly small number of societies (perhaps 4 percent), married people preferentially lived with or near the man's mother's brother. **Avunculocality** was essentially an adaptation to male property rights in a society that traced group membership through women (see below). In such a system, a man's maternal uncle was a kinsman in a way that his paternal uncle was not; the effect was to live with the most important male relative in the kinship universe.

4. **Ambilocality** (*ambi* for both or either). Somewhat more often (9 percent), married people were either free to choose which household to live with or elected to divide their time between the two households. **Ambilocality** was a useful adaptation for societies that lived in difficult environments or low-yield economies, which gave them maximal flexibility in their living arrangements. One place we might expect to find it, then, was in foraging societies, where nuclear families may need to travel and camp with the man's family at certain times and the woman's family at others.

5. **Neolocality** (*neo* for new). In a surprisingly small minority of societies (5 percent), married people were expected or preferred to start a new household on their own, apart from either family. While this is the norm in most Western societies, that fact simply reinforces the awareness that those ways, although they are familiar and "right" to Westerners, are often quite exceptional among the cultures of the world. **Neolocal** residence tends to produce small households, since families "fission" into

Patrilocality
The residence practice of living with or near the husband's family after marriage.

Matrilocality
The residence practice of living with or near the wife's family after marriage.

Avunculocality
A residence practice in which a married couple lives with or near an uncle, often a mother's brother.

Ambilocality
A residence practice in which individuals may live after marriage with both "sides" of the family (perhaps alternating between them), or optionally with one or the other.

Neolocality
The residence practice in which married people start their own household apart from their parents' or families' households.

nuclear units, and it also requires or breeds a unique mentality that values privacy, individuality, and mobility. It further requires a fair amount of wealth, since it is not cheap to own and supply a home for each marital couple. Accordingly, neolocal residence is suited to intensive agriculture and perhaps even more to industrial and post-industrial societies. Not only are individuals and nuclear families fairly rich and independent, but labor needs to be mobile, since the family may be called upon to relocate in search of work. Neolocal households also maximize consumption, since each household requires a complete set of furnishings.

Within these ideal types, considerable variation and complication exists. According to their ethnographers, neither the Ulithi (Pacific Islands) nor the Dani (New Guinea) had residential nuclear families. The Ulithi nuclear family was not a "commensal" group; that is, they did not eat together; eating arrangements and living arrangements did not overlap in any serious way (Lessa 1966). Heider asserts that the Dani lived in multi-family compounds and that it was "hopeless even to try to generalize about the composition's population. One can find unrelated nuclear families, polygynous families, families extended vertically into three or even four generations or laterally with siblings and cousins, as well as the odd singleton unrelated to anyone" (1979: 76). Cheyenne nuclear or conjugal families were organized into what Hoebel called kindreds, which were matrilocal groups that camped together; these kindreds were further aggregated into "bands," of which there were ten, each of which would set up camp in its own area when the whole society gathered.

Descent

Descent

The kinship principle of tracing membership in a kin-based corporate group through a sequence of ancestors.

Descent is the third principle in the system of kinship. We described this as the vertical or chronological relationship between the generations, "coming down" from parents to children and beyond. In this sense, descent is an absolutely physical thing; children really are related to their parents and their ancestors. However, what societies choose to do with it – how they construct it to create corporate groups – is cultural and therefore culturally relative.

Societies can create all kinds of different kinship arrangements, but anthropologists have found that they can represent the entire spectrum of such relationships with a kit of only a few symbols and abbreviations. In fact, only six are required to represent most kinship relationships (Figure 8.1).

Δ	a male
○	a female
□	a person of nonspecific gender
=	a marriage
≠	a divorce
|	descent or connection between parents and children (can be "branched" to additional children)

FIGURE 8.1 Kinship notation

Thus, in order to diagram a simple nuclear family, we can draw a triangle linked to a circle by two parallel lines, with a descent line down to one or more children, which can "branch" as often as necessary. In order to show siblings for the parents we can draw branches above them; and in order to show multiple generations (say, the grandparents or grandchildren) we can add descent lines above or below the nuclear generations depicted. To represent a deceased kinsperson, anthropologists place a slash mark through that person's symbol.

It is also useful to have shorthand abbreviations for the "absolute" relationships between people, rather than invoking ethnocentric and loaded kinship terms like "uncle" or "cousin." For more complex and inclusive kinship diagrams, we can describe literal relationships with a limited set of letters (Figure 8.2).

M	for mother	H	for husband	MBW	for mother's brother's wife
F	for father	W	for wife		
S	for son	MBD	for mother's brother's daughter	FF	for father's father
D	for daughter			and so on	
B	for brother	FZS	for father's sister's son		
Z	for sister				

FIGURE 8.2 Kinship abbreviations

With this vocabulary, it is possible to specify relationships like "father's brother" (FB) or "mother's brother" (MB) instead of "uncle" – which might be an important difference in a society. Likewise, it is possible to distinguish precisely between "cousins" – "father's brother's son" (FBS) versus "mother's sister's daughter" (MZD) – or any other combination of relationships.

All societies use descent in at least some way to assign children to parents and to assign children and their parents to corporate groups. However, not all societies formalize descent into exclusive groups such that an individual belongs to one such group and not to another. When such exclusive groups are created and used, anthropologists call them descent groups. The easiest and most common way for a society to do this is through **unilineal descent**, that is, tracing a single "line" of related ancestors based on a shared characteristic, particularly sex. Not all, but a majority (around 60 percent), of societies utilize the concept of unilineal descent to create corporate groups that include some people and exclude others. The disadvantage of such systems is that they do exclude some kin; the advantage is that they draw incredibly sharp lines of distinction between who is and who is not a "member" of the group. The two obvious alternatives in unilineal descent are patrilineal and matrilineal.

Patrilineal descent is where membership in the kin corporate group is reckoned through a line of male ancestors. That is to say, children belong to their father's corporate group, not to their mother's. They of course know who their mother is, and they recognize her as a close relative, but she is not a member of "their group" as is their father. All siblings will belong to the same group – called a **lineage** – since they

Unilineal descent
A principle in which individuals trace their ancestry through a "line" of related kin (typically a male or a female line) such that some "blood" relatives are included in the descent group or lineage and other relatives are excluded from it.

Patrilineal descent
A descent system in which lineage relations are traced through a line of related males. Children belong to their father's corporate group.

Lineage
A kinship-based corporate group composed of members related by descent from a known ancestor.

all have the same father. All other relatives who can trace their relationships through the same line of related men are also members of the lineage, in this case the patrilineage. Thus, all of the father's brothers (FB) are lineage members, as are all of their children (FBS and FBD alike). Females belong to the lineage too, but they do not perpetuate it: a woman's children belong to *their* father's (her husband's) lineage, not her own. Anglo-Americans do not have a formal lineage system, but they do take their surname "patrilineally," at least traditionally. Thus, males continue the "family name" but females do not. Of unilineal descent systems, this is by far the most common (85 percent).

Matrilineal descent is where membership in the kin corporate group is traced through a line of female ancestors. In a reverse image of the patrilineal system, children belong to their mother's group or matrilineage but not to their father's. Siblings belong to the same lineage, but only females will continue it; a man's children belong to *their* mother's lineage. Since the father is not part of his children's lineage, the most important male relative may be their mother's brother (MB), their maternal uncle, who is a member of their matrilineage. However, MB's own children will not be part of the lineage, since they will belong to his wife's lineage. This is a much less common way of reckoning descent (15 percent) but occurs in societies where female-centered families make sense. Ulithi practiced a matrilineal descent system, in which lineages owned land and houses, maintained cooking hearths, and attended to their own ghosts at their own shrines; however, they also practiced patrilocal residence.

In a few, rare instances, societies may employ the descent relationship to create corporate groups but not in a unilineal manner. We refer to such systems as **double descent**, where an individual belongs to both mother's and father's group, sometimes for different purposes. For example, among the Yako of Nigeria, people obtained access to land and forest goods through their father's group but access to other kinds of resources (such as animals and money) through their mother's. About 5 percent of societies did this.

Two other possibilities include **ambilineal descent**, in which, like ambilocal residence, children may be assigned to either group by their parents or may move freely between groups during their lifetimes, and **bilateral descent**, in which children are considered to belong to both "sides" of their family equally. Ambilineal descent, also like ambilocal residence, provides the most flexibility for individuals and families, while bilateral descent is not "lineal" at all in an important sense. That is, this kinship system – which most resembles the American form – does not create "lines" of kin at all but rather "sides" of families and makes the least distinction between them. Some individuals might like their mother's or father's people more than the other, but there is no institutionalized preference. Thus, no "lineage" results at all, but rather the outcome is a kindred – a group of relatives reckoned from the individual's point of view. Like neolocal residence, this form of kinship provides the most independence and mobility.

It is possible for societies to extend the descent principle for creating even larger and more inclusive kinship groupings. The term **clan** is sometimes used to name a corporate group of related lineages, often one which cannot actually specify all of

---

Matrilineal descent

A descent system in which lineage relations are traced through a line of related females. Children belong to their mother's corporate group.

Double descent

The kinship practice of reckoning one's membership in kinship-based corporate groups through two lines of descent, ordinarily the mother's and the father's.

Ambilineal descent

A descent system in which individuals trace their membership through both "sides" or "lines" of the family, or optionally through one or the other.

Bilateral descent

Relating to both "sides," as in a kinship system, in which individuals regard kin related to the mother and to the father as socially equivalent.

Clan

A kinship group, sometimes an assortment of lineages, whether or not it can trace its descent back to a common ancestor.

the lineal links between the members; the "founding" member may also not be remembered or may be "mythical" (a spirit or animal, for instance). When two or more clans are conjoined, we have a **phratry**. And in a few cases, the various kin groups of a society may be agglomerated into two halves such that the entire society is bifurcated for at least some (perhaps ritual) purposes. We refer to such a "half of a society," the highest possible level of corporateness short of an entire society, as a **moiety**, which is often exogamous.

These institutions can also be surprisingly diverse. Dani society contained fifty clan-like entities, which were not territorial but did share corporate interests in marriage and ritual. These clans were combined into two named patrimoieties, called *Wida* and *Waija*. The moieties were exogamous, but strangely all children were born into the *Wida* side; around puberty, children of the other moiety were transferred to it (Heider 1979: 64). Barabaig patrlineages were organized into clans called *dosht* which Klima describes as territorial "mutual aid societies" that looked after their members (39). The sixty or so named clans were mostly autonomous, sharing few interests or institutions, and were divided into two types (not moieties), the five priestly *Daremgadyeg* clans and the fifty-five secular or "commoner" *Homat'k* clans. We will mention Warlpiri moieties later.

Phratry
A kinship-based corporate group composed of two or more clans that recognize common ancestry.

Moiety
One of the "halves" of a society, when kin groups are combined in such a way as to create a binary division within society.

See Seeing Culture as a Whole #2

Kinship terminologies

Since societies vary so widely in how they understand and use kinship relations, it figures that they would vary in how they talk about kin. Every society has a set of kinship terms or names, such as the English "father," "mother," "uncle," "cousin," and so on. Of course, what one society calls a "cousin" might not be called, or treated like, a cousin in another. The physical relationships that underlie any set of terms are the same; however, how those "blood" or physical relationships are valued and used diverges greatly by culture.

There is an almost infinite variety of permutations on kinship terminology, but there is a basic set of six systems that societies then modify or customize according to their local needs and interests. Use the kinship chart (Figure 8.3) to make sense of these systems described below.

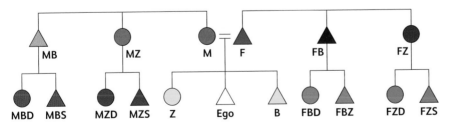

FIGURE 8.3 A generic kinship chart

1. **Hawaiian**. This common (about one-third of societies) terminology is nearly the simplest possible one, in which a very limited set of terms is used to make a very

limited set of distinctions. There are only four main terms – two for the parent's generation (one male, one female, approximately equivalent to "father" and "mother") and two for one's own generation (again, one male, one female, roughly "brother" and "sister"). So, what English speakers would call "uncle" (both MB and FB) would be called by the same term as father, "aunt" (MZ and FZ) would be called by the same term as mother, and all "cousins" would be called by the terms for brother and sister.

2. **Omaha**. This system represents a patrilineal naming convention. Parallel cousins are called by the same term as brothers and sisters, but cross-cousins are called by different terms. Even more, cross-cousins on the mother's side (MBS and MBD) are called by different terms – the same as for M and MB, respectively – than those on the father's side (FBS and FBD). Finally, FB is called by the same term as F, and MZ is called by the same term as M, but FZ and MB are called by different terms, roughly equivalent to "aunt" and "uncle."

3. **Crow**. The Crow system is the prototype of a matrilineal naming convention. The same basic logic applies as in the Omaha, but in mirror reversal. Mother and MZ are termed the same, father and FB are termed the same, and FZ and MB each get a unique term. Parallel cousins are all called "brother" or "sister," and FZ's children are referred to by the same term as FB and FZ.

4. **Iroquois**. This system is similar to the two unilineal systems above, with one major exception. Cross-cousins on both sides (MB's children and FZ's children) are called by the same two terms – essentially, what we might translate as "male cousin" and "female cousin." Parallel cousins are still designated as "brother" and "sister."

5. **Sudanese**. This "descriptive" system is the hardest to commit to memory but the easiest to understand. It makes the most possible distinctions, using a different term for each relationship and collapsing no relationships into others; MB is not the same as FB, and so on, and every possible variation of "cousin" is given a different name (that is, FBS and FZS are termed differently, *ad infinitum*).

6. **Eskimo**. Fairly uncommon (at about 10 percent of societies) is the system that most resembles the Anglo-American one. Here, no distinctions are made between cross- and parallel cousins (that is, between "sides" of the family) nor between their parents. FB and MB are called by the same term (e.g., "uncle"), as are FZ and MZ (e.g., "aunt"). All cousins are distinguished by only one feature, sex (and in English not even by that – there are no English words that distinguish "male cousin" from "female cousin," like the French *cousin* and *cousine* or the Spanish *primo* and *prima*). The key kinship unit based on the terminology is the nuclear family.

These diverse systems may seem odd and impenetrable, yet each is a "language" for talking about the society's kinship reality. The key point is to appreciate that different societies have reasons to make the terminological distinctions that they do. That is, the kinship terminology of a society is a way of expressing things that are important (or not expressing things that are unimportant or not even "there") for them.

We can think, therefore, of a kinship terminology as a kind of language or code for important cultural aspects of family and kinship. Rather than naming people, they are naming relationships: the "cousin" relationship or the "uncle" relationship indicates a certain kind of role, feeling, and even social duty. A person would expect to feel generally the same and behave generally the same toward two different "cousins." However, s/he might feel and behave differently toward an "uncle" than toward a cousin, and definitely toward a "father" or "mother" than toward a cousin. So, ultimately, we may think of a kinship terminology system as naming the different socially recognized and socially important kinship roles in society. If an individual calls two different people by the same term, then that individual's role toward them should be the same and their role toward him or her should be the same. On the other hand, if an individual calls two different people by two different terms, then his or her and their roles should be different. This is what we meant by "collapsing" different kin into the same term: if I call MB and FB by the same term, then they are culturally equivalent for me. I know that they are not the same person, but what is important is how I am supposed to act toward them and they toward me. And if I call MB and FB by different terms, that indicates a culturally relevant distinction between those two kinsmen.

Some of the factors that are "coded" into a system of terms – or more significantly, the statuses they name – are:

■ Generation – are they in my own, my parents', my children's generation?
■ Sex or gender – are they male or female? Or, in some cases, are they the same sex as me or the opposite sex than me (relative gender)? For instance, Ulithi did not have terms that mean "brother" or "sister" but rather "sibling of my sex" or "sibling not of my sex."
■ Blood vs. marriage – are they kin by descent or by marriage? In the American system, members do not even distinguish between, say, MB and MZH.
■ "Side of the family" – are they on the mother's side or the father's side? This is not a very important distinction in American society. However, when laterality becomes lineality, it is important in a society to know which side the kinsman falls on. This is seen in the Omaha and Crow systems, where who is "in my lineage" and who is not is a serious concern.
■ Age or relative age – are they older or younger? Or are they older or younger than me? Warlpiri, for example, has distinct terms for older brother (*papardi*) and younger brother (*kukurnu*).
■ Marital status – are they married, single, widowed?

In other words, the "logic" of a kinship system can be decoded – the kinship terminology can be "read" – if we realize what social and kinship distinctions are made and are central in a society. Or, by reading the system, we can decipher what distinctions are made and central. In the U.S.A., for instance, the same terms are applied identically to both "sides." Americans do not care about age in particular, so they do not encode that distinction. In this, the American kinship system reflects the same social order that American language and honorifics does: social distinctions are not very extensive and not very important. If a society does make big distinctions (like lineage-mates and nonlineage-mates), it must and will have a way to talk about them.

NON-KINSHIP-BASED CORPORATE GROUPS

The "facts" and principles of marriage, residence, and descent exist in (nearly) all societies, and those societies use them – in unique and creative ways – to assign people to groups and to give those groups common tasks, common interests, and common identity. An observer might think that this would be enough structure for a society, but even in the smallest societies, other groupings are used too. Why would a society go on to elaborate non-kinship kinds of corporate groups too? There are probably at least three reasons.

1. Kinship-based corporate groups may not be large enough or dispersed enough to handle all the tasks and "corporate duties" required in a society.
2. Kinship-based corporate groups alone might tend to fragment society into horizontally divided identity and interest groups with little common identity or interest, turning them into competitive or even conflictual groups. Of course, this can happen anyway, but a society may benefit from "cross-cutting" groups that bring together members of divergent kinship groups in various kinds of non-kinship collectivities. Such cross-cutting or "vertical" groups provide more social "glue" or integration.
3. Other non-kinship kinds of traits and identities exist, so society may as well use them. In other words, all humans have characteristics besides kinship that they share with other humans and by which they may be classified and organized.

There are many such traits or categories available in any society and many ways to exploit them where they are found. The following are some of these traits and some of the kinds of corporate groups that are constructed around them. In addition to those groups and traits discussed below, race and ethnicity are also vital organizing factors.

See Chapter 6

Sex or gender

The most universal and fundamental social distinction across cultures is based on sex or gender: the "gender division of labor," for example, creates productive groups out of the sexes. Men or women widely comprise sex-specific work details, as when foraging men ventured together to hunt or foraging women formed parties to gather. Among the Abkhasians of Georgia, a territory in the Caucasus and formerly part of the Soviet Union, local men assembled into voluntary work cooperatives or *kiaraz* (literally "self-help") to tend each other's fields in order of need (e.g., ripeness of crop, weediness of land). According to Benet (1974), each task that the *kiaraz* performed had a name and a song, and the group would divide into teams to compete in races and contests during work breaks; also, if it passed a widow's land, it would tend her fields for her. Finally, the group also functioned as a militia and as a lawcourt, with powers to confiscate property or even assign the death penalty.

In other societies, men and women would each have their particular spaces and prerogatives. We saw how the Sambia kept a men's house in the village. The Konyak Nagas in India, like many others around the world, also had a men's house institution, or *ban*, which functioned as a dormitory for older boys and unmarried men. Actually, each village might have several of these, associated with a neighborhood or ward of the village; some were large and ornate, with fancy carvings and a large drum or gong. Women were not totally forbidden from entering and in fact did enter on ceremonial occasions. Otherwise, the *ban* was corporate in many ways, including social, economic, legal, and ritual. It held joint ownership of land as well as of "symbolic property" such as songs, dances, and decorations; it cultivated land together, defended and avenged its interests, and collected wealth for tribute. It also made up the core of the political system, sending officials (*niengba*) from each *ban* to sit with the chief as a village council, while other officers (*benba*) conducted rituals and sacrifices. Women also had a site, the *yo*, that served as a dormitory for young unmarried girls (Von Fuerer-Haimendorf 1969).

See Chapter 5

The Cheyenne offered an assortment of military associations for men. In the early nineteenth century there were five named associations (Fox, Elk, Shield, Dog, and Bow-String or "Contrary"), with two more added later (Wolf and Crazy Dogs). Young males were free to join any of the groups, which were not formally stratified (although they might rise and fall in prestige based on their achievements). Each group was essentially a private army, with its own symbols, dances, songs, history, and internal organization; they could in fact conduct private raids and wars, or act together as a tribal police force and army (Hoebel 1960).

Not all societies have demonstrated the same degree of segregation and stratification between the sexes, but some degree of "camaraderie" between sex-mates is common if not universal. From the National Organization of Women or the League of Women Voters to sex-specific sports teams to the modern "women's spirituality" movement, women in modern societies often meet and act corporately, as do men, who have done so for a very long time in their "old boy networks" and "smoke-filled rooms."

Age

The second natural characteristic on which to build groups or to develop affiliation is age, and all societies employ it to some extent: every society has "adult" and "child" roles and rights. Americans consider child labor, child alcohol consumption, child sexuality, and child driving inappropriate or even illegal. There is a virtual "youth subculture" in the West (and increasingly around the world) that is very influential in cultural trends and tastes. And of course young people are assembled into age-based groups or "grades" or "classes" in school, which may affect their entire lives. Many graduates of educational institutions feel an attachment to their classmates long after school is over, and many societies mark the transition from one stage of life to another with ceremonies and rituals, or "rites of passage." From the Jewish tradition of *bar mitzvah* for boys to the Australian Aboriginal (and other) ceremony of circumcision, rituals especially relate to the attainment of adulthood; recall that some societies, like the Sambia, believed that a boy could not become a man "naturally" but only through cultural and ritual intervention.

Age grade system

A non-kinship-based corporate system in which members, usually of one sex, are organized into groups or "grades" according to age and assigned roles and values as a group.

Other societies have elaborated and formalized the idea of age-based corporateness, as in the so-called **age grade system**. Particularly common in pastoral societies, boys might be assigned in their early childhood to an age set along with their peers. At a certain age, depending on the society, they moved together as a group into the next stage or grade of life, sometimes given new labors to perform, new tools to use, and even new names. The transition between grades might be ritualized, especially the transition to the grade of adult, which was often the grade of warriors. The Maasai (east Africa) possessed a basic system with three grades, roughly equivalent to "youth," "warrior" (*moran*), and "elder." Males in the *moran* grade lived apart in a *manyatta* where they acted as the standing army of the society (Leakey 1930).

PLATE 8.3 At age fifteen, a Mexican girl would traditionally celebrate her *quinceañera*, at which she was introduced to adult society

The Dinka (east Africa) held an initiation ceremony for males around age 16, at which time they were assigned to an age set with a designated "father" for the group who named it, thus bringing it into existence. During the initiation, boys received deep cuts across their foreheads and moved into a separate village for several months. They received new rights, including the right to dance and flirt with girls, as well as new responsibilities, including adult expectations of courage and aggressiveness tempered with dignity and self-control. Most importantly, they became warriors. As they matured they remained forever connected to their age set, although its corporateness faded over time; marriage weakened it, as corporateness was transferred to the kin unit, and by old age it had almost disappeared. Women also had age sets, but they ceased to act corporately at marriage (Deng 1972).

PLATE 8.4 Members of the *moran* or warrior age-set among the Samburu of Kenya

---

BOX 8.2 FEMALE AGE GRADES IN HIDATSA CULTURE

The Hidatsa, a people of the Northern Plains of North America, had formal age grades for both men and women in which the latter were at least as important as the former. As a horticultural, matrilocal, and matrilineal society, they placed more emphasis on women than did many other societies. Accordingly, there were four named grades for women (each with a male counterpart), starting with the "Skunk Society" at age 12 and extending to about age 20, whose main role was to dance following successful wars. Young married women (age 20 to 30) moved into the "Enemy Society," which also had responsibilities following wars. From age 30 to 40, women joined the "Goose Society," a prestigious level concerned with fertility, farming success, and the annual return of migratory birds. Women who attained seniority were eligible for the "White Buffalo Society," charged with caring for certain sacred objects (medicine bundles) and with bringing the buffalo to the people. Altogether, this system not only conferred status on women but served as a social network through which they enjoyed guidance while youths, and comradeship and support while adults.

Common interest

Any number of other shared traits or interests might form the basis for grouping of a more or less corporate nature. In modern societies these are frequently fairly trivial and short term; a person might belong to a service organization, fraternity/sorority, professional association, labor union, activist group, political party, church congregation, and so on. Some of these might have deep and abiding meaning for members, some might not. They are for the most part voluntary groupings, which one is not compelled to join (although there may be real social pressure to join a particular group or at least some group). And of course individuals can belong to more than one common interest group simultaneously – this church, that club, the other professional association. This situates each individual at a unique intersection of group identities and interests.

In a certain sense, all human groups are interest groups, since, among other things, they all have shared interests too. Although it is controversial among scholars and activists, it is at least partly appropriate to regard ethnic and racial and nationalist groups as interest groups, since they may definitely feel and/or be treated like "one people" and act accordingly to advance the corporate interests. Often, if not usually, the discourse of such groups is that of "family," of a large, natural kinship group linked by "blood" and history – a kind of super-clan – but this is not always the factual situation; instead, like other mega-groups such as nations or ethnic groups, these collectivities are often what Anderson (1983) called "imagined communities." That is, while the group identities are founded on some shared "real" physical or historical characteristics, the meanings and values of those characteristics are culturally defined and deployed, and almost certainly the group is too large to ever meet or interact as one. Nevertheless, membership in or assignment to such a group, or to a category on which such a group is based, can significantly affect the quality of one's life.

Socio-economic status or class

One last major social characteristic that individuals may share and orient themselves around is **class** or socio-economic status. Class is different from the other traits and groupings we have discussed in that it tends to be, if not by definition, "vertical" or socially hierarchical. Again, not all societies exhibit this quality, but most did and do, from the moment of the appearance of the first economic surplus and the social and political distinctions that arise from it. This economic, social, and political inequality results in a system of **social stratification**, in which society is divided into discrete and unequal groups in terms of their access to wealth, power, and prestige. Each "position" or level within a stratified society is identifiable as a class, with its social and economic characteristics and opportunities and burdens. Societies that evidence this stratification are called stratified societies, and those that do not are called egalitarian societies.

Exactly how many classes exist in a society and their respective rules and roles vary and are subject to dispute. The U.S.A. is commonly regarded as much less class-conscious than the U.K.: only the U.K. has a "royal" class. Some analysts in the U.S.A., when they even acknowledge a class division, break it down into lower, middle, and upper classes, sometimes with a lower, middle, and upper substratum within each class (hence, "lower middle class" or "upper lower class"). The details depend on the definitions of each. The greater point is that individuals do face different life chances based on their position in the socio-economic system and that their position is in turn determined by other social and cultural factors, such as education, age, race, gender, and so on. In fact, we can speak of two general ways in which one's position or status is determined in a stratified society:

1. **Ascribed status** – The status is determined by "birth" or by "nature" – literally "written on" the individual (although it is of course still given cultural sig-

---

See Chapters 6 and 13

Anderson, Benedict. 1983. *Imagined Communities: Reflections of the Origin and Spread of Nationalism.* London: Verso.

Class

An (at least ideally) open socio-economic status, which members can change through their own achievements.

Social stratification

The division of a society into distinct and unequal groups or classes.

Ascribed status

A social characteristic that is attributed to a person without any effort on their part, either innate (e.g., sex or race) or acquired in the normal course of development (e.g., age).

nificance). An ascribed status cannot be changed much, if at all, through the efforts of the individual.

2. **Achieved status** – The status is the result of some effort or action of the individual. It can, therefore, at least in principle be changed in a person's lifetime, although this possibility may be difficult to realize.

Any individual will occupy at one time a combination of ascribed and achieved statuses: for example, one may be female, white, and a certain age (ascribed) while simultaneously being married, college-educated, and an anthropologist (achieved). The sum or product of these statuses and their relative weight in a given society will place the individual in a particular socio-economic status.

The important question is which status(es) most powerfully determine one's place in society, i.e., whether the ascribed statuses outweigh or trump the achieved statuses or vice versa. The answer to this question will define the **social mobility** in the society; that is, the extent to which one can change one's position in the stratification system. If there are few, or few meaningful, statuses that one can achieve, then one is socially immobile and one's position is settled once and for all. We refer to societies organized in this way as "closed societies," and the positions within them are "closed classes" or even **castes**. If there are many and meaningful achieved statuses, then people can be quite socially mobile and one's socio-economic position is a momentary result of those achievements. We call such societies "open societies" and the positions within them "open classes" or simply classes. Of course, one's ideal mobility is up, but social mobility includes the possibility of negative mobility – moving down in the stratification system.

Achieved status
A social position or role that a person acquires through some effort or accomplishment of his or her own.

Social mobility
The possibility or ease with which one may change position in the social stratification system.

Caste
A closed socio-economic status, often ascribed by birth.

BOX 8.3 THE INDIAN CASTE SYSTEM

The best-known closed or caste system is that of India, in which caste membership is ascribed at birth. It would not be quite correct to say that membership is ascribed "by" birth, although usually one belongs to the caste of one's parents. However, you are not in your caste because you are born to certain parents; rather, you are born to certain parents because you are in your caste. Castes, or *jatis*, represent a combination of economic, kinship, political, and religious elements. You do share your caste with your kin and most immediately inherit it from them. Your occupation or economic contribution is also defined by caste: castes are, in fact, occupational groups. Beals (1980) reports that Gopalpur had fifty different *jatis* resident in or passing through the village, each with its own role, including priest, farmer, blacksmith, salt-maker, barber, butcher, stoneworker, leatherworker, and so on. While these were clearly economic roles, he notes that there was no direct correlation between the wealth of an individual or group and his or her or its caste: any person in any *jati* might be rich or poor, and there were as many rich shepherds and farmers as there were rich priests in the village. Rather, the defining feature of a *jati* was its spiritual condition – its ritual purity and spiritual cleanliness. Humans who were "purer" as a result of behaviors in their past lives were born into higher *jatis*, and those who were more "impure" were born into lower ones. The lowest castes did the dirtiest work, including handling dead (animals and human) bodies and other unclean substances. Castes might live in separate neighborhoods and observe different social rules and restrictions (like the eating rules in the prior chapter), and members of the same *jati* might consider themselves to be – and often were – kin.

In their individualistic and achievement-oriented society, Americans like to think that everyone can "make it" and that all it takes is hard work but that if a person does not succeed then this is somehow his or her own fault. Their "rugged individualism" suggests to them that each person can and does rise and fall on his or her own merits. This attitude has been diluted somewhat by the creation of a "welfare" system in which those who "have" contribute to the maintenance of those who "have not" – a kind of formal and obligatory "mutual support system" based, at least in part, on a notion of common "kinship" as Americans, of being "a family" that takes care of its own.

The real controversy in the U.S.A. over social mobility is whether or not some real persistent social factors prevent some individuals as members of groups from achieving the "American dream." The most overt of these factors is race or ethnicity, leading to calls for "affirmative action" to correct the "closed" nature of racial/ethnic stratification and counter-calls of "reverse discrimination." This is not an easy problem to settle. There seems to be little doubt that there are still differences of opportunity that lead to differences of outcome, based on ascribed characteristics not only of race and ethnicity but of gender and age and even of physical appearance (so-called "lookism") as well. But the question is much broader than that. The "ideology" of social mobility may not match the reality, and this is a general and important cultural fact. Societies do not always entirely see or understand themselves clearly and may take ideals for actualities. A study of American incomes from 1967 to 1991 (Gittleman and Joyce 1995) came to two conclusions – that the income gap between rich and poor had actually widened during those years, and that mobility was actually less common than one would think. While it is possible to change one's position in the social stratification system (at least as indicated by wealth), it was not easy to improve one's situation and it did not happen all that often. Unhappily but not surprisingly, those who were most likely to be and to stay in the lower ranks of the system were the young, the uneducated, and the non-white. So, while the class structure of the United States is not "closed," it is "stiff" – and more so for some than for others.

BOX 8.4 CONTEMPORARY CULTURAL CONTROVERSIES: GAY MARRIAGE IN THE U.S.A.

One of the most intense cultural debates in the United States, as in some other Western societies, concerns the institution of marriage, particularly the access of homosexual couples to the institution. The dispute has many sources, including cultural opposition to the very idea of homosexuality: the Judeo-Christian scriptures do in fact provide passages condemning the practice; until 1973 the American Psychiatric Association listed it as a mental disorder; and in 1971 twenty U.S. states still had laws making it a crime. Today, many gay couples live openly in long-term committed, loving relationships and assert the individual right to marry, but opponents of gay marriage often claim to be "protecting marriage" by restricting it to heterosexuals. Some even seek to use the political system to establish kinship regulations by, for instance, adding an amendment to the Constitution defining marriage. Advocates of so-called "traditional marriage," while frequently missing the facts of "traditional" marriage in Western society (see above), also miss the fact that marriage, like every other institution in society, is a cultural construction: marriage was defined and practiced differently in the past and elsewhere in the world, and it will be defined and practiced differently in the future. Marriage is, more literally than most, a "social contract" which humans make and modify; the struggle is over how precisely a society will make or modify it. What do you think?

SUMMARY

A society must assign individuals names, identities, roles, interests, and statuses. This entails establishing and perpetuating corporate groups. Kinship is one universal way of making and maintaining such groups but not the only way. A kinship system is a confluence of three principles:

- Marriage
- Residence
- Descent.

Within each of these principles are numerous sub-issues with considerable area for diversity in each, and the forms they take and the interconnections they make significantly shape the experience of the society, in particular gender, domestic, and property relations.

In addition to kinship principles, non-kinship characteristics and commonalities can be and are widely used to create corporate groups and allot tasks, roles, and social meaning and values. Some of the traits that humans share and that can be used to build groups and categories include:

- Sex or gender
- Age

- Race
- Common interest
- Class or socio-economic status.

Any individual in a society will occupy a complex and sometimes contradictory constellation of positions with regard to all of these kin and non-kin categories, which will affect their opportunities and often their outcomes in social life.

Key Terms

Achieved status	Levirate
Age grade system	Lineage
Ambilineal descent	Marriage
Ambilocality	Matrilineal descent
Arranged marriage	Matrilocality
Ascribed status	Moiety
Avunculocality	Monogamy
Bilateral descent	Neolocality
Bride service	Patrilineal descent
Bridewealth/brideprice	Patrilocality
Caste	Phratry
Clan	Polyandry
Class	Polygyny
Corporate group	Preferential cousin marriage
Descent	Residence
Double descent	Serial monogamy
Dowry	Social mobility
Endogamy	Social reproduction
Exogamy	Social stratification
Household	Sororal polygyny
Hypergamy	Sororate
Incest taboo	Unilineal descent
Kindred	

Politics: Social Order and Social Control

Among the Semai, a reportedly non-violent people, the very idea of seeking authority over other individuals violated the spirit of their culture. According to Dentan (1968) they said that to pressure others was to *persusah* them, and this led to the unpleasant experience of *punan* for both parties. This extended to children: adults did not pester them with commands any more than adults pestered each other. This did not lead to social chaos, however, since members of the society shared basic standards of behavior not to mention values about power (or the lack thereof). People generally acted well because they learned that it was important, for others as for themselves, to act well. And people respected even if they did not always obey their elders or *rana'*; obedience was not necessary for the smooth operation of their society. In such small and egalitarian groups, personal relations and public opinion were as effective as anything in maintaining order. Kinship was one process by which people were made to do the right thing. In terms of influencing others, two critical dimensions were generosity and verbal skill. A generous person was a popular person, although even a generous person had to be subtle and not too overt, or else people would suspect his or her motives. And speaking abilities – proficiency with metaphors and jokes and proverbs and irony – could make or break one's "political" position.

When Westerners think of politics they usually think of governments and laws and police and courts – all of the formal institutions of power and authority in modern societies. These, like the factories and markets and money of economics, are one type or manifestation of politics but not the essence or definition of it. That is, governments and courts are one way but not the only or universal way of doing politics. In fact, as we will discover below, they may not be the predominant form of politics even in complex modern "political" societies.

The word "politics" originally derives from the ancient Greek *polis* or city, referring to the proper organization of the city or city-state and the proper behavior of its citizens. Not all societies, of course, have lived in cities, but that is beside the point. The city in ancient Greece was the total society, and politics was the total way of life in that society. This is why Aristotle called humans a "political" species – because humans live in societies and must order themselves to be able to co-exist and cooperate in social groups.

Politics broadly conceived, then, refers to the cultural ideas, norms, values, and practices that regulate how people interact in an orderly and (more or less) mutually beneficial manner. This may involve formal, specialized, and large-scale institutions, like a congress or parliament, where the rules and laws of the society are formulated and propagated; it may involve informal, generalized, and nearly socially invisible norms and relationships that do not appear "political" at first glance. In most – or all – cases, it will involve both, and often the latter more than the former.

It may be more profitable to think of "political functions" than of "politics" proper, since in many societies (like the Semai) politics may not be distinguished from other social and cultural rules and roles, and in no society is it *totally* distinguished from them. Other parts of culture, including kinship and potentially economics – and certainly religion – and even language and gender, have political functions and implications as well, if by that we mean informing people of the expected ways to behave and enforcing those ways. Thus, while we identify politics as a distinct "floor" or domain of our house of culture, we must remember that its functions may be and by and large are distributed throughout the social system – and that politics probably works better for being so distributed. Therefore, our job in this chapter is to consider the political functions that any society must accomplish, the various ways in which a society may accomplish them, and the relations between the "political" aspects of the culture and all its other components.

SOCIAL CONTROL: THE FUNCTIONS OF POLITICS

Culture is by definition learned and shared ways of thinking, feeling, and behaving. Without these shared ways, members of society could not interact effectively, since they would not be able to anticipate what others are going to do, to interpret what they actually do, or to respond appropriately. Culture is a shared communicative and behavioral environment – a kind of all-embracing language of social life and social reality. In the normal course of social living, various kinds of problems and challenges arise that demand attention and resolution, if the society is to continue living harmoniously, if at all. These issues include:

- decision-making
- norm/rule/law creation
- dispute resolution
- norm/rule/law enforcement
- deviance punishment
- social integration
- defense of community and society
- aggression/offense against other communities and societies.

We might think of all of these issues in tandem as the problem of "social control" – directing members of the group to perform their duties, follow the established norms, and do "the right thing" as defined by the society. (Who does the defining is a prime concern for anthropology as well as for the members of the society.)

Social control refers to the various types and sources of social pressures that are brought to bear on individuals to get them to do, as individuals or as members of specific groups and categories, what the society demands and expects them to do. In its more sinister guise, which really exists often enough in the human world, social control is the imposition of one person's or group's will on others: inducing members of society (the ones under the "political control" of the dominant person or group) to do what the "leadership" wants them to do. In other, more benign versions, it is simply what is necessary for successful communal co-existence.

Social control can take two very different though related forms. The logically and chronologically prior form involves the actions of others upon the individual. Before any particular individual is born, the rules and norms and institutions of society already exist, and humans, for the most part, conform to them. Therefore, the other people who came before us and who introduced us and enculturated us into social expectations are the "authorities" of the society. They control – or perhaps it would be more accurate to say, they represent – the terms of the society, and they, like all of culture, are "before" and "outside" of us. Anthropologists refer to this factor as **externalized control**, the creation and enforcement of socially appropriate behavior by persons, groups, or institutions outside of the individual. Such persons, groups, or institutions are **agents of social control**, and every society abounds with them. They consist of such roles or positions as parents, peers, priests, professors, police, prison guards, parole officers, and presidents and prime ministers. When a person does "right," these agents can provide positive responses, but when a person does "wrong," the agents can give negative feedback, from instruction to punishment. Hopefully and usually, the individual gets the idea and begins to voluntarily conform to expectations, even to accept and believe in them. However, in every society in some way or another, agents of social control stand over society to make sure that compliance occurs.

The second source of control, one that is related to and dependent on the first, is **internalized control**, the process by which the individual controls his or her own behavior in conformity with rules or norms or standards. This is by far the most efficient form of social control, since no society can have a policeman or a guard

Social control
The political and general social function of getting members of a group to conform to expectations and rules and to obey authorities. Includes inculcating of social values as well as punishment of deviance from expectations.

Externalized control
The source of social control that lies outside of the individual, in the form of individuals, groups, and institutions with the power to sanction behavior, such as parents, teachers, police, governments, and so on.

Agents of social control
Individuals, groups, or roles that play a part in instilling social norms in members and protecting and perpetuating those norms through the use of their powers and sanctions.

Internalized control
A form or source of social control in which individuals make themselves conform to social expectations through the internalization of rules and norms; by enculturation, social rules and norms become part of the personalities of members.

See Chapter 2

See Chapter 5

monitoring every member every moment of the day. Fortunately, most people most of the time do not require monitoring to ensure their compliance. They conform quite voluntarily – because they come to think it is the right thing to do. The key to internalized control is enculturation. The whole point of enculturation is the learning or acquisition of one's culture. What this "acquisition" means is that society's rules, norms, values, beliefs, and so on get "inside" the individual; they become part of that individual's personality.

As a result of enculturation and the internalization of culture, the individual "has" or "is" (some expression of) the society's culture – not a carbon copy to be sure, but a culturally informed product. S/he shares the sense that what the society deems as right really is right, that what the society deems as reprehensible really is reprehensible. Ideally, no further control would be necessary, since members of the group would not allow themselves to do, perhaps could not imagine themselves doing, those things that they have learned are wrong or evil or shameful. A "conscience" (in Freudian theory, a superego), in other words, some part of the personality or self, stands watch over the individual and makes each one of us feel good when we do (socially) right and bad when we do (socially) wrong. If this form of social control is complete and effective, then little other social control is required.

See Chapter 2

However, internalized social control is often not complete or completely effective. There are many reasons for this. For instance, given the "guided reinvention" quality of culture, it is possible that the individual may be exposed to all the normal rules and pressures and still not learn or internalize the preferred things; s/he might learn or construct an idiosyncratic lesson from cultural experience. In another case, the individual may be exposed to "abnormal" experiences, such as violence or abuse in home life, internalizing a lesson that society would prefer s/he not to do. Individuals may even be enculturated into what some researchers call a "culture of deviance" (for instance, a gang or a criminal environment), in which they acquire "alternate norms" that are deviant by society's standard but "normal" by the subculture's standard. Finally, an individual may internalize all the right norms and values but find that social circumstances do not allow him or her to conduct normal, socially appropriate behavior. As an example, one may possess the "good" values of hard work and frugality and so on, but find oneself in a class or race or ethnic or gender situation where these values do not apply or "work" – where, for example, opportunities for employment or education are absent or blocked.

Sanction

Any type of social pressure in the form of "reward" or "punishment" that can be imposed on people to influence and control their behavior.

When individuals, through their own choices or through social constraints, violate the norms and rules of the group, the agents of social control have specific tools they can utilize, depending on the particular agent, the particular society, and the particular deviance. These tools are called **sanctions**. English speakers tend to think of sanctions as negative things: when the U.S.A. imposes sanctions on a country like Cuba or North Korea, a punishment is intended, which is meant to impel the belligerent countries to change their behavior in more favorable (from the sanctioning agent's point of view) directions. In reality, there are both positive and negative sanctions. Sanctions are merely reactions or responses by others that are intended to affect the sanctioned individual's or group's behavior. Positive sanctions are intended to encourage the individual to repeat "good" behavior, while negative sanctions are intended to discourage them from "bad" behavior.

Sanctions can also be more or less formal. A **formal sanction** is one that is explicit, even "official," and perhaps written down; normally it applies to more serious social infractions, and usually members know exactly what behaviors will unleash it, exactly what the sanction will be, and exactly what agents of social control have the right to impose it. An **informal sanction** is more vague, implicit, and usually not written down. Individuals may have some general sense of what behaviors produce what sanctions, but there may be no specialized agents to administer them. In fact, the right to impose informal sanctions may exist for every member of society.

There are then four possible varieties of sanctions, not all of which are familiar as "political":

- formal positive – for example, rewards and prizes and promotions
- formal negative – for example, jail and fines and, at the extreme, capital punishment
- informal positive – for example, praise and smiles and thanks and inclusion in the group
- informal negative – for example, insults and dirty looks and gossip/ridicule and ostracism.

In trying to think of other examples, the reader may be inclined to conclude that there are more negative sanctions than positive ones; after all, the police seldom stop a driver to congratulate him or her for driving at exactly the speed limit. It may be the case that there are more negative sanctions, depending on the society. It may also be that good behavior, being the ideal and the norm, draws less attention and intervention than bad behavior. Another important point is that members of a society tend to overlook all of the little ways in which they all sanction each other, positively and negatively, every moment of every day. All humans are continuously administering, and having administered to them, sanctions intended to shape the flow of behavior. The classic study of this process is the "elevator experiment," in which subjects intentionally break some minor norm such as standing facing the wrong way in an elevator; it becomes immediately apparent how many norms there are in society, how much people assume that everyone knows and follows them, and the ways in which they can show their disapproval or discomfort when those norms are broken.

The point is that politics is not just something that police and presidents do. Politics in any society is mostly informal and interpersonal, and only secondarily formal and institutional. As humans we live constantly in a "political" environment in which we press others – and they press us – to do the normal, expected, and valued things. We are all agents of social control to the other people in our society, and they are all agents of social control to us. Only when these pervasive political pressures fail, or when someone (like a dictator) appears who wants to change and control the course of society, do we experience clearly and directly the formal side of politics.

Formal sanction
A method of social control employing rewards and punishments that are explicit and well known, often written down, and administered by special agents of control who possess the authority to administer them (such as the police or courts).

Informal sanction
A "reward" or "punishment" that is widely understood in a society but is not precisely defined, usually not written down, and for which no specialized role exists to administer the sanction.

POWER

Every type and instance of sanction is an expression of power. Power is one person's or group's or institution's ability to influence and affect the behavior of others, as well as to influence and affect the disposition of the resources (material and symbolic) of society; power then becomes the capacity to influence the course and outcome of social interactions. When most people think of power, they tend to think of force, but not all exercise of power involves force. In fact, anthropologists have identified three quite different types or sources of power, which are independent but which may simultaneously exist in any society or in any specific role or agent of power. All of these variations of power are social phenomena which depend at least in part on the complicity of those under power, as Hannah Arendt reminds us.

BOX 9.1 HARRAH ARENDT ON POWER AND AUTHORITY

Arendt, Hannah. 1969.
On Violence. New York:
Harcourt, Brace, &
World, Inc.

In her book *On Violence* (1969) Arendt uses the word "power" to mean what we mean by authority in the present discussion, arguing that authority/power is always a relationship between those "in" power and those "under" that power.

> Power corresponds to the human ability not just to act but to act in concert. Power is never the property of an individual; it belongs to a group and remains in existence only so long as the group keeps together. When we say of somebody that he is "in power" we actually refer to his being empowered by a certain number of people to act in their name. The moment the group, from which the power originated to begin with ... disappears, "his power" also vanishes. In current usage, when we speak of a "powerful man" or a "powerful personality," we already use the word "power" metaphorically; what we refer to without metaphor is "strength."

> Authority, relating to the most elusive of these phenomena and therefore, as a term, most frequently abused, can be vested in persons – there is such a thing as personal authority, as, for instance, in the relation between parent and child, between teacher and pupil – or it can be vested in offices, as, for instance, in the Roman senate ... or in the hierarchical offices of the Church. .... Its hallmark is unquestioning recognition by those who are asked to obey; neither coercion nor persuasion is needed. (A father can lose his authority either by beating his child or by starting to argue with him, that is, either by behaving to him like a tyrant or by treating him as an equal.) To remain in authority requires respect for the person or the office, and the surest way to undermine it is laughter.

(44–5)

Authority

Authority may be thought of as "legitimate" power, power that a person or group or institution possesses and uses "rightfully"; Morton Fried defined it as "the ability to channel the behavior of others in the absence of the threat or use of sanctions" (1967: 13). Followers recognize the authority's right to this power and respect and obey it. Authority itself derives from a variety of sources, including physical strength, skill or knowledge, age, education, charisma, or office. Most of these qualities belong to the individual; s/he is strong or knowledgable or has "charisma" or charm. Some individuals seem to possess "charisma" and some do not: President John F. Kennedy was said to be charismatic, as was President Ronald Reagan, whereas presidential candidate Al Gore in 2000 was regarded as lacking it, being "wooden" in his personal style. The twentieth century was unfortunately distinguished by the large number of leaders who effectively and often intentionally advanced "personality" as a foundation or manifestation of their power, fostering what has been named the "cult of personality." Huge posters of and constant references to Josef Stalin or Kim Jong-Il or Saddam Hussein created and maintained an aura of authority as all-wise or fatherly (which was backed up with other forms of power as well).

Office, on the other hand, is not a characteristic of an individual but bestows authority on the individual. An **office** is a position or role of power in a society. "Police officer" is an office, as is "teacher" or "boss" or "president." The power belongs to the role, not the individual. Any person who occupies the office has the authority. As long as an individual occupies the role or position, he or she exercises the authority of the office; however, when the office is lost or vacated, the power is lost too.

Often the authority of leaders has a supernatural base as well. In his study of the Madagascar kingdom of Merina, Maurice Bloch (1989) discusses the central concept of *hasina* that energizes the entire system. *Hasina* is a mystical power associated with nature and reproduction; it is supposedly inherent in some people and not in others. In the Merina worldview, it is inherent in the kings and not in the commoners; commoners need kings to guarantee the continued fertility of the earth, and the subjects repay the kings with respect, obedience, and wealth.

One important characteristic of authority as a type of power is its limitation. It is limited both in scope and duration. A person of authority in one area of society may have no authority in another; you might recognize a stockbroker's authority in investing but not in medicine. And the stockbroker usually cannot compel you to invest the way s/he recommends; if you respect his or her opinion, you will follow the advice, but if you do not you will not. In terms of duration, an authority figure loses his or her power when his or her strength, skill, charisma, office, or whatever justification for that original authority disappears or is terminated. Authority is not permanent but lasts only as long as the grounds for it.

Authority
Legitimate power or power that an individual, group, or institution is felt to rightly possess and exercise on the grounds of age, knowledge, office, and so on.

Fried, Morton H. 1967. *The Evolution of Political Society: An Essay in Political Anthropology.* New York: Random House.

Office
A more or less formal social position with specific rights and responsibilities. One source of "political" authority and social control.

Persuasion

A source of social and political power, based on the ability to move people to agree with or obey the persuader. Often exercised through linguistic skill (e.g., the ability to "give a good speech") and the manipulation of resources and social relationships.

See Chapter 4

Symbolic capital

"Resources" that humans can use to influence situations and affect other people's behavior that are not "material" or "economic." These can include knowledge, social relationships/debts, prestige, and so on.

Geertz, Clifford. 1980. *Negara: The Theatre State in Nineteenth-Century Bali.* Princeton: Princeton University Press.

Persuasion

Persuasion is an intermediate type of power, based on one's ability to influence or manipulate people into obedience or compliance, typically through skillful use of language or control of resources. One of the most familiar forms of persuasion is "talking people into" doing what the persuader wants them to do. In all societies, there are specific linguistic skills of oratory or "speech-making" that give certain individuals more persuasive power than others. In the United States, "political speaking" or speech-making is a special and highly elaborated and valued style of language, and leaders who can speak "well" are more effective – ultimately "more powerful" – than those who cannot.

The other foundation of persuasion is control or manipulation of cultural resources. These resources can obviously include money or property; if someone is rich – or, say, the boss – then people may tend to find his or her opinions and directions more compelling than other people's. The "big man" discussed below has persuasive power by virtue of his central position in the redistribution system. A teacher has a certain persuasive power by virtue of his or her control over grades. However, the control may not necessarily involve "economic" resources but may rest on what the French anthropologist Pierre Bourdieu (1977) called cultural or symbolic capital. **Symbolic capital** can include things like flags and other physical symbols, key terminology (in the U.S.A., "freedom" or "rights"), specific pieces of cultural knowledge, myths, rituals, and other often overtly religious things. Like the Madagascar *hasina* concept, as in most royal circumstances, kings and queens demonstrated and reproduced their power through ritual performances such as coronations, state marriages, and state funerals. Geertz claims that precolonial Bali took this principle even further, establishing a "theater state" in which the rituals and demonstrations were the very basis and expression of power. Politics itself was display and acting:

> the kings and princes were the impresarios, the priests the directors, and the peasants the supporting cast, stage crew, and audience. The stupendous cremations, tooth filings, temple dedications, pilgrimages, and blood sacrifices, mobilizing hundreds and even thousands of people and great quantities of wealth, were not means to particular ends: they were the ends themselves, they were what the state was for. Court ceremonialism was the driving force of court politics; and mass ritual was not a device to shore up the state, but rather the state, even in its final gasp, was a device for the enactment of mass ritual. Power served pomp, not pomp power.
>
> (Geertz 1980: 13)

Contemporary politicians often criticize their opponents for engaging in "political theater" without realizing (or at least acknowledging) that they themselves do so as well and that all politics is theater to an extent.

Coercion

When all else fails – or often in conjunction with other sources of power – a would-be leader may resort to coercion. **Coercion** is power based on the threat or use of force or violence. Arendt argues that coercion or violence is the very opposite or absence of authority: individuals only use force when authority is questioned or lost. There is no doubt that coercion can escalate as the legitimacy of the political leader declines, but it is probably not correct to see them as antithetical and foreign principles. A police officer combines authority, persuasion, and coercion in his or her power, and most members of a society recognize some form of "legitimate force," whether in the criminal justice system, in the military, or in personal self-defense.

As the sole basis of power, coercion can be very effective in the short term: if a police officer needs to subdue a suspect, physical force – up to and including deadly force – can get the job done. However, if Arendt is correct, coercion alone cannot control a society over the long term, and even coercive leaders attempt to project an aura of legitimacy on their actions. They may suggest that they are eliminating a threat to the society, preserving "law and order," or actually improving that society in some way. The leaders of the French Revolution, particularly in the period known as the Terror, explicitly used violence and terror (the term "terror" or "terrorism" was invented at that moment) as a political device. In attempting to create a perfect society, deadly violence was a method or tool, as Robespierre stated:

> We desire an order of things in which all base and cruel feelings are suppressed by the laws, and all beneficent and generous feelings evoked; in which ambition means the desire to merit glory and to serve one's country. In which distinctions arise only from equality itself . . . in which all minds are enlarged by the continued conviction of republican sentiments and by the endeavor to win the respect of a great people. . . . We must crush both the internal and foreign enemies of the Republic, or perish with it. And in this situation, the first maxim of your policy should be to guide the people by reason and repress the enemies of the people by terror.
>
> (quoted in Gershoy 1957: 159–60)

Coercion can and often does include guillotines and clubs and dogs, but there is also "soft coercion," as anthropologists, political scientists, and interrogators and advertisers are discovering. People do not have to be beaten or threatened to have their behavior largely determined for them. There are ways to bend them to another's will, from "strong" soft coercion like sleep deprivation, starvation, cold-water dousings, and emotional and informational manipulation to "weak" soft coercion like invasive advertising, product placement, and a host of marketing tricks that opinion-shapers have learned from decades of close observation of consumer habits and tendencies. Human voting behavior, buying behavior, and most other forms of behavior can be shaped quite effectively – and without the victim's knowledge – through much more subtle devices than torture. In fact, often such devices only work, or at least work best, when they are not seen or felt at all. Some of these

Coercion
Power based on the threat or use of force.

techniques may perhaps belong in the persuasion category, but when options are denied or hidden, they begin to cross over into coercion, albeit "soft" coercion.

A final point is that, of course, any single person or group or institution of power may have one or two or all three of these types of power. Teachers probably have authority and a bit of persuasion. Police officers have all three. Coercion does not automatically invalidate all other sources of power in an agent of social control, but too much reliance on coercion at the expense of all others and the leadership begins to draw complaints, for instance, of "police brutality."

THE ANTHROPOLOGY OF POLITICAL SYSTEMS

As in the domains of economics and kinship, anthropological inquiry has identified a variety of political systems, which can be organized along a rough continuum in terms of their level of political integration. By this phrase, anthropologists mean the extent to which politics "integrates" or literally "makes one out of" a society. This can be expressed as a combination of at least five variables.

1. Size of society. A small society is less integrated than a large one, since more people, groups, and institutions are "made one" and incorporated into a single polity or political community in a large one than in a small one. Size of society may be measured in terms of population and/or in terms of the number of local groups (families, villages, towns) encompassed by the political system.

2. Complexity of society. A society that contains internal differentiations, such as class distinctions, is more integrated or requires more integration than one that does not. This internal complexity may also include multiple linguistic or religious or racial or ethnic communities.

3. Centralization of power. If there is no "center" of power – that is, if power is dispersed widely or evenly through society – then there is little political integration. The more that power is collected into a few hands (maybe as few as one), the more integrated the system. If power is distributed absolutely evenly in a society, then there is no real power at all, since no one has more power than anyone else and cannot really make anyone else do anything.

4. Amount of coercion. The more force that is available to the political system and its agents, the more integrated the society. Again, coercion by itself has a finite life span, but without coercion no leader or would-be leader can guarantee or compel obedience and integration; followers or would-be followers could detach themselves from the leader and disregard his or her mandates (which amounts to a "revolution").

5. Formality of power. The more explicit and specialized the agents and institutions of power and politics are, the more integrated the system. Societies in which rules, sanctions, and roles of enforcement are implicit or embedded in other non-political relationships and institutions are less integrated.

On a spectrum of political integration, different anthropologists have proposed different typologies for political systems. Fried, for instance, suggests a four-type classification including egalitarian, rank, stratified, and state societies. An egalitarian society is "one in which there are as many positions of prestige in any given age-sex grade as there are persons capable of filling them" (1967: 33); that is, political power is not limited to a few individuals in a competitive way. A rank society results "when there are fewer positions of valued status than persons capable of filling them. A rank society has means of limiting the access of its members to status positions that they would otherwise hold on the basis of sex, age, or personal attributes" (52); individuals must then jockey for rank. A stratified society "is one in which members of the same sex and equivalent age status do not have equal access to the basic resources that sustain life" and this unequal access is formalized into hierarchical (and often hereditary) strata or classes (186). Finally, a state is "the complex of institutions by means of which the power of the society is organized on a basis superior to kinship" (229). Put another way, a state is "a collection of specialized institutions and agencies, some formal and others informal, that maintains an order of stratification" (235) and thus strives for and defends its "sovereignty" or "monopoly of permanent control over a population and an area" (237).

Despite the utility of this typology, the one advanced by Elman Service in his 1962 book *Primitive Social Organization* has achieved the widest adoption. No typology is, of course, true or perfect, but since Service's is the best known, it is the one we will discuss in more detail (see Figure 9.1).

Service, Elman R. 1962. *Primitive Social Organization: An Evolutionary Perspective.* New York: Random House.

| BAND | TRIBE | CHIEFDOM | STATE |

FIGURE 9.1 Political systems by level of political integration (following Service 1962)

The band

The **band** is the lowest level of political integration short of solitary individuals, which never happens in society (in fact, it would be the antithesis of society). A band tended to comprise a remarkably small number of people over a very local area, sometimes no more than a handful and seldom more than a hundred or so, typically averaging between thirty and fifty. This number was clearly too small to constitute an entire society; indeed, bands tended to be local subunits of societies, dispersed over the territorial range of the society. Essentially a residential subset of a society, it was often simply an extended family that moved and camped on its own.

The decentralization of power was manifested in two ways. First, within the band, there was no single individual with a great amount of power compared to other members. Since the "political" and residential group was essentially a kinship group, then kinship organization and power was the political organization and

Band
A political system or "level of political integration" where small, autonomous, and typically leaderless groups constitute local segments of a decentralized society.

power. Elders, often both male and female, exercised nominally more power than youngsters, but this power was limited to authority and persuasion (with occasional coercion) and was not "total." It was not much more than "head of the household" power, like any father or mother would enjoy. Actually, it may actually have been less than most fathers and mothers enjoy: many band-level societies, like the Australian Aboriginals, the Ju/hoansi, or Inuit/Eskimo societies, did little in the way of disciplining or controlling the behavior of children, often explicitly believing that young humans lacked the "reason" or "maturity" to take instruction and discipline. Some, like the Semai, found it positively offensive to be told what to do.

The highest position of "leadership" in bands was sometimes referred to as the "headman," but even this man had little formal power. His authority came from age, kinship relation, experience and knowledge hopefully, and perhaps ritual role. Members of the band deferred to him in decision-making, but they were not bound to follow him and could follow other members whose authority exceeded the headman's in specific arenas like hunting. And the headman's power was overtly circumscribed. The general and often self-conscious ethic was to maintain equality between individuals; any man who tried to get too "big" was reminded in no uncertain terms that he was out of line. This phenomenon, known as a **leveling mechanism**, intentionally prevents anyone from becoming more important, dominant, or prestigious than anyone else.

Leveling mechanism

A practice to establish or re-establish social equality or parity, usually by "bringing down" individuals or groups that threaten to get "above" or "better than" others.

BOX 9.2 TO BE OR NOT TO BE A HEADMAN

The term "headman" may be inappropriately attributed to societies where they themselves do not really recognize the role. Among the Ju/hoansi, Lee (1984) encountered the term //kaiha which translates as headman (or even worse, chief), but he found that many members denied that such a person actually existed. When asked about it, one informant said, "In fact, we are all headman. Each one of us is headman over himself!" (89). Dentan (1968) also found a headman concept among the Semai, but he reports that only in around 1900 did the external political authority, the Sultan of Perak, invent the office and start to invest elders with it through "letters of authority." Even so, some Semai during his research had begun to obey these "headmen" and even grant magical powers to the official letters. Among the Tiwi of Northern Australia, a few (but not all) old men would achieve a status above others, based on their marriages and children and the successful personal alliances they formed throughout their lives. Hart and Pilling (1960) refer to this as a "primitive oligarchy" because it was very much an accomplishment of the few, not the elderly as a class or category, based on a "game" of "trying to win friends and increase prestige and influence over others" (52), by marrying "well" and arranging "good" marriages for their sons and daughters. In the economically more marginal desert area, the Warlpiri lacked anything recognizable as a headman. In fact, they consciously downplayed individual status and power. Teachers in the Yuendumu community school told me that children found public praise and accolades uncomfortable: if a teacher singled out a student for praise in front of peers, the child would often intentionally misbehave the next day, to "announce" to other students that s/he was not really trying to be better than everyone else.

The general absence of coercion made bands fluid and temporary. People moved and resided together while it was desirable to do so. If anyone did attempt to climb to higher power, his alleged followers would either knock him on the head with a club or just wander off and join another band or start their own band. The environment also played a prominent part in the life of bands. Bands lived dispersed mostly because it was necessary, their environments being difficult and relatively unproductive. In times of plenty, multiple bands might gather and reside together for a while, often conducting their ritual affairs. However, these larger aggregations were always short-lived, either through environmental constraints or the social frictions they caused, and bands soon disbanded and headed their separate ways.

This raises the second manifestation of decentralization, which is the lack of any sustained coordination or integration above the band level. Just as the headman did not have much power even within his band, there was no one with power over multiple bands. That is, there was no "pan-band" or "super-band" leadership. Diverse bands usually shared kinship or non-kin organization (for example, members of the same family or ritual group might cross bands), and of course they shared a common language and religion and culture, but that was as far as inter-band cooperation went. This lack of higher level integration, which served them well enough in their traditional circumstances, was often a severe handicap upon contact with Western societies; band societies were unable to mount an organized resistance to colonial invaders and were often swept aside like wildlife – which is often how the invaders regarded them – in the path of settlement and agriculture.

Not surprisingly, the fluid, egalitarian, unspecialized, disintegrated ways of the band fit most closely with the foraging mode of production. Foraging peoples typically organized themselves into band systems, or rather, foraging organization *was* band organization. Especially in less productive environments, groups had to be small and dispersed, each band hunting and gathering within a specific "country" inside the society's territory. The band was typically a family unit, among whom distribution of food and other goods was accomplished mainly through reciprocity, although some long-distance trading might be conducted. Kinship expectations, economic exigencies, and religious beliefs and values tended to shape and integrate the society and accomplish the political functions.

BOX 9.3 THE TIWI BAND

According the Hart and Pilling (1980), the Tiwi – whom I briefly visited myself in 1982 – were organized into nine named bands or "hordes" across the two islands (Bathurst and Melville) that they inhabited. In a subtropical and relatively productive environment, the bands ranged between 100 and 300 members, and each was connected to a particular territory. Hart and Pilling describe the bands as "small tribelets or semisovereign groups," since the various bands almost never gathered together and each conducted its own foraging and marrying and warring independent of the others. Band membership was not fixed and static; members, especially women, would often shift band residence. Thus, they concluded that the homeland of the band was permanent, but the people who actually occupied that homeland and made up the band changed continuously. As we saw above, no real headman of a band existed, and certainly no "central authority" over all the bands existed. The closest thing to an authority was the handful of old men who happened to achieve some prominence and influence through the accidents of living a long time, marrying into the "right" families, and marrying their sons and daughters into the right families as well. Thus, no person was assured power as a function of old age, and no inheritable or transferable power exists at all.

Actually, in Service's original formulation, he distinguishes (following Julian Steward's earlier ecological analysis) between the patrilocal band (the smallest type, basically a male-centered exogamous kin group), the composite band (lacking band exogamy or definite residence rules, and therefore "more of an expedient agglomeration than a structured society (60)), and the anomalous band (a fragmented system which did not fit into either category).

Tribe

Tribe

A political system or level of integration in which multiple local communities may be organized into a single system but in which political power is still relatively informal and usually flows from institutions that are not specifically political (such as elders, lineages, age sets, religious specialists, and so on).

Non-anthropologists often use the word "tribe" to designate any small-scale, traditional society (such as the "Warlpiri tribe" or the "Ju/hoansi tribe"), but this is technically incorrect. A **tribe** is a very particular kind of society or polity; some pre-modern peoples lived in tribe-level societies and some did not. The word derives from ancient Roman politics, which divided the population into *tribua* or political/economic units (which paid taxes or "tribute" as a group). In contemporary anthropology, we use "tribe" to refer to a small-scale – but larger than band – political system, often encompassing multiple local residential groups that lose some of their local autonomy in a larger polity, with some at least incipient overarching political institutions. The organization of tribes may not be very extensive or very recognizably "political," but we begin to see what may justifiably be called "pan-tribal" politics.

Tribe-level politics is associated most closely with pastoralism and horticulture, which, as we know, yielded larger economic surpluses, more populous and settled social units, and more specialization of labor and other roles than foraging economies. They also produced more social inequalities and disputes (over property and the uses of property, such as bridewealth). The net result was more interpersonal friction in the society together with comparatively ranked or stratified individuals or groups who began to add other kinds of power than authority to their means of social control.

These new means of social control were what we meant above by "incipient overarching political institutions." There is usually nothing in tribe-level integration that equates to the Western conception of "government," but there are individuals or groups or institutions that exert various kinds of power on various grounds across one or more communities within a tribe, up to and including the entire tribal population. Some of the possible forms that tribal political institutions can take are:

- Age grade system and age sets. In some tribal settings, especially east African pastoralism, the male age grade system constituted a political arrangement. Men in the warrior set provided the defensive and "law enforcement" arm of politics, while the elder set provided the decision-making and/or problem-settling branch.

  See Chapter 8

- Council of elders. Even in the absence of a formal age grade system, elder members of the tribe, sometimes as representatives of families, lineages, clans, or villages, met as an ad hoc decision-making or problem-settling body. This council was not a full-time government but assembled only when there was a specific pan-tribal issue to address. At other times, disparate families, lineages, clans, or villages handled their own affairs.

- Descent groups. As mentioned above, kinship corporate groups could serve a political function, perhaps by providing representatives to some political body. Another way that descent groups, like lineages and clans, could contribute to political integration was by having members resident in diverse local communities or villages. In this way, the group could preside over issues that concerned more than one local community and give some structure to the wider social life of the tribe. Specific families or lineages might function as "segments" of a larger kinship corporate group, making for what we call a segmentary lineage system. As with the council of elders, for the most part each lineage segment functioned autonomously, but when an inter-segment problem arose, or an external threat challenged multiple segments, they could pull together at least temporarily, although they tended to fall apart again when the problem was solved or the threat was past.

  See Chapter 8

- The "big man." The big man was a type of tribal leader whose power flowed from his central position in the redistribution system. Redistribution was only possible in economic settings of greater surplus and greater control of that surplus. The big man did not in most cases have formal, permanent, or coercive power, but he did have both authority and persuasion. He was in a constant status competition with other rivals who may have their own entourage and their own power within the tribe – the very essence of a rank system. Collectively, the various big men in a village or tribe provided an amount of political structure to the society.

  See Chapter 7

- Common interest groups. These non-kinship corporate groups could also add political structure to a society. Like the Cheyenne warrior clubs, they were often law enforcers and agents of social control, although not quite a "government." Still, their existence and the sanctions they could impose – including physical force – made them potent intra-society and inter-society political forces. Cheyenne warrior clubs, for example, were "police" of the buffalo hunts as well as private armies for defense of their own interests as well as the whole tribe (when they acted in unison).

  See Chapter 8

See Chapter 10

■ Religious specialists. In many tribal societies, men or women of distinguished religious or spiritual power and skill had a substantial political role to play. These specialists, who were usually "part-time," could act as mediators, "consultants" (like oracles and diviners, whom individuals might consult before making important decisions), problem-solvers, and sanctuaries to whom disputants and defendants could turn to seek temporary protection from violence until a more pro-social solution could be found to arguments or "crimes" (crimes sometimes including murder).

PLATE 9.1 In many societies, religious specialists like this *mara'acame* of the Huichol Indians provide political leadership

What these and similar roles, institutions, and mechanisms have in common is (1) that they were "political" even while they also arose and drew power from other aspects of culture (economics, kinship, non-kin corporateness, and religion); (2) that they were part-time or ad hoc (that is, they only assembled or served when needed, unlike a permanent full-time sitting government); and (3) that their ability to dictate decisions and solutions to the society and its members was fairly circumscribed. Such was the nature of "politics" in societies of only limited size, surplus, wealth, and socio-economic and power distinctions.

BOX 9.4 CHEYENNE TRIBAL POLITICS

The Cheyenne warrior clubs constituted a "backbone" of political and military organization that, while ordinarily not unified, could be unified for pan-tribal purposes. However, the real "government" of the tribe was the Council of Forty-four, the committee of representatives from the various subunits or "bands" of the tribe. The Council consisted of forty-four "peace chiefs," elder men who were proven warriors in their younger days. Each was selected for a formal, ten-year term, and they possessed a sacred character. Hoebel (1960) writes that they were expected to resign their positions in any warrior clubs and demonstrate other qualities, in particular "an even-tempered nature, energy, wisdom, kindliness, concern for the well-being of others, courage, generosity, and altruism" (37). They were addressed as "father" and "protector of the people." The head of the Council was the Sweet Medicine Chief, a religiously significant office referred to as *heum* or center of the universe, and he was joined by five other medicine chiefs and four sacred assistants, representing four supernatural beings. The political prerogatives of the Council were limited but specific: they deliberated on issues of concern to the entire tribe, such as camp moves, alliances or wars with other tribes, and criminal affairs, particularly murders (which were rare) and violations of protocol for buffalo hunts.

See Chapter 8

Chiefdom

In larger and higher surplus pastoral and horticultural societies, a more formal, full-time, and recognizably "political" system could develop, which anthropologists refer to as a chiefdom. A **chiefdom** is a polity usually consisting of multiple local communities over which an individual or a hierarchy of individuals exercises authority, persuasion, and at least some coercion. Since the chief and his "court" are full-time political specialists, they will be exempted from economic/productive activity, so obviously the economic system of the society must be productive enough to support this new "ruling class." Sometimes the role of chief is a ritual or ceremonial one; in other situations it is a distinctly political one.

Besides – and based on – the economic aspect of chiefdom-level integration, the system depends on a clear, consistent, and often hereditary conception of rank, in which individuals, families, lineages, even entire villages or sets of villages are more or less literally and explicitly "ordered" from first to last in a prestige and power ladder (a kind of "pecking order"). Chiefs of course come from the "premier" families or lineages of society, and/or control the premier resources of the society. This phenomenon should be familiar to Westerners in the form of European royal families; the next king or queen of England will, for example, come from the current ruling

Chiefdom

A political system or "level of integration" in which a central office, often hereditary, possesses formal political power and social prestige through some degree of redistributive control over surplus and the ability to organize and manage labor.

family (the Windsors), who are regarded as "higher" in some way than even other royal families (the dukes, earls, and princes), let alone the "commoners." This is why royalty is often addressed as "your highness." Pre-modern and feudal European society was an elaborate set of ranked individuals and families, with middle-level office-holders in the system both a "lord" to somebody below them and a "serf" or "client" to somebody above them (a higher lord and ultimately the king).

Before colonialism Rwanda and Burundi were traditional chiefdoms, with a multi-layered hierarchy of small chiefs leading up to the paramount chief, who approximated a king. There were chiefs of villages, chiefs of particular hills, chiefs of districts, and chiefs of other chiefs, in interlocking allegiance and competition with each other. Individuals and families "below" a particular chief would pay gifts to their chief, who used that wealth both to "take care of his people" and to pay his own gifts to his higher chief. The paramount chief accepted gifts from the chiefs immediately below him, who accepted gifts from the chiefs below them, and so on, so that ultimately everyone was contributing indirectly to the paramount chief. When Europeans encountered this system, they found it quite convenient to exploit and manipulate for their own purposes, actually in some ways *increasing* chiefly power rather than dismantling it.

PLATE 9.2 The king or Asantehene of the Ashanti Kingdom (present-day Ghana)

Chiefdoms were thus definitely more formal and explicit political relationships than anything we have seen before. Chiefs were not always such overt political and economic masters of their societies – in some societies the chief was a symbolic or even ritual figure, perhaps even one who did not venture out of his "royal" compound and whose existence and health supposedly symbolized and determined the fate of the society – but most of the time their concrete effect on society was unquestionable. Chiefs obviously lived off the surplus of the economy, and they could in many cases compel (although this compulsion often took the form of personal or religious obligation) contribution to it. A chief often "held court," where important decisions were made and important problems settled: "subjects" would "come to court" to get a hearing and a decision. The chief frequently even maintained a fighting force loyal to him, which he used for external aggression as well as "control" of his own people. Some large and advanced chiefdoms, like the one on traditional Hawaii, were shading into the next and final level of integration, the state.

BOX 9.5 INTERNAL AND EXTERNAL POLITICS IN THE ULITHI CHIEFDOM

Ulithi, a group of islands in the northwest Pacific (today part of Micronesia), was at the time of Lessa's research (1966) a thoroughly ranked society with a paramount chief over the entire island complex.

Not only were lineages and villages ranked, but particular parcels of land and the resources on them were ranked as well. Each habitable island (some were too small for permanent settlement but might still be owned and used as farmland) contained one or more villages, and each village was headed by a council of elders, and the village council was headed by a *metang* or village chief. The villages were organized into eight districts, each of which contained a village and one or more outlying islands, and was overseen by a district chief. Over all of the districts sat a top or paramount chief, who always came from the Lamathakh lineage. The chief of all Ulithi had some general powers in areas of justice and intra-Ulithi affairs, although his was not a role of command over the island chain. His main responsibility was in "external" political relations, particularly with the dominant island of Yap. Not only was Ulithi ranked internally, but it was part of a much larger ranking system that spanned many island chains and culminated in Yap, where "regional" power sat. In a kind of feudal relation, Yap was the lord of Ulithi, and Ulithi was the lord of even smaller islands to its east (Yap being the western-most end-point of the "empire"). Yap itself was a caste society, with an exogamous upper caste that owned the land. Apparently the caste concept had spread from Yap to shape the relations between entire islands and island systems, in which Ulithi became the subordinate, and paid respect and tribute to its overlord and in turn received respect and tribute from its own subordinates. Lessa suggests that these were not always happy relationships and that struggle and even war may have marked their pre-contact form.

Lessa, William A. 1966. *Ulithi: A Micronesian Design for Living.* New York: Holt, Rinehart, & Winston.

State

The highest level of political integration achieved by humans (so far) is the state, which is the system with which Westerners are most familiar and under which they

State

A political system or level of integration in which a formal centralized government has power over a delimited territory to make and enforce laws, to establish currency and collect taxes, and to maintain an army and declare war.

See Chapter 13

– and essentially all people of the world ultimately – live. By state, anthropologists do not mean the entities such as New York or Texas or California that Americans ordinarily call "states." These are not states in the technical use of the term but rather "provinces" or "administrative units." Instead, the U.S.A. is a state, the U.K. is a state, Mexico, Canada, Australia, Japan, France, Russia, Nigeria, India, and the other "countries" or "nations" that one finds on "political maps" are states.

For the purposes of anthropology a state is a centralized political system with a formal government that has monopolistic power over a specific territory, including the power to make and enforce laws, to print money and collect taxes, and to maintain an army and declare war. This is why New York or California is not a state: while it can make some laws, it is under a "higher" power – the U.S. federal government – and cannot print its own money or declare its own wars, either on another state (e.g., Mexico) or another "state" (e.g., Pennsylvania or Oregon). A state is "sovereign"; that is, it is self-ruling or "self-determining" or autonomous. There is no higher political power to which it must answer, certainly not the United Nations. (In fact, the United Nations might be better named the "United States," since all of its members are states, not necessarily nations.) If someday an ultra-state polity is created – as some observers think the European Union is or may come to be – then there will be an even higher level of integration, perhaps even to the level of a "world government," but no such thing exists today, and there are those who are opposed to such a development on both nationalistic and religious grounds.

States, which can achieve great power and great size (up to hundreds of millions of people), depend on the most productive economic practice, namely intensive agriculture. In fact, the first states (often small ones, nothing more than independent cities or "city-states") appeared with the emergence of intensive agriculture in places

PLATE 9.3 State-level political systems, like the Italian one headed by Prime Minister Silvio Berlusconi (pictured here May 2008), combine power and pageantry to control large, complex, and wealthy societies

like Mesopotamia, Egypt, India, and China, and later in Central America and Peru. What all of these societies had in common was a highly productive economy controlled by a powerful central government, often integrating military and religious power for the purpose of controlling territory and wealth. The size and density of society, especially the new social phenomenon called the "city" plus the elaborate stratification and specialization of society, was possible only because the new food-production methods were incredibly productive, yielding more than enough food for the farmers themselves. Now there was enough for a significant number of non-productive "specialists," including specialists in politics, religion, and war. Not surprisingly, with the stockpiles of surplus in these societies and the male-dominated and hierarchical organization of politics, war was an inevitable and regular outcome.

See Chapter 7

State leaders still depend on their position as the center of a redistribution system, in which they can command not only production and labor but the contribution of that production and labor in the form of taxes or tribute or work on "public" projects like palaces, pyramids, roads, and city walls. In addition, the market plays a key role in state societies, and the state may exercise power over the market as well. Certainly Western governments manage their market economies (despite the ideology of "free markets") with centrally controlled monetary and banking institutions, like the Federal Reserve and the Federal Deposit Insurance Corporation, as well as domestic subsidies and international trade policies. States make rules and regulations for market players, tax those players, and protect them from players from other states.

See Chapter 7

Not all states have seen their primary business as business. In fact, the first states were probably more religious than economic institutions. The early Mesopotamian cities were "temple communities" where the priests and kings lived and which not only served as the religious and ritual center of society but lived off of the religious contributions of outlying rural inhabitants. This raises a critical idea, which concerns the "legitimation" of this new social arrangement. Why would laborers, who work hard out in the countryside, participate in a system in which their labor and wealth are expropriated from them – in fact, in which they often constitute a poor and lower or "peasant" class? One answer to this question is religion. As political power was centralized in the city and its ruler(s), so religious power was centralized as well, and the two were closely identified. The king was often the chief priest (the ancient Roman ruler was also the *pontifex maximus*, from which the term "pontiff," a title for the Pope, is derived) or, in the case of ancient Egypt, an actual god himself. The diffuse and spiritualized religion of earlier societies became a centralized and ritualized religion of state power and prestige. Subjects participated in the political system because that was what the god(s) ordained; religion became a source of authority for the (new) political institutions.

Since state political integration is comparatively new to the human world, we need to see it as a specifically social and relative phenomenon. No states existed before 5,000 or 6,000 years ago, and many states have come and gone since then. States tend to emerge from social practices like war and political/cultural expansion; the early modern European states coalesced when local or regional rulers began to exercise their power and authority over larger areas and integrate them into a single political, economic, and cultural system, including things like a common currency, language, and sets of weights and measures. Local communities and polities often resisted – and continue to resist – this "unification" and centralization. Even today, there are some disputes (some of international proportions) over what is or is not a state. Tibet is one example: many Tibetans consider their land to be a sovereign state, but China regards it as an historical part of China. Probably the most ominous debate is over the status of Taiwan, which was settled by refugees from Nationalist China when the Communists took control of the mainland in 1949. Today, Taiwan is less than a state but more than a territory of a larger state, with mutual defense treaties with the United States. However, China sees Taiwan as a rogue and separatist province of China (much as the U.S.A. saw the southern Confederacy during the Civil War) and intends to reintegrate it some day. When that day comes, there will be serious international ramifications. But the general point is that states are social concepts and social accomplishments, not "natural" or "real" entities.

State politics can take many forms, from monarchy and totalitarianism to democracy, from capitalist to socialist and communist. These are all merely ways of organizing state power and function. All of them – Mesopotamian and Greek city-states, empires, kingdoms, constitutional monarchies, capitalist democracies, socialist democracies, communist "people's republics," brutal autocracies, and even theocracies (like Khomeini's Iran or the Taliban's Afghanistan) – actually have much more in common with each other than with bands and tribes and chiefdoms. None of them contemplates doing away with borders, laws, capitals, taxes, or armies. Rather, they merely value different ways of arranging those social and political realities. Whether the state is one person (France's King Louis XIV famously uttering "I am the state") or "the people" (the U.S. Constitution starting with the words, "We the People"), states are the dominant ideas and forces in the modern world – at least until multinational corporations and ideologically based "civilizations"

See Chapter 15

surfaced.

BOX 9.6 THE QEMANT IN THE ETHIOPIAN STATE

While the term "peasant" is a problematic one in anthropology and economics, there are local communities and peoples who live within but at the margins of larger political systems in which they have little status or power. This reminds us that states are often composites of various societies or strata in complex and unequal relations. The Qemant were described by Gamst (1969) as a "peasantry" in modern Ethiopia, socially and politically distinct from the Amhara and Tegre, to whom they had been politically subordinate for 600 years. They were farmers who produced for their own subsistence and for selling at market as well as for paying taxes to the central government. Within their communities they had their own three-level political system, including a council of elders at the bottom who ruled on most day-to-day matters of law and administration. There were both formal regular and informal ad hoc councils. Above that was a body of higher and lower priests, who mostly advised and assisted the highest level, the *wambar*, a religious/political leader who not only assessed political penalties like fines and even death but also spiritual ones like curses. The *wambar*, however, was subservient to the officials of the central government, and the entire local system enjoyed its autonomy at the indulgence of the Ethiopian state; in fact, Gamst noted that at any moment in history the freedom of the Qemant political institutions had depended inversely on the strength of central power, making the relationship an unstable and constantly moving one.

MAINTAINING INTERNAL ORDER AND "SOCIAL HARMONY"

One of the major functions of politics is dispute resolution, whether these disputes arise from "normal" social differences and conflicts (e.g., disagreements over wealth and property or women) or from deviant behavior (e.g., robbery or murder). Regardless of the details of a society's economic, kinship, and political arrangements, these kinds of problems can arise, and the society is faced with two issues – the type of response it will make, and the overall goal or end that it seeks in its response.

There are a number of such possible responses cross-culturally, but anthropologists can broadly distinguish two overall approaches: punishment or the assignment of guilt versus restoration of social order and social harmony. In the modern Western context, the first often takes precedence over the second. The main thrust of the American legal system, for example, is to determine "who is guilty" and to punish that person; American judicial practices are overtly adversarial, based on a notion of a "winner" and a "loser." There may be a secondary interest in the "rehabilitation" of the offender, and recently the "victim's rights" movement has placed emphasis on helping or compensating the victim, but the essential thing is to assess blame, usually in an all-or-nothing way, and penalize it. One concern that has come increasingly to American attention is what happens when these "convicts," particularly sexual criminals, are returned to society, as they almost always are.

For all societies, this is a real concern. But in large societies like the U.S.A. or U.K., people sometimes can (or think they can) ignore the problem to a large extent. Because the societies are large, former outlaws might seem remote or invisible. In addition, in large complex societies, politics and criminal justice are "professionalized," such that most members think that someone else will handle it – police, parole officers, "halfway houses," and so on. Like so much of modern life, the legal system often seems distant and impersonal.

In small societies and communities, this attitude cannot be taken. Difficult or deviant individuals cannot be "sent away" (often there is nowhere to send them), so they must reside within the society. In such societies – and to an extent in all societies – social harmony is a crucial interest, and restoring social harmony becomes a central goal. Restoring social harmony means making it possible for both or all parties to walk away from the dispute or infraction with some dignity, maybe some shared blame, and some possibility of an ongoing social life. Different societies have arrived at different solutions, with varying degrees of success. Some of the solutions they have devised to determine the "truth" and to dispose of social disputes and to restore social harmony include the following.

1. Trials or ordeals. When most people think of a trial, they think of a court room and its gravity and rules of evidence and logic. The original meaning and form of a "trial," however, was literally an onerous task that one or more party performed to reveal the "facts" of the case. In many if not most situations, the facts are not perfectly clear and indisputable, so who is telling the truth? One means of "collecting evidence" was to subject claimants to a test, on the premise that truth-tellers would pass and liars would fail. This is why "witch trials," for instance, involved physical tests like being submerged in water: an innocent person should respond differently from a guilty one. Sometimes a special officiate like a diviner or oracle was employed to administer and interpret the test.

See Chapter 10

2. Oaths. Again, when facts are uncertain or unavailable, many societies (including contemporary U.S. society) demand oaths or "sworn statements," which often invoke a spiritual power and punishment, as a guarantee of truthfulness.

3. Duels. One form that a "legal test" may take, either at the behest of some officials or as a private matter between them, is an actual confrontation between the parties. Such a duel might be a physical one, as when Europeans would pull guns or swords on each other and fight it out, or the archetypal "showdown" in the imagery of the western United States. Australian Aboriginals would conduct spear duels in which parties threw spears at each other until blood was drawn; then the duel was over and satisfaction was achieved. In other settings the duels were more symbolic, as when Inuit/Eskimo people held "song duels" in which they competed to insult and chastise each other, the "winner" chosen by popular reaction. In all but the deadliest of these confrontations, the point is more the ritualized nature of the event than the actual damage done.

4. Feuds and raids. Sometimes, raids were conducted for purely economic purposes (e.g., to steal property). However, at least as often if not more so, attacks and counter-attacks were about social disputes between groups, especially disputes over women or deaths (not to mention past raids, in other words, revenge). If one village or tribe dealt dishonestly with marriage or bridewealth or some other social matter, the aggrieved man or his family or village might raid the other for satisfaction, perhaps taking some women or wealth. Deaths, both what Westerners would consider murders and accidental or even natural deaths, might call for a response; many traditional societies believed that few if any deaths were ever "natural," particularly those that involved young and apparently healthy people. "Guilt" for the death might be assigned (in whatever manner) and compensation or vengeance sought. Feuds are a particular problem in societies that lack overarching political institutions and authorities, so that no one has the place or authority to intervene and suggest, let alone impose, a settlement.

BOX 9.7 HONOR AND FEUD IN ALBANIA

While social harmony may seem like the ideal, not all societies share the same sense or value of it. Or perhaps we should say that societies can live in a state of "dynamic disharmony" in which conflicts never truly end. In Albania (Schwandner-Sievers 2001), the concept of *kanun* embodies an honor code in which loss of honor can only be addressed by gestures, including violence, that restore honor. Traditional *kanun* morality is expressed in proverbs like "Blood for blood," "The soap of a man is his gunpowder," and "The wolf licks his own flesh but eats the flesh of others." Accordingly, if another man or family or village starts a conflict, especially if the blood of one's own family or village is spilled, then revenge attacks are necessary and appropriate to restore the "balance of blood." Sometimes young men organize violence against other villages simply to acquire prestige and prove their honor, guaranteeing feelings of dishonor in the subject village if not a subsequent counter-attack. Individuals and groups who have been so dishonored are fair targets for public ridicule, ostracism, and assault – the perception of weakness inviting more abuse. This game of honor and dishonor is often played in terms of women; for example, a woman whose family has been dishonored or has shown itself unable to protect its own will have her marriage prospects significantly limited. Nobody wants to marry into a family without honor. If honor is lost, there are two main ways to restore it. The first is a ritual of forgiveness, in which the dishonored family or group must show extreme generosity. By making such a gesture, their honor rises in the eyes of witnesses. The other obvious course is counter-violence, in which the dishonored party "washes his blackened face," especially by killing a member of another group during a feud.

5. **Moots**. Some societies have developed their own "legal" or "court" systems, often with quite different procedures and quite different ends than the Western version. A moot was one form of court in which disputes and charges were publicly heard and decided, always by members of the society and often by members of the families. It tended to be a more "informal" proceeding than the Western court process, and it might drag up complaints or grievances from past years or even past generations (e.g., someone's grandfather who never finished paying his bridewealth). Perhaps most importantly and characteristically, a moot did not attempt to find one party exclusively at fault and responsible for damages, nor did it use imprisonment as its penalty. The social relations between disputants and their backers were more important than "guilt" and punishment, so rather than separate the innocent from the guilty, the moot prepared them to be reintegrated. The "penalty" could be a fine, a public statement of apology or remorse, or even a "party" at the expense of the "guilty" person to which the aggrieved person was invited. The individual or family "at fault" would have to brew a large amount of beer or provide a large amount of food, and everyone attended, got drunk or full, and came away (hopefully) in a forgiving mood.

AN ANTHROPOLOGY OF WAR

One of the most important external or inter-societal political relations is, unfortunately, war. It is by no means the only relationship between any two societies (many live in peace, or in tense mutual co-existence, or in occasional brief outbreaks of conflict, like raids and border skirmishes), nor is war the only form of political violence, which includes feuds, persecution, genocide, ethnic conflict, and others. There are those who might assert that an anthropology of war is unnecessary – war being simply a natural and instinctive trait of humans – or impossible – war being not a social phenomenon but the *breakdown* of society. But of course, whatever the status of the first claim, it is untrue that war is the absence or failure of social life or politics; after all, according to Clausewitz' classic study, war is the continuation of politics by other (deadly) means.

Anthropologists have, not surprisingly, devoted some attention to war. Malinowski himself wrote an essay entitled "An Anthropological Analysis of War" in which he defined it as "an armed contest between two independent political units, by means of organized military force, in the pursuit of a tribal or national policy" (1964: 247). Such an activity clearly requires at least two societies, with political interests and goals ("policies") and with sufficient social and political organization to field an army and prosecute an extended struggle. This raises an obvious question: have all human societies practiced war or been warlike? One immediate answer is no, since some societies, like the Semai and Utku, reject violence more or less completely. However, precisely how widespread war is in human society and history depends on how we further describe war's essential qualities.

Harry Turney-High, for instance, distinguishes between what he calls "modern" or "true" war and "primitive" or pre-modern or tribal war. True war, he insists, includes tactical operations, command and control processes, "the ability to conduct a campaign for the reduction of enemy resistance if the first battle fails" (in other words, the ability to support a protracted military conflict, which involves a military institution like an army), a collective motive rather than a personal one, and "an adequate supply" which involves the organization of the entire society for the purpose and provisioning of war (1971: 30). By these standards, most pre-modern inter-society violence did not rise to the level of war. Combat practices of the Plains Indians of North America, who were more interested in "counting coup" by striking an enemy and retreating or stealing an enemy's horse than conquering or exterminating the enemy, would disqualify them. Raids or attacks out of personal interests like vengeance, jealousy, theft, or suspected witchcraft would also not constitute war; a classic example would be the Ok of highlands New Guinea, for whom "war" consisted of

> small-scale ambushes and raids, which probably produce the majority of casualties, as well as the rarer large-scale confrontations . . . and battles that are circumscribed by rules and conventions, such as the use of traditional fighting grounds. Confrontations or "nothing fights" escalate to all-out fighting with

Turney-High, Harry H. 1971. *Primitive War: Its Practice and Concepts.* Columbia: University of South Carolina Press.

heavy casualties only infrequently. The proximate cause of particular incidents is the perceived need to retaliate for past wrongs summarized in the phrase *blood revenge*, often the murder or putative murder (by sorcery) of a group member by members of a neighboring group.

(Morren 1984: 173)

Such are the reasons that Turney-High considers the pre-modern fighter to be more of a "warrior" than a "soldier," the latter being a disciplined member of an extended military enterprise.

That war is a social institution or phenomenon is also evidenced in the amount of "social support" that it requires. This includes not only the logistics of war: the recruitment of large numbers of soldiers, the contributions of the non-combatants to the "war effort," the military and political decision-making systems, and the supply procedures to keep the armies fed and fueled in the field. As Turney-High rightly acknowledges, war depends on the social acceptance of war, established through warrior values, attitudes, and rules. Among the martial values are high-minded principles like honor, bravery, patriotism, and self-defense, and lower minded ones like vengeance and the acquisition of war profits and trophies. Until very recently, war was regularly seen as a glorious and manly undertaking; war preparedness is a virtue, and participation in war is still widely regarded as "service to one's country." In addition, contrary to the image of war as antisocial chaos, there are indeed "rules of war" (codified in institutions like the Geneva Conventions) and standards for a "just war," such as not harming non-combatants and treating war prisoners humanely.

Finally, we cannot overlook the cultural, even mythical, quality of war. War itself is a cultural or mythical condition, one that plays upon and activates the deepest meanings of a society. Chris Hedges has gone so far as to stress, as his book is titled, that war is a force that gives us meaning: "It can give us purpose, meaning, a reason for living. Only when we are in the midst of conflict does the shallowness and vapidness of much of our lives become apparent" (2002: 3). At such times, individuals transcend the individual existence and truly become part of a grander, sometimes even cosmic, endeavor.

BOX 9.8 CONTEMPORARY CULTURE CONTROVERSIES: IS WAR INEVITABLE?

Anthropologists, like the general public, have wondered whether war is an unavoidable, even instinctive, fact of human life. The discovery that some species of chimpanzee engage in "patrols" and deadly attacks against their own kind (but of "other groups") has led some to the depressing conclusion that humans have evolved to be warlike and aggressive. Steven Le Blanc, for instance, has claimed to find war at the very roots of human society; he writes that "We need to recognize and accept the idea of a nonpeaceful past for the entire time of human existence. . . . People in the past were in conflict and competition most of the time" (2003: 8). Others, like Douglas Fry, use the cross-cultural variation in violence – and the apparent absence of violence in some societies – to argue against the inevitability of war and even to show that a belief in war's inevitability is itself a dreadful thing: "The assumption that all societies are necessarily aggressive not only is incorrect but also poses a danger to world peace" (2006: xi), since, if war is "seen as natural, then there is little point in trying to prevent, reduce, or abolish it" (2). Here, perhaps more than almost anywhere else, the final conclusion from the anthropological evidence has profound consequences. What do you think?

SUMMARY

Every society has political functions that must be fulfilled, but not all have distinct and formal political institutions, separate from the economic and kinship and non-kin and religious roles and institutions of the society. The various functions can be encapsulated into social order and social control. Social control is achieved by a combination of

- externalized controls
- internalized controls.

The agents of social control who make up the external controls have a variety of sanctions at their disposal, and, while formal agents can and do impose heavy pressures for proper behavior, most sanctions are informal and personal. In fact, all members of a society are informal agents of social control on each other.

Politics is the exercise of power, with different sources and different qualities:

- authority
- persuasion
- coercion.

Therefore, based on their level of political integration, including the types and roles of power, political systems may be distinguished into:

- band
- tribe
- chiefdom
- state.

Finally, any society must meet and solve recurrent social problems, such as dispute resolution and deviance or crime. There are many practices and institutions available to do so, depending on the society's values, roles, and goals, but they may be distinguished along two broad lines:

- determination and punishment of guilt
- restoration of social harmony.

Key Terms

Agents of social control

Authority

Band

Chiefdom

Coercion

Externalized control

Formal sanction

Informal sanction

Internalized control

Leveling mechanism

Office

Peasant

Persuasion

Sanction

Social control

State

Symbolic capital

Tribe

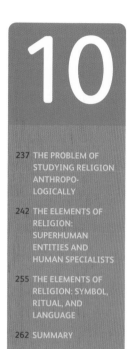

10 Religion: Interacting with the Non-human World

On Mayotte island between Madagascar and the African mainland, spirits were not "spiritual" in the familiar sense of the word. As Lambek (1981) describes them, what English speakers would call spirits were "decidedly phenomena of this world. . . . They exist in space and they have physical characteristics that can be apprehended by human perception and described by the categories of human cognition" (26). They were governed by the same physical laws that pertain to humans; they could be seen or sensed. In fact, they were distinctly human-like in many ways – living in their own villages, raising their own families, even taking an interest in mundane economic matters like food. *Lulu*, the general name for such "spirits," were distinguished into various classes or types which were referred to as *kabila* or "ethnic groups." Some were indigenous to the island, and others were foreigners and migrants. The "native" spirits, called *patros*, had gender and skin color and their own language and music and dance. Lambek concludes that it is inappropriate to call Mayotte spirits "supernatural phenomena. Rather, they are extracultural, that is, beyond the bounds of human culture as the people of Mayotte conceive it" (29).

The final domain of culture, and one that has received extraordinary attention from anthropologists and the general public alike, is religion. One reason why religion has held such fascination for Western observers is its drama and color, if not its "strangeness." If anything, religion cross-culturally takes an even more dizzying array of shapes than the other areas of human thought and action, which might be expected since, in our model of culture, it is the least constrained by practical or material concerns. This is not to say that anthropologists cannot examine religion scientifically and holistically, as a part of culture interconnected with all other parts. Rather, it is to say that, at its more abstract level, religion is less determined – although still powerfully influenced and shaped – than are other levels of culture.

Another reason why religion has attracted observers, while simultaneously repelling them, is the way in which it challenges one's own most basic conceptions of what is true and real, one's "ontology." Geertz (1973) has even characterized religion as the realm of the "really real," those beliefs and behaviors and imperatives and institutions that are most important, most permanent, most "given" (literally, often given or ordained by the religious beings themselves), and most compulsory. However, scholars studying religion cross-culturally could not help but notice that different societies have different notions of what is religiously real and even that one's familiar ways of talking about religion and the real, as in the Mayotte case, often do not apply. In other words, it is not just a matter of what gods or spirits *those* people believe in but of whether they believe in a god at all or whether their spirits are "spiritual" at all.

The anthropology of religion, then, more than any other area of culture, not only has the task of describing and explaining the diversity of its forms and manifestations but also of reflecting back on our own practices and concepts. Just as the analysis of kinship forces us to ponder the definition and diversity of marriage, or the analysis of politics forces us to ponder the definition and diversity of power, so the analysis of religion forces us to ponder the definition and diversity of god(s) and spirit(s) and supernatural and the very notion of "belief" itself.

THE PROBLEM OF STUDYING RELIGION ANTHROPOLOGICALLY

The anthropological approach to religion, as to all other facets of culture, involves a cross-cultural, holistic, and relativistic perspective. That is, we must consider all the variations of religion found in the human world, search for the interconnections between religion and the rest of culture (not the least of which are language, politics, and gender), and understand and judge religion only in the terms of the society in which we find it and never merely our own. This is more difficult for religion than for any other facet of culture, precisely because religion *does* seem to deal with the "real," for both the observer and the observed, in ways that the rest of culture does not. That is, it is hard to imagine someone (at least someone having reached this stage of their anthropological experience) saying that their language is "true" or that their economic practices or political systems are "true." Language is easily recognized as culturally relative; it makes no sense to claim that English is "truer" or "better" than Spanish or Japanese or Warlpiri. However, people are much more comfortable asserting that their religion is "true"; in fact, it may be hard to imagine otherwise.

Early (and not so early) researchers were attracted to but at the same time distanced themselves from the religious beliefs and practices they viewed and reported, in a way that is unusual if not unthinkable for most cultural behaviors. For example, James Frazer, the author of the massive comparative mythology *The Golden Bough*, testified that "I look upon [the myths] not merely as false but as preposterous and absurd" (1958: vii). Of magic he concluded that "every single profession and claim put forward by the magician as such is false" (53). E. E. Evans-Pritchard, writing on witchcraft among the Azande of Africa, asserted: "Witches, as the Azande conceive them, cannot exist" (1937: 63). They follow a long tradition, back to the historian Herodotus, who wrote: "My duty is to report all that is said, but I am not obliged to believe it all" (1942: 556).

It is obviously not an anthropological attitude to refute, let alone to disparage as "absurd," another culture's ideas and behaviors. Religion, then, has proven to be a place where relativism and objectivity are most challenged. Unlike other parts of culture, religion appears to make truth claims about the world: this or that god or spirit or force or being, such as a witch, "really exists." For those who do not share the truth claim – who think, as Evans-Pritchard did, that witches do not exist – the beliefs they investigate are false. So the "contents" of religion, as mutually incompatible truth claims, clash in ways that differing languages or economic systems do not; *your* language or economic system does not render *mine* false.

More than any other area of culture, we must be especially careful about forcing other societies' beliefs into one's own conceptual mold. As the Mayotte case shows, the term "spirit" or "spiritual" may not be appropriate to apply to every religion. The same is true for "god" and "soul" and "heaven," and so on. Anthropologists have realized that these are *cultural concepts deployed as scientific tools* – that is, terms and concepts that belong to one religious tradition (generally, Christianity) and are not neutral analytical tools. Even worse, Rodney Needham has suggested that the very notion of "belief" itself is culturally relative and that not all cultures have it with the same meaning – or have it at all. "We have discovered grounds to conclude that the concept of belief is not expressed in all languages," therefore "we are not sharing their apprehension and are not understanding their thought if we foist this typically Western distinction on to them" when they do not possess it themselves (1972: 175).

Defining religion

The first problem in the anthropological study of religion is determining what religion is; that is, defining religion. E. B. Tylor offered what he considered to be the "minimal" definition that could apply to all observed cases of religion: *belief in spiritual beings*. A simpler and more compact definition can hardly be conceived, but it faces at least one problem: it introduces another term, "spiritual being," that requires a definition. If by this we mean "beings without a physical body," then Mayotte spirits would not count as spirits and therefore Mayotte religion would not count as religion.

Evans-Pritchard. E. E. 1937. *Witchcraft, Oracles, and Magic Among the Azande.* New York: Oxford University Press.

Needham, Rodney. 1972. *Belief, Language, and Experience.* Chicago: The University of Chicago Press.

Since Tylor's day, anthropologists have produced a plethora of definitions for religion, sometimes focusing on belief, sometimes on behavior, sometimes on myth or ritual, and so on. They are too numerous to count or recount here, but three influential ones include the following:

> a unified system of beliefs and practices relative to sacred things, that is to say, things set aside and forbidden – beliefs and practices which unite into one single moral community called a Church, all those who adhere to them.
>
> (Durkheim 1965 [1915]: 62)

Durkheim, Emile. 1965 [1915]. *The Elementary Forms of the Religious Life*. New York: The Free Press.

> a set of rituals, rationalized by myth, which mobilizes supernatural powers for the purpose of achieving or preventing transformations of state in man and nature.
>
> (Wallace 1966: 107)

Wallace, Anthony. 1966. *Religion: An Anthropological View*. New York: Random House.

> a system of symbols which act to establish powerful, pervasive, and long-lasting moods and motivations in men by formulating conceptions of a general order of existence and clothing these conceptions with such an aura of factuality that the moods and motivations seem uniquely realistic.
>
> (Geertz 1973: 90)

Even more, Wallace inaugurated a view that religion is not even a "thing" or a distinct and unitary entity at all but a composite of lower level building blocks, built upon the "supernatural premise" that supernatural beings or forces exist. Then, thirteen "categories of religious behavior" (such as prayer, music, myth, sacrifice, physical "exercises" – many or all of which have their non-religious counterparts) are combined in particular ways in any given religion. These are further combined

PLATE 10.1 Religions convey belief and meaning in symbols, like this golden Buddha in Thailand

into religious or "cult" institutions which are finally combined into "a religion." Thus religion is "essentially a summative notion and cannot be taken uncritically to imply that one single unifying, internally coherent, carefully programmed set of rituals and beliefs characterizes the religious behavior or the society or is equally followed by all its members" (78). Contemporary scholars like Boyer (2001) and Atran (2002) have expanded on this approach, Boyer, for instance, asserting that religion is a "by-product" of "mental systems and capacities that are there anyway, religious concepts or not" (311). If this is the case, then like belief for Needham, the "notion of religion as a special domain is not just unfounded but in fact rather ethnocentric" (ibid.).

We cannot settle these questions here. What we need to do is to place religion in its proper cultural and adaptive context – not so much to see what it *is* as what it does and the various ways that it manages to do what it does. Therefore, let us offer the following not as a definition of religion but as an orienting statement for further study and discussion: *Religion is the parts of culture that involve ideas, and the associated actions and objects and institutions, about non-human and often "super"-human being(s) and/or force(s) that enter into "social" relationships with humans.* This statement is intentionally vague about the types of ideas, actions, objects, and institutions as well as their causal connection (i.e., which comes first). It also avoids slippery qualities like "spiritual" or "divine" and allows for maximum flexibility and inclusiveness. Perhaps most importantly, it emphasizes that there is some reciprocal relationship between humans and the entities of religious interest. Humans must be able to interact with them, and them with us, in some ways, for good or ill. Humans must be able to communicate their desires, understandings, and problems to those entities and they to us.

In this sense, the relationship between humans and their religious entities is a *social relationship*. It is a relationship of agency, communication, intention, reciprocity, respect, avoidance, control, and so on. The being(s) and/or force(s) *are like us* in some ways, despite the fact that they are greatly unlike us in others. They may have a language (usually ours), personality or will, desires and interests and likes and dislikes. They can be approached and influenced. This takes us to the significance of religion as a cultural factor and its critical distinction from the other domains of culture. Economics, kinship, politics – these are comprised of humans. People produce, distribute, and consume food. Kin are people. Political leaders are people, and the powers they have and the rules they make are human ones. But the entities that populate the religious world are not humans. They are non-humans: plants or animals or natural objects (the sun and the moon) or natural forces (the wind and the rain), or the dead ancestors, or non-human spirits or gods. Yet *they are social, they are part of society*. As Robin Horton phrased it, "In short, Religion can be looked upon as an extension of the field of people's social relationships beyond the confines of purely human society" (1960: 211).

In other words, religion is the system or the discourse through which human society and culture is expanded to include the non-human. Or, ultimately, it projects humanness on the non-human world, so that humans are not the "only people in the universe." Irving Hallowell told a story of an Ojibwa informant who, when asked if all rocks and trees are people, answered, "No, but some are" (1967: 28). A friend of mine, a senior Osage Indian, told another story of accompanying a spiritual leader to gather stones for a ceremony; asked how the leader would know which stones to gather, he responded, "The stones will tell me."

Hallowell, A. Irving. 1967 [1955]. *Culture and Experience*. New York: Schocken Books.

Throughout this book we have talked about how human actions and symbols and meanings "culturize" nature (e.g., sex and gender). Now we may conclude that religion takes this process further, perhaps as far as it can go, in "culturizing" super-nature and simultaneously "supernaturalizing" culture. Human behavior and culture are seen in some ways to apply to the supernatural realm, while human behavior and culture are seen to depend on or come from the supernatural realm as well. The two – human and non/super-human – become interdependent and mutually defining and sustaining.

Functions of religion

Why do humans have such a thing as religion, and what does it do for them? We can identify a diverse set of potential functions, each of which spawns a particular theoretical angle on religion. Malinowski emphasized religion's role in filling individual needs, especially psychological or emotional, such as comfort, hope, perhaps love, definitely a sense of control, and relief from fear and despair. A. R. Radcliffe-Brown, in a position known as structural functionalism, insisted that society has its own needs, particularly the need for cohesion, solidarity, integration, and perpetuation. So, in times of crisis, or just in the ordinary course of events, people might drift apart or even blow apart, ending "society" altogether. Religion's shared beliefs, shared values, and shared activities (prayers, rituals, sacrifices) not only provide things to do together to get through the hard times, but make them more alike, give them a sense of shared identity and shared destiny. Partly this position is derived from Durkheim, who focused on the social force which results from ritual behavior, creating almost a "group mind," a collective conscience, or at least a common experience.

Assessing these and other functions of religion, we can condense them into three main categories:

1. **Explanation, especially of origins or causes**. Humans wonder why things are as they are. How did the world start? How did humans start? How did society start? Most religions not only include cosmogony (the creation of the world) but the origin of specific cultural institutions, like marriage, language, technology, politics, and the like. Religions also explain why things happen in the present. Why do we get sick? Why do bad things happen to us? Why do we die? In some societies, much if not all of sickness and misfortune is attributed to religious causes, as was true in Western society not so very long ago and still is for some people.

2. **Control, both of culture and of nature**. Religion has, in all societies, an inherently "political" function, to guide human behavior in certain directions; which directions

in particular depends on the society and religion. So, religion provides rules and standards, sometimes quite explicit and formal ones (like the Judeo-Christian "Ten Commandments") as well as implicit and informal ones. It also provides models or paradigms of behavior: Christians are taught to imitate Christ (many literally determine their behavior based on WWJD – what would Jesus do?), and Muslims hold up Muhammad as the paragon of human virtue. Finally, it provides sanctions and agents and institutions (human and non-human) to impose those sanctions, from sickness or misfortune to excommunication and eternal damnation. Religion also asserts itself as a means to control the physical world, including the human body. Religion may offer processes to control the wind and the rain, the fertility of land or animals, and the health of humans: curing rituals really are intended to drive out illness, and "black magic" really is intended to harm one's enemies.

3. Legitimation, of cultural and natural realities. Humans appear to need to legitimate or justify the arrangements of society and nature to themselves; that is, not merely to explain why some fact exists (like death or kingship) but *why it should exist, why it is right and good*. Why is it not only true but proper that women suffer in childbirth? Why is it not only true but desirable to have a king? Christianity has answered these questions with doctrines like the sin of Eve and the divine right of kings. In each case, either a spirit or ancestor set the precedent, or a supernatural figure made the choice. All religions meet the challenge of legitimating the reigning order by containing some element of "order establishment" or "culture establishment." This is the *charter* function of religion as identified by Malinowski (see below): it acts as the guideline or authority or "charter" by which humans organize themselves in particular ways and follow particular standards. Of course, there are many types of legitimation, such as popular opinion or majority vote. But religious legitimation is superior to any human legitimation, since the supernatural beings or forces – the "authors" of the religiously given order – have the "authority" to create order and are not subject to the imperfections and indecisions of humans.

In terms of these three functions, religion may be seen as a generally conservative force. Yet, with its rules, authorities, and institutions in place, it can also be a powerful medium for change and protest – for adjusting to, challenging, resisting, and creating social relations. As we will see below, often the first change or resistance movements in a society take a religious form, and many of the most important movements for cultural change in the world today are religious in character.

See Chapters 11 and 15

THE ELEMENTS OF RELIGION: SUPERHUMAN ENTITIES AND HUMAN SPECIALISTS

Compared to economics and kinship and politics, typologies of religion are even less useful, since actual religions tend to defy or mix types in ways that make the typology fruitless; the conventional "types" of religion are not mutually exclusive and in fact may and often do co-exist. Following the suggestion of Wallace and Boyer and Atran, it may be more productive to consider the "elements" out of which any particular religion is constructed, rather than to attempt to find "essences" of different religious types. Therefore, this section presents two broad and interlinked categories of components of religion – supernatural entities and human specialists – within which vast diversity is possible and between which complex relationships are common.

Religious entities: beings and forces

The qualities of a religion will depend largely on what kinds of entities it posits as real and important. This area is often referred to as the "beliefs" of the religion, but that term is misleading and potentially ethnocentric, as we noted above. There are two general subcategories of religious entities – beings and forces – which may and often do appear together in any actual religion.

Beings

Tylor's minimal definition of religion depended on spiritual beings. Now, all of the beings that humans ordinarily meet and interact with are "physical" or "material" – that is, they have corporeal bodies, they occupy space, they are constrained by laws of motion, they age and die, and so on. Spiritual beings are different in some (but not necessarily every) way. In some versions they do not have physical bodies, or they may not occupy space or may be able to share the same space as physical bodies, or they can move and act in ways that defy natural law, or they may not age or die (i.e., are "immortal" or at least "less mortal"). That leaves much room for elaboration across religions. But the one thing that spiritual beings have in common is that they are *beings*; that is, they are individuals with some degree of will and mind and personality of their own. One possible distinction among spiritual beings is whether they are or once were human or whether they are fundamentally non-human – although the human/non-human boundary is a permeable one too.

One of the most persistent ideas across cultures is that humans themselves have a spiritual part or parts, which cohabits with the body to some extent and which survives the body after death. In the Christian tradition, the **soul** is an eternal, immaterial, indivisible, personal (that is, it preserves the person's individuality) entity. Not all religions have such a concept, and those that have it often have very different notions about it. According to the Buddhist teaching of *anatta* or "no soul," the human spiritual part is not a permanent unchanging essence but rather is in constant flux. Other religions speak of multiple souls or a soul with multiple parts. The Tausug of the Philippines said that humans were composed of four parts: the body, the mind, the "liver" or emotion, and the "soul." The soul also had four parts: the transcendent soul, which was all-good and always in the spiritual realm, even while one was alive; the life soul, which was related to the blood and attached to the body but which wandered from the body in dreams; the breath, which was the essence of life and always attached to the body; and the spirit soul, the person's "shadow" (Kiefer 1972).

Soul

A religious concept of a non-material component or components of a living human. It is widely believed that a soul survives the death of the body, at least temporarily, and continues in another form of existence.

The Huron of North America talked of two souls or *atisken*. Both were the same size and shape as the body, and one remained with the body after death while the other departed (Trigger 1969). The Konyak Nagas of India identified several different soul parts that separated at death: the *yaha* contained the individual's personality and went off to the land of the dead, while the *mia* stayed attached to the skull (which explains their practice of headhunting), and the *hiba* became a ghost if the person died a violent death (Von Fuerer-Haimendorf 1969). Finally, the Dusun of Borneo mentioned seven soul parts, one inside the other, the smallest the width of the little finger and the largest the thickness of the thumb. They were not "born" full-sized but grew as the body grew. The six "outside" souls or *magalugulu* were visible in human form, but the innermost soul or *gadagada* was formless and invisible (Williams 1965).

The spiritual fate of deceased humans also varies from society to society. Even in technologically advanced societies, many people believe that the dead can become ghosts. **Ghosts** are spiritual parts of dead humans that continue to exist and participate in the human world, usually to our detriment. Downs (1972) says that among the Navajo a ghost was the evil part of a dead person, so there were no good ghosts by definition. In Spiro's renowned study of Burmese religion (1978), he finds that the dead could become *leikpya* if they did not receive a proper funeral or if they were powerful and ambitious people in their lifetime (e.g. government officials), in which case they haunted their former house or village. Among the Anuta of the Solomon Islands, ghosts were one type of *atua* or "common spirits" that were recently deceased humans and looked like humans, only bigger and stronger (Feinberg 1996). In other cases, humans may be dead but still "active" in the physical world, as in the case of the vampire or the zombie, both of whom are dead individuals who have somehow been reanimated but without a soul.

Ghosts and similar manifestations are therefore one possible destination for deceased humans. In other cases, dead people may carry on as **ancestor spirits**, although there is no clear dividing line between the two. Ancestor spirits may be benevolent or malevolent; it is not always correct to speak of "ancestor worship," since not all societies worshipped their dead ancestors, or even particularly liked them. The Swazi of South Africa regarded their ancestors as possessing "greater wisdom, foresight, and power" than the living but not divine or omnipotent; they were still "practical beings" (Kuper 1963: 60). She also notes that ancestors were not as important to the Swazi as nature spirits. For the Dinka as for many peoples with strong lineage systems, the clan spirits or *yieth* were their prime concern, even more so than their god and their "independent spirits" or *jak*. *Yieth* spirits tended to be "partial [to humans] and protective," but they could also be punitive, in which case they recruited the *jak* to do their dirty work. In other words, "there is much crisscrossing in which spirits protect or injure people with justification, or as their whims may dictate" (Deng 1972: 123). On the other hand, the Huron of North America, who did not keep detailed genealogies, did not appear to have any ancestor spirit concepts at all (Trigger 1969).

Ghost

A religious or spiritual being, generally regarded to be the disembodied spiritual part of a deceased human.

Spiro, Melford. 1978 [1967]. *Burmese Supernaturalism* (expanded edn). Philadelphia: Institute for the Study of Human Issues.

Ancestor spirits

The spirits of dead family members who are believed to continue to reside near and interact with their living kin.

BOX 10.1 THE AMBIGUOUS ANCESTORS OF THE JU/HOANSI

Ju/hoansi religion was a complicated mixture of virtually all of the entity types discussed in this chapter. At the center of their focus were the *//gangwasi* or *//gauwasi* spirits of their dead kin. According to Lee (1984) and Katz (1982), the Ju/hoansi came close to dreading their ancestors, for two reasons. First, the gods tended to work through the ancestors as intermediaries, so that much divine punishment or misfortune came by way of the ancestors. Second, they thought that the *//gangwasi* caused a great deal of misfortune directly. Some Ju/hoansi reported that there were good and bad spirits, but others said that it was the position of the dead *vis-à-vis* the living that was the problem. As one woman expressed it,

Longing of the living is what drives the dead to make people sick. When they go on the road that leads to the village of the *//gangwasi* they are very, very sad. Even though they will have food and company and everything they need there, they are not content. They miss their people on earth. And so they come back to get us. They hover near the villages and put sickness into people, saying, "Come, come here to me."

(Lee 1984: 109)

Hence much of Ju/hoansi curing activity was aimed at the ancestors, who may be fought off in curing ceremonies with words like "What business do you have here tonight? This man is not ready to go. He wants to remain with those who love him" (Katz 1982: 41).

Finally, in other cases, it may not be one's own kin that inhabited the ancestral realm. For the Anuta, chiefs and other powerful individuals continued to be powerful after death. Such beings were named and venerated through prayer, song, and story, the greatest among them being Tearakura, an ancient chief turned culture hero and virtual deity (thus closing the gap between human spirits and "gods") (Feinberg 1996).

Many other kinds of spiritual beings were not humans (although, as we saw above, this can be a porous boundary). Perhaps the most common of these are the "nature spirits," the spirits that "are" or "are in" plants and/or animals and/or natural objects and/or natural forces. This was the observation that led Tylor to formulate his definition of religion, which he termed **animism**. Animism, derived from the Latin *anima* for soul or more literally "alive" or "moving," is the general conception that non-human beings can and do have spiritual parts too. It is not always the case that every non-human thing is "animated." For the Warlpiri, some trees and rocks have spirit and some do not; they can point at one tree and say that it is "just a tree," while another (that looks identical) is a spirit, just as the Ojibwa man told Hallowell that some rocks are persons. Also, in any society some animal and plant species were spiritual, while others were just natural beings. This relationship between humans and non-human material objects has sometimes been called **totemism**, a word that is not much used any more. The idea of totemism was usually that an individual or

Animism

A type of religious belief in which non-human species and phenomena have spiritual components that interact with and sanction humans.

Totemism

A religious conception that human individuals or groups have a symbolic or spiritual connection with particular natural species, objects, or phenomena.

social group (family, clan, village) had a spiritual association with a particular species or object, such that the person's or group's "totem" was that species or object. Humans and their totems may be believed to share the same spirit or substance, and sometimes taboos against harming or eating the totem existed.

The animistic spirits of plants and animals, and so on, may be individual or collective – that is, each individual being may have a spirit, or there may be a spirit of all of them (say, a generic "bear spirit"). Ainu religion contained a vast number of spirits; in fact, they regarded all species (and practically all objects) as "soul-owning." Even artifacts like tools and utensils had souls. Accordingly, those beings and objects had to be treated with respect, like the "people" that they were. Hunting was thus never a purely material activity, since it involved interacting with spirits that could anger and withdraw cooperation; in other words, hunting was seen as a kind of "reciprocity" between human and animals/spirits. Also, at the end of its "life" a soul-owning being – human or otherwise – deserved a decent burial. For animals, a proper location, a bone pile or *keyohniusi*, was maintained for each species, and even household objects had a "final resting place." Rituals had to be performed as part of the disposal, "since their negligence brings forth much suffering, mostly in the form of illness" (Ohnuki-Tierney 1974: 87).

Sometimes the spirits had personal names; sometimes they were only vaguely and collectively known. Sometimes they were associated with specific locations or physical objects; sometimes they were diffuse and amorphous. They may be good, bad, or indifferent from a human point of view; they may be helpful, harmful, mischievous, or even unaware of their effect on humans. The Burmese villagers in Spiro's research told him about the *nat* spirits, which included three categories. The first were native spirits that resided in trees and hills and fields and bodies of water. The basic idea was that they guarded their domains, were "petty and irascible," and overall made the world a more dangerous place (1978: 47). The second category were the *devas* or Buddhist spirits who were good and moral; the higher *devas* were too distant to be matters of ritual or speculation, but the lower ones took a positive interest in humans. (Spiro states that some of these lower *devas* were "gods" in the Western sense and that they were the spirits of former especially pious humans, bridging all four types of beings – humans, ancestors, spirits, and gods.) Finally, the "thirty-seven *nats*" were regarded as evil. Each was known by its name and myth, and each had to be appeased with offerings of food.

The volume and diversity of spirit concepts are too great to discuss here in detail. Such beings included demons, devils, and any of a wide array of culturally local characters such as ogres (*bilus* in Spiro's Burmese village, which might be the spirits of deformed babies), fairies, elves, sprites, muses, furies, *jinns* or genies, and many others.

A final type of religious being is a god. There is no perfect, universal definition for a god, but they tend to be extremely powerful, usually creative, and comparatively remote spiritual beings. Many societies that recognized gods (and not all did) did not attempt to communicate or relate directly to those gods because they were so distant, but rather approached them through lower level spiritual intermediaries. The

Ju/hoansi, for instance, included two gods in their religious system, a high god *Gao Na* and a lower god *Kauha*; however, most attention was directed to the ancestors. Across religions, some gods were highly personal and moral, while others were not. The sky god of the Konyak Nagas intervened in the moral affairs of humans; the god of the Azande, named *Mboli* or *Mbori*, was morally neutral and uninvolved in human moral business.

A religion that focuses primarily on god(s) is called a **theism** (from the Greek *theo-* or *deo-* for god, which also gives English the word "deity"). In any particular theism there may be one or more than one god, and gods are seldom if ever the only spiritual beings in the system, i.e., gods typically co-exist in a religion with human spirits, nature spirits, ancestor spirits, and other supernatural entities (e.g., angels or devils). A theistic religion that contains multiple gods is a **polytheism**, and a theistic religion that contains one god is a **monotheism**. Ancient Greek religion is a familiar example of polytheism, with its "pantheon" (from *pan-* for all) of gods residing on Mount Olympus. The Greek gods were not always good or "moral" (some of them did very reprehensible things, even in Greek eyes), nor were they always eternal or immortal (many Greek gods were born, often from other Greek gods, and many died). Judaism, Christianity, and Islam constitute the dominant monotheisms in the world, although there are other smaller and newer religions that hold the notion of a single god (e.g., Baha'i).

Theism can take a few other forms. For instance, many of the colonial American leaders practiced **deism**, the position that there is or was a god who created the world and put it in motion but then withdrew from it; this god is more or less "impersonal" and may take no active part in the daily affairs of humans at all (thus Azande theism resembles deism). Finally, some thinkers have come to the conclusion that god is everything and everything is god, a belief known as **pantheism**. Some mystical traditions within larger religious systems, and to an extent the entire system of Hinduism, maintain that the whole universe is really god or the "mind of god" or one great cosmic soul (the *brahman* in Hinduism), of which the human soul (*atman*) is a small, alienated piece.

Theism
The religious belief in one or more god(s).

Polytheism
The religious belief in two or more gods.

Monotheism
The form of theism that includes belief in only one god/goddess.

Deism
The form of theism or belief in god(s) which posits a creator god that does not take an active role or moral interest in human affairs.

Pantheism
A form of theism in which it is believed that "everything" is God, that the universe and all of the material world is the same thing as God, that God is "immanent" in and co-extensive with the physical world.

BOX 10.2 THE GODS OF ULITHI

On the Pacific atoll of Ulithi, people knew many different gods, none of which, however, were active in the creation of the universe. In fact, Lessa (1966) proclaims that there was not even a creation story in Ulithi religion. The highest god was *Ialulep*, who was seen as a very large white-haired person, old and feeble; he controlled the lives of humans by holding their "thread of life" and determined their death by breaking the thread. His son *Lugeilang* was not a paragon of virtue: he lusted after human women and sired the trickster god *Iolofath* who had many misadventures. A pantheon of other gods – earth gods – existed in a kind of supernatural division of labor. For instance, *Palulap* was the Great Navigator, the god of ocean navigation. His son *Ialulwe* (a being with four or more eyes) was the patron of sailors. *Solang* was the god or patron of canoe-building. *Ligafas*, a goddess and daughter of *Palulap*, ruined the canoe that her divine family was riding in, leading to the human restriction that menstruating women should not sail the sea. Finally, there was *Solal*, the god of the underworld as well as patron of certain magicians. On other islands in the Carolines he was held to be equal to the great god *Ialulep*, although Ulithians did not grant him such high status.

Forces

Animatism

A type of religious belief where impersonal spiritual forces exist in the world and affect human life and behavior.

Not all religions include beings, and many of those that do include beings include other entities as well. There are also recurring conceptions of impersonal spiritual forces – ones that do not necessarily have an individual "mind" or "will." Often these forces are more like "spiritual water" or "spiritual electricity" – a (super)naturally occurring power that exists in and flows through nature, giving it the qualities that we find there. The usual name given to this religious conception is **animatism**.

The classic example of a spiritual force is *mana* as understood in numerous Melanesian cultures. Mana was an energy or power that presented itself in material objects, including people, but was not inherent in them; that is, it was a separate "thing" from them and could come and go. It was in the interest of a person, then, to know, use, and accumulate mana if possible, since luck, strength, virtue, and many good results came from having or controlling it. Likewise, a person without mana was destined to be unlucky, weak, and unsuccessful. Most English speakers have also heard of the Chinese animatistic principle of *chi*. It is probably a very old idea but it is most clearly and poetically described in the *Tao Te Ching*, a book attributed to a sage named Lao Tze about the *tao* or the "way" or "path" of nature and the *chi* that informs it. The *tao* flows like water (water is the most often-used analogy for it), taking the path of least resistance. Thus, the person who would live well should go with the *tao*, leading to such insights as "Do nothing and leave nothing undone" or "The best ruler is he who rules least." The general idea is that human will, when it goes against the *tao* (as it usually does), ends in struggle, difficulty, and wasted effort; it is like trying to swim upstream. The wise person "goes with the flow," letting the force of (super)nature take him or her where it will.

Spiritual forces can take many other shapes. The Dusun worried about "luck" which was a finite spiritual resource of each individual that, if spent in one area of life, could endanger other areas (e.g., acquisition of property, success in disputes). Luck was also finite in society, making one person's gain in it another person's loss; this naturally led to arguments about surreptitious efforts to steal or damage each other's luck. In Apache religion the power was known as *diyi*, which was in infinite supply. Many forms of this power were recognized, related to different animals or natural phenomena. And unlike many such forces, *diyi* did in fact have some "personal" attributes, including the ability to seek out people to attach to (individuals could also seek *diyi*) and to experience anger, which could of course harm humans (Basso 1970). The Menomini of North America spoke of a power called *tatahkesewen* ("that which has energy"), *meskowesan* ("that which has strength"), or *ahpehtesewesen* ("that which is valuable"). They described it as non-material and invisible but like a bright light that could be sought and mastered through dreams, vision quests, and the guidance of guardian spirits.

As one of the most religiously eclectic societies, the Ju/hoansi also had a concept of spiritual energy called *n/um*. Richard Lee defines it as a "substance that lies in the pit of the stomach of men and women . . . and becomes active during a healing dance. The !Kung believe that the movements of the dancers heat the *n/um* up and when it boils it rises up the spinal cord and explodes in the brain" (1984: 109). The Ju/hoansi shaman (see below) mastered this force and called upon it in healing rituals to transfer power and wellness to patients.

Religious specialists

As in all other walks of human life, there are always some individuals who have more ability or power in religion than others. This facility may come from knowledge, skill, practice, training, personal experience, office, or other such factors. Hence, when the layman had a problem or an interest to which religion applies, s/he would turn to a specialist for assistance or intervention with the spiritual. Predictably, there is a variety of religious specialists across cultures, who vary in what they do, how they do it, and for what purposes they do it.

Shaman

One of the most celebrated of all religious characters is the **shaman**, sometimes popularly known as the witch doctor or medicine man because shamans often use their abilities to help people who are suffering from physical, emotional, or social misfortune. The unique and important thing about shamans is that they were distinctly spiritually powerful individuals, that is to say, their specialist talents came from some quality of their own individual personality or biography. With this personal power, shamans could do spiritual things that other "normal" people could not.

A potential shaman did not go to "shaman school" or take a test to get a "shaman license." The process was both more informal and more profound than that. A person typically showed a propensity or tendency toward shamanic abilities early in life, such as talent for singing or ability to enter into trances or have visions. One very common element of the life story of a shaman was a serious illness in youth, from which the person dramatically or miraculously recovered. This was evidence that s/he "had the power," and it was also often the first significant contact with the spirit world, since to be sick – and especially to die – was to interact with (and overcome) spirits.

The aspiring shaman often then became a student or apprentice to a senior shaman, who "taught" the novice. The master would seldom lecture to him or her

Shaman
A religious specialist, often part-time, who has personal power, based on unique life experiences or apprenticeship to a senior shaman, to communicate, interact, and sometimes struggle with supernatural beings or forces. Often a healer.

about how to be a shaman; rather, the apprentice received "hands-on" training. The teacher might subject the student to trials, like sleep deprivation, long hours of chanting, drug ingestion, seclusion, quests of various kinds, and other difficult and even painful ordeals. One of the common factors in becoming a full-fledged shaman was acquiring a helper spirit, sometimes called a "spirit familiar," which would show the trainee things that cannot be known any other way. It would teach him or her about the spirits and give him or her a personalized set of songs, dances, symbols, and other spiritual tools. That is why a shaman could not simply copy the knowledge of past shamans; each must have his or her own "kit." Paramount in many of these kits was the skill to enter into a trance-like state, during which the most "spiritual" of shamanic work was done.

Ju/hoansi shamans, for example, were called upon when a member of the band was sick or troubled. The shaman began his work (most were male) by singing and chanting until he fell, literally, into a trance; his body collapsed on the ground, because his "soul" had left it and was sojourning in the spiritual dimension. The entranced shaman regained his senses and conducted "operations" that included rubbing his own sweat on the patient, which was thought to contain "boiling energy" or n/um. The shaman eventually literally "swam" back to consciousness, having performed the cure that the patient sought.

In Australian Aboriginal societies, shamans would often accomplish their cures by removing objects – like stones or feathers – from the body of the victim. (In many cultures, shamans themselves were thought to have supernatural objects in their bodies, which may be implanted as part of their training.) Elsewhere, shamans purportedly visited spirits while in trance and either questioned them or on occasion engaged them in combat; a shaman really could be a spiritual warrior. Shamans might also incorporate more "mundane" items into their cures, like potions, charms, sacrifices, and such. What Spiro translates as shaman in his Burmese study was nat kadow or "nat wife" and was a role almost entirely occupied by women. He argues that they did not journey to the spirit world or cure sickness at all but functioned through spirit possession by their nat husband who told them the nature of the spiritual offense that plagued the patient.

One of the last key features of shamanism is that the role was typically a "part-time" one. The shaman might take some form of compensation for his or her efforts, but this never amounted to an income. Furthermore, shamanism was not a formal position, certainly not an "office." One was a shaman if one had spiritual power; if one lost that power, one was no longer regarded as a shaman. There might be multiple shamans in a community or society depending on how many people wanted to and were able to master shamanic techniques. Shamans were often a little feared and distrusted for their power and their personal oddity; being a shaman could be a lonely and uncomfortable existence. Finally, shamanism could not be truly or dependably inherited; sometimes the children of shamans became shamans too, but that was because they also "had the power," not because of who their parents were. Each would-be shaman had to prove his or her ability and gather his or her own spiritual resources.

Priest

For most English speakers, the term "priest" conjures up an image of a man (usually a man) in a black robe leading a church service. That is definitely one variety of priestly activity but not the definition of priesthood. The **priest** is, in a word, all of the things that a shaman is not. S/he is often a full-time specialist occupying a formal office achieved by study, testing, and "ordination" by a religious institution or structure with the power and authority to invest priests. Priests may or may not be powerful individuals – some are quite ordinary people – but they hold a powerful office.

Priest
A religious specialist, often full-time, who is trained in a religious tradition and acts as a functionary of a religious institution to lead ritual and perpetuate the religious institution.

One becomes a priest by very different means than one becomes a shaman. Commonly, acquiring a priesthood means mastering a body of knowledge and dogma, becoming an "expert" in some orthodoxy (from the roots *ortho* and *doxa* for "correct/straight" and "opinion"). Individuals with deviant or "heretical" ideas do not tend to receive priestly offices; thus, priests tend to be agents of conservatism. In fact, they represent the institution in which they belong, rather than being "free agents" like shamans. The activities of priests tend to differ as well. The occasional priest may engage in curing practices, but more often priests are ritual leaders, functionaries who organize, conduct, and preside over ritual situations with more or less formulaic words and gestures. Priests are not generally encouraged to "improvise" or to receive their own private spiritual instructions or resources. Ideally, every time a priest performs or leads a ritual, it should be exactly the same, down to the finest detail. The efficacy of the ritual may depend on each bit of it being correctly done.

The priesthood, while not always hereditary, may have a hereditary component. In various societies there are priestly lineages or classes, most explicitly the Brahman caste in Hinduism. In traditional Judaism the Levite line provided the priests of the group and, as we commented, in Barabaig society five of the clans were priestly (the *Daremgadyeg*) and fifty-five of the clans were purely secular. So, priesthood tends to be associated with social stratification as well as "institutionalization" or "formalization" of religion and the conflation of religious with political power. The high officers of the Cheyenne Council of Forty-four were religious personages too. Priests, especially in larger, richer, and more centralized societies, tend to be full-time employees of the religious establishment (depending on a considerable surplus to support them), and they often exercise "secular" or political power as well as religious power. Many top political offices, like the kingship under Henry VIII, have had religious power or significance, and many religious offices, like Pope of the Catholic Church, have had political power or significance. Often, it is impossible to separate the two functions.

See Chapter 8

Sorcerer

Sorcerers were generally people understood to exercise spiritual power, typically for the worse, through specific "technical" means. That is, sorcery might be classed as

Sorcerer
A religious specialist who uses techniques, including spells and potions, to achieve supernatural effects.

a subset of *magic*, which is normally thought of as an instrumental action in which certain gestures or behaviors "automatically" lead to certain results. The line between magic and religion is thin and controversial, and we will not explore it here; there is no doubt that there is much magic in any religion and some religion in all magic, but we can perhaps distinguish them usefully, as anthropologists from Frazer and Malinowski have attempted to do. Frazer in particular made a further distinction, between what he called contagious magic and sympathetic or imitative magic. **Contagious magic** is the spiritual consequence of bringing two things together, sometimes literally touching. For example, if I do some kind of ceremonial act on or store up some kind of spiritual power in a wand or other object and touch you with it, that power will be transferred to you. Australian Aboriginal sorcerers would focus their power through a magical bone, which they would point at a victim to "shoot" the magic at them. The use of a strand of a person's hair or a piece of fingernail on a "voodoo doll" follows the same logic: the body part was in contact with the person, so there is still a magical connection. **Sympathetic or imitative magic** relies on some similarity between the action or the object and its target; so, if I want to make rain, I might pour water on to the ground, simulating rain. Or, if I want to guarantee fertility, I might incorporate a particularly fertile animal (perhaps a rabbit, or a symbol of fertility, like an egg) into my technique. In all of these behaviors, the idea is that the behavior is sufficient to achieve the result. One does not have to pray or ask for results; the magical ritual has an almost "technological" relation to its outcome – do this action or say these words and get that result. The sorcerer, then, may be regarded as a person who performed such activities ordinarily for the purpose of evil or harm.

According to Basso, an Apache sorcerer had to learn the techniques of negative magic, and most sorcerers were men, since men were thought to feel more *kedn* or hatred than women. Potential sorcerers would have to pay a senior expert, usually a maternal kinsman, for the knowledge and skills, which took three main forms – making and administering poisons, casting spells, and shooting objects "into" the victim's body. The result of successful sorcery was a specific set of symptoms that appeared suddenly and without warning; further, the corpses of victims were distinguished by "swollen tongues and bluish markings around the face and neck. They are also reported to decompose at an unusually rapid rate" (Basso 1970: 76). On Mayotte, sorcerers worked through evil spirits, literally "hiring" them to do harm; the greatest sorcerers met spirits in person and used the souls of the recently deceased. Lambek explains that the cure for sorcery was to find and remove

> a small, rotting cloth packet filled with dirt, nail clippings, hair, broken glass, and the like from either the body of the patient, his house floor, or the ground of his compound or fields. This packet of dirt is the physical representation of the harm caused by the spirit itself.

(1981: 44)

Contagious magic

The belief and practice that objects that come into contact with each other have some supernatural connection with each other.

Sympathetic magic

The belief and practice that objects which have something in common with each other (e.g., same shape or texture) have some supernatural connection with each other.

Witch

Many societies were quite sure that **witches** were at work in the community all the time. As a cultural concept witchcraft is very diverse, but the common thread across cultures is that witches were responsible for bad things that happened to people – often all bad things. In one of the classic studies of witchcraft, Evans-Pritchard argues that the Azande of the Sudan saw the action of witches everywhere:

> If blight seizes the ground-nut crop it is witchcraft; if the bush is vaingloriously scoured for game it is witchcraft; if women laboriously bale water out of a pool and are rewarded by but a few small fish it is witchcraft; if termites do not rise when their swarming is due and a cold useless night is spent in waiting for their flight it is witchcraft; if a wife is sulky and unresponsive to her husband it is witchcraft; if a prince is cold and distant with his subjects it is witchcraft; if a magical rite fails to achieve its purpose it is witchcraft; if, in fact, any failure or misfortune falls upon anyone at any time and in relation to any of the manifold activities of his life it may be due to witchcraft.
>
> (1937: 18–19)

Some societies held that a witch was a person with an innate, even anatomical, power to do harm; the witch may have an extra organ in his or her chest containing negative spiritual power, or the witch's emotions simply radiate some malevolent force. Witch power may actually be involuntary to the witch, at least initially; they may simply exude negativity in ways that even they did not understand or control. The Kaguru also said that witches (*wahai*) were congenitally evil people, the ontological opposite of normal human beings (Beidelman 1971). Or they may practice, sharpen, and intentionally employ their power for their benefit, especially against rivals, including rival witches.

Anthropological discussions of witches and witchcraft, and of sorcery, turn on the particular concepts and how they function in a particular society. One function of witch concepts, as of sorcery concepts, is explanatory: they explained why unfortunate things occurred. In addition, fear of witches or of being branded as a witch had a strong social control function. If one did things to make other people angry or unhappy, the witch among them might afflict the perpetrator. Or, if one was accused of witchcraft, the social (and mortal) consequences could be severe, including ostracism, condemnation, or even death. The Swazi recognized witches as well as sorcerers, which they categorized together as *batsakatsi* or "evil-doers." On the other hand, the Menomini said that witches were not antisocial deviants but the group in society with the most power and prestige, namely the elders. Spindler and Spindler write that "social control is achieved . . . by the threat of witchcraft by power figures rather than through accusation of the witch by the community" (1971: 73). All elders were potential witches which, in a society of relative equals, was one of the few "power relations" available.

According to Spiro, some informants in Burma claimed that witches were not even human but evil spirits in a human guise; also they did not make a sharp distinction between sorcery and witchcraft. A witch might have innate evil powers

Witch
A religious specialist, often conceived as a human with a supernatural ability to harm others, sometimes through possession of an unnatural bodily organ or an unnatural personality. Sometimes viewed as an antisocial and even anti-human type who causes misfortune out of excessive greed or anger or jealousy.

or the learned and acquired power more usually associated with a sorcerer. The two main types were the witch (*soun*) and the master witch (*aulan hsaya*). A *soun* was almost always female, recognizable by her dimly colored eyes; her power could be inherent or learned, although the learned witches were less powerful but more deliberately evil (since they sought out the ability actively). They were believed to cause various illnesses and to eat feces by detaching their heads and rolling along the ground. They might also work in conjunction with bad spirits. The master witch was much more powerful and always male. He did his dirty work by controlling evil spirits, feeding them raw meat until they became dependent on him. Interestingly, though, there were also good master witches (*ahtelan hsaya*) who could counteract the malice of *aulan hsaya*.

Diviner/oracle

Diviner
A religious specialist who uses one of many techniques to "read" information from the supernatural world.

Oracle
A religious specialist (or any religious object or process) with the power to forecast the future or answer questions through communication with or manipulation of supernatural forces.

Especially in societies with gods or powerful and well-known spirits, it is extremely valuable to know what those beings want or intend. The **diviner** or **oracle** had the ability to read or interpret the will of spirits, sometimes by asking direction questions and inspecting some material manifestation of an answer. Astrology has traditionally been a divining activity, looking for traces of "divine" communication in the stars. Any number of other kinds of signs have been read for spiritual meaning, from tea-leaves and coins to the bones or entrails of animals; a diviner may put a question or request to the spirits, then kill and study the body of an animal for indications of an answer. The Barabaig diviner or *sitetehid* manipulated a pile of stones and examined the patterns for messages, usually involving witches or angry ancestor spirits, although he did not actually perform the cure, which was turned over to another specialist. Probably the most famous oracle in Western history was the Greek oracle at Delphi, where citizens – including kings, generals, and philosophers – would ask advice from young priestesses who gave cryptic responses while in a trance. Decisions to go to war and other epoch-making decisions were sometimes made in this way.

Prophet

Prophet
A human who speaks for or receives messages from spirits.

Across cultures, spirits and gods are notoriously silent, so a **prophet** was an individual who received direct communication from the spirits, often quite involuntarily (recall how Moses and other Hebrew prophets were reluctant to take on the role), and was then charged to pass that communication along to other humans. "Prophecy," which is often confused with telling the future, is a bulwark in the Judeo-Christian tradition, and Muhammad is revered among Muslims for being not only a prophet but "the seal of prophets" – the final and authoritative one. His prophecy, received as a recitation or *Qur'an* from Allah and his angels themselves, was intended to complete and correct all previous prophecies. Obviously, though, there are those who think that new prophets continue to appear, both inside and outside the Judeo-Christian-Muslim world.

THE ELEMENTS OF RELIGION: SYMBOL, RITUAL, AND LANGUAGE

In addition to the beings and forces and the human specialists who interact with them, any religion has numerous other components. Many of these components can rightfully be called symbols because they "stand for" the spirits or forces or convey meaning in some way, although members of the religion would often disagree that they are merely symbolic. In fact, from the member's point of view, some "symbols" are symbolic and some are not. For a Warlpiri, a *churinga* stone or board is not a symbol of an ancestral spirit but a *manifestation* of that spirit – what the eminent scholar of comparative religion Mircea Eliade called a "hierophany" or appearance of the sacred in the material world.

Various such "symbolic" objects, places, and behaviors exist in the religious domain. Every religion, for instance, has sacred spaces, either sacralized by humans or by the spirits who live(d) there. A ceremonial ground, a mountain, a building, or an entire city may be a sacred space. Religions contain sacred objects as well, such as the medicine arrows of the Cheyenne, and carvings, paintings, masks and many other examples across cultures. Relics (pieces of the bodies of important human figures) have religious significance in some societies. Finally, symbolic or sacred behaviors are key to religion, in particular behaviors that are intended as communication between humans and their non/superhuman partners. Because the religious beings and forces are powerful and real, it is of central importance for humans to get information from or give information to these entities, to show them respect, and to determine and follow their bidding. In this and other ways, the relationships between humans and non/superhumans are analogous to the relationships between humans themselves; they are social and (hopefully) reciprocal relations, predictable and controllable (to some extent) and shaped by the same roles, values, practices, and institutions as human interactions.

These religious behaviors can take diverse forms or be expressed in diverse media. Two obvious and not entirely separable media are language and "action" or bodily motion, although language ultimately is action and most religious behaviors feature both. Under these two major headings are a variety of types of behaviors, which, as Wallace and Boyer and Atran have noted, often also have their non-religious counterparts.

Religious behavior: ritual

Ritual is not an exclusively religious phenomenon; people can be ritualistic about anything, and even animals have rituals (e.g., mating rituals, fighting rituals). A ritual most generally is a highly stylized and formalized behavior pattern that is thought to be effective if performed properly. Humans engage in all kinds of rituals that are not religious in any manner of speaking, from ritual greetings (some much more extensive and formalized than the English "How are you? Fine, how are you?") to

Ritual
Any type of formal, repetitive behavior that is felt to have significance beyond the actions themselves. In particular, religious ritual is often composed of symbols, re-enacts supernatural/ mythical events, and is believed to have efficacy if performed correctly.

obsessive-compulsive rituals like hand-washing and "good luck" routines to "ritual murder." Anything that an individual – and even more so, a society – does repeatedly in the same way is a ritual. In this sense, most or all of culture is ritual or ritualistic, because it depends on people knowing and doing the "right things" in particular social situations, from saying "Good morning" when you see someone for the first time of the day to saying "I do" when you officially marry someone. Rituals, then, have been characterized by the philosopher John Skorupski in his study of anthropology as part of the *interaction code*, which he defines as behavior intended "to establish or maintain (or destroy) an equilibrium, or mutual agreement, among the people involved in an interaction as to their relative standing or roles, and their reciprocal commitments and obligations" (1976: 77). Interaction between humans is routinized and culturized by the elaboration of an interaction code that contains such elements as honor and politeness. Accordingly, with non/superhumans also now inside the interactional universe of humans, the interaction code extends to them – and they tend to receive the "highest," most formal, and most "ritualized" behavior of all.

Religious rituals can take many forms, and Wallace (1966) has suggested a typology, including the following:

Skorupski, John. 1976.
*Symbol and Theory: A
Philosophical Study of
Theories of Religion in
Social Anthropology.*
Cambridge: Cambridge
University Press.

- ■ Technical rituals – rituals that are intended to achieve certain specific ends, like divination or rites of intensification (see below).
- ■ Therapeutic or anti-therapeutic rituals – rituals that are intended to cure illness and misfortune, such as shamanic healing, or to cause it, such as sorcery and witchcraft.

PLATE 10.2 Warlpiri women lead girls in a dance ritual

■ Ideological rituals – rituals that are intended to express or achieve social goals, including rites of passage (see below), taboos, and rituals of rebellion or transgression (e.g., carnival).

■ Salvation rituals – rituals that are intended to work changes in individuals, particularly at moments of personal crisis, such as spirit possession or mystical experiences.

■ Revitalization rituals – rituals that are intended to work changes in society, particularly at moments of social crisis.

See Chapter 15

Within these types, a few specific ritual actions or general "ritual processes" demand more attention. One of these is **rites of intensification** which are activated to "intensify" nature or society at specific times or on a regular schedule. A reason for intensifying nature is, for instance, to guarantee or increase the fertility of plants, animals, and even humans (leading to what are sometimes called "increase rituals"). Thus, a society may perform a ritual to increase the number or health or reproductive capacity of wild species or domesticated herds. A reason for intensifying society may be a crisis or shock that threatens to disorient or even disintegrate society, such as a natural disaster, a death, or a defeat in war. A ritual at such times could bring people back together as a society and strengthen the bonds that unite them. Some rites of intensification are ad hoc, while others are "calendrical," that is, are part of a society's ritual calendar. For farmers, a harvest will occur every year around the same time, so a harvest ritual can occur every year around the same time. Americans find remnants of this in the observance of Halloween, a version of a harvest (and death, which is often associated with the harvest and the approach of winter) festival. Some American rituals combine natural and historical occurrences (Thanksgiving), while some are purely historical (Fourth of July).

Rite of intensification
A form of ritual in which members of the society are brought into greater communion, in which social bonds are intensified.

Sacrifice is not a specific kind of ritual so much as a recurring ingredient in rituals. A sacrifice is the voluntary loss of something valuable, usually through destruction, usually as a way of communicating with spirits in the sense of offering a gift or "payment" to them. In many cases, the central notion is that the spirit world in some way provides the resources that humans enjoy in their lives; since the spirits give humans so much, the least humans can do is to give a small amount back. It is essentially religious reciprocity. In some systems, it is told that the spirits demand such sacrifices or else they will withhold their providence; in others, it is thought to be a good and generous gesture, as when various societies set a small portion of their meal aside in honor of the gods. Sometimes it is a matter of giving thanks. In other cases, as in Aztec religion, the sacrifice (including of humans) was believed to be necessary for the continued functioning of the universe (i.e., the hungry sun-god required sacrifices of human hearts and blood to make it return each day).

Sacrifice
A ritual behavior in which something is destroyed or killed, in the belief that supernatural powers are somehow unleashed.

Finally, the anthropologist Victor Turner (1969, 1981) identified a "ritual process" which follows a common pattern or progression. Turner noticed that many rituals have a recurrent structure, in which individuals undergoing the ritual are transformed – socially or even physically – from one condition or status to another. Following Van Gennup's suggestion, he called these **rites of passage**, indicating that

Rite of passage
A form of ritual intended to accompany or accomplish a change of status or role of the participants, such as initiation (change from youth to adult) or marriage.

Turner, Victor. 1969. *The Ritual Process: Structure and Anti-Structure.* Chicago: Aldine Publishing.

the subjects "pass" from one social state to another. Familiar examples of rites of passage include weddings and graduations and (at least in some interpretations) funerals. Before a wedding ceremony, each party is a "single person," but after – and *because of* – the ceremony, each party is a "married person." They are moved from one social position or status to another, with different social roles and expectations.

Societies and religions are replete with rites of passage. Initiation rituals are one prominent example; ordination rituals of priests or training rituals of shamans are others. The key to the process of ritual passage is the removal of the subject person from his or her previous role or status and re-placement into a new role or status; however, "in between" there is a period of "rolelessness," or non-identity, or undifferentiated status, which Turner called **liminality**. In the liminal phase, the person is neither this nor that but is between statuses and therefore without status. For most Western/Christian rituals this moment is usually fleeting, but some religions or rituals sustain it for a long period. In Australian Aboriginal initiations, boys or young men would literally be isolated from society for weeks or months, following a ritual "capture" that was treated and mourned like a death. During the isolation they might undergo deprivations like silence and nakedness, as well as physical operations like circumcision and also some learning about or at least exposure to sacred knowledge and objects. Upon their return to society, they were "new people"; symbolically, the boy had died and a man had been made in his place, with an altered body to mark his transformation.

Liminality

The condition of being "in between" or "on the margins" of social roles, in particular of being in transition (as during ritual) between one social role and another.

Religious language: myth

Myth

A narrative, usually of the activities of supernatural beings, often telling of how some or all of the natural or social world was established. In addition to an "explanation" of origins, it also provides a "charter" or model for how humans should live today.

When most English speakers use the word "**myth**," they imply a disbelief in or disdain for some story or claim (e.g., the "myths" of weight loss or the "myths" of ancient Greek religion). People do not usually apply the word "myth" to their own cherished and accepted beliefs, since the word feels pejorative: Christians do not call the story of Adam and Eve a myth. Anthropologically, myth does not suggest or denote falsity. Rather, we should think of a myth as simply a form of religious communication, a narrative (story) of sacred quality that has some explanatory function or effect. That is, a myth tends to be an account of how some aspect of the known world – the universe as a whole, the Earth or the society's particular environment, human beings, or social institutions, for example – came into existence. The "creation" may be an act of god(s), animal or plant spirits, or human ancestors ("culture heroes") and can be as diverse across cultures as may possibly be imagined.

Socially, then, myths are a way in which members of a society communicate their ideas about the sacred and about their own "holy history"; as such, myths are a manifestation of the general human tendency to turn our lives and worlds into stories. Humans are story-telling beings; that is, we aim to "make sense" of the flow of events and facts by organizing the details into a continuous and meaningful narrative, one that usually has a message or "moral" of some sort. Myths then are "instructional" in the strongest possible sense of the word – they put "structure in" human thought and human social life. They have been described as "charters" or "models" for how humans should live their lives today, and of course for how they should think about their lives and their world. As Bronislaw Malinowski wrote in one of the most oft-quoted passages in anthropology:

> Studied alive, myth . . . is not symbolic, but a direct expression of its subject matter; it is not an explanation in satisfaction of a scientific interest, but a narrative resurrection of a primeval reality, told in satisfaction of deep religious wants, moral cravings, social submissions, assertions, even practical requirements. Myth fulfills in primitive culture an indispensable function; it expresses, enhances, and codifies belief; it safeguards and enforces morality; it vouches for the efficiency of ritual and contains practical rules for the guidance of man. Myth is thus a vital ingredient of human civilization; it is not an idle tale, but a hard-worked active force; it is not an intellectual explanation or an artistic imagery, but a pragmatic charter of primitive faith and moral wisdom.
>
> (1948: 101)

Malinowski, Bronislaw. 1948. Magic, Science, and Religion and Other Essays. Garden City, NY: Doubleday Anchor Books.

Religious language: prayer

Prayer is a type of religious speech directed specifically to supernatural beings. The form and intent of prayer depends intimately on the nature of the spirit being prayed to. Sam Gill (1981) conducted a major analysis of Navajo prayer, which cannot be understood apart from the concepts and myths of the society. He writes that "prayers are considered to be complex ritual acts whose performances engage and are informed by elements of mythology and the cultural contexts in which they are performed" (xxii). In fact, this context is critical, since any particular prayer may be used in different ways with different meanings, for instance, "in one context to request and effect a smooth and healthy birth and in another to request and effect rainfall in a period of drought" (xxiii).

Prayer
A form of linguistic religious ritual in which humans are believed to speak to and interact with supernatural beings.

Gill, Sam D. 1981. Sacred Words: A Study of Navajo Religion and Prayer. Westport, CT: Greenwood Press.

Reviewing 300 different accounts of Navajo prayers, Gill arrives at eight general types: blessings, prayers of restoration/recovery by reidentification/reassociation with the means of health, prayers of restoration by expulsion of foreign malevolence, prayers of restoration by expulsion of the malevolent influence of native ghosts or witches, prayers of restoration by the removal of the malevolent influence of Holy People, prayers of restoration by the recovery, return, and reassociation with the means of health, prayers of procurement of protection against potential attack, and prayers of restoration by remaking/redressing the Holy Person's means of health and life. Even more, each prayer type has a standard structure of elements in a particular order. For example, an Enemyway prayer, which is part of a ritual to expel a foreign evil, opens with a place reference, which is followed by naming one or more sacred beings called Holy People, then a section asking for the removal of the evil force, and finally one or more references to an eventual state of blessing.

Religious language: specialized ritual speech

In many societies and religions, one way of indicating the special and "set-apart" nature of the religious occasion is through the use of forms of speech not used at any other time. For instance, until the Second Vatican Council (1962–1965), the Catholic mass was performed exclusively in Latin, the language of religion and "high culture," and reformers like Martin Luther met with great resistance in efforts to translate the Bible into vernacular languages. (Many Catholics continue to reject the changes enacted at the Second Vatican Council, perhaps most famously Mel Gibson.) Likewise, Islamic tradition insists that the Qur'an can only be presented in Arabic and that all translations are misinterpretations at best and betrayals at worst.

See Chapter 4

As we mentioned already, special speech styles and formats are distinguishable by unique properties, including vocabularies that are not employed in any other type of speech, voice qualities (like chanting or singing), the use of metaphor, and specific formulas such as standard openings or endings. For example, Parks (1996), in his study of myths and narratives of the Arikara of South Dakota, proposes six areas in which their religious language differs from other, more mundane language forms:

1. Characters. Myths and tales often employ a cast of well-known characters like Lucky Man, Stays in the Lodge Dressed in Finery, Bloody Hands, Scalped Man, and so on.
2. "Style." Myths and stories are often told in the third person, using quotation and a verb form which indicates that the teller did not witness the events himself or herself. Actions are frequently described after the results of the actions, with

PLATE 10.3 A sacred site: the inside of a spirit-house in Papua New Guinea

the actor identified last. Tellings use repetition, indeterminacy (e.g., words like *niikohna-* meaning "whoever/whichever"), and introductions like "This is what he said."

3. Morphology and syntax. Narratives contain many special words, phrases, and constructions, such as "introducers" and "connectors" like *nawah* and *wah* (for "now" or "well"), demonstratives and exclamatives, and "decedents" that refer to deceased characters (like *nuuxU* for "the one who was"). In addition, sentences alternate between long and short.

4. Narrative structure. Stories often open with formulaic phrases like *kuwiteetu-unu'a'* or *nuuneesawatuuNU*, for "the village was coming in a long procession" or "there over the hill," respectively (akin to the English "Once upon a time"). Specific stock episodes may be added or subtracted, or more or less elaborated. Explanations or "morals" may be given, and stories that are regarded as "factual" may end with a credit for the source, such as "Now this is what I used to hear when my grandmother told the story."

5. Context. Myths and tales must also be told and received properly in social terms. The teller must be shown respect and offered a gift of food or tobacco. References to directions and colors are part of the telling, and themes of power acquisition and sympathy for the unfortunate – orphans, the poor, the sick – are common.

6. Performance. Religious language, like all other forms of language and of social behavior, is a *performance* with its own rules and norms. There are proper ways and times to do it, and circumstances that distinguish it as one kind of behavior or narrative rather than another. Myths and tales, for example, were traditionally only told in the winter, preferably during the evening and mostly by men. The audience would interject with words like *hini* or "go on," and speakers might take turns adding an episode or telling a new version. When one was finished speaking, he would say something like *wetAhneesi'it* or "Now I am letting go of the gut."

BOX 10.3 CONTEMPORARY CULTURAL CONTROVERSIES: "CIVIL RELIGION" IN THE U.S.A.

Robert Bellah suggests that the United States has a second religion alongside Christianity, which he calls, following Rousseau, the "civil religion." According to Bellah, the central concept of American civil religion is "God," "a word that almost all Americans can accept but that means so many different things to so many different people that it is almost an empty sign" (1967: 3). However, it does not make reference to Jesus or other specifically Christian beliefs. Even more, the god of civil religion "is also on the austere side, much more related to order, law, and right than to salvation and love" (7). Why does America – or

Bellah, Robert N. 1967. "Civil Religion in America." *Daedalus* 96 (1): 1–21.

Kosmin, Barry A., Egon
Mayer, and Ariela Keysar.
2001. *American Religious
Identification Survey*.
New York: The Graduate
Center of the City
University of New York.

any society – need a civil religion? Bellah's answer is that the religion gives the society and its institutions, policies, and leadership "legitimation" and "transcendental goals." But why a religion other than or in addition to Christianity? At least one reason is America's dazzling religious diversity: approximately 75 percent of Americans are Christians, but that number contains hundreds if not thousands of sects and denominations with different doctrines, and the remaining 25 percent are non-Christian – either religions other than Christianity or non-religious (14 percent, according to the *American Religious Identification Survey* [Kosmin et al. 2001]). The civil religion is intended to be "non-sectarian," something that all Americans can agree on. But in a ruling on the civil religion practice of including "one nation under God" in the U.S. Pledge of Allegiance, a federal court declared that saying "'under God' is identical, for Establishment Clause [i.e. constitutional] purposes, to a profession that we are a nation 'under Jesus,' a nation 'under Vishnu' [or] a nation 'under Zeus'" (U.S. Court of Appeals of the Ninth Circuit 2002: 9123). What do you think?

SUMMARY

Religion is part of human culture, but it presents unique problems for anthropology, not only because both members of societies and anthropologists themselves often take it more seriously and literally than other parts but because it poses profound challenges to the terms and concepts that we use to understand and analyze cross-cultural belief and behavior. A firm and authoritative definition is difficult to determine, but an essential feature is that it includes conceptions of non-human and superhuman beings and forces that are in social and cultural relationships with humans. Society and its prerogatives and meanings are thus expanded to include humans and other kinds of "persons." We can also identify social functions that religion fulfills, from explanation to individual emotional needs to social integration and social control.

A religion is a loose system of different kinds of concepts, roles, and behaviors. Every religion appears to include:

■ "spiritual" being(s) and/or force(s), including a "spiritual" part of humans;
■ roles for human specialists;
■ behavioral or "ritual" activity;
■ language or religious speech, usually as part of – or itself being – ritual activity.

Within the category of beings and forces is a wide variety of overlapping conceptions, with permeable boundaries, such that humans can become spirits or demons or even gods and vice versa. Some beings and forces are intimately known, while others are vague and amorphous.

Religious ideas and practices help to explain, control, and legitimize the social and natural world. They also, like myths, linguistic "performatives," and rites of passage, are meant to affect the human and non-human world and to bring about actual changes in individuals, society, and the universe.

Key Terms

Ancestor spirit	Prayer
Animatism	Priest
Animism	Prophet
Contagious magic	Rite of intensification
Deism	Rite of passage
Diviner	Ritual
Ghost	Sacrifice
Liminality	Shaman
Monotheism	Sorcerer
Myth	Soul
Oracle	Theism
Pantheism	Totemism
Polytheism	Witch

Seeing Culture as a Whole #2: The Integration of Culture in Warlpiri Society

Prior to the 1940s, when they were settled into communities by government and missionary authorities, the Warlpiri were a foraging society inhabiting the Central Desert of Australia, northwest of present-day Alice Springs. The environment was and is forbidding, with little standing water, small and sparse trees, hot summer days and cold winter nights, and no great abundance of animal or plant foods. The Warlpiri survived with minimal technology (spears and boomerangs but no bow and arrow, and certainly no houses or writing) through intimate knowledge of the land and the species on it, and food was usually adequate. However, they lived in small, dispersed, mobile family units, usually a man and his wives and children, and seldom gathered in larger groups except in times of plenty or on ritual occasions. The men hunted kangaroos and other larger animals, while the women gathered plant materials and the children caught small species like goannas (a type of lizard). They walked continuously, dividing into gender-specific teams and reassembling at the end of day, when they camped at named sites such as waterholes and hills. Everything that was collected during the day was cooked and eaten communally. There was relative tranquility and equality within the group.

While Warlpiri material culture was simple, the abstract and conceptual parts of the culture were highly developed. Kinship was one area of elaboration. All Warlpiri (and visitors like myself) belong to one of eight named kinship categories, called "skin names" in English; if you want to ask a Warlpiri what his or her skin name is, you ask "*Nyiya nyiya nyuntuju?*" or "What are you really?" (literally, what-what-you). The eight categories come in two gender variations, with J-terms for men and N-terms for women:

Jakamarra/Nakamarra	Japaljarri/Napaljarri
Jupurrula/Naparrula	Japanangka/Napanangka
Jangala/Nangala	Jungarrayi/Nungarrayi
Jampijinpa/Nampijinpa	Japangardi/Napangardi

The terms orient every member of the social universe. Gender pairs are brother and sister, and all individuals with the same skin name are siblings, metaphorically if not literally. Skin name is determined by one's father in alternating pairs: a Jakamarra man has Jupurrula/Napurrula children, and a Jupurrula man has Jakamarra and Nakamarra children. All other skin names are in some kin relation to the individual.

Skin name also determines who is a good choice for marriage partner. The ideal wife for a Jakamarra is a Napaljarri (in fact, each of the horizontal pairings in the list above is an ideal marriage pairing). In addition, Jakamarras and Japaljarris (like each horizontal pair of males) can and often do exchange sisters in marriage, creating the *bunji* or brother-in-law relationship between them, a particularly warm and friendly one. However, some marriages are especially avoided, say, between a Jakamarra and a Napanangka (who would be his mother) or Nangala (who would be his mother-in-law). Traditionally, they practiced a strong version of mother-in-law avoidance, although in the present it seems to be fading.

Warlpiri society did not include formal lineages or clans. However, the eight kinship groups were organized into two sets of four, making a system of two exogamous moieties. The main functions of the moieties were religious and ritual, as discussed below.

The pre-contact political system of the Warlpiri was not distinguished from the economic, kinship, and religious domains. There was no real "headman," although older men tended to have more prestige than younger ones and than women. Men were "graded" mainly in terms of religious and ceremonial knowledge, although no man could hope to possess it all, given the geographic and social distribution of such knowledge. Still, a man could rise up through the "ranks" of knowledge to become an important ritual leader, although this did not convey any real "political" power. Even prestigious men had to hunt and could not compel the labor of others.

Two recognizably political institutions – agents of social control – outside of the family unit were the *kurdaitja* and the Red Ochre Men. *Kurdaitja* or "feather feet" were men who, as supernatural beings, would walk among camps without leaving footprints and punish other men for transgressions, particularly ritual improprieties like showing sacred objects to women or uninitiated men. The Red Ochre Men were another association of powerful ritual leaders who patrolled the society and administered similar punishments, largely through fear; I watched people run in every direction when they heard the Red Ochre Men were coming.

Warlpiri religion, like that of all Aboriginal peoples, is based on a concept translated into English as "Dreaming" or "Dreamtime." Called *jukurrpa* in Warlpiri, it refers to the creation time at the Beginning when the ancestral spirits emerged from the ground, took physical form, and had adventures. Their actions produced the landscape as well as the social institutions of the Warlpiri. Places where the ancestors sat or lived are *jukurrpa* today, as are the rituals in which these events are re-enacted and the dreams in which they are experienced anew. Each Warlpiri person is one of these spirits or *pirlirrpa* in a human body, depending on where s/he was conceived or where the mother first discovered her pregnancy. A person traditionally lived his or her life learning about and "looking after" his or her dreaming, including the "country" associated with it. Warlpiri country, and all of Australia, was criss-crossed by "Dreaming tracks" that sometimes passed through the territory of multiple societies. Members would gather in appropriate groupings to perform their ritual duties, which involved singing and dancing and the fashioning of ceremonial objects. Perhaps the most important ceremony was the initiation and circumcision of young males.

For purposes of ritual, the two moieties had complementary functions. The "side" that comprised the primary "owners" and performers of the ritual was *kirda* and did the singing and dancing. The other side acted as assistants or *kurdungurlu*, helping with preparations and food and such. On other occasions, the roles would be reversed.

At death, a person's "spirit" returned to the earth, to be reborn into another human in the future. Death, however, except for the very old and young, was not considered a "natural" event but a social or supernatural one (or both) and was often the occasion for angry duels and real bloodshed. It was also a time for "sorry business," which included funeral rituals, self-mutilations (such as bashing one's head or cutting one's face), and restrictions on the name or image of the dead. The person's name or any word that sounded like it could not be spoken, and was replaced with the word *kumanjayi* or "no name."

The cycle of Warlpiri birth, initiation, and death linked humans individually and collectively to a spiritual world that was manifest in and not separable from a natural world. Thus, in the final analysis, the natural, the human/social, and the spiritual were one continuous system.

Cultural Dynamics: Continuity and Change

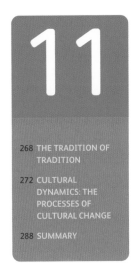

After several weeks on the ground in Australia, I arrived at my first Australian Aboriginal community, Bamyili in northeast Northern Territory, one evening after dark. Waking up the next morning, the first thing I heard outside was the sound of heavy equipment. I looked out of the window and saw Aboriginal people driving bulldozers and backhoes. My immediate reaction was, "This is not what I came here to see!" I wanted, and I suppose expected, to see "traditional people" doing traditional things – going "walkabout," throwing spears, and doing mystical rituals. Like many people, I had been raised on a diet of "traditional cultures" in which "traditional" means "authentic" and anything else is somewhere between corrupted and false. Since that time, I have observed Aboriginal people driving cars, speaking fine English, reading a book on the life of Gandhi, playing the guitar, and watching and even making their own radio and television programs, as well as going walkabout, throwing spears, and doing mystical rituals. Aboriginal people, I had to realize, are like all other people – citizens of the modern world, whose ways of thinking and behaving are a complex blend of "traditional" and "non-traditional," local and global. I have also realized that it was always this way, that no culture is or ever has been frozen in time or preserved under glass.

Cultural anthropology is the study of the diversity of human behavior in the present. This is true enough, but it hardly conveys the depth or the urgency of the discipline. Even worse, anthropology has long and often had, and helped perpetuate, the reputation that it is exclusively concerned with small or traditional societies, remote tribes and such. The influential A. R. Radcliffe-Brown actually described anthropology not long ago as "the study of what are called primitive or backward people" (1965: 2). Aside from the fact that "primitive" and "backward" are harsh and judgmental terms which we do not use today, the statement itself is false in the twenty-first century and has been for decades – if it was ever true. If anthropology were seriously to consider itself, or to be considered, the science of the primitive and the traditional, then it would be finished, since there are no primitive or purely traditional people in the world to study. On the other hand, new "traditions" are emerging all the time and diversity remains and thrives, giving anthropology an endless supply of cultural phenomena to investigate, along with the basic processes of culture and tradition themselves.

If modern professional anthropology, marked by the innovations of Boas and Malinowski, could maintain an innocent and naive attitude toward culture and tradition through the first half of the twentieth century (and, on close inspection, it did not always), it certainly had shed that attitude by the second half of the twentieth century. As early as 1945 (the end of World War II), books like *The Science of Man in the World Crisis* (Linton 1945) and Malinowski's own *The Dynamics of Culture Change* (1945) illustrated that the discipline had become aware of the changes that were occurring in their chosen subject societies, in the world around them, and in the discipline itself. It was Stanley Diamond who, in anthropology's soul-searching phase in the late 1960s and early 1970s, finally recast it as "the study of man in crisis by man in crisis" (1972: 401). This is profoundly true and profoundly important but not profoundly new. In a certain sense, the human world has probably always been in crisis in some way or another, whether it was the Native Americans confronting the first European settlers, the ancient Israelites confronting the first Roman conquerors, or Neandertals confronting the first *Homo sapiens*.

So, anthropology has changed, and *had* to change, because the groups that it aims to study have changed. It has also come to see change as not "corruption" or "de-traditionalization" but as an inherent part of the cultural process, of the dynamic nature of culture and human ways of living. It has also, as a result of these realizations, taken a look at itself in new ways and come away from the experience better for it.

THE TRADITION OF TRADITION

Many people (and perhaps a few anthropologists) still think of anthropology as the study of traditional cultures. Outside of anthropology, the "tradition" word has taken on major cultural and political significance, as American citizens, for instance, debate issues of "traditional marriage" or "traditional values," and so on. "**Tradition**" is not just a term or concept of interest to anthropologists but to the general public, and in fact it is or was an anthropological concept because it is a general concept, not unlike "belief" or even "culture," as we have seen in past chapters. Anthropology is, or at least has been, a product of its own culture too.

Linton, Ralph, ed. 1945. *The Science of Man in the World Crisis*. New York: Columbia University Press.

Malinowski, Bronislaw. 1945. *The Dynamics of Culture Change: An Inquiry into Race Relations in Africa*. New Haven and London: Yale University Press.

Tradition
Some practice or idea or object that is (at least believed to be) continuous or associated with "the past." A tradition may be very ancient or very recent, but as an ideological element it is often assumed to be important, authentic, and even "superior" to non-traditional (especially foreign) practices, ideas, and objects.

The discussion of tradition – or the discussion *in terms of tradition* – is not so much false as vacuous. What precisely is tradition? It implies something that exists and continues "from way back" or "following old ways." "Traditional," therefore, suggests continuity with the past, something that is rooted in and even the same as the past. But of course, no societies today are carrying on the past exactly as it was. First, no society is a living fossil, and no society resides in the past. All existing societies live in the present. Second, no society is or ever has been in such complete isolation from the "outside world" that it did not have some exposure to other societies and incorporate some elements of those other cultures into its own. Certainly many if not all of these societies have incorporated influences from the "modern" world, like cars and cell phones and blue jeans. But they have also absorbed influences from neighboring "traditional peoples" that were "changing" them long before the "modern world" arrived.

There is a third issue that makes the term and idea of tradition even more problematic: if "tradition" refers to the past, then which particular moment of the past and which particular parts of that moment? When you think, for instance, of the "traditional cuisine" of Italy, you probably think of pasta and tomato sauce. And indeed, for the past few hundred years, pasta and tomato sauce have been staples of the Italian kitchen – but only for the past few hundred years. Further back in the past, 500 or 600 or 1,000 years ago, these dishes were not and could not have been Italian traditions. Tomatoes were not native to Europe; rather, they were domesticated by ancient Native American societies and introduced to Europe only after contact following 1492. Even pasta was not a local creation of Europe but was developed in China and brought to the attention of Europeans through the voyages of Marco Polo and others in the 1300s and 1400s. Travelers carried the practice of noodle-making back to Europe, modified it using local ingredients (wheat instead of rice), and came up with pasta. Later, tomato sauces were added to create a "traditional" cuisine that had never existed before.

We could multiply examples infinitely. When, say, Protestant Christians talk about their "religious traditions," those traditions cannot extend back more than 500 years (and often much less), since Protestantism only originated in the early 1500s. And "Christian tradition" as such cannot reach back more than 2,000 years, since there was no Christianity at all before that time. Every tradition has its starting point, before which it could not be "traditional" and immediately after which it was not traditional but innovative, even radical.

The upshot of this discussion is that, like so much else in the cultural world, *tradition is relative*. It is relative to the particular society or social matter at hand (that is, there are Christian traditions and Jewish traditions and Muslim traditions and Warlpiri traditions). It is relative to the particular time period to which "traditionalists" point (fifty years ago, 500 years ago, 5,000 years ago?). And it is relative to the particular elements of that time period which the "traditionalists" want to emphasize or celebrate. In other words, when Americans talk about preserving or returning to "traditional values," they usually mean not only a particular moment – usually around the 1950s, not the 1850s or 1750s – but only certain aspects of that moment. Presumably, they are not talking about returning to racial segregation or black-and-white television. And presumably, they are not talking about living without cell phones and computers and modern medicine. They are, in other words, picking and choosing from among the shards of the past to imagine a "traditional culture."

There is no such thing as a "traditional" culture – not today and probably not ever – because the very meaning of the term is so vague and relative. If by "traditional" we mean "living in some primordial unchanged condition," then the idea is not just wrong but nonsensical: no society lives the way it did "in the beginning." More importantly still for us, anthropology too has its "traditions." Doing fieldwork and writing ethnographies are anthropological traditions. Focusing on small-scale and remote societies is an anthropological tradition. And treating these societies as if they were "traditional" is an anthropological tradition. It has even been argued that the very notions of "society" and "culture" are anthropological traditions (Kuper 1988; Wagner 1975). It is well to recall that anthropology emerged at a specific place and time with specific interests. Anthropology's initial interests were in origins and history: how did culture start, what was the first kind of culture, what was the first religion or kinship system or other parts of culture, and how has culture "progressed" to its present state? These were the questions that informed the early approach of cultural evolutionism, looking for the "stages" of cultural evolution from "primitive" to "civilized." This perspective was roundly and thoroughly rejected by later

See Chapter 3

anthropologists like Bronislaw Malinowski and Franz Boas as both speculative and ethnocentric.

Because the project of Culture history (with a capital C) required "survivals" from past cultural eras in order to fill in the line of progression, and because the researchers who arrived to study the "primitive societies" necessarily had no data on the prior state of those societies, it was easy and natural to conclude or assume that they had no history, that they were living "in some primordial unchanged condition." More, it was useful: only if those remote societies were preserved fossils of a lost cultural past could they play their role as exemplars of former and lower cultural formations. Eric Wolf, in his epic treatise on the contact between Europeans and non-European peoples, made light of this notion in the title of his book, *Europe and the People without History* (1982). As a result of the apparent dearth of historical information and of the obvious excesses of the Culture history approach, Malinowski and Boas advised on avoiding historical questions at all, probably perpetuating the impression that non-European societies really were ahistorical and static.

Interestingly, Malinowski, the father of ahistorical "functionalism," is wrongly accused of being unaware of or unconcerned with history and change. In fact, he was one of the first major scholars to draw attention to both, in his 1945 book mentioned above and excerpted below.

BOX 11.1   MALINOWSKI ON THE "CHANGING NATIVE"

The following passages from *The Dynamics of Culture Change* (1945) demonstrate Malinowski's aware-ness of the changing nature of "traditional culture" and its importance to anthropology.

The figment of the "uncontaminated" Native has to be dropped from research in field and study. The cogent reason for this is that the "uncontaminated" Native does not exist anywhere. The man of science has to study what is, and not what might have been (2–3).

The scientific anthropologist must be the anthropologist of the changing Native. Why? Because what exists nowadays is not a primitive culture in isolation but one in contact and process of change (6).

The nature of culture change is determined by factors and circumstances which cannot be assessed by the study of either [European or traditional] culture alone, or of both of them as lumber rooms of elements. The clash and interplay of the two cultures produce new things (25).

To the student of culture change, what really matters is not the objectively true past, scientifically reconstructed and all-important to the antiquarian, but the psychological reality of today (29).

[T]he retrospective vision, however erroneous, is more important than the myth unknown or forgotten by old informants (31).

What the "old men of the tribe" tell us about the past can never be scientific or historical truth, since it is always affected by sentiment, by retrospective regrets and longings (154).

[E]lements of the old culture . . . are being revived with a secondary, almost ethnographic interest in racial history, customary law, and the artistic and intellectual achievements of their race. . . . This sophisticated nationalism or tribalism can still draw full strength from the enormous residues of old tradition (158).

Later anthropologists took this insight much further, pondering whether the very concepts of "culture" and "society" might be impositions on social reality. Edmund Leach was perhaps the first to question the objectivity of terms like "society," calling clearly bounded and distinguishable societies an "academic fiction": the anthro-pologist, he wrote, "has often only managed to discern the existence of [a society] because he took it as axiomatic that this kind of cultural entity must exist" (1954: 291). This awareness led to a flood of publications with titles like *Reinventing Anthropology* (Hymes 1972), *The Invention of Culture* (Wagner 1975), *The Invention of Primitive Society* (Kuper 1988), and ultimately *The Invention of Tradition* (Hobsbawm and Ranger 1983). Roy Wagner, for instance, argued that we assume that culture is "a concrete entity, a 'thing' that has rules, 'works' in a certain way, and can

Hymes, Dell, ed. 1972 [1969]. *Reinventing Anthropology*. New York: Random House, Inc.

Wagner, Roy. 1975. *The Invention of Culture*. Englewood Cliffs, NJ: Prentice-Hall, Inc.

Kuper, Adam. 1988. *The Invention of Primitive Society: Transformations of an Illusion*. London: Routledge.

Hobsbawm, Eric and
Terence Ranger, eds.
1983. *The Invention of
Tradition.* Cambridge:
Cambridge University
Press.

be learned" and then go out and find what we expected to find (1975: 8). Kuper added the observation that the concept of society, especially primitive society, supported certain preconceptions and prejudices of Europeans of their day with regard to their own origins and to the relation of cultural "essentials" to identity. In other words, he said that

> the idea of primitive society fed the common belief that societies were based either on blood or on soil, and that these principles of descent and territoriality may be equated with race and citizenship, the contrasting components of every imperialism and every nationalism.
>
> (1988: 9)

Since those days of the "crisis in anthropology," brought about partly by the crisis in the subject peoples of anthropology, the discipline has become even more self-reflective. In a way, anthropology itself is not as "traditional" as it once was, just as the societies we examine are not as "traditional" either. Clifford and Marcus' (1986) *Writing Culture: The Poetics and Politics of Ethnography*, Marcus and Fischer's (1986) *Anthropology as Cultural Critique*, Crapanzano's (1992) *Hermes' Dilemma and Hamlet's Desire: On the Epistemology of Interpretation*, and most scathingly Sandall's (2001) *The Culture Cult* have questioned the objectivity, the scientific-ness, and even the motivations of anthropologists and others who use "traditional culture" for various purposes. Clifford and Marcus in particular point to the "literary" and even poetic quality of anthropological works, that they are "fictions" or "narratives" instead of or in addition to "factual accounts," and Sandall savagely criticizes the romantic and destructive "designer tribalism" he sees in much professional and popular thinking about culture. What all of these authors, and the entire history of anthropology and the encounter with cultural difference, show is that the description of, analysis of, and participation in culture and culture change are much more problematic and subjective – in the end, more human – than was once thought.

Clifford, James and George
Marcus, eds. 1986.
*Writing Culture: The
Poetics and Politics of
Ethnography.* Berkeley:
University of California
Press.

CULTURAL DYNAMICS: THE PROCESSES OF CULTURAL CHANGE

Cultures and societies are not easy things to grasp and portray, because they are complex, living, and developing things with inexact borders and histories. This is why it is unprofitable to speak of "culture change" as if it is foreign, almost unnatural or hostile, to "traditional culture." In fact, as we have said, "culture change" is a constant and natural quality of culture, not something that only appeared in recent years or centuries with colonialism and globalization. Just as a living body does not stay the same throughout its lifetime, neither does a society or culture. This is why we will talk about the "processes of culture change" under the more general heading of cultural dynamics – dynamics meaning action, movement, growth, and generation. Culture never stands still but moves and develops continuously. Any actual culture is a complicated and sometimes contradictory fusion of continuity and change.

Innovation and diffusion

What the "original" form of culture was, or where it came from, we will probably never know. Primate studies suggest some indication of what pre-cultural or proto-cultural but highly social and imitative beings can be like, but non-human primates are just that – not human. So their study can answer some questions but not the most fundamental question: what is human culture and how did humans get it? Therefore, a better question to ask is: what are the means by which cultural novelty enters, and then affects, a society? Again, as we said above, cultures do undoubtedly tend to be "conservative" in the sense that they try to preserve and repeat what they have done in the past. However, new elements do enter cultures, or else we would all still be sitting in caves making stone tools – which were themselves cultural novelties at first.

See Chapter 2

There are two main sources of novelty in any particular society: **innovation** and **diffusion**. Innovation is the ultimate source of all cultural novelty: at some point in time, somebody has to think of or start doing something different. An innovation (literally, "to make/do new") can take the form of an invention or a discovery, as well as the form of a **primary innovation** (the development of a completely new principle or object) or a **secondary innovation** (a novel application or combination of already-existing principles or objects, i.e., using old components in new arrangements, such as attaching wires and vacuum tubes to invent a television). In whatever form, the key characteristic of innovation is that it is internal to the society: a member of the society introduces it into the society.

Innovation is not only the ultimate source of cultural novelty but it tends to be a very individual or personal source. In other words, most if not all innovations (perhaps less so today, in the age of research teams) tend to be the work or inspiration of a single person or at most a small group of people. When fire was first made and controlled, or plants and animals were first domesticated, or the wheel was first invented, it was quite probably discovered by one person or a few people. We know that when a new religion like Christianity or Islam is introduced, it tends to be the idea of one or at most a few individuals – a prophetic figure like Jesus or Muhammad. Others of course helped shape and promote it (like Paul in the case of Christianity), but the original innovators were most often single individuals or at most small numbers of individuals.

Innovation may be the ultimate source of culture change, but it is not the most common source. For example, every modern Westerner knows how to write, but none of them created writing. Humans are very inventive, to be sure, but humans are above all else imitative. And thank goodness for it: if every person invented his or her own writing system, or language, or clothing style, or religion, there would be precious little communication possible between people. Most Americans, then, speak English not because Americans invented English but because the English language was carried to America by English speakers. This process is diffusion, the spread of some cultural practice – an idea, an object or technology, a word or symbol or meaning – from one society to another.

Innovation
The invention or discovery of a new cultural concept, idea, behavior, or object.

Diffusion
The spread of a cultural trait (object, idea, practice, institution) from one society to another.

Primary innovation
The invention or discovery of a totally original cultural item, as opposed to *secondary innovation*.

Secondary innovation
An invention or discovery that uses or combines existing ideas, objects, or techniques in novel arrangements.

Diffusion is orders of magnitude more common than innovation. There is good reason to believe that humans, for instance, invented writing at most three or four times in human history, and almost all of them quite long ago. But virtually all societies write today. That is because not only the notion of writing but a specific notation for writing diffused from another society to theirs; that is why there are so few major scripts or writing systems in the world today.

BOX 11.2 THE INVENTION OF CHEROKEE WRITING

One of the only, if not the only, case of the invention of a writing system in recorded history (since recorded history could not start until writing existed) occurred in the 1800s among the Cherokee. According to the Manataka American Indian Council, a man named Sequoyah single-handedly developed a system for writing the Cherokee language where no such system had ever existed (although an ancient legend tells of a lost script). Sequoyah was born between two cultures himself, with a Cherokee mother named Wu-the and a white father named Nathaniel Gist or Guest. He was raised in Cherokee society, married a Cherokee woman, and learned to craft iron and silver. He was also exposed to the American practice of writing, although he supposedly never learned to read and write in English; however, he did witness the phenomenon of making marks on paper to represent sounds. Between 1809 and 1821 he worked on a set of language symbols for Cherokee and finally introduced it in 1821. It was not an alphabet but a syllabary, with "letters" for syllables rather than for individual sounds or phonemes. The Cherokee elders accepted the system after a demonstration by Sequoyah, and by 1825 the Bible and several other documents including religious and legal writings had been rendered into the new script. In 1828, after acquiring their own printing press, the Cherokee Nation began to produce their own newspaper, *Tsa la gi Tsu lehisanunhi* or "Cherokee Phoenix," with parallel columns of Cherokee and English. Whether this case constitutes an innovation or a diffusion, or something in between, is open to interpretation.

THE CHEROKEE SYLLABARY

D a	R e	T i	Ꭳ o	Ꭴ u	i v
Ꮝ ga	Ꮎ ka	Ꮁ ge	Ꭹ gi	A go	J gu	Ꭼ gv
Ꮤ ha	Ꭾ he	Ꮀ hi	Ꮅ ho	Ꮁ hu	Ꮂ hv
W la	Ꮆ le	Ꮅ li	Ꮈ lo	M lu	Ꮑ lv
Ꮊ ma	Ꮉ me	H mi	Ꮒ mo	Ꭹ mu
Ꮻ na hna	Ꮅ ne	Ꮑ ni	Z no	Ꮕ nu	Ꮒ nv
Ꮖ qua	Ꮙ que	Ꮗ qui	quo	quu	quv
Ꮗ sa	Ꮝ s	Ꮞ se	Ꮟ si	Ꮠ so	Ꮡ su	R sv
Ꮣ da	W ta	Ꮥ de	Ꮦ te	Ꮧ di	Ꮨ ti	V do	S du	Ꮫ dv
Ꮬ dla	Ꮯ tla	L tle	C tli	Ꮮ tlo	Ꮰ tlu	P tlv
Ꮳ tsa	V tse	Ꮵ tsi	K tso	Ꮷ tsu	Ꮸ tsv
Ꮹ wa	Ꮺ we	Ꮻ wi	Ꮼ wo	Ꮽ wu	Ꮾ wv
Ꮿ ya	Ᏸ ye	Ᏹ yi	Ᏺ yo	Ᏻ yu	B yv

Whether the specific process of novelty is innovation or diffusion, the introduction of the new cultural element is not the end of the story but just the beginning. For, if Sequoyah or anyone else "invents" a new word or language or religion or clothing style or cuisine, is it culture now? What makes something "culture"? The simple criterion is learned and shared behavior. So, if someone starts a new language or religion, it is not "cultural" unless and until other people observe it, adopt it, practice it, and ideally pass it along to still others, especially their children. If no one ever learns and shares the innovation or diffusion, it never achieves "cultural" status. When the innovator dies, the innovation dies with him or her, since culture exists only so long as it is known and practiced. But as soon as it is learned and shared, it is cultural.

See Chapter 2

There is, as we said elsewhere, no precise quantifiable dimension to culture; that is, it is not necessary that all or even most or any specific percentage of society adopts the new behavior. Every innovation or diffusion originally starts as "individual peculiarities" on Linton's spectrum of the distribution of culture. If it never catches on or spreads any further, then it will remain a peculiarity and ultimately disappear from the culture. If it spreads a little further it can become a cultural specialty; a little further and it could achieve the rank of an alternative. If it becomes widely held and used, it may eventually become a "universal" within that society. Of course, any particular cultural item can get "lodged" at one of these stages and remain there, or even begin to decline again. Similarly, a cultural practice of age and prestige, even a universal one, can over time fade until it becomes a peculiarity of a few people or vanishes completely.

So the question is what makes a cultural novelty "catch on" or not. Or, to put it in more technical terms, after an innovation or diffusion is introduced to a society, a process begins, which can end in any of three outcomes: acceptance, rejection, or acceptance-with-modification. Probably most cultural innovations fail, and virtually all alter from their initial form before they are widely distributed. What kinds of factors lead a society to accept, modify, or ultimately reject some new cultural offering? Some of the criteria that affect the future of new phenomena are:

- how well it fits with already-existing preferences and tastes;
- what local materials or ingredients are available;
- how difficult or expensive it will be to implement;
- what symbolic or social meaning or value exists in society;
- how well it performs relative to competing items already in the culture;
- how much it enhances or threatens other aspects of the culture;
- how much power those who resist the change can muster;
- how important it is that the phenomenon is "new" or "foreign";
- how much status the innovator or diffuser himself or herself possesses.

The basic issue in any case of adoption of cultural novelty is whether it fits with the culture that already exists. For example, if Americans already like to eat meat but not insects, then there is small chance that a new dish based on grasshoppers or cockroaches will gain very wide acceptance. If a society prefers that men wear pants and women wear dresses, then a dress for men will probably not catch on; this could also be a matter of symbolic or social meaning – of a behavior "appropriate for" one type of person but not for another. One common factor is local tastes and ingredients; when I cook international foods, I often substitute exotic ingredients with local ones that I already have in my kitchen. When I was in Japan some years ago I found a pizza restaurant in my neighborhood that served not only pepperoni pizza and sausage pizza but seaweed pizza and shrimp pizza. My Japanese restaurateurs had simply adapted pizza to local tastes, using local ingredients, to make a "Japanese pizza."

The issue of expense or difficulty is illustrated well in the American resistance to the metric system. As useful and precise as it is, the changes involved in trying to convert the entire society and economy to another system of measure make it prohibitively difficult. Every machine, every tool, every cup and container, every thermometer would have to be replaced, at great cost both for the technology and the training. It is easier just to leave things as they are. The English typewriter keyboard is another prime example. The familiar "QWERTY" keyboard (so named for the row of keys across the upper left) was in fact originally laid out to be as incon-venient as possible. In the days of mechanical typewriters, fast typists could jam the keys since they could type faster than the machine could respond. It was necessary to slow down these speed typists to compensate for the limitations of the devices. Today, electronic keyboards have no such mechanical limitations, so more "natural" keyboards, including the proposed Dvorak style, could be effectively used. However, again, the cost of replacement and of retraining would be so exorbitant that nobody seriously considers a change. The lesson from this discussion is that cultural elements are not always chosen or preserved because they are the best but because they are the most familiar or the "easiest" in the sense of requiring the least bother.

One other issue to consider is the impact on a society and culture of the adoption of a new item, whether by innovation or diffusion. It can and often does happen that a modification in one area of culture, even a small one, can have ramifications, frequently unexpected and sometimes serious, in other areas of culture. The simple reason for this effect is that culture is an integrated entity; by the fact of holism, the consequences of change in one realm may be felt in other and seemingly "unrelated" realms – except that nothing in culture is unrelated. The effects can, in the end, be widespread and disastrous.

BOX 11.3 STONE VERSUS STEEL AXES IN AN ABORIGINAL SOCIETY

The Yir Yoront of Cape York Peninsula, northeast Australia, used stone axes long before contact with Europeans. The tools were relatively easy to make, and men (but not women or children) could produce them for themselves. Women in fact were the primary users of the tools, for chopping firewood; however, men owned and kept them, and women or youths had to ask a man's permission to use one and return it promptly. Lauriston Sharp (1952) writes that access to axes was part of a general status system in which people were ranked by age, sex, and clan membership. The axe was a symbol of masculine power, an important trade good for establishing interpersonal relations, and a ritual object. When European Australians arrived and introduced steel axes, one might think that the impact would be minimal – perhaps cutting down more trees with less effort. However, the effects rippled through the society, from gender and political relations to religion. Aboriginals could not make their own steel axes, so they were dependent for them on whites, especially administrators and missionaries. Aboriginals who interacted with whites – and were perceived as "good" Aboriginals by the whites – had better access to the technology. This meant that older and more "traditional" men were more often excluded.

Further, whites often gave the tools directly to women or children, unaware of, unconcerned about, or actively opposed to the gender segregation in the culture. Women and youths were freed from dependence on men for the property, depriving men of a practical and symbolic expression of power. Exchange relations between the Yir Yoront and other tribes broke down, as the Yir Yoront could not acquire steel axes from them and did not desire to trade steel axes to them. Sharp argues that the greatest effects were in the arena of "ideas, sentiments, and values," which radiated rapidly and contributed to the "collapse" of their society. Concepts of ownership, status, and even religion, myth, and ritual underwent stresses and transformations, "hacking," as he concludes, "at the supports of the entire cultural system" (22).

Cultural loss

Cultural loss

The process by which elements of a culture disappear over time, through natural/ environmental changes, social pressures, or individual choices.

Deculturation

See cultural loss.

Ideally, innovation or diffusion would result in at worst a substitution of one cultural practice for another and at best an addition to the cultural repertoire – a new specialty or alternative. However, culture does not proceed by addition and substitution alone but also by subtraction. In some cases, cultural elements are lost and not replaced by anything. The net result is an impoverishment of culture. It is important to remember that culture exists only so long as somebody is learning it, doing it, and transmitting it. When that process stops, culture ceases to be. This is why **cultural loss** is sometimes also referred to as **deculturation**.

This is a major problem in the world today, especially in the context of the passing of culture between the generations. In many societies, young people often have little interest in the ways of the elders. Among the Gaguju people of Australia, as told in a recent *National Geographic* program entitled "Australia's Twilight of the Dreamtime," there are no longer enough men who know the traditional dances to conduct them in the old way; the Gaguju must invite men from other tribes to fill the required roles. The cause is a combination of the interests of the young and the decisions of the old. The young often do not care about the old ways, and frequently they are not even available much of the time due to new demands of work and new opportunities for travel and play (not to mention plagues like alcohol and drugs). At the same time, the elders assess the readiness of the next generation before they share their secret-sacred knowledge. In Australia, religious knowledge is not for just

PLATE 11.1 Foragers are often forced to settle down, as in these concrete houses built for the formerly nomadic Warlpiri

anyone, and only men who are properly initiated and committed to and advanced in the traditions can receive it. If the elders never consider the youngsters qualified to get the knowledge, then the elders will keep it to themselves, and when they die it will die with them.

From the perspective of the young, there is sometimes a voluntary or involuntary detachment from their culture. In a changing and modernizing world, the young may see little use for or value in "traditional" knowledge or skills, from hunting or horticulture to music or language or religion. On the other hand, outside agents may intentionally or unintentionally interrupt the culture transfer process, as with boarding-schools, forced separation of families, and even involuntary adoptions. In some cases, other groups or classes, including the state government under which a society lives, have explicitly forbidden the use of some or all parts of a culture; for example, in the second half of the twentieth century, Turkish authorities literally outlawed the use of Kurdish language and symbols in an effort to eliminate not only Kurdish culture but even Kurdish identity as a distinct culture-bearing group.

See Chapter 13

All of these things have already happened in many parts of the world to many parts of culture – and in some cases, to entire cultures. By some counts there are hundreds of traditional languages, for instance, that are endangered today, and we can never know how many have already become extinct. An alarming number of languages are on the verge of disappearance, some with less than 100 surviving speakers. The Ainu language, spoken by natives of northern Japan, is one of the worst cases: with the youngest remaining speaker already 65 years old in the 1990s, such a language has little future.

See Chapter 15

It is of course not just language that is in the process of being lost. Religions, music, and other kinds of irreplaceable knowledge, including potentially important botanical and medicinal knowledge, are in danger. When these cultural things are dead, some will "live on" in the ethnographies of anthropologists, but some will be lost to humanity forever.

Acculturation

Enculturation is the name for the process of acquiring one's culture, ordinarily as a child, from the other members of one's society. It is the learning and teaching process by which Americans get their American culture, Warlpiri get their Warlpiri culture, and so on. Acculturation as a word sounds very similar, and conceptually it is very similar, but with a profound twist.

Acculturation

The process of acquiring a "second culture," usually as an effect of sustained and imbalanced contact between two societies. Members of the "weaker" society are compelled to adopt aspects of the dominant society.

Acculturation may be thought of as the exposure to a second culture other than one's own, although this is too simple to be completely accurate: in the case of Sequoyah, which culture was "his own" culture? In a way, having two cultures may sound like a good thing, a kind of "multiculturalism" or cultural "bilingualism." No doubt in some cases and in some ways it is a good thing. However, it can also be disruptive and it can also be coercive. In essence, acculturation is the process of culture change that occurs as a result of intense and sustained contact between two societies. Whenever there is such contact, there is going to be a circulation or flow of culture (and sometimes genes too) between the two societies; after all, that is how Europe got noodles and gunpowder and the compass and the zero and tomatoes and potatoes. Cultural exchange can bring benefits for both sides.

However, one crucial issue in acculturation is that there is usually a power differential between the two societies. In such cases, the smaller or weaker society is changed much more extensively than the larger or more powerful society, although both are changed in some ways. When the first English settlers arrived at Massachusetts Bay, there is no doubt that they learned some critical things from the Native Americans, and there are many elements of Indian culture in American culture today. Even so, no one can dispute that the changes for Native American societies were immeasurably greater and more negative than for the European immigrants.

One of the fascinating aspects of acculturation is that it is often extremely personal. That is, it is less true to say that a society is acculturated than that individual people are acculturated. Usually the first to feel the pressure are those in the most intimate and prolonged contact with the foreigners, including those engaged in trade or in political relationships. Others who feel the clutch of acculturation earliest are the children of mixed couples, like Sequoyah, who find themselves physically and culturally "in between." Sometimes referred to in the early anthropological literature as "marginal people," they often experience the personal sting of acculturation by being partly in each culture but not completely in either. They are the harbingers of the future.

As members of the dominated society (which may actually be larger demographically, as in the case of India under British rule) succumb to the pressures and lures of the new society, they may become in some ways more like this new society – that

See Chapter 6

is, assimilate to it. They may learn its language, adopt some of its practices (clothing, firearms, and alcohol are three familiar ones), and emulate the new models in various ways. This process is partly natural and spontaneous, but it is also sometimes artificial and compulsory. In such cases, we can rightly speak of repressive acculturation or forced acculturation.

There are many known (and probably even more unknown) instances of forced acculturation. They are basically implementations of ethnocentric beliefs and attitudes. The activities of missionaries is one of the prime examples. Missionaries often did good work, bringing food and even peace to conflicting societies. However, the "mission" behind these works was always to change the society, most obviously (but not exclusively) its religion. Missionaries would naturally attempt to introduce foreign beliefs into the society, but they would often do so by ridiculing, condemning, or even punishing the "traditionalists" or at least by favoring the "converts." They were not above using the influence of their resources, including food and water, as weapons in this conversion effort, nor did they refrain from using corporal punishment or destroying native religious artifacts and buildings. In some places, missions became virtual prisons, from which natives were not permitted to leave once they arrived and where the missionary's will was law (see Tinker 1993). Obviously, too, the missionary's interests were not limited to religion as such, seeing as how all the domains of culture are integrated and that religion provides the rules and the sanctions for conduct in other regards. So, missionaries often imposed their (that is, Western or European) values and practices in the areas of kinship, gender roles, language, and economics on the local people too, forbidding, for instance, polygyny or child marriages or nakedness or gender equality or nomadism, and so on.

In addition (and often connected) to the missionaries were the institutions of education, most notably boarding-schools. In America and Australia as elsewhere, native – and especially mixed-race – children were rounded up into these schools, sometimes by force, where they were compelled to change their appearance, their language, and their religion and where they were expected to receive "civilization and Christianity" including a new name, a "modern" education, and a trade. (The feature film *Rabbit-proof Fence* is a splendid portrayal of this process in early twentieth-century Australia.) Boys were taught conventional white male roles and girls conventional white female roles. No matter what, they were subjected to acculturation pressures which neither they nor their parents could resist and which the dominant society thoroughly approved. Often, at the end of their stay, the children were turned back out into the bigger world, where they did not have the skills and knowledge to be Indians or Aboriginals nor the acceptance to be whites. They were literally marginalized.

These more overt methods to acculturate American Indian and Australian Aboriginal children were not the only ones employed. Children were sometimes actually seized from their parents and placed in white foster homes, to give them the benefits of white culture. Other, more indirect means were used too, some of which were ostensibly in the natives' "best interests." For example, in 1887, after most Native American societies had been pacified and placed on reservations, some white

PLATE 11.2 Native American children were often acculturated through the use of boarding schools, like the Carlisle School

Americans thought they were doing the Indians a favor (while others had different motivations) by breaking up communal tribal land and assigning it as private property to individual people or families. Known as "allotment," the intention was not only to turn Native Americans into private landowners and farmers like other Americans but also to tear down any communal identity and to destroy any vestiges of traditional economies and politics. After all, people could not practice foraging or pastoralism on sixteen acres of land. Individual Indians on their little plots would cease thinking of themselves as "Indians" and assimilate to the white "individual landholder" model (and "excess" land could be sold to or seized by non-Indians).

Genocide and ethnocide

Genocide

The destruction of a group or society by harming, killing, or preventing the birth of its members.

Acculturation can be forceful and repressive, but it tends to leave people alive, more or less. However, when one society desires and seeks the complete eradication of another society, this is known as **genocide** (from the Greek *gens* for a people or group and *cide* for kill). Genocide as a practice has been formally identified and defined by the United Nations, which described it in Article II of the 1948 UN Genocide Convention as "acts committed with intent to destroy, in whole or in part, a national, ethnical, racial, or religious group, as such:

(a) Killing members of the group;
(b) Causing serious bodily or mental harm to members of the group;

PLATE 11.3 A newspaper image protesting political oppression in Mongolia: main text reads "Don't forget . . . This repression shouldn't be repeated"

(c) Deliberately inflicting on the group conditions of life calculated to bring about its physical destruction in whole or in part;

(d) Imposing measures intended to prevent births within the group;

(e) Forcibly transferring children of the group to another group."

By this definition, there have been many genocides over human history, most occurring in ancient times but plenty in contemporary history. It is indisputable that many societies and their cultures have vanished from the Earth or had their remnants absorbed into other larger societies, without a trace or a memory. In recent historical times, the Nazi "final solution" against European Jews is the very face of genocide for most people, but it is by no means the only one. Around the turn of the twentieth century, the Turks committed genocide against the Armenians, while in the 1990s the Serbs conducted "ethnic cleansing" against Bosnian Muslims in Yugoslavia and the Hutus killed vast numbers of Tutsis in Rwanda.

BOX 11.4　GENOCIDE IN RWANDA 1994

Genocide takes many forms and has many motivations. While "weapons of mass destruction" like poison gas and concentration camps can kill thousands or millions, handheld weapons like machetes can kill masses if enough of them

See Chapter 12

See Chapter 6

are placed in enough hands. Through such face-to-face means, some 800,000 Tutsis and their supporters were exterminated in one hundred days in the spring of 1994 by Hutu vigilantes and militias. The violence was not unexpected or unprecedented – or uncoordinated. As recounted elsewhere, at the time of European invasion (late 1800s), Rwanda was a composite society, containing a dominant Tutsi minority (approximately 15 percent) and a subordinated Hutu majority (about 85 percent), plus a minuscule number of Twa bushmen. German and then Belgian colonial administration had perpetuated the power of the Tutsi nobility, even expanding their powers of taxation and labor recruitment; the Tutsis were inevitably favored in education and religion as well. As independence approached in the 1950s, the Hutus (formerly arguably more a class or caste than a "race" or "ethnic group" or "tribe") – in a classic case of ethnogenesis – began to organize and identify as a unified identity and interest group. After the proclamation of the "Manifesto of the Bahutu" in 1957, which declared the Tutsi and the Hutu to be distinct races and the Tutsi to be responsible for Hutu poverty and oppression, a Hutu political party, PARMEHUTU or Parti du Mouvement de l'Emancipation Hutu, was formed. In response, Tutsi leaders started their own party, UNAR or Union Nationale Rwandaise. Riots in 1959 led PARMEHUTU to become more militant and seize political power in 1961, establishing what one observer called "a racial dictatorship of one party" in which the Tutsi minority "may find itself defenseless in the face of abuses" (quoted in Lemarchand 1970: 194–5). Indeed, physical attacks on Tutsis drove some 120,000 (up to or more than half their population) into refuge outside the country. From those locations, they and their descendants organized paramilitary bands (known as *inyenzi* or cockroaches) to raid across the border in anticipation of their eventual return – and return to power. By 1993 the Rwandan government of Juvenal Habyarimana was in peace negotiations with Tutsi insurgents; however, hard-line Hutus in units called *interahamwe* ("those who attack as one") opposed such initiatives. In April 1994, when Habyarimana's airplane was shot down, the Tutsi were instantly blamed for the assassination, and the bloodbath began. The violence was not totally spontaneous however. Government radio urged Hutus to destroy Tutsis and even broadcast the locations of Tutsis in hiding. Weapons and preprepared death lists were distributed, and prominent Hutu citizens joined in or promoted the killing. Some Tutsis were targeted as ethnic leaders, some for their wealth and property, some out of vengeance for past actions; Hutus who sympathized with or protected Tutsis were likely to be annihilated with them. Victims were often slashed along the neck or ankle and left alive, to be killed when the attackers returned, sometimes a day or more later, prowling for more prey.

The first or familiar impression of genocide is violence against "them," outsiders to a society or members of other societies. However, "them" is a relative term too, and some societies, or at least contingents within societies, have committed what we may call "auto-genocide" against what we would normally think of as "their own people." Cambodia under the Khmer Rouge party and then government is perhaps the most familiar instance. Pol Pot, the head of the Communist Khmer Rouge (as told in the popular media, like the movie *The Killing Fields*) was responsible for the death of up to one-third of the population of his own country under various programs aimed at forced culture change. That is, in order to realize the desired communist workers' utopia, "enemies of the revolution" and counter-revolutionaries had to die, and this tended to include the intelligentsia, the urban population, and anyone who disagreed with official policy.

Genocide can be effective, but it is horribly expensive, messy, and unpopular; while the world does not always rush to stop it, it does usually rise up to condemn it. Genocide leaves evidence, literally in the form of corpses. However, it is not necessary to kill people in order to achieve the same basic result – the elimination of a social group. A much "cleaner" method that has proven just as effective is ethnocide. **Ethnocide** (from the Greek *ethno* for a culture or way of life) means destroying the culture or institutions of a group rather than the people themselves. It often masquerades as any other "educational" endeavor. The missions and boarding-schools described above could and perhaps should be understood as ethnocidal projects and are often viewed as such by the indigenous people. The goal was, and was sometimes even stated as, the eradication of one kind of person and the replacement with another kind. This sentiment was expressed directly in the late nineteenth-century American slogan, "Kill the Indian to save the man." This meant rooting out the Indianness from Indian people, so that they would become "regular Americans." And many white Americans thought they were doing the Indians a favor – giving them a "modern" culture by means of which they could participate in broader American society and life.

Unlike genocide, ethnocide leaves living victims. The aftermath is people who "look like" Indians or Aboriginals, but who do not act, think, or live like them. They are, culturally, indistinguishable from the dominant society. They have in effect been deculturated and then re-enculturated as members of the dominant society. The consequences can be and have been so abrupt, however, that some people refer to ethnocide as "cultural genocide."

Ethnocide
The destruction of a group's culture, without necessarily killing any of the members of the culture.

Directed change

As we have acknowledged, culture change is inevitable in situations of culture contact, which has been the normal condition of human societies as long as there have been human societies. Even without that contact, individuals or groups continuously modify their cultures. Environmental changes may call for new behavioral adaptations over the short or long term. Innovations introduce new material, and reinterpretations shift the meaning of previous material. The mere passing of generations brings new individuals with new perspectives on their "traditions." In all of these ways, culture change is normal and natural. Cultures are always "in process."

Even in situations of culture contact, the changes induced are often unplanned, spontaneous, and uncoordinated. People observe this or that, transfer this or that, accept or modify or reject this or that in the normal course of cultural development without any specific goals in mind and without anybody dominating or driving the process. However, sometimes this change is not spontaneous and voluntary at all, and more and more in the modern world, such change is highly planned and even highly coercive.

Directed change

A cultural process in which internal or external agents make more or less intentional, coordinated, and sustained modifications or reforms to a society and culture.

Let us define **directed change**, then, as planned, coordinated, and sustained efforts to make changes to a part or all of a culture. There are two directions from which this initiative may come. In one case, changes are imposed "from the outside," by a foreign society that is aiming to change the culture of another society for the benefit of the former (and occasionally, at least the perception of the benefit of the latter). In the other case, changes are imposed "from the inside," by one element (class, religion, race, ethnic group) or region (e.g., urban versus rural, north versus south) of a society on another element or region of the same society. This distinction can be a little blurred, however, since in practice, "on the ground," it might not be quite clear when a group or society is "inside" or "outside." This too can be relative. When the United States wanted to encourage settlers into the Oklahoma territory in the nineteenth century, this could be regarded as promoting changes *inside American society and territory* or as imposing changes *on non-American, namely Indian societies*. Or, in actuality, it can and should be regarded as both simultaneously, depending on the point of view. The same would be the situation in discussions of "developing" the Amazon rainforest, which is inside and under the control of the Brazilian state but also inhabited by societies that do not identify themselves as "Brazilian," as well as in many other parts of the world.

See Chapter 12

See Chapter 13

See Chapter 14

For our purposes, directed change will come in four major, world-historical manifestations, which will comprise the remainder of this book. The first is colonialism, a prime example of directed change from the outside; although modern European colonialism began as a piecemeal and even accidental project, it eventually coalesced into a very intentional and organized enterprise, with profound international repercussions that are still felt today. The second is nationalism, a type of cultural and political movement to unify and empower a social group, often with the ultimate goal of achieving sovereign political power and an independent state for the group. Closely associated with nationalism is ethnicity, a different but related form of cultural movement that may have political and/or other goals. The third is development, usually conceived as coordinated changes to the economy of a (most often poor) society, often along with or for the purpose of changes in the standard and quality of life as well. Development is an example of directed change that can come from the outside or the inside, and often both simultaneously, since states frequently propose and direct development efforts within their territory with the assistance (financial and technical) of foreign states, corporations, or organizations.

The fourth and final directed change is what we will call generally "revitalization movements," including efforts to "reform" elements or institutions of a society as well as initiatives (particularly in the case of small, indigenous groups) to protect and preserve and in some instances revive cultural practices. These revitalization movements often, but not always, emphasize "tradition" but in a modern and "non-traditional" way and are not above using non-traditional media (like the internet) to achieve their objectives. All in all, they and the other types of directed change illustrate the power and pervasiveness of cultural innovation and diffusion and of the "invention of tradition" – which can become a "real tradition" tomorrow.

See Chapter 15

BOX 11.5 CONTEMPORARY CULTURAL CONTROVERSIES: IMPOSING REGIME CHANGE

Societies frequently think that they know what is best for other societies and the entire world. During the French Revolution (starting in 1789), enthusiastic revolutionaries believed that theirs was not a national event but a world event, the beginning of an idealistic global transformation – an end to tyranny and injustice and crime, a regeneration and salvation of humanity – of which France would be the agent. The revolutionaries, and later Napoleon, invaded neighboring countries from Spain to Russia to "liberate" them from their backward and uncivilized conditions. In 1917, another idealistic regime came to power, this time in Russia. The Soviet Union also saw itself as a vanguard of world revolution, a liberation from the abusive international systems of colonialism and capitalism. It too exported war and a "democratic" ideology around the world, allegedly to assist other societies to shed the bonds of political oppression and slavish conformity to tradition – promising "self-determination" but more often, and for over half a century, imposing communist rule on states from Poland to Cuba to Vietnam. Both the Soviet Union and the First French Republic are no more. When one society, even if it means well (and that is a relative term), attempts to reshape the political or other aspects of another, it inevitably meets with a variety of resistances. The targeted society may feel more invaded and occupied than liberated; it certainly did not choose the change. It may regard even beneficial changes as objectionable foreign interference – and of course, changes may be beneficial to some members of the society and not to others. And finally, the best-intended and best-laid plans for change always encounter the integration of the pre-existing culture: one cannot modify or remove elements of politics or tradition without affecting, sometimes quite negatively, other aspects of the culture. Whether or not a society should engage in regime change, nation-building, and the spread of its own values and institutions is one question; how most effectively to do so is another. What do you think?

SUMMARY

Anthropology has often been thought of, and thought of itself, as the study of "traditional societies," but no society today is perfectly "traditional," and "tradition" is a relative concept in itself. Anthropology has grown and changed, as the societies that interest it have grown and changed, into the study of cultural processes by which human groups adjust to changing internal and external realities, including contact with societies that are very different from and in very unequal power relationships with them. As it has done so, anthropology has become more self-aware of its own practices and of the entire project of conceptualizing and describing cultures.

Cultures are never static and unchanging. Even when they appear "continuous," this is an achievement of ongoing active cultural processes. In fact, every culture at every moment of its existence is a complicated alloy of continuity and change, and that is normal. Some of the processes that function in the dynamics of culture are:

- innovation
- diffusion
- cultural loss or deculturation
- acculturation
- genocide and ethnocide
- directed change.

Whatever the original source of the cultural novelty, a process of circulation and distribution within the society is begun, which can end in three general outcomes:

- acceptance
- rejection
- acceptance with modification.

It is also possible that the new cultural element may achieve a certain limited distribution and "stall" there. Culture, thus, emerges as a living system of elements that are differentially distributed throughout the society and moving (growing or shrinking) within that society. This process is often spontaneous and unintentional, or even unnoticed, but it can be – and in the modern world increasingly is – very intentional as well as very contentious.

Key Terms

Acculturation

Cultural loss

Deculturation

Diffusion

Directed change

Ethnocide

Genocide

Innovation

Primary innovation

Secondary innovation

Tradition

12

Colonialism and the Origin of Globalization

Lemarchand, Réné. 1970.
Rwanda and Burundi. New
York: Praeger.

After the Congress of Berlin (1884–1885), at which the European governments decided how they would mutually handle the occupation and exploitation of Africa, the various European states began to explore and settle the areas they had awarded themselves, often without ever having set foot in them. Germany had received a large portion of eastern Africa, including what would become Tanzania. It was only in 1892 that Germany began what Lemarchand (1970) calls its "explorations of possession" in the small African kingdom that would be named Ruanda-Urundi and eventually become the neighboring states of Rwanda and Burundi. Germany did not hold the territory for long, since it was stripped of colonies following World War I, and in 1923 the League of Nations handed control of the tiny region to Belgium, which ruled it until independence in 1962. During its colonial occupation, the Belgians introduced changes intended to increase economic production and improve administrative efficiency. Ruling "indirectly" through local chiefs and the king (*mwami*), the colonial authorities reorganized the pre-contact political system (reducing the number of chiefs but often enhancing their powers), redefined, eliminated, or created economic relationships (such as "traditional" patron/client relations and "modern" wage labor), and powerfully affected intergroup identities and relations, in such a way as to exacerbate "ethnic" frictions. This is particularly important because Rwanda and Burundi had been heterogeneous societies for a very long time prior to European arrival. Historical analyses indicate that the "original" population

was a "pygmy" foraging people known as the Twa. By around 1000 CE Bantu horticulturists began to penetrate the region, settling among and displacing the Twa. Finally,
Tutsi pastoralists from the north had invaded the area starting around 1500 CE, a
process which was not complete upon the arrival of Europeans. The result is that
European authority, and with it anthropology, stepped into a scene in which three
distinguishable groups, alternately referred to as "tribes" or "classes" or "castes,"
shared social space in a stratified system. The result was an unsettled and unstable
cultural system, still developing as the era of colonialism dawned: as Lemarchand
said, the invading Germans discovered "a situation bordering on chaos" (1970: 49),
and Ress suggests that the Germans were led "to conclude that these Tutsi people
were predominant" (1988: 70).

The nearly 500-year-long enterprise of European colonialism profoundly
changed the cultural course of the world. Societies that had never been in contact
with another group so vastly different and so far away from themselves were more
or less suddenly cast into a social system of global proportions and interconnections.
However, as should be clear from this introduction, the phenomenon of culture
contact, culture change, and unequal cultural relationships was not a new thing
invented by Europeans or modern colonialism. Even the Aboriginals on the northern
shore of Australia had been in contact with Macassan or Malay fishermen who came
annually to trawl the waters off the continent, and groups like the Qemant in Ethiopia
had been surrounded and engulfed by foreign social and political systems for
centuries. Complex, hierarchical, and multicultural societies and empires had risen
and fallen throughout history, and no area of the Earth was immune from culture
contact and the effects of long-distance trade and unequal power relations. In fact,
societies that are associated with one area or way of life, such as the Cheyenne of
the Great Plains of North America, have frequently been shown through historical,
archaeological, and ethnographic evidence to have reached these places and social
patterns only recently in time (obviously, there was no horse-riding culture in the
American Plains before the European introduction of horses).

See Chapter 9

Modern European colonialism in certain senses perpetuated long-standing and
familiar cultural processes of innovation and diffusion and acculturation. In some
ways it merely escalated and intensified these processes, while in other ways it
represented a radically new moment in world cultural history. For the first time,
cultural contacts and political and economic relationships were not merely local or
regional but truly global. And the impact on the local societies was complex and
contradictory: sometimes it appeared to freeze their "traditional" cultures at a particular moment in time, while it also altered those traditions or even destroyed them
and generated entirely novel ones. The two things we cannot say any longer are that
societies had no history – were stable and homeostatic – before colonialism or that
societies can be meaningfully described and understood in isolation from their wider
social context. In other words, by 500 years ago we see the seeds of contemporary
globalization, in which distant societies would become connected economically,
politically, technologically, and "culturally." Societies were increasingly integrated into
state, regional, and ultimately global systems that preserved, challenged, and changed

them simultaneously. The events, decisions, and policies of any one society, state, or region can now affect other and perhaps all societies. In fact, that wider social context *becomes part of their contemporary culture*.

THE CULTURE OF COLONIALISM

Colonialism

The more or less organized system of occupation and exploitation of foreign territories through settlement and conquest, especially as practiced by Western states since 1492.

Colony

A segment of a population (not exclusively a human population) that moves into and occupies territory not previously occupied by the population, often displacing or subduing the previous occupants.

In 1492, when Christopher Columbus and his expedition made landfall in the "New World," he inaugurated an unprecedented expansion of cultural processes that would come to be known as **colonialism**. Colonialism, as a world system of occupation and exploitation of foreign territories within a European capitalist market economy, and eventually as a world system of territorial empire, had unprecedented effects. However, the practice of establishing and controlling colonies was not new at all. In fact, colonies are not even unique to humans. The word "**colony**" comes from the Latin *colonia* which derives from *colonus* or farmer, which further derives from *colere* or to cultivate (also related to the root of the term "culture"). A colony is a segment of a population that moves into and occupies a new territory; as such, there can be not only colonies of humans but of animals, trees, or bacteria. To "colonize" is merely to expand into areas previously unoccupied by the population, and the offshoot of the original population that pioneers this new occupation is the colony.

So humans did not invent colonization, let alone modern humans. Societies were colonizing new lands in the ancient and prehistoric past. Greek cities colonized the Mediterranean coast, "planting" colonies of Greeks as far afield as present-day Turkey and Spain. When Alexander the Great swept through the Middle East and Central Asia, he intentionally left behind colonies, often named Alexandria, with the full complement of Greek social, intellectual, and artistic institutions. At one time or another humans colonized the Pacific Islands and North America itself, and modern-day European societies are the product of multiple waves of colonization of that continent, from the first Neandertals and later *Homo sapiens* to Greek and Roman and Germanic, Slavic, Celtic, Nordic, and other peoples (again refuting the "pure race"

PLATE 12.1
Colonialism was a political and personal relationship between colonizers – like the British officer depicted here in colonial India – and colonized

image of Europeans). Later, these products of ancient colonization reached out to colonize a world that had itself been shaped, like Rwanda and Burundi, by successive waves of occupation.

See Chapter 6

The worldwide phenomenon that was sparked by the explorations of fifteenth-century travelers was to evolve into something quite extraordinary, however. In scale and impact it was unmatched, since no society had ever flung its colonies so broadly nor wrought such grand changes on the colonized regions. And in intentionality it was unrivaled, since, at least by late in the colonial endeavor, the acquisition and exploitation of colonies was consciously sought and managed. This represents a shift from mere colonization to a deliberate and sustained policy of colonialism. Colonialism then is a form of directed change, a deliberate and concerted attempt to place settlements in new territories for the purpose of economic and political domination of those territories and of the peoples who already live there. This domination was, of course, primarily for the benefit of the transplanted foreigners (the colonists) or even of the "mother country" from which the colonists were sent, rather than of the local indigenous people. In fact, the interests of the colonists and the locals or "indigenous peoples" were usually if not invariably at odds, leading to serious and often violent conflict.

See Chapter 15

Something as long-lasting and widespread as European colonialism could not possibly be a one-dimensional affair. It varied along a number of lines, depending on the historical period involved, the particular colonizing country, the particular colonized region, and the types of colonies established there. **Colonies of settlement** were those where large numbers of foreign colonists flocked into the colonies, in some cases to the point that they outnumbered the native population. The United States is a classic case of a colony of settlement, or actually several colonies of settlement that eventually united into a single polity. In such cases, the native peoples were typically displaced – through treaty or conquest or disease and depopulation – and the colonists' culture was substituted for the native culture. Coincidental or coercive acculturation of native peoples normally occurred. Other colonies of settlement included Canada, Australia, New Zealand, South Africa, and Southern Rhodesia (Zimbabwe today), although the European population never reached majority status in the last two colonies.

It was not necessary to outnumber the natives in order to dominate them. In many if not most cases, relatively few colonists actually lived in the colonies, and the colonies were treated more as sources of wealth than as places to live. Such **colonies of exploitation** never acquired large European populations, sometimes because the climate was unwelcoming, sometimes because large-scale settlement was too expensive, and sometimes because it was simply unnecessary. After all, if the purpose of the colony was to supply cheap sources of primary products like cotton or rubber or coffee, the colonizers did not need or perhaps even want a lot of settlers. Organizing the native population into "productive" labor was sufficient and often more desirable.

Internal colonialism was – and in some cases still is – a situation in which one region or group dominates the land, population, and resources of another region

Colonies of settlement
Colonies in which many foreigners immigrate, sometimes such that they and their descendants become the majority population of the territory.

Colonies of exploitation
Colonies in which few foreigners immigrate but the territory is still used for its resources, wealth, labor, markets, and/or strategic location.

Internal colonialism
The practice in which a society (usually a state) penetrates and occupies territory within its jurisdiction (normally inside its borders) but that contains peoples who do not identify as and with the occupying society. In some usages, it can also refer to the condition in which colonized peoples internalize in their own minds and personalities the institutions and values of colonialism.

Sphere of influence

In European colonial practice, an area of foreign territory where the power and authority of one European state was recognized.

or group within the same polity. The United States prior to the Civil War has been described as a case of internal colonialism, with the industrial North exploiting the agrarian South. Brazil and its exploitation of the Amazonian region for the benefit of the eastern and southern urban regions could be another example, as could England with its historical domination of the Scottish, Welsh, and Irish lands and people. As such, internal colonialism is probably very common. Finally, when colonialism does not reach its completion, **spheres of influence** may result. This was the case in China, which was simply too large and too powerful to be controlled in its entirety or by any single foreign power. Instead, the local society is weakened to the point at which it cannot prevent foreign interference and penetration, and chunks of territory are occupied or dominated by various foreign powers. Hong Kong, where British occupation only recently ended, was one such chunk; other states including France, Germany, Japan, and even the United States also had their pieces or "spheres," in which foreign law and culture was more or less formally instituted (the concept of "extraterritoriality").

The colonial experience also diverged according to the era in which it was practiced. When Europe launched its colonial adventure, just prior to 1500, it was still a relatively weak continent in comparison to the great empires of the day – Ottoman, Chinese, Mughal (Indian), and others. Its goals and its capabilities were fairly limited, as was its range: North and South America came under its sway, as did parts of the "East Indies" or the so-called Spice Islands (largely, present-day Indonesia) and a very few coastal patches of Africa and India. This phase, which has been called **mercantilism**, focused essentially on trade monopolies between states and their colonies and the accumulation of wealth, particularly gold. Colonies were often like remote farms and mines for the mother country to harvest and tap.

Mercantilism

An early modern European economic and political system in which wealth and power were determined by possession of gold and a favorable balance of trade with each other.

Imperialism

The pursuit of territorial and political domination of foreign lands and peoples (building an "empire"), known since ancient history but reaching its greatest extent in the late phase of European colonialism.

Many of these early mercantile colonies achieved independence from their overlords in the mid- to late 1800s. Subsequently, European colonialism was reconstituted in a modern and more systematic and exploitative form, which we will call **imperialism**. Imperialism sought more than the old colonialism ever did, including territorial possession, efficient administration, and enhanced wealth production and extraction, all related to the political competitions between the "Great Powers" of Europe and their industrial and military needs and interests. In this later period, the final and complete occupation of the world was accomplished, with enormous colonial holdings, especially for England, in Africa, India, Asia, and the Middle East. For instance, following the Congress of Berlin mentioned above, a "scramble for Africa" commenced which ended within a few years by the carving of what King Leopold of Belgium referred to as the "magnificent African cake," every "piece" of which was colonized except Ethiopia and Liberia – and Liberia had been founded by the American Colonization Society in 1821 in the first place.

Agents of colonialism

At its outset in the late 1400s, colonialism was not an organized project for European states but rather a hit-and-miss patchwork of individual and corporate exploration, investment, and settlement, with many false starts and failures. Various "agents" pursuing their own interests – economic, political, religious – were involved, and the results of these first forays into new worlds were only later coordinated and integrated into a few great national enterprises.

In most locations, explorers and missionaries were the first point of contact between Europe and the non-European world. Explorers were obviously often the first foreigners to set foot on unknown lands, to map them, report information back to the home country, and claim the territories in the name of the home country. Sometimes arriving with the explorers, and soon traveling and exploring on their own, were the missionaries. One of the most energetic missionary groups was The Society of Jesus, best known as the Jesuits, a Catholic organization formed in response to the Protestant Reformation. By the late 1500s and early 1600s, missionaries – Catholic and later Protestant – were blazing trails to the interior of the Americas, often ahead of explorers and other colonizers. While they did impose many changes on indigenous cultures, they often conducted important descriptive work too, in places where acculturation and cultural loss sometimes made subsequent study difficult or impossible. One of their main contributions was in the area of language, which they studied principally for the purpose of translating the Christian Bible into local languages; still, some of those linguistic analyses – dictionaries, grammars, and translated documents – are the oldest or only records of native cultures.

Not far behind the explorers and the missionaries were the traders, planters, and administrators. Some traders were individual men (and occasionally women) who came to conduct economic exchanges with the native populations. They often lived relatively "native" lives, acculturating to native ways to the point of wearing native clothing, speaking native languages, and occasionally marrying native women. They thus often produced the first generation of mixed-blood children. Other traders were representatives of large formal organizations, like the official British East India Company, Dutch East Indies Company, or other similar chartered business ventures. They were hardly interested in acculturating to local customs but merely wanted to make money.

Where land was good and plentiful, planters or settlers were soon to arrive. Various settler colonies were attempted along the North American coast, particularly in present-day Virginia and Massachusetts, like Raleigh, Roanoke, and Plymouth. Some of these failed, but others survived and became the bridgehead of the British invasion. Similarly, Spanish and Portuguese settlers migrated to South and Central America, and other nationalities – Dutch, German, French, and Russian – moved into areas where they were the only settlers or where they shared colonial space with competing settlers. New York, for instance, was originally claimed by Holland but was wrested away by England, and the province of Quebec, a French colony, was also

PLATE 12.2 Colonialism typically involved the military defeat and conquest of native peoples, like these Apache women held captive by American soldiers

acquired by England as part of the resolution of the global colonial struggle that ended in 1763 (and was, in a way, the "first world war").

Administrators, from governors and regents to accountants and tax collectors, as well as soldiers to secure peace and compliance, were sometimes among the last to arrive, since the governments often did not take much interest until the colonies were functioning and profitable. However, it was inevitable that European law and politics would eventually prevail in these colonies and that even the natives themselves would be brought under their jurisdiction. In some cases this involved little more than military campaigns to "pacify" restless and resistant locals, while in others it involved cooptation of indigenous authorities as part of colonial administration. At one extreme, formal "intergovernmental" relations with the locals were established, up to the point of actual "treaties" between governments and indigenous leaders. This practice was most common in English territories and the United States, where treaties still significantly shape U.S./Indian relations today, setting the precedent of Indian tribal sovereignty.

BOX 12.1   A U.S. INDIAN TREATY: THE TREATY OF CANANDAIGUA, 1794

The President of the United States having determined to hold a conference with the Six Nations of Indians [Iroquois], for the purpose of removing from their minds all causes of complaint, and establishing a firm and permanent friendship with them; and Timothy Pickering being appointed sole agent for that purpose; and the agent having met and conferred with the Sachems, Chiefs, and

Warriors of the Six Nations in a general council. Now, in order to accomplish the good design of this conference, the parties have agreed on the following articles; which . . . shall be binding on them and the Six Nations.

Article 1. Peace and friendship are hereby firmly established, and shall be perpetual, between the United States and the Six Nations.

Article 2. The United States acknowledges the lands reserved to the Oneida, Onondaga, and Cayuga Nations, in their respective treaties with the State of New York, and called their reservations, to be their property; and the United States will never claim the same, nor disturb them or either of the Six Nations, nor their Indian friends residing thereon and united with them, in the free use and enjoyment thereof: but the said reservations shall remain theirs, until they choose to sell the same to the people of the United States, who have the right to purchase.

Article 3. [describes the exact location of the land] Now, the United States acknowledge all the land within the aforementioned boundaries, to be the property of the Seneca nation; and the United States will never claim the same, nor disturb the Seneca nation, nor any of the Six Nations, or of their Indian friends residing thereon and united with them, in the free use and enjoyment thereof: but it shall remain theirs, until they choose to sell the same to the people of the United States, who have the right to purchase.

Article 4. The United States having thus described and acknowledged what lands belong to the Oneidas, Onondagas, Cayugas, and Senecas, and engaged never to claim the same, nor to disturb them, or any of the Six Nations, or their Indian friends residing thereon and united with them, in the free use and enjoyment thereof: Now, the Six Nations, and each of them, hereby engage that they will never claim any other lands within the boundaries of the United States; nor ever disturb the people of the United States in the free use and enjoyment thereof.

Article 5. The Seneca Nation, all others of the Six Nations concurring, cede to the United States, the right of making a wagon road from Fort Schlosser to Lake Erie, as far south as Buffalo Creek; and the people of the United States shall have the free and undisturbed use of this road, for the purpose of traveling and transportation. And the Six Nations, and each of them, will forever allow to the people of the United States, a free passage through their lands, and the free use of the harbors and rivers adjoining and within their respective tracts of land, for passing and securing of vessels and boats, and liberty to land their cargoes where necessary for their safety.

Article 6. In consideration of the peace and friendship hereby established, and of the engagements entered into by the Six Nations; and because the United States desire, with humility and kindness, to contribute to their comfortable support; and to render the peace and friendship hereby established, strong and perpetual; the United States now deliver to the Six Nations, and the Indians of the other nations residing among and united with them, a quantity of goods of the value of $10,000. And for the same considerations, and with a view to promote the future welfare of the Six Nations and of their Indian friends aforesaid, the United States will add the sum of $3,000 to the $1,500, heretofore allowed them by an article ratified by the President, on the 23rd day of April, 1792; making the whole, $4,500; which shall be expended yearly forever, in purchasing clothing, domestic animals, implements of husbandry and other utensils suited to their circumstances, and in compensating useful artificer [*sic*] who shall reside with or near them, and be employed for their benefit. The immediate application of the whole annual allowance now stipulated, to be made by the superintendent appointed by the President for the affairs of the Six Nations, and their Indian friends aforesaid.

Article 7. Lest the firm peace and friendship now established should be interrupted by the misconduct of individuals, the United States and Six Nations agree, that for injuries done by individuals on either side no private revenge or retaliation shall take place; but, instead thereof, complaint shall be made by the party injured, to the other. By the Six Nations or any of them, to the President of the United States, or the Superintendent by him appointed: and by the Superintendent, or other person appointed by the President, to the principal chiefs of the Six Nations, or of the nation to which the offender belongs: and such prudent measures shall then be pursued as shall be necessary to preserve our peace and friendship unbroken; until the legislature (or great council) of the United States shall make other equitable provision for the purpose.

NOTE: It is clearly understood by the parties to this treaty, that the annuity stipulated in the sixth article, is to be applied to the benefit of such of the Six Nations and of their Indian friends united with them as aforesaid, as do or shall reside within the boundaries of the United States: For the United States do not interfere with nations, tribes or families, of Indians elsewhere resident. In witness whereof, the said Timothy Pickering, and the sachems and War chiefs of the Six Nations, have hereto set their hands and seals.

Goals and methods of colonialism

Colonialism in both its mercantile and imperialist phases had certain basic goals, as well as methods to achieve those goals. At the most fundamental level, these goals were economic (the enrichment of the colonialist society and of the colonists who emigrated to the colonies) and political (the empowerment of the colonialist society through expansion of its dominion and blockage of expansion by its rivals). We can identify the following specific purposes and practices.

1. **Wealth**. Colonialist/imperialist societies sought wealth, first portable wealth that they could expropriate and carry back to their home countries. This was of course at the very heart of the mercantile system, which was based on the acquisition of precious metals – particularly gold and silver – and a favorable balance of trade that led to further accumulation of these metals. Accordingly, when Columbus set off for the "Indies," his eyes were fixed on gold (along with God, government, and glory). Later expeditions to the Americas criss-crossed the continent searching for El Dorado,

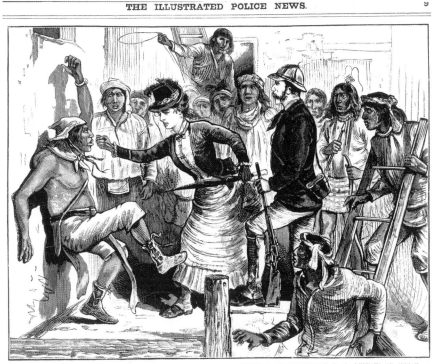

THE ILLUSTRATED POLICE NEWS.

AN ASSASSIN RED-DEVIL COWED BY A WHITE HEROINE- MRS. COL. STEVENSON, OF WASHINGTON, D. C., DEFEATS AN INDIAN ASSASSINATION CONSPIRACY IN ARIZONA.

PLATE 12.3 Public opinion typically supported colonial conquest, demonizing and dehumanizing native peoples: here a white woman confronts an "assassin red-devil"

the legendary city and society of gold. Where gold was found – either in use or at the source – it was theirs for the taking. The story of the gold of the Incas is only atypical in its ferocity: Spanish conquistadors, having penetrated Inca society, took the Emperor Atahualpa hostage and demanded that his subjects fill an entire room with gold as his ransom. When the room was filled to the brim, the Spanish christened Atahualpa with a Spanish name and garroted (strangled) him to death. Then they melted the priceless gold artifacts into bullion and shipped it to Europe. How all of this appeared to the native peoples of the Americas is best expressed in *The Indian Chronicles*: "I believe the gold makes them crazy. . . . That is truly their god. Gold is more important to them than their own people. . . . The Castilla [Spanish] worship only one God, his name is Gold" (Barreiro 1993: 191).

2. **Access to resources, especially at the source**. Perhaps the main motivation was to find a path to the sources of goods including spices like cinnamon, ginger, nutmeg, and so on, which originated in the Pacific "Spice Islands." Other valued goods included unique scented woods, silks and porcelains, and products that would become staples of Western life such as coffee and tea. Before 1500, some Europeans had traveled east to the sources of some of these goods, particularly China. However, for most purposes, especially for the island trade, they depended on the overland Central Asian trade system, dominated by the Muslims. This was a major problem for the Europeans, though, for two reasons: religio-political (trading with and

enriching their enemies) and sheer economic (paying a middleman for their supply). If Europeans could make their own connections to the source, they could "cut out the middleman" and enhance their profits. Thus, the first tentative ventures away from Europe, starting in the mid-1400s, tended to hug the coastline of Africa, where they occasionally landed to plant a trading post; once they rounded the southern tip of Africa they proceeded east to the islands. In many places, they found strong societies and established traders and posts; however, unlike Arab and other traders before them, Europeans soon aimed to monopolize and to own. Accessing and controlling the sources of valuable goods involved finding and, where possible, taking possession of, farms, mines, forests, and any other means of production. And of course, as in the New World, nothing stood in their way. Europeans seized mines, like the great silver mines of central South America, or farmland or rivers, or anything of any value to them.

3. Land. Colonists claimed and occupied land and then put it to whatever use they could discover or develop there. Even more, colonists needed to find a way to justify to themselves this expropriation of native land. Two concepts, "legal fictions" if you will, emerged to solve the problem – the "doctrine of discovery" and the notion of *terra nullius*. The **doctrine of discovery** stipulated that any state that could discover and claim a hitherto unknown or unclaimed land could have undisputed title to it. The doctrine of discovery therefore gave the discovering power the first right of occupation if there were no previous inhabitants. If there were inhabitants, the discovering power had the first right to trade with them and to negotiate political relations with them, normally taking the form of subordination and/or war. This doctrine alone, though, did not justify taking away land other than by agreement or aggression. Here, the idea of *terra nullius* served well. Latin for "empty land," it suggested that the lands discovered and claimed by Europeans were unoccupied and therefore available to anyone who could squat on them. The only problem was that virtually no land anywhere in the world was unoccupied. If it could not be argued that the land was void of human beings, it could be argued that it was void of *completely* human beings or of *civilized* human beings. The mark of civilization was permanent settlements and cultivated farmland after the European fashion. Natives who were foragers or nomads were treated as little more than "beasts of the field," who by this logic surely did not own the lands they wandered and grazed on. Thus, since such people never established title to the land, original title could be claimed by the European arrivals. In other cases, title to land could be created by treaty, which extinguished native claims and invented the first "deed" for it.

4. Labor. There was much work to be done in the colonies, but usually there were not enough European immigrants to do it; besides, many colonists did not want to do this grueling work but rather to profit from the work of others. So the system needed more than the dispossessed property of the natives; they needed their labor too. Hence, native labor became a valuable commodity, since it produced (at little or no cost) the wealth of the colony. Indians were "employed" in the mines or farms or ports of the Americas, and in more powerful and resistant societies (e.g., African

Doctrine of discovery
The European colonial principle that the state which "discovered" or arrived first in a new territory had the right to occupy and administer it without interference from other states.

Terra nullius
The colonial doctrine of "empty land," that colonized land was empty of human inhabitants and therefore could be claimed and settled by colonists.

and Indonesian ones) increasingly imbalanced and exploitative relations were established with the producers, who were converted into European employees and serfs. Europeans devised many methods to achieve the "employment" they needed, including force and enslavement. In some cases, a system of **corvée** labor was instituted, which required that every able-bodied person provide a certain number of days or months of labor each year. Large private farms or plantations were quick to appear. In Spanish territories, these farms were known as *encomiendas* and *haciendas* (in Portuguese Brazil, the name was *fazendas*). **Encomiendas** were essentially grants of land to conquerors and explorers, much like medieval estates; as such, control of land meant control of the people and wealth on the land. Therefore, unlucky Indians who had *encomiendas* organized under their feet found themselves changed into serfs who owed labor and tribute to their new lords. This institution was eventually replaced by a more modern but thereby more exploitative arrangement called the *hacienda*. A **hacienda** was less feudal but was truly owned by the *haciendados* who acquired workers or tenants through indebtedness and sharecropping. Mines and other interests were organized on basically the same principles: Europeans controlled or owned, and natives worked. In many cases, the natives failed to do the work satisfactorily, either because the ordeals of the work simply killed them or because they could escape and run away, like the Suriname Maroons. This led to the introduction of a new institution, the slave trade. Slaves, mostly but not exclusively from Africa, were collected (with the cooperation of African rulers and entrepreneurs) and sold to plantation owners throughout the Americas. Of course, Europeans did not invent slavery, and long after they abolished it, other societies continued (and continue today) to practice it, but the scale of the European slave trade was truly unique. In addition, Africans were not the only peoples to be enslaved. In a practice known as **blackbirding**, European sailors would often land on small Pacific islands and carry off virtually the entire populations to work on some far-off colonial project in India or Southeast Asia.

5. Taxation. European colonialists introduced taxation in their colonies for two reasons. One was to pay the administrative costs of the colony itself. Colonies were not always profitable ventures; colonialism was inefficient compared to some of the more "modern" means of exploitation. Rather than bearing these costs themselves, the colonialists shifted the burden to the natives. Arguably, some improvements in the quality of life were subsidized this way, including schools and hospitals and such, but none of it was the choice of the natives. Yet another reason for taxation was to compel natives to participate in the colonial economy. The colonial administration would order that all inhabitants had to pay a cash tax on their houses, their livestock, their own heads, and so on. But natives had no cash, and the only place they could obtain it was from wage labor for European businesses. Thus colonialists got the natives' land and their wealth and their work and at least some of their wages.

6. Markets. Colonialism was above all things about the economic growth of the colonizing societies. During the mercantile age, domestic European production was on the increase, first in the agricultural and then in the "light industrial" (especially

Corvée
A colonial practice in which local people were required to provide a period of labor to the administration as a sort of "tax."

Encomienda
In Latin American colonial history, a grant of land to a conqueror and explorer, much like medieval estates, which gave the grant-holder control over the land and its inhabitants.

Hacienda
The Spanish colonial practice in which land was granted as private property and in which these estates were run both for subsistence production and for the production of cash and export crops.

See Chapter 6

Blackbirding
The colonial practice of abducting the populations of areas, often islands, and resettling them as a labor force in some other part of the world.

See Chapter 14

textile) sectors; in England, for example, corn and wool were in abundant supply in the early 1600s, causing economic and social turmoil as prices dropped, dragging down the wages of workers and the profits of producers. But there was a limit to the sales that could occur within the domestic market. The colonies became a profitable new place to make these sales. Next, colonial administrations could sell the exotic products of the colonies (coffee, tea, sugar, rubber) to the home country or to each other. Colonial trading monopolies meant that colonies could only sell to the home country or to other colonies of the home country. Further, this growth in markets helped pay for the continuing and expanding growth of business and industry back home. Colonial powers could acquire raw materials cheaply, manufacture those materials into finished products, and sell those products to their own people, to other Europeans, or to the colonies. The wealth that was accumulated by England and France in particular was reinvested into expansion and technical innovation, ultimately financing their industrial revolutions. Of course, much of this wealth also went into military ventures and other less productive enterprises.

Geopolitics

The use of geographical territory for purposes of maintenance and projection of power; the control of strategic locations in the pursuit of political goals.

7. Geopolitics. **Geopolitics** means control and use of important or strategic locations of the globe. Although originally targeted principally at the Muslims, geopolitics naturally and quickly pitted European states against each other. In fact, as early as 1494, Spain and Portugal claimed, by right of a papal decree, to divide the entire New World between their two empires. Of course, England, Holland, France, and other ambitious states would not accept this arrangement for long and sought to undermine it immediately – in some cases first as pirates, then as rivals. By 1588 Spain was sufficiently tired of English interference to sail its armada to invade England but was summarily crushed. Dominating the sources of valuable trade goods was only the first step in the geopolitical game. Soon Europeans wanted to control territory, and for long, slow, intercontinental voyages, refueling and resupplying stations were necessary; therefore, claiming and occupying intermediate spots, especially Pacific island ports, was critical. Colonial competition became so fierce that, by 1756, England and France were fighting around the globe for political dominance in what American history remembers as the French and Indian War but world history calls the Seven Years War (1756–1763), which England won. Yet, just at this moment, the independence movements from this first phase of colonialism were approaching. As a result, Europeans had to find new lands to colonize (hence the "scramble for Africa"). Sometimes, the point was simply to prevent anyone else from getting a territory, even if it was not particularly valuable to the colonizers. The case of the Gambia River is one of the clearest and most absurd examples. England invaded and occupied a few miles of land on both banks of this northwest African waterway. France, however, occupying the surrounding territory of Senegal, suggested a land swap, offering larger and richer regions like the Ivory Coast in exchange. England refused and retained a tiny sliver of territory deep in the heart of French Africa (which went on to become a tiny sliver of an independent state). The same scenario was played out around the world, from Hong Kong and Singapore to Hawaii to Cuba.

THE LEGACY OF COLONIALISM

Eventually, the formal colonial system came to an end, and the entities that were formerly – for the period of a few decades or a few centuries – colonies became "independent." This does not mean, of course, that everything returned to pre-colonial conditions, nor that everything had a happy ending. It certainly does not mean that external and global forces ceased to impact and indeed to be intimately enmeshed with local groups and cultures. In some ways, new intercultural realities emerged that were not all that different from the colonial relationships. The one thing that would never again be true, if it ever was, was the possibility of thinking in terms of bounded and discrete societies in isolation from each other.

While modern Western colonialism was not utterly unprecedented, its long-term effects were: it wrought changes on a scale and of types that would not be rolled back by the simple end of the system. In fact, in a variety of ways, the colonial project was not completed when it "ended." In North America, for example, British and French colonial administrations departed the scene, but local governments – American and Canadian – continued to "colonize" the territories to which they laid claim. The U.S.A. asserted possession and control of the western regions of its continent, but it still had the challenge of moving colonies of settlers into those regions and making good its assertions; the people who traveled in wagon trains along the Oregon Trail and other western routes ought rightly to be thought of as colonists too. This process goes on today in many parts of the world. Some of the changes introduced by this colonial process, old and new, are environmental, some are cultural, others are demographic, and still others are "economic" and "political"

TABLE 12.1   Dates of independence from colonialism, selected countries

First (mercantile) phase		Second (imperialist) phase	
United States	1776	Iraq	1932
Brazil	1815	Jordan, Syria, Lebanon	1946
Peru	1821	India, Pakistan	1947
Mexico	1821	Indonesia	1949
Argentina	1815	Ghana (Gold Coast)	1957
Bolivia	1825	Mali, Niger, Chad	1960
Venezuela	1830	Sudan	1956
Guatemala	1838	Nigeria, Cameroon, Senegal	1960
Honduras	1838	Libya	1951
El Salvador	1838	Zaire/Congo	1960
Costa Rica	1838	Malaysia	1963
Chile	1818	Algeria	1962
Ecuador	1803	Kenya	1963
Paraguay	1811	Angola, Mozambique	1975
Uruguay	1828	Zimbabwe	1980

in the familiar sense. All of them are of concern not only to anthropologists but to all citizens of the world.

Depopulation

In all colonial settings, there had been extensive loss of life. In some, huge numbers of native people died from diseases like smallpox, syphilis, and other plagues that were lethal to but controllable in European societies. Some estimates suggest that as much as 90 percent of the Native American population died in the early decades of contact, many before they ever saw a white person. Where disease did not ravage the local people, war often did. Many colonized people fought long and hard struggles to resist European invasion; however, in practically every case, European war technology was superior to local weapons, and where weapons alone could not suffice, economic and political pressures eventually brought the peoples to heel. In many places there were declared wars prosecuted by professional soldiers, including the "Indian wars" in the United States. However, an untold number of native people died from unofficial and personal violence perpetrated by settlers. In Africa, armed homesteaders often killed locals in "self-defense" when those locals attempted to defend their land.

In Australia, which was entirely inhabited by band-level foraging societies, English settlers often considered the Aboriginals little more than vermin to be exterminated, like any other native wildlife that stood in the way of farming and ranching. Massacres took place from the earliest days of Australian settlement (1788) until the early 1900s. When settlement ships arrived with the first 800 or so English convicts, it took only a year for an Aboriginal leader, Pemulwuy, to be captured and beheaded. As Euro-Australians pushed their way into central Australia, they encountered more foragers occupying land in "non-productive" activities and displaced them. The settlers who followed behind them, with the aid of the territorial police, "protected" whites against the predations of the Aboriginals, who merely saw themselves as acting in self-defense. By the mid-1800s, the era of massacres was well under way. Entire Aboriginal communities were rounded up and executed for the deaths of whites or of the cattle of whites, regardless of whether or not those particular Aboriginals were the culprits. Some of the most notorious killings occurred in the 1900s, such as the 1928 Coniston massacre, in which police and settlers killed fifty-one Aboriginals (most of them probably innocent of any wrongdoing); the whites were never found guilty of any crime for these acts. In the same year, police captured another whole society of Aboriginal hunters, chained them by the neck, and killed all of them except three women. They killed and burned all the men. Neck-chaining continued to be practiced in Australia until 1960.

Most infamously in Africa, but in other locations as well, large populations were deported into slavery. It is estimated that as many as thirty million Africans were removed, mostly bound for South America, although many fewer than that number ever arrived alive. "Blackbirding," as we noted above, also wiped out whole island societies. And where slavery as such was not practiced, people were often transferred from one area to another as labor, like the Tamils of India who were imported into highland Ceylon (Sri Lanka) as agricultural workers. Finally, many native people died from the living conditions in the colonies, including overwork, poor diet, alcoholism, internecine fighting, seizure of women and children, the difficulty of making culturally correct marriages, and the sheer hopelessness that comes with the destruction of one's traditions and culture.

Acculturation and deculturation

Native peoples were often unable to continue their pre-colonial ways of life, due to inadvertent factors or intentional policy. Indigenous societies, especially foragers and pastoralists, were often settled more or less forcibly in villages. Efforts were made to convert all locals into wage laborers and tax payers, and all production was integrated into the colonial and global economy, producing for export rather than for local consumption. Furthermore, if people were compelled to toil on plantations or in mines, there was precious little time left for traditional social or religious activities, which were often discouraged or forbidden anyway. When men were required to travel far distances to work, traditional family structures suffered and occasionally collapsed. Kinship practices were altered, often by law, particularly when it came to matters of polygyny or child marriage. European-style marriage and sexual rules were enforced on natives, and European gender roles were imposed, often to the impoverishment of women who in some cases enjoyed better status before colonialism than afterwards. Enforced Western-style education, boarding-schools, and separation of native children from their parents and societies interrupted cultural transmission and introduced competing values and institutions. Pre-colonial political systems were modified in sometimes contradictory ways: political roles and offices were often consolidated or eliminated, even while the powers of the remaining authorities expanded, strengthened by colonial administrations and armies and given new prerogatives like tax collecting and the right to compel labor. Simultaneously, colonial administrators and courts claimed the final right to intervene in matters of law. Religion was a particular target for change and "conversion," discrediting local spirits and gods and prohibiting or coopting local practices and institutions. Often, key artifacts and symbols were appropriated by travelers, traders, and collectors. Finally, particularly in colonies of settlement, indigenous societies were literally swamped by people with foreign cultures, although even a small number of settlers could radically reshape cultural relations.

Acculturation was not always a simple and direct acquisition of a foreign culture; on more than a few occasions it was a fascinating process of invention and acceptance of a novel or reinterpreted version of "tradition." Colonial authorities, some presumably well-meaning, would often try to base colonial policy on "traditional culture" – or what they thought was traditional culture. Since what was actually encountered on the ground was a messy and complicated blend of different social systems varying more or less from their own ideals, outsiders, including anthropologists, occasionally "found" more order and non-ambiguity than really existed and fed it back to the natives, inventing a "traditional" culture that had never existed – but which might *become* tradition in persuasive and powerful ways.

BOX 12.2   INVENTING TRADITION IN COLONIAL FIJI

According to Clammer (1973), at the inception of colonialism the islands of Fiji were home to around 100 different language groups. In 1912 G. V. Maxwell was appointed Native Lands Commissioner of Fiji and commenced a study of native land tenure and social organization, so as to run the colony more authentically and efficiently. After six months, he arrived at a clear-cut model that featured land-right holding units called *tokatoka* which were organized into higher level groups called *mataqali* which were further organized into top-level kinship groups called *yavusa* based on direct descent from a divine ancestor. Along the way, even Maxwell had noticed how contradictory Fijian social organization was, commenting that "the people are absolutely incapable of classifying themselves without assistance" (203). So Maxwell gave them a clean classification that was not only previously unknown on the islands but that was "immediately enshrined as the 'official' doctrine of native social structure" (202). Oddly enough, the locals had been complicit in its invention: when they heard he was coming to study them they would either meet in advance to iron out disagreements in their social and landowning arrangements "which could be represented to the Commission as immemorially sanctioned by tradition" (202) or just make up social units and relations that had never existed. This invention of Fijian tradition included other aspects, such as language (one dialect, Mbauan, was advanced as "traditional Fijian language," and the very social terms used by Maxwell are Mbauan) and economic/labor relations, particularly "communalism." It was determined by colonial authorities that Fijians had "traditionally" worked together communally, so land was assigned to *mataqali* groups as communal property, although land had actually previously been owned individually. Clammer concludes that "modern communalism is entirely the child of Colonial administration" (213). Almost a century later, with colonialism long abolished, "many Fijians are 'ignorant' of the *mataqali* and *yavusa* units to which they are supposed to belong. Yet, while in village life the system is ignored or evaded wherever possible, it is, at the national level, lauded and defended as being at the very foundation of Fijian social order" (218).

Loss of economic independence

Native peoples were no longer free to make their own decisions about production or distribution; they were now working for systems over which they had no control and often little understanding. Land, resources, and other means of production had been taken into foreign hands, and this would not change with mere political "independence." Even if the colonial administration went home, this did not mean that ownership and control of land and resources suddenly – if ever – reverted back to the natives. In reality, it was not governments that owned and controlled most of

See Chapter 14

the wealth and property but companies and individuals, and these did not give up their power, or even leave the territory, when colonialism officially ended. In addition, naturally, since they did not want the competition, most colonial administrations had discouraged the development of local industry. Colonies had few factories or other facilities to produce manufactured goods. Colonies were still suppliers of primary goods or raw materials, which were transported to Western factories for processing into finished goods and then sold back to the colonies. And since "value-added" goods (like manufactures) are almost always more expensive than primary ones, colonized peoples lost on both ends of the transaction. Finally, colonies had often been made to "specialize" in one or a few products for which each particular colony was best suited; farming colonies were often marshaled into **monoculture** agriculture, in which one single crop constituted the main if not the sole product of the colony, particularly if the crop could not be grown in Europe, such as sugar, coffee, tea, rubber, cocoa, bananas, and so on (hence the term "banana republic"). This left the colony vulnerable to food dependency, as well as to international prices and demand; a drop in prices or demand could impoverish an entire colony and its people.

Monoculture
The specialization of production of only one crop or product for which a territory is particularly suited. This can involve food crops like corn or rice, or raw materials like lumber, coffee, rubber, tea, and so on.

Forced settlement

Part of colonial policy was to compel local people to live according to patterns that met the economic and political needs of colonialism. In particular, colonialists (and contemporary state-level government) detested nomads and tried to settle them as aggressively as possible. Nomads like foragers and pastoralists were hard to control, hard to count, and hard to tax. They occupied large tracts of land but produced little of value to the colonial economy. Whether in America, Australia, Africa, or Amazonia, their land was a prime attraction to settlers and entrepreneurs who saw little opposition to exploiting those untapped resources. So, these societies were particular targets for "pacification" and acculturation efforts, when they were not, like many Aboriginal or many American Indian societies, simply wiped out. In addition to forced settlement of nomadic peoples, wholesale population transfers were conducted, moving people from where they were to where colonial interests wanted them. Colonialism needed labor, if not from slavery then from other means. So colonial administrations would shift populations, either to fill jobs or to populate "underpopulated" regions. And as in other cases, this policy did not end with the colonial era; in Indonesia under its *transmigrasi* program in the 1960s and 1970s, people from high-density areas like the city of Jakarta were encouraged to relocate to less dense lands like Sumatra and Kalimantan. Of course, the underpopulated places were seldom if ever *unpopulated*, and such human transfers tended to create social conflicts. As long as there was a net improvement on the balance sheet of the colony or state, other considerations were secondary.

See Chapter 14

Creation of "plural societies" and mixing of cultures

One of the most enduring and significant characteristics of colonies was their *artificiality*. Before colonialism, the political entities that became colonies usually did not exist. The colonies were "artificial" in the sense that someone (a foreign power) drew lines on a map to create administrative boundaries. Suddenly there was a thing called, for example, Gambia, where there was no such thing before; there had never been a state or other polity called Gambia. However, the political aspect of this colonial artificiality is less profound than the social aspect. Not only had there never been a state called Gambia, but there had never been a society that called itself Gambian. After all, Gambia is the name of a river, not of a society. There were people living near the Gambia River, but they had various cultures and languages and religions. There was no such thing as "Gambian culture" or "Gambian language" – and in many former colonies there still is not. So colonies like Gambia were created with little knowledge of – and quite frankly, little concern for – which people were circumscribed by its borders. The borders were administrative, not cultural. Colonial policy was sometimes explicitly to seize territory and, as much as possible, to rule it as if there were no people there at all. The result was that, in virtually all colonies, diverse peoples were thrust together in unprecedented ways (Figure 12.1).

This non-traditional creation and administration of multicultural social systems posed a managerial problem. J.S. Furnivall wrote one of the most important and influential studies on the subject, *Colonial Policy and Practice* (1956), in which he analyzed the social realities of two colonies, Burma and the Dutch East Indies (Indonesia). What he noted was that these colonies were by no means homogeneous – made up of one kind of people – but highly heterogeneous and "enclaved." In other words, the groups were not fully or even nearly integrated but rather occupied very discrete social, and in some instances physical, spaces in the colony. In Burma, he found, in addition to the "Burmese" (who themselves were a diverse group),

Furnivall, J.S. 1956. *Colonial Policy and Practice: A Comparative Study of Burma and Netherlands India.* New York: New York University Press.

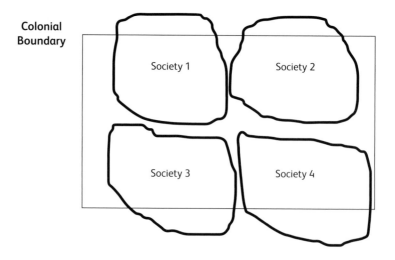

FIGURE 12.1

A hypothetical colonial boundary, in relation to societies within

Indians, Chinese, and of course Europeans, as well as "mixed-blood" individuals of every combination. Each group fitted into the colony in a different way, and its communal identity led to intergroup violence in the 1920s and 1930s. To describe this situation, Furnivall coined the term "**plural society**," which has two characteristics. The first or political characteristic of a plural society is that it contains separate cultural or social sections that "mix but do not combine." They live side by side in the same political unit but do not form an integrated "society" in any significant way. Social and political life is therefore "atomized" or incomplete: the cultural sections of the society are not coherent groups themselves but mere "aggregates of individuals." Each "is a crowd and not a community." One prime reason for this fact is the second or economic characteristic of plural societies; that is, that they are purely economic arrangements, not true societies or cultures at all. In what he calls "the process of the survival of the cheapest," market forces function "to eliminate all non-economic values," leaving only economic interests and relations with no other common social interests or causes (299). Society is stripped of cultural significance, and only jobs and money drive the system or unify people.

Plural society
A society that contains various cultural groups. Such groups often occupy "niches" in the broader social system, such that the groups do not interact with each other except in limited and often mutually exploitive ways.

Introduction of race concept and racism

Race, at least in the way that it is understood and practiced in Western societies, is not a concept shared by all societies. When colonialists began to have prolonged contact with non-Western peoples, their reactions to those peoples were at first not entirely negative. Columbus was rather impressed with the appearance and personality of the natives he saw. Even Captain James Cook, one of the first Europeans to lay eyes on Australian Aboriginals, commented in the 1770s that they were tranquil, non-materialistic, and happy people (Reed 1969: 136). However, as European domination of these peoples grew more widespread, it became more common to berate them as, if not reduce them to, abject savages worthy of no better treatment than they were getting. The social Darwinism of the time suggested the inferiority of some groups to others, evidenced by the "success" of some and the "failure" of others. However, it could be argued that Western racism was not so much a cause as an *effect* of colonialism. How else to justify the conduct and policies of colonialists toward the native peoples? If the natives were inferior – a lower race, a primitive species, a sort of half-human/half-animal – then what better consideration did they deserve? Racism in this sense indicated the dissonant feelings of the conquerors and their attempt to assuage these feelings by rationalizing their behavior.

See Chapter 6

If racism helped the whites to legitimize colonialism, it did not do much good for the locals. It exposed them to unprecedented levels of cruelty and exploitation. But even more, it penetrated their own thinking about the identity of and relations among groups, with profound effect. In some colonies, Europeans found some peoples with whom they felt more commonality than others; the Tutsi in Rwanda, the Sikhs in northern India, and the Sinhalese in Sri Lanka are three examples. The Tutsi were the dominant segment of Rwandan society. A chiefly class or caste, they were ascribed physical traits as well – taller, thinner, and more "Caucasian" in some ways. The Hutu were seen as more "African" or Bantu. Accordingly, the European opinion of the Hutu was much lower. One colonial observer in 1925 characterized the Hutu as "generally short and thick-set with a big head, a jovial expression, a wide nose and enormous lips," whereas the Tutsi

> has nothing of the negro, apart from his color. He is usually very tall. . . . He is very thin. . . . His features are very fine: a high brow, thin nose and fine lips framing beautiful shining teeth. Batutsi women are usually lighter-skinned than their husbands, very slender and pretty in their youth, although they tend to thicken with age.
>
> (quoted in Prunier 1995: 6)

It was claimed that each had a racially specific personality too: Hutu tended to be "hardworking, not very clever, extrovert, irascible, unmannerly, obedient" – suitable to the lower class they occupied – while the Tutsi were "intelligent (in the sense of astute in political intrigues), capable of command, refined, courageous, and cruel" (Maquet 1961: 164). The 1925 observer went so far as to applaud the Tutsi for displaying "a refinement of feelings which is rare among primitive peoples." Not surprisingly, the Tutsi were preferred by the European colonialists for political service and education. This created a new dimension of animosity between them and the Hutu majority (around 85 percent), which could only make for trouble at a later date.

Maquet, Jacques. 1961. The Premise of Inequality in Rwanda: A Study of Political Relations in a Central African Kingdom. London: Oxford University Press.

The same was true in colonial Ceylon (Sri Lanka), where the dominant Buddhist Sinhalese, whose history and mythology told of a northern India origin, absorbed the British concept of and preference for "Aryan" peoples, which they fancied themselves. They used this distinction against the south Indian, non-Aryan, or "Dravidian" Hindu Tamils on the island to assert their own similarity to the Europeans and their superiority to the minority Tamils. Thus, the Sinhalese came to regard themselves as a race in the European sense and as a higher race than their fellow natives, creating again a new type and degree of distinction between the two local groups that never existed in pre-colonial times. As the Sinhalese apologist Dharmapala put it:

> the Aryan race is the only race with noble customs handed down from tradition . . . [therefore] the Sinhalese (who are Aryans) should cultivate ancient codes of conduct. Aryan customs and Aryan dresses and ornaments. . . . The Sinhalese first came to this country from Bengal and the Bengalis are superior in their intelligence to other communities in India.
>
> (quoted in Dharmadasa 1992: 145–6)

Racism, then, was not only a virulent force in relations between white colonizers and non-white colonized peoples but also often enough between various non-white peoples themselves. In fact, the concept of race and its inherent hierarchy helped to exacerbate intergroup differences and hostilities when such forms of distinct identities already existed or sometimes to create the very notion of disparate native "peoples" where no such distinctions had previously existed. This too would bear fruit long after colonialism was gone.

Environmental degradation and declining living conditions

In many colonial settings, the rapacious exploitation of local resources and labor left huge environmental disruption. Entire forests were cut down (and are still being cut down) to make room for farms and towns, for export of the wood, and for the production of charcoal. Erosion and pollution occurred. Squalid shantytowns rose up, often where local people had never congregated in large numbers before. In places where indigenous people had always lived in small mobile groups, settlement only aggravated their social and physical complaints and caused despoliation of the land. Colonial officials did make certain attempts to clean up the messes they created, such as establishing hospitals and Western-style medical care. However, one unintended and undesired consequence of this humanitarianism was an enormous explosion of population. People who improved their infant mortality rates and life expectancies but did not curb their reproduction soon found themselves with up to a 10 percent annual population growth rate, resulting in doubling the population every seven years or so. In the villages, the land – already expropriated by colonial interests – simply could not support the burden of population growth. People had no choice but to gather in burgeoning new cities, without the infrastructure or economy to handle such large inflows. Literally millions of people ended up and still end up as squatters on the fringes of cities, without adequate (or sometimes any) fresh water, sewerage, electricity, and other amenities, consuming the environment on a profligate scale. Forests were denuded for firewood, farmland was overworked to the point of exhaustion, and water and food supplies became inadequate or prohibitively expensive, as evidenced by the worldwide food riots of 2008. Meanwhile, communicable disease (e.g., dysentery and malaria and most recently AIDS) ran rampant. Still the population grew, composed of people with lots of complaints and little to lose – a recipe for political disaster.

See Chapter 14

BOX 12.3 CONTEMPORARY CULTURAL CONTROVERSIES: "SOVEREIGN FARMS" IN SUDAN

Colonization did not begin with Western expansion; neither, apparently, did it end with Western decolonization. Indeed, any society that is rich and powerful enough to commandeer another society's resources, and with a sufficient need for those resources, is likely to engage in colonialism. According to the Sudanese Media Center (http://english.smc.sd/enmain/entopic/?artID=13513), the small Persian Gulf state of Abu Dhabi has begun acquiring land in Sudan as "the first step towards ensuring food security" for Abu Dhabi's people. With a population of four million and virtually no arable land, and with the price and availability of food in serious question, with great oil wealth – and with Sudan's significant unexploited resources and profound weakness and poverty – the Arab state has established so-called "sovereign farms," developed by government and private companies, to fill its food needs. This means, of course, that the land will not be used to fill Sudan's, or anyone else's, needs. Other oil-rich states like Saudi Arabia and Bahrain have taken similar steps, "locking up land" in Thailand, India, Ukraine, and Brazil; Pakistan offered hundreds of thousands of acres to Saudi Arabia in exchange for oil and cash. The government of Sudan hopes to benefit from the relationship with Abu Dhabi and other interested wealthy states, and the director-general of the Abu Dhabi Fund for Development has announced that the current land acquisitions "will not be the last project." What do you think?

SUMMARY

The spread of colonies into new territories is not a uniquely modern or even human phenomenon, but modern colonialism (from the fifteenth to the twentieth centuries) escalated the process and its impact to unknown levels. It not only brought far-flung societies into prolonged contact with each other but began the centuries-long project of linking all societies into a truly global cultural network, a project that is just now reaching its fulfillment. Anthropologists who had previously looked for discrete, homogeneous, and static "traditional societies" began to understand that societies are often internally complex and even contradictory, that discrete boundaries are often lacking, and that even "traditional" societies had their histories – of which Western colonialism and even anthropology itself would now and forever more be parts.

The goals and methods of colonialism varied by time period, colonizing power, colonized area, and other such factors, but tended to include

■ expropriation of wealth
■ access to resources at the source
■ land
■ labor
■ taxation
■ markets
■ geopolitics.

These interests and the political and economic institutions that were instated to achieve them imposed extensive changes on colonized societies, many of which did not disappear when colonialism officially ended. These changes included

■ depopulation
■ acculturation and deculturation

- loss of economic independence
- forced settlement
- creation of "plural societies" with artificial boundaries
- the concept of race and racism
- environmental degradation and declining living conditions.

At the most extreme, but not uncommonly, old cultures and identities were given new interpretations and valuations, or new cultures and identities were invented outright from a combination of indigenous cultural materials, colonial imperatives, and human imagination.

Key Terms

Blackbirding	*Hacienda*
Colonialism	Imperialism
Colonies of exploitation	Internal colonialism
Colonies of settlement	Mercantilism
Colony	Monoculture
Corvée	Plural society
Doctrine of discovery	Sphere of influence
Encomienda	*Terra nullius*
Geopolitics	

13

The Struggle for Political Identity: Nationalism, Ethnicity, and Conflict

In the fifteenth century, a Muslim government had ruled over northern India for centuries, bringing Islam and Hinduism into sustained and awkward contact – awkward, at least partly, because of Islam's rejection of perceived polytheism and caste distinctions. Various individuals offered various messages of accommodation and resistance, among them Guru Nanak (1469–1539) who taught that there was no such thing as Muslim or Hindu but only those who worship the one true divinity. His followers, known as *sikhs* or "disciples," were at first mostly Hindu converts who rejected the caste and ascetic strictures of Indian religion. By 1600 the movement had grown into a major force in the Punjab region of north India, where a temple was built at Amritsar housing the scriptures known as *Adi Granth* or "Original Book." However, a new, less tolerant Muslim dynasty had come to power and executed the current guru, Arjan, giving the new community its first martyr. Hostility between Sikh and Muslim authorities increased until the tenth guru, Gobind Singh (1675–1708), inaugurated a military branch within the group, the Khalsa or "Company of the Pure," who would wear the symbols of Sikh identity (including a sword) and evolve into a militant community-within-the-community. Soon, two events galvanized Sikh identity and opposition to the reigning authorities – the "Lesser Holocaust" of 1746 and the "Greater Holocaust" of 1762. The power of the Sikhs grew in northern India as Europeans began to penetrate the subcontinent, until by 1800 they ruled the region but came into conflict with the British in two wars

(1845–1846 and 1848–1849), which led to the disbanding of the Khalsa army. Another threat emerged in the late 1880s in the form of the Hindu missionary society *Arya Samaj* that sought to "reconvert" Sikhs to Hinduism. By 1920 Sikhs had established a body to protect and manage their sacred places, called the *Shiromani Gurdwara Prabhandak* Committee (SGPC) or Central Gurdwara Management Committee; also a new political-military organization, the Akali Dal or "Army of Immortals," was instituted. At independence in 1947, India and Pakistan divided Punjab between them, splitting Sikhs across two states. Almost immediately the Sikhs began advocating reunification of their community in its own sovereign state. Hostility and direct violence between Sikhs and the Indian government escalated into hijacking and terrorism until June 1, 1984, when Indian forces stormed the Golden Temple at Amritsar. In response, Sikhs killed Indian Prime Minister Indira Gandhi on October 21, 1984 and declared the independent state of Khalistan on April 29, 1986. Since then, an on-and-off struggle between the Sikh and Indian communities has existed, which Mahmood characterizes as "a resistance movement against the perceived injustices of the Indian state and a political movement aimed at sovereign rule, but . . . also . . . an existentially meaningful way to be a Sikh and a human being independent of instrumental political goals" (1994: 12).

Long before modern colonialism, human groups were confronting each other, challenging each other, and dominating, absorbing, or destroying each other. Out of this constant agitation old societies have disappeared, new societies have emerged, separate societies have coalesced into mixed (and often stratified) systems, and cultural elements have been circulated, interpreted, and invented. Thus, there has always been a kind of "cultural crisis" of the sort referred to by Linton and Diamond, which was not new to modern colonialism but was greatly accelerated and globalized during that period. Group boundaries, identities, and cultures, which were forever coming into and going out of existence – but which Western observers at first took as "finished" and timeless and "traditional" – became a conspicuously obvious feature and problem of human life.

See Chapter 11

One of the key manifestations of the cultural crisis hastened by colonialism and also by the end of colonialism is the struggle for order and control among social groups, among social groups and the states in which they live, and among states themselves. We can properly refer to this as a "political" matter in the widest possible sense – in terms of how humans in groups manage their affairs, settle their disputes, institute their laws, defend their interests, and so on. And politics is certainly a domain of culture, so political matters are cultural matters. However, particularly in the contemporary era culture is especially political, as cultural differences become the basis and resource for political organization, operation, and opposition. Differences of value or interest can flare into real competition and violence, leading to death and displacement of people. Above all, issues of power, order, and control cannot be detached from questions of *identity*, which is attached to questions of *authenticity* ("who we really are"), which is often attached integrally to questions of culture. In the modern world – not simply because of but substantially related to colonialism and the course of post-colonial events – politics and identity are

Identity politics

The organization and mobilization of groups and parties on the basis of shared cultural characteristics, such that these groups and parties are seen to share an "identity" and to pursue economic, political, and cultural goals for and in the name of those who share that identity.

Taylor, Charles. 1994. "The Politics of Recognition." In Amy Gutman, ed. *Multiculturalism: Examining the Politics of Recognition*. Princeton: Princeton University Press, 25–73.

inseparable, so that anthropologists can and must speak of "**identity politics**" or "the politics of identity" (Taylor 1994). And both identity and politics are increasingly inseparable from culture.

The notion of individual and collective identity being rooted in culture is not a new one. The German historian and philosopher Johann Herder (1744–1803) believed that every "nation" (*Volk*, as in the English word "folk") of humanity had its own unique "spirit" (*Geist*) or "soul" (*Seele*), expressed in its language and culture. For Herder, all Germans were one nation or people, united by the essence of their common history and culture, even if they were not aware of or did not identify with the shared "Germanness." However, he vehemently recommended that the German nation – and every other nation – recognize its true identity and cultivate and preserve its special cultural genius. This interpretation of culture and identity was influential in Europe, as Germany and Italy, for instance, forged national states and former multinational empires (like the Austrian and Ottoman Turkish) collapsed and fragmented into their local pieces. During and particularly after colonialism, non-Western peoples were compelled to determine how to organize and govern themselves – after significant mixing of peoples and the introduction of the Western concepts of culture, nation, and state. The result has been and continues to be a contested field of constructed identities, often if not always built on (the rubble of) culture. And too often, these struggles have made further rubble of culture, of the physical environment, and of people's lives.

POLITICS, IDENTITY, AND POST-COLONIALISM

While the relationship between politics, "traditional culture," and identity is not exclusive to the post-colonial period, it is acute in that period – in terms of the legacies that colonialism left, the path that each colony took to independence, and the choices and incidents that occurred subsequently. Especially because former colonies had been carved artificially out of indigenous territories, creating "plural" or "multicultural" entities, and because these entities had further been integrated into regional, imperial, and global systems, the cultural and political situation was complicated and fraught with tension. In addition, the political and cultural situation was anything but a continuation of "traditional" forms, nor was it a straightforward absorption of Western forms. Rather, as Malinowski commented, it was an innovative amalgamation of both traditional and Western and other elements as well.

See Chapter 12

The path to independence

The immediate fate of the colonies after independence was largely set by the colony's path to independence. There were three main avenues: more or less gradual and orderly transition to native self-government, more or less gradual and orderly transition to rule by resident Europeans or descendants of Europeans, and more or less violent resistance and revolution, with natives fighting to dislodge Europeans and establish self-government. It may seem on the surface that the first of these processes would be preferable and would lead to greater long-term stability, but such was not always the case.

Transition to native self-government

Some colonial powers were better than others about preparing their colonies for eventual independence. England was perhaps the best. By the end of World War II, as independence for the last colonies seemed inevitable, England adjusted to the fact and began to hand over power to native representatives who would become the first government after independence. This is not to say that England did not initially resist independence movements (often violently, as in India), but the success of their policy of transition is evidenced by the good relations between the mother country and the "children," many of whom still belong to the British Commonwealth. France did not share the English attitude toward transition to independence, mainly because of the fundamentally different French view of colonies. For England, the colonies were part of the British Empire but not part of Britain itself; the colonized people were subjects of England but were not and could not be "English." For France, colonies were more than subjects of a French Empire but *overseas parts of France* (as Hawaii or Alaska is to the U.S.A.), so independence was not prepared because it was essentially unthinkable; native resistance to colonialism amounted to civil war. Other colonial powers did little or no preparation and pulled out of their colonies abruptly, leaving a power vacuum that was not easily or painlessly filled, as in the case of the Belgian Congo. Others fought bitterly into very recent history to prevent their colonies from escaping, like Portugal's prolonged wars to stop separatist movements in Angola and Mozambique until 1975.

The peaceful transition course had common and often ultimately troubled effects in the newly independent colonies. One of the main questions was how power would be shared and with whom. Colonies composed of multiple cultural groups – as most were – faced challenges of power-sharing and co-existence that went down to the smallest details of life: what language(s) would be spoken, what symbols (e.g., flags) would be used, what religious holidays would be celebrated, and so on. Dividing power equally among groups would alienate the majority group, but dividing it proportionally, or leaving it to the results of "democratic" elections, would disempower the minority group(s). Beyond that, the introduction of Western cultural, legal, economic, and educational institutions often created a small but influential class of acculturated native people who did not identify with any traditional groups but with either the colonial "nation" or with European culture. In the colony of Ceylon (present-day Sri Lanka) this acculturated elite, referred to as "educated Ceylonese," numbered at most 4 or 5 percent of the population and came from both of the main cultural groups on the island, Sinhalese and Tamils. The Ceylon National Congress (CNC), formed in 1919, was dominated by this group and offered a non-ethnic alternative to culture-based politics: members regarded themselves not as

Communal representation

The political procedure of guaranteeing that groups (ethnic groups, language groups, races, religions) will have representation in governments by setting aside offices in the government specifically for those groups.

Sinhalese or Tamils but as Ceylonese, and the president of the party was a (minority) Tamil, Sir Ponnambalam Arunachalam. Up until this time, ethnic Sinhalese and Tamils had been guaranteed equal representation in the Legislative Council, but reforms in 1920 replaced **communal representation** (that is, reserving seats for representatives of specific cultural groups) with the more familiar "one man, one vote" policy. As a result, ethnic Sinhalese, making up about 75 percent of the island's population, soon outnumbered Tamils in the administration thirteen to three. As serious preparations for independence began in the 1940s, a new Tamil party, the Ceylon Tamil Congress, argued for fifty/fifty representation for Tamils and Sinhalese, which was rejected. Elections were held in the summer of 1947 for the new government, and the "multicultural" party of "educated Ceylonese" (which had been reconstituted into the United National Party) won.

The problem with such transition was twofold. First, in a sense nothing much really changed immediately after independence. Given the choice, Western colonialists preferred to transfer power to acculturated "Westernized" natives, not the more "traditional" (and often militant) components of society. Second, the acculturated natives often did not understand the feelings and interests of the more traditional citizens of the former colony and were often soon replaced by more "nativistic" leaders and parties that played on communal identities and grievances. So, often enough, this first native government was truly a "transitional" one, on the way to more native – and many times, more violent – politics at a later stage.

Government by expatriate Europeans

In many cases independence did not mean devolution of power to "natives" at all, if by natives we mean non-whites and descendants of the originally colonized peoples. In colonies where large numbers of Europeans immigrated (like the United States), there was often a sufficient political base of local whites to constitute a white-dominated post-colonial government. The territory that would become the U.S.A. was colonized from the early 1600s. By the late 1700s, local white immigrants and their progeny fought for independence from England. However, this was not a struggle by or for the "native peoples" of North America; rather, a seed or branch of European society simply formed in a new region and carried on many of the accustomed Western policies toward the native inhabitants. Most of South and Central America followed suit. Perhaps the most extreme case was Brazil, which first claimed independence as a kingdom when members of the Portuguese royal family resettled there after the Napoleonic wars – literally transplanting Portugal to Brazil. The Brazilian indigenous people were certainly not part of the independence declaration, nor were they included in the first (or any subsequent) government. The best-known example is South Africa, where 10 percent of the population (white) ruled 90 percent of the population (black) until about 1990. In this and similar cases, independence meant fairly little – or worse – for the colonized peoples.

See Chapter 6

Native resistance and revolution

In virtually all colonial cases, even the ones where a relatively impressive amount of preparation for independence was allowed, a degree of resistance to colonial rule occurred. Ceylon might be the case of the least struggle and violence prior to independence – which makes the extensive violence since independence all the more ironic. Elsewhere, resistance took many forms. In India, Mohandas "Mahatma" Gandhi's principle of "passive resistance" and non-violent, morality-based struggle guided the process. But it was resistance all the same and was occasionally met with violence, nor was it the only process occurring within India at the time. In most instances the anti-colonial resistance was more violent. Algeria in the 1950s was one of the first societies to practice modern terrorism in pursuit of anti-colonial goals, in this case against the French occupiers. In Vietnam and Angola and elsewhere "guerrilla" armies fought protracted wars against European administrations to dislodge them from native homelands. In addition, in Vietnam and Angola as in many other colonies, communist ideology and even soldiers from other communist states defined the course of the struggle. It must be remembered that all colonial struggles in the twentieth century took place in the context of international communist revolutions and the "Cold War." Communism was attractive to colonized peoples for two reasons – as a way to distinguish themselves from their European oppressors and as a "language" or "theory" of resistance and of the political and cultural future after victory. As a distinction, European/Western culture was equated to capitalism which was equated to colonialism and oppression by many colonized peoples – that is, capitalism seemed naturally to lead to or include colonialism. As non-Europeans, the rebels would then naturally be non-capitalists and non-colonialists, and the opposite or antithesis of capitalism was seen to be communism.

The specific doctrines of communism also seemed to explain the global colonial system, and to offer an alternative and a means to reach that alternative. Marxism explains all of history and society by class conflict. Lenin, the first leader of the Soviet Union, explicitly applied Marxian philosophy to colonialism and imperialism. Already by the turn of the twentieth century, he argued, imperialism had internationalized capitalism and transformed non-Western people into a global "lower class" or proletariat. Lenin hoped and predicted, and worked to achieve the aim, that the awareness and understanding of this oppression would awaken their "class consciousness" and stimulate them to fight for economic and cultural freedom; that is, self-determination. So communism offered itself as a natural ally in the struggle against colonialism, in two senses. First, it "accounted for" colonialism – it gave colonized people a way to understand it and its role in history and in the future. Second, it offered powerful allies, with the Soviet Union and the People's Republic of China (and their satellites) actively supporting such independence struggles. This is why Cuban soldiers fought alongside Angolan rebels against Portuguese colonialists into the 1970s, why China sent armies into North Korea to resist American forces in the 1950s, and why the USSR supplied North Vietnam in its war.

Self-determination

The concept that groups with a distinct culture and identity have a right to choose their own political arrangements and their own collective destiny.

Fanon, Frantz. 1963.
The Wretched of the Earth,
trans. Constance
Farrington. New York:
Grove Press, Inc.

For many, resistance and revolution not only were but had to be violent processes. Practically speaking, the superior power of colonizing states meant that they would not leave without a fight. Theoretically or philosophically speaking, colonized peoples, especially when inspired by communist ideology, saw violent revolution as the completion of the predicted world system and also as a kind of "cleansing" of the souls of the colonized. No one represents this position better than Frantz Fanon, author of *The Wretched of the Earth*. In this influential book, he maintains that "decolonization is always a violent phenomenon" because colonialism itself is a violent phenomenon. The colonialists' and colonized's "first encounter was marked by violence and their existence together – that is to say the exploitation of the native by the settler – was carried on by dint of a great array of bayonets and cannons." He continues:

> The violence which has ruled over the ordering of the colonial world, which has ceaselessly drummed the rhythm for the destruction of native social forms and broken up without reserve the systems of reference of the economy, the customs of dress and external life, that same violence will be claimed and taken over by the native at the moment when, deciding to embody history in his own person, he surges into forbidden quarters. To wreck the colonial world is henceforward a mental picture of action which is very clear, very easy to understand and which may be assumed by each one of the individuals which constitute the colonized people. To break up the colonial world does not mean that after the frontiers have been abolished lines of communication will be set up between the two zones. The destruction of the colonial world is no more and no less than the abolition of one zone, its burial in the depths of the earth or its expulsion from the country.
>
> (1963: 40–1)

The politics of the "new states"

Whatever the process(es), the formal system of colonialism eventually ended, which had to be followed by something. One conceivable possibility was a return to pre-colonial arrangements – the dissolution of the colony and its replacement with "traditional" social and political systems – but that was virtually impossible and never happened in reality. Instead, the colonial entity, regardless of its form and composition, almost always became a sovereign entity – a "state." In fact, the path to independence, as well as the entire colonial enterprise, essentially guaranteed this outcome. Where a colony had been established (artificially, even irrationally), internal institutions were established – schools, markets, transportation systems, courts – which would not disappear overnight. Furthermore, legislatures and parties were organized, especially when a peaceful transition was planned, such that the colony was intentionally groomed to become a state, with a functioning central government and the same borders, the same multicultural make-up, and usually the same name as the former colony. Little would change in actuality. In fact, Fanon quotes the president of the new state of Gabon, a former French colony in Africa, who said to officials in Paris, "Gabon is independent, but between Gabon and France nothing has changed; everything goes on as before" (67).

The main internal problem faced by what were called the "new states," aside from the economic conditions that perpetuated their poverty and dependence, was the mixed and confused demographic situation of plural societies becoming self-governing states. A state, as we know, is merely a political system with a centralized government empowered to exercise certain authority over a specific territory. There is no particular claim made about who lives in and under the state and its government. European states had taken centuries to coalesce out of the fragments of personal kingdoms and principalities and regional tribal and village cultures, and the process had not been peaceful – nor complete, as the ongoing struggles of the Basque and Irish, to name only two, attest. In the "new states" this was a keen problem because the internal diversity was even greater and fresher and the time scale to achieve unity shorter. By the 1960s anthropologists and others thought they were witnessing just such a unification process, an "integrative revolution," in which old "primordial" and "tribal" identities were being swapped for new "modern" and "national" ones (e.g. Geertz 1963). Some referred to this as "nation-building."

The terms *state*, *nation*, and *country* are often used synonymously in English, but anthropologists make some careful and useful distinctions. A state is a political system, whatever its constituency may be. A **nation** (from the Latin *nasci* for "to be born") is a group of humans who identify as a group, frequently using the idioms of birth and kinship. **Country** refers to the *territory* that a group occupies. The three concepts need not be, and routinely are not, coterminous. As explained before, a state is not an objective or natural entity but a social product, an accomplishment, of specific and typically modern political processes. States are "artificial" in the sense that they are human artifices. The laws and institutions of states change and evolve over time. The boundaries of states fluctuate, as land is annexed to and lost from the state, often by war. The populations of states also fluctuate, as groups are absorbed by conquest of land or by immigration or assimilation, or lost through military defeat or emigration. States rise and fall over time, disappearing where once they reigned. And states can be contested, as in the cases of Tibet and Taiwan, or of Israel by (at least some of) its Arab neighbors.

A **state** is a political system, but a nation is people – or more accurately, *a people*. The "people" or social unit may or may not be politically integrated or sovereign. Anthony Smith (1991) lists the main characteristics of a nation as including a name, a historic territory or homeland, common myths and historical memory, a mass public culture, an integrated economy, and an integrated politics with common rights and duties for members. A nation, then, is first and foremost an identity group – the named unit with which an individual primarily identifies. This identity is often based on history or "tradition," but one of its key dynamics is its future orientation, its *shared sense of purpose or destiny*. The members of a nation are "in it together." They tend to think of themselves, metaphorically if not literally, as a kind of family. Benedict Anderson (1983) has noted aptly that this is an imaginary kind of kinship,

See Chapter 14

Geertz, Clifford, ed. 1963. *Old Societies and New States: The Quest for Modernity in Asia and Africa*. New York: The Free Press.

Nation
A corporate group that shares an identity based on such traits as history, culture, territory, and so on, and that recognizes a shared political destiny. A group that is politically mobilized to achieve certain goals, usually including political recognition, rights, and sometimes an independent state.

See Chapter 9

Country
Commonly used as a synonym for "nation" or "state," more properly refers to the territory that a society or polity inhabits.

State
A political system or level of integration in which a formal centralized government has power over a delimited territory to make and enforce laws, to establish currency and collect taxes, and to maintain an army and declare war.

Smith, Anthony. 1991.
National Identity. Reno:
University of Nevada
Press.

Anderson, Benedict. 1983.
*Imagined Communities:
Reflections of the Origin and
Spread of Nationalism*.
London: Verso.

Nation-state

A people with a shared
identity and culture
(a nation) who possess their
own territory and state
government, or a state-level
political system that
contains all and only
members of one nation.

Multinational state

A state that contains some
or all of two or more
distinct nations or cultural
groups.

Multi-state nation

A nation or cultural group
that is divided across two or
more state borders.

and he has accordingly called nations "imagined communities." Not everyone in the nation is actually related to or actually knows everyone else; the point is that members feel closer to each other than to other people in the world. Fellow nation-members are "us."

There is no necessary relationship between a state and a nation. However, in the modern world, one political ideal has become the **nation-state**, which does align the political and social. A nation-state is a state that consists of all of and only one nation, or a nation that has its own state (territory and government). Many nations aspire to be or to have a state. At the same time, many states aspire to be a nation. This is important because *so few states are nations*. Most states and nations find themselves in more contradictory and tortuous relationships. One such relationship is the **multinational state**, in which two or more (and sometimes many more) nations share the same state. Most modern states are multinational states, including virtually all of the states born from colonialism. Another and often enough parallel relationship is the **multi-state nation**, in which one nation is split across two or more state boundaries, with parts of the nation living in different states. This was also regularly an outcome of colonialism, in which political boundaries were drawn with little knowledge of or interest in social boundaries.

Clearly, this is a sensitive problem for new post-colonial states, but not only for them. Many if not all older states, including Western ones, find themselves in similarly complicated social positions. The Basque people in Spain comprise a distinct and often fractious minority in that state, and the various nationalities in the United Kingdom under English authority – the Welsh, Scottish, Irish, and even Breton – have

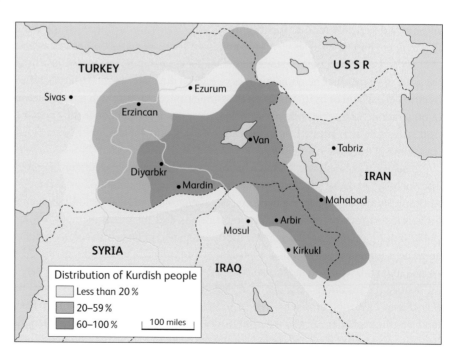

MAP 13.1 Distribution of Kurdish people

at times lived uncomfortably or violently together. The United States, Canada, Australia, and most states include within their boundaries groups that maintain other substate or national identities, such as the various Indian or Aboriginal groups, not to mention immigrant populations.

BOX 13.1   POLITICS, CULTURE, AND IDENTITY IN CANADA

Canada has an image as a venerable and stable democratic society, but it has faced and still faces its own "national" crisis. In 1980 the province of Quebec held a referendum on whether the provincial government should begin negotiations on separation from the Canadian federal state. The issue failed, but it returned in 1995, when a sovereignty referendum was more narrowly defeated. At stake was the perceived identity and rights of the French-speaking majority of Quebec (which forms a minority of Canada) – to be recognized as a people and to govern themselves as one. The French colony of Quebec had been conquered by England in the global Seven Years War (1756–1763) and integrated into English Canada in 1763. Throughout its history, some individuals had held that Canada was in fact two peoples trapped in one state, like Alexis de Tocqueville, who commented in 1831 that

> it is easy to see that the French are the vanquished people. The rich classes belong for the most part to the English race . . . [The French] have come to feel strongly about their subordinate position. The French newspapers that I read maintain a constant and lively opposition to *les anglais*. . . . I cannot believe that they will ever fuse together, or that there can be an indissoluble union between them.
>
> (quoted in Johnson 1994: 11)

As early as 1834 Louis-Joseph Papineau and John Nielson had organized the *Parti Canadien* to protest and resist English domination, but their uprising was quashed. The Prime Minister in 1890, Sir Wilfrid Laurier, saw this cultural dualism so clearly that he concluded, "We have come to a period in the history of this young country when premature dissolution seems to be at hand" (quoted in Lamont 1994: 52). The divisions simmered until the 1960s, when French-Canadian activists like Réné Lévesque took up the fight. In his words,

> French Canadians are more than a collection of individuals; they form a national community with its own culture and history, and today they prefer to call themselves a nation. . . . [Therefore, in Quebec] French-Canadians form a political society with its own powers and institutions and, above all, a state whose machinery and direction they control.
>
> (1968: 89–90)

Such thinking led to a militant movement known as the *Front de Liberation du Quebec* (FLQ). The FLQ's manifesto, which appeared in April 1963, contains such statements as these:

Quebec is a colony!

We are a colonized people, politically, socially, and economically. Politically, because we do not have any hold on the political instruments necessary for our survival. . . .

Socially, too, Quebec is a colony. We represent 80 percent of the population, and yet the English language prevails in many fields. French is gradually relegated to the realm of folklore. . . .

. . . it is no longer enough to want independence, to work within the existing political separatist parties. . . .

Only a full-fledged revolution can build up the necessary power to achieve the vital changes that will be needed in an independent Quebec. . . .

QUEBEC PATRIOTS, TO ARMS! THE HOUR OF NATIONAL REVOLUTION HAS STRUCK!

(quoted in Scott and Oliver 1964: 83–7)

While states are conspicuously new and artificial in most cases, there is a common impression that nations are more ancient and authentic. However, just as anthropology has become suspicious of the "reality" of concepts like "tradition" and "belief" and "culture" and "society," so we have found reasons to question the concreteness and objectivity of "nation." First, not all nations are ancient; some, like "French-Canadian," are quite modern and must be so, as there were no French in Canada – in fact, there was no Canada – in ancient times. In addition, nations change throughout their history, emphasizing different parts of their culture, taking on different identities, advancing different demands. And the fact that nations do make demands transforms such entities from mere identity groups into *interest groups*, groups that have interests *as a group* and that act to achieve those interests. Among these national goals and interests are:

- above all else, survival
- prosperity, including rights to wealth, property, jobs, and so on
- equality with – and sometimes superiority to – other groups within the state
- recognition by the state and possibly the world of their existence and identity
- cultural rights; that is, the right and freedom to practice their culture
- self-determination; that is, the right and freedom to choose their own future
- in the most extreme case, political independence and their own state.

Thus, one of the goals of a nation may be precisely its own state, envisioned as a nation-state, a place where it can be, as the Quebecois say, *maître chez nous*, "master of our own house." We can refer to such a cause and movement as **nationalism**. Nationalism, it would seem, is the kind of movement that is intended to promote the interests of a "real" nation; however, observers have noted that it can *create* the nation in the first place by proposing an identity and a set of interests for a group that ostensibly is, or eventually becomes, "a people." This can be what Guidieri and Pellizi (1988: 11) have called "a process of collective becoming" which involves, above all other things, a transfer of corporateness from other, perhaps older and

Nationalism

A social movement to achieve recognition, rights, and sometimes an independent state for a nation.

usually smaller or more local, collectivities and identities to the new "nation." A process of collective becoming, a national genesis, is what Geertz and others meant by the "integrative revolution" – the phenomenon of integrating individuals and groups (families, villages, classes, societies) into larger "national" units by *dis-integrating* them from sectarian and often "traditional" units and identities. It may be seen, in Benedict Anderson's terms, as an exercise in "reimagining" a community on the basis of more or less "traditional" – or sometimes outright modern or even invented – cultural materials. Nationalism is, in the final analysis, itself "a *form of culture* – an ideology, a language, mythology, symbolism, and consciousness" (Smith 1991: 91) premised on the notion that nations exist, are important, and are more "real" or "organic" or "authentic" than other means of organization and action.

BOX 13.2 DEFINING THE NATION IN "YUGOSLAVIA"

Yugoslavia was a new state that emerged not from colonialism but from the dissolution of multinational empires after World War I. The Slavic peoples who shared it – including Serbs, Croats, Slovenes – began to migrate into southeastern Europe in the sixth or seventh centuries CE from farther east, perhaps as far as Central Asia, mixing with or displacing the previous Illyrian and Goth inhabitants. By the 900s a Croat kingdom appeared, and by the 1100s a Serb kingdom formed in the region that is Montenegro and Kosovo today. In the inland area around the Bosna River a principality arose as well. Catholicism was influential in the northwest (Slovene and Croat) regions, while the southeastern area came under Eastern Orthodox influence, and the Bosna area never effectively converted to any one religion. In the 1300s, autonomous Slav cultural development was interrupted by Ottoman invasion from the south, culminating in the Battle of Kosovo (1389) and defeat of the Slavs. Until the 1800s the Balkans region was under Ottoman authority, and many Slavs, especially in Bosnia, adopted the new religion. As European states grew in power, Ottoman control of southeast Europe declined, until the northern lands of the Slavs were integrated into the Austrian Empire. However, as throughout Europe where peoples under "foreign" domination were becoming restive for "self-determination," the Balkan Slavs struggled under their Austrian and Ottoman lords. The question was what would replace them. Divergent answers were offered. In Austria, some Slavs suggested a policy of "trialism," in which Slavs would be recognized as a "third" nation in the state (in addition to Austrians and Hungarians). Others proposed "Illyrianism," harking back to the ancient (in fact, pre-Slavic) days of an independent Balkans. "Nationalists" of each constituent nation promoted the particularistic identity and interests of their group, but what made "their group" a group was unclear. Some argued that religion was the source of identity – for instance, Croats were Catholic, Serbs were Orthodox, and Bosnians were Muslim. To achieve this supposedly "authentic" identity, activists like Teofil Petranovic traveled around Orthodox villages trying to convince locals to call themselves Serbs, while in 1844 Ilija Garasanin published the *Nacertanije* or Outline calling for the unification of all Serbs in a single national state. Even more remarkable were the claims that *all* Slavs were really one nation and that "ethnic" differences were false. This too took many forms: Croat nationalists like Ante Starcevic and Josip Frank insisted that all Slavs were really Croats, while Vuk Karadzic in his 1849 document "Serbs All and

Everywhere" asserted that all Slavs were Serbs. After World War I, the state of Yugoslavia was established on the basis of yet another notion, that all southern (*yugo*) Slav peoples were related as a family of nations. This pan-Slavic state, as recent history evinces, was ultimately torn apart by rival "nationalisms" that pitted one "people" or "nation" against another and resulted in the formation of several small "nation-states" — each with more or less sizable "ethnic" minority groups within it.

Prenational group

A social group that has not yet achieved the mobilization and self-awareness that characterize a nation.

Potential nation

A group that has not yet achieved national integration and self-consciousness but that is in the process of achieving them or has the characteristics necessary to achieve them.

Connor, Walker. 1994.
 *Ethnonationalism: The
 Quest for Understanding.*
 Princeton: Princeton
 University Press.

Offshoot nation

A national group that emerges as a local or historical branch of an older and larger group, eventually pursuing its own cultural and political identity and interests.

Ethnic group

A corporate group based on some shared cultural traits – language, religion, history – which finds itself in competition with other groups for wealth, power, opportunity, and recognition. An ethnic group shares an identity and a destiny and therefore competes as a group.

FLUID, FRAGMENTED, AND FRACTIOUS CULTURES IN THE MODERN WORLD

By this point, terms like "society," "culture," and "nation" have become almost impossibly blurred, since the three concepts are not synonymous or homogeneous. That is, in the twenty-first century, and possibly throughout human history, it is important to understand that

- *a* society does not necessarily have *a* culture, i.e., a society may embrace significant cultural diversity
- a society is not necessarily "bounded" or distinguishable from other societies in regard to culture or territory; in particular the notion that a society or culture occupies a single unified "home area" is no longer appropriate
- a society is not necessarily politically organized as a nation or a state.

A nation is one kind of society or social organization, a kind that is *culturally self-aware* and *politically mobilized*. Walker Connor (1994) has identified a number of other forms of socio-political organization as well, including **prenational groups** or **potential nations** that have not attained a national-political level of integration or identity but have the cultural raw materials to do so (like many indigenous societies and modern race groups); **offshoot nations** that are fragments of nations that have been separated from the main body long enough to begin to form a separate identity (such as the French-Canadians or *Quebecois* above, or the Afrikaners in southern Africa), and diasporas that have been scattered from their ancestral territories and perhaps affiliate with their host-society while still retaining some identification with their past home and group. In the twenty-first century, the most familiar and significant cultural identity type may be the **ethnic group**, a cultural/racial group sharing a society and competing for resources (practical and symbolic) with one or more other groups. Clearly, the lines between these categories are not clear or complete either.

Diasporas

Whatever geographical isolation existed between societies ended long ago with the advent of long-distance travel and trade. In fact, the spatial boundaries between societies were never permanent and impenetrable: objects, ideas, genes, and people always flowed across social boundaries, whether in Aboriginal Australia, Native America, or pre-modern Europe. James Clifford, who has written extensively about cultural circulation and movement, notes that there is an "unruly crowd" of concepts relating to "the contact zones of nations, cultures, and regions: terms such as *border*, *travel*, *creolization*, *transculturation*, *hybridity*, and *diaspora*" (1994: 302). In short, the old "localizing strategies" of anthropology, aimed at assigning one person or artifact or practice to one society or culture occupying one homeland, is hopelessly obsolete.

Clifford, James. 1994. "Diasporas." *Cultural Anthropology* 9 (3): 302–8.

One particularly common and important cultural arrangement is the **diaspora**, the dispersion of a cultural group across multiple social territories and states, potentially even globally. As coined by the ancient Greeks, diaspora (from *speiro* for "to sow" and *dia* for "over") referred to the generally voluntary movement of Greek settlers into the islands and remote mainlands of the Mediterranean. Other and later diasporas were often involuntary. Whatever their form and motivation, Clifford regards the key characteristics of a diaspora to be "a history of dispersal, myths/memories of the homeland, alienation in the host (bad host?) country, desire for eventual return, ongoing support of the homeland, and a collective identity importantly defined by this relationship" (305).

Diaspora

The dispersion of a social group from its historical homeland (often applied specifically to the Jewish community).

There are obviously multiple ways for a society to find itself in a diasporic condition. One, as with the ancient Jews, is forced eviction from their land and transplantation into another land; another, as with the modern Africans, is an international trade and trafficking in humans, transporting them afar for labor. In other cases, members of a society may voluntarily migrate – permanently or cyclically – in search of work or other advantages. People may also flee their homeland to escape natural disasters (e.g., droughts, floods) or, more frequently, wars – in which case they become not only a diaspora but a refugee population (see below). They may, finally, become diasporic through the drawing of political/state borders, which divide the people without the people actually moving. Robin Cohen (1997) in particular distinguishes between *victim*, *labor*, *trade*, *imperial*, and *cultural* diasporas, with the spread of British settlers and colonists around the world an example of the imperial type.

Many, many societies exist in a diasporic condition today, including Chinese, Armenians, Asian Indians, Sikhs, Tamils, Somalis, and an endless list of others. Ultimately, it may be true that virtually all societies are to some degree diasporic, their members tossed around the world – increasingly so with expanding globalization and incessant political conflict. Indeed, as Levy emphasizes, diasporas "evolve within transnational politics and are related to them, individuals within the diasporic scene are influenced by such politics. . . . [Therefore] the 'larger picture' of transnationalism and global processes affects and even transforms the informants' lives and, by implication, shapes the ethnographer's perspectives" (2000: 146).

The diasporic condition has become increasingly relevant to anthropology and other social sciences (including a journal called *Diaspora* launched in the 1990s), partly because the phenomenon is increasingly common but also because of the light it sheds on cultural processes. First, it means that we cannot study local societies in isolation: as Paul Gilroy argues in *The Black Atlantic* (1993), the entire Atlantic region, from West Africa to the Americas, must be seen as one large cultural area when considering slavery and African culture. Accordingly, diasporic cultures are a natural candidate for multi-sited ethnography. Further, groups in diaspora may attempt to preserve their "traditional" culture and identity, or they may strive to assimilate to their host society/state, but diasporic culture and identity is never simple or given. Remembering a homeland is not the same as residing in a homeland; people in diaspora therefore stand in a problematic relation to "their culture" and "their country." As Malinowski noted decades ago, and as numerous scholars have noted since, people distanced from their homeland and home culture tend to develop an "ethnographic" perspective on both: culture or identity or origin can no longer be taken for granted but must be "worked on," constructed, intentionally practiced and perpetuated – which usually means *selectively* practiced and perpetuated. The very notion of what it means to be a Jew or an African or an Armenian, and who counts as one, becomes a cultural-political issue.

See Chapter 2

See Seeing Culture as a Whole #3

See Chapter 11

Ethnic groups

See Chapter 6

Ethnicity
The phenomenon of organizing around some aspect of shared culture to integrate an identity group, differentiate it from other groups, and compete in a multi-ethnic context for resources.

Barth, Fredrik, ed. 1969. *Ethnic Groups and Boundaries*. Boston: Little, Brown & Co.

Ethnicity and ethnic groups were introduced earlier in this book, as a form, along with race, of contrasting or differentiating cultural groups from each other. DeVos defined ethnicity to highlight the distinctions between groups but also the integration of groups by so distinguishing and maintaining those differences. Ethnicity, in short, is a "boundary-creating" and a "boundary-maintaining" phenomenon (Barth 1969), which is only necessary or possible when multiple groups share the same social-political space – which is especially possible and common in post-colonial, globalized contexts.

Ethnic groups are "cultural" but in a highly specific and problematic way. If we think of the "ethnic groups" in Northern Ireland, for instance, it is apparent that the two groups have many cultural aspects in common: Northern Irish Catholics and Protestants are both Christian, both mostly white, and both mostly English-speaking. Yet they thought of each other as sufficiently unalike not only to separate but to fight. In other words, there is no one-to-one correspondence between the number or strength of cultural similarities or differences and the degree of ethnic identity and mobilization. One small difference, despite several large similarities, can be the ground for ethnic differentiation, whereas relatively large cultural differences might make no "ethnic" difference at all. In the United States there are Catholics and Protestants, but they do not regard themselves as ethnic groups as in Northern Ireland. Thus, a cultural difference does not automatically make "ethnicity."

The key question is when a cultural difference – even a "factual" difference like ancestry – makes an *ethnic* difference. The main answer is competition. Ethnic groups by definition inhabit a "multicultural" or "multiethnic" social space, usually one in which there is a real or perceived inequity in the distribution of some valued

PLATE 13.1 A mural in Ulster/Northern Ireland depicting the "struggle" of Loyalists against Irish-Catholic Nationalists

commodity. This may include "real" commodities like land, money, jobs, political offices, and educational seats as well as "symbolic" commodities like respect, cultural rights, autonomy, and power. It is the inequalities in these "goods" that mobilize cultural groups into ethnic groups and that convert identity groups into interest groups.

So, ethnic groups are not only groups *in contrast* but groups *in competition*. Ethnicity, in the modern context, is a particularly effective way to compete in multi-cultural circumstances. For one thing, "cultural" identities have proven to be much more persistent and powerful than social theorists, from Marx to Geertz, thought they would; many scholars expected cultural interests to wane in favor of political/national/state or class interests, but that has not generally happened. For another, culture and ethnicity carry an aura of authenticity that is difficult to refute; if a group has a "real" and "ancient" identity and culture, that culture seems to convey certain rights. This is a perfect illustration of identity politics, characterized by Kauffman as "the belief that identity itself – its elaboration, expression, or affirmation – is and should be a fundamental focus of political work" (1990: 67). As such, ethnicity is cultural politics twice over: first, in using culture for political purposes; and second, for fomenting the political strategy that culture can and should be used for political purposes.

Like nationalism, ethnicity may be seen as a form of culture, one that uses culture more or less self-consciously. The consequence is that ethnic groups do not so much compete about culture as they compete with culture. Ethnicity is certainly not about proving who is "right" or has the "better" culture, since, after all, "our" culture is "for us" and "yours" is "for you." It is about making claims to valuable resources and about legitimizing those claims. In other words, a group can say, "We demand X because we are Y." The Y, the name of the group or part(s) of the culture of the group then function(s) as the banner or flag or marker of the group – as well as a stick with which to beat the other group(s).

See Chapter 11

As a tool or weapon in contemporary political, economic, and cultural struggles, ethnicity has a complex relationship with culture or tradition. Ethnic groups typically draw their inspiration, their "sense of self," from the past in some fashion; but like tradition in general, this is not a simple past or even a past brought into the present. It is not merely "the past remembered," any more than diasporic history or culture is. Rather, in every case, ethnicity is a combination of remembering, forgetting, interpreting, and inventing "the past." The same may be said for tradition and even for culture in general. Ethnic groups tend to look backward for signs or symbols or indicators of their "true" identity or culture. They find these in stories and myths, in historic battles (both victories and losses), and customs and practices (often long lost). However, no group does or can remember all of its past; some forget spontaneously, and some forget strategically. Sinhalese in Sri Lanka "remember" that they were the first people to settle the island but forget that there were also historical Tamil kingdoms and rulers and that maybe Tamils were there before. Serbs remember that their traditional homeland was the area of Kosovo but forget that most Serbs abandoned it over 600 years ago. An important part of this memory is a history of "hurt" or grievances, as we discuss below.

Groups also cannot help but interpret their past through the lenses of the present. Things that were small then might be big today, and vice versa. French speakers in Quebec interpret their historical claims to a francophone homeland in Canada through the lens of modern-day Quebec; they claim modern Quebec as the "traditional home" of francophones without considering that francophones never occupied all of modern Quebec, that not all francophones live in Quebec today, and that not all of Quebec today is francophone. Serbs during the Yugoslavian conflicts of the 1990s often cast the struggle in terms of modern-day Christianity versus militant Islam, although the Bosnian Muslims were hardly militant Muslims. And, in the extreme case, the ethnic culture or past is simply made up. "Tradition" may be centuries old or days old. The classic case of "invented tradition" was Nazi Germany, which borrowed elements from pre-Christian Europe, Central Asia (the swastika), and other sources including occultism, and added purely fanciful bits and promoted this ersatz invention as "traditional German culture."

FROM CULTURE TO COMPETITION TO CONFLICT

Ethnicity is probably best known in the modern world in the form of serious, sometimes genocidal, conflict. The competitions between cultural and identity groups over scarce and valued resources can turn deadly and have repeatedly done so, from Rwanda to Bosnia to Sri Lanka and Punjab and far beyond. The problem is only intensified by the various relationships between the ethnic group(s) and the state with its apparatus of control and coercion.

PLATE 13.2 During the 1994 genocide, Ugandan fishermen found themselves pulling dozens of bodies out of Lake Victoria. The badly decomposed bodies had traveled hundreds of miles by river from Rwanda

State terrorism
The use of force and terror by a state government against its own people – either a particular group or minority within the state or the entire population.

Separatism
A movement that has as its goal the cultural and/or political disengagement of two groups or societies. A separatist movement often struggles to detach its territory from a multicultural or plural state and establish its own state.

Civil war
A violent conflict within a particular state or between corporate or identity groups within the state.

Revolution
A more or less sudden, complete, and often violent movement to change a political or social system.

In one possible situation, the state applies pressure to groups living within its territory. The state may seek to assimilate groups to state political or economic or cultural policies, or to force them to evacuate land coveted by the state or other groups, or to annihilate the groups altogether; all of these motivations are found in the historical encounter between the U.S.A. and its indigenous populations. At the extreme, state pressures can turn into state oppression and **state terrorism**, in which the state victimizes "its own citizens" (who may not be fully participating or voluntary members of the state). Particularly when the state is associated with or dominated by one of the resident ethnic groups, this situation can be lethal.

In other cases, ethnic groups not in power or actually disempowered by the state may resist it violently. Their goals may be cultural empowerment, local cultural autonomy, or literal **separatism** from the state and the formation of their own state, sometimes in unison with their co-members on the other side of state boundaries. Such conditions often lead to **civil war** or **revolution**, to change, topple, or assume control over the state regime. At least it may appear like civil war from the outside, whereas the parties involved in the conflict may have never been or felt integrated into the state system in the first place. The Tamil struggle against the Sinhalese-dominated state of Sri Lanka is a good example. Finally, two or more ethnic groups, none of which holds the reins of state power, may fight each other, or all of these conditions may obtain simultaneously.

Two other points are worth mentioning. First, relations between groups seldom start with conflict and war; this outcome is usually the end of a long process of escalation of grievances and responses. In Sri Lanka, Tamils began with demands for inclusion and power-sharing in the new state. When the Sinhalese-dominated government enacted discriminatory laws (such as an official language act) or adopted divisive political symbols (like a state flag with Buddhist imagery), tempers rose, and with them demands. When those demands went unmet or were overtly rejected, anger increased and local outbreaks of violence occurred. A heavy-handed reaction to those uprisings resulted in demands for separation and for an independent Tamil state (Tamil Eelam), and war. In a word, then, ethnic conflict is one outcome of the identity politics process of "the recognition of a collective hurt" (Gitlin 1995: 147) allegedly delivered by the other group for which one's own group is merely seeking justice or restitution or revenge. Ironically, a hurt, even a decisive defeat, can be equally or more effective than a triumph in organizing and mobilizing a cultural/political identity group, since a defeat or humiliation is particularly "usable" in motivating people to take action and make history right.

The second point is that conflict and violence of course need not be related exclusively to ethnicity; in the twentieth century, violence was frequently related to class and "party" divisions (which were often connected with other types of cultural identities, since marginal ethnic groups tended also to be poor and "revolutionary," especially when they embraced communist ideologies). Some of the most savage violence of the century was committed by or against "left-wing" movements with goals of social reform and revolution. Cambodia under Pol Pot is a classic example: up to one-third of the population of the state was killed by the communist government as part of a program of enforced social change. From the other side, the perception of such threats often brought violent "right-wing" forces to power, which used all their means to suppress these movements, even after the leftists ceased to be a threat or to exist at all. Argentina in the 1970s is a good illustration: from the 1960s there had been a violent leftist guerrilla movement that killed police, soldiers, government officials, business figures, journalists, and scholars. The former President General Aramburu himself was kidnapped and executed. Rightist paramilitary groups formed to oppose these actions, like *Asociacion Anticomunista Argentina* which used virtually the same tactics in the opposite direction. A military coup brought a right-wing government to power in 1976 which "perpetuated and carefully fed the myth of a subversive threat, *even after the armed left had been virtually annihilated in the field*" (Suarez-Orozco 1992: 232). In fact, Suarez-Orozco argues that the regime soon developed a "paranoid ethos" that saw Argentina at the center of an international attack on Western civilization and which gave rise to metaphors of "cleansing" and "curing" the society of dirty or unhealthy influences. Among these influences were the 10,000 to 30,000 citizens who were "disappeared" during the period.

Refugees

In a world of dwindling resources, escalating globalizing pressures, and seemingly continuous hostility and conflict, it is no wonder that a considerable number of people are displaced from their homelands and cultural settings. As noted above, people "leave home" for a number of reasons, from job opportunities to natural disasters to political oppression and war in their region, creating a significant international flow of refugees. In a certain sense, refugee status is one kind of, or one process in, diaspora.

The United Nations High Commissioner for Refugees, which was created by international agreement in 1951, defined a refugee in its founding document as a person who

www.unhcr.org

> owing to well-founded fear of being persecuted for reasons of race, religion, nationality, membership of a particular social group or political opinion, is outside the country of his nationality and is unable or, owing to such fear, is unwilling to avail himself of the protection of that country; or who, not having a nationality and being outside the country of his former habitual residence as a result of such events, is unable or, owing to such fear, is unwilling to return to it.
>
> (2007b: 17)

While this definition focuses on political displacement, the UNHCR has added other categories of displaced persons or "persons of concern," including

PLATE 13.3 A refugee camp in Somalia, east Africa

- Asylum seekers – "persons who have applied for asylum or refugee status, but who have not yet received a final decision on their application" (2007a: 16).
- Internally displaced persons (IDPs) – those "who have been forced or obliged to flee or to leave their homes or places of habitual residence, in particular as a result of or in order to avoid the effects of armed conflict, situations of generalized violence, violations of human rights or natural- or human-made disasters, and who have not crossed an international border" (ibid.).
- Returnees – "displaced populations (mainly refugees and IDPs) who have returned to their country or place of origin," who are to be reintegrated into their former homeland (17).
- Stateless persons – people who are "not considered as a national by any State under the operation of its law" (ibid.).

According to these criteria, the UNHCR reported that there were 32.9 million persons of concern to the agency at the end of 2006, including 9.9 million refugees, 744,000 asylum seekers, 12.8 million internally displaced persons, 2.6 million returned persons, and 5.8 million stateless persons. This number, they concluded, represented a 56 percent growth over the previous year, with an 89 percent increase in Africa alone. Of the total, the single largest contingent originated from Asia (with the Middle East included in the Asian count) at 34 percent, followed by Africa (31 percent), Latin America and the Caribbean (11 percent), and Europe (5 percent). The 2006 total was especially high owing to the 1.2 million Iraqis seeking refuge in neighboring states; of all states hosting refugees, Pakistan and Iran led with about one million each.

While the sheer scale of the refugee problem necessarily attracts scholarly attention, anthropology takes an interest in quite specific ways. First, as Harrell-Bond and Voutira suggest, refugee status – living apart from one's land and society, often in poverty and squalor, frequently unwelcome and disliked in their host country – requires that displaced persons "adapt to radically new social and material conditions. Documenting and interpreting the variety and diversity [of such responses] is the work of anthropology" (1992: 7). Further, the international relief effort directed at refugees itself forms a social system, what they call "the machinery of humanitarian assistance." For studying the humanitarian response itself, then – that is, how aid is doled out, how refugee camps are administered, how the goals and policies of assistance are determined and implemented – "anthropologists' insights into power, and their expertise on the structure of authority, place them in an advantageous position." Anthropology can advise policy-makers, investigate the needs of refugees, and assess the impact of assistance programs on the recipients. Harrell-Bond's own study of the humanitarian system, *Imposing Aid: Emergency Assistance to Refugees* (1986), is a model for such research.

Anthropology can also examine the forces that drive people from their homes. War is one obvious cause; natural disasters are another. However, as we will discuss later, human-made but not intentionally violent conditions can force many people into refugee and exile status, including resettlement programs (explicitly to move them from one place to another) and development schemes (incidentally requiring

Harrell-Bond, Barbara E. 1986. *Imposing Aid: Emergency Assistance to Refugees*. Oxford: Oxford University Press.

See Chapter 14

them to move). Dam projects, for instance, in India and elsewhere have flooded vast tracts of land and with it entire villages; the current Three Gorges project in China promises to do so on an epic scale.

Finally and most significantly for anthropology, the processes that create and perpetuate refugee status also lay bare some of the most basic processes that create, perpetuate, reinterpret, and modify culture itself. As Harrell-Bond and Voutira explain, and as may be observed in diasporas and other forms of modern transnational community, "One of the gains for anthropology in studying refugees is that it offers the chance to record the processes of social change, not merely as a process of transition within a cultural enclave, but in the dramatic context of uprootedness where a people's quest for survival becomes a model of social change" (9). One of the most fascinating and profound aspects of this change-and-survival process is the manipulation of culture and tradition – of memory and history themselves – for specific purposes and in reaction to specific pressures for dispersed and displaced groups. Indeed, the

> creation of a shared history, a founding myth, is such a common phenomenon among both refugees and others forced from home that it needs probing. It has powerful creative functions, but is no sign that the uprooted have put their experience behind them and moved on to other things. . . . Resettlement does not wipe out memory, but rather provides a medium through which it is reworked, and the memory of shared experience of uprooting helps to create new forms of identity.
>
> (Colson 2003: 9)

A number of anthropologists have accepted the challenge to study how culture and memory function in refugee and other diasporic communities, perhaps most famously Liisa Malkki (1995) in her fieldwork in a Rwandan refugee camp who found that residents engage in a kind of mythico-history intended not to remember the "facts" of the past but to select, marshal, and employ history, tradition, and culture to understand and solve problems of their current social predicament. We return to this issue in the final extended case-study at the end of this book.

Finally and most soberly, refugees, diasporas, ethnic conflicts, and other forms of modern suffering demand that anthropology take seriously and contribute something not only to the cultural roots of suffering but to the possible reduction of it. This is why Davis argued almost two decades ago for "an anthropology of suffering" (1992). Anthropology cannot be merely the science of "social organizations [when they are] working more or less normally" but also a solemn science of the "breakdown and repair" of societies. He called therefore for the unification of "two kinds of anthropology: the comfortable anthropology of social organization, and the painful anthropology of disruption and despair" (149). Anything less, he suggested, is not a complete or respectful account of the current human condition.

Malkki, Liisa. 1995. *Purity and Exile: Violence, Memory, and National Cosmology among Hutu Refugees in Tanzania*. Chicago and London: The University of Chicago Press.

BOX 13.3 CONTEMPORARY CULTURAL CONTROVERSIES: THE REPUBLIC OF LAKOTAH

On December 17, 2007 the Lakotah nation (popularly known as the Sioux) notified the government of the United States that it was withdrawing from all of its treaties with the federal government. Essentially a declaration of independence from the U.S.A. the decision was the realization of the promise, made in the "Declaration of Continuing Independence" promulgated in 1974 after the failed uprising at Wounded Knee, South Dakota. According to the website of the Lakotah people they were driven to this act by the "continuing violations of these treaties' terms [which] have resulted in the near annihilation of our people physically, spiritually, and culturally." The "colonial apartheid conditions imposed on Lakotah people" have led, they assert, to a life expectancy of 44 years, high infant mortality and teen suicide, rampant alcoholism and drug addiction, dramatic rates of crime and incarceration, disease, poverty, and unemployment, as well as the loss of culture and language (only 14 percent of Lakotah members speak the native tongue). By this declaration, they have claimed a huge chunk of the American Plains as a sovereign state, the Republic of Lakotah, including half of South Dakota, most of Nebraska, and large parts of North Dakota, Wyoming, and Montana. What do you think?

www.republicoflakotah.com

SUMMARY

Politics, concerning order and control and power and at the profoundest level identity, is an acute problem in the modern world, not only but especially for people in the post-colonial phase of their societies. The processes by which colonialism ended in any single colony set the tone for immediate political opportunities or challenges, whether by

- transition to native self-government
- transition to expatriate European government
- violent resistance and revolution.

Any of these processes might yield a temporary transitional state and a struggle for political control and cultural definition in the future. Communism was a frequent and attractive element in the battle against colonialism because it seemed to offer an explanation or theory of colonialism and anti-colonial resistance as well as a plan for the future.

The "new states" formed from independence movements faced the distinction between state, nation, and nation-state. Virtually none of them were nation-states, but rather

- multinational states and/or
- multi-state nations.

This reality set up conditions of cultural competition and conflict between groups sharing the state. In these contests, culture itself became a useful tool for differentiating groups from each other and making and legitimizing demands. Out of "traditional" cultures came cultural movements such as:

- nationalism
- ethnicity

with their varying cultural bases and goals, including sometimes separation and sovereignty as a group. These conflicts all too often escalated into real shooting wars, with sometimes genocidal consequences. Some of the results, of anthropological significance, have been:

- ethnic conflicts
- diasporas
- refugees.

These painful contemporary developments call for a re-examination of concepts like culture and identity – and potentially for a re-examination of the culture and identity of anthropology.

Key Terms

Civil war	Nationalism
Communal representation	Nation-state
Country	Offshoot nation
Diaspora	Potential nation
Ethnic group	Prenational group
Ethnicity	Revolution
Identity politics	Self-determination
Multinational state	Separatism
Multi-state nation	State
Nation	State terrorism

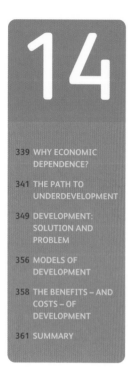

The Struggle for Economic Independence: Development, Modernization, and Globalization

In early 2000, the government of Zimbabwe (formerly the British colony of Southern Rhodesia) began a "land reform" policy of returning farms to black Zimbabweans. The vast majority of land had been seized and occupied by white settlers during the colonial period; in 2000, the white segment of the population – less than 1 percent – controlled 70 percent of the fertile farmland. When Robert Mugabe became president of newly independent Zimbabwe in 1980, he had accepted a ten-year moratorium on land reform, guaranteeing preservation of the economic conditions created by colonialism. By the 1990s he was speaking out against the perceived injustice of continued monopolization of land by a tiny post-colonial minority. When a white- and British-funded organization, Movement for Democratic Change (MDC), was formed in the late 1990s to oppose land reform, tensions escalated. Many local people saw the 2000 land seizure as a long-overdue reversal of colonialism: "The land belongs to us. The foreigners should not own land here. There is no black Zimbabwean who owns land in England. Why should any European own land here?" (quoted in Chua 2003: 10). President Mugabe himself stated, "We are taking our land. We cannot be expected to buy back our land that was never bought from us, never bought from our ancestors!" (quoted in ibid.: 127). The slogans of his re-election campaign in 2002 were "Down with the whites. Down with colonialism. Down with the MDC. Down with Britain" (quoted in ibid: 129). So, land was "liberated" for poor landless squatters, with more than a dozen whites killed while resisting the transfer, many more chased off their farms or out of the country, and fields and houses and other property burnt or destroyed. The immediate consequences were negative for the economy: by some estimates, 150,000 black farm workers (out of a total population of around 6.7 million) became unemployed, agricultural production fell, tourism dried up, and the state's financial institutions collapsed. Whether or not it recovers in the near future, the immediate course of "decolonization" has been no less painful than the original course of colonization.

When the formal relationship of colonialism ended, each former colony became a politically independent state. However, as we have already discussed, many negative effects of the colonial period lingered long past this independence, up until the present day. Some of these effects are primarily political. Others are more fundamentally economic – involving ownership of wealth and resources, production, distribution, and the international system of trade – although these cannot be entirely separated from politics. Ownership and control of productive resources confers political power, and political power grants influence over the economy. The upshot of the legacy of economic arrangements during and after independence highlights the point that political independence does not equal economic independence, and it certainly does not equal economic prosperity.

See Chapter 12

See Chapter 13

In this chapter we will examine the ongoing economic challenges facing the newly independent states and the societies within them as they emerged from colonialism. We will also look at some of the policies and practices which have been intended to "correct" the perceived problems, economic and social, especially what is referred to as "development." Finally, we will see the mixed effects of contemporary development activities and globalization, not only at the state level but at the level of the small indigenous groups within those states. As we have emphasized in our earlier discussion of economics and throughout this book, societies seldom if ever operated in total economic isolation. But with the arrival of colonialism and then state and global cultural processes, it is impossible to understand the situation in any society – even the small and allegedly "traditional" ones – apart from its surrounding and interpenetrating context. At the same time, we can consider the contribution of anthropology to understanding, delivering, and critiquing these development and culture change activities.

See Chapter 7

WHY ECONOMIC DEPENDENCE?

Political independence from colonialism only meant the departure of foreign administrators and armies and the establishment of an internal government with its own army. It did not always mean, as the case of Zimbabwe illustrates, changes in the economic realities on the ground; often independence was intentionally not meant to change those realities. If a colony had a large number of landless people before independence, it still had them afterwards. If it had an economy dependent on **primary production** (producing raw materials rather than manufactured goods), it still had it afterwards. And if non-local or non-indigenous interests (individuals or

Primary production
The production of raw materials in the form of farming, mining, foresting, and so on.

corporations) owned resources or possessed wealth before independence, they still did afterwards. In fact, because political independence was a modification of relations between governments (new state and former colonizing state) and not necessarily between individuals or classes or businesses, it could not address those other issues – at least not until later, as the case of Zimbabwe also shows.

There are a number of reasons why economic conditions changed more slowly, if at all, compared to political ones. In many former colonies, large or at least significant foreign populations stayed behind. The United States is a good example. When the U.S.A. became independent, power and control hardly reverted to the native peoples. Rather, expatriate Europeans and their descendants, who now identified as and called themselves "Americans," created an offshoot of Western culture, politics, and economics on new soil. Therefore, white, European-descended landholders continued to hold land and gradually increased their holdings at the further expense of the native populations. Australia and Canada and New Zealand were the same. South Africa is the most dramatic case, where local whites, a mere 10 percent of the population, dominated the government of the state long after independence in 1910 and actually enacted discriminatory laws (**apartheid**) to disenfranchise and restrict non-whites in many ways. When multiracial elections were held for the first time in 1994 and a black government was elected, headed by Nelson Mandela, even this did not change basic economic facts, such as the extreme poverty of many black South Africans.

In other former colonies, with or without major white segments, independence was often merely a transfer of power from one group of elites (white) to another (native). But, in the cases of Sri Lanka and Rwanda, these native elites were commonly enculturated to Western ways and did not challenge the status quo, at least initially. In some cases, the outgoing colonizers actually set up the future government, as in Iraq, where a pro-Western king was installed in 1932 who was not overthrown until 1958. These native elites sometimes continued to take inspiration, if not direction, from former colonizers, and as often as not they aimed to enrich themselves by exploiting the population no less than the colonizers had done. In fact, we might call this stage in the history of "new states" **internal colonialism**, as one section of the society – sometimes a regional group, sometimes an ethnic or "national" group, sometimes just an individual and his family or party – ran the state like private property. Zaire under Joseph Mobuto (later Mobuto Sese Seko) is a prime example, since Mobuto was reported to have accumulated $5 billion in personal wealth while his state slid into poverty, repression, and chaos.

Finally and most crucially, nothing did or perhaps even could change "on the ground" and in regard to the states' external relations with the global capitalist system. During colonialism, entire colonies had been turned into **monoculture** plantations, producing one crop (such as coffee, tea, rubber, sugar, cocoa, peanuts) for export. On the day after independence the new states did not simply plow under the coffee fields and plant food crops for local consumption – or build factories to manufacture cars and computers. For one thing, the land was usually still owned by individuals or corporations (resident in the state or not) who wanted it to continue to produce

Apartheid
In twentieth-century South Africa, the official policy of separating the races within their society legally and socially.

See Chapter 6

Internal colonialism
The practice in which a society (usually a state) penetrates and occupies territory within its jurisdiction (normally inside its borders) but that contains peoples who do not identify as and with the occupying society. In some usages, it can also refer to the condition in which colonized peoples internalize in their own minds and personalities the institutions and values of colonialism.

Monoculture
The specialization of production of only one crop or product for which a territory is particularly suited. This can involve food crops like corn or rice, or raw materials like lumber, coffee, rubber, tea, and so on.

export products. Even if the resources were controlled by native elites, they too typically wanted to perpetuate the export economy and its income stream. Finally, even if the local government had wanted to alter fundamentally the economy of the state, the process would have been difficult if not impossible for financial reasons. The new states were often quite poor, as they had never been allowed to amass any wealth for their own use. Even more, they still had production contracts and other economic obligations. Many had debts to repay, and their only means of earning cash to pay their debts was exporting their existing products. Foreign banks, companies, and other agencies influenced the internal economic decisions. Finally, it cannot be overlooked that powerful forces, including the United States and European countries, pressured new states to leave their economies as is, offering assistance or even convincing them that production for export was the road to economic freedom and success. The result is that the damage and injustice of colonialism was usually not reversed with the arrival of political independence but was rather perpetuated by new and less overt (and also less expensive) means.

THE PATH TO UNDERDEVELOPMENT

So, colonialism left a constellation of economic legacies that would not be soon erased in most new states – even in those that made any serious effort to erase them. The economic conditions of the new states were marked most conspicuously by poverty. In its 2000 to 2001 report the World Bank asserted that almost half of the world's population lived on less than $2 per day and that 20 percent lived on less than $1 per day. Of these desperately poor people, 43.5 percent lived in South Asia, 24.3 percent in sub-Saharan Africa, 23.3 percent in East Asia and the Pacific, 6.5 percent in Latin America and the Caribbean, and only 2 percent in Europe and Central Asia (World Bank 2001: 3–4). The situation had actually deteriorated in South Asia and sub-Saharan Africa, which in 1987 accounted for 40.1 percent and 18.4 percent, respectively, of those living on less than $1 per day. Other economic characteristics in addition to or underlying this condition of poverty include:

www.worldbank.org

- primary production (the production of raw materials, like food, lumber, metals, fuels) as the predominant element of the state economy;
- a high proportion of the population engaged in agricultural activities;
- low incomes, individually and nationally;
- an unfavorable distribution of the national income, such that a small minority received or controlled most of the wealth and the vast majority were relatively – or sometimes absolutely – impoverished;
- little or no industrial production;
- dependence on foreign sources for money, skills, and manufactured goods;
- dependence on foreign markets for their primary goods, with prices out of their control.

Perhaps equally if not more significant and negative are the social consequences of these factors, affecting the quality of life in the new states:

- a mostly rural population;
- very high birth and death rates, combining short life expectancies and high infant mortality with high fertility to produce a population explosion;
- insufficient diet and poor nutrition;
- high incidence of (preventable) diseases, both infectious/parasitic and nutrition related;
- low education and high illiteracy;
- poor housing and services, combined with urban overcrowding as people attempt to escape rural conditions, creating a huge urban slum-dwelling population;
- often quite low status for women.

Gross national product (GNP)

The total value of goods and services produced by a society or state.

Gross national product per capita

The GNP of a state divided by its population.

A few numbers are necessary and sufficient to communicate the scale of the problem. The wealth and economic health of a state can be measured in numerous ways, each with its distinct significance and associated pros and cons. One common measure is **gross national product (GNP)**, roughly defined as the total value of the goods and services produced by the state, domestically and by overseas investment. However, since it does not tell us much to compare the production of a large state with that of a small state, a more meaningful statistic is **GNP per capita** or the GNP divided by the population, which suggests how much wealth is produced per inhabitant. This does not mean that every person in the state actually earns this much income per year; some have much more and many much less, making the distribution of this

TABLE 14.1   GNP per capita 2007

Highest ten countries		Lowest ten countries	
1. Norway	$76,450	1. Liberia	$290
2. Luxembourg	$75,880	2. Dem Rep of Congo	$290
3. Switzerland	$59,880	3. Burundi	$330
4. Denmark	$54,910	4. Guinea-Bissau	$470
5. Iceland	$54,100	5. Eritrea	$530
6. Ireland	$48,140	6. Niger	$630
7. Sweden	$46,060	7. Sierra Leone	$660
8. United States	$46,040	8. Mozambique	$690
9. Netherlands	$45,820	9. Central African Rep	$740
10. Finland	$44,400	10. Malawi	$750

Note: World Bank calculates gross national *income* per capita using Atlas method. This listing does not include states for which precise dollar amounts were unavailable (of which there were five in the World Bank top-ten ranking – Liechtenstein, Bermuda, Qatar, Channel Islands, Andorra).

Source: World Bank

wealth a critical issue. In addition, individuals may have access to other forms of livelihood than cash, such as subsistence agriculture, but these other forms will not ordinarily allow them to participate in the cash-based economy, where they might acquire manufactured goods, medical care, and education.

It is clear from this information that the "richest" states in the world are Western or Westernized states (Japan is the top non-Western state, in nineteenth place with $37,670), while the "poorest" states in the world are non-Western states. In fact, all of the lowest ten state economies are found in Africa. But average income figures do not tell the whole story, since the average may be quite high while large proportions of people live in poverty. Therefore, we must also consider income distribution figures.

TABLE 14.2   Income disparity, selected states

State	Survey year	GINI index	% of income (bottom 10% of population)	% of income (middle 20% of population)	% of income (top 10% of population)
Burundi	1998	33.3	1.7	15.1	32.8
Ethiopia	1999–2000	30.0	3.9	16.8	25.5
Guinea-Bissau	1993	47.0	2.1	13.1	39.3
Malawi	1997	50.3	1.9	12.3	42.2
Sierra Leone	1989	62.9	0.5	9.8	43.6
Rwanda	1983–1985	28.9	4.2	16.5	24.2
Niger	1995	50.5	0.8	13.9	35.4
United States	2000	40.8	1.9	15.7	29.9
Japan	1993	24.9	4.8	17.6	21.7
Sweden	2000	25.0	3.6	17.6	22.2
Brazil	2001	59.3	0.7	10.4	46.0
Namibia	1993	70.7	0.5	5.4	64.5

Note: GINI index is measure of deviation from perfect equality.

Source: World Bank

You will notice that some of the poorest states also have some of the worst distribution of wealth: in Malawi and Sierra Leone, the tenth and seventh poorest states respectively by World Bank calculations, the richest 10 percent of the citizens monopolize 42.2 percent and 43.6 percent of the income respectively. Notice also that the United States does not have the most equitable distribution of wealth but is actually worse than Burundi, Ethiopia, and Rwanda; Japan and Sweden have the most even distributions. Brazil, on these results, has the greatest concentration of wealth in the hands of the rich, and Namibia has the worst overall index of inequality.

We cannot measure the living conditions in a state by economic data alone; we must also consider standard-of-living indicators that measure health and education and other quality-of-life issues. Infant mortality (the rate of deaths of infants before 1 year of age) and life expectancy (the average length of life) are two telling indicators.

TABLE 14.3   Infant mortality (per 1,000 births), 2008

Lowest ten states		Highest ten states	
1. Singapore	2.30	1. Angola	184.44
2. Sweden	2.76	2. Sierra Leone	158.27
3. Japan	2.80	3. Afghanistan	157.43
4. Hong Kong	2.94	4. Liberia	149.73
5. Iceland	3.27	5. Niger	116.83
6. France	3.41	6. Somalia	113.08
7. Finland	3.52	7. Mozambique	109.93
8. Norway	3.64	8. Mali	105.65
9. Malta	3.82	9. Guinea-Bissau	103.50
10. Czech Republic	3.86	10. Chad	102.07

Source: *CIA World Factbook*

As a point of interest, the U.K. comes in thirty-first (at 4.85) and the U.S.A. forty-fourth (at 6.26) out of 222 states, but considerably better than some parts of Africa, where between 10 percent and 19 percent of all infants die. Things at the other end of life are no better.

TABLE 14.4   Life expectancy (in years), 2009 estimated

Highest ten states		Lowest ten states	
1. Macau	84.36	1. Swaziland	31.88
2. Andorra	82.51	2. Angola	38.20
3. Japan	82.12	3. Zambia	38.63
4. Singapore	81.98	4. Lesotho	40.38
5. San Marino	81.97	5. Mozambique	41.18
6. Hong Kong	81.86	6. Sierra Leone	41.24
7. Australia	81.63	7. Liberia	41.84
8. Canada	81.23	8. Djibouti	43.37
9. France	80.98	9. Malawi	43.82
10. Sweden	80.86	10. Central African Republic	44.47

Source: *CIA World Factbook*

The U.K. comes in at thirty-sixth place (79.01 years) and the U.S.A. at fiftieth (78.11 years), which is still about twice the life span of some African states. While longevity is not necessarily a proof of quality of life, it can only be surmised that people who live half as long do not live very well. Notice yet again that in both of these measures Africa provides most of the unfortunate cases. Examples could be multiplied, and the reader is encouraged to look up data on education, literacy, health, access to clean water, and women's rights. The picture will remain consistent throughout.

Finally, the U.N. Human Development Index is a composite score of the "livability" of various states based on life expectancy, adult literacy, school enrollment, educational attainment, and per capita national income. On these data, the most livable and least livable states in the world in 2005 are shown in Table 14.5.

TABLE 14.5   Most and least livable states, 2008

Most	Least
1. Iceland	1. Sierra Leone
2. Norway	2. Central African Republic
3. Canada	3. Democratic Republic of Congo
4. Australia	4. Liberia
5. Ireland	5. Mozambique
6. Netherlands	6. Niger
7. Sweden	7. Burkina Faso
8. Japan	8. Burundi
9. Luxembourg	9. Guinea-Bissau
10. Switzerland	10. Chad

The United States ranked fifteenth and the United Kingdom twenty-first.

As we have come to expect, all of the "best places to live" were Western or Westernized, and all of the "worst" were non-Western states – all in Africa. In fact, the bottom twenty states, and all but one of the bottom thirty states (Timor), were in Africa.

It is easy to understand, then, why observers and scholars have divided the world's states into different "classes." One of the most familiar "class systems" is the **First World/Third World** division. The Third World is the assortment of poor states, mostly if not exclusively recent colonies, with all or most of the traits listed above in terms of economic and social difficulties. The term "Third World" was actually coined by a set of states including India, Egypt, and Yugoslavia in the mid-1950s to describe their position relative to the other "worlds" of the era. Not only were they poorer than some of the other states, but they also desired to remain "non-aligned" in terms of the primary division of the world in the 1950s – the capitalist-versus-communist division. They explicitly aligned themselves with neither Cold War camp (hence the Third World movement began as and sometimes referred to itself as the "non-aligned movement") and suggested that their positions and problems were not those of either the capitalist or the communist world. They were a distinct, third world.

This international "lower class" of states has other distinct – and unsettling – characteristics. A line drawn to separate the Third World from the rest of the world highlights two facts. The first is that there is a "north/south" quality to the inequality, such that virtually all of the Third World states lie in the Southern Hemisphere or

First World

A term not commonly used anymore for the rich, powerful states in the world that dominate the international political and economic arena and consist basically of the former colonial powers.

Third World

A term sometimes used to refer to the economically poor, politically and militarily weak, relatively unstable, and dependent states of the world, most of which emerged from colonialism in fairly recent history.

at least south of the rich states; in the southern half of the Earth, only Australia, New Zealand, and South Africa fall out of the Third World. Second, virtually all of these Third World states are majority non-white – Asian, African, and other non-European. It is as if the apartheid system (mentioned above) applies to the system of states too – as if there is a color-based stratification of states internationally, not just of races within particular states. This phenomenon has been termed **global apartheid**, which does not suggest a deliberate or formal/legal system of international racial discrimination but rather a (for the most part) unintentional and informal/situational outcome based on historical, environmental, political, and economic factors.

Global apartheid
The de facto division of the world's states into rich, powerful, majority-white states and poor, weak and dependent majority-non-white states.

Another way to look at the distinction between the rich and the poor states is in terms of "developed" on the one hand and "undeveloped" or "underdeveloped" or "developing" on the other. The latter group has all the characteristics listed above. The "developed" group tends to have exactly the opposite characteristics:

- high GNP and income;
- wealth is often comparatively evenly distributed;
- agriculture provides a very small (as little as 2 percent) part of the economy;
- manufacturing ("secondary sector") and services ("tertiary sector") make up the bulk of the economy;
- predominantly urban;
- high life expectancy, low birth and death rates;
- adequate food supplies, mostly self-sufficient;
- generally good health care situation, high education and literacy, and adequate social services and standard of living;
- relatively high women's status.

PLATE 14.1 Many of the world's poor live in squalid conditions, like this crowded *favela* or slum in Brazil

Because of these traits, developed states are for the most part able to meet the needs of their populations to a reasonable level. While there are of course poor and hungry people in the richest of states, the proportion of these people is low and the "level of poverty" is relative rather than absolute. In other words, in conditions of **relative poverty**, poor people do not have as much food or as many comforts as do others in their society, but in **absolute poverty**, poor people do not have enough food and other resources to live reasonably if at all. Famine and starvation are common sights.

Underdevelopment and the "Third World"

It is tempting and all too easy to dismiss the underdeveloped states as perpetual failures – as societies that have always been unable to feed themselves or to provide their own basic needs and therefore always will be unable to do so. However, the fact is that most "traditional" societies, in pre-colonial times, were self-sufficient and fairly successful, at least by their own standards. They may not have had two automobiles and a larder full of food for every family, but there is little question that most pre-colonial societies were able to provide their own basic sustenance. They produced what they needed with what they had, and they did it autonomously. Trade occurred, but peoples did not trade away their basic needs, only their (minimal) excess. Thus, it could be said that traditional societies were not "underdeveloped" in their pre-colonial condition, but rather that they *were underdeveloped by* historical political and economic forces. In other words, it might be preferable to use "under-developed" as a verb, not as an adjective, and as a passive verb at that: many poor states became underdeveloped as a result of some external force or system.

The process of underdevelopment parallels the process of colonialism, and in many instances it was the process of colonialism. As we saw, colonialism stripped traditional peoples of their wealth, dispossessed them of their land, deprived them of their own labor and the fruits of that labor, entangled them in the interests of foreign societies, bled them in the form of taxes, and rendered them dependent on foreign products to replace their lost self-sufficiency. In the cases of small, less polit-ically integrated societies (bands, tribes, and even some chiefdoms) this was a simple process: colonizers arrived with weapons, religious convictions, economic institu-tions, and adequate populations to overpower natives and compel their participation in the new regime.

We know by now that not all pre-colonial societies were living in "tribal" arrangements. India and China had their own organized states, and they and parts of Africa had flourishing traditions of enterprise and "mass production" (although not modern industrial mass production) long before Europeans arrived. In addition to the colonial methods previously described, colonialists had to devise more mus-cular means to crack open and wear down these societies. Native "industries" had to be eliminated, sometimes by unfair competition (for example, dumping products on to their markets at unnaturally low prices), sometimes by creating hostile financial

Relative poverty
The possession of less money than others in the same society, or the inability to afford the standard of living of more comfortable individuals or that is believed to be possible or appropriate.

Absolute poverty
A level of income below what is required to have a decent standard of living, sometimes measured at less than $1 per day.

See Chapter 12

and business environments. The British textile industry, for instance, could not compete with the local Indian one at the outset and had to suppress and destroy it before it could underdevelop India in this regard. African native trading and financial institutions also had to be crushed.

China presents probably the most interesting and shameful case of the destruction of local enterprise and independence. It is well known that China had achieved a high level of literacy and prosperity while the West was still suffering through its "dark ages." Travelers like Marco Polo were dazzled by the wealth of imperial China in the 1300s and 1400s, and many Europeans could not believe the tales of a non-Christian society more advanced than their own. Chinese goods, such as silk and porcelain, were highly prized by European consumers, who traded gold to acquire them, but there was nothing that China cared to import in exchange. The Chinese emperor said it well himself in 1793 in a communication to the King of England: "As your Ambassador can see for himself, we possess all things. I set no value on objects strange or ingenious, and have no use for your country's manufactures." Three hundred years earlier a raja from India had expressed similar sentiments to the head of Portugal: "In my kingdom there is abundance. . . . What I seek from thy country is gold, silver, coral and scarlet" (quoted in Frank 1979: 18). European businessmen tried furiously for years to find a product that the Chinese especially would purchase or to imitate Chinese crafts for themselves in Europe.

European inventors finally discovered the secrets of silk, porcelain, and other Chinese goods, but the net flow of wealth was still from Europe to China: Europe bought Chinese goods for gold but sold no goods in exchange. This "negative balance of trade" was not permanently sustainable (Americans complained bitterly about the same issue in relation to Japan in the 1990s, and increasingly again with China in the twenty-first century), until a product was discovered that Chinese would buy – opium. In the early 1800s, Western traders began to unload opium on Chinese markets, at great profit and with destructive consequences for Chinese society. The government of China, still independent at this time, outlawed the opium trade, but when England's profits and property were threatened, it fought a war (1839–1842) to protect its drug trade. This first major defeat for China opened it up to further exploitation, resulting in territorial loss (for example, Hong Kong was ceded away by treaty, a treaty that only expired in 1997) and more war (a second "opium war" was waged by England and France against China in 1856 to 1860). Eventually, Beijing was occupied and the carve-up of Chinese land began, with many European states claiming their "sphere of influence" (no one state could ever hold the entire territory of China) and introducing their laws, economic practices, and people. The whole process was facilitated by being drug-pushers to the Chinese.

Underdevelopment, then, was not the original or "traditional" condition of most non-Western societies. It was, rather, a product or outcome of specific historical and cultural processes. These practices impoverished the local people, made them dependent, and then set them loose on post-independence courses which were almost certainly doomed to be difficult if not insurmountable economically. The very political facts of the new states – that they were artificial, divided, conflicted, not to

See Chapter 13

mention too small in many cases to be economically viable – only added to the legacy of colonialism and the challenges of the future.

DEVELOPMENT: SOLUTION AND PROBLEM

For most people – former colonies and former colonizers alike – the answer to the "problem" of underdevelopment has been, naturally, **development**. Development is a form of directed change intended to correct the inadequacies and failures of the existing economic systems – their poverty, dependence on primary production, lack of industry, and low standard of living. Development then consists of planned and coordinated efforts, usually by the government of a state but sometimes by agents outside of the state, to change or improve the economy of the state – and as necessary the culture of the state – so as to provide greater wealth and a higher standard of living.

Various social scientists, including historians, political scientists, and economists, have offered various definitions or understandings of the notion of development, generally recognizing that economic change cannot occur without more widespread cultural and social change. Gunnar Myrdal (1968: 1869) characterized it simply as "upward movement of the entire social system" and not just the economy (although "upward" is a vague and relative term). Wilbert Moore called it the "total transformation of a traditional or pre-modern society into the types of technology and associated social organization that characterize the 'advanced,' economically prosperous, and relatively politically stable nations of the Western world" (1963: 93). Surveying various definitions, David Apter (1968) identifies some common elements: differentiation or increasing specialization of roles, stability or the ability to institute changes without causing greater problems, choice or the freedom of innovation and flexibility, and emulation or the imitation of foreign/Western models.

Riall Nolan, a contemporary anthropologist involved in development issues, views development as "attempts to improve the conditions of life for people, focusing on raising standards of living, building local capacity, and encouraging local participation and decision making. Development almost always involves multiple groups, and therefore, multiple cultural perspectives" (2002: 309). This reminds us that development, like any other initiative of directed change, is ideally first and foremost about people. The 1986 U.N. General Assembly's Declaration on the Right to Development (GA Res 41/128) related development to "human rights and fundamental freedoms." Furthermore, since development is about changing how people live and work, it is also cultural to the core: it introduces new cultural ideas and practices to people and brings cultures into contact in critical ways – not only Western and non-Western cultures but various disparate cultures within the development zone. It cannot be conceived as a sheer economic or political process and takes place at multiple social levels simultaneously, including individual, household/family/kin group, community, nation/state, and international/global.

Development
A form of directed change in which a state tries to change its internal economy and society, and/or foreign states and institutions try to change it, to promote economic growth, industrialize and urbanize, and ideally achieve a higher standard of living for its inhabitants.

Myrdal, Gunnar. 1968. *Asian Drama: An Inquiry into the Poverty of Nations*. New York: Pantheon.

Nolan, Riall. 2002. *Development Anthropology: Encounters in the Real World*. Boulder: Westview Press.

Development policy
The general priorities and decisions set by a state or by development agencies to achieve economic, political, and social goals.

Import substitution
A development policy aimed at producing domestically what the state or society currently imports from other states (i.e., substituting its own local products for imported products).

Structural adjustment
A development policy requiring that the governments which receive development aid must make certain changes to their economic and political practices, such as cutting spending, abolishing subsidies, deregulating business, privatizing previously state-run enterprises, and removing price controls.

Development planning and projects

In the modern context, development is to be understood as something that a society, ordinarily a state and its government, chooses to do and directs at "itself." We say "itself" in quotation marks because, as we have seen and will explore again below, the state and its dominant group(s) may target areas that are within its jurisdiction but not inhabited by those groups themselves or entirely integrated into the state political/economic system. At any rate, development ordinarily exhibits the traits of large-scale, planned, and sustained decision-making and implementation.

Perhaps the first thing to understand is that development is business – big business. It starts, as all rational economic decision-making does, with the perception of a problem to solve. It then entails the formulation of a **development policy**, the broad principles or goals of the effort. Among the common development policies are "economic growth," especially as determined by rising GNP. Some states have adopted the policy of **import substitution**, in which they aim to produce domestically what they have previously had to import from abroad (i.e., substituting local production for foreign-made products). In recent decades, development policies have increasingly focused on market principles and "free trade." In fact, development policies, either internally or internationally, have turned since 1980 toward what is called **structural adjustment** (also known as "neoliberalism"), which requires state governments to control or limit spending, abolish most or all subsidies, deregulate businesses, privatize operations previously owned or run by the state, allow prices to rise to market levels (i.e., removing price controls), and keep the currency

PLATE 14.2 This Gunjari village in India was submerged because of a dam project

exchange rate low or "realistic" (which often means devaluation of currency). Such adjustments have at times been explicit conditions for international support of the state's development schemes.

A state's development policy dictates the specific **development projects** that it will undertake. Development projects are pinpointed actions that the state wishes to take to achieve its development goals, which are expected to deliver specific returns and ideally serve as the basis for additional development beyond the scope of the project itself. This means that such projects tend to emphasize "infrastructure" which provides multiple benefits, a platform for subsequent development, and ultimately self-sustaining economic growth. Therefore, some of the typical development projects include:

Development project
A specific activity or task settled upon to achieve the economic, political, and social goals of a development policy. Such projects often include transportation, energy (especially hydro-electric), agricultural, and resettlement schemes.

- ■ energy projects, especially hydroelectric dams if appropriate rivers are available;
- ■ transportation projects, especially roads and railroads;
- ■ agricultural projects, to increase the yield of agriculture and/or to open up new land for farming;
- ■ settlement projects, to move people to less populous or underproducing territories or to move people off territories that are marked for "development" (e.g., flooding from a dam project);
- ■ industrial projects, to increase (or in many cases start) the manufacturing sector of the economy and provide a new source of export income and local self-sufficiency.

In a sense, the fifth type of project is the ultimate goal of development, but it is not possible without the preceding four types. There must be power to run the factories, transportation for workers and materials to get in and manufactures to get out, adequate agriculture to feed the workers while freeing laborers from farm work to shift them to factory work, and adequate income and capital for investment which is usually skimmed off the agricultural sector. In addition, there must be people where the state needs them – which may or may not be where they are now and were traditionally.

BOX 14.1 IRRIGATION AND AGRICULTURE IN A SENEGAL DEVELOPMENT PROJECT

Waldstein (1986) offers the SAED (Société d'Amenagement et d'Exploitation des Terres du Delta) project in Senegal as an "archetype" of development. The agency was formed in 1965 for the purpose of "developing land for hydro-agricultural production; controlling, transforming, and marketing produce; and promoting cooperative organization among the peasants working on the land" (121). The Senegal River delta area was practically uninhabited prior to the 1960s, when SAED created five new villages there. It also constructed an irrigation system and established land-use and work-, cost-, and profit-sharing arrangements for the settlers. In the Kassak region, cooperatives were set up, with presidents and "weighers" and quartermasters to distribute supplies. SAED determined what was to be grown and the prices paid to the farmers, and all produce that was not approved for local use was handed over to the agency. Farm land was allotted to households on the basis of the number of able-bodied adult members, and households in the cooperative worked side by side. The mid-range results were less than inspiring. In 1975 to 1976 the average household in the three villages under study lost money, and in 1976 to 1977 the average household in two of the three villages earned less than $16 (127). A variety of problems were noted, not the least of which was that the location was not really suitable for agriculture; as Waldstein writes, "the decisions regarding where and how to develop Kassak were based on political rather than ecological considerations" (133). In addition, the technical and social organization of the work involved "major departures from customary production practices in producers' home areas" (133), such as outside decision-making, powerful "internal" offices like president, and forced cooperative labor and production; together, these factors "led to much intragroup conflict and factionalization. . . . In Kassak, [cooperative members] hardly knew one another; yet, they were forced by the technical design of the works to labor side by side" (125). The overall effect was a very low return on the investment in development as well as "social disorganization."

Social impact analysis
A fieldwork study of the consequences that a development project or other social change policies have on the affected peoples.

Sociocultural appraisal
A study examining the appropriateness of a development or other social change project, its likely impact on the various groups affected by it, and the distribution of the benefits that accrue from it.

As may be seen, development entails much planning, but often not the correct kind; decisions are often made for economic and political reasons but with little knowledge of or concern for the environmental or social/cultural variables and consequences of the plan. One possible remedy for this problem is **social impact analysis** or **sociocultural appraisal**, which introduces the human and cultural dimension back into the planning. Such a study examines the project and the areas and peoples affected, looking into the appropriateness of the project, its likely impact on the various groups implicated in it (including, for example, the people who will be moved, the people who will not be moved, the people already living where the new people will be moved to, extended families, women, local authorities, and state officials), and the distribution of the benefits that accrue from it (see below for a discussion of costs and benefits).

BOX 14.2   APPRAISING DEVELOPMENT: A ROLE FOR ANTHROPOLOGISTS

Hoben (1986) and Grayzel (1986) offer contrasting but mutually informing portraits of development projects and their relation to indigenous cultures, as well as the value of "applied anthropology." Hoben's research was lucky enough to come before the project, in this case to resettle 80,000 people from a heavily populated mountain region of Cameroon to a thinly populated plateau to the south. He discovered that there were as many as twenty-seven cultural or ethnic groups in the source region, in two clusters of cultures. The more northern cluster was distinguished by a denser population and higher fertility rate. They lived in scattered households with no villages but rather "sprawling hamlets" of twenty-five to fifty households, which were further aggregated into units of up to a thousand households. Worse still, these non-Muslim mountaineers were looked down upon by the local Muslims as *kirdi* or "pagan, naked, poor, backward, and lack[ing] government" (180). In the target region, Hoben found 70,000 people already in residence, divided into ten or more groups with the Fulani comprising over 50 percent. As noted, there were standing hostilities between the Muslims of the plateau and the incoming *kirdi*, and the relocation of the latter appeared to be not quite voluntary anyway. Finally, the amount of quality land did not match the number of proposed settlers, almost guaranteeing environmental degradation and the gradual drifting of the settlers back to their home region. He therefore concluded that the project should not be undertaken, and the decision-makers took his advice.

Meanwhile, Grayzel investigated a land- and cattle-management project in Mali, where the Doukoloma Forest Reserve was being developed for use by Bamana (Bambara) horticulturalists and FulBe (Fulani) pastoralists. Here he found a cultural mismatch between the values of the project and those of the FulBe people. Decision-makers had assumed that the people would appreciate a plan to graze and fatten their cattle for sale to the market, but they did not understand FulBe practices. More important than owning cattle (which not all FulBe did) was a FulBe code of life called *pulaade* "which they guarded more fiercely than their animals" and which included notions of intelligence, beauty, wealth, and above all else independence. Intelligence, for instance, involved displays of cunning and calculation. The pursuit of beauty, especially female beauty, could lead a man to make certain economic choices, including selling his whole herd. And independence meant not taking orders from or being beholden to anybody. The project threatened all of these values: government planning and control deprived them of their opportunity to display intelligence and was a direct affront to independence. As far as cattle went, FulBe had never regarded them as a "fixed source of income" but rather as "convertible capital" which they could accumulate or liquidate as they saw fit, including their pursuits of beauty, intelligence, and independence. What planners had failed to consider was the "aesthetic" or "emotional" core of life for people swept into projects, for which "development projects have failed and will continue to fail" (Grayzel 1986: 160).

Development financing

Like all major business ventures, development costs money – lots of money. Often, states propose and prefer huge projects like dam or dam-system construction schemes. Poor states do not have the wealth to pay for such projects themselves, so they turn to various external sources of funding. Among these are foreign governments, **multilateral development institutions**, and private enterprise, including multinational corporations. Foreign governments, particularly rich Western ones, provide a certain amount of "foreign aid" for development purposes, either in the form of loans or outright grants. The United States, for instance, gives billions of dollars in foreign aid, although much less than previously; according to Hook (1996), in the 1950s in the heyday of development the U.S.A. accounted for 60 percent of total international aid but by the 1990s this fell to 17 percent. In real terms, the U.S. contribution of 3 percent of its GNP to foreign aid dropped to 0.1 percent in the late 1990s, lower than any major Western state. Among the institutions through which the United States funnels assistance to poor countries is the U.S. Agency for International Development (USAID). Large corporations may elect to invest in particular places to take advantage of tax breaks, cheap labor, access to resources, or access to local markets; theirs is of course always a business decision, not a humanitarian effort.

Multilateral development institutions were mostly created around the end of World War II, originally to help rebuild Europe. Out of a meeting held at Bretton Woods, New Hampshire in 1944, two important institutions – the International Monetary Fund (IMF) and the International Bank for Reconstruction and Development (IBRD, better known as the World Bank) – emerged. The IMF was designed primarily to assist states with balance-of-payment problems, although it also offers some advisory and technical assistance. The World Bank was designed to be just that, a bank, with deposits of cash from rich states that could be loaned for particular purposes to poor states and repaid by them.

The World Bank may be the prime mover in international development financing. Underdeveloped states come to it with formal proposals for projects, which the Bank evaluates and agrees to support or not. The Bank's decision-making process, as that of all lending and aid institutions, is affected by various internal criteria, in this case:

■ The control of the Bank, which is determined by the financial contribution made by the member state. The United States is by far the largest single contributor and therefore largest single influence on decisions. Up to 50 percent of the voting power in the World Bank is held by half-a-dozen rich states.

■ The mission of the World Bank to lend money. It is in the business of lending, and it has annual lending targets, so it is inclined toward supporting projects rather than rejecting them.

■ The organization and staffing of the Bank. Kardam wrote that "Sociological issues do not fit naturally into the goals and procedures of the World Bank" (1993:

Multilateral development institutions
Organizations like the World Bank (officially the International Bank for Reconstruction and Development) and the International Monetary Fund that were established and are funded and operated by more than one government for the purpose of disbursing money, advice, and technology in the pursuit of development.

1777), which at that time was composed of about 70 percent economists while the remainder were mostly engineers. Only some fifty or sixty anthropologists and sociologists were employed there.

BOX 14.3   MICROFINANCING – A NEW DEVELOPMENT STRATEGY

As described above, development is not only business but big business, usually involving governments, banks, large corporations, and huge sums of money. An innovative and promising direction in development is to make small loans, sometimes only a few hundred dollars, directly to poor but industrious individuals and families which they can invest in their own products or businesses. Known as **microfinancing** or microcredit, it was first organized by Bangladeshi economist Muhammad Yunus (b. 1940) in 1976 after his tour of impoverished and war-ravaged rural Bangladesh suggested that minimal credit and loans offered to struggling households could yield dramatic positive results. (His first loan, $27 of his own money, went to forty-two women in the village of Jobra; interestingly, many of microfinance's borrowers are women.) Since major banks were reluctant to loan such trivial amounts to "non-credit-worthy" borrowers, Yunus eventually formed his own bank, the Grameen ("village/rural") Bank, in 1983. Grameen Bank has continued to make money available to individuals and families, as well as supporting irrigation, telecommunications, and other local projects. Grameen is today one of numerous microfinance institutions which interact directly with poor rural people. Some, like Kiva, allow citizens from around the world to contribute to – and even to select specific projects or individuals to receive – small-scale self-development in needy countries.

Microfinancing

A recent development approach which provides very small loans directly to poor individuals or families in poor states so that they can start small businesses or expand their already-existing businesses.

www.kiva.org

PLATE 14.3 Indian women attending a presentation on microfinancing

MODELS OF DEVELOPMENT

Like the solution to any problem, the approach to and general policies of development depend largely on how the problem is understood. What are the causes of underdevelopment, and therefore what are the proper areas and activities for intervention? Two prominent "models" or "theories" of underdevelopment and development are modernization theory and dependency/world system theory, with very different analyses of the source of the problem and very different recommendations to improve conditions.

Modernization theory comes from the work of W.W. Rostow (1965), who examined the mechanisms by which the first societies in history developed from "pre-industrial" or "pre-modern" to "industrial" and "modern," and therefore suggested the same course of action for contemporary underdeveloped states. His theory basically sees the fault for underdevelopment as internal, in particular "backward" traditional values and practices. The development process, he theorizes, involves a sequence of stages. Stage One is the *Traditional culture stage*, the initial undeveloped condition in which the economy is stagnant and at a standstill. The society is characterized (and plagued) by "traditional culture," consisting of values and attitudes that represent roadblocks to development. Traditional culture results in a kind of "cultural inertia." Nothing changes, no one takes any risks, people simply repeat old behaviors, and there is no growth. In Stage Two, the *Culture-change stage*, certain cultural preconditions must be established before growth can take place. These preconditions include a belief in and commitment to progress, a "forward-looking" attitude (planning for the future rather than repeating the past), an emphasis on individuality and the freedom and right to accumulate private property and wealth without "sharing" it with family and community, an entrepreneurial/risk-taking spirit, and education.

Like an airplane on a runway gathering momentum, in Stage Three, the *Take-off stage*, the economy finally "gets off the ground." Individuals commence building the economic structures necessary for a modern economy. They will start businesses, make money, save money, and invest money. Foreign aid and investment will almost certainly be necessary. With all of these pieces in place, the economy will reach "take-off" velocity and begin to grow. Stage Four, the *"Drive to maturity" or self-sustained growth stage*, finds the economy "in the air," lifted by industrialization and technology. Profits from the buoyant economy can be reinvested in additional infrastructure as well as in mass education and modern skills. By the end of this stage, "tradition" has been largely displaced in favor of "modern culture." The final goal is Stage Five, the *Mature economy/high mass consumption stage*, in which economic growth becomes self-sustaining and permanent, "cruising" on continuous profit and reinvestment. A high standard of living is achieved, mass production and consumption characterize the economy, and people have become fully "modern."

Other scholars have disagreed that the obstacles to development are internal, even suggesting that this attitude "blames the victim" of underdevelopment. They further argue that modernization in this model essentially means "Westernization"

Modernization theory
The theory that the improvement of economic and social conditions in poor states entails the creation of "modern" (generally understood as Western-like) institutions, values, and habits. Also, the specific processes or policies by which this form of social change can occur. W.W. Rostow offers one of the most complete and well-known modernization theories.

Rostow, W.W. 1965. *The Stages of Economic Growth: A Non-Communist Manifesto.* New York: Cambridge University Press.

– that non-Western societies must imitate the West to succeed. "Traditional culture," rather than being lauded, is condemned. Finally, they remind us that the "modernization" of early modern Western societies was a slow and painful process and that many of the conditions that existed then – such as territories to colonize and exploit, as well as wide-open markets with few competitors – no longer exist.

A second type of model, then, identifies the barriers to development *outside* the underdeveloped society or state. It views underdevelopment as a product of complex external relationships and factors, instituted by colonialism but perpetuated by post-colonial international systems. **Dependency theory** (André Gunder Frank) and **world systems theory** (Immanuel Wallerstein) both fit within this approach. Dependency/world systems theory posits that underdeveloped states face serious external challenges to their development efforts in the form of global systems of inequality as a result of historical exploitation of their societies by foreign societies and continuing structures, rules, and practices of imbalance. There really is a "world economy" or a global economic system, created and dominated by a few states for their own benefit. This economy, including its international "aid institutions," serves to perpetuate the existing dependency relations in which poor new states find themselves.

Frank's version of the theory (1966, 1979) divides the world into two components – the "metropole" and the "satellites," with the metropole (roughly the First World) using the satellites (roughly the Third World) for raw materials and cheap labor. He argues that this relationship began in the 1500s and that political independence has had no effect on the fundamental economic realities. Surplus value flows from the poor, primary-producing states to the rich, manufacturing states. Accordingly, the rich get richer and the poor get poorer. Wallerstein's theory (1974) distinguishes the world into **core**, **periphery**, and **semi-periphery**. The core of the world system is, again, the First World, embodied in its multilateral organizations designed to shape and control the world economy. These organizations include the World Trade Organization (WTO), the G-8, GATT (the General Agreement on Tariffs and Trade), and even the World Bank and IMF. It is the same leaders of the same states who sit down in all of these forums to design and manage the world economy in their own interests. The periphery is the Third World, which is not invited to sit with the G-8 and does not have much clout in the World Bank. The periphery merely feeds the core and takes orders from it. It is dependent. The semi-periphery is composed of the states "in the middle" or "in transition." Thus, this theory is a little more dynamic, since it is possible (though not at all easy) to move from one category to another. States that have been successful in their industrialization, like South Korea or Taiwan or Indonesia and especially China and India, are moving from periphery to semi-periphery, while states that were formerly core have moved out to semi-periphery, like Spain and Portugal.

The point of dependency/world systems theory is that Third World states do not have themselves solely to blame for their lot, nor are they totally free agents to extricate themselves from dependency. Their most profound challenges are "structural" at the international level, rather than "cultural" at the local level. No doubt,

Dependency theory
The theory of "Third World" underdevelopment that attributes the poverty and weakness of certain states to their ongoing unfavorable relationship to richer and more powerful states. Poor/weak states continue to be dependent on rich/powerful (mostly Western) ones for capital, manufactured goods, and other key economic resources.

World systems theory
The theory that explains the ongoing poverty and low standard of living in Third World states as the effect of external arrangements and relationships, specifically the global economic and political practices and institutions set up by the "core" of rich, powerful, industrialized states that function to their own advantage but to the disadvantage of the poor, weak, "peripheral" states.

Frank, André Gunder. 1979. *Dependent Accumulation and Underdevelopment.* New York and London: Monthly Review Press.
Wallerstein, Immanuel. 1974. *The Modern World-System: Capitalist Agriculture and the Origins of the European World-Economy in the Sixteenth Century.* New York: Academic Press.

Core
In dependency/world systems theory, the states that make up the power center of the world system – essentially the rich industrial states and former colonialists.

Periphery
In dependency or world systems theory, the societies and states that have the least wealth and power and the least influence on the practices and policies in the global economy.

Semi-periphery
In world systems theory, the category of states that are not as poor and dependent as the periphery states but that are not as rich and influential as the core states.

Claxton, Nicholas. 1989. *The Price of Progress*. Oley, PA: Bullfrog Films.

Bodley, John. 1975. *Victims of Progress*. Menlo Park, CA: Cummings.

in the end, the reality will probably be somewhere in between or in combination, but, as we have insisted, it is no longer possible or profitable to consider societies, or even states or entire world regions, in isolation from each other and the global system.

THE BENEFITS – AND COSTS – OF DEVELOPMENT

Finally, like any business venture, development involves the measuring and weighing of benefits and costs. There is no dispute that development can confer benefits, financial and otherwise. The question is what kinds of costs are incurred, who pays the costs, and how the benefits are distributed. Obvious costs include the expense of the projects themselves, for instance, the price of concrete to build a dam. As an economic exercise, development planners assign dollar values to costs and benefits and move ahead with projects that appear to have a favorable "cost/benefit ratio." However, there are other kinds of costs that are not always or easily factored into the calculations. There is the cost of cultural displacement, social disorganization, and acculturation or deculturation; these costs are paid for much more dearly by the poor and "traditional" peoples whose lands are regularly targeted for development. These people often pay the cost for benefits that go to other, often distant, people, as when the aforementioned dam is constructed and electrical power is sent to remote cities or factories. The local people may find their land submerged, their previous way of life destroyed, their culture threatened. How does one put a number on that?

No one is unaware of the costs of development. In the film *The Price of Progress*, one World Bank official admits, "You can't have development without someone getting hurt" (Claxton 1989). Environmentalists are particularly attuned to the environmental costs. Anthropologists are particularly attuned to the cultural costs. Many observers and critics – and observers-turned-critics – like John Bodley in his *Victims of Progress* (1975; see also 1985) have chronicled the negative and destructive consequences of development, a few of which are as follows.

1. **Poverty**. Ironically, while development is intended and designed to raise net economic wealth, it often has the opposite effect, at least for segments of the population. Groups whose lands and livelihoods are lost end up more impoverished than when they started. Wealth may be transferred from one physical or social segment of the society/state to another, so that even improved GNP numbers do not mean prosperity for all.

2. **More difficult working conditions**. Development often brings not only different work but a different work ethic that demands eight or more (sometimes ten- or twelve-) hour workdays away from home. This work is also often more arduous and dangerous than any traditional activity; jobs like mining and manufacturing can mean more effort for proportionately less gain. Post-development economies are frequently more exploitative than pre-development ones, not less.

3. **Poor health**. New populations in previously unpopulated or underpopulated areas, new living conditions (e.g., inadequate sanitation or clean water, overcrowding), and new practices can add up to a more unhealthy life. The gains from modern medicine are often offset by the losses to degraded health and social standards. Diet may decline; people may eat absolutely less, or they may eat less well, including over-processed foods like sugar, flour, canned food, and junk food. "Developing" peoples regularly experience the **diseases of development** – high blood pressure, tooth decay, obesity, diabetes, and other degenerative diseases like cancer – previously unknown to them. Parasites and bacteria may flourish. People may come into contact with previously isolated pathogens like the Ebola virus, or they may spread pathogens more effectively than ever, like the HIV virus in Africa and India.

4. **Loss of land and forced resettlement**. States routinely look to their "least developed" regions for development schemes, which tend to be inhabited by the least efficient producers in the state – usually foragers or pastoralists – who must get out of the way of development. Lands are opened up to settlers and prospectors when roads are built. Lands are submerged when dams are built. And lands are claimed by immigrating groups when poor urban people move or are moved into "lower density" areas, as in the Indonesian *transmigrasi* project in Indonesia or the Cameroon resettlement scheme above.

5. **Debt**. Developing states can find themselves in horrendous debt to foreign institutions. Debt restricts freedom of operation and consumes future earnings. The fallout is less money for today's and tomorrow's needs. In addition, as too often occurs, if a development project fails to deliver its promises, the state still holds the obligation of repayment. Poor states struggle under significant debt burdens, as much as 4 or 5 percent of their total yearly GNP. When the burden gets too great, the state may default and refuse to repay the debt, as Argentina did in late 2002. It borrowed over $800 million from the World Bank and owed more than $77 million in interest payments alone. As a result, after sixty days of non-payment, Argentina would become ineligible for any additional development loans.

6. **Social disorder**. Changes of these types and magnitude have all kinds of socially negative consequences. People under the pressures of development tend to suffer social breakdown, as their traditional orders are replaced by new orders – or sometimes what seems like no order. Crime, alcoholism, violence, suicide, juvenile delinquency, and so on appear in previously relatively well-balanced societies and sometimes destroy those societies. Ironically, Chua (2003) suggests that the much-vaunted "free market" policies underlying much contemporary development planning can actually lead to escalated violence, when these reforms interact with multicultural societies in which there is a **market-dominant minority** which benefits disproportionately. The result can be protests and violence directed at the market reforms and the wealth of the minority, democracy and the power and rights of the majority, the minority group itself, or the majority group(s) – all of which have been witnessed in recent years.

Diseases of development
The lifestyle-related diseases that are common in developed industrial societies and increasingly common in developing societies, such as high blood pressure, heart disease, diabetes, tooth decay, and obesity.

Chua, Amy. 2003. *World on Fire: How Exporting Free Market Democracy Breeds Ethnic Hatred and Global Instability*. New York: Anchor Books.

Market-dominant minority
"Ethnic minorities who, for widely varying reasons, tend under market conditions to dominate economically, often to a startling extent, the 'indigenous' majorities around them" (Chua 2003: 6).

Overurbanization

The growth of large cities without the infrastructure to handle the urban populations, especially when a disproportionate amount of the state's population lives in one or a few such cities.

7. Overurbanization. As people flee or are driven from rural areas, they tend to congregate in cities, which can result in **overurbanization**. In a few extreme cases, a single sprawling city may be home to 10 percent or more of the entire state's population, such as Luanda, Angola (20 percent of the state's total population), Brazzaville, Republic of Congo (30 percent), Buenos Aires, Argentina (30 percent), and Montevideo, Uruguay (over 33 percent). Cities in developing states, especially such densely populated ones, often lack the infrastructure – water, electricity, sewerage, housing – or the jobs to support large, dense populations, leaving people who were already marginalized now living on the margins of urban society, in shanty towns or squatter communities. The city of Mumbai in India houses 60 percent of its population in slums, and the United Nations has warned that one-third of the entire human population may inhabit slums by the year 2030.

8. Environmental degradation. Pollution, loss of forests, exhaustion of sometimes-fragile soils, destruction of habitat for animals, and general accumulation of the "garbage of development" can scar a state's territory almost irretrievably. Developing states often declare that they can and must "develop" their own resources, but the rate of disappearance of their and the world's valuable resources has become much more than a local problem. (Third World states sometimes complain that Western states were free to exploit their own – as well as the Third World's – resources but that now they are being denied the same freedom.)

BOX 14.4   CONTEMPORARY CULTURAL CONTROVERSIES: RESISTING DEVELOPMENT – THE JAMES BAY CREE

Indigenous people are no longer passive victims of development. In 1971 the government of Quebec announced a project to build ten dams and 500 miles of road in its far north, stimulating $6 billion in economic activity, creating 125,000 jobs, and generating enough electricity to power the entire northeastern United States. The targeted land, however, was the home of the Cree, a native Canadian population who call themselves *Eeyouch*. Traditional hunters and trappers, they had long been in contact with Western traders, and *Eeyouch* language and culture were alive and well, although the people had been settled into "bands" around trading posts and drawn into wage labor. In June 1971, the *Eeyouch* opened their legal fight against the dam with an unusual petition to the Minister of Indian Affairs, asserting that "only the beavers had the right to build dams in our territory" (quoted in Richardson 1991: 82). The case went to federal court in late 1972, with the government arguing that the Cree had no title to the land and the *Eeyouch* responding that they held "aboriginal title." The court, to everyone's surprise, ruled in favor of the *Eeyouch*; however, rather than see the decision reversed on appeal, the Cree accepted a settlement in 1974 called The James Bay and Northern Quebec Agreement (JBNQA). Essentially a treaty with Quebec (and an ultimatum to the Cree), it allowed development to continue while enshrining certain native rights to land. Lands were divided into three categories, one of which the *Eeyouch* were said to "own," one of which was set aside for their use, and the third of which was opened to the public. Looking back on the agreement, *Eeyouch* have expressed very mixed feelings: it did establish their legal right to some of their homeland and produce other benefits, but it also flooded 4,400 square miles of territory (almost twice as much as the total of Cree "owned" land). Many of the other touted benefits have not materialized, and negative effects on *Eeyouch* health and social organization have been seen. The most positive result from the indigenous perspective is a new and strong sense of identity *as* a people, represented by novel formal institutions like the Grand Council of the Cree and various "corporations" for self-management. As Salisbury put it, "They have turned seven 'home villages' into one 'homeland'" (1986: 8). Other peoples have also fought to preserve their lands and cultures. What do you think?

SUMMARY

The arrival of political independence and the replacement of colonies with independent states did not necessarily or usually bring economic independence with it. The old economic relations of ownership, control, production, and export did not change substantially if at all, because economic and financial institutions were already in place, settlement was not reversed, and ownership did not change hands. The result was continued economic dependence on foreign individuals, corporations, governments, markets, and agencies.

The consequences of economic dependence add up to underdevelopment, characterized by:

- poverty
- low standards of living, including housing, health, and education
- mainly rural populations and agricultural or "primary" production.

These and other undesirable conditions distinguish the "Third World."

To alleviate these problems, development has been seen as the solution, with public and private development institutions created to guide and fund the process. The business of development, premised on policies and implemented in projects, seeks to build up the infrastructure and productive capacity of a poor state to the point where economic growth and improved living standards are possible. Development planning, often undertaken by politicians, economists, and business interests, has not always considered the environmental and social impact of their ideas, which is where anthropologists can contribute and have contributed.

The general approach to development has been informed by theories and models of development and underdevelopment, including:

- modernization theory
- dependency/world systems theory,

each with its distinct emphasis and focus and with its pros and cons. However, one thing that all observers can agree on is that development is, from start to finish, a cultural and not purely economic or political affair and that many of its costs have offset its benefits, including such costs as:

- displacement of people
- social disorganization
- declining health and living standards for some
- acculturation and deculturation
- destruction of the environment.

However, groups "in the way" of development have begun to organize to resist or shape development, as we will consider further in the next chapter.

Key Terms

Absolute poverty

Apartheid

Core

Dependency theory

Development

Development policy

Development project

Diseases of development

First World

Global apartheid

Gross national product (GNP)

Gross national product per capita

Import substitution

Internal colonialism

Market-dominant minority

Microfinancing

Modernization theory

Monoculture

Multilateral development institutions

Overurbanization

Periphery

Primary production

Relative poverty

Social impact analysis

Sociocultural appraisal

Third World

World systems theory

The Struggle for Cultural Survival, Revival, and Revitalization

In 1975, indigenous groups from all over the world gathered for a conference in British Columbia, Canada to form what would become the World Council of Indigenous Peoples. In addition to "practical" goals including seeking representation at the United Nations; drafting the charter for the new organization; advocating social, economic, and political justice; and demanding rights to land, cultural identity, and natural resources, the conference produced a Solemn Declaration in which they stated:

www.csiw.org

> We the Indigenous Peoples of the world, united in this corner of our Mother the Earth in a great assembly of men of wisdom, declare to all nations:
>
> We glory in our proud past:
> when the earth was our nurturing mother,
> when the night sky formed our common roof,
> when Sun and Moon were our parents,
> when all were brothers and sisters,
> when our great civilizations grew under the sun,
> when our chiefs and elders were great leaders,
> when justice ruled the Law and its execution.

Then other peoples arrived:
>
> thirsting for blood, for gold, for land and all its wealth,
> carrying the cross and the sword, one in each hand,
> without knowing or waiting to learn the ways of our worlds,
> they considered us to be lower than the animals,
> they stole our lands from us and took us from our lands,
> they made slaves of the Sons of the sun.

However, they have never been able to eliminate us,
>
> nor to erase our memories of what we were,
> because we are the culture of the earth and the sky,
> we are of ancient descent and we are millions,
> and although our whole universe may be ravaged,
> our people will live on
> for longer than even the kingdom of death.

Now, we come from the four corners of the earth,
>
> we protest before the concert of nations
> that, "we are the Indigenous Peoples, we who
> have a consciousness of culture and peoplehood
> on the edge of each country's borders and
> marginal to each country's citizenship."

And rising up after centuries of oppression,
>
> evoking the greatness of our ancestors,
> in the memory of our Indigenous martyrs,
> and in homage to the counsel of our wise elders:

We vow to control again our own destiny and recover our complete humanity and pride in being Indigenous People.

(quoted in Sanders 1980)

For years and centuries, most of the world's societies have labored under dual burdens, one of which has been the system of invasion and intervention, expropriation and even extermination, that was colonialism. This system affected every part of their culture and left lasting and probably permanent legacies. The other has been a "burden of silence," in which such peoples have not been able or allowed to speak for themselves or have not been heard when they did. Early modern anthropologists, in the days of Franz Boas and Margaret Mead, felt that their duty was to "salvage" as much of "traditional" culture as possible before it all disappeared and was silenced forever. And many did disappear forever. Others that survived, however, acquired their own voice, understood their own plight, and expressed their own perspectives on their life and culture, on the global dimension of colonialism and international culture, and even on anthropology itself.

As societies newly integrated by global processes have struggled to come to grips with them, they have responded in various important ways. At times they have retreated into or revived their "traditional" culture, while in other situations they have abandoned "tradition" and dived headlong, voluntarily or not, into modern (often Western) culture. More likely, though, they have made modifications and interpretations – creative and complex ones – based on memory of the past, understanding of the present, and anticipation of the future. We are no longer witness to "traditional culture" (if we ever were) but to an accelerating – and acceleratingly self-conscious and intentional – dynamism of culture, in which "culture" itself becomes a resource or discourse in a cause or movement.

VOICES FROM ANOTHER WORLD

The previous chapter described the First and Third Worlds of the rich Western or Westernized states and the poorer, mostly post-colonial states (the "Second World" was the now nearly defunct socialist/communist bloc of states). The one thing these worlds share is that they are all composed of states. However, these categories do not capture the experience of non-state peoples like the various Native American and Australian Aboriginal societies, the !Kung or Ju/hoansi, and so many of the world's other societies that have always been the primary subject of anthropology. These groups are sometimes designated as the **Fourth World** or indigenous peoples or First Peoples. Unlike the First and Third Worlds, the Fourth World consists of the small-scale, "traditional," mostly non-state or pre-state societies that dwell within states – states that they did not create and do not control and that ordinarily do not operate in their interest. Usually the original occupants of the territory held by the state, they are often the poorest and weakest citizens of the state – when they are granted citizenship at all (Australia only bestowed citizenship on Aboriginals in 1967). Because they tend to be small and not highly politically integrated, they could mount limited resistance to colonialism then and to state power and encroachment today.

Many of the non-state societies that existed 500 years ago have long since become extinct. Still, by some counts, there are as many as 6,000 distinct cultural or linguistic groups on Earth today. Of these groups, approximately half have fewer than 5,000 members. Some, on the other hand, are quite large; there may be 350 or more Fourth World societies with over a million members each. Africa alone had 104 indigenous societies of greater than one million people in 1993, and Asia 164. Papua New Guinea was the most culturally diverse area on the planet, with over 800 identifiable language groups, the overwhelming majority being quite small.

In the early 1990s, an alarming number of indigenous societies were already considered endangered – either of absolute extinction or of loss of their culture or language. In Venezuela the Piaroa had declined to 500 members, in Brazil the Uru Eu Wau Wau and the Waimiri-Atroari numbered only 300 each, and in the U.S.A. the Alaskan Eyak had been reduced to one last survivor. In some cases, while the group was large, its language and culture were disappearing. The Ainu of Japan still numbered about 25,000, but fewer than 100 of them still spoke their own language (Verrengia 1993). In fact, a recent UNESCO study entitled "Atlas of the World's

Fourth World

A collective term for the "traditional," often small-scale and indigenous non-state societies that live inside states (frequently created by colonialism) that they do not control and in which they are the minority and typically the poorest group

TABLE 15.1 Indigenous languages and peoples

Number of languages/societies by population size and world region

Location	1–5,000	5,000–50,000	50,000–250,000	250,000–1 million	over 1 million
Africa	486	803	422	190	104
North America	303	133	17	5	0
South America	442	67	12	4	6
Asia	871	628	269	142	164
Europe	43	47	54	34	61
Pacific	1131	169	10	2	0
Papua New Guinea	685	129	6	na	na
Total	3296	1890	798	379	335

Source: Miller 1993

http://portal.unesco.org/ci/en/ev.php URL_ID=18853& URL_DO=DO_TOPIC&URL_SECTION=201.html

Languages in Danger of Disappearing" listed 3,000 of the 6,000 extant languages as threatened. In Australia, hundreds were already gone, in the U.S.A. less than 150 Indian languages have survived out of several hundred pre-Columbian tongues, and in Africa about one-third of today's languages (550 out of 1,400) are declining, with 250 in dire conditions. Only in the Pacific region – with more than 2,000 living languages – is linguistic and cultural diversity fairly secure.

The threats to these groups are multiple. Frequently remote, they are removed from the view of most people within their state and the wider world. Their comparatively low population density and economic productivity makes them prime

PLATE 15.1 Many indigenous societies are in danger of extinction, like the Akuntsu of South America, who are down to their last six survivors

candidates for development. Their lack of modern weapons and (but not always) political integration makes armed resistance futile, and their lack of political clout makes political resistance difficult though not impossible (as with the Cree). Their susceptibility to some of the diseases and vices of development has crippled many of them. Malaria, cholera, influenza, smallpox, AIDS, not to mention alcoholism and other social problems, have taken a great toll.

See Chapter 14

Indigenous people have lost much in the advance of colonialism, development, state integration, and globalization. These losses have involved two kinds of "property" – literal physical property or real estate (their land) and other physical or symbolical property, such as their artifacts, knowledge, and the very bodies of their ancestors. In former days, anthropologists and archaeologists would collect objects and human remains virtually at will and carry them away for study and storage. However, in both domains indigenous people have made gains in re-establishing control. For instance, in 1990 the Native American Graves Protection and Repatriation Act (NAGPRA) went into effect, requiring that all federally funded organizations (including universities and museums) in the U.S.A. catalog their holdings of Indian human remains and artifacts, inform the societies that provided the materials, and return the materials if requested. It also outlawed trafficking in illegal human or cultural materials. In Australia in 1992 a court decision called *Mabo and Others v. Queensland* declared that Eddie Mabo and his Aboriginal co-plaintiffs had property rights to their traditional homelands; instead of the presumption of *terra nullius* and state ownership, courts would have to presume native ownership unless the state could prove that there were no traditional owners or that they had voluntarily relinquished ownership (for example, through a treaty, of which there were none in Australia).

Meanwhile, both individually and collectively, indigenous peoples have raised their voices in all sorts of media. A few have even been trained as anthropologists. Others have used song and writing, both fiction and non-fiction, to convey facts, feelings, and fears. Chinua Achebe's *Things Fall Apart* about the traditions and contact experiences of an African society, Leslie Marmon Silko's *Ceremony* about Pueblo Indian life and culture, and Sherman Alexie's *The Lone Ranger and Tonto Fistfight in Heaven* about life on the reservation are just three well-known examples. Anthropologists too have found ways to assist native peoples in telling their stories and speaking indirectly to the world, as in Griaule's (1965) conversations with Dogon elder Ogotemelli, Shostak's (1983) life of the Ju/hoansi woman Nisa, or John Neihardt's (1961) account of the life and visions of Lakotah elder Black Elk.

Griaule, Marcel. 1965. *Conversations with Ogotemelli: An Introduction to Dogon Religious Ideas.* London: Oxford University Press.

Shostak, Marjorie. 1983 [1981]. *Nisa: The Life and Words of a !Kung Woman.* New York: Vintage Books.

Neihardt, John G. 1961. *Black Elk Speaks: Being the Life Story of a Holy Man of the Oglala Sioux.* Lincoln: University of Nebraska Press.

BOX 15.1   SHERMAN ALEXIE ON "IMAGINING THE RESERVATION"

Imagine Crazy Horse invented the atom bomb in 1876 and detonated it over Washington, D.C. Would the urban Indians still be sprawled around the one-room apartment in the cable television reservation? Imagine a loaf of bread could feed the entire tribe. Didn't you know Jesus Christ was a Spokane Indian? Imagine Columbus landed in 1492 and some tribe or another drowned him in the ocean. Would Lester FallsApart still be shoplifting in the 7–11?

Survival = Anger × Imagination. Imagination is the only weapon on the reservation.

The reservation doesn't sing anymore but the songs still hang in the air. Every molecule waits for a drumbeat; every element dreams lyrics. Today I am walking between water, two parts hydrogen, one part oxygen, and the energy expelled is named *Forgiveness*.

What do you believe in? Does every Indian depend on Hollywood for a twentieth-century vision? Listen: when I was young, living on the reservation, eating potatoes every day of my life, I imagined the potatoes grew larger, filled my stomach, reversed the emptiness. My sisters saved up a few quarters and bought food coloring. For weeks we ate red potatoes, green potatoes, blue potatoes. In the dark, 'The Tonight Show' on the television, my father and I telling stories about the food we wanted most. We imagined oranges, Pepsi-Cola, chocolate, deer jerky. We imagined the salt on our skin could change the world.

July 4th and all is hell. Adrian, I am waiting for someone to tell the truth. . . . But, Adrian, it's the same old story, whispered past the same false teeth. How can we imagine a new language when the language of the enemy keeps our dismembered tongues tied to his belt? How can we imagine a new alphabet when the old jumps off billboards down into our stomachs?

There are so many possibilities in the reservation 7–11, so many methods of survival. Imagine every Skin on the reservation is the new lead guitarist for the Rolling Stones, on the cover of a rock-and-roll magazine. Imagine forgiveness is sold 2 for 1. Imagine every Indian is a video game with braids. Do you believe laughter can save us? All I know is that I count coyotes to help me sleep. Didn't you know? Imagination is the politics of dreams; imagination turns every word into a bottle rocket. Adrian, imagine every day is Independence Day and save us from traveling the river changed; save us from hitchhiking the long road home. Imagine an escape. Imagine that your own shadow on the wall is a perfect door. Imagine a song stronger than penicillin. Imagine a spring with water that mends broken bones. Imagine a drum which wraps itself around your heart. Imagine a story that puts wood in the fireplace.

(Alexie 1994: 149–53)

Alexie, Sherman. 1994. *The Lone Ranger and Tonto Fistfight in Heaven*. New York: HarperPerennial.

FROM CULTURE TO CULTURAL MOVEMENT

Hopefully this book has demonstrated that culture was never static, closed, and homogeneous; rather, it has always been (more or less, depending on the place and time) dynamic, open, and complex and heterogeneous. As a system of *adaptation*, it only stands to reason that humans would adapt ever-changing cultural forms and expressions as circumstances or simply membership changed over time. And when circumstances changed especially rapidly or unfavorably, the form of those new adaptations would be more dramatic and total.

Bronislaw Malinowski, despite his reputation as a functionalist and at a time when colonialism seemed to be in the ascendant, foresaw these profound cultural effects. The unprecedented cultural forces and experiences in the twentieth century were leading to novel cultural outcomes, which were not a mere continuation of "tradition," a passive adoption of Western styles and practices, or a simple mingling of the two. Rather, the cultural changes were eruptions of something original; commenting on the scene in Africa, he wrote, "They are one and all entirely new products [with] no antecedents in Europe or in African tribalism" (1961: 25), although of course the same could be said about the entire world. What he observed were "new cultural realities" – but even more, cultural developments with a new attitude toward "culture." Even when culture appeared to be changing in the direction of "tradition," he noted that the "elements of the old culture [were] being revived with a secondary, almost *ethnographic* interest in racial history, customary law, and the artistic and intellectual achievements of their race" (158, emphasis added). In other words, "natives" were becoming like anthropologists and observers of their own culture – which meant that their "traditional culture" was already somewhat "foreign" to them.

In many of the circumstances in which they found themselves, people (and not just indigenous people) experienced dissatisfaction and frustration, from mild to extreme. Their land, livelihood, liberty, and very lives were under attack. Worst of all, often, was the sense that their *identity* was eroding or disappearing; hence the urge to protect or re-establish identity on the basis of culture. But a culture or identity re-established is not quite the same as a pristine or "traditional" one. A common result was and is a "cultural movement" in which the group actively picks, preserves, and promotes part(s) of its culture. And while culture is continuously in motion, there is a major difference between "culture in motion" and "a cultural movement." Cultural movements are much more self-conscious, even "ethnographic," as the groups engaging in them experience their cultures in new ways – particularly as "problems" and "resources." In addition, cultural movements tend to be more argumentative and mobilized than mere cultures-in-motion. They can be positively militant. "Genuine continuity of cultural identity is seldom as strident or as dramatic as artificial revivals," write Guidieri and Pellizi (1988: 29).

Cultural movements aimed at "reviving" or repairing a damaged culture or identity are sometimes called **revitalization movements**. Revitalization movements, as described by Anthony Wallace (1956: 265), are conscious, deliberate, and organized

See Chapter 11

Malinowski, Bronislaw. 1961 [1945]. *The Dynamics of Culture Change: An Inquiry into Race Relations in Africa.* New Haven and London: Yale University Press.

Revitalization movement
According to Wallace, the deliberate, organized, and self-conscious effort of a society to create a more satisfying culture.

Wallace, Anthony F. C. 1956. "Revitalization Movements." *American Anthropologist* 58 (2): 264–81.

efforts on the part of some member(s) of a society to create a new, better, and more satisfying culture. As such, they are a special type of self-directed change. Like all other instances of change, whether arising from innovation or diffusion, revitalization efforts have certain regular characteristics:

1. They appear at moments of cultural stress – when past ideas and actions no longer produce satisfactory results, especially when foreign influences or persons have disturbed the balance of the society.
2. They are usually the inspiration of one person or at most a few people. Certain individuals feel the "culture crisis" before others, and their inspiration often comes in the form of a dream, a vision, or a "near-death" experience.
3. They go through a process of acceptance, rejection, or modification. Members of the society may join or ignore the movement, and elders and traditionalists may actively oppose it. Outside forces may also oppose it as a threat to their domination.
4. They begin as unfamiliar, often "heretical" or "cultish" phenomena, but if they catch on they become "mainstream."
5. They can have unanticipated, undesired, and even undesirable consequences.
6. There may be more than one such movement occurring in the same society at the same time, sometimes with opposite goals. Differing and rival movements and movement leaders may vie for the attention and loyalty of the society, each offering a solution to the society's troubles.

PLATE 15.2 Indigenous Aymara of Bolivia marching in support of new president Evo Morales

7.   The movement, if it survives, will "routinize" and institutionalize – either as the new "mainstream" or as a more constricted alternative or specialty within the society.

Revitalization movements can take many forms. Very often, especially in their early manifestations, they are religious in nature (see below). Subsequently or in combination, they can take a political shape; in fact, all such movements are probably "political" in a sense, since they seek to modify the order of society, including its power arrangements and norms and rules. Groups may literally organize political parties or "congresses," like the African National Congress (South Africa), the Indian National Congress, or the Australian Aboriginal National Congress. Nationalism and ethnicity may be expressions of politicized culture and identity. Groups may generate their own media, starting newsletters or newspapers, radio and television stations, and more recently internet websites. Even more common, and sometimes equally important, are "cultural organizations" that promote and advance aspects of culture, such as language, music and dance, arts, food, or religion.

See Chapter 13

   There are a few recurring components or qualities of cultural/revitalization movements. Any actual movement may exhibit one or more of these qualities or "types," but enough movements have been observed to distill some common patterns among them.

Syncretism

Syncretism (from the Greek *syn* for "with" or "same") means the mixing or blending of elements from two or more cultural sources to produce a new, third, better culture or system. In a very real sense, all culture, and certainly all religion, is syncretistic; humans are forever borrowing from various sources and combining them in ways to produce whatever it is they call "their culture" or "their tradition." Of course, this borrowing and combining is not always deliberate or clearly perceived, but no culture, religion, or any other human activity is "pure" or "original" in any significant or meaningful way. All humans live in a melting-pot of culture.

Syncretism
A type of revitalization movement in which elements of two or more cultural sources are blended into a new and more satisfying cultural arrangement.

   Among the most colorful syncretistic movements in the anthropological literature are the so-called "cargo cults" that swept through the Pacific Islands, particularly Melanesia and the southwest regions, between about 1900 and 1950 (see Worsley 1968; Lawrence 1964). During the two World Wars, thousands of Western soldiers came ashore and, even more remarkably, unloaded caches of goods the likes of which no local had ever seen. Islanders could have no idea where these people and their goods came from; the one thing they knew was that the strangers had a lot of "cargo" and that they never seemed to work for any of it. They stood around, marched around, sat around, but they never produced anything – yet they had this inconceivable largesse.

Worsley, Peter. 1968. *The Trumpet Shall Sound: A Study of "Cargo Cults" in Melanesia*. New York: Shocken Books.
Lawrence, Peter. 1964. *Road Belong Cargo*. Manchester: Manchester University Press.

   Cargo cults were an indigenous attempt to make sense of this new situation and to, quite literally, get some cargo for themselves. One of the first and best-known examples is the "Vailala madness" that "broke out" in 1917 among the Elema people of Papua. The Elema first tried to incorporate the foreigners into their native economic system of reciprocity by giving them gifts, expecting that the invaders would reciprocate by sharing some of their wealth. When that failed, a man named Evara originated the notion that people needed to practice specific religious observances, including trances and jerky body movement and speech, which seemed so pathological to observers that it was dubbed "madness." More to the point was the content and expectation of the movement: if people destroyed parts of their traditional culture and replaced them with parts of the foreign culture, they could conjure cargo ships of their own. Accordingly, traditional religious and ceremonial items were discarded, gardens and animals were untended or destroyed, and imitative gestures toward Western culture were made (for instance, a pretend radio was built to talk to the phantom cargo ship). It was believed that these changes would bring forth a ship laden with cargo piloted by their dead ancestors, who would establish a better and happier culture for the Elema. Needless to say, it did not happen.

One other example of a syncretistic movement, during which twenty or thirty million people died, was the Taiping Rebellion in China (1850–1864), one of a number of such movements after the Opium Wars and full-scale establishment of colonialism in China. The Taiping movement (from the Chinese *Taiping tien-quo* for Heavenly Kingdom of Great Peace) began with one man, Hung Xiuquan (also Hsiu-chuan), who had a vision of the future and his role in it. After a personal crisis and a near-death experience, he received a series of visions of an old man (supposedly God) who warned that people had stopped worshipping Him and taken to the worship of demons. Hung was to battle these demons, as he was in fact the younger son of God and the younger brother of Jesus. In the 1840s his religious community was reorganized into a holy army, and in 1851 he announced the Taiping tien-quo, a theocratic state with himself as the Heavenly King. His heavenly army marched against the government, capturing the city of Nanking in 1853 and from there attacking Beijing. The imperial government fought back for a decade until in June 1864 Hung died, and a conflict that claimed millions of lives in the hopes of a better day ended.

Millenarianism

Millenarianism

A type of revitalization movement aimed at preparing for and perhaps bringing about the end of the "present era," however that era is understood, and replacing it with a new and better existence.

Millenarianism (from the Latin *mille* for thousand) is a familiar concept to Western culture and Christianity, which think in terms of a thousand because their number system is based on ten. The point of millenarianism is not literally a thousand-year period (since not all cultures use base-ten) but the notion that the world does proceed through periods, the current one of which will end soon. Thus, **millenarianism** is a type of movement based on the conception that the present era of the world (an inferior, unhappy, or wicked one) is about to end and that a superior era is approaching. The followers of the movement must either prepare for the coming change or actively set the change in motion.

Millenarianism is common in movements among large-scale modern societies as well as small-scale traditional ones. The cargo cults and the Taiping rebellion had millenarian aspects, as did the well-known "Ghost Dance" movement among Native Americans in the late 1800s. Ghost Dancers believed that performing the special dance and wearing particular symbols and clothing would make the dancers impervious to white weapons, bring back their dead ancestors, and ultimately restore their land and independence to them. The failed armageddons of the Aum Shinrikyo and Heaven's Gate are only two of the more recent instances.

BOX 15.2 MILLENNIUM ON THE SUBWAY: AUM SHINRIKYO

Aum Shinrikyo, a Japanese movement headed by Shoko Asahara, believed in and sought to ignite a doomsday scenario one day in 1995 when it released poison gas into the Tokyo subways. Aum Shinrikyo is a name that combines the Hindu mantra "om" with *shinri* (Japanese for "supreme truth") and *kyo* ("religious teaching"). It was a millenarian syncretistic movement, blending parts of Hindu/Buddhist, Japanese, Christian, and secular/technological cultures into one explosive system. It predicted an apocalyptic end of the world, which was referred to as Armageddon or World War III. The expected apocalypse was at least partly a function of a vast international conspiracy, which involved the Freemasons and the American government. Early in the sect's history, the goal was to prevent this event from occurring. The work of the group, then, was to intercept the negative energy in the world and transform it into positive energy; for this work, 30,000 members were needed, who had achieved their own enlightenment through the teachings of the guru. However, as prevention began to seem more and more unlikely, the goal shifted to survival through and after it. The only avenue to such survival was participation in Aum Shinrikyo. By 1990 the sect was talking about and constructing communes and bomb shelters where they could isolate themselves from the ignorant society and prepare for and be saved from the inevitable conflagration. These few survivors could then emerge to rebuild civilization – Aum Shinrikyo civilization. The conflagration and the forthcoming world-to-be were vague in description, but it was claimed that evil forces would attack the world with their ultimate weapons, including nuclear, biological, and chemical weapons, and gases like sarin. The group even began manufacturing, stockpiling, and testing its own supply of these weapons, releasing sarin gas on the population of Matsumoto Nagano prefecture in Japan a year before the Tokyo attack (June 1994), with almost equally deadly results – seven fatalities, 600 injuries. The assault on the Tokyo subway in 1995 might have been an effort to jump-start Armageddon, or it might have been an attempt to make their prediction appear true, perhaps as a recruiting effort. The latter interpretation seems likely in view of Asahara's claim immediately following the attack that it was actually committed by the United States, which had begun its war against Japan and already seized the Japanese government.

Irredentism

Irredentism (from the Italian *irredenta* for unredeemed) is any movement intended to reclaim and reoccupy a lost homeland. As such, irredentism is at the heart of

Irredentism
A revitalization movement to reclaim a lost homeland.

See Chapter 13

many "ethnic conflicts" in the modern world. The Tamil struggle in Sri Lanka is a sort of irredentist movement, to (re)create and (re)occupy the homeland of Tamil Eelam. At least part of the motivation for the Yugoslavian wars of the 1990s was irredentist, Serbs reclaiming Serb territory, especially the heartland of Kosovo lost in 1389. The Zionist movement, beginning officially in the late 1800s but with much older roots, claimed as its goal the re-creation of a Jewish national state in the Jewish "holy land." Zionists like Theodore Herzl, author of the *The Jewish State*, worked toward returning to their lost homeland, from which they had been dispersed for nearly 2,000 years. The subsequent establishment of the modern state of Israel in Palestine in 1948 was the end result of this movement. Contemporary irredentists like the Jewish fundamentalist group *Gush Emunim* (The Bloc of the Faithful) not only support the recovery of their ancient homeland but seek to expand it, ideally "from the Euphrates River in Iraq to the Brook of Egypt" (Aran 1991: 268).

Modernism/vitalism

Modernism

A type of revitalization movement intended to adopt the characteristics of a foreign and "modern" society, in the process abandoning some or all of the "traditional" characteristics of the society undergoing the movement.

Modernism, also termed **vitalism**, includes movements to import and accept alien cultural ways, in part or in total. Some societies, when they encountered Western colonial power, determined that the best course was to imitate the foreign culture, at least in its essential aspects, to empower themselves to resist and perhaps even join the international political system. Japan is probably the best example of a successful vitalistic movement. Japan was almost completely isolated from the external world before the mid-1800s. However, its rulers watched with interest as Europeans forced the Opium Wars and then colonialism and "spheres of influence" on the defeated Chinese. When American Commodore Matthew Perry arrived with his flotilla of gunships in Tokyo harbor in 1854, the shogun of Japan accepted trade and relations with America. Very quickly, Japan began to adapt itself to this new contact, sending observers to Europe and America to study Western culture and technology, particularly railroad and military technologies. Japanese students were sent to foreign schools and colleges. English was widely learned, and Western-style music and dress were adopted. By 1868, a "revolution" was underway, known as the Meiji (Japanese for enlightenment) revolution. A modern-style constitution was written, the feudal system was abolished, mass state-sponsored education was established, and concentrated efforts to industrialize and to modernize the army were made. Even symbolic gestures like Western haircuts became important; instead of the long hair of the traditional samurai, barbered hair was the fashion. (A saying of the time was, "If you slap a barbered head, it rings 'civilization and enlightenment.'") This modernist/vitalist movement was so successful that, within forty years of the Meiji revolution, Japan became the first non-European state to defeat a European state in war (Russia in 1904–1905). Of course, like all vitalistic movements, there was not a wholesale replacement of local culture with foreign culture. Japan did not jettison the Japanese language, nor Japanese political, economic, or social values. Its "modernization" and industrialization pursued a distinctly Japanese path, emphasizing social duty over individualism, order over competition, and government/business cooperation over disengagement and regulation (see below).

Nativism/fundamentalism

At the opposite end of the spectrum are nativist or fundamentalist movements. **Nativism** or **fundamentalism** emphasizes local or "traditional" culture and values and resistance to or even elimination of alien culture and values. The Chinese response to foreign contact was nativistic. Chinese society considered itself superior to European in every imaginable way, and they could not conceive of themselves falling prey to such backward barbarians. The emperor showed no interest in and strictly forbade European toys like trains and clocks, and the Chinese leadership was sure that it could strengthen itself by relying on completely native resources. In other words, while in a sense the Japanese response was to become more modern, the Chinese (and many other societies') response was to become more "traditional." In the late twentieth and early twenty-first centuries, some societies and states have gone so far as to isolate themselves totally from the outside world. Burma (or Myanmar today) is a tightly closed society, North Korea cuts itself off effectively, and Cambodia under the Khmer Rouge and Pol Pot attempted to eradicate foreign and modern influences, including urbanization, education, and eyeglasses, as portrayed in the movie *The Killing Fields*. However, as these cases illustrate, extreme nativist or isolationist societies tend to end up impoverished, paranoid, and dangerous (to others and to themselves).

Fundamentalism typically has a special religious connotation, but this need not be so; a group can be "fundamentalist" about any aspect of its culture or tradition. The term merely refers to efforts to return to the "fundamentals" of that society, whatever they may be. Many societies and states have viewed this as returning to the rural or village culture of the society, far from the cosmopolitan and thus "mongrel" or "polluted" culture of the city. By definition, it implies an orientation to the *past*, to what the society used to do and be. In the fundamentalist vision, "we" are most crucially "who we were." But fundamentalism or nativism is not about the past, any more than ethnicity is. Rather, all of these movement types use the past to imagine and construct the future.

Nativism or fundamentalism, even more so than the other types of revitalization, is a resistance movement based on difference – the rejection of modern, foreign, or secular influences and the advancement or exaggeration of what makes the group unique or authentic. It is a way of distancing the "external" by emphasizing the "internal." Along with or because of its resistant nature, it can be distinctly militant or violent. George Marsden (1990) in fact characterizes it as traditionalism that is angry about something. What is it angry about? Different groups find different things to oppose in the current cultural condition of the world. From a non-Western perspective it is often Western culture itself, as early twentieth-century Islamic fundamentalist Hasan al-Banna said:

Nativism
A type of revitalization movement aimed at perpetuating, restoring, or reviving "traditional" cultural practices or characteristics, which are thought to be the source of the group's strength and to be threatened or lost.

Fundamentalism
A type of cultural/ revitalization movement in which members attempt to address perceived social problems or disadvantages by restoring the perceived "fundamentals" or oldest, most important, and most "genuine" elements of culture.

Just after the First World War and during my stay in Cairo, the wave of atheism and lewdness engulfed Egypt. It started the devastation of religion and morality on the pretext of individual and intellectual freedom. Nothing could stop this storm.

[Westerners introduced] their half-naked women . . . , their liquors, their theaters, their dance halls, their amusements, their stories, their newspapers, their novels, their whims, their silly games, and their vices [as well as] schools and scientific and cultural institutions in the very heart of the Islamic domain, which cast doubt and heresy into the souls of its sons and taught them how to demean themselves, disparage their religion and their fatherland, divest themselves of their traditions and beliefs, and to regard as sacred anything Western.

(quoted in Voll 1991: 360–1)

See Chapter 11

One interesting and ironic fact is that nativism/fundamentalism too is culturally relative, which is entirely contrary to its claims and ideology. However, since we now know that "tradition" is culturally relative, it is necessarily true that "militant tradition" is relative too. First, any culture or cultural tradition can be fundamentalist; there are Christian fundamentalisms and Islamic fundamentalisms and Jewish fundamentalisms and Hindu fundamentalisms, and so on. Second, each fundamentalist movement has different goals or elevates different parts of doctrine or history or culture as the defining fundamental of the group or tradition. Some, like the original "fundamentalists" in early twentieth-century America, sought only religious revival and purification, but some in the late twentieth and early twenty-first centuries add social and political goals to their change agendas. All create barriers around themselves; many scholars have characterized fundamentalism as a form of boundary maintenance.

BOX 15.3   POLITICS AND CHRISTIAN FUNDAMENTALISM IN THE U.S.A.

Between 1910 and 1915 a series of publications entitled *The Fundamentals: A Testimony to the Truth* appeared in the U.S.A., touching off the modern fundamentalist movement in favor of biblical literalism and religious activism and against "modernizing" and "liberalizing" influences such as "Darwinism." During the first fifty years of the movement fundamentalists saw their calling as more spiritual than political – to save souls, not change laws. Billy Graham represents this earlier approach and might better be called an "evangelical" than a "fundamentalist." However, with perceived "cultural setbacks" in the 1960s and 1970s, such as the removal of official prayers from schools and most critically the enshrinement of abortion rights, fundamentalism turned political. The 1979 formation of the Moral Majority and the increased political activity of Christian groups like Focus on the Family marked a new era in the mingling of politics and religion: since political leaders and decisions had taken America down this "wrong road," it was politics that would return it to the right path. Some, however, think that American culture is too far gone for strictly political solutions and seek a radical re-creation along Christian lines. The "Christian Reconstructionism" movement, as the name suggests, wants to reconstruct American society in absolute conformity with (its version of) biblical principles. It would

> replace democracy with a theocratic elite that would govern by imposing their interpretation of "Biblical Law." Reconstructionism would eliminate not only democracy but many of its manifestations, such as labor unions, civil rights laws, and public schools. Women would be generally relegated to hearth and home. Insufficiently Christian men would be denied citizenship, perhaps executed. So severe is this theocracy that it would extend capital punishment beyond such crimes as kidnapping, rape, and murder to include, among other things, blasphemy, heresy, adultery, and homosexuality.
>
> (Clarkson 2005)

While that is a long-term and unlikely goal, others have set their sights on more immediate and achievable results. The "Christian Exodus" movement plans to found its own Christian-based state and society. As its own website declares, it has given up on America and intends to physically relocate members to a place where they can "reestablish constitutionally limited government founded upon Christian principles." This place – which has been decided will be South Carolina – will be a new Christian homeland with members "electing State and local officials who will interpose on behalf of the people and refuse to enforce illegal federal acts" such as abortion rights and gay marriage. And if need be, they are prepared to secede from the Union altogether.

www.christianexodus.org

THE FUTURE OF CULTURE, AND THE CULTURE OF THE FUTURE

All cultural movements show in starker contrast what the study of "normal" (or non-crisis) cultural dynamics shows – that if humans make their culture, if culture is in the end a social construct, not a given fact, then humans can and will remake their culture again and again. In fact humans have remade and continue to remake their cultures, without an end in sight. Whether it is colonialism or development or syncretism or fundamentalism, culture is always on the move, as humans think of new things to do, reinterpret old things to do, encounter new things from other groups, and respond to new situations and circumstances. The fiction that culture is static can no longer be believed.

"Culture" and "tradition" seem oriented to the past. However, today we can see that this is more ideology than reality. Culture and tradition refer to the past, but humans are really oriented toward the future, not toward the past. The main question for humans is always "who are we today and who will we be tomorrow?" The main answer to this question, or the main resource for thinking about the answer, is the past. As humans grapple toward and construct their future, they inevitably pick up, examine, and assemble the bits and shards of broken and vanished pasts to create that future – partly because those pasts constitute the lenses with which they view the present and future, and partly because those pasts constitute the primary, though not only, raw materials with which to build.

Once upon a time, and still in many locations for many individuals, the construction of culture was an "invisible," spontaneous, or unselfconscious process. Increasingly in the world today, cultural construction is conspicuous, self-conscious, and even belligerent, as we have just seen. Individuals, groups, parties, classes, races, genders, and so on assert that the culture is theirs to make – that culture is not just a construction, nor even just a "negotiation," but a contest and a struggle. In the process, even many non-anthropologists have achieved what Malinowski called an "ethnographic" attitude toward their own culture, seeing it "as culture" and not just as what they have always been or done unproblematically.

The culture of modernity and after

Anthropologists, historians, and other social scientists have considered Western society to be in a condition referred to as "modernity" for at least a couple or as many as several hundred years. Since the European Enlightenment (1700s) and arguably as far back as the Renaissance (1400s–1500s), a certain distinct cultural complex dubbed "modern" has been in effect, with some specific qualities:

- *Rationalism* – The world, including the human/social world, is rationally knowable, and rationally controllable, because it is seen as orderly, consistent, and therefore predictable.
- *Progress* – The general ethos, fueled by advances in knowledge and science and by growth in economic and political power, is that things get better over time. Progress is not only desirable but inevitable, and improvement in the human condition is the natural course of things.
- *Optimism* – Therefore, modernity is characterized by an overall positive outlook: what we do not know today we will know tomorrow, and what we know tomorrow will aid us in making a better world the day after. Particularly in the "social sciences" that arose in the 1700s and 1800s, the attitude was that, by manipulating culture, we could construct a better society composed of better people.

- *Integration* – The early modern period leaned toward ever larger (and happier) conglomerations of humans. This involved the creation of "modern" states out of disparate polities and societies. Societies that were already "integral," like England for the most part, were internally connected with new systems of canals, roads, and ultimately railroads. Other societies that were not yet integral but that shared cultural commonalities, like Germans or Italians, struggled toward integration with "culture" as their guide. Colonialism represented the largest possible integration, into a few imperial systems or even a single world system. The expectation was that small, independent, "traditional" identities and allegiances would give way to the larger, interdependent "modern" ones.

- *Bureaucratization* – Instead of the subjective and "personal" leadership of kings, princes, chiefs, or headmen, society would become more "organized" and impersonal, with various departments headed by professionals making decisions relevant to their jurisdiction and expertise. All aspects of society, from law to the economy to the family, would become more "rational" and less arbitrary.

- *Secularization* – A final but perhaps pervasive assumption is an inherent secularization or detachment of "civil" society, especially the government and the economy, from religion. It was widely believed that religion would lose its importance and perhaps disappear altogether.

Thus, the net direction of "modern" society is/was toward a more rational, more progressive, more integrated, more bureaucratic, and less religious way of life.

Things did not quite work out that way. Even by the late 1800s, a few sensitive types were questioning the triumph of modernity. Nietzsche, Freud, and others began to criticize rationalism, objectivity, mass integration, and all the other conceits of modern society. They emphasized the irrational in human life (the "will to power" or the "unconscious") as inescapable forces, and they often despaired of the homogenization that was occurring under capitalism, democracy, and mass culture. What seemed to be proof of human irrationality and of the danger of modernity came in the form of World War I (1914–1918), which shocked people more than we can comprehend in our own time. Citizens who prized their rationality, their progressivism, their optimism, and so on were horrified at their behavior in the trenches, at their capacity and even thirst for destruction. The Spanish Civil War (1936–1939) and World War II (1939–1945) completed the experience. It became increasingly more difficult to believe in the rosy picture painted by modernity. In fact, it was in the arts, such as painting, that much of the soul-searching occurred: artists like Picasso gave humanity disturbing irrational/emotional depictions of itself, Dali made time and space melt, and Munch captured the mood of the epoch with perhaps the best-known work of the period, *The Scream* (1893).

By the early 1900s, at least in some fields and some circles, people could no longer sustain a belief in modernity. To them, the project had failed, and humanity had moved on to another phase of culture, which could only be called "post-modern." Post-modernity, or **post-modernism**, emphasizes the irrational (even the unconscious), the subjective, the spontaneous (as opposed to the bureaucratic), the

Post-modernism
A form of life or way of thinking, and the theory of these, of the mid- to late twentieth century, in which earlier notions of unity, progress, reason, and the increasing integration of peoples and societies break down and are replaced by plurality, "irrationality" or emotion or tradition, decentering, and cultural disintegration.

Decentered

The absence or denial of a particular society's or culture's perspective from which to view the world, usually associated with moving away from a Western or Eurocentric perspective. Could potentially imply the absence of any central perspective.

Anderson, Walter Truett. 1990. *Reality Isn't What It Used to Be: Theatrical Politics, Ready-to-wear Religion, Global Myths, Primitive Chic, and Other Wonders of the Postmodern World.* New York: Harper.

Cultural tourism

The practice of "consuming" culture as a form of entertainment and education. Traveling to foreign societies to observe their ways of life (not always "traditional" but sometimes designed for the tourist) in an informal manner.

Popular culture

Often contrasted with "high" or "official" culture, the cultural practices and creations of "the people." Often used as a pejorative term to indicate the poor quality and low intelligence of such culture, in the contemporary world it has also become an important and vibrant form of culture, although one that is not entirely "of the people," in the sense that large corporations often create and disseminate it.

superficial. It doubts progress and is considerably more pessimistic, while at the same time in a sense more "playful." Since in many formulations there is no "ultimate reality," no "knowable truth," no "absolute center," all things are mere representation, surface, perspective, or image. Science becomes a "culture," history becomes a "point of view," and all things become relative, so humans can mix and match fragments of this or that subjective experience into an ersatz creation that amuses, whether or not it informs. Reality becomes something like MTV (perhaps the fulfillment of post-modernism) with rapidly changing images that are not meant to communicate but to evoke or merely dazzle. What could humans in the end communicate, since the "meaning" of the work according to the viewer may not and probably will not be the "meaning" of the author? Meaning becomes **decentered**; there is no "true" meaning, just *your* meaning or *my* meaning, and either of us can choose or create any meaning we want. The detachment gained from one's own culture creates the condition that Malinowski called "ethnographic." As Walter Truett Anderson expressed it, in the pre-modern condition humans did not choose their culture; rather, "If you choose, you are at least modern. If you know you are choosing, you are postmodern" (1990: 112).

The commodification of culture

The contemporary world is a place not only where culture is chosen and created but also where it is commodified and consumed. A commodity is something that is bought and sold, to which a price can be attached. We easily think of clothes and food and manufactured goods as commodities; culture, it might seem, is something that you *are*, not something you buy and consume. However, not only is "the consumption of culture" a more and more common occurrence, but it is a prime opportunity to observe the process of the construction of culture.

In a world in which business and "the market" increasingly define human inter-actions, it should be no surprise that culture becomes a business as well. In fact, a "culture industry" exists to make, distribute, and sell culture. Two of its main forms are **cultural tourism** and **popular culture**. Neither is a brand-new idea, but each has become bigger, more deliberate, and more influential than ever, like all of the other intentional forms of culture we have discussed.

Cultural tourism entails seeking out a "cultural" experience as entertainment and education. Former president of the National Tourism Association, Bruce Beckham, stated that the modern American vacationer is "more into life-seeing than into sight-seeing" (Brown 2000). This often means seeing someone else's life, someone exotic, someone "anthropological." The thrust of Brown's article is that cultural tourism is big business, whether it involves visiting a museum or a "heritage exhibit" like an ethnic festival or a performance of "traditional" music or dance. In fact, the National Trust for Historic Preservation helped formulate the first "strategic plan" for cultural/heritage tourism, which it defined as "traveling to experience the places, artifacts, and activities that authentically represent the stories and people of the past and present" (ibid.). The key word here is "authentically."

PLATE 15.3 Cultural tourists strolling through Aztec ruins in central Mexico

Naturally, if someone is going to consume culture, someone else must produce and distribute it for them. This is why there are "native dance shows" and "native arts centers" and adventure/culture camps and get-aways. In Australia, one can take an "authentic" Aboriginal excursion, complete with an Aboriginal guide, during which tourists hike in the bush, eat over a campfire, and learn to throw a boomerang; never mind that most Aboriginal peoples, like the Warlpiri, never made or used returning boomerangs. Australia is one of many countries that have discovered that visitors want to consume "traditional culture": a 1993 survey of international travelers indicated that almost half wanted to see Aboriginal culture and that more than one-third actually did include such an activity in their plans. Other travelers seek out "authentic" cultural experiences on African safaris or anywhere else in the world.

The problem, of course, is that these experiences are seldom if ever "authentic." They are selected, and sometimes invented, for tourists. They perpetuate stereotypes (who would go on an Aboriginal tour without a boomerang?). Worse, they actually change the culture of the host people; for instance, "native artists" begin producing small (portable) trinkets in styles that they know tourists will buy. And they expose the providers of these cultural experiences to the vagaries of world (mostly Western) tastes and trends.

If other societies produce "tradition for sale," American society produces "popular culture" in abundance. In a sense, popular culture is culture by and for the people, but then all culture is by and for people. Popular culture as a distinct phenomenon tends to mean three things: not "high culture" like opera or symphony, culture for sale and disposal, and culture mass produced and mass marketed. In all of these ways, it is distinct from high or elite culture as well as from "folk culture." High/elite culture was allegedly noble (i.e., only for the upper classes) and non-commercial, whereas folk culture was supposedly crude but authentic and traditional and also non-commercial. Popular culture, a commodity for the masses, is largely seen as cheap, low quality, even "ghastly" (Rosenberg 1957: 9). And often it is. But it is also important, if only because it is a significant part of what people make, do, and think. More than this, though, it gives anthropologists important insights into contemporary society and the culture-making process.

Popular culture of the contemporary sort is related to other cultural factors. It could not exist without mass production, disposable income to buy it, leisure time to enjoy it, and a "mass society" to sell it to. Some observers have considered this a uniformly bad thing: Ortega y Gasset famously declared that "the masses, by definition, neither should nor can direct their own personal experience, and still less rule society in general" (1932: 11) – an elitist attitude. It also has social consequences, including the "leveling" of social distinctions and the establishment of a common "language" and experience – or even the creation of new communities and institutions (as *Star Wars* and *Star Trek* have done). Popular culture can be conservative or subversive. As advertising and propaganda, it can manipulate people for the enrichment and empowerment of others. At the same time, with the machinery of cultural production in their own hands – whether the printing press, the television camera, or the internet – people can comment on and protest against social institutions and offer alternative perspectives. It is not without significance that the Warlpiri, for instance, now have their own television studio.

Finally, as trivial and banal as much popular culture seems, like all other cultural forms it communicates meaningful messages. Underneath the transitory characters and stories are the deep myths, values, and symbols of the society. Popular culture is, after all, one way that a society tells itself its stories over and over again. As one brief example, Gary Engle's essay called "What Makes Superman So Darned American?" (1987) suggests that the Superman character and story embody several key American values and narratives, including immigration and the experience of being an "alien" in one's own country, the "problem" of identity, social mobility, the transformation from rural to urban life, and of course "truth, justice, and the American way." Other thinkers have conducted similar analyses of Batman, Barbie, the Simpsons, and various genres like the Western movie or the horror movie. Each is a spotlight on the society that produces it and consumes it; after all, popular culture is popular for a reason.

Four views of the future of culture

Where does culture go from here? This is the new framing question of cultural anthropology. Long ago anthropology ceased to be the "science of the primitive," the study of the "uncontaminated Native." As Malinowski instructed, anthropology must be the study of what is, not an antiquarian (and essentially fanciful or impossible) reconstruction of the past. Anthropology not only can but must be relevant to seeing the possibilities for the future and the advantages and disadvantages of those various possibilities, as well as to constructing that future. Various observers have offered at least four potential visions for the future.

One-world culture

Some observers foresee a future in which the human world will integrate into one vast single culture on the basis of globalization. Already in the first days of Western colonialism, events or decisions or consumption choices in one part of the world tied together other and potentially all parts. Decades ago people were speaking of the "global village" in which all humans would be citizens (although it would more likely be a "global city" with many neighborhoods and enclaves). Developments in those decades – in trade, technology, media, and the environment – have helped to hasten the dictum to "think globally." Many people herald the coming of a single global cultural system as the inevitable, if not perfectly positive, destination of integrative processes.

There are two different versions of how a **one-world culture** might evolve. The first is a hybridization of all the world's cultures, in which societies big and small contribute toward a new system that includes, affirms, and addresses all of them. Two rather obvious problems confront this view. A new syncretistic global culture that affirms local "traditional" cultures is essentially a contradiction, since it would be non-traditional – indeed, the most non-traditional culture ever devised by humans. Whether societies would be willing to embrace the new culture in place of their "old" one is a contentious question. In addition, it seems patently unlikely that all societies would be able to make an equal contribution to this global culture, or that the contribution of some would be felt at all. What language would it speak? A polyglot of English, Spanish, Japanese, Warlpiri, and the 5,997 other world languages? Not likely. Rather, a few languages and cultures or even a single language and culture would be liable to dominate this new world. Therefore, the second version of a one-world culture is a "globalization" of one or a few dominant culture(s). The most likely candidates for global dominance at present are Western culture as a whole or American culture alone, as expressed in Francis Fukuyama's popular book *The End of History and the Last Man* (1992). Today, English reigns as the language of trade and diplomacy, and American popular culture (movies, music, celebrities) pervades the world. The one-world culture could be nothing more than American culture writ large. On the other hand, former dominant cultures have come and gone; French is no longer the lingua franca. Some see China poised to be a major international political, economic, and cultural force in the twenty-first century, which would alter the winds of cultural change and globalization yet again – and in ways not advantageous to English speakers or the West in general.

One-world culture
The idea that all of the peoples and cultures of the world are becoming (or should become) more similar, to the point at which all humans share a single culture. Often attributed to globalization and the universal access to technology and cultural images (like American movies), it assumes that disparate groups will continue to become more similar until all groups share the same basic values, tastes, and media.

Jihad versus McWorld

Partly out of appreciation for the obstacles to globalization, Benjamin Barber (1995) reports two opposing tendencies operating simultaneously in the contemporary

Jihad versus McWorld

Benjamin Barber's notion that two opposing but related forces operate in the modern world, one to integrate the world into a single market dominated by a few multinational corporations, and the other to disintegrate the world into exclusivist and often hostile cultural or national groups.

Barber, Benjamin. 1995. *Jihad versus McWorld*. New York: Times Books.

world, **jihad versus McWorld**. "Jihad," the Arabic word for struggle and sometimes violent struggle, Barber adopts to stand for all of the "local," tradition-oriented, frequently angry and militant, "identity-based" groups and movements in the world. It represents the fragmentation of the world, the disengagement from and even hostility toward the world system and the "integrative revolution" that scholars once watched and applauded and declared victorious. It talks the talk of culture and tradition, but this is remembered tradition as well as aggravated, mobilized, and often armed tradition.

Barber's jihad is innately hostile to the "outside" world, whether that "outside" is other societies in its midst or the foreign and globalizing and modernizing influences of the world economic and cultural system. These influences come in many shapes and from many quarters, but Barber calls one key aspect "McWorld." McWorld is the culture and power of the multinational corporations and their "development" orientation. These corporations include all of the famous names that modern people know so well, like Nike, Microsoft, Pepsi-Cola and Coca-Cola (and others that we do not know so well), although the most representative may be Disney. McWorld has two critical characteristics: it is nakedly economic in focus, and it is culturally invasive. By nakedly economic, Barber means that it has only one interest – profit. It is not concerned to any degree with social relationships or environmental issues or "tradition." All of those things can be impediments to profit and are to be minimized. Since these corporations "fly under the radar" when they can, this is not as difficult as it seems. They often come to non-Western states bearing the gift of development – jobs, income, training, "modernization," and increased GNP – but this comes with all of the costs discussed in earlier chapters, and most of the benefits accrue to the corporations themselves.

McWorld is culturally invasive in two senses – that it brings a message from another culture which is at best foreign and at worst corrosive to the host society, and that it acts, sometimes consciously, to undermine the culture of the host society. An important part of McWorld is American popular culture, embodied in Hollywood. The messages and images of the American culture and entertainment industry are seductive but also anathema to many of the values and beliefs of other societies. No wonder a few societies with the power to do so have banned satellite dishes and the internet; they consider the content of this McCulture to be decadent and disruptive. That McWorld is even intentionally "hostile" toward local cultures is evident from the fundamental requirement to "adjust" a culture so that the corporations, their products, and their values can penetrate it. Before a society will drink Coke, its local tastes and preferences must be changed. Before a society will wear Nikes or Mickey Mouse T-shirts, its sense of style and perceived needs must be altered.

Barber roughly equates jihad with tribalism (although militant tribalism) and McWorld with globalization. The one thing he does not equate either with is democracy, cultural pluralism, or cultural relativism. Both are exclusivist, in a curious way. It is easy to see the exclusivism in jihad: "our" cultural group is right and good and "yours" is wrong and bad. Groups with this mindset tend to find it undesirable if not impossible to co-exist. The only option is separation, and the path to separation is often conflict. But McWorld is exclusivist too: Microsoft tolerates but hardly enjoys having Macintosh in the world, and Coke and Pepsi do not really like each other, nor, even more so, local "traditional" drinks. If jihad is about separatism, McWorld is about monopoly. Neither has a taste for competition. Neither is, therefore, about choice in the end. Wherever you go in the world, the options are to be exactly the same, with local variation or "flavor" eradicated. Americans already know what that looks like in "mall America"; the goal of McWorld is "mall world." In jihad, choice is also inconceivable. One is born a Basque or a Tamil or a Serb or a Christian, and these are inescapable, "natural" identities. Decisions and behaviors are "given," and individualism is not encouraged or desired.

Clash of civilizations

Samuel Huntington (1996) emphasizes a different aspect of the cultural future but one that is no more heartening and that is part of the same general cultural dynamic – a **clash of civilizations**. Huntington suggests that the primary actors on the stage of world history and culture in the future will not be states or even societies. Prior to the modern period, he argues, history was basically the story of the struggle of powerful individuals – kings, princes, emperors – and the populations they could drag along with them. Beginning in the 1600s or 1700s, the agents in cultural history became "nations" and the states within which they could wrap themselves. However, there is something else going on today, and it was there all the time – the phenomenon of "civilization," which Huntington defines as a sort of "super-society" or "super-culture," a family of closely related cultures that share certain basic beliefs and values, often religious.

To understand his notion of civilization it is useful to think about American and British and Canadian and Australian cultures. The four are no doubt different in a number of ways; at the same time, they are also similar (for instance, English speaking) and part of a yet larger, European, Christian, "Western" culture that Huntington would call a civilization. A civilization, then, is the largest cultural community known to humans. Within a civilization are many cultural variations, but the differences between civilizations are much more profound – and potentially insurmountable – than the differences within.

Civilizations have been there throughout the modern era; they were merely obfuscated or forgotten in the excitement of colonialism, modernization, and globalization. Western scholars believed or assumed that modern movements – communism, liberalism, progressivism, capitalism – were or would become the true forces of cultural history, and they ignored (when they even knew about) the movements that local peoples formed for themselves or the cultural "narratives" that local peoples told to themselves. If Westerners were aware of other civilizations and their worldviews, they fully expected that Western worldviews would replace them. But as the smoke of demolished colonialism and communism clears, we see the old structures of the civilizations looming from the haze. Today and tomorrow, the world's main civilizations – Western/Christian, Islamic, Chinese, South Asian/Indian,

Clash of civilizations
Huntington's notion that the key forces in the future will not be societies or states but regional cultural entities (e.g., "Western civilization" or "Islam"); within a civilization a variety of cultural attitudes are shared, but between civilizations differences of attitude and interest will breed conflict.

Huntington, Samuel. 1996. *The Clash of Civilizations and the Remaking of World Order*. New York: Simon & Schuster.

Multiple modernities
The perspective that
"modernity" as known in
the Western tradition is not
the only possible form of
modern society, and that
other societies can and will
devise their own particular
experience of and response
to modern/global forces.

Eisenstadt, S.N. 2000.
   "Multiple Modernities."
   Daedalus 129 (1): 1–29.
Hefner, Robert W. 1998.
   "Multiple Modernities:
   Christianity, Islam, and
   Hinduism in a Globalizing
   Age." *Annual Review of
   Anthropology* 27: 83–104.

"African" – are back, although they had never really gone. And they were "back with a vengeance," as Huntington predicts that the conflicts and wars of the near future will be between these civilizations (for instance, "the West" versus "Islam") or along the fault-lines where they meet (for instance, the Middle East and Israel or Taiwan).

Multiple modernities

Some may find in Huntington's vision, and perhaps Barber's too, a failure of modernity, but in an important way, modernity was another Western worldview and movement like colonialism and development. Accordingly, one of the most interesting, and anthropological, commentaries on the present and future of cultures – one which explicitly opposes Huntington's and Fukuyama's analysis – has recognized multiple paths to this cultural future, multiple ways to be "modern"; that is, **multiple modernities** (Eisenstadt 2000; Hefner 1998).

S. N. Eisenstadt notes that all of the dominant theories and predictions regarding culture assumed "that the cultural program of modernity as it developed in modern Europe and the basic institutional constellations that emerged there would ultimately take over in all modernizing and modern societies; with the expansion of modernity, they would prevail throughout the world" (2000: 1). However, as he notes generally, and as Hefner notes specifically concerning religion,

> The actual developments in modernizing societies have refuted the homogenizing and hegemonic assumptions of this Western program of modernity. While a general trend toward structural differentiation developed across the wide range of institutions in most of these societies . . . the ways in which these arenas were defined and organized varied greatly, in different periods of their development, giving rise to multiple institutional and ideological patterns. Significantly, these patterns did not constitute simple continuations in the modern era of traditions of their respective societies. Such patterns were distinctively modern, though greatly influenced by specific cultural premises, traditions, and historical experiences. . . . Many of the movements that developed in non-Western societies articulate strong anti-Western or even antimodern themes, yet all were distinctively modern.
>
> (Hefner 1998: 1–2)

In other words, while Eisenstadt acknowledges elsewhere that Western civilization represents "the 'original' modernity" (1999: 284), the Western version of "modern culture" is neither the only possible one nor the only existing one. Rather, each society can and will find its own form of or response to the common yet unevenly distributed global processes; the future can and will hold "attempts by various groups and movements to reappropriate and redefine the discourse of modernity in their own new terms" (Eisenstadt 2000: 24), based on their particular pre-modern cultures, their particular experiences of modernization, and the particular choices of leaders and members alike. This perspective aligns well with the notion of "glocalization", in which global processes cannot help but take locally specific shapes. In the end,

See Chapter 1

then, there would not be one cultural future, not two, not even several, but many diverse and continually emerging and changing ones – precisely the sort of future that cultural anthropology should expect and is uniquely poised to understand.

BOX 15.4   CONTEMPORARY CULTURAL CONTROVERSIES: WHO OWNS CULTURE?

The contemporary Western world is familiar with the concept of "intellectual property," that ideas and images can be owned. As societies, including and especially indigenous societies, become increasingly integrated into a global system and market, a new and difficult question emerges: who owns and controls "traditional culture," and which – or whose – laws will govern its production and sale? In 1997, an Aboriginal artist named Johnny Bulun Bulun sued a company called R & T Textiles for copyright infringement, claiming that the company used unauthorized images of his work on its products. As recounted by Michael Brown in his book *Who Owns Native Culture?*, Bulun Bulun was no pure traditionalist: he was an accomplished modern painter whose most famous work, *Magpie Geese and Waterlilies at the Waterhole*, hung in the Museum and Art Gallery of the Northern Territory in Australia. Therefore, when R & T Textiles printed his designs on their materials, they were "stealing" his property and violating his ownership rights. However, as even Bulun Bulun would admit, images like his are not entirely private but communal, some-where between "art" and "folklore," derived from "designs [that] belong not only to him but to his clan" (Brown 2003: 45). In a sense, then, Bulun Bulun did not exactly "own" his images; he was a sort of traditional caretaker and reproducer of them. This problem is not unique to Australia or to visual culture. In other countries, words or names or objects or other bits of culture are used commercially; think of the automobile called Dodge Cherokee, not to mention the mass production of Indian dolls, Mexican blankets, or toy bows and arrows. Many indigenous societies do not quite have concepts to deal with such uses of their cultural heritage; at the same time, modern state societies do not quite have the appropriate concepts either. In fact, note that the debate, and the litigation, is ordinarily conducted in modern/Western, not indigenous terms – about "copyright" and "property" and so on. Money is at stake, as well as cultural pride and issues of authenticity. What do you think?

Brown, Michael. 2003.
Who Owns Native Culture?
Cambridge MA and
London: Harvard
University Press.

SUMMARY

While world-altering processes like colonialism, globalization, nationalism, and development have affected many peoples negatively, those peoples have not been passive victims of cultural changes. Increasingly in the contemporary world, indigenous people have raised their voices to state their demands, reclaim their cultures, and speak on their own behalf. Formerly "traditional societies" have mastered the modern tools of arts, media, politics, and organization to present formidable challenges to perceived injustices and inequalities. Along the way, anthropology has changed to reflect and study these changed cultural realities.

One of the most important aspects of culture in the twentieth and twenty-first centuries is the adaptation of culture into cultural movements intended to address some aspect of cultural frustration and dissatisfaction. A cultural movement, however, is a new kind or formation of culture itself and not merely a continuation of traditional culture or an abandonment of it. These revitalization movements have taken many shapes and are not unique to small, "traditional" societies but are an increasing part of the life of all societies. Some of the types or qualities of movements include:

- syncretism
- millenarianism
- irredentism
- modernism or vitalism
- nativism or fundamentalism.

All of these movements are modern manifestations of the "culture-making" phenomenon. In the post-modern world, culture is perceived more or less clearly as a product and a construction, rather than as a "thing" or an "essence." People in all sorts of societies have developed a nearly "ethnographic" or anthropological understanding of their own culture. At the same time, the processes of culture creation and consumption have expanded and accelerated, to include cultural tourism and popular culture. Where the culture of the future will take us, we cannot say. We can, however, appreciate that it will be a construction too – one emerging from multiple and contradictory forces and one to which anthropology has something to contribute as observer and participant.

Key Terms

Clash of civilizations

Cultural tourism

Decentered

Fourth World

Fundamentalism

Irredentism

Jihad versus McWorld

Millenarianism

Modernism

Multiple modernities

Nativism

One-world culture

Popular culture

Post-modernism

Revitalization movement

Syncretism

Vitalism

Seeing Culture as a Whole #3: Exile, Refuge, and Culture

Distance from one's own culture may be a necessary ingredient in seeing one's culture as "a culture." A "break" from lived and spontaneous culture can make culture a *problem* and an *object* in a way that continuity cannot, resulting in new senses of "identity" and "ethnicity" and "cultural movements." As Guidieri and Pellizi suggest, "Exile creates 'ethnicities.' No people truly is, *chez soi*, an ethnic group, because that which defines ethnicity is Difference" (1988: 155) – and distance established difference.

If exile, the loss of "natural" or "genuine" culture, is a foundation for cultural self-awareness, then there are two populations who experience this exile most exquisitely. One is the refugees, those people who are literally driven from their homes and home-lands by war, famine, disaster, or other crises. Anthropologists have begun to notice that refugees, whether in temporary camps or in their new resettled lives, are overt prac-titioners of social dynamics and of interpretation and imagination. Liisa Malkki, who conducted fieldwork in the Tanzanian camps for Hutu refugees from the 1972 ethnic clash in Burundi, writes that the "most unusual and prominent social fact about the camp was that its inhabitants were continually engaged in an impassioned construction and reconstruction of their history as 'a people'" (1995: 3). In such environments people must reconstruct a life out of memories and imaginings, because their old taken-for-granted life really is lost. In particular, she describes the "mythico-history" they create, especially in the stories they tell about the recent and ancient past. In these stories they explore recurrent themes of their ancient origins and a "golden past" before the Tutsi came, or the evil of the Tutsi and their own subordination, of the purported physical and psycho-logical differences between "them" and "us," and of course of the apocalypse that was the 1972 war and its atrocities. These accounts are not always "factual," nor is that their function: for instance, when a refugee tells that "It was one hundred years before Jesus Christ that we [the Hutu] came to Burundi" (60), that claim is not to be taken as fact or history nor even as memory but as polemic and paradigmatic act. What it says is that the Hutu were there before the Tutsi and therefore have certain rights that Tutsi lack. As paradigms, such accounts explain and legitimize present and future social arrange-ments by projecting them back into the past. Concurrently, she observes them forming the allegories of the present that shape the image of the past. Past, present, and future – exile and home – are all subjected to an interpretation and invention that yields something at once old and new.

Among Cambodian refugees resettled in the United States, Mortland (1994) finds their notion of "traditional identity" to be allegedly "natural, *a priori*, and without dispute. But Cambodians fear that their 'natural' identity as Cambodians will fade if they do not do the things that make them Cambodian" (6). This is a new challenge because, in their pre-refugee lives, they had not been aware of their culture in the same way; Khmer-ness was taken-for-granted if not unconscious. "They were not aware of having 'ethnic identity'; they were instead defined by their work, education, family, and village" (8). Relocated to the U.S.A., culture and identity were problems that required effort. It was necessary to determine precisely what "Khmer-ness" entailed, and extensive discus-sions were held within the group about "the necessity, advantage, disadvantage, and impossibility of 'being Cambodian,' 'being American,' or some integration of the two" (11). Out of these discussions emerged certain "criteria" of Cambodian identity – some ways to measure their own cultural authenticity as well as that of their children and others in the community, including language and (Buddhist) religion. They came to view Cambodian-ness as a concrete quality, "quantifiable, observable," but one that was "distributed unequally among them" (13) – some were more "Cambodian" than others.

The heart of the invention and perpetuation of Cambodian-ness was the myth of pre-refugee Cambodia, "about what Cambodia was like before in order to contrast traditional Cambodian and modern American customs, to describe ideal and actual Cambodian behavior, and the gap between the two" (15). Key to the myth of Cambodia was the essentialization or reification – the identification of an essence or fundamental reality – of "traditional" Cambodia, a place and culture that was viewed as "unchanging, indeed unchangeable" (20). Interestingly, while their lived reality in America became looser and less "traditional," their sense of tradition – what "used to be" and "ought to be" – became "more rigid, more stolidly asserted" (21). This "remembered tradition" was thus very different in fact and feel from the former "lived tradition." In the end, Mortland concludes, once they lose "home" and the taken-for-granted quality of life before exile, "they can never return unscathed to the certainty of traditional beliefs and rituals" (24).

We said that there are two kinds of exiled souls in the world. One is the involuntary exile. The other is the voluntary exile, including the anthropologist himself or herself. Anthropologists are not only voluntary but *eager* exiles, literally and physically leaving their culture if only temporarily, but changed permanently by the experience. Anthropologists seek this disorientation, this distancing from the familiar, this loss of a taken-for-granted "home" and cultural reality. Once they have experienced it, they can never quite go home again.

Anthropologists do one more thing. They do not keep their experiences to themselves. Rather, they share news from other worlds with members of their own and every other society. And this is not the only way that people encounter "difference": in their own everyday lives, they are faced with humans of differing languages, religions, values, and bodies. Human diversity, the reality of "difference," follows them home. Even people who never leave home experience that, in a way, home – the simple, certain, unquestioned truth and goodness of things – has left them.

Glossary

Absolute poverty A level of income below what is required to have a decent standard of living, sometimes measured at less than $1 per day.

Acculturation The process of acquiring a "second culture," usually as an effect of sustained and imbalanced contact between two societies. Members of the "weaker" society are compelled to adopt aspects of the dominant society.

Acheulian The stone tool technology associated with *Homo erectus*, which involves a more complex flaking of bifacial implements.

Achieved status A social position or role that a person acquires through some effort or accomplishment of his or her own.

Adaptation Changes in a system, including a species, in response to changes in its context or environment so as to make that system or species more fit to survive in the context or environment.

Age grade system A non-kinship-based corporate system in which members, usually of one sex, are organized into groups or "grades" according to age and assigned roles and values as a group.

Agents of social control Individuals, groups, or roles that play a part in instilling social norms in members and protecting and perpetuating those norms through the use of their powers and sanctions.

Ambilineal descent A descent system in which individuals trace their membership through both "sides" or "lines" of the family, or optionally through one or the other.

Ambilocality A residence practice in which individuals may live after marriage with both "sides" of the family (perhaps alternating between them), or optionally with one or the other.

Ancestor spirits The spirits of dead family members who are believed to continue to reside near and interact with their living kin.

Animatism A type of religious belief where impersonal spiritual forces exist in the world and affect human life and behavior.

Animism A type of religious belief in which non-human species and phenomena have spiritual components that interact with and sanction humans.

Anthropological perspective The unique "angle" or point of view of anthropology, consisting of cross-cultural or comparative study, holism, and cultural relativism.

Anthropometry The measurement of human bodies to determine individual and group ("racial") physical characteristics.

Anti-language A speech style used by individuals or groups in the performance of roles opposing or inverting the society outside of their group.

Apartheid In twentieth-century South Africa, the official policy of separating the races within their society legally and socially.

Archaeology The study of the diversity of human behavior in the past, based on the traces left behind by past humans or societies.

Arranged marriage A practice where family members (often parents) choose the partner for marriageable youths, sometimes with little or no input from or option for the partners themselves.

Artifacts Physical objects created by humans, often specifically the "portable" objects like tools, pottery, and jewelry (as opposed to the non-portable ones like buildings and roads).

Ascribed status A social characteristic that is attributed to a person without any effort on their part, either innate (e.g., sex or race) or acquired in the normal course of development (e.g., age).

Assimilation The social process by which individuals and groups are absorbed into another, usually dominant, cultural group.

Australopithecus A genus of the category Hominid, closely related to and earlier than genus Homo, to which modern humans belong.

Authority Legitimate power or power that an individual, group, or institution is felt to rightly possess and exercise on the grounds of age, knowledge, office, and so on.

Avunculocality A residence practice in which a married couple lives with or near an uncle, often a mother's brother.

Band A political system or "level of political integration" where small, autonomous, and typically leaderless groups constitute local segments of a decentralized society.

Basic personality The psychological traits common to most or all of the members of a society (roughly synonymous with modal personality).

Berdache A gender concept in some Native American societies for biological males who adopt certain behavioral and personality characteristics of females.

Bilateral descent Relating to both "sides," as in a kinship system, in which individuals regard kin related to the mother and to the father as socially equivalent.

Biocultural The mutual interaction between physical/biological and behavioral/cultural factors, in which physical traits make certain behaviors possible, and behavior feeds back to influence physical traits.

Bipedalism The ability and tendency to walk on two feet.

Blackbirding The colonial practice of abducting the populations of areas, often islands, and resettling them as a labor force in some other part of the world.

Bound morpheme A morpheme that has meaning but only when it is used in conjunction with a word.

Brideprice *See bridewealth*.

Bride service The marriage wealth-exchange practice in which a man must labor for his wife's kin for a certain period of time before he may assume rights over his wife.

Bridewealth The marriage wealth-exchange practice in which a man or his family must pay an amount of property to his wife's kin before he may assume rights over his wife.

Caste A closed socio-economic status, often ascribed by birth.

Cephalic index A measurement of the skull/brain volume and shape, based on a ratio of the width of the head from ear to ear relative to the depth of the head from front to back.

Chiefdom A political system or "level of integration" in which a central office, often hereditary, possesses formal political power and social prestige through some degree of redistributive control over surplus and the ability to organize and manage labor.

Childrearing practices The methods employed by members of a society to care for children and to prepare those children to become future members of that society.

Civil war A violent conflict within a particular state or between corporate or identity groups within the state.

Civilization A form of society based on cities as the centers of administration and the focus of social life, usually dependent on intensive agriculture in the surrounding countryside.

Clan A kinship group, sometimes an assortment of lineages, whether or not it can trace its descent back to a common ancestor.

Clash of civilizations Huntington's notion that the key forces in the future will not be societies or states but regional cultural entities (e.g., "Western civilization" or "Islam"); within a civilization a variety of cultural attitudes are shared, but between civilizations differences of attitude and interest will breed conflict.

Class An (at least ideally) open socio-economic status, which members can change through their own achievements.

Coercion Power based on the threat or use of force.

Colonialism The more or less organized system of occupation and exploitation of foreign territories through settlement and conquest, especially as practiced by Western states since 1492.

Colonies of exploitation Colonies in which few foreigners immigrate but the territory is still used for its resources, wealth, labor, markets, and/or strategic location.

Colonies of settlement Colonies in which many foreigners immigrate, sometimes such that they and their descendants become the majority population of the territory.

Colony A segment of a population (not exclusively a human population) that moves into and occupies territory not previously occupied by the population, often displacing or subduing the previous occupants.

Communal representation The political procedure of guaranteeing that groups (ethnic groups, language groups, races, religions) will have representation in governments by setting aside offices in the government specifically for those groups.

Competence In language, the mastery of the elements (sounds, semantics, and grammar) of a language to be able to make intelligible utterances.

Contagious magic The belief and practice that objects that come into contact with each other have some supernatural connection with each other.

Core In dependency/world systems theory, the states that make up the power center of the world system – essentially the rich industrial states and former colonialists.

Corporate group A social group that shares some degree of practical interest, identity, residence, and destiny.

Corvée A colonial practice in which local people were required to provide a period of labor to the administration as a sort of "tax."

Counterculture A group or subset within a society that more or less intentionally adopts behaviors, beliefs, or practices that are at odds with or opposed to the mainstream of society.

Country Commonly used as a synonym for "nation" or "state," more properly refers to the territory that a society or polity inhabits.

Creole A pidgin language that has become elaborated into a multi-functional language and distributed into a first language of the community.

Cross-cultural study The examination of a wide variety of societies when considering any particular cultural question, for purposes of comparison.

Cultural anthropology The study of the diversity of human behavior in the present.

Cultural assimilation A type of assimilation which refers specifically to the loss of distinctive cultural traits, such as language or religion.

Cultural evolutionism The early ethnological or anthropological position or theory that Culture started at some moment in the past and evolved from its "primitive" beginnings through a series of stages to achieve its "higher" or more modern form.

Cultural loss The process by which elements of a culture disappear over time, through natural/environmental changes, social pressures, or individual choices.

Cultural materialism The theory that practical/material/economic factors can explain some or all cultural phenomena.

Cultural ontology A society's system of notions about what kinds of things (including kinds of people) exist in the world and their characteristics and social value. A socially specific way of categorizing and valuing the physical and social world.

Cultural relativism The reaction to the fact of cultural diversity in which one attempts to understand and judge the behavior of another culture in terms of its standards of good, normal, moral, legal, etc. rather than one's own.

Cultural tourism The practice of "consuming" culture as a form of entertainment and education. Traveling to foreign societies to observe their ways of life (not always "traditional" but sometimes designed for the tourist) in an informal manner.

Culture and personality An early twentieth-century school of anthropology which investigated the relationship between individual/psychological processes and culture, often but not always from a psychoanalytic perspective, focusing on childhood experiences and childrearing practices.

Culture shock The surprise, confusion, and pain we feel when we encounter a way of life that is very foreign to our own.

Decentered The absence or denial of a particular society's or culture's perspective from which to view the world, usually associated with moving away from a Western or Eurocentric perspective. Could potentially imply the absence of any central perspective.

Deculturation *See cultural loss.*

Deism The form of theism or belief in god(s) which posits a creator god that does not take an active role or moral interest in human affairs.

Dependency theory The theory of "Third World" underdevelopment that attributes the poverty and weakness of certain states to their ongoing unfavorable relationship to richer and more powerful states. Poor/weak states continue to be dependent on rich/powerful (mostly Western) ones for capital, manufactured goods, and other key economic resources.

Descent The kinship principle of tracing membership in a kin-based corporate group through a sequence of ancestors.

Development A form of directed change in which a state tries to change its internal economy and society, and/or foreign states and institutions try to change it, to promote economic growth, industrialize and urbanize, and ideally achieve a higher standard of living for its inhabitants.

Development policy The general priorities and decisions set by a state or by development agencies to achieve economic, political, and social goals.

Development project A specific activity or task settled upon to achieve the economic, political, and social goals of a development policy. Such projects often include transportation, energy (especially hydro-electric), agricultural, and resettlement schemes.

Diaspora The dispersion of a social group from its historical homeland (often applied specifically to the Jewish community).

Diffusion The spread of a cultural trait (object, idea, practice, institution) from one society to another.

Diffusionism The early ethnological or anthropological position or theory that Culture, or specific cultural practices, objects, or institutions had appeared once or at most a few times and spread out from their original center.

Diglossia   The use of two varieties of a language by members of a society for distinct functions or by distinct groups or classes of people.

Directed change   A cultural process in which internal or external agents make more or less intentional, coordinated, and sustained modifications or reforms to a society and culture.

Displacement   The linguistic feature that allows for communication about things that are "not here" in the sense of absent or out of view, past or future, conceptual or even imaginary.

Diseases of development   The lifestyle-related diseases that are common in developed industrial societies and increasingly common in developing societies, such as high blood pressure, heart disease, diabetes, tooth decay, and obesity.

Diviner   A religious specialist who uses one of many techniques to "read" information from the supernatural world.

Division of labor   The differentiation of the economy into a set of distinct production tasks, which are assigned to different individuals, groups, or classes, usually creating economic and political inequalities.

Doctrine of discovery   The European colonial principle that the state which "discovered" or arrived first in a new territory had the right to occupy and administer it without interference from other states.

Domestication   The process of modification of plants and/or animals to establish human control over them, leading to agriculture and pastoralism.

Dominance   The social relationship in which certain individuals have higher prestige or power in the group, allowing them to enjoy more or better resources as well as the deference of lower ranked members.

Double descent   The kinship practice of reckoning one's membership in kinship-based corporate groups through two lines of descent, ordinarily the mother's and the father's.

Dowry   The marriage wealth-exchange practice in which the woman's family is required to provide the husband with property (e.g., money, land, household goods) in order to make the marriage.

Dowry death   The killing of wives because the husbands were not satisfied with the dowry payment they received, or else to free them to marry again and collect another dowry.

Ecofacts   The environmental remains from past human social contexts, including wood, seeds, pollen, animal bones, and shells.

Encomienda   In Latin American colonial history, a grant of land to a conqueror and explorer, much like medieval estates, which gave the grant-holder control over the land and its inhabitants.

Enculturation   The process by which a person learns or acquires his or her culture, usually as a child. *Also known as socialization.*

Endogamy   The marriage principle in which an individual marries someone who is in the same cultural category as himself or herself (e.g., marrying someone in one's own race or religion).

Erectness The tendency to have an "upright" posture based on a spine that is vertical rather than parallel to the ground.

Ethnic group A corporate group based on some shared cultural traits – language, religion, history – which finds itself in competition with other groups for wealth, power, opportunity, and recognition. An ethnic group shares an identity and a destiny and therefore competes as a group.

Ethnicity The phenomenon of organizing around some aspect of shared culture to integrate an identity group, differentiate it from other groups, and compete in a multi-ethnic context for resources.

Ethnocentrism The attitude or belief that one's own culture is the best or only one, and that one can understand or judge another culture in terms of one's own.

Ethnocide The destruction of a group's culture, without necessarily killing any of the members of the culture.

Ethnogenesis The process by which ethnic groups come into being and/or attain their cultural characteristics.

Ethnography A written account or description of a particular culture, usually including its environment, economic system, kinship arrangements, political systems, and religious beliefs, and often including some discussion of culture change.

Ethnoscience The anthropological theory or approach that investigates the native classification systems of societies to discover the concepts, terms, and categories by which they understand their world.

Eugenics The scientific practice of "improving" a population or species by selective breeding or genetic engineering, to breed out "bad" traits and breed in "good" ones.

Eunuch A gender category involving non-sexual individuals (usually men), who may be castrated or merely celibate, sterile, or lacking sexual desire.

Exogamy The marriage principle in which an individual marries someone who is not in the same cultural category as himself or herself (e.g., marrying someone of a different sex/gender).

Externalized control The source of social control that lies outside of the individual, in the form of individuals, groups, and institutions with the power to sanction behavior, such as parents, teachers, police, governments, and so on.

Facial angle The slope of the lower face and jaw away from the flatness of the forehead, used by "scientific racists" to measure the difference between races (the sharper the angle, the more "primitive" the face).

Features In archaeology, the large and non-portable objects or structures created and left by humans, including walls, buildings, roads, canals, and so on.

Female circumcision Also known as female genital mutilation, the practice of cutting off some or all of a female's external genitalia, for purposes of "beauty" or the regulation of sexual sensations.

Female infanticide The overt killing or neglect until death of female babies. It may also take the form of preferential abortion.

Feminist anthropology The anthropological theory or approach that focuses on how gender relations are constructed in society and how those relations subsequently shape the society. Also examines how gender concepts have affected the science of anthropology itself – the questions it asks and the issues it emphasizes.

Fieldwork The anthropological method of traveling to the society one wants to study and living there for a prolonged period of time to collect data first hand.

First World A term not commonly used anymore for the rich, powerful states in the world that dominate the international political and economic arena and consist basically of the former colonial powers.

Folklore The "traditional," usually oral literature of a society, consisting of various genres such as myth, legend, folktale, song, proverb, and many others.

Foot-binding A traditional Chinese practice of tying a young girl's feet tightly so that her feet remained small (and often painful) into adulthood.

Foraging Also known as hunting and gathering, the production of food by collecting wild (undomesticated) animals and plants.

Formal sanction A method of social control employing rewards and punishments that are explicit and well known, often written down, and administered by special agents of control who possess the authority to administer them (such as the police or courts).

Fourth World A collective term for the "traditional," often small-scale and indigenous non-state societies that live inside states (frequently created by colonialism) that they do not control and in which they are the minority and typically the poorest group.

Free morpheme A morpheme that has meaning in its own right, that can stand alone as a meaningful sound (for the most part, a word).

Functionalism The method, and eventually the theory, that a cultural trait can be investigated for the contribution it makes to the survival of individual humans, the operation of other cultural items, or the culture as a whole.

Fundamentalism A type of cultural/revitalization movement in which members attempt to address perceived social problems or disadvantages by restoring the perceived "fundamentals" or oldest, most important, and most "genuine" elements of culture.

Garbalogy The study of contemporary trash to examine how humans make, consume, and discard material objects in the present.

Gender The social categories based on physical sexual characteristics and the meanings, behaviors, and values associated with these categories.

Genealogy Kinship or "blood" and "marriage" information about a society.

Genocide The destruction of a group or society by harming, killing, or preventing the birth of its members.

Geopolitics The use of geographical territory for purposes of maintenance and projection of power; the control of strategic locations in the pursuit of political goals.

Ghost A religious or spiritual being, generally regarded to be the disembodied spiritual part of a deceased human.

Global apartheid The de facto division of the world's states into rich, powerful, majority-white states and poor, weak and dependent majority-non-white states.

Glocalization A combination of the words "globalization" and "local," which suggests the unique local and situated forms and effects of widespread and even global processes.

Grammar *See syntax.*

Gross national product (GNP) The total value of goods and services produced by a society or state.

Gross national product per capita The GNP of a state divided by its population.

Guided reinvention of culture The process by which individuals, ordinarily children, "acquire" ideas, concepts, and skills actively by observing the behavior of others, extracting meanings and rules, and testing those meanings and rules in social situations; fully competent members "guide" the learning by providing models of behavior and correction for inappropriate behaviors.

Hacienda The Spanish colonial practice in which land was granted as private property and in which these estates were run both for subsistence production and for the production of cash and export crops.

Hijra A gender concept in India for biological males who regard themselves as neither male nor female; they often play a social role at weddings and childbirths.

Holism The part of the "anthropological perspective" that involves consideration of every part of a culture in relation to every other part and to the whole.

Homo The genus that contains the modern human species (*Homo sapiens*) as well as several other extinct human species.

Homo erectus An extinct human species that lived from approximately 1.8 million years ago until a few hundred thousand years ago or perhaps even more recently.

Homo habilis An extinct human species that lived from over 2 million years ago until less than 2 million years ago. They are also known as the first stone toolmakers.

Homo sapiens The species name for modern humans.

Honor killing The killing, usually of females, when their behavior has brought shame or dishonor on a family, such as premarital sex or "dating" outside the preferred categories.

Honorifics Language forms specialized to indicate the relative social status or relationship of the speakers.

Horticulture A production system based on low-technology farming or gardening, without the use of plows, draft animals, irrigation, or fertilizers.

Household All the people who live in the same house or compound of houses and act for some or all purposes as a corporate group.

Hypergamy The marriage practice of marrying "up" with a spouse in a higher status, class, or caste than oneself.

Identity politics The organization and mobilization of groups and parties on the basis of shared cultural characteristics, such that these groups and parties are seen to share an "identity" and to pursue economic, political, and cultural goals for and in the name of those who share that identity.

Imperialism   The pursuit of territorial and political domination of foreign lands and peoples (building an "empire"), known since ancient history but reaching its greatest extent in the late phase of European colonialism.

Import substitution   A development policy aimed at producing domestically what the state or society currently imports from other states (i.e., substituting its own local products for imported products).

Incest taboo   The near universal rule against marrying or having sex with "kin."

Informal sanction   A "reward" or "punishment" that is widely understood in a society but is not precisely defined, usually not written down, and for which no specialized role exists to administer the sanction.

Innovation   The invention or discovery of a new cultural concept, idea, behavior, or object.

Intensive agriculture   The production of food by use of complex and high-yield methods like irrigation, fertilizer, draft animals, and permanent fields.

Internal colonialism   The practice in which a society (usually a state) penetrates and occupies territory within its jurisdiction (normally inside its borders) but that contains peoples who do not identify as and with the occupying society. In some usages, it can also refer to the condition in which colonized peoples internalize in their own minds and personalities the institutions and values of colonialism.

Internalized control   A form or source of social control in which individuals make themselves conform to social expectations through the internalization of rules and norms; by enculturation, social rules and norms become part of the personalities of members.

Irredentism   A revitalization movement to reclaim a lost homeland.

Jihad versus McWorld   Benjamin Barber's notion that two opposing but related forces operate in the modern world, one to integrate the world into a single market dominated by a few multinational corporations, and the other to disintegrate the world into exclusivist and often hostile cultural or national groups.

Kindred   An ego-centered (that is, reckoned from the perspective of some particular individual) category of persons related by kinship, especially in bilateral societies, including members from "both sides" of the family in older and younger generations.

Kinesics   The study of how body movements are used to communicate social information, sometimes referred to as "body language."

Leveling mechanism   A practice to establish or re-establish social equality or parity, usually by "bringing down" individuals or groups that threaten to get "above" or "better than" others.

Levirate   A marriage practice in which the brother of a deceased man is expected to marry his brother's widow.

Liminality   The condition of being "in between" or "on the margins" of social roles, in particular of being in transition (as during ritual) between one social role and another.

Lineage A kinship-based corporate group composed of members related by descent from a known ancestor.

Linguistic anthropology The study of the diversity of human language in the past and present, and its relationship to social groups, practices, and values.

Linguistic relativity hypothesis The claim that language is not only a medium for communication about experience but actually a more or less powerful constituent of that experience. Language consists of concepts, relations, and values, and speakers of different languages approach and interpret reality through different sets of concepts, relations, and values. Also known as the Sapir-Whorf hypothesis.

Market-dominant minority "Ethnic minorities who, for widely varying reasons, tend under market conditions to dominate economically, often to a startling extent, the 'indigenous' majorities around them" (Chua 2003: 6).

Market exchange A form of distribution based on the use of a specialized location (the "marketplace") and relatively impersonal principles of supply and demand and the pursuit of profit.

Marriage A cultural institution joining two or more persons into a socially recognized, long-term relationship for personal, sexual, childbearing, political, and/or economic purposes.

Marxist/critical anthropology The theory, based on the work of Karl Marx, which emphasizes the material and economic forces that underlie society, relying on notions of power and inequality, modes of production, and class relations and conflicts.

Matrilineal descent A descent system in which lineage relations are traced through a line of related females. Children belong to their mother's corporate group.

Matrilocality The residence practice of living with or near the wife's family after marriage.

Mercantilism An early modern European economic and political system in which wealth and power were determined by possession of gold and a favorable balance of trade with each other.

Microfinancing A recent development approach which provides very small loans directly to poor individuals or families in poor states so that they can start small businesses or expand their already-existing businesses.

Millenarianism A type of revitalization movement aimed at preparing for and perhaps bringing about the end of the "present era," however that era is understood, and replacing it with a new and better existence.

Miscegenation A term for the undesirable effects of the mixing of different genetic types or populations, especially race groups. Often refers to the very notion of mixing the races.

Modal personality The statistically most commonly occurring personality traits in a society.

Mode of production The activities and tools a society employs to satisfy its material needs. The form of "work" or "labor" that is performed in a society.

Modernism   A type of revitalization movement intended to adopt the characteristics of a foreign and "modern" society, in the process abandoning some or all of the "traditional" characteristics of the society undergoing the movement.

Modernization theory   The theory that the improvement of economic and social conditions in poor states entails the creation of "modern" (generally understood as Western-like) institutions, values, and habits. Also, the specific processes or policies by which this form of social change can occur. W. W. Rostow offers one of the most complete and well-known modernization theories.

Moiety   One of the "halves" of a society, when kin groups are combined in such a way as to create a binary division within society.

Monoculture   The specialization of production of only one crop or product for which a territory is particularly suited. This can involve food crops like corn or rice, or raw materials like lumber, coffee, rubber, tea, and so on.

Monogamy   The marriage rule in which an individual may have only one spouse.

Monotheism   The form of theism that includes belief in only one god/goddess.

Morpheme   The smallest bit of meaningful sound in a language, usually a word but also a prefix or suffix or other meaning-conveying sound that may be used in conjunction with a word.

Morphology   The area of language dealing with how meaningful bits (usually but not exclusively words) are created and manipulated by the combination of language sounds.

Mousterian   The stone tool technology associated with Neandertals, first appearing less than 130,000 years ago.

Multilateral development institutions   Organizations like the World Bank (officially the International Bank for Reconstruction and Development) and the International Monetary Fund that were established and are funded and operated by more than one government for the purpose of disbursing money, advice, and technology in the pursuit of development.

Multinational state   A state that contains some or all of two or more distinct nations or cultural groups.

Multiple modernities   The perspective that "modernity" as known in the Western tradition is not the only possible form of modern society, and that other societies can and will devise their own particular experience of and response to modern/global forces.

Multi-state nation   A nation or cultural group that is divided across two or more state borders.

Myth   A narrative, usually of the activities of supernatural beings, often telling of how some or all of the natural or social world was established. In addition to an "explanation" of origins, it also provides a "charter" or model for how humans should live today.

Nation   A corporate group that shares an identity based on such traits as history, culture, territory, and so on, and that recognizes a shared political destiny. A group that is politically mobilized to achieve certain goals, usually including political recognition, rights, and sometimes an independent state.

Nation-state A people with a shared identity and culture (a nation) who possess their own territory and state government, or a state-level political system that contains all and only members of one nation.

National character The alleged common personality characteristics of an entire society or country; especially applied to modern societies or nation-states.

Nationalism A social movement to achieve recognition, rights, and sometimes an independent state for a nation.

Nativism A type of revitalization movement aimed at perpetuating, restoring, or reviving "traditional" cultural practices or characteristics, which are thought to be the source of the group's strength and to be threatened or lost.

Neandertal The species or subspecies of Homo that first appeared around 130,000 years ago and is associated with the cold climate of Europe. They became extinct in the last 35,000 to 40,000 years and are generally not regarded as direct human ancestors, although this interpretation is still somewhat controversial.

Neo-evolutionism The mid-twentieth-century revival of focus on the historical development of cultures and societies, as in the work of Leslie White and Julian Steward, which generally sought to repair the failings of nineteenth-century evolutionism by proposing specific processes and a "multilinear" path of change.

Neolithic The "New Stone" age, beginning around 10,000 to 12,000 years ago with the first animal and plant domestication.

Neolocality The residence practice in which married people start their own household apart from their parents' or families' households.

Noble savage The notion, often associated with Rousseau, that non-Western or "primitive" people are actually happier and more virtuous than Westerners. Based on the idea that humans are free and equal in "a state of nature" but that social institutions deprive them of that freedom and equality.

Office A more or less formal social position with specific rights and responsibilities. One source of "political" authority and social control.

Offshoot nation A national group that emerges as a local or historical branch of an older and larger group, eventually pursuing its own cultural and political identity and interests.

Oldowan The earliest known stone tool technology, associated with *Homo habilis* and named for the location of its discovery, Olduvai Gorge in East Africa.

One-world culture The idea that all of the peoples and cultures of the world are becoming (or should become) more similar, to the point at which all humans share a single culture. Often attributed to globalization and the universal access to technology and cultural images (like American movies), it assumes that disparate groups will continue to become more similar until all groups share the same basic values, tastes, and media.

Oracle A religious specialist (or any religious object or process) with the power to forecast the future or answer questions through communication with or manipulation of supernatural forces.

Overurbanization   The growth of large cities without the infrastructure to handle the urban populations, especially when a disproportionate amount of the state's population lives in one or a few such cities.

Pantheism   A form of theism in which it is believed that "everything" is God, that the universe and all of the material world is the same thing as God, that God is "immanent" in and co-extensive with the physical world.

Paralanguage   The qualities which speakers can add to language to modify the factual or social meaning of speech, such as tone of voice, volume, pitch, speed and cadence, and "non-linguistic" sounds like grunts and snickers.

Participant observation   The anthropological field method in which we travel to the society we want to study and spend long periods of time there, not only watching but joining in their culture as much as possible.

Pastoralism   A productive system based on domesticated animals as the main source of food.

Patrilineal descent   A descent system in which lineage relations are traced through a line of related males. Children belong to their father's corporate group.

Patrilocality   The residence practice of living with or near the husband's family after marriage.

Peasant   An out-of-favor term for rural and agricultural peoples who live in but are peripheral to a centralized and often urbanized society. The peasants provide the food for the society but generally have the least power and wealth in the society.

Performatives   Linguistic utterances that do not merely describe but actually accomplish a transformation in the social world.

Periphery   In dependency or world systems theory, the societies and states that have the least wealth and power and the least influence on the practices and policies in the global economy.

Personality   The ways of thinking, feeling, and behaving characteristic of a particular individual.

Persuasion   A source of social and political power, based on the ability to move people to agree with or obey the persuader. Often exercised through linguistic skill (e.g., the ability to "give a good speech") and the manipulation of resources and social relationships.

Phenotype   The observable physical traits of an individual, based on the expression of the internal and not directly observable genetic make-up of the individual (the genotype).

Phoneme   The smallest bit of sound in a language.

Phonology   The study of the sounds used in a language.

Phratry   A kinship-based corporate group composed of two or more clans that recognize common ancestry.

Physical anthropology   The study of the diversity of human bodies in the past and present, including physical adaptation, group or "race" characteristics, and human evolution.

Pidgin A simplified version of a language that is usually used for limited purposes, such as trade and economic interactions, by non-native speakers of the language (as in Melanesian pidgin versions of English). Usually an incomplete language that is not the "first" language of any group.

Plural society A society that contains various cultural groups. Such groups often occupy "niches" in the broader social system, such that the groups do not interact with each other except in limited and often mutually exploitive ways.

Pluralism The co-existence of multiple social/cultural groups in the same society or state.

Polyandry The marriage rule in which a woman marries two or more men.

Polygyny The marriage rule in which a man marries two or more women.

Polytheism The religious belief in two or more gods.

Popular culture Often contrasted with "high" or "official" culture, the cultural practices and creations of "the people." Often used as a pejorative term to indicate the poor quality and low intelligence of such culture, in the contemporary world it has also become an important and vibrant form of culture, although one that is not entirely "of the people," in the sense that large corporations often create and disseminate it.

Post-modernism A form of life or way of thinking, and the theory of these, of the mid- to late twentieth century, in which earlier notions of unity, progress, reason, and the increasing integration of peoples and societies break down and are replaced by plurality, "irrationality" or emotion or tradition, decentering, and cultural disintegration.

Potential nation A group that has not yet achieved national integration and self-consciousness but that is in the process of achieving them or has the characteristics necessary to achieve them.

Pragmatics The rules or practices regarding how language is used in particular social situations to convey particular social information, such as the relative status or power of the speakers.

Prayer A form of linguistic religious ritual in which humans are believed to speak to and interact with supernatural beings.

Preferential cousin marriage The marriage principle that a person ought to marry a "cousin," that is, a child of one's mother's sibling or one's father's sibling.

Prenational group A social group that has not yet achieved the mobilization and self-awareness that characterize a nation.

Priest A religious specialist, often full-time, who is trained in a religious tradition and acts as a functionary of a religious institution to lead ritual and perpetuate the religious institution.

Primary innovation The invention or discovery of a totally original cultural item, as opposed to *secondary innovation*.

Primary production The production of raw materials in the form of farming, mining, foresting, and so on.

Primate The term for the classification of mammals, including prosimians, monkeys, apes, and humans, that share a collection of physical characteristics including a distinct tooth pattern, five-fingered hands, a tendency toward erectness of the spine, large eyes and good vision, and a relatively large brain in relation to body weight, among others.

Primatology The study of the physical and behavioral characteristics of the category of species called primates.

Primitive mentality The idea, associated with Lucien Lévy-Bruhl, that non-Western and "primitive" peoples possessed a distinctly different, "pre-logical" mode of thought.

Productivity The capacity of language to combine meaningless sounds to create new words or to combine words to create new utterances.

Prophet A human who speaks for or receives messages from spirits.

Prosimian The category with the classification *Primate* that includes the least derived or "most primitive" species, such as lemurs, lorises, bush babies, galagas, and so on. Most have long tails and protruding snouts, but they exhibit other basic features of primates.

Proxemics The study of how cultures use personal space (or "proximity").

Psychic unity of humanity The attitude that all humans regardless of culture share the same basic thought processes.

Psychological anthropology The subdiscipline within anthropology which explores the relationship between mental processes and cultural processes.

Purdah The practice of "wearing the veil" in many Muslim countries, in which women are expected to keep some parts of their body covered in public – in some instances the head, in other instances the entire body other than the eyes.

Racial assimilation A form of assimilation in which the physical traits of a group are lost through intermarriage.

Reciprocity A form of exchange that involves giving and receiving between relative equals and as part of a larger ongoing social relationship.

Redistribution A form of exchange that involves collection of surplus or wealth by a "central" individual, group, or institution that controls how the wealth is redistributed and used.

Relations of production In Marxist theory, the social roles and relationships that are generated by the mode of production, including such things as class, ownership, "management," and in some lines of thinking "family."

Relative poverty The possession of less money than others in the same society, or the inability to afford the standard of living of more comfortable individuals or that is believed to be possible or appropriate.

Residence The kinship principle concerning where people live, especially after marriage, and therefore what kinds of residential and corporate groups are found in the society and what tasks and values they are assigned.

Revitalization movement According to Wallace, the deliberate, organized, and self-conscious effort of a society to create a more satisfying culture.

Revolution A more or less sudden, complete, and often violent movement to change a political or social system.

Rite of intensification A form of ritual in which members of the society are brought into greater communion, in which social bonds are intensified.

Rite of passage A form of ritual intended to accompany or accomplish a change of status or role of the participants, such as initiation (change from youth to adult) or marriage.

Ritual Any type of formal, repetitive behavior that is felt to have significance beyond the actions themselves. In particular, religious ritual is often composed of symbols, re-enacts supernatural/mythical events, and is believed to have efficacy if performed correctly.

Sacrifice A ritual behavior in which something is destroyed or killed, in the belief that supernatural powers are somehow unleashed.

Sanction Any type of social pressure in the form of "reward" or "punishment" that can be imposed on people to influence and control their behavior.

Sati The traditional Indian practice in which a widow commits suicide by throwing herself on her dead husband's funeral pyre.

Secondary innovation An invention or discovery that uses or combines existing ideas, objects, or techniques in novel arrangements.

Self The more or less enduring, bounded, and discrete part of an individual's identity or personality, and the reflexive awareness of this aspect of oneself.

Self-determination The concept that groups with a distinct culture and identity have a right to choose their own political arrangements and their own collective destiny.

Semantics The study of meaning in language. *See morphology*.

Semi-periphery In world systems theory, the category of states that are not as poor and dependent as the periphery states but that are not as rich and influential as the core states.

Separatism A movement that has as its goal the cultural and/or political disengagement of two groups or societies. A separatist movement often struggles to detach its territory from a multicultural or plural state and establish its own state.

Serial monogamy The marriage practice of having only one spouse at a time but perhaps having more than one spouse, at different times, during one's life.

Sexual dimorphism The occurrence of two physically distinct forms of a species, based on sexual characteristics as well as non-sexual ones such as body size.

Shaman A religious specialist, often part-time, who has personal power, based on unique life experiences or apprenticeship to a senior shaman, to communicate, interact, and sometimes struggle with supernatural beings or forces. Often a healer.

Slash-and-burn A horticultural practice in which trees and underbrush are cut, left to dry, and then burned as preparation for planting a garden. Also known as *swidden*.

Social assimilation A form of assimilation in which groups are integrated into the society (for instance, sharing the same jobs or the same neighborhoods), whether or not they share the same culture.

Social control   The political and general social function of getting members of a group to conform to expectations and rules and to obey authorities. Includes inculcating of social values as well as punishment of deviance from expectations.

Social impact analysis   A fieldwork study of the consequences that a development project or other social change policies have on the affected peoples.

Social mobility   The possibility or ease with which one may change position in the social stratification system.

Social reproduction   The maintenance and perpetuation of society beyond mere childbearing, including enculturation and teaching of members to take their place in society and day-to-day activities to allow members of the society to perform their specified tasks (including what is sometimes called "housework").

Social stratification   The division of a society into distinct and unequal groups or classes.

Socialization   From an anthropological point of view, a synonym for enculturation.

Society   A group of humans who live in relative proximity to each other, tend to marry each other more than people outside the group, and share a set of beliefs and behaviors.

Sociocultural appraisal   A study examining the *appropriateness* of a development or other social change project, its likely *impact* on the various groups affected by it, and the distribution of the benefits that accrue from it.

Sociolinguistics   *See pragmatics.*

Sorcerer   A religious specialist who uses techniques, including spells and potions, to achieve supernatural effects.

Sororal polygyny   The marriage practice in which a man marries two or more sisters.

Sororate   A marriage practice in which a woman is expected to marry the husband of her sister in the event of the married sister's death.

Soul   A religious concept of a non-material component or components of a living human. It is widely believed that a soul survives the death of the body, at least temporarily, and continues in another form of existence.

Sphere of influence   In European colonial practice, an area of foreign territory where the power and authority of one European state was recognized.

State   A political system or level of integration in which a formal centralized government has power over a delimited territory to make and enforce laws, to establish currency and collect taxes, and to maintain an army and declare war.

State terrorism   The use of force and terror by a state government against its own people – either a particular group or minority within the state or the entire population.

Structural assimilation   *See social assimilation.*

Structural adjustment   A development policy requiring that the governments which receive development aid must make certain changes to their economic and political practices, such as cutting spending, abolishing subsidies, deregulating business, privatizing previously state-run enterprises, and removing price controls.

Structural functionalism The theory that the function of a cultural trait, particularly an institution, is the creation and preservation of social order and social integration.

Structuralism The theory (associated most closely with Claude Lévi-Strauss) that the significance of an item (word, role, practice, belief) is not so much in the particular item but in its relationship to others. In other words, the "structure" of multiple items and the location of any one in relation to others is most important.

Structured interview A fieldwork method in which the anthropologist administers a prepared set of questions to an informant/consultant.

Subculture A group or subset within a society that is distinguished by some unique aspects of its behavior (such as clothing styles, linguistic usages, or beliefs and values).

Swidden *See slash-and-burn.*

Symbol An object, gesture, sound, or image that "stands for" some other idea or concept or object. Something that has "meaning," particularly when the meaning is arbitrary and conventional, and thus culturally relative.

Symbolic anthropology The school of thought (often associated with Clifford Geertz and Victor Turner) that the main goal of anthropology is to elucidate the meanings within which humans live and behave. Rather than focusing on institutions and rules, it focuses on symbols and how symbols shape our experience and are manipulated by people in social situations.

Symbolic capital "Resources" that humans can use to influence situations and affect other people's behavior that are not "material" or "economic." These can include knowledge, social relationships/debts, prestige, and so on.

Sympathetic magic The belief and practice that objects which have something in common with each other (e.g., same shape or texture) have some supernatural connection with each other.

Syncretism A type of revitalization movement in which elements of two or more cultural sources are blended into a new and more satisfying cultural arrangement.

Syntax The rules in a language for how words are combined to make intelligible utterances of speech acts (for example, sentences). Also known as grammar.

Terra nullius The colonial doctrine of "empty land," that colonized land was empty of human inhabitants and therefore could be claimed and settled by colonists.

Theism The religious belief in one or more god(s).

Third World A term sometimes used to refer to the economically poor, politically and militarily weak, relatively unstable, and dependent states of the world, most of which emerged from colonialism in fairly recent history.

Totemism A religious conception that human individuals or groups have a symbolic or spiritual connection with particular natural species, objects, or phenomena.

Tradition Some practice or idea or object that is (at least believed to be) continuous or associated with "the past." A tradition may be very ancient or very recent, but as an ideological element it is often assumed to be important, authentic, and even "superior" to non-traditional (especially foreign) practices, ideas, and objects.

Travesti An alternate gender role in Brazil, in which males take on certain physical traits and sexual behaviors typically associated with females.

Tribe A political system or level of integration in which multiple local communities may be organized into a single system but in which political power is still relatively informal and usually flows from institutions that are not specifically political (such as elders, lineages, age sets, religious specialists, and so on).

Unilineal descent A principle in which individuals trace their ancestry through a "line" of related kin (typically a male or a female line) such that some "blood" relatives are included in the descent group or lineage and other relatives are excluded from it.

Unstructured interview A fieldwork method in which the anthropologist conducts a relatively free-flowing conversation with an informant/consultant, either without prepared questions or unconstrained by these questions.

Vitalism *See modernism.*

Vocalizations Non-linguistic sounds that can accompany and affect the meaning of speech.

Witch A religious specialist, often conceived as a human with a supernatural ability to harm others, sometimes through possession of an unnatural bodily organ or an unnatural personality. Sometimes viewed as an antisocial and even anti-human type who causes misfortune out of excessive greed or anger or jealousy.

World anthropologies The perspective that anthropology as developed and practiced in the West is not the only form of anthropology, and that other societies may develop and practice other types of anthropology based on their specific experiences and interests.

World systems theory The theory that explains the ongoing poverty and low standard of living in Third World states as the effect of external arrangements and relationships, specifically the global economic and political practices and institutions set up by the "core" of rich, powerful, industrialized states that function to their own advantage but to the disadvantage of the poor, weak, "peripheral" states.

Bibliography

Abu-Lughod, Lila. 1985. "Honor and Sentiments of Loss in a Bedouin Society." *American Ethnologist* 12 (2): 245–61.

Alexie, Sherman. 1994. *The Lone Ranger and Tonto Fistfight in Heaven*. New York: HarperPerennial.

Allison, Anne. 1997. "Japanese Mothers and *Obentos*: The Lunch-box as Ideological State Apparatus." In Carole Counihan and Penny van Esterick, eds. *Food and Culture: A Reader*. New York and London: Routledge, 296–314.

American Anthropological Association. 1939 [1938]. "Resolution of December 1938." *Science* 89 (2298): 30.

American Anthropological Association. 1998. "AAA Statement on Race." *American Anthropologist* 100 (3): 712–13.

Anderson, Benedict. 1983. *Imagined Communities: Reflections of the Origin and Spread of Nationalism*. London: Verso.

Anderson, Walter Truett. 1990. *Reality Isn't What It Used to Be: Theatrical Politics, Ready-to-wear Religion, Global Myths, Primitive Chic, and Other Wonders of the Postmodern World*. New York: Harper.

Apter, David E. 1968. *Some Conceptual Approaches to the Study of Modernization*. Englewood Cliffs, NJ: Prentice Hall.

Aran, Gideon. 1991. "Jewish Zionist Fundamentalism: The Bloc of the Faithful in Israel (Gush Emunim)." In Martin Marty and R. Scott Appleby, eds. *Fundamentalisms Observed*. Chicago: The University of Chicago Press, 265–344.

Arendt, Hannah. 1969. *On Violence*. New York: Harcourt, Brace, & World.

Arnold, Matthew. 1971 [1869]. *Culture and Anarchy: An Essay in Political and Social Criticism*. Indianapolis: Bobbs-Merrill.

Askew, Kelly and Richard R. Wilk, eds. 2002. *The Anthropology of Media: A Reader*. London: Blackwell Publishing.

Atkinson, Jane Monnig. 1984. "'Wrapped Words': Poetry and Politics among the Wana of Central Sulawesi, Indonesia." In Donald Brenneis and Fred R. Myers, eds. *Dangerous Words: Language and Politics in the Pacific*. Prospect Heights, IL: Waveland Press, 33–68.

Atran, Scott. 2002. *In Gods We Trust: The Evolutionary Landscape of Religion*. Oxford: Oxford University Press.

Auster, Lawrence. 1994. "The U.S. Must Restrict Immigration to Prevent Cultural Disintegration." In Fred Whitehead, ed. *Culture Wars: Opposing Viewpoints*. San Diego, CA: Greenhaven Press, 56–62.

Austin, J.L. 1962. *How To Do Things with Words*. Oxford: Clarendon Press.

Axtell, Roger E. 1991. *Gestures: The Do's and Taboos of Body Language Around the World*. New York: John Wiley & Sons.

Banton, Michael. 1987. *Racial Theories*. Cambridge: Cambridge University Press.

Barber, Benjamin. 1995. *Jihad versus McWorld*. New York: Times Books.

Barreiro, Jose. 1993. *The Indian Chronicles*. Houston: Arte Publico Press.

Barth, Fredrik. 1965. *Nomads of South Persia: The Basseri Tribe of the Khamseh Confederacy*. New York: Humanities Press.

Barth, Fredrik, ed. 1969. *Ethnic Groups and Boundaries*. Boston: Little, Brown & Co.

Barthes, Roland. 1997. "Toward a Psychosociology of Contemporary Food Consumption." In Carole Counihan and Penny van Esterick, eds. *Food and Culture: A Reader*. New York and London: Routledge, 20–7.

Basso, Keith H. 1970. *The Cibecue Apache*. New York: Holt, Rinehart, & Winston.

Bauman, Richard. 2001. "Verbal Art in Performance." In Alessandro Duranti, ed. *Linguistic Anthropology: A Reader*. Malden, MA, and Oxford: Blackwell Publishing, 165–88.

Beals, Alan R. 1980. *Gopalpur: A South Indian Village*. New York: Holt, Rinehart, & Winston.

Beidelman, T.O. 1971. *The Kaguru: A Matrilineal People of East Africa*. New York: Holt, Rinehart, & Winston.

Bell, Diane. 1993. *Daughters of the Dreaming*, 2nd edn. Minneapolis: University of Minnesota Press.

Bellah, Robert N. 1967. "Civil Religion in America." *Daedalus* 96 (1): 1–21.

Benedict, Ruth. 1934. *Patterns of Culture*. New York: The New American Library.

Benedict, Ruth. 1946. *The Chrysanthemum and the Sword*. Boston: Houghton Mifflin.

Benet, Sula. 1974. *Abkhasians: The Long-living People of the Caucasus*. New York: Holt, Rinehart, & Winston.

Berlin, Brent and Paul Kay. 1969. *Basic Color Terms: Their Universality and Evolution*. Berkeley: University of California Press.

Beuchat, P.D. 1957. "Riddles in Bantu." *African Studies* 16: 133–49.

Bloch, Maurice. 1983. *Marxism and Anthropology: The History of a Relationship*. Oxford: Clarendon Press.

Bloch, Maurice. 1989 [1979]. *Ritual, History, and Power: Selected Papers in Anthropology*. London: Athlone Press.

Boas, Franz. 1896. "The Limitations of the Comparative Method of Anthropology." *Science* 4: 901–8.

Boas, Franz. 1928. *Anthropology and Modern Life*. New York: W. W. Norton & Co.

Bodley, John. 1975. *Victims of Progress*. Menlo Park, CA: Cummings.

Bodley, John. 1985. *Anthropology and Contemporary Human Problems*, 2nd edn. Palo Alto and London: Mayfield Publishing Co.

Bogardus, Emory. 1933. "A Social Distance Scale." *Sociology and Social Research* 17: 65–71.

Boites, Salvadore Z., Pamela Geller, and Thomas C. Patterson. n.d. "The Growth and Changing Composition of Anthropology 1966–2002." www.aaanet.org/ar/changing_composition.pdf, accessed November 21, 2005.

Bonta, Bruce. 1997. "Cooperation and Competition in Peaceful Societies." *Psychological Bulletin* 121: 299–320.

Boswell, John. 1994. *Same-sex Union in Premodern Europe*. New York: Villard Books.

Bourdieu, Pierre. 1977. *Outline of a Theory of Practice*. Cambridge, MA: Cambridge University Press.

Boyer, Pascal. 2001. *Religion Explained: The Evolutionary Origins of Religious Thought*. New York: Basic Books.

Brenneis, Donald. 1984. "Straight Talk and Sweet Talk: Political Discourse in an Occasionally Egalitarian Community." In Donald Brenneis and Fred R. Myers, eds. *Dangerous Words: Language and Politics in the Pacific*. Prospect Heights, IL: Waveland Press, 69–84.

Briggs, Jean. 1970. *Never in Anger: Portrait of an Eskimo Family*. Cambridge, MA: Harvard University Press.

Brown, Judith K. 1975. "Iroquois Women: An Ethnohistoric Note." In Rayna R. Reiter, ed. *Toward an Anthropology of Women*. New York and London: Monthly Review Press, 235–51.

Brown, Katherine Tandy. 2000. "Cultural or Heritage – This Tourism is Hot!" http://www.grouptraveler.com/roundups/6-00.html, accessed July 26, 2005.

Brown, Michael. 2003. *Who Owns Native Culture?* Cambridge, MA, and London: Harvard University Press.

Budiansky, Stephen. 2005. "Truth Extraction." *The Atlantic Monthly* June: 32–5.

Burgess, M. Elaine. 1978. "The Resurgence of Ethnicity: Myth or Reality?" *Ethnic and Racial Studies* 1: 265–85.

Cassirer, Ernst. 1954. *An Essay on Man: An Introduction to a Philosophy of Human Culture*. Garden City, NY: Doubleday & Co.

Chagnon, Napoleon. 1992. *Yanomamo*, 4th edn. Fort Worth, TX: Harcourt Brace College Publishers.

Chatters, James C. 2002. *Ancient Encounters: Kennewick Man and the First Americans*. New York: Simon & Schuster.

Chavez, Leo R. 1998. *Shadowed Lives: Undocumented Immigrants in American Society*. Fort Worth, TX: Harcourt Brace College Publishers.

Chua, Amy. 2003. *World on Fire: How Exporting Free Market Democracy Breeds Ethnic Hatred and Global Instability*. New York: Anchor Books.

Clammer, John. 1973. "Colonialism and the Perception of Tradition in Fiji." In Talal Asad, ed. *Anthropology and the Colonial Encounter*. New York: Humanities Press, 199–220.

Clarkson, Frederick. 2005. "Christian Reconstructionism: Theocratic Dominionism Gains Influence." http://www.axisoflogic.com/artman/publish/article_18836.shtml, accessed July 26, 2005.

Claxton, Nicholas. 1989. *The Price of Progress*. Oley, PA: Bullfrog Films.

Clifford, James. 1994. "Diasporas." *Cultural Anthropology* 9 (3): 302–38.

Clifford, James and George Marcus, eds. 1986. *Writing Culture: The Poetics and Politics of Ethnography*. Berkeley: University of California Press.

Cohen, Lawrence. 2005. "The Kothi Wars: AIDS and Cosmopolitanism and the Morality of Classification." In Vincanne Adams and Stacy Leigh Pigg, eds. *Sex in Development: Science, Sexuality, and Morality in Global Perspective*. Durham, NC, and London: Duke University Press, 269–303.

Cohen, Robin. 1997. *Global Diasporas: An Introduction*. Seattle: University of Washington Press.

Collins, Francis S. 2004. "What We Do and Don't Know about 'Race,' 'Ethnicity,' Genetics, and Health at the Dawn of the Genome Era." *Nature Genetics* Supplement 36 (11): S 13–15.

Colson, Elizabeth. 2003. "Forced Migration and the Anthropological Response." *Journal of Refugee Studies* 16 (1): 1–18.

Connor, Walker. 1994. *Ethnonationalism: The Quest for Understanding*. Princeton: Princeton University Press.

Conover, Ted. 1987. *Coyotes: A Journey Through the Secret World of America's Illegal Aliens*. New York: Vintage.

Conover, Ted. 2001. *New Jack: Guarding Sing Sing*. New York: Random House.

Coontz, Stephanie. 1992. *The Way We Never Were: American Families and the Nostalgia Trap*. New York: Basic Books.

Counihan, Carole and Penny Van Esterick, eds. 1997. *Food and Culture: A Reader*. New York: Routledge.

Coupland, Nikolas. 2007. *Style: Language Variation and Identity*. Cambridge: Cambridge University Press.

Crapanzano, Vincent. 1992. *Hermes' Dilemma and Hamlet's Desire: On the Epistemology of Interpretation*. Cambridge, MA: Harvard University Press.

Crystal, David. 1987. *The Cambridge Encyclopedia of Language*. Cambridge and New York: Cambridge University Press.

Daniel, G. Reginald. 2005. "White into Black: Race and National Identity in Contemporary Brazil." In Paul Spickard, ed. *Race and Nation: Ethnic Systems in the Modern World*. New York and London: Routledge, 87–113.

Darian-Smith, Eve. 2004. *New Capitalists: Law, Politics, and Identity Surrounding Casino Gambling on Native American Land*. Belmont, CA: Wadsworth Publishing.

Davis, J. 1992. "The Anthropology of Suffering." *Journal of Refugee Studies* 5 (2): 149–61.

De Caro, F.A. 1986. "Riddles and Proverbs." In Elliott Oring, ed. *Folk Groups and Folklore Genres: An Introduction*. Logan: Utah State University Press, 175–97.

Deger, Jennifer. 2006. *Shimmering Screens: Making Media in an Aboriginal Community*. Minneapolis: University of Minnesota Press.

Deng, Francis Mading. 1972. *The Dinka of the Sudan*. New York: Holt, Rinehart, & Winston.

Dentan, Robert Knox. 1968. *The Semai: A Non-violent People of Malaya*. New York: Holt, Rinehart, & Winston.

DeVos, George. 1975. "Ethnic Pluralism: Conflict and Accommodation." In George DeVos and Lola Romanucci-Ross, eds. *Ethnic Identity: Cultural Continuities and Change*. Palo Alto: Mayfield Publishing, 5–41.

DeVos, George and Hiroshi Wagatsumo. 1966. *Japan's Invisible Race: Caste in Culture and Personality*. Berkeley: University of California Press.

Dharmadasa, K.N.O. 1992. *Language, Religion, and Ethnic Assertiveness: The Growth of Sinhalese Nationalism in Sri Lanka*. Ann Arbor: University of Michigan Press.

Diamond, Stanley. 1972 [1969]. "Anthropology in Question." In Dell Hymes, ed. *Reinventing Anthropology*. New York: Random House, 401–29.

Douglas, Mary. 1966. *Purity and Danger: An Analysis of the Concepts of Pollution and Taboo*. London: Routledge & Kegan Paul.

Douglas, Mary. 1975. *Implicit Meanings: Essays in Anthropology*. London and Boston: Routledge & Kegan Paul.

Downs, James F. 1972. *The Navajo*. New York: Holt, Rinehart, & Winston.

Dundes, Alan. 1965. "What is Folklore?" In Alan Dundes, ed. *The Study of Folklore*. Englewood Cliffs, NJ: Prentice-Hall, 1–3.

Durkheim, Emile. 1965 [1915]. *The Elementary Forms of the Religious Life*. New York: The Free Press.

Dussart, Francoise. 2000. *The Politics of Ritual in an Aboriginal Settlement: Kinship, Gender, and the Currency of Knowledge*. Washington, DC, and London: Smithsonian Institution Press.

Eisenstadt, N.S. 1999. "Multiple Modernities in an Age of Globalization." *Canadian Journal of Sociology* 24 (2): 283–95.

Eisenstadt, N.S. 2000. "Multiple Modernities." *Daedalus* 129 (1): 1–29.

Eissenstat, Howard. 2005. "Metaphors of Race and Discourse of Nation: Racial Theory and State Nationalism in the First Decades of the Turkish Republic." In Paul Spickard, ed. *Race and Nation: Ethnic Systems in the Modern World*. New York and London: Routledge, 239–56.

Eller, Jack David. 1999. *From Culture to Ethnicity to Conflict: An Anthropological Perspective on International Ethnic Conflict*. Ann Arbor: University of Michigan Press.

Eller, Jack David. 2005. *Violence and Culture: A Cross-cultural and Interdisciplinary Approach*. Belmont, CA: Wadsworth Publishing.

Engle, Gary. 1987. "What Makes Superman So Darned American?" In Gary Engle and Dennis Dooley, eds. *Superman at Fifty: The Persistence of a Legend*. Cleveland: Octavia Press, 79–87.

Ehrenreich, Barbara. 2002. *Nickel and Dimed: On (Not) Getting By in America*. New York: Owl Books/Henry Holt.

Eriksen, Thomas Hylland. 2002 [1993]. *Ethnicity and Nationalism: Anthropological Perspectives*. London: Pluto Press.

Ervin, Alexander M. 2000. *Applied Anthropology: Tools and Perspectives for Contemporary Practice*. Boston, MA: Allyn and Bacon.

Estioko-Griffin, Agnes and P. Bion Griffin. 2002. "Woman the Hunter: The Agta." In Caroline Brettell and Carolyn Sargent, eds. *Gender in Cross-cultural Perspective*. Englewood Cliffs, NJ: Prentice-Hall, 206–15.

Evans-Pritchard, E.E. 1937. *Witchcraft, Oracles, and Magic Among the Azande*. New York: Oxford University Press.

Evans-Pritchard, E.E. 1951. *Kinship and Marriage among the Nuer*. New York: Oxford University Press.

Evans-Pritchard, E.E. 1956. *Nuer Religion*. Oxford: Oxford University Press.

Evans-Pritchard, E.E. 1962. *Social Anthropology and Other Essays*. New York: The Free Press.

Fanon, Frantz. 1963. *The Wretched of the Earth*. trans. Constance Farrington. New York: Grove Press.

Feinberg, Richard. 1996. "Spirit Encounters on a Polynesian Outlier: Anuta, Solomon Islands." In Jeannette Marie Mageo and Alan Howard, eds. *Spirits in Culture, History, and Mind*. New York and London: Routledge, 99–120.

Finkelstein, Marni. 2005. *With No Direction Home: Homeless Youth on the Road and in the Streets*. Belmont, CA: Wadsworth Publishing.

Firth, Raymond. 1975. "Speech-making and Authority in Tikopia." In Maurice Bloch, ed. *Political Language and Oratory in Traditional Society*. London: Academic Press, 29–43.

Foley, William A. 1997. *Anthropological Linguistics: An Introduction*. London: Blackwell Publishers.

Fortes, Meyer and E.E. Evans-Pritchard, eds. 1940. *African Political Systems*. London: Oxford University Press.

Frake, Charles. 1962. *The Ethnographic Study of Cognitive Systems. Anthropology and Human Behavior*. Washington, DC: Society of Washington.

Frank, André Gundar. 1966. "The Development of Underdevelopment." *Monthly Review* 18: 17–31.

Frank, André Gundar. 1979. *Dependent Accumulation and Underdevelopment*. New York and London: Monthly Review Press.

Frazer, James George. 1958 [1922]. *The Golden Bough: A Study in Magic and Religion*. New York: Macmillan.

Freudenthal, Hans. 1973. *Mathematics as an Educational Task*. Dordrecht: Reidel.

Fried, Morton H. 1967. *The Evolution of Political Society: An Essay in Political Anthropology*. New York: Random House.

Friedl, Ernestine. 1975. *Women and Men*. New York: Holt, Rinehart, & Winston.

Friedl, Ernestine. 1978. "Society and Sex Roles." *Human Nature* 1 (6): 68–75.

Friedman, John Block. 2000. *The Monstrous Races in Medieval Art and Thought*. Syracuse: Syracuse University Press.

Friedman, Thomas. 2005. *The World is Flat: A Brief History of the Twenty-first Century*. New York: Farrar, Straus, & Giroux.

Fry, Douglas P. 2006. *The Human Potential for Peace: An Anthropological Challenge to Assumptions about War and Violence*. New York and Oxford: Oxford University Press.

Fukuyama, Francis. 1992. *The End of History and the Last Man*. New York: The Free Press.

Furnivall, J.S. 1956. *Colonial Policy and Practice: A Comparative Study of Burma and Netherlands India*. New York: New York University Press.

Gallup, Jr., Gordon G. 1970. "Chimpanzee Self-recognition." *Science* 167: 86–7.

Gamst, Frederick C. 1969. *The Qemant: A Pagan-Hebraic Peasantry of Ethiopia*. New York: Holt, Rinehart, & Winston.

Garfinkel, Harold. 1967. *Studies in Ethnomethodology*. Englewood Cliffs, NJ: Prentice-Hall.

Geertz, Clifford, ed. 1963. *Old Societies and New States: The Quest for Modernity in Asia and Africa*. New York: The Free Press.

Geertz, Clifford. 1973. *The Interpretation of Cultures*. New York: Basic Books.

Geertz, Clifford. 1976. "'From the Native's Point of View': On the Nature of Anthropological Understanding." In Keith Basso and Henry A. Selby, eds. *Meaning in Anthropology*. Albuquerque: University of New Mexico Press, 221–37.

Geertz, Clifford. 1980. *Negara: The Theatre State in Nineteenth-century Bali*. Princeton: Princeton University Press.

Gellner, Ernest. 1988. *Plough, Sword, and Book: The Structure of Human History*. Chicago: The University of Chicago Press.

Gershoy, Leo. 1957. *The Era of the French Revolution 1789–1799*. Princeton, NJ: D. Van Nostrand Co.

Gill, Sam D. 1981. *Sacred Words: A Study of Navajo Religion and Prayer*. Westport, CT: Greenwood Press.

Gilroy, Paul. 1993. *The Black Atlantic: Modernity and Double*

Consciousness. Cambridge, MA: Harvard University Press.

Gitlin, Todd. 1995. *The Twilight of Common Dreams: Why America is Wracked by Culture Wars*. New York: Metropolitan.

Gittleman, Maury and Mary Joyce. 1995. "Earnings Mobility in the United States, 1967–91." *Monthly Labor Review* September: 3–13.

Givens, David B., Patsy Evans, and Timothy Jablonski. 2000. "1997 American Anthropological Association Summary of Anthropology Ph.D.s." www.aaanet.org/surveys/97survey.htm, accessed November 21, 2005.

Gluckman, Max. 1956. *Custom and Conflict in Africa*. Oxford: Blackwell.

Godelier, Maurice. 1978. *Perspectives in Marxist Anthropology*. Cambridge: Cambridge University Press.

Goldman, Irving. 2004. *Cubeo Hehenewa Religious Thought: Metaphysics of a Northwestern Amazonian People*. New York: Columbia University Press.

Goodall, Jane. 1986. *The Chimpanzees of Gombe: Patterns of Behavior*. Cambridge, MA: Harvard University Press.

Goodenough, Ward H. 1956. "Componential Analysis and The Study of Meaning." *Language* 32: 195–216.

Gould, Drusilla and Christopher Loether. 2002. *An Introduction to the Shoshoni Language*. Salt Lake City: The University of Utah Press.

Grant, Madison. 1916. *The Passing of the Great Race; Or the Racial Basis of European History*. New York: Charles Scribner's Sons.

Gray, John. 1992. *Men are from Mars, Women are from Venus: A Practical Guide for Improving Communication and Getting What You Want in Your Relationships*. New York: HarperCollins Publishers.

Grayzel, John. 1986. "Libido and Development: The Importance of Emotions in Development Work." In Michael M. Horowitz and Thomas M. Painter, eds. *Anthropology and Rural Development in West Africa*. Boulder: Westview Press, 147–65.

Greeley, Andrew. 1971. *Why Can't They Be Like Us?: America's White Ethnic Groups*. New York: E.P. Dutton & Co.

Green, John C. 1959. *The Death of Adam: Evolution and its Impact on Western Thought*. Ames, IA: The Iowa State University Press.

Gregory, C.A. 1982. *Gifts and Commodities*. London: Academic Press.

Grémaux, Réné. 1994. "Woman Becomes Man in the Balkans." In Gilbert Herdt, ed. *Third Sex, Third Gender: Beyond Sexual Dimorphism in Culture and History*. New York: Zone Books, 241–81.

Griaule, Marcel. 1965. *Conversations with Ogotemelli: An Introduction to Dogon Religious Ideas*. London: Oxford University Press.

Guidieri, Remo and Francesco Pellizi. 1988. "Introduction: 'Smoking Mirrors' – Modern Polity and Ethnicity." In Remo Guidieri, Francesco Pellizi, and Stanley Tambiah, eds. *Ethnicities and Nations: Processes of Interethnic Relations in Latin America, Southeast Asia, and the Pacific*. Austin: University of Texas Press, 7–38.

Gurr, Ted Robert and Barbara Harff. 1994. *Ethnic Conflict in World Politics*. Boulder: Westview Press.

Haller Jr., John S. 1971. *Outcasts from Evolution: Scientific Attitudes of Racial Inferiority, 1859–1900*. Carbondale and Edwardsville: Southern Illinois University Press.

Halliday, M.A.K. 1976. "Anti-languages." *American Anthropologist* 78: 570–84.

Hallowell, A. Irving. 1967 [1955]. *Culture and Experience*. New York: Schocken Books.

Harlow, Harry. 1959. "Love in Infant Monkeys." *Scientific American* 200 (6): 68–74.

Harrell-Bond, Barbara E. 1986. *Imposing Aid: Emergency Assistance to Refugees*. Oxford: Oxford University Press.

Harrell-Bond, Barbara E. and E. Voutira. 1992. "Anthropology and the Study of Refugees." *Anthropology Today* 8 (4): 6–10.

Harris, Marvin. 1968. *The Rise of Anthropological Theory*. New York: Thomas Y. Crowell.

Harris, Marvin. 1974. *Cows, Pigs, Wars, and Witches: The Riddles of Culture*. New York: Random House.

Harris, Marvin. 1979. *Cultural Materialism: The Struggle for a Science of Culture*. New York: Random House.

Hart, C.W.M. and Arnold R. Pilling. 1960. *The Tiwi of North Australia*. New York: Holt, Rinehart, & Winston.

Heald, Suzette. 1986. "The Ritual Use of Violence: Circumcision among the Gisu of Uganda." In David Riches, ed. *The Anthropology of Violence*. Oxford: Blackwell, 70–85.

Hedges, Chris. 2002. *War is a Force that Gives Us Meaning*. New York: Public Affairs.

Hefner, Robert W. 1998. "Multiple Modernities: Christianity, Islam, and Hinduism in a Globalizing Age." *Annual Review of Anthropology* 27: 83–104.

Heider, Karl. 1979. *Grand Valley Dani: Peaceful Warriors*. New York: Holt, Rinehart, & Winston.

Herdt, Gilbert. 1987 [1981]. *Guardians of the Flutes: Idioms of Masculinity*. New York: Columbia University Press.

Herdt, Gilbert. 1994. "Introduction: Third Sexes and Third Genders." In Gilbert Herdt, ed. *Third Sex, Third Gender: Beyond Sexual Dimorphism in Culture and History*. New York: Zone Books, 21–81.

Herodotus. 1942. *The Persian Wars*, trans. George Rawlinson. New York: Modern Library.

Herodotus. 1972. *The Histories*, trans. Aubrey de Selincourt. Revised with introduction and notes by A.R. Burn. London: Penguin Books.

Herskovits, Melville J. 1958 [1941]. *The Myth of the Negro Past*. Boston: Beacon Press.

Himpele, Jeff D. 2008. *Circuits of Culture: Media, Politics, and Indigenous Identity in the Andes*. Minneapolis: University of Minnesota Press.

Hine, Thomas. 2003. *I Want That!: How We All Became Shoppers*. New York: Perennial.

Hoben, Allan. 1986. "Assessing the Social Feasibility of a Settlement Project in North Cameroon." In Michael M. Horowitz and Thomas M. Painter, eds. *Anthropology and Rural Development in West Africa*. Boulder: Westview Press, 169–94.

Hobsbawm, Eric and Terence Ranger, eds. 1983. *The Invention of Tradition*. Cambridge: Cambridge University Press.

Hockett, Charles F. 1958. *A Course in Modern Linguistics*. New York: Macmillan.

Hockett, Charles F. 1977. *The View from Language: Selected Essays, 1948–1974*. Athens: University of Georgia Press.

Hoebel, E. Adamson. 1960. *The Cheyennes Indians of the Great Plains*. New York: Holt, Rinehart, & Winston.

Hoffman, Susanna M. and Anthony Oliver-Smith, eds. 2002. *Catastrophe and Culture: The Anthropology of Disaster*. Santa Fe: School of American Research Press.

Hook, Stephen. 1996. "Introduction: Foreign Aid in a Transformed World." In Stephen Hook, ed. *Foreign Aid Toward the Millennium*. Boulder: Lynne Rienner, 1–16.

Horowitz, David. 1985. *Ethnic Groups in Conflict*. Berkeley: University of California Press.

Horton, Robin. 1960. "A Definition of Religion, and its Uses." *The Journal of the Royal Anthropological Institute of Great Britain and Ireland* 90 (2): 201–26.

Howes, David, ed. 1996. *Cross-cultural Consumption: Global Markets, Local Realities*. London and New York: Routledge.

Hua Cai. 2001 [1997]. *A Society without Fathers or Husbands: The Na of China*, trans. Asti Hustvedt. New York: Zone Books.

Huntington, Samuel. 1996. *The Clash of Civilizations and the Remaking of World Order*. New York: Simon & Schuster.

Huxley, Julian and A.C. Haddon. 1935. *We Europeans: A Survey of 'Racial' Problems*. London: Jonathan Cape.

Hymes, Dell, ed. 1972 [1969]. *Reinventing Anthropology*. New York: Random House.

Igoe, Jim. 2004. *Conservation and Globalization: A Study of National Parks and Indigenous Communities from East Africa to South Dakota*. Belmont, CA: Wadsworth Publishing.

Johnson, William. 1994. *A Canadian Myth: Quebec, Between Canada and the Illusion of Utopia*. Montreal: R. Davies.

Kardam, Nuket. 1993. "Development Approaches and the Role of Policy Advocacy: The Case of the World Bank." *World Development* 21 (11): 1773–86.

Katz, Richard. 1982. *Boiling Energy: Community Healing Among the Kalahari Kung*. Cambridge, MA, and London: Harvard University Press.

Kauffman, L.A. 1990. "The Anti-politics of Identity." *Socialist Review* 90 (1): 67–80.

Kawai, Masao. 1965. "Newly-acquired Pre-cultural Behavior of the Natural Troops of Japanese Monkeys on Koshima Islet." *Primates* 6: 1–30.

Kearney, M. 1995. "The Local and the Global: The Anthropology of Globalization and Transnationalism." *Annual Review of Anthropology* 24: 547–65.

Keeler, Ward. 1983. "Shame and Stage Fright in Java." *Ethos* 11 (3): 152–65.

Keen, Ian. 1994. *Knowledge and Secrecy in an Aboriginal Religion*. Melbourne and Oxford: Oxford University Press.

Kelly, Raymond. 1977. *Etoro Social Structure*. Ann Arbor: University of Michigan Press.

Kiefer, Thomas M. 1972. *The Tausug: Violence and Law in a Philippine Moslem Society*. New York: Holt, Rinehart, & Winston.

Klima, George J. 1970. *The Barabaig: East Africa Cattle-herders*. New York: Holt, Rinehart, & Winston.

Kosmin, Barry A., Egon Mayer, and Ariela Keysar. 2001. *American Religious Identification Survey*. New York: The Graduate Center of the City University of New York.

Kulick, Don. 1997. "The Gender of Brazilian Transgendered Prostitutes." *American Anthropologist* 95: 574–85.

Kummer, Hans. 1995. *In Quest of the Sacred Baboon*. Princeton: Princeton University Press.

Kuper, Adam. 1983. *Anthropology and Anthropologists: The Modern British School*, revised edn. London and New York: Routledge.

Kuper, Adam. 1988. *The Invention of Primitive Society: Transformations of an Illusion*. London: Routledge.

Kuper, Hilda. 1963. *The Swazi: A South African Kingdom*. New York: Holt, Rinehart, & Winston.

Lakoff, Robin. 1975. *Language and Woman's Place*. New York: Harper.

Lambek, Michael. 1981. *Human Spirits: A Cultural Account of Trance in Mayotte*. Cambridge: Cambridge University Press.

Lamont, Lansing. 1994. *Breakup: The Coming End of Canada and the Stakes for America*. New York: Norton.

Lane, Harlan. 1977. *The Wild Boy of Aveyron*. New York: Bantam Books.

Lane, Harlan, Robert Hoffmeister, and Ben Bahan. 1996. *A Journey into Deaf-world*. San Diego: Dawn Sign Press.

Langer, Suzanne K. 1942. *Philosophy in a New Key: A Study in the Symbolism of Reason, Rite, and Art*. New York: Mentor Books.

Laqueur, Thomas. 1990. *Making Sex: Body and Gender from the Greeks to Freud*. Cambridge, MA: Harvard University Press.

Lawrence, Peter. 1964. *Road Belong Cargo*. Manchester: Manchester University Press.

Leach, Edmund R. 1954. *Political Systems of Highland Burma*. Boston: Beacon Press.

Leakey, Louis S.B. 1930. *Some Notes on the Masai of Kenya Colony*. London: Royal Anthropological Institute of Great Britain and Ireland 60: 185–209.

Le Blanc, Steven A., with Katherine E. Register. 2003. *Constant Battles: The Myth of the Peaceful, Noble Savage*. New York: St. Martin's Press.

Lee, Dorothy. 1959. *Freedom and Culture*. Englewood Cliffs, NJ: Prentice-Hall.

Lee, Richard. 1984. *The Dobe !Kung*. New York: Holt, Rinehart, & Winston.

Lemarchand, René. 1970. *Rwanda and Burundi*. New York: Praeger.

Lenski, Gerhard and Jean Lenski. 1982. *Human Societies: An Introduction to Macrosociology*, 4th edn. New York: McGraw-Hill.

Lerner, Jimmy A. 2002. *You Got Nothing Coming: Notes from a Prison Fish*. New York: Broadway Books.

Lessa, William A. 1966. *Ulithi: A Micronesian Design for Living*. New York: Holt, Rinehart, & Winston.

Lévesque, René. 1968. *An Option for Quebec*. London: McClelland & Stewart.

Lévi-Strauss, Claude. 1978. *The Origin of Table Manners*. New York: Harper & Row.

Levison, Iain. 2002. *A Working Stiff's Manifesto: Confessions of a Wage Slave*. New York: Soho Press.

Levy, Andre. 2000. "Diasporas through Anthropological Lenses: Contexts of Postmodernity." *Diaspora* 9 (1): 137–57.

Lewellen, Ted C. 2002. *The Anthropology of Globalization: Cultural Anthropology Enters the 21st Century*. Westport, CT: Bergin & Garvey.

Lewontin, Richard C. 1972. "The Apportionment of Human Diversity." *Evolutionary Biology* 6: 381–98.

Lie, John. 2001. *Multiethnic Japan*. Cambridge, MA, and London: Harvard University Press.

Linton, Ralph. 1936. *The Study of Man*. New York: Appleton-Century.

Linton, Ralph, ed. 1945. *The Science of Man in the World Crisis*. New York: Columbia University Press.

Livingstone, Frank B. 1962. "On the Non-existence of Human Races." *Current Anthropology* 3 (3): 279–81.

Lorenz, Konrad. 1963. *On Aggression*, trans. Marjorie Kerr Wilson. New York: Bantam Books.

Lutz, Catherine A. 1998. *Unnatural Emotions: Everyday Sentiments on a Micronesian Atoll and their Challenge to Western Theory*. Chicago and London: The University of Chicago Press.

Maclean, Charles. 1979. *The Wolf Children: Fact or Fantasy?* Harmondsworth, UK: Penguin Books.

Mahmood, Cynthia Keppley. 1994. "Why Sikhs Fight." In Alvin W. Wolfe and Honggang Yang, eds. *Anthropological Contributions to Conflict Resolution*. Athens and London: The University of Georgia Press, 11–30.

Malinowski, Bronislaw. 1948. *Magic, Science, and Religion and Other Essays*. Garden City, NY: Doubleday Anchor Books.

Malinowski, Bronislaw. 1961 [1945]. *The Dynamics of Culture Change: An Inquiry into Race Relations in Africa*. New Haven and London: Yale University Press.

Malinowski, Bronislaw. 1964. "An Anthropological Analysis of War." In L. Bramson and G. Goethals, eds. *War: Studies from Psychology, Sociology, Anthropology*. New York: Basic Books, 245–68.

Malinowski, Bronislaw. 1984 [1922]. *Argonauts of the Western Pacific*. Long Grove, IL: Waveland Press.

Malkki, Liisa. 1995. *Purity and Exile: Violence, Memory, and National Cosmology among Hutu Refugees in Tanzania*. Chicago and London: The University of Chicago Press.

Maltz, Daniel N. and Ruth A. Borker. 1996. "A Cultural Approach to Male–Female Miscommunication." In Donald Brenneis and Ronald K. S. Macaulay, eds. *The Matrix of Language: Contemporary Linguistic Anthropology*. Boulder: Westview Press, 81–98.

Maquet, Jacques. 1961. *The Premise of Inequality in Rwanda: A Study of Political Relations in a Central African Kingdom*. London: Oxford University Press.

Marcus, George E. 1995. "Ethnography In/Of the World: The Emergence of Multi-sited Ethnography." *Annual Review of Anthropology* 24: 95–117.

Marcus, George E. and Michael M.J. Fischer. 1986. *Anthropology as Cultural Critique: An Experimental Moment in the Human Sciences*. Chicago: The University of Chicago Press.

Marsden, George M. 1990. "Defining American Fundamentalism." In Norman J. Cohen, ed. *The Fundamentalist Phenomenon: A View from Within, A Response from Without*. Grand Rapids: William B. Eerdmans Publishing Company, 22–37.

Maybury-Lewis, David. 2002. *Indigenous Peoples, Ethnic Groups, and the State*, 2nd edn. Boston: Allyn & Bacon.

McDowall, David. 1996. *A Modern History of the Kurds.* London: I.B. Tauris.

Mead, Margaret. 1928. *Coming of Age in Samoa: A Psychological Study of Primitive Youth for Western Civilization.* New York: W.W. Morrow.

Meigs, Anna. 1997. "Food as a Cultural Construction." In Carole Counihan and Penny van Esterick, eds. *Food and Culture: A Reader.* New York and London: Routledge, 95–106.

Messenger, Jr., John C. 1965. "The Role of Proverbs in a Nigerian Judicial System." In Alan Dundes, ed. *The Study of Folklore.* Englewood Cliffs, NJ: Prentice-Hall, 299–307.

Michaels, Eric. 1986. *The Aboriginal Invention of Television in Central Australia, 1982–1986.* Canberra: Australian Institute of Aboriginal Studies.

Miller, Daniel. 1998. *A Theory of Shopping.* Ithaca, NY: Cornell University Press.

Miller, Marc S., ed. 1993. *State of the Peoples: A Global Human Rights Report on Societies in Danger.* Boston: Beacon Press.

Mills, C. Wright. 1959. *The Sociological Imagination.* New York: Oxford University Press.

Montagu, M.F. Ashley. 1945. *Man's Most Dangerous Myth: The Fallacy of Race,* 2nd edn. New York: Columbia University Press.

Moodie, T. Dunbar. 2005. "Race and Ethnicity in South Africa." In Paul Spickard, ed. *Race and Nation: Ethnic Systems in the Modern World.* New York and London: Routledge, 319–35.

Moore, Wilbert E. 1963. *Social Change.* Englewood Cliffs, NJ: Prentice-Hall.

Morgan, Lewis Henry. 1877. *Ancient Society, or Researches in the Lines of Human Progress from Savagery, through Barbarism to Civilization.* New York: Henry Holt & Co.

Morphy, Howard. 1991. *Ancestral Connections: Art and An Aboriginal System of Knowledge.* Chicago: The University of Chicago Press.

Morren Jr., George E.B. 1984. "Warfare on the Highland Fringe of New Guinea: The Case of the Mountain Ok." In R. Brian Ferguson, ed. *Warfare, Culture, and Environment.* Orlando, FL: Academic Press, 169–207.

Mortland, Carol A. 1994. "Cambodian Refugees and Identity in the United States." In Linda A. Camino and Ruth M. Krulfeld, eds. *Reconstructing Lives, Recapturing Meaning: Refugee Identity, Gender, and Culture Change.* Basel, Switzerland: Gordon and Breach Science Publishers, 5–28.

Munn, Nancy D. 1973. *Walbiri Iconography: Graphic Representations and Cultural Symbolism in a Central Australian Society.* Chicago: The University of Chicago Press.

Murphy, Richard McGill. 2005. "Getting to Know You: Microsoft Dispatches Anthropologists into the Field to Study Small Businesses Like Yours. Here's Why." *Fortune Small Business* June 2005. http://www.fortune.com/fortune/smallbusiness/technology/articles/0,15114,1062892-1,00.html, accessed June 15, 2005.

Myrdal, Gunnar. 1968. *Asian Drama: An Inquiry into the Poverty of Nations.* New York: Pantheon.

Nanda, Serena. 1999. *Neither Man nor Woman: The Hijras of India,* 2nd edn. Belmont, CA: Wadsworth Publishing.

Naphy, William. 2004. *Born to Be Gay: A History of Homosexuality.* Gloucestershire, UK: Tempus Publishing.

Nash, Manning. 1962. "Race and the Ideology of Race." *Current Anthropology* 3 (3): 285–8.

Nash, Manning. 1989. *The Cauldron of Ethnicity in the Modern World.* Chicago: The University of Chicago Press.

Needham, Rodney. 1972. *Belief, Language, and Experience.* Chicago: The University of Chicago Press.

Neihardt, John G. 1961. *Black Elk Speaks: Being the Life Story of a Holy Man of the Oglala Sioux.* Lincoln: University of Nebraska Press.

Nelson, Cynthia. 1974. "Public and Private Politics: Women in the Middle Eastern World." *American Ethnologist* 1: 551–63.

Nguyen, Vinh-Kim. 2005. "Uses and Pleasures: Sexual Modernity, HIV/AIDS, and Confessional Technologies in a West African Metropolis." In Vincanne Adams and Stacy Leigh Pigg, eds. *Sex in Development: Science, Sexuality, and Morality in Global Perspective.* Durham, NC, and London: Duke University Press, 245–68.

Nolan, Riall. 2002. *Development Anthropology: Encounters in the Real World.* Boulder: Westview Press.

Obeyesekere, Gananath. 1981. *Medusa's Hair: An Essay on Personal Symbols and Religious Experience.* Chicago: The University of Chicago Press.

Ochs, Elinor Keenan. 1996. "Norm-makers, Norm-breakers: Uses of Speech in Men and Women in a Malagasy Community." In Donald Brenneis and Ronald K.S. Macaulay, eds. *The Matrix of Language: Contemporary Linguistic Anthropology.* Boulder: Westview Press, 99–115.

Ohnuki-Tierney, Emiko. 1974. *The Ainu of the Northwest Coast of Southern Sakhalin.* New York: Holt, Rinehart, & Winston.

Ortega y Gasset, Jose. 1932. *The Revolt of the Masses.* New York: W. W. Norton and Company.

Ortner, Sherry. 1973. "On Key Symbols." *American Anthropologist* 75: 1338–46.

Padden, Carol A. and Tom L. Humphries. 2005. *Inside Deaf*

Culture. Cambridge, MA, and London: Harvard University Press.

Parks, Douglas. 1996. *Myths and Traditions of the Arikara Indians.* Lincoln and London: University of Nebraska Press.

Patterson, Orlando. 1975. "Context and Choice in Ethnic Allegiance: A Theoretical Framework and Caribbean Case Study." In Nathan Glazer and Daniel Patrick Moynihan, eds. *Ethnicity: Theory and Experience.* Cambridge, MA: Harvard University Press, 305–49.

Pearce, Roy Harvey. 1965 [1953]. *Savagism and Civilization: A Study of the Indian and the American Mind.* Baltimore and London: The Johns Hopkins University Press.

Pena, Sergio D.J. and Telma de Souza Birchal. 2005–6. "The Biological Non-existence versus the Social Existence of Human Races: Can Science Instruct the Social Ethos?" http://www.fhi.ox.ac.uk/teaching%20and%20posters/TT08/Birchal_paper_29_04.pdf, accessed October 29, 2008.

Peterson, Richard A. and N. Anand. 2004. "The Production of Culture Perspective." *Annual Review of Sociology* 30: 311–34.

Philippine Center for Language Study. 1965. *Beginning Tagalog: A Course for Speakers of English.* Berkeley: University of California Press.

Pigg, Stacy Leigh and Vincanne Adams. 2005. "Introduction: The Moral Object of Sex." In Vincanne Adams and Stacy Leigh Pigg, eds. *Sex in Development: Science, Sexuality, and Morality in Global Perspective.* Durham, NC, and London: Duke University Press, 1–38.

Polanyi, Karl. 1957. "The Economy as Instituted Process." In Karl Polanyi, Conrad M. Arenberg, and Harry W. Pearson, eds. *Trade and Market in the Early Empires: Economies in History and Theory.* New York and London: The Free Press and Collier-Macmillan Limited, 243–70.

Prunier, Gerard. 1995. *The Rwandan Crisis: History of a Genocide.* New York: Columbia University Press.

Puzzo, Dante. 1964. "Racism and the Western Tradition." *Journal of the History of Ideas* 25 (4): 579–86.

Radcliffe-Brown, A.R. 1965 [1952]. *Structure and Function in Primitive Society.* New York: The Free Press.

Ramirez-Esparza, Nairan, Samuel D. Gosling, Veronica Benet-Martinez, Jeffrey P. Potter, and James W. Pennebaker. 2006. "Do Bilinguals have Two Personalities? A Special Case of Cultural Frame Switching." *Journal of Research in Personality* 40: 99–120.

Reagan, Bernice Johnson. 1993. "'Battle Stancing': To Do Cultural Work in America." In Marta Moreno Vega and Cheryl Y. Greene, eds. *Voices from the Battlefront: Achieving Cultural Equity.* Trenton, NJ: Africa World Press, 69–82.

Reed, A.W., ed. 1969. *Captain Cook in Australia: Extracts from the Journals of Captain James Cook.* Wellington, New Zealand: A.H. & A.W. Reed.

Reiter, Rayna. 1975a. "Men and Women in the South of France: Public and Private Domains." In Rayna Reiter, ed. *Toward an Anthropology of Women.* New York: Monthly Review Press, 252–82.

Reiter, Rayna, ed. 1975b. *Toward an Anthropology of Women.* New York: Monthly Review Press.

Ress, David. 1988. *The Burundi Ethnic Massacres, 1988.* San Francisco: Mellon Research University Press.

Ribeiro, Gustavo Lins and Arturo Escobar. 2006. "World Anthropologies: Disciplinary Transformations with Systems of Power." In Gustavo Lins Ribeiro and Arturo Escobar, eds. *World Anthropologies: Disciplinary Transformations within Systems of Power.* Oxford and New York: Berg, 1–25.

Richardson, Boyce. 1991. *Strangers Devour the Land.* Post Mills, VT: Chelsea Green Publishing.

Ringrose, Kathryn M. 1994. "Living in the Shadows: Eunuchs and Gender in Byzantium." In Gilbert Herdt, ed. *Third Sex, Third Gender: Beyond Sexual Dimorphism in Culture and History.* New York: Zone Books, 85–109.

Ritzer, George. 2003. *Enchanting a Disenchanted World: Revolutionizing the Means of Consumption,* 2nd edn. Thousand Oaks, CA, and London: Pine Forge Press.

Roheim, Geza. 1974. *The Children of the Desert: The Western Tribes of Central Australia.* New York: Basic Books.

Rosaldo, Michelle. 1974. "Woman, Culture, and Society: A Theoretical Overview." In Michelle Rosaldo and Louise Lamphere, eds. *Woman, Culture, and Society.* Stanford: Stanford University Press, 17–42.

Rosaldo, Michelle. 1980. *Knowledge and Passion: Ilongot Notions of Self and Social Life.* Cambridge: Cambridge University Press.

Rosaldo, Michelle. 1984. "Words that are Moving: The Social Meanings of Ilongot Verbal Art." In Donald Brenneis and Fred R. Myers, eds. *Dangerous Words: Language and Politics in the Pacific.* Prospect Heights, IL: Waveland Press, 131–60.

Rosaldo, Michelle and Louise Lamphere, eds. 1974. *Women, Culture, and Society.* Stanford: Stanford University Press.

Roscoe, Will. 1994. "How to Become a Berdache: Toward a Unified Analysis of Gender Diversity." In Gilbert Herdt, ed. *Third Sex, Third Gender: Beyond Sexual Dimorphism in Culture and History.* New York: Zone Books, 329–72.

Roscoe, Will. 1998. *Changing Ones: Third and Fourth Genders in Native North America.* New York: St. Martin's Press.

Rosenberg, Bernard. 1957. "Mass Culture in America." In Bernard Rosenberg and David Manning White, eds.

Mass Culture: The Popular Arts in America. New York: The Free Press, 3–12.

Ross, Michael, W.Q. Elaine Xun, and Anne E. Wilson. 2002. "Language and the Bicultural Self." *Personality and Social Psychology Bulletin* 28: 1040–50.

Rostow, W.W. 1965. *The Stages of Economic Growth: A Non-Communist Manifesto*. New York: Cambridge University Press.

Sahlins, Marshall. 1976. *The Use and Abuse of Biology: An Anthropological Critique of Sociobiology*. Ann Arbor: University of Michigan Press.

Salisbury, Richard. 1986. *A Homeland for the Cree: Regional Development in James Bay 1971–1981*. Kingston and Montreal: McGill-Queen's University Press.

Sandall, Roger. 2001. *The Culture Cult: Designer Tribalism and Other Essays*. Boulder: Westview Press.

Sanders, Douglas. 1980. "The Formation of the World Council of Indigenous Peoples." http://www.cwis.org/wcipinfo.txt, accessed July 22, 2005.

Sapir, Edward. 1949. *Selected Writings*. Berkeley: University of California Press.

Scheper-Hughes, Nancy. 1992. *Death without Weeping: The Violence of Everyday Life in Brazil*. Berkeley: University of California Press.

Scheper-Hughes, Nancy and Philippe Bourgois, eds. 2004. *Violence in War and Peace: An Anthology*. London: Blackwell Publishing.

Schieffelin, Edward L. 1983. "Anger and Shame in the Tropical Forest: On Affect as a Cultural System in Papua New Guinea." *Ethos* 11 (3): 181–91.

Schlesinger, Arthur. 1992. *The Disuniting of America*. New York: W.W. Norton and Co.

Schwandner-Sievers, Stephanie. 2001. "The Enactment of 'Tradition': Albanian Constructions of Identity, Violence, and Power in Times of Crisis." In Bettina Schmidt and Ingo Schroder, eds. *Anthropology of Violence and Conflict*. London: Routledge, 97–120.

Schwimmer, Eric. 1984. "Male Couples in New Guinea." In Gilbert Herdt, ed. *Ritualized Homosexuality in Melanesia*. Berkeley: University of California Press.

Scott, Frank and Michael Oliver, eds. 1964. *Quebec States Her Case*. Toronto: Macmillan Company of Canada.

Sen, Amartya. 2006. *Identity and Violence: The Illusion of Destiny*. New York and London: W.W. Norton & Co.

Sen, Mala. 2001. *Death by Fire: Sati, Dowry Death, and Female Infanticide in Modern India*. New Brunswick, NJ: Rutgers University Press.

Service, Elman R. 1962. *Primitive Social Organization: An Evolutionary Perspective*. New York: Random House.

Sharp, Lauriston. 1952. "Steel Axes for Stone-age Australians." *Human Organization* summer: 17–22.

Sherzer, Joel. 1983. *Kuna Ways of Speaking*. Austin: University of Texas Press.

Shostak, Marjorie. 1983 [1981]. *Nisa: The Life and Words of a !Kung Woman*. New York: Vintage Books.

Sillitoe, Paul. 1998. *An Introduction to the Anthropology of Melanesia: Culture and Tradition*. Cambridge: Cambridge University Press.

Simpson, George E. and J. Milton Yinger. 1972. *Racial and Cultural Minorities*, 4th edn. New York: Harper & Row.

Skorupski, John. 1976. *Symbol and Theory: A Philosophical Study of Theories of Religion in Social Anthropology*. Cambridge: Cambridge University Press.

Slotkin, J.S., ed. 1965. *Readings in Early Anthropology*. London: Methuen & Co.

Smedley, Audrey. 1999. *Race in North America: Origin and Evolution of a Worldview*, 2nd edn. Boulder, CO: Westview Press.

Smith, Anthony. 1991. *National Identity*. Reno: University of Nevada Press.

Spindler, George and Louise Spindler. 1971. *Dreamers without Power: The Menomini Indians*. New York: Holt, Rinehart, & Winston.

Spiro, Melford. 1978 [1967]. *Burmese Supernaturalism*, expanded edn. Philadelphia: Institute for the Study of Human Issues.

Steward, Julian. 1950. *Area Research: Theory and Practice*. New York: Social Science Research Council, Bulletin 63.

Steward, Julian. 1953. "Evolution and Process." In Alfred Kroeber, ed. *Anthropology Today*. Chicago: The University of Chicago Press, 313–26.

Stull, Donald D. and Michael J. Broadway. 2004. *Slaughterhouse Blues: The Meat and Poultry Industry in North America*. Belmont, CA: Wadsworth Publishing.

Suarez-Orozco, Marcelo. 1992. "A Grammar of Terror: Psychocultural Responses to State Terrorism in Dirty War and Post-dirty War Argentina." In Carolyn Nordstrom and JoAnn Martin, eds. *The Paths to Domination, Resistance, and Terror*. Berkeley: University of California Press, 219–59.

Taylor, Charles. 1994. "The Politics of Recognition." In Amy Gutman, ed. *Multiculturalism: Examining the Politics of Recognition*. Princeton: Princeton University Press, 25–73.

Tilley, Virginia Q. 2005. "*Mestizaje* and the 'Ethnicization of Race in Latin America." In Paul Spickard, ed. *Race and Nation: Ethnic Systems in the Modern World*. New York and London: Routledge, 53-68.

Tinker, George E. 1993. *Missionary Conquest: The Gospel and Native American Cultural Genocide*. Minneapolis: Fortress Press.

Tocqueville, Alexis de. 1969. *Democracy in America*, trans. J.P. Mayer. Anchor City, NY: Doubleday & Co.

Trigger, Bruce G. 1969. *The Huron: Farmers of the North*. New York: Holt, Rinehart, & Winston.

Trouillot, Michel-Rolph. 1991. "Anthropology and the Savage Slot: The Poetics and Politics of Otherness." In R. Fox, ed. *Recapturing Anthropology: Working in the Present*. Santa Fe, NM: School of American Research Press, 18–44.

Turnbull, Colin. 1962. *The Forest People*. New York: Simon & Schuster.

Turner, Victor W. 1967. *The Forest of Symbols: Aspects of Ndembu Ritual*. Ithaca and London: Cornell University Press.

Turner, Victor W. 1969. *The Ritual Process: Structure and Anti-Structure*. Chicago: Aldine Publishing.

Turner, Victor W. 1981 [1968]. *The Drums of Affliction: A Study of Religious Processes among the Ndembu of Zambia*. London: Hutchinson University Library for Africa.

Turney-High, Harry H. 1971. *Primitive War: Its Practice and Concepts*. Columbia: University of South Carolina Press.

Tyler, Stephen A., ed. 1969. *Cognitive Anthropology*. New York: Holt, Rinehart, & Winston.

Tylor, E.B. 1958 [1871]. *Primitive Culture*. New York: Harper Torchbooks.

Uchendu, Victor C. 1965. *The Igbo of Southeast Nigeria*. New York: Holt, Rinehart, & Winston.

United Nations High Commissioner for Refugees. 2007a. *2006 Statistical Yearbook*. Geneva: United Nations High Commissioner for Refugees.

United Nations High Commissioner for Refugees. 2007b. "Convention and Protocol Relating to the Status of Refugees." Geneva: United Nations High Commissioner for Refugees.

U.S. Court of Appeals for the Ninth Circuit. 2002. "Michael A. Newdow v U.S. Congress, United States of America, George W. Bush, et al." http://www.ca9.uscourts.gov/ca9/newopinions.nsf/FE05EEE79C2A97B688256BE3007FEE32/$file/0016423.pdf, accessed June 27, 2002.

Valentine, Lisa Philips. 1995. *Making It Their Own: Severn Ojibwe Communicative Practices*. Toronto: University of Toronto Press.

van den Berghe, Pierre L. 1967. *Race and Racism: A Comparative Perspective*. New York: John Wiley & Sons.

van den Berghe, Pierre L. 1987 [1981]. *The Ethnic Phenomenon*. New York: Praeger.

van der Dennen, Johan M.G. 2002. "Nonhuman Intergroup Agonistic Behavior and 'Warfare.'" http://rint.rechten.rug.nl/rth/dennen/animwar.htm, accessed May 29, 2002.

van Velzen, H.U.E. Thoden and W. van Wetering. 2004. *In the Shadow of the Oracle: Religion as Politics in a Suriname Maroon Society*. Long Grove, IL: Waveland Press.

Vasconcelos, José. 1979 [1925]. *The Cosmic Race*. trans. Didier T. Jaen. Baltimore and London: The Johns Hopkins University Press.

Veblen, Thorstein. 1934 [1899]. *Theory of the Leisure Class: An Economic Study of Institutions*. New York: Modern Library.

Verrengia, Joseph B. 1993. "Vanishing Tribes." *Rocky Mountain News*, December 12.

Voll, John O. 1991. "Fundamentalism in the Sunni Arab World: Egypt and the Sudan." In Martin Marty and R. Scott Appleby, eds. *Fundamentalisms Observed*. Chicago: The University of Chicago Press, 345–402.

Von Fuerer-Haimendorf, Christoph. 1969. *The Konyak Nagas: An Indian Frontier Tribe*. New York: Holt, Rinehart, & Winston.

Waal, Frans de. 1998 [1982]. *Chimpanzee Politics: Power and Sex among Apes*, revised edn. Baltimore: Johns Hopkins University Press.

Wagner, Roy. 1975. *The Invention of Culture*. Englewood Cliffs, NJ: Prentice-Hall.

Waldstein, Alfred S. 1986. "Irrigated Agriculture as an Archetypal Development Project: Senegal." In Michael M. Horowitz and Thomas M. Painter, eds. *Anthropology and Rural Development in West Africa*. Boulder: Westview Press, 119–43.

Wallace, Anthony F.C. 1956. "Revitalization Movements." *American Anthropologist* 58 (2): 264–81.

Wallace, Anthony F.C. 1961. *Culture and Personality*. New York: Random House.

Wallace, Anthony F.C. 1966. *Religion: An Anthropological View*. New York: Random House.

Wallerstein, Immanuel. 1974. *The Modern World-system: Capitalist Agriculture and the Origins of the European World-economy in the Sixteenth Century*. New York: Academic Press.

Washburn, Sherwood. 1963. "The Study of Race." *American Anthropologist* 65 (3): 521–31.

Weber, Max. 1968. *Economy and Society*, Vol. 1, ed. Guenther Roth and Claus Wittich. New York: Bedminster Press.

Wheelwright, Philip, ed. 1966. *The Presocratics*. New York: The Odyssey Press.

White, Leslie. 1940. "The Symbol: The Origin and Basis of Human Behavior." *Philosophy of Science* 7 (4): 451–63.

White, Leslie. 1949. *The Science of Culture*. New York: Grove Press.

White, Leslie. 1959a. "The Concept of Evolution in Cultural Anthropology." In Betty Meggers, ed. *Evolution and Anthropology: A Centennial Appraisal*. Washington, DC: The Anthropological Society of Washington, 106–25.

White, Leslie. 1959b. *The Evolution of Culture*. New York: McGraw-Hill.

Whiting, Beatrice, ed. 1963. *Six Cultures: Studies of Child Rearing*. New York: John Wiley & Sons.

Whiting, John W.M. and Irvin L. Child. 1953. *Child Training and Personality*. New Haven: Yale University Press.

Whorf, Benjamin Lee. 1940. "Science and Linguistics." *Technology Review* 43: 229–31, 247–8.

Whorf, Benjamin Lee. 1956. *Language, Thought, and Reality: Selected Writings of Benjamin Lee Whorf*. Cambridge: The Massachusetts Institute of Technology Press.

Williams, Thomas Rhys. 1965. *The Dusun: A North Borneo Society*. New York: Holt, Rinehart, & Winston.

Wolf, Eric. 1982. *Europe and the People without History*. Berkeley: University of California Press.

Wolf, Eric. 1994. "Perilous Ideas: Race, Culture, People." *Current Anthropology* 35 (1): 1–12.

Wolfe, Alvin W. and Honggang Yang, eds. 1996. *Anthropological Contributions to Conflict Resolution*. Athens and London: The University of Georgia Press.

Woodburn, James. 1968. "Stability and Flexibility in Hadza Residential Groups." In Richard Lee and Irven DeVore, eds. *Man the Hunter*. Chicago: Aldine, 103–11.

World Bank. 2001. *World Development Report 2000/20001: Attacking Poverty*. Oxford: Oxford University Press.

Worsley, Peter. 1968. *The Trumpet Shall Sound: A Study of "Cargo Cults" in Melanesia*. New York: Shocken Books.

Wrangham, Richard and Dale Peterson. 1996. *Demonic Males: Apes and the Origins of Human Violence*. Boston: Houghton Mifflin Company.

Wrigley, Owen. 1996. *The Politics of Deafness*. Washington, DC: Gallaudet University Press.

Yonezawa, Miyuki. 2005. "Memories of Japanese Identity and Racial Hierarchy." In Paul Spickard, ed. *Race and Nation: Ethnic Systems in the Modern World*. New York and London: Routledge, 115–32.

Index